Steering the Senate

The Senate majority and minority leaders stand at the pinnacle of American national government—as important to Congress as the speaker of the House. However, the invention of Senate floor leadership has, until now, been entirely unknown. Providing a sweeping account of the emergence of party organization and leadership in the U.S. Senate, *Steering the Senate* is the first-ever study to examine the development of the Senate's main governing institutions. It argues that three forces—party competition, intraparty factionalism, and entrepreneurship—have driven innovation in the Senate. The book details how the position of floor leader was invented in 1890 and then strengthened through the twentieth and twenty-first centuries. Drawing on the full history of the Senate, this book immediately becomes the authoritative source for understanding the institutional development of the Senate—uncovering the origins of the Senate party caucuses, steering committees, and floor leadership. This title is also available as Open Access on Cambridge Core.

Gerald Gamm is Professor of Political Science and of History at the University of Rochester. He is a Fellow of the Massachusetts Historical Society, and he began the research that led to this book as a Fellow at the Woodrow Wilson International Center for Scholars. He is the author of *The Making of New Deal Democrats: Voting Behavior and Realignment in Boston, 1920–1940* (1989) and *Urban Exodus: Why the Jews Left Boston and the Catholics Stayed* (1999). His recent articles have appeared in *American Political Science Review, Legislative Studies Quarterly,* and *Studies in American Political Development.*

Steven S. Smith is Professor in the School of Politics and Global Studies at Arizona State University and Kate M. Gregg Emeritus Professor at Washington University in St. Louis. He is the 2023 winner of the Barbara Sinclair Lecture Award for his achievement in promoting the understanding of the U.S. Congress and legislative politics. He is the author of *Politics over Process: Partisan Conflict and Post-Passage Processes in the U.S. Congress* (2017), *The American Congress* (10 editions, 1995–2019), *The Senate Syndrome: The Evolution of Parliamentary Warfare in the Modern U.S. Senate* (2014), *Party Influence in Congress* (2007), *The Politics of Institutional Choice: The Formation of the Russian State Duma* (2001), and more.

Steering the Senate

The Emergence of Party Organization and Leadership, 1789–2024

GERALD GAMM
University of Rochester

STEVEN S. SMITH
Arizona State University
and
Washington University in St. Louis

 CAMBRIDGE
UNIVERSITY PRESS

Shaftesbury Road, Cambridge CB2 8EA, United Kingdom

One Liberty Plaza, 20th Floor, New York, NY 10006, USA

477 Williamstown Road, Port Melbourne, VIC 3207, Australia

314–321, 3rd Floor, Plot 3, Splendor Forum, Jasola District Centre, New Delhi—110025, India

103 Penang Road, #05-06/07, Visioncrest Commercial, Singapore 238467

Cambridge University Press is part of Cambridge University Press & Assessment, a department of the University of Cambridge.

We share the University's mission to contribute to society through the pursuit of education, learning and research at the highest international levels of excellence.

www.cambridge.org
Information on this title: www.cambridge.org/9780521883528

DOI: 10.1017/9781139029926

First published 2025

Cover image: Berryman, Clifford K. "The Kellogg Pact does not apply to the Senate tariff arena." Published in *The Evening Star* (Washington, D.C.), September 4, 1929.

Library of Congress Cataloging-in-Publication Data

NAMES: Gamm, Gerald H., author. | Smith, Steven S., 1953–, author.
TITLE: Steering the Senate : the emergence of party organization and leadership, 1789-2024 / Gerald Gamm, University of Rochester; Steven S. Smith, Arizona State University and Washington University in St. Louis.
DESCRIPTION: New York, NY : Cambridge University Press, 2025. | Includes bibliographical references and index. | Contents: Individual goals and Senate party organization – Presiding officer, 1789-1914 – Caucus, 1789-1879 – Steering committee, 1856-1913 – Arthur Pue Gorman, the federal elections bill, and the invention of elected floor leadership, 1890-1913 – Leaders and whips, 1913-1924 – Divergent paths and the consolidation of leadership structures, 1923-1944 – Party infrastructure, 1945-1980 – Polarization, competition, and centralization, 1981-2024 – Conclusion.
IDENTIFIERS: LCCN 2025024517 (print) | LCCN 2025024518 (ebook) | ISBN 9780521883528 (hardback) | ISBN 9780521709866 (paperback) | ISBN 9781139029926 (epub)
SUBJECTS: LCSH: United States. Congress. Senate–Leadership. | United States. Congress. Senate–Majority Leaders–History. | United States. Congress. Senate–Caucuses. | United States. Congress. Senate–History. | Republican Party (U.S. : 1854-)–History. | Democratic Party (U.S.)–History.
CLASSIFICATION: LCC JK1161 .G36 2025 (print) | LCC JK1161 (ebook) |
DDC 328.73/0769–dc23/eng/20250722
LC record available at https://lccn.loc.gov/2025024517
LC ebook record available at https://lccn.loc.gov/2025024518

ISBN 978-0-521-88352-8 Hardback
ISBN 978-0-521-70986-6 Paperback

....

In memory of Dick Fenno

Contents

Figures

Tables

Preface and Acknowledgments

This book has been germinating in the background of our lives—and, at critical moments, in the foreground—for much of our careers. The origins of this project go back to 1995. Strom Thurmond, Robert Byrd, Ted Kennedy, Daniel Patrick Moynihan, and Joe Biden were all sitting senators. Bob Dole was the long-time Senate Republican leader, Tom Daschle had just become the Democratic leader, Newt Gingrich was the new speaker of the House, and Bill Clinton was in his first term as president. It was hard for us, or for anyone we knew, to imagine the Senate—or Washington—growing any more polarized along partisan lines than it had already become.

Steve was at Minnesota in 1995, trying to track down an account of Senate party development for a book he was writing, and Gerald, a young assistant professor at Rochester, had become interested in congressional history. Dick Fenno connected the two of us, thinking there might be a promising collaboration somewhere in there, perhaps a paper or two.

The Senate, we both knew, was not an easy institution to study. It is a small body and a continuing body, tracing its membership, without interruption, to 1789. Its rules are few and change slowly. "The rules of the Senate are practically unchanged from what they were at the beginning," Henry Cabot Lodge had written in 1893 (526), and, apart from the adoption of a cloture rule, little substantial had shifted over the next century. The Senate's members are famously independent and undisciplined. The presiding officer is a ceremonial position. Its party leaders struggle to corral their fellow senators. And its primary feature often seems to be a sturdy resistance to simple majority rule. The Senate, in short, has never been the modern House with its strong speaker, powerful rules empowering the majority party, and, depending on the historical moment, either a vigorous committee system or strong parties. Whatever the era, the Senate is a chamber where leadership institutions heave and buckle under pressures of partisan competition and factionalism. The Senate's unending story is the struggle of the majority party to govern.

So three decades ago, we set out to solve two interlocked mysteries: How did the main features of Senate party organization and leadership emerge and develop over time? And what explains the broad process of institutional innovation in the Senate and, more generally, in legislatures? This book represents our best effort to solve these puzzles, which we contend are fundamental to understanding the institutional development of what has often been called, sometimes without irony, the world's greatest deliberative body.

Thus we uncover the origins of the central leaders of the modern Senate—the majority and minority leaders—showing that these positions trace their beginning to Arthur Pue Gorman, a Democratic senator who in 1890 mustered his caucus on the floor to obstruct and ultimately defeat passage of a landmark voting rights bill. Since party leadership grew out of the party caucuses, we reconstruct the origins of the party caucus. We find that the caucuses emerged in 1841, when Henry Clay brought discipline and cohesion to his fellow Whig senators—and we excavate the beginnings of what became the Republican steering committee, which, led by Nelson Aldrich and William Allison, managed the Senate at the turn of the last century. And we show how the institutions forged in the nineteenth century were consolidated, strengthened, extended, and fortified by innovations through the twentieth and into the twenty-first centuries.

Every major institutional innovation, we contend, represented a rational response, by individual senators and by the Senate parties, to moments that demanded coordination and collective action. These moments, we find, were frequently created by factional tensions within parties and exploited by entrepreneurial politicians. But always, we conclude, institutional innovation in the Senate—dramatic new changes in party structure, organization, and leadership—represented responses to periods of intense competition between closely balanced parties. It was in those times, when control of the Senate was in doubt, that majority and especially minority parties were most likely to innovate. Once new institutions emerged, they rarely disappeared. So each generation in the Senate inherited a set of institutional solutions and then built new institutions on top of the old foundation stones. The Senate of 2025, we conclude—highly centralized, with an unprecedented network of party organs—is the apotheosis of more than two centuries of institutional change.

For sources for this project, we ranged widely—to official Senate publications, to the minutes of the two Senate parties, to contemporary books and journals, to biographies of senators, to personal papers, to extensive studies by historians, journalists, and political scientists. But our most important source by far proved to be newspapers. Since the first decades of the nineteenth century, newspapers across the country, but especially in big cities, covered the House and Senate in great detail. While they may have covered Congress through different partisan lenses, they almost never disagreed on the basic facts of what was happening on Capitol Hill. And the best newspapers—in Washington, New York, Boston, Baltimore, Chicago, and other cities—posted their finest journalists to Congress, who competed with one another to present the fullest accounts of what was happening behind the closed doors of caucus meetings. Ultimately, we (and our research assistants) read tens of thousands of these stories, which together detail the behind-the-scenes construction of Senate party organization and leadership.

Doing this research in the 1990s and early 2000s was an act of brute force. It meant tracking down newspapers on microfilm and then sitting for hours in front of microfilm readers to find stories on Senate party organization. This necessitated a focus on the first weeks of each Congress, when organizational decisions were likeliest to be made, and allowed little attention to the remainder of each two-year period. Apart from the *New York Times*, no newspaper in the nineteenth century or first half of the twentieth century had a published index, so there was usually no way to sift through stories without reading every page of every newspaper.

The digital revolution transformed our research and allowed us to discover deeper, more compelling, and more convincing accounts than we ever could have done in the age of microfilm, paper, and a paucity of indexes. The origins of party caucuses, the emergence of steering committees, the invention of floor leadership, and most of what we know about the twentieth-century Senate: all of this is grounded in digitized newspapers, where we could search using keywords and find stories and newspapers that were otherwise lost. We have drawn on many databases, but the most important, especially for the nineteenth- and early twentieth-century chapters, have been ProQuest Historical Newspapers, America's Historical Newspapers, and Chronicling America: Historic American Newspapers. We are both in great debt to our respective university libraries for providing access to these rich databases in the 2010s and 2020s, but also for all they did in those olden days when we relied on interlibrary loan and reels of microfilm.

We have accumulated abundant debts in writing this book. Legions of undergraduates at the University of Rochester have worked as research assistants through the years, reading microfilm and searching through digitized databases, and we are grateful to all of them. A handful, who did work in the last stages of this project, we single out by name—Redd Brown, Hugh Curran, Alec Ellison, Zach Lawlor—but our gratitude extends to every student who assisted it. At the University of Minnesota and Washington University in St. Louis, we were assisted by an extremely talented set of graduate students:

Eric Lawrence, Anthony Madonna, Ian Ostrander, Hong Min Park, Jason Roberts, Elizabeth Rybicki, and Ryan Vander Wielen. During Gerald's year at the Woodrow Wilson Center, in many ways the project's formative year, he relied on the generosity of the center, the excellent help of Brian Roraff, and the work that Sarah Binder, Eric Lawrence, and Forrest Maltzman did in welcoming him into the fellowship of congressional scholars.

For three decades, we have benefited from the patience and support of a superb community of scholars whose work focuses on Congress, with many specializing in the history of Congress. We have learned from many people through the years—and at multiple meetings of the American Political Science Association, the Midwest Political Science Association, and the Congress and History conference, as well as in talks we have been invited to give at universities and opportunities to discuss drafts of this manuscript with students and faculty. We have also enjoyed unstinting support from experts on Capitol Hill—Stanley Bach and Elizabeth Rybicki, at the Congressional Research Service; and Richard Baker, Daniel Holt, Betty Koed, Heather Moore, Donald Ritchie, and Wendy Wolff, all in the Senate Historical Office. Finally, we are grateful to Reb Brownell for welcoming us to the Capitol, sharing research with us, and arranging for two meetings between us and Senator Mitch McConnell.

Our colleagues and students—at Minnesota, Washington University, Arizona State, and Rochester—have had our backs these thirty years. They have heard innumerable stories about this book and only sometimes appeared to lose their patience with our interminable timelines. During these years, Steve directed the Weidenbaum Center, Gerald chaired his department, and both of them made time almost every Friday morning to check in with each other with updates big and small. Our colleagues, our friends—in our departments and throughout the profession— kept believing in our capacity to see this work to fruition.

Of course, we owe our greatest debts to the ones we love.

For Gerald, the support of his family has sustained him all these years. His father, Stephen, and stepmother, Celia, have been with him every step of the way, along with his siblings, their spouses and kids, and the rest of his extended family. Now Tahmede brings kindness and courage to every day. But more than anyone it has been Charles on whom Gerald has come to rely—his best friend, his true love, his support, the person who challenges Gerald constantly to do new things and get old things completed at last.

For Steve, the love and encouragement of his wife, Liz, motivates him every day. Liz is a brilliant scholar, wonderful mom, and the best friend anyone could have. Tyler, Shannon, Maxine, Alice, and Ruby, whose lives are simply inspiring, have provided the love and joy that he always carries with him.

We dedicate this book to Dick. He was the single greatest congressional scholar and teacher of the last century, probably of all time. But that is not why we make this dedication. It is instead to Dick as we knew him for so many years. He was a colleague, a mentor, someone always in our corner, and, with his wife, Nancy, a true and constant friend to us both. We miss his generous spirit and we remember, no matter how many years pass, the sound of him whistling as we walk down the third-floor corridor of Harkness Hall.

Majority Leader Joe Robinson (D, Ark.) in May 1937. He served as Democratic leader for almost 14 years.

Individual Goals and Senate Party Organization

Nelson Aldrich (R, R.I.) dominated the Senate at the turn of the last century, known, by his admirers as much as his critics, as the "General Manager of the United States."[1] He held three formal positions of consequence—he chaired the Senate Rules Committee, 1887–93 and 1895–99; he chaired the Senate Finance Committee, 1899–1911; and he sat on the Republican steering committee, 1893–1911—but he never served as caucus chairman or as elected floor leader. Indeed, at least on the Republican side of the aisle, the position of elected floor leader had yet to be invented during Aldrich's time as a senator. When he announced plans to retire from the Senate, Aldrich told his friends that he had grown tired of being a "pack-horse" for his colleagues. In the recent battle over revisions to the tariff, Aldrich had "labored incessantly, day and night," the *New York Times* reported in the spring of 1910. "There were innumerable conferences, in which he took part, at his committee rooms, at the White House, and elsewhere. He was always on duty, and the strain was tremendous."[2]

But the power of any senator in those years, even of Aldrich, was limited. "The public now and again picks out a Senator who seems to act and to speak with true instinct of statesmanship and who unmistakably merits the confidence of colleagues and of people," Woodrow Wilson wrote in 1885 (213), in his classic book *Congressional Government*. "But such a man, however eminent, is never more than *a* Senator. No one is *the* Senator." Aldrich's leadership was at

---

[1] "'General Manager' Aldrich," *Boston Globe*, Mar. 25, 1904, 6; "The Boston Herald speaks of ... ," *Atlanta Constitution*, Oct. 8, 1904, 6; "It was hardly necessary ... ," *Atlanta Constitution*, June 4, 1905, A4; "New Political Boss of Rhode Island," *Boston Globe*, Jan. 22, 1911, 51. See also "Political Gossip," *Washington Post*, May 15, 1904, E7; A. Maurice Low, "'Manager of the Senate'—Aldrich of Rhode Island," *Boston Globe*, Jan. 7, 1906, SM5.

[2] "Aldrich To Retire at End of His Term," *New York Times*, Apr. 16, 1910, 1.

its greatest on financial issues—even the *Boston Herald*, which appears to have popularized the notion of Aldrich as "General Manager," confined the epithet to the matters of "trade and commerce and finance"³—and he was reminded often of the constraints on his ability to shape outcomes in other realms. In 1890–91, when Democrats launched a historic filibuster to frustrate the Republican effort to pass the Federal Elections Bill, Aldrich announced plans to use majority cloture to end the debate and bring the bill to a vote.⁴ Thomas Reed, speaker of the House of Representatives, had already acted decisively to reform his chamber's rules and to pass the landmark bill protecting voting rights for Black men in the South, and Republican senators, who controlled the Senate, were on record supporting the bill. Aldrich faltered in the effort, and the Federal Elections Bill failed.⁵ A decade later, in 1900, in a news story meant to demonstrate his skill in managing the Senate, the *Washington Post* inadvertently exposed the weakness of Aldrich's position. Titling its story "Mr. Aldrich's Clever Move," the *Post* reported how he took advantage of a nearly empty Senate chamber to secure a "'unanimous' agreement" that the gold standard bill would be considered to the exclusion of all other business until it came to a vote eight days later.⁶ That Aldrich was most effective when he had the chamber largely to himself suggests the challenges he faced in managing currency legislation, let alone the rest of the Senate's business.

In the 2020s, the power wielded by the Senate majority leader is, in contrast, immense and in public view. It is visible in historic procedural decisions. First Harry Reid (D, Nev.) in 2013, then Mitch McConnell (R, Ky.) in 2017, mobilized their caucuses to end the filibuster and adopt majority cloture for judicial and executive branch confirmation votes, in the face of determined minority obstructionism. That power is visible in unprecedented actions taken to block or confirm nominees to the Supreme Court. When Justice Antonin Scalia unexpectedly died in February 2016, McConnell, on vacation with his wife in the Caribbean, immediately announced that the Senate would not consider any nominee by President Barack Obama. "I had members all over

---

³ "General Manager of United States," *Boston Herald*, Mar. 25, 1904, 6.

⁴ "With Partisan Aims Only," *New York Times*, Dec. 23, 1890, 5; "The Cloture Talk," *Atlanta Constitution*, Dec. 24, 1890, 1; "From Washington—The 'Gag Law' Change Introduced in the Senate," *Baltimore Sun*, Dec. 24, 1890, 1; "The Cloture Rule Is In," *Washington Post*, Dec. 24, 1890, 1; "Mr. Aldrich's Gag Rule," *New York Times*, Dec. 26, 1890, 1; "Fight at Hand," *Boston Globe*, Dec. 30, 1890, 1; "Will Mr. Morton Do It," *Washington Post*, Jan. 19, 1891, 1; "By Aid of the Chair," *Washington Post*, Jan. 23, 1891, 2; "To Close the Debate," *Washington Post*, Jan. 26, 1891, 1; Frederic J. Haskin, "The American Congress: IX. The Force Bill and Cloture," *Washington Post*, Dec. 1, 1909, 4.

⁵ "Black Eye to Cloture," *Washington Post*, Jan. 27, 1891, 1; "May It Rest in Peace," *Washington Post*, Jan. 27, 1891, 4; "A Constitutional Gossip," *Atlanta Constitution*, Jan. 28, 1891, 4; Frederic J. Haskin, "The American Congress: IX. The Force Bill and Cloture," *Washington Post*, Dec. 1, 1909, 4.

⁶ "Mr. Aldrich's Clever Move," *Washington Post*, Feb. 7, 1900, 4.

the country and all over the world. I didn't want to deal with 52 different opinions when we got back about how we were going to handle it," McConnell explained later. "And so I decided to lay down a marker and hope that people would fall in line. And with few exceptions, they did."[7] Four years later, in 2020, when Justice Ruth Bader Ginsburg died six weeks before the November elections, McConnell also acted swiftly, declaring that the Senate majority would confirm a nominee by President Donald Trump. And that power is visible in legislation—as Reid in 2009 worked "behind closed doors," in his office, to determine the final shape of the Affordable Care Act and build support from the 60 Democrats whose votes he needed to pass the bill without minority support; as McConnell in 2017 brought a handful of senators into his office and helped manage the negotiations that led to massive changes in the tax code, with the bill passing by a 51–48 vote; and as Charles E. Schumer (D, N.Y.), "the cordial collaborator who always keeps his flip phone nearby to start a new discussion toward sealing the deal," negotiated, over many months and in secret, with Joe Manchin (D, W.Va.) to secure passage of a historic climate package, the Inflation Reduction Act, in the summer of 2022 by a 51–50 vote.[8]

Leadership of the Senate was an afterthought at the Constitutional Convention. It took more than a century's time before senators began to find an enduring solution to that problem. The Constitution, of course, provided the Senate with a leader—"The Vice President of the United States shall be President of the Senate"—but "president" in this case simply meant presiding officer, and it was a presiding officer without a vote (except in cases of ties) and a leader imposed on the Senate from the outside, neither chosen by senators nor accountable to them. The framers of the Constitution assigned presiding officer duties to the vice president to give vice presidents something to do with their abundant free time, not to empower the Senate to govern itself. For its first hundred years, as we will show, the Senate struggled with a variety of organizational challenges and experimented with various institutional solutions: granting powers to the presiding officer, inventing party caucuses, organizing an array of ad hoc caucus committees, and establishing powerful campaign committees, committees on committees, and steering committees. Only in 1890 did senators in the Democratic caucus create a position that would become the ancestor of the modern posts of majority and minority leaders,

---

[7] Tyler Olson, "What Mitch McConnell Did in the Immediate Aftermath of Justice Scalia's Death," *Fox News*, Sept. 18, 2020. See also Burgess Everett and Glenn Thrush, "McConnell Throws Down the Gauntlet: No Scalia Replacement Under Obama," *Politico*, Feb. 13, 2016.

[8] Glenn Kessler, "History Lesson: How the Democrats Pushed Obamacare Through the Senate," *Washington Post*, June 22, 2017; Paul Kane, "Schumer Isn't Harry Reid or LBJ: How His Style Helped Land Democrats a String of Wins," *Washington Post*, Aug. 9, 2022. See also Jim Tankersley and Alan Rappeport, "How Republicans Rallied Together to Deliver a Tax Plan," *New York Times*, Dec. 19, 2017.

and it was a position that was not adopted by the Republican caucus until 1913. Republicans, after all, had Aldrich and the Republican steering committee. Elected floor leadership developed late in the Senate's history, fitfully, in the shadows.

Our account in this book is largely new and original. The course of Senate party development—including the origins of caucuses, steering committees, other caucus committees, and floor leadership—has long been obscure. Before we began this research, no accurate lists of early floor leaders or caucus chairs existed. The standard narrative identified the 1920s as the moment when recognized floor leaders appeared in the Senate. Until recently, in fact, when it drew on early drafts of this book to update its records, even the Senate Historical Office reported on its website and in its reports that "the positions of party floor leaders ... developed gradually in the 20th century," identifying 1920 (for Democrats) and 1925 (for Republicans) as the date when each party first named a formally designated leader.[9] But that timeline was off by a generation. We will show that the origins of party floor leadership, including formal caucus designation, came in the 1890s—when Maryland senator Arthur Pue Gorman led the minority Democrats in their successful effort to defeat the landmark Federal Elections Bill of 1890, the last serious effort by Congress, until the modern civil rights era, to protect Black voting rights in the South.

The majority and minority leaders of the twentieth and twenty-first centuries are, first and foremost, party leaders. Unlike the president, elected by a nation-spanning electoral college, and the speaker, chosen by the full membership of the House, the Senate leaders are selected in caucus, designated by members of their party to lead them on the chamber floor. In the early years that this position was created, few understood its significance. It was simply one among many party institutions with which senators were experimenting. But by the 1930s, it was well established that the majority and minority leaders of the Senate were consequential, and the significance of these positions has only grown in recent decades.

Our main concern is to understand Senate party development. What are the problems that individual legislators encounter in the absence of leadership? How do they set out to solve problems of coordination and collective action? How do they assign members to committees, organize campaigns, and set legislative agendas? At which moments do individual legislators decide to delegate some of their powers to a collective group of legislators and, ultimately, to a single leader? How and when, over time, do they decide to grant that single leader greater authority? Because the invention of entirely new party structures in the Senate stretched over a century's time, from 1789 to the 1890s—and the powers of floor leaders have then been elaborated over the

---

[9] As we go to press, both the *Biographical Directory of the United States Congress* and various websites maintained by the Senate have been updated to incorporate the research reflected in this book: see, for example, U.S. Senate Historical Office (2024a, 2024b).

course of more than another century, from the 1890s to the 2020s—the U.S. Senate offers an outstanding laboratory for answering these questions. Time after time, senators have turned to new institutions and new forms of party organization, which gives us multiple opportunities to ask what distinguishes those moments.

Our answer, and our central argument, focuses on three factors: *party competition, factionalism,* and *entrepreneurship.* In the Senate, where leadership and institutional organization rest in the two parties rather than in the presiding officer, members adopt innovative structures when parties are most closely balanced. It has been at those moments when parties are battling for control of the Senate, often just after a shift in majority control, that one party (or both) adopts organizational innovations. New institutions are the products of tenuous majorities and hopeful or disappointed minority parties. But these innovations are adopted not only in response to moments of party competition but to address factionalism within parties. Factions often seek organizational and procedural changes within parties to gain an advantage. Moreover, divided parties and unified parties demand different forms of organization. And entrepreneurship matters. Whether it was Thomas Hart Benton (D, Mo.) and Henry Clay (W, Ky.) in the 1840s, Aldrich and Gorman in the 1890s, Charles Curtis (R, Kans.) and Joseph Robinson (D, Ark.) in the 1920s, Robert Taft (R, Ohio) and Lyndon B. Johnson (D, Tex.) in the 1950s, or Schumer and McConnell in the 2020s, individual entrepreneurs are the ones who take the lead in constructing new institutions in response to competitive parties or factionalized coalitions.

THE UNDERSTUDIED SENATE

The longstanding individualism and informality of Senate proceedings have limited scholarly interest in the development of Senate party leadership and organization. Both the contemporary Senate and the historical Senate have been underexamined by scholars. Most major studies of Congress have been studies of the House of Representatives, and the House speakership alone has been the subject of several books. Traditionally viewed as a less rules-bound body, with weaker leadership and more powerful individual members, the Senate has languished in congressional scholarship from the nineteenth century until the present day. In the 1970s, Jones (1976, 19–20), reflecting on the modern Senate, made the uncontroversial observation that "strong substance-oriented policy leadership by party leaders is neither possible nor desirable in the United States Senate." The rules of the Senate, it has been commonly observed, protect the rights of senators to debate and offer proposals on the floor of the Senate and grant few special privileges to its presiding officer or to the leader of the majority party. And Senate rules rarely change from Congress to Congress.

The few existing studies of Senate party development present competing accounts of when and how centralized parties emerged. A set of studies from the 1960s and 1970s, three published and two unpublished, offer outstanding examples of this scholarship. The three published accounts have had a lasting impact on congressional studies, yet their main features are difficult to reconcile with one another. Rothman's *Politics and Power* (1966), the most important book-length study of the Senate's institutional development, focuses on the collective governance structures, dominated by senior senators, that emerged in both parties in the late 1890s—institutions that Rothman regards as the foundation of modern, disciplined Senate party organization—but Rothman's account focuses on the turn of the last century, failing to note that these oligarchical institutions did not survive the early 1910s. Munk, in a dissertation (1970) and published article (1974), emphasizes an entirely different institution, the position of floor leader. In her dissertation, she lays out a nuanced, gradual process of institutional change, examining the ascendancy and collapse of the Republican oligarchy in the 1890s, 1900s, and 1910s, alongside the steady development of the floor leadership position from the 1890s to the 1960s—remarkably similar to the account in Kravitz (ca. 1971), an unpublished book manuscript. However, in refining her argument for publication, Munk argues that floor leadership remained a primitive position until 1913, when John W. Kern (D, Ind.) became the Senate's first widely recognized majority leader. "The existence of majority and minority floor leaders," Munk (1974, 23) contends in her article, "can be traced with assurance only back to the second decade of the twentieth century." That crisp contention, rather than the subtle argument of her dissertation, had lasting resonance for subsequent scholarship. Meanwhile, Riddick (1971), drawing directly on surviving minutes of the two Senate caucuses, which exist for the Democrats since 1903 and the Republicans since 1911, concluded from his research that designated floor leaders emerged only in the 1920s.

The tensions between these accounts create obvious challenges for generating and testing theories of institutional change in the Senate. These scholars, each a careful student of Senate history, disagreed on which institutions, whether the Republican oligarchy of the 1890s or the floor leaders of the first decades of the twentieth century, best reflected a centralized structure of Senate party organization. For those emphasizing the role of floor leaders, they disagreed on timing—whether this was a gradual process of development, a dramatic break in 1913, or a new institution in the 1920s. Consequently, as they and subsequent political scientists sought to explain the rise of party institutions in the Senate, their efforts were hobbled by the elusiveness of their dependent variable.

Careerism, for example, has been cited by scholars as critical to Senate party development, but they disagree about the role careerism has played. Rothman (1966) contends that the centralization of Senate parties in the late nineteenth century resulted from the increasing number of senators who regarded Senate service as a career and owed their advancement to state party organizations. Yet Ripley (1969b) insists that, until the 1880s, careerism slowed the elaboration of Senate party organization and central leadership posts because career-minded senators, unlike less career-oriented members of the House, were unwilling to tolerate strong central leaders. And Brady et al. (Brady, Brody, and Epstein 1989; Brady and Epstein 1997) assert that it was the dominance of "noncareerists" in the Senate that facilitated the centralization of power in the late nineteenth century in the Aldrich oligarchy.

The Senate's workload and size are natural candidates as factors that shaped party organization. McConachie (1898, 313–21) observes in the 1890s how the Senate's increasing workload compelled adjustments in procedure and practice. Similarly, Baker and Davidson (1991, 2) argue that the independent power of committee chairs eroded sharply in the 1910s when the Senate reorganized its affairs to respond to the Great War and to an increasingly powerful president. Looking at the development of new party leadership positions in the Senate in this era, they conclude that the new conditions "necessitated a coordinated Senate leadership quite beyond the capacity of individual committee chairmen."[10] A war effort, domestic emergencies, a large policy agenda, or even new forms of press coverage may create new demands for coordination, particularly from within the majority party, which is likely to be blamed by outsiders if the Senate fails to act on desired legislation.

The Senate's size, too, may create coordination and collective action problems that can be addressed by party organization, including the creation of formal leadership positions. For decades, social scientists have emphasized the importance of *group size* as a factor that influences the severity of the collective action problem and the effect of individual efforts to address it. The larger the group, the smaller the contribution of the individual, the greater the incentive to be a "free rider," the greater the transaction costs, and the more inefficient the pursuit of collective interests. Members of small groups tend to recognize the importance of their individual contributions to their personal interests and make an effort to achieve collective goals (Olson 1965; Frohlich, Oppenheimer, and Young 1971). In the case of the Senate, the addition of states to the Union led the Senate to grow from 48 seats in 1821 to 66 seats in 1857, to 88 seats in 1889, and to 96 seats in 1911. It may seem more than coincidental that leadership emerged when the Senate approached 90 members.

In practice, we seldom find that increases in workload and size, by themselves, stimulate organizational innovation. While size and workload surely set the context for the activities of Senate parties, we rarely find that increases in size and workload per se are mentioned by senators as their motivation for organizational innovations. Nor does either workload or size change sharply in the short term. Instead, when more directly partisan or political factors

---

[10] This perspective stands in sharp contrast to the argument of Brady and Epstein (1997, 33), who assert that the 1910s was a period "in which the House and Senate became more committee- and less party-oriented and leadership style changed from command to bargaining."

motivate senators to improve their organizational effectiveness, workload and size may condition the form that innovation takes. For example, a sizable workload makes effective floor leadership important, particularly for the majority party, but the emergence of floor leadership occurred first in the minority party and was a by-product of the need for a coordinated strategy rather than an increase in the Senate's legislative workload or size. Moreover, the free-rider problem is not severe in Senate parties. They are neither very large nor very small. They are large enough to make building coalitions and other legislative activities expensive in time and other resources. But the Senate remains small enough that the efforts of individual senators and factions can make a difference.

In her account, Munk argues that modern Senate floor leadership was the product of President Wilson's need for a lieutenant to push his program through a factionalized, filibuster-prone Senate (Munk 1974). With a small Democratic majority behind him in 1913 and a large legislative program, Wilson recognized that his chances of success were undermined by having a party divided between progressive and conservative forces. In the House, the speaker was the recognized party leader and a ready-made champion of the president's cause. But the Senate majority party, without a central leader, promised to be ineffective. Wilson's obvious solution, according to Munk, was to endorse a senator for a leadership role who shared his views on key issues and then rely on that senator to represent administration interests. Subsequent presidents then followed Wilson's example, giving the floor leadership a distinctive role as a partner to the president. Relations with the president are one of the main responsibilities of Senate floor leaders, but, as we contend below, it is one of several duties attached to this position, and a focus on this one aspect of the position fails to account for the substantial development of this position in the years before the Wilson presidency and in realms beyond executive relationships.

Other scholars point out that an influx of new members can drive institutional change (Davidson and Oleszek 1977; Evans and Oleszek 1997; Fenno 1997). According to this perspective, new members have no vested interest in the existing institutional arrangements and may even perceive a mandate to change the way their chamber and party operate. Large numbers of new members, too, can upset preexisting balances within or between the parties. As we lay out our own theory below, we draw on this insight too, considering how changes in the membership of the two parties can give rise to new forms of party organization.

Finally, a large body of legislative research argues that the influence of central party leaders over the policymaking process is related to the extent of ideological or policy differences between the parties (Cooper and Brady 1981; Sinclair 1983, 1995; Brady 1988; Brady, Brody, and Epstein 1989; Smith and Deering 1990; Rohde 1991; Aldrich and Rohde 1997, 1998; Brady and Epstein 1997; Aldrich, Berger, and Rohde 2002). This perspective holds that congressional parties are preeminently policy coalitions of varying degrees of cohesiveness and polarization (Aldrich and Rohde 1997, 1998). When intra-party cohesiveness is high and the distance between the parties is great, legisla-tors are eager to license aggressive party leaders who will coordinate strategy in their interest. Members of internally divided parties, in contrast, tend to distrust strong leaders and prefer a more decentralized, committee-oriented policymak-ing process. The argument, usually termed "conditional party government," was developed for the House of Representatives but has been extended to the Senate.

This attention to variation in party polarization influences our approach, but we diverge in emphasizing the creation and development of party institutions—caucuses, steering committees, leadership positions, and other forms of partisan organization—rather than how leaders make use of their powers, as is the focus in studies grounded in the conditional party government perspective. We also, of course, are examining a legislative body that lacks the majoritarian features of the House. In the House of Representatives, the speaker is selected by the full chamber and a simple majority controls the agenda, so, as power in the majority party becomes more concentrated, power within the House becomes more concentrated. But in the Senate changes within a party caucus, even within the majority party caucus, do not translate automatically to shifts of power within the chamber.

A theory of Senate institutional development requires understanding how Senate parties and leaders help solve the problems of collective action and coordination for their membership, problems long recognized by social scien-tists as basic to understanding human organizations and leadership (Frohlich, Oppenheimer, and Young 1971; Calvert 1987; Rohde and Shepsle 1987). Senators require means to coordinate activities such as setting the agenda, drafting legislation, mobilizing majorities, assigning members to committees, and winning elections. When senators' political interests are differentiated by party, as they were from the early years of the Congress, solutions will be organized by party. But what form those party-based solutions take—and at what moments in time—is what needs elaboration.

INDIVIDUAL AND COLLECTIVE GOALS

In developing a theory of institutional change in the Senate, we begin with the premise that legislators have goals not only as individuals—reelection, good public policy, and influence (Fenno 1973; Bullock 1976; Smith and Deering 1990)—but also as members of an organized party. Each of the individual goals has a correlative collective goal:

1. As individuals value *reelection*, the party values a favorable *reputation*.
2. As individuals value *good public policy*, the party values the *ability to shape legislative outcomes*.
3. As individuals value *influence*, the party values *majority control* of the chamber.

The collective goals are grounded in the individual-level goals. Legislators seeking to enact certain policies are advantaged if their party wins majority control of Congress, its committees, and scheduling mechanisms. Legislators seeking reelection are advantaged if the public has a favorable view of their party's legislative record and their party's reputation. For parties, these collective goals are central to their creation and development, they justify the elaboration of party organizations, and they motivate the strategies of party leaders.

There is no one-to-one correspondence between individual and party goals. To be sure, we would expect changes in the relative importance of reelection and policy goals among party members to be reflected in a party leader's priorities. Critically, however, the electoral and policy goals of the party are interdependent. A party's reputation influences its electoral success, its electoral success influences its legislative record, and its legislative record influences its popularity. Winning elections helps a party create the coalitions necessary for passing or blocking legislation, and a legislative record helps generate the desired reputation essential to winning elections. The interdependence of party goals, whatever their origin in senators' goals, requires that party leaders be attentive to a full array of party goals. In this way, the emergence of new party institutions, like the caucus and steering committees, and the creation of leadership positions all represent non-incremental changes in Senate party organization.

Interdependence of goals means that parties will pursue all three goals even if one of the personal goals that underpins them loses some of its importance to rank-and-file senators. Conversely, it means that party leaders will continue to pursue all three goals even if one of the personal goals gains greater importance for senators. In fact, an even stronger argument can be made: *leaders will pursue all three party goals even if rank-and-file senators are motivated exclusively by one of the personal goals.* Thus, the priority given to any of the party goals by party leaders will show more stability than variation in the importance or compatibility of individual goals might suggest. Even if we treat legislators as individually motivated by the desire to see their policy preferences reflected in law, fellow partisans would share an interest in both enacting their common policy interests and in maintaining or securing majority party status. They would care about the electoral fortunes of other party members. Consequently, they might be willing to exchange some of their policy aspirations for the electoral benefit of their party as a whole. It is precisely such exchanges that each party must address collectively, doing so by taking into account the broad electoral environment and expected behavior of the other party.

OBSTACLES TO ACHIEVING PARTY GOALS

Party efforts to acquire public goods—that is, to achieve collective party goals—are subject to collective action and coordination problems (Baumol 1952; Coase 1960; Olson 1965; Frohlich, Oppenheimer, and Young 1971). The *collective action problem* arises when the successful achievement of party goals is not greatly influenced by the actions of any individual legislator. Consequently, the incentive for individuals to contribute a fair share to collective party efforts is small (Olson 1965). With respect to passing or blocking legislation, the party needs a majority of legislators' votes to win, so the effort is necessarily a collective effort. But the leadership necessary for corralling votes is concentrated in a small number of members. Considering their own reelection, the ordinary legislator cannot reasonably expect to materially affect the reputation of their party and would therefore focus their energies on campaigning at home rather than working on Capitol Hill to enhance the party reputation (Mayhew 1974). A legislator might even reasonably expect a net gain in votes from criticizing or standing apart from their own party.

Senate parties must also address *coordination* and *transaction costs*. The party's members must somehow coordinate their strategies or, alternatively, create a mechanism that will produce a choice from one of a few acceptable strategies. Coordination is costly. Meetings must be organized, responsibilities delegated, information disseminated, and leaders held accountable. Indeed, high transaction costs, relative to the expected gains from coordination, can prevent a collective choice and the realization of benefits from a public good (Coase 1960; North 1990). Organizational innovations, such as arranging for regular meetings of committees to make decisions for the larger party caucus, may reduce transaction costs and improve the collective efforts of a party.

Transaction costs vary over time. In a world in which the Senate has a modest workload and senators have time to spare, party caucus meetings can be held frequently and issues discussed at length without taking away from other efforts. As the volume of legislative business that is processed by committees and on the floor increases and as legislative and electoral activities take up more of senators' time, members are likely to seek relief by relying on party leaders, committees, and staff to manage some matters on their behalf. Over the span of many decades, increasing transaction costs create incentives for senators to propose organizational responses to address them.[11] Moreover, the need for quick action by a party to assert or protect its interests may lead party leaders to take more initiative and suppress demands for full deliberations of the caucus. Institutional innovation is costly—in time and money, but also in transferring powers from individual members to collective party organizations and leaders. For senators to acquiesce in this delegation, they must be convinced of its necessity to further their own personal goals.

---

[11] Increasing transaction costs also may be exploited by senators. As Oppenheimer (1985) argues persuasively, the legislative burdens on the Senate in the last half of the twentieth century made obstructionist tactics more useful, encouraged filibusters and holds, and led to organizational and procedural responses by floor leaders.

LEADERS

If legislators operated independently, party goals would be pursued inefficiently. At least in the long run, then, competitive pressures from the other party encourage legislators to invent ways of organizing their party for collective action, and successful innovations in one party are readily adopted by the other. Parties create committees, task forces, and leadership positions, and they assign responsibility for achieving collective party goals to the legislators appointed or elected to those posts. Legislators need to be motivated to pursue these efforts, but the same mix of goals that motivate others—additional influence over policy outcomes, visibility useful in the pursuit of reelection or higher office, the sheer satisfaction of being in the middle of important events—may motivate at least a few legislators to attend to the collective interests of the party.

Of course, legislators may not fully trust their leaders and party committees. After all, power delegated to leaders and committees to pursue party interests might instead be used in pursuit of personal interests (Ross 1973; Mitnick 1975). Like all organizations, congressional parties address this threat—called the *principal-agent problem* or, more simply, the agency problem—in a variety of ways, such as by defining the responsibilities and jurisdictions of committees and leaders, assigning some decisions to multi-member committees or leadership groups rather than to individuals, subjecting leaders to periodic election, and requiring leaders to justify their strategies at caucuses or other party meetings (Kiewiet and McCubbins 1991). All these venues give the party rank-and-file an opportunity to define how party goals should be defined and pursued. As in other settings, though, leaders acquire advantages that give them considerable influence over the direction of party strategy.

Variation in individuals' electoral and policy objectives and uncertainty about how events will unfold give rise to squabbles about party strategy. These arguments are articulated in contests for leadership positions, party meetings, and everyday conversations. The responsibility of party leaders is to further party goals while minimizing the severity of the trade-offs that are required. Giving priority to some legislation over other measures, at least until after the next election, is a common strategic choice of parties. This type of strategic choice is manifested in the activities of party leaders—managing the party organization, coordinating with the president or leaders of the other chamber, speaking on behalf of the party for the media and other audiences, setting staff priorities, managing floor activity, negotiating legislation within the chamber and with leaders of the other policymaking institutions, and even taking the lead in writing legislation and building majorities.

WHY PARTIES INNOVATE

This brings us to our central question: What political conditions are associated with the elaboration of Senate party organizations? The general condition that promotes innovation in Senate party organizations is keen *interparty competition* in the legislative and electoral arenas (Gamm and Smith 2000, 2002a, 2002b;

Smith and Gamm 2001, 2020; Lee 2016; Koger and Lebo 2017). The payoff for organizational innovation is likely to be greatest when the two parties are close to parity—when the parties are of nearly equal size and when party strength, due to the parties' relative cohesiveness, is nearly equal. These are the times, we contend, that a party is most likely to make innovations in party organization, rules, or leadership to gain advantage over the opposing party. For a minority party, especially one with reasonable hope of attaining majority status, the drive to overcome its limitations with more effective legislative and electoral strategies stimulates innovations. For a majority party clinging to power, or having just come to power, we predict similar attention to organizational change.

Within the Senate, the most important obstacle to achieving party goals is the other party. Party competition is at the root of most major organizational developments in congressional parties. The incentive to innovate often is greatest in the minority party, which looks to improve its ability to compete in the legislative and electoral arenas and gain majority status. But beyond challenges from the other party, legislators' goals often entail trade-offs that must be resolved or managed. Not all members of a legislative party share the same political interests, and a party's policy and electoral goals may require setting priorities.[12] Even partially conflicting interests and priorities often generate *factionalism*, and resolving the conflicts entails collective action and coordination (Smith 2007). Evolving challenges in pursuing party goals determine the functions that party organizations and leaders perform.

The focus on party competition and factions is not new, of course. Historians of American political parties have long made the interplay of the parties and the maneuvering of factions a central feature of their narratives. Holt's magisterial history of the Whigs, to cite just one prominent study, begins with the observation that "no political party can be fully understood in terms of its own beliefs, actions, and internal quarrels. Its relationships with rival parties must also be incorporated into the analysis" (Holt 1999, ix). Moreover, the Whigs, even more than mid-twentieth-century Democrats, struggled with factionalism that eventually made them the only mass major party to disappear. We, too, make interparty and factional relations central to our story.

Individual senators matter, too. *Entrepreneurs*—senators motivated by ambition or who simply take joy from deep engagement in the legislative process—attain leadership positions and, at times when the party is ready to accept organizational changes, champion innovations that advance both party and personal interests. Opportunism underlies many innovations in Senate party organization. A senator, or perhaps a small group of senators, recognizing that their party interests align with their personal or factional interests, invents new organizational forms, often (at least in modern times) advocating for these reforms in campaigns to win leadership elections. These entrepreneurs

---

[12] For background and theoretical perspectives on congressional party factions, see Bawn (1998) and DiSalvo (2009).

exploit occasions in which their party colleagues are open to redistributing power within the party caucus in order to serve collective goals. We are not arguing that great senators have, on their own, molded Senate parties. On the contrary, party competition and factionalism create opportunities and constraints that shape the incentives for individuals to promote their own electoral, policy, and career interests. The greater the opportunities and the looser the constraints, the more room for senators' varied interests, backgrounds, and skills to affect organizational choices.

Organizational innovation in Senate parties is not continuous because it is costly. Structural change, after all, often creates winners and losers among the members and factions of a party, may take considerable time and effort to work out, and may harm interpersonal relations. It is most likely to occur when the short-term payoff, in terms of the goals of majority party control and winning legislative battles, is substantial. In fact, as we will show, competition in the legislative and electoral arenas often are closely connected and pursued in tandem. A party seeking electoral victories may seek to get credit, or avoid blame, with the electorate by passing legislation, blocking bills, or keeping issues off the Senate agenda entirely. It also may pursue its legislative goals by persuading the electorate to support its legislative initiatives.

There is nothing automatic about parties becoming organized to perform these tasks, in parties becoming "cartels" (Cox and McCubbins 1993, 2005). When the majority party is united, it can control the agenda-setting processes of a legislative body, produce legislation, and choose the officers and staff of the chamber. Jenkins and Stewart (2013) demonstrate that it took decades for House majority parties to do this. Seemingly simple matters like the choice of a House speaker or a printer were not resolved within meetings of the majority party until the mid-nineteenth century. Control of the House floor by a recognized leader of the majority party, the speaker, was not established until the end of that century.

As we examine 235 years of Senate history, we find that the development of its party organizations has tended to be cumulative. There have been dead ends, to be sure—the effort to invest committee appointment powers in the presiding officer, as we will show, or the concentration of chamber leadership in the Republican steering committee at the turn of the last century. Complete party failure was experienced by the Federalists and the Whigs. But, most often, as new challenges generate new institutional arrangements, these are built upon inherited structures (Schickler 2001). The floor leadership position, invented in obscurity in the 1890s, has proved to be remarkably durable. As long as an innovation continues to serve the party's interest, it will survive long beyond the life span of the senators who initially were most advantaged by it and well past the competitive circumstances of its origins. And imitation is a Senate party's highest form of flattery. As parties have competed through the years, successful innovations initiated by one party are embraced and extended by the other party—a coevolutionary process. Competition between the parties, over many generations, has created in the U.S. Senate a remarkable hothouse of institutional tinkering and experimentation, and neither party has held a patent on its best discoveries.

The earliest photograph (a daguerreotype) of the Capitol. Taken in 1846, it shows the building before the new House and Senate wings were constructed during the 1850s and the new dome was completed in the 1860s.

Library of Congress, Prints & Photographs Division, reproduction number LC-USZ62-110213

OVERVIEW

The book proceeds chronologically, which allows us to emphasize the context, sequence, and timing of important developments in Senate party organization. In each chapter, our focus is on identifying those developments, providing detailed evidence, much of it newly discovered, to document each innovation. Crucially, given our theoretical approach, we specify when each new institution is created. Chapter by chapter, we examine, too, how institutional innovation relates to periods of competitive parties and, where relevant, the roles played by factions and entrepreneurs. The generally cumulative nature of party organizational development quickly becomes obvious. The political context evolves and leaders adapt, but some important elements of modern Senate party organization—above all, the primacy of the caucus, over both the floor and the rostrum, for solving collective action problems—can be traced back to the first half of the nineteenth century.

Senate party organization emerged and has changed in response to the challenge of securing common goals. For most of the nineteenth century, that meant simply achieving a measure of cooperation within the caucus. But, over time, solving collective action and coordination problems meant developing institutions that could provide active leadership on the Senate floor and extend the reach of the caucus beyond the chamber entirely. Since the middle of the twentieth century, modern Senate leadership has been defined by a set of discrete functions or activities (Ripley 1969a, 1969b):

Party management. Each party has conference meetings that must be organized and led; a staff, budget, and office space that must be managed; and party committees that must be appointed.

Floor management. Each party has assigned responsibilities for planning a floor schedule, making motions on behalf of the party, and overseeing floor activity.

Intermediary with the president and House. Each party is represented in regular and irregular meetings at the White House and in relations with other administration officials, House leaders, and others.

Party spokespersonship. Each party's leaders serve as spokespersons in public and media venues and maintain a public relations operation, sometimes in the form of a party committee or task force.

Coalition building. Each party's leaders seek to build coalitions to pass or block legislation, often in alliance with the president, interest groups, and others.

These activities are how leaders promote the party's collective goals of enhancing the party's reputation, gaining or holding majority status, and pursuing a legislative agenda. As the book proceeds, we are attentive to these different functions. In early chapters, our emphasis, like that of senators through most of the nineteenth century, is on the tasks of party management and coalition building, primarily in the legislative realm. Starting in the 1890s, however, senators created leadership positions that began to assume responsibility for all five functions and expanded their reach to elections and the party brand, so, in examining Senate organization since the late nineteenth century, we focus on how new institutions came to perform these activities.

We begin our account with the presiding officer, in Chapter 2. The failure of the vice president—even more, the failure of the president pro tempore, who unlike the vice president is elected by the Senate—to become a party leader is a puzzle. Perhaps the weakness of the vice president was preordained by the inability of senators to hold him accountable, but, even so, this development took decades. However, as someone chosen by their fellow senators—selected, like the speaker of the House, and eventually by the majority party's caucus and ratified by the full chamber—it is not immediately clear why the president pro tempore did not consolidate in the Senate powers comparable to those of the House speaker. Indeed, in the late 1830s and early 1840s, a full half-century after the first Congress, the president pro tempore, like the speaker, was routinely exercising the power to name the chairs and members of all standing committees; elections for president pro tempore were contested and closely watched; and no seniority rule existed. But, as we show in Chapter 2, the influence of the president pro tempore over the Senate's affairs reached its zenith in the early 1840s. Although senators continued to refine the office's responsibilities for maintaining order and enforcing rules, the position of the Senate's presiding officer never fulfilled its early promise.

In its place, the party caucus emerged. As we show in Chapter 3, senators met in caucus only infrequently in the first half-century of the chamber's history. From the 1790s through the 1830s, caucus meetings were controversial affairs, seen by many as illegal assemblies of public officials, and meetings rarely focused on legislative business. The most notable use of early caucuses was by Republicans in the two chambers, who gathered on a quadrennial basis to nominate their presidential candidate. But, in 1841–45, led by the Whigs, the modern Senate party caucuses were born. In that brief period of time, senators began utilizing caucuses on a regular basis, both to conduct legislative business and to organize the membership of the Senate's standing committees. In later years, first in 1856–62, then in the 1870s, Republicans and Democrats gave new structure and permanence to their caucuses. They created formal positions in the caucus, such as a regular caucus chairman, and caucus committees, including committees on committees, campaign committees, and ad hoc committees on the order of business. From time to time, individual senators emerged as de facto leaders in the chamber, but these senators—people like Thomas Hart Benton (Mo.), Henry Clay (Ky.), John C. Calhoun (S.C.), and Daniel Webster (Mass.)—did not serve their caucuses in any formal, elected capacity.

The emergence of the Senate caucus in 1841–45 coincided with the rise of a competitive two-party system, both in the electorate and in the Senate. Whigs gained their first Senate majority with the 1840 elections, and, as they organized the Senate in 1841, they relied heavily on the caucus as an institution. As Figure 1.1 shows, the early and mid-1840s was a time of intense party competition between the nation's first two broad-based political parties, the Democrats and the Whigs. Between 1839 and 1847, the majority party never held more than 34 seats and the minority party never had fewer than 22 seats. The Democrats controlled the Senate until 1841, then the Whigs were in the majority for four years, and then the Democrats regained control in 1845. From 1845 through the late 1850s, the Senate was dominated by the Democratic party. Opposition parties—whether Whigs, Know-Nothings, Free Soilers, or early Republicans—represented a small minority in those years. But, with the invention of the Republican party in the mid-1850s, Democrats came to face a new threat. Republicans, who held one seat in the 34th Congress (1855–57), held 20 seats in the 35th Congress (1857–59), 26 seats in the 36th Congress (1859–61), and, with the secession of southern states, a large majority starting in 1861.

Figure 1.2 shows the relative size of Senate parties from the organization of the Republican party in the 1850s through the present day. Several periods, scattered over time, exhibited near parity in party strength. The first came in the aftermath of Reconstruction, from the mid-1870s through the mid-1890s. Then, in the 1911–21 decade, came a second era of close competition, with

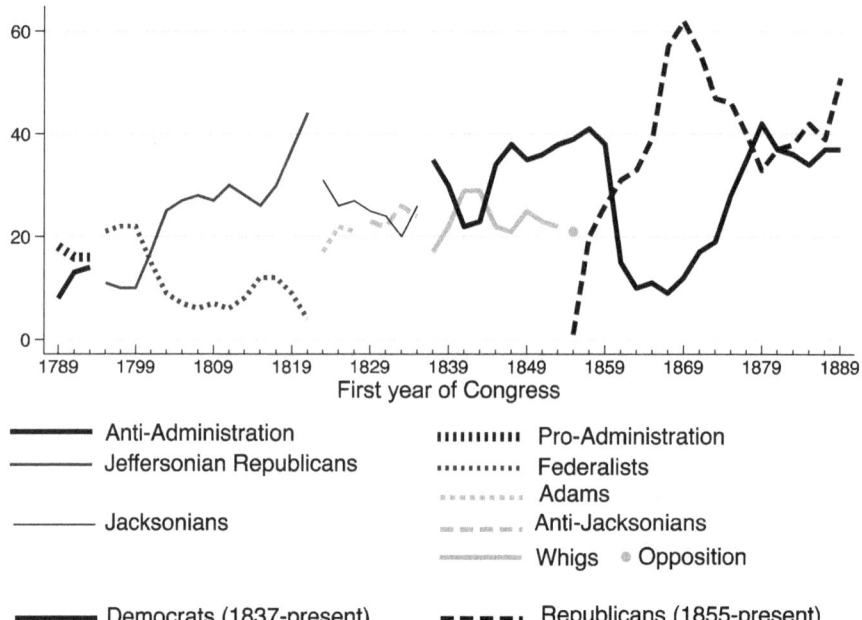

First year of Congress

────	Anti-Administration	ııııııııı	Pro-Administration
────	Jeffersonian Republicans	··········	Federalists
		·········	Adams
────	Jacksonians	── ── ── ·	Anti-Jacksonians
		════════	Whigs ● Opposition
────	Democrats (1837-present)	── ── ── ·	Republicans (1855-present)

FIGURE 1.1 Size of Senate parties, 1789–1889

Source: www.senate.gov

three Democratic majorities and two Republican majorities, all of them narrow. Small Republican majorities in 1927–29 and 1931–33 were surrounded by larger majorities in the 1920s and large Democratic majorities in the 1930s and early 1940s. Republican election victories in 1946 then initiated a period of intense competition and small majorities lasting through the 1950s. Democrats controlled the chamber by large margins in the 1960s and 1970s. The 1980 election proved to be a dramatic turning point: for more than 40 years since then, the parties have regularly alternated control of a Senate in which the majority party has never exceeded 60 seats and averaged fewer than 54 seats.

As Chapter 4 discusses, the closely divided Senates between the late 1870s and early 1890s was a period of remarkable innovation in the Senate. In 1881, each party controlled the same number of seats, something that had never before occurred in Senate history. It was in that Senate, in 1882–83, that Republicans invented a wholly new institution, which they gave the name "steering committee." As we show, the Republican steering committee built on precedents established by both parties, but the institution that emerged in 1882–83 was truly novel. Over the next decade, both parties, but especially Republicans, regularly turned to steering committees to manage their caucus's business. Then, in 1892–93, the Republican steering committee was strengthened and redefined, making it the dominant institution of the dominant Senate party for the next two decades. Facing the prospect of losing their majority following the 1892 elections, Republican senators mobilized, first to try to influence the state

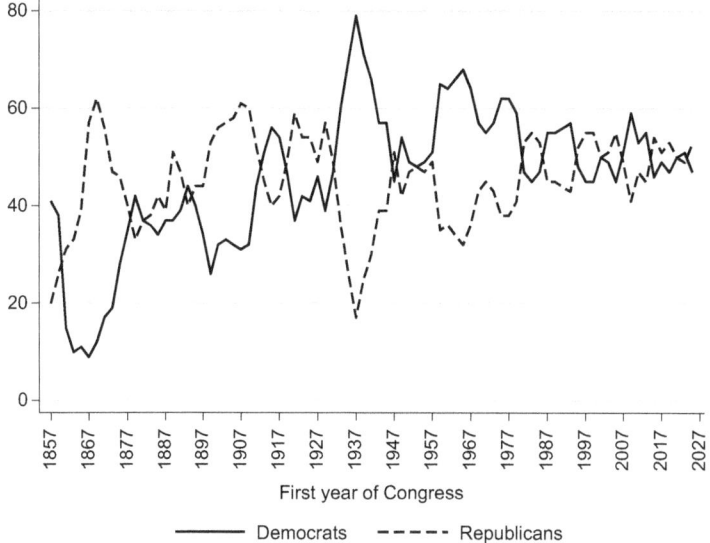

FIGURE 1.2 Size of major Senate parties, 1857–2025

Source: www.senate.gov. Independents and minor party senators counted in the major party with which they caucused; minor party senators not caucusing with major parties excluded.

legislatures picking new senators and then to manage the legislative process. In Chapter 4, we detail the reorganization of the steering committee in 1892–93 as a permanent, ongoing standing committee of the Republican caucus. Created by a competitive party suddenly in the minority, the committee came to eclipse the caucus itself once Republicans regained majority status in 1895. During these years, Republican leadership in the Senate was centered in a handful of men: Nelson Aldrich (R, R.I.), William Allison (R, Iowa), Orville Platt (R, Conn.), Eugene Hale (R, Maine), and John Spooner (R, Wisc.). The group functioned as an interlocking directorate of Republican committee and party leaders, with Allison and Hale serving as caucus chairmen for most of this period and all but Platt serving regularly on the steering committee.

The Senate parties had been competitive since the 1870s, but, in the early 1890s, the intensity of competition was exacerbated by the waning battle by Republicans to secure voting rights for Black men in the South. For years, white southerners had worked to erect new structures of white supremacy and racist oppression, undermining Reconstruction-era gains for civil and political rights for southern Blacks. The Federal Elections Bill of 1890–91 represented the last attempt, for the next two-thirds of a century, to protect the right to vote. Chapter 5 examines this battle and its transformative impact for the Senate. Faced with the prospect of reenfranchised Black voters, an overwhelmingly Republican group, and thus the end of Democratic hegemony in the South, Senate Democrats regarded the battle against the bill as an existential fight. Leading them in battle was Arthur Pue Gorman (D, Md.), who, in the process of defeating the Federal Elections Bill, honed the filibuster as a weapon of minority obstruction and transformed the position of caucus chairman, at least for the minority Democratic party, into a position of elected floor leadership. Modern party leadership in the Senate, we show, traces its birth to Gorman and to this battle.

With the 1912 elections, 18 years of Republican control of the Senate came to an abrupt end. In Chapter 6, we examine the institutional inventions of the 63rd Congress (1913–15), when, in a newly competitive world, the Democratic floor leader—John W. Kern (D, Ind.), a progressive senator closely allied with the newly elected president Woodrow Wilson—became the first person widely regarded as an elected majority leader of the Senate, with responsibility for devising and implementing party strategy. The Republicans, now in the minority, created their own position of elected floor leader in 1913, following the generation-old Democratic model, and both parties invented the position of whip. Other developments, such as the emergence of the modern use of unanimous consent agreements, the creation of party floor staff, and, for the Democrats, the practice of entrusting committee assignments to their leadership, were accomplished in the 1910s and 1920s.

Between the mid-1920s and mid-1940s, the two Senate parties strengthened the position of floor leadership, building on the foundations laid by Gorman in the 1890s and on the innovations of the 1910s. This era of consolidation—a period first of Republican dominance, then of extended Democratic dominance, interrupted by a short period of competitiveness—is the subject of Chapter 7. Charles Curtis (R, Kans.), who became Republican leader in 1924, elaborated leadership posts as he navigated factionalism within his party. The New Deal elections left the Republican conference depleted—down to 16 members in 1937—so they minimized their formal organization in the 1930s and waited until 1944 to reinvent it. Democrats in this era were led by Joe Robinson (D, Ark.) and Alben Barkley (D, Ky.), who centralized power in the floor leadership position and wielded it effectively but otherwise made few organizational changes.

Informed observers of the Senate may view the 1945–80 period as the doldrums of Senate party history, a period of stasis, the unchanging "textbook Congress" (Shepsle 1989). The study of Congress in these years has long emphasized the role of weak parties and a decentralized policymaking process dominated by committees and their chairmen. However, as we discover in Chapter 8, the parties under Robert Taft (R, Ohio) and Lyndon Johnson (D, Tex.) were dynamic, establishing organizational foundations that shaped future developments and patterns of leadership behavior. We emphasize four developments, none of which have been emphasized in other accounts: evolving new venues for collective decision-making, expanding staff resources, adopting new committee assignment practices, and establishing more consequential campaign committees. These developments were responses to the parties' electoral challenges, factional problems, and personal interests of key leaders.

The 1970s and 1980s proved to be transitional years. At first, it appeared that individualism had taken hold in the Senate, undermining the influence of both leaders and standing committees, but, as Chapter 9 shows, partisan conflict intensified during the 1980s and senators began demanding more effective party organizations and leadership. The Democratic leader, Robert Byrd (D, W.Va.), was challenged for Democratic floor leader in 1986 and two years later gave up his post because he was not meeting his colleagues' expectations as a team leader and party spokesman. By the mid-1990s, party leaders not only served as their parties' chief strategists on floor procedure but increasingly guided the tandem tasks of writing important legislation and fashioning media strategies. Procedural maneuvering intensified on the Senate floor, which placed floor leaders in the middle of every legislative battle. By the 2020s, Senate policymaking was remarkably centralized in the two floor leaders, Mitch McConnell and Chuck Schumer. The Senate reached 2024 with stronger central party leaders and more elaborate organizations than ever before.

CONCLUSION

The ability of Senate floor leaders to marshal legislative, public relations, and campaign resources on behalf of their parties has never been greater than it is today. The two floor leaders are the central players in performing each of the major functions of their parties, and the organizational apparatus of each party centers on them. No earlier senator, not Henry Clay or Nelson Aldrich or Lyndon Johnson, had an array of resources comparable to those available to Reid, McConnell, and Schumer. How modern floor leaders use their resources and perform those functions remains contingent and circumscribed, conditioned in large part by the demands placed on them by party colleagues. In recent decades, intensifying partisan polarization and political competition has produced demands for effective party strategies that leaders are expected to devise and implement, which has prompted leader-generated legislative agendas, leader-led negotiations on major legislation, and leader-centered public relations efforts, all backed by enlarged leadership staffs.

Party organization and leadership roles have a cumulative character. In this regard, we diverge from the literature on conditional party government, which suggests that powers accumulate when parties are strong and polarized, and then dissipate when partisan coalitions overlap. As we argue instead, leaders rarely give up resources that they have inherited. They use what they are given and make incremental improvements, and then, occasionally, exhibit a willingness to remodel party organization and resources when their colleagues allow or even demand it. Today's Senate leaders, as a consequence, benefit not only from an era of minimal factionalism and high levels of party competition but also from the accretion of earlier innovations. On the House side of the Capitol, party leadership rests in the speakership, in a position defined in the Constitution of 1787 and well-developed as a party institution by the time of the Civil War. Senate party organization and leadership, in contrast, are endogenous to the Senate itself. The floor leaders of the 2020s are inheritors of 235 years of tinkering, of dead ends long abandoned, of lessons learned and remembered, and of a multitude of useful scraps that are now part of the institution's warp and woof.

View of the Senate of the United States in Session.

The Old Senate Chamber in the U.S. Capitol in 1850, from an engraving. The Senate used this chamber from 1810 until 1859, when it moved into the newly completed Senate wing of the Capitol.

View of the Senate in Session, by J. Rodgers (artist) and Edward Anthony (publisher), ca. 1850, hand-colored engraving, Office of the Senate Curator, Accession No. 38.00911.001

2

Presiding Officer, 1789–1914

In the final days of the Constitutional Convention, the framers placed the vice president at the head of the Senate. The framers had given little thought to the creation of the vice presidency; the office itself was a by-product of the process for choosing a president. They gave even less attention to the consequences of naming the vice president as the Senate's presiding officer. "If the vice-President were not to be President of the Senate, he would be without employment," Roger Sherman (Conn.) explained. Following such reasoning and by a vote of eight states to two, delegates adopted the provision (Farrand 1966, ii: 537). Within a few days, and apparently without discussion, the delegates adopted the provision that "the Senate shall choose their other officers, and also a President pro tempore, in the absence of the Vice-President, or when he shall exercise the office of President of the United States" (Farrand 1966, ii: 592).

Their hasty decisions—and the corresponding constitutional clause that "the House of Representatives shall chuse their Speaker"—is a major reason why the House and Senate are radically different in their internal organization, their leadership structures, and their rules. George Mason (Va.), who opposed the provision at the Constitutional Convention, "thought the office of vice-President an encroachment on the rights of the Senate" (Farrand 1966, ii: 537). More than two centuries of evidence have confirmed Mason's fear. Because senators cannot choose their regular presiding officer, they could never trust their chair with the powers that the House assigned to the speaker. "The differences between the two houses," Kravitz (ca. 1971, v: 1) wrote, "is nowhere more striking than in the comparative stature of their presiding officers." As Woodrow Wilson (1885, 241) wrote, in reference to the vice president, "The chief embarrassment in discussing his office is, that in explaining how little there is to be said about it one has evidently said all there is to say."

Joseph Bailey (D, Tex.) stated the matter plainly, addressing Vice President James S. Sherman in 1910. "We do not choose our Presiding Officer. He is chosen, as the President is chosen, by the electoral college, and we have no power ourselves to depose him," Bailey explained on the Senate floor (*Cong. Rec.*, December 19, 1910, 473, as cited in Nelson 1980, 4–5). "Remembering that he is put over us without our consent, and often over our protest, the Senate can not be too resolutely insistent that he shall merely execute the rules, not as he may think they ought to be read and administered, but as they have been read and as they have been understood by this body from time out of mind." Charles Curtis (R, Kans.), who had served as the Senate Republican leader before becoming vice president, understood the limitations of the new role. "My service among you has impressed me with the responsibilities of every Senator, and at the same time it has given me a clear understanding of the duties and obligations of the Vice President," Curtis stated in March 1929, upon assuming his new position (*Cong. Rec.*, March 4, 1929, 3, as cited in Nelson 1980, 5). "He is not one of the makers of the law, nor is he consulted about the rules adopted to govern your actions."

The failure of the vice president as a Senate leader was nearly preordained by the inability of senators to hold him accountable, but the failure of the president pro tempore presents an intriguing puzzle. Chosen by the Senate—selected, like the speaker of the House, by the majority party's caucus and ratified by the full chamber—the president pro tempore might have emerged as a powerful leader. Indeed, in the late 1830s and early 1840s, a full half-century after the first Congress, the president pro tempore, like the speaker, was routinely exercising the power to name the chairs and members of all standing committees. Elections for president pro tempore were contested and closely watched. No seniority rule existed. But the influence of the president pro tempore over the Senate's affairs reached its zenith in the early 1840s. Although senators continued to refine the office's responsibilities for maintaining order and enforcing rules, the office of president pro tempore never fulfilled its early promise.

Political scientists offer two principal explanations—the instability of the office and the place of the president pro tempore in the line of presidential succession—in accounting for this failure. Both explanations are useful and they call attention to long-term weaknesses in the position of the president pro tempore relative to that of the House speaker. But institutional change is not a matter of inevitability.

What these conventional explanations cannot convey is the extent to which senators looked to the president pro tempore for leadership in the first decades of the nineteenth century. Until the 1840s, granting powers to the president pro tempore was a principal vehicle for solving collective action problems in the Senate. Understanding the failure of the president pro tempore to sustain these powers means reckoning with the extent to which institutional change is a consequence of short-term political calculations. It means reckoning, too, with the overriding need of senators to solve collective action and coordination problems. Not until senators devised an alternative method for solving these problems could they permanently turn away from the president pro tempore as a potential solution. Consequently, the events of 1845 represented a watershed in Senate development not because senators removed committee-naming power from their presiding officer—this they had done twice before, only to restore it quickly—but because they constructed an alternative mechanism, the caucus, that could effectively assign members to committees.

In assuming this power in 1845, the party caucus created a new path for solving one of the Senate's central, persistent collective action problems. Five decades later, the president pro tempore no longer suffered from the disabilities identified by previous scholars: he now held his position at the pleasure of the Senate and he no longer stood after the vice president in the line of presidential succession. Given the president pro tempore's constitutional stature, the new permanence of his position and his accountability to the Senate, the assertion in 1890 of broad new powers by the House's presiding officer, and the lack of any other prominent elected leader in the Senate, circumstances at the turn of the century would seem to have favored the emergence of the president pro tempore as a strong Senate leader. Yet the obvious did not happen. As senators grappled to resolve a variety of collective action problems in the late nineteenth and early twentieth centuries, they did not look to the president pro tempore for leadership. Instead, they continued to turn to the caucus and its still-obscure officers, establishing steering committees and inventing the office of floor leader. The existence of this alternate arena rendered stillborn any effort to vest power in the president pro tempore.

THE SELECTION OF PRESIDENTS PRO TEMPORE

In March 1890, senators resolved to place the office of president pro tempore on a permanent footing. Until then, the rules and practice of the Senate had stated that the position of president pro tempore existed only in the absence of the vice president. Not only did a senator cease to exercise the duties of presiding officer when the vice president reappeared in the chamber, but the office itself was instantly dissolved. As late as 1876, senators had even questioned their own ability to remove a president pro tempore from office, with many of them arguing that only the vice president's arrival could terminate the term of a president pro tempore. With the 1890 resolution, the Senate declared that the president pro tempore held his office at the pleasure of the Senate and that the office existed without regard to the presence or absence of the vice president. Four years before, in 1886, Congress had removed the president pro tempore and speaker from the line of presidential succession.

Explaining the failure of the president pro tempore to become the leader of the Senate, scholars have called attention to the pre-1886 succession act, which placed the president pro tempore immediately after the vice president in line for the presidency (McConachie 1898, 332; Wilson 1908, 132; Haynes 1938, i:

256–59; McConnell and Brownell 2019, 45). This law generated various maneuvers by the vice president and the Senate majority that were unrelated to the business of leading the Senate. The usual, and least pernicious, effect of the old succession act was to encourage vice presidents to leave the Senate before a session ended, so that senators could elect a president pro tempore for the ensuing recess. But when vice presidents did not enjoy the support of the Senate majority, vice presidents often refused to leave their posts, which created anxiety and occasional conflict.

More significant than the succession act for the presiding officer's weakness was the pre-1890 understanding that presidents pro tempore did not exist when the vice president was in the Senate chamber (Kerr 1895, 24–25; McConachie 1898, 332–38; Wilson 1908, 132–33; Riddick 1949, 60; Kravitz ca. 1971, v: 49–54; Swanstrom 1988, 257–58; Byrd 1991, 175–76; Swift 1996, 76–77; McConnell and Brownell 2019, 45). However, the effect of the non-continuous term of the office is easily exaggerated. Although nineteenth-century senators understood that official "terms" ended with the appearance of the vice president, a presumptive president pro tempore existed throughout a Congress. Solomon Foot (R, Vt.) was chosen 12 consecutive times in 1861–64, Lafayette Foster (R, Conn.) served continuously from 1865 to 1867, Benjamin Wade (R, Ohio) served continuously from 1867 to 1869, and Henry B. Anthony (R, R.I.) was chosen 15 consecutive times between 1869 and 1873. Discussing possible successors to Anthony in March 1873, the *New York Times* described Anthony's tenure as a continuous four-year term—rather than as 15 terms interrupted by appearances of the vice president. "Senator Anthony, after having been unanimously chosen for four years to fill the office of President pro tempore of the Senate, has declined re-election, and Senator Carpenter was designated by the caucus to succeed him," the *Times* reported. "It has been usual for the same Senator to hold this position only through one Congress. Mr. Foote [sic] was President two [sic] years, and Foster, of Connecticut, two years. Mr. Anthony was paid the unusual compliment of an election for four years, and would have been chosen for two years more if he had not himself declined."[1]

Table A.3 lists every president pro tempore in Senate history, with their terms of office; to create the table, we examined the entire run of *Senate Journals* as well as records of Senate debates and the signatures on several enrolled bills.[2] From the vantage point of 1890—one century into the Senate's history—the position of president pro tempore had already been reduced to an

---

[1] "Senator Anthony Declines Re-Election," *New York Times*, Mar. 9, 1873, 1.
[2] No list of presidents pro tempore with dates of service has previously existed. Most of the research for this table was done by Scott Amrozowicz and Jeff Jackson. Drawing on an unpublished draft of the table we present here, the Senate Historical Office updated its own records and website. The table now appears online at: www.senate.gov/artandhistory/history/common/briefing/President_Pro_Tempore.htm#5, website accessed February 9, 2025.

honorific position. The term of office had been made continuous, and the post had been removed from the line of presidential succession. But in 1890 it bore no comparison to the extraordinary office that the House speakership had become under Thomas B. Reed. There was no seniority system—of 13 senators elected president pro tempore between 1870 and 1900, just two ranked first in their party—but senators instead tended to elect men who were distinguished, popular, and familiar with parliamentary law. According to the *New York Times*, John J. Ingalls (R, Kans.) was elected in 1887 because he is "one of the best parliamentarians in the Senate, and he has the ability to put business through with neatness and dispatch." Moreover, the *Times* noted, Ingalls "has also the not unimportant advantage of a voice that can be heard in every nook and cranny of the chamber."[3] Charles F. Manderson (R, Nebr.), chosen four years later, possessed similar gifts. As the *Times* reported, "He is a gentleman of attractive manners, a good orator, is familiar with the rules of the Senate, and is popular among his associates."[4] Geographical considerations also mattered, at least at the margins, as senators attempted to balance the regions of the president pro tempore with both the majority caucus chairman (Haynes 1938, i: 255) and the vice president.[5]

Presidents pro tempore in the late nineteenth century recognized that the office was an honor that carried with it more burdens than responsibility. "It has one or two places in its gift more than ordinary Senators have, and the salary is $8,000 a year, against $5,000 for an ordinary Senator," the *New York Times* observed in 1887. "These and the supposed honor of the office are all the advantages of the Senate Presidency."[6] William Allison (R, Iowa), indicated in 1883 that he had no interest in serving as president pro tempore, since the office would take him away from the far more interesting work of chairing the Appropriations Committee.[7] That same year, the *Times* indicated that, because of his seniority and popularity, Henry B. Anthony was the obvious candidate for president pro tempore. His age and poor health made it unlikely that Anthony could actively preside, but this was no impediment to the honor. "He may receive the title out of the consideration and esteem in which he is held by both sides of the Chamber," according to the *Times*, "but younger men will have to hold the gavel through the long hours of droning debate."[8]

---

[3] "An effort will be made by the Republican senators . . . ," *New York Times*, Feb. 24, 1887, 1.
[4] "The Expiring Congress," *New York Times*, Mar. 2, 1891, 5.
[5] "The President Pro Tem," *New York Times*, Mar. 9, 1875, 1. In fact, there was a tendency for the caucus chairs and presidents pro tempore to come from different regions of the country, although we have not found explicit references by senators to this consideration.
[6] "An effort will be made by the Republican senators . . . ," *New York Times*, Feb. 24, 1887, 1.
[7] "Avoiding a Special Session," *New York Times*, Feb. 28, 1883, 1.
[8] "Senator Anthony," *New York Times*, Oct. 30, 1883, 1.

Vice President George M. Dallas. In the 1840s he was presiding over the Senate when senators rejected his authority to name a temporary presiding officer and also when they first turned to their caucuses to make committee assignments.

Harry T. Peters, "America on Stone" Lithography Collection

Until the 1850s, the right of vice presidents and presidents pro tempore to designate temporary presiding officers was not generally recognized. When Vice President George M. Dallas notified the Senate in December 1845 that he would be absent and that he had asked Ambrose Sevier (D, Ark.) to preside in his place for the day, John J. Crittenden (W, Ky.) immediately challenged the vice president's authority. "He had no kind of personal objection to the honorable Senator who was in the chair—very far from it," Crittenden declared. "But it occurred to him that the Vice President had no right to commission any one to preside over the body. It was a matter for the Senate itself to determine, in the absence of the presiding officer" (*Cong. Globe*, December 27, 1845, 95–96, as quoted in Gilfry 1911, 22–23). Although Crittenden agreed to withdraw his motion, he objected again in January 1847, the next time that Dallas attempted to appoint a presiding officer for a day. This time, a majority of the Senate supported Crittenden's position and firmly rejected Dallas's right to name David R. Atchison (D, Mo.) to the chair. In a series of votes, senators first refused to pass a resolution appointing Atchison president pro tempore, then approved a resolution to hold an election for president pro tempore, and then finally chose Atchison themselves in the election (*Senate Journal*, January 11, 1847, 91–92, as cited in Gilfry 1911, 24–25; see also Kravitz ca. 1971, v: 29). Senators defending the vice president's right to name a temporary presiding officer cited Samuel Southard (W, N.J.), who as president pro tempore had exercised this right several times in the early 1840s. But George Badger (W, N.C.) rejected this as precedent, arguing that the status of the vice president, who was not a member of the Senate, differed fundamentally from that of the president pro tempore (*Cong. Globe*, January 11, 1847, 161–64, as cited in Gilfry 1911, 27). Other senators, however, rejected Badger's distinction between the two offices. "They are regarded as the same in the rule," William Allen (D, Ohio) observed. "They are treated precisely alike" (*Cong. Globe*, January 11, 1847, 161–64, as cited in Gilfry 1911, 28).

Although presidents pro tempore occasionally appointed temporary presiding officers in the 1840s and the early 1850s, their right to do so remained unsettled. On three different days in June 1856, Jesse D. Bright (D, Ind.), the president pro tempore, asked Charles E. Stuart (D, Mich.) to preside in his absence. On the first two occasions, senators offered no objection. But, on the third day, Crittenden rose in protest. "I deny that the President of the Senate has any right, by letter, to delegate his power to preside over this body," Crittenden stated. "It is a small affair now, but I think the Senate ought to have a little care of its own rights" (*Cong. Globe*, June 9, 1856, 1368). After a brief discussion, in which only the temporary chair himself attempted to justify Bright's action, the Senate rejected the appointment and then immediately elected Stuart president pro tempore. When Bright returned to the Senate two days later, he expressed his surprise at the dispute. "In requesting the honorable Senator from Michigan [Mr. Stuart] to preside during my absence," Bright explained from the chair, "I but followed precedent after precedent to be found in the Journal of the Senate's proceedings" (*Cong. Globe*, June 11, 1856, 1385).

Bright's explanation in June 1856 seems to have satisfied senators. Beginning that year, the *Congressional Globe* began regularly identifying the "presiding officers" who temporarily occupied the chair during a daily session. But presidents pro tempore and vice presidents appear to have used this right sparingly until the late 1870s. Not until 1879 does Gilfry (1911, 111) identify another instance of a president pro tempore naming a presiding officer to serve an entire day. In 1882, when the practice was challenged again, the Senate amended its rules to authorize the president pro tempore to "designate, in writing, a Senator to perform the duties of the Chair" (Furber 1893, 167, 188–89). Increased reliance on this practice probably reflected the widespread understanding that the work of the presiding officer had grown tiresome. Distinguished senators accepted the honor with gratitude, but, beginning in the 1840s—when the office of president pro tempore declined in importance—they began asking others to perform the actual work.

To analyze changing patterns in the occupancy of the chair, we examined a full week in every fourth Congress. From the 1850s through the 1940s, either the vice president or the president pro tempore personally occupied the chair at the start of nearly every daily session; on average, they named one or two temporary presiding officers to relieve them in the course of a typical day. From the 1950s until the 1970s, both the president pro tempore and vice president continued to sit in the chair at least once or twice in a week, but "acting presidents pro tempore" began to appear on a frequent basis in the place of the two constitutional officers. An average of five temporary presiding officers served each day. In the sample weeks since the 1980s, the vice president does not sit in the chair, presidents pro tempore and "acting presidents pro tempore" open daily sessions, and an average of eight other senators sit in the chair each day.

The growing reliance on temporary presiding officers since the 1940s reflects not only the weakness of the office but the development of a seniority system. As Table A.3 shows, seniority did not become a determining consideration until the 1940s, with the election of Kenneth McKellar (D, Tenn.). Since McKellar's election, presidents pro tempore have been selected on a strict seniority basis (McConnell and Brownell 2019, 47). Senators adopted a seniority system for the president pro tempore two decades after the Senate Republican conference had abandoned seniority as its rule for selecting a caucus chairman and floor leader. In electing Charles Curtis (R, Kans.) as majority leader in 1924, Republicans broke with a half-century of precedent, recognizing the need for vigor and ability in the office. The caucus chair—now also the floor leader—was no longer an elderly, distinguished senator who quietly presided over the boisterous, powerful caucus. The caucus chair had real work to do, and the distinguished, long-serving gentlewoman or gentleman now presided over the Senate.

COLLECTIVE ACTION PROBLEMS AND THE LEADERSHIP OF THE CHAIR, 1816–56

From the start, senators struggled to balance their individual prerogatives against the need for chamber-wide coordination. They kept agenda-setting power on the Senate floor. But they gave their presiding officer—above all, the president pro tempore, whom they elected—significant powers in the first half of the nineteenth century. During three different periods, they entrusted the presiding officer with the power to name standing committees. And they also initially empowered their presiding officer to enforce order, decorum, and relevancy in debate. Presiding officers themselves abdicated their role in judging relevancy and diminished their ability to maintain order. And, responding to short-term concerns, senators, on three occasions, reclaimed the power to make committee assignments. The third occasion proved decisive, as senators of both parties transferred the power to their caucuses.

More than any deficiency inherent in the office of president pro tempore, the rise of party organization and the ability of the caucuses to coordinate the Senate's business precluded the restoration of these powers to the president pro tempore. "Caucuses with their chairmen and their committee machinery," McConachie observed in 1898 (343), "have been [the Senate's] only escape from dire confusion and weakness of leadership due to Constitutional difficulties." Wilson, writing a decade later, also recognized that caucuses, caucus committees, and caucus chairs had become the real leaders of the Senate. The president pro tempore "is not in fact in command in debate or in the direction of party tactics," Wilson (1908, 133) contended. "The leader of the Senate is the chairman of the majority caucus. Each party in the Senate finds its real, its permanent, its effective organization in its caucus, and follows the leadership, in all important parliamentary battles, of the chairman of that caucus, its organization and its leadership alike resting upon arrangements quite outside the Constitution."

Although Wilson exaggerated the influence of the caucus chair—not until the 1910s, as we show later, did both parties begin recognizing their caucus chairmen as their floor leaders—he understood that the Senate's collective action problems were resolved in caucus and not by the presiding officer. What neither McConachie nor Wilson explored, though, was the extent to which party organization was both consequence and cause of the weakness of the presiding officer: consequence, because the instability of the president pro tempore's office in 1845 helped lay the groundwork for the modern caucus; cause, because the modern caucus, once created, proved more reliable than the presiding officer for solving collective action problems of any political importance.

Committee Assignments

The Senate standing committee system was born in December 1816, at the start of the second session of the 14th Congress (Gamm and Shepsle 1989, 53–57).

James Barbour (R, Va.) proposed that the Senate adopt a rule "to appoint at each session certain standing Committees"—"the same as are now appointed by the House of Representatives," the *New York Evening Post* explained in a parenthetical aside—and the resolution was adopted.[9] After approving the resolution, senators elected the committees, balloting separately for each member. This was time-consuming work. "The sitting of the Senate, yesterday," the *Daily National Intelligencer* reported a few days later, "was almost entirely occupied in balloting for the numerous committees they have determined to establish."[10]

Since then, the Senate has named its standing committees on a routine, regular basis. Table 2.1—based on the *Senate Journal* for each session, as well as the *Annals*, the *Register of Debates*, the *Congressional Globe*, and newspaper accounts—identifies the method of committee assignment for each regular session of Congress between 1816, when committees were first named, and 1865, when the modern system of assignment was well established.

As Table 2.1 shows, the Senate delegated committee assignment power to its presiding officer at three different times (not including 1850): 1823–25, 1829–32, and 1837–44. With the exceptions of vice presidents John C. Calhoun in 1825 and Richard M. Johnson in 1837, all the assignments in regular sessions were made by presidents pro tempore. Calhoun's exercise of this power prompted senators to remove the power altogether from the chair for the next four sessions. And, as the only vice president in American history who was elected by the Senate (Kravitz ca. 1971, v: 19; McConnell and Brownell 2019, 19), Johnson was no typical vice president. (Indeed, in the case of Johnson, senators specifically noted in debate "that the arrangement should not be considered as a precedent."[11]) At the start of the 18th Congress in 1823, as Table 2.1 shows, senators had grown accustomed to their presidents pro tempore occupying the chair at the start of Congress; this had been the experience of four full Congresses. They regularly had presidents pro tempore preside throughout every session, as is illustrated in Figure 2.1. The message of the Senate was unmistakable: when they gave the power of committee appointments to the chair, they intended to give it only to an officer of their choosing. Most vice presidents understood that they were not welcome on the opening days of a new session. They left their chair before the previous session adjourned to permit the Senate to elect a president pro tempore. This practice, as the *New York Evening Post* explained in 1833, was designed not only to protect the succession to the presidency during the recess, but also to permit the president pro tempore to assume "the Chair at the beginning of the session, for the purpose of organizing the body, and to appoint Committees."[12]

[9] "Congress," *New York Evening Post*, Dec. 9, 1816, 2.

[10] "The sitting of the Senate . . . ," *Daily National Intelligencer*, Dec. 14, 1816, 2.

[11] "Twenty-fifth Congress," *Columbian Centinel*, Dec. 9, 1837, 2.

[12] "The opposition party in the Senate . . . ," *Evening Post* (New York, N.Y.), Dec. 12, 1833, 2, quoting the Washington *Globe*. See also Kravitz ca. 1971, v: 54–55; Niven 1983, 356.

TABLE 2.1 *Methods for Senate committee assignments, 1815–64*

Congress	Date	Vice president	V.P. opens session	Method for committee assignment
14th	Dec. 1815	None		No major committees
	Dec. 1816	None		Ballot
15th	Dec. 1817	Daniel D. Tompkins		Ballot
	Nov. 1818	Daniel D. Tompkins		Ballot
16th	Dec. 1819	Daniel D. Tompkins		Ballot
	Nov. 1820	Daniel D. Tompkins		Ballot
17th	Dec. 1821	Daniel D. Tompkins		Ballot
	Dec. 1822	Daniel D. Tompkins		Ballot
18th	Dec. 1823	Daniel D. Tompkins		President pro tempore
	Dec. 1824	Daniel D. Tompkins		President pro tempore
19th	Dec. 1825	John Calhoun	✓	Vice president
	Dec. 1826	John Calhoun	✓	Ballot
20th	Dec. 1827	John Calhoun	✓	Ballot
	Dec. 1828	John Calhoun		Ballot
21st	Dec. 1829	John Calhoun		President pro tempore
	Dec. 1830	John Calhoun		President pro tempore
22nd	Dec. 1831	John Calhoun		President pro tempore
	Dec. 1832	John Calhoun		President pro tempore
23rd	Dec. 1833	Martin Van Buren		Ballot
	Dec. 1834	Martin Van Buren	✓	Ballot
24th	Dec. 1835	Martin Van Buren	✓	Ballot
	Dec. 1836	Martin Van Buren	✓	Ballot
25th	Sept. 1837	Richard M. Johnson*	✓	Ballot; Vice president
	Dec. 1837	Richard M. Johnson	✓	Vice president
	Dec. 1838	Richard M. Johnson		President pro tempore
26th	Dec. 1839	Richard M. Johnson		President pro tempore
	Dec. 1840	Richard M. Johnson		President pro tempore
27th	June 1841	None		Ballot; President pro tempore
	Dec. 1841	None		President pro tempore
	Dec. 1842	None		President pro tempore
28th	Dec. 1843	None		President pro tempore
	Dec. 1844	None		President pro tempore
29th	Dec. 1845	George M. Dallas	✓	Ballot; Resolution
	Dec. 1846	George M. Dallas	✓	Ballot; Resolution
30th	Dec. 1847	George M. Dallas	✓	Resolution
	Dec. 1848	George M. Dallas		Resolution
31st	Dec. 1849	Millard Fillmore	✓	Ballot; Resolution
	Dec. 1850	None		President pro tempore
32nd	Dec. 1851	None		Resolution
	Dec. 1852	None		Resolution
33rd	Dec. 1853	None		Resolution
	Dec. 1854	None		Resolution

(*continued*)

TABLE 2.1 *(continued)*

Congress	Date	Vice president	V.P. opens session	Method for committee assignment
34th	Dec. 1855	None		Ballot; Resolution
	Aug. 1856	None		Resolution
	Dec. 1856	None		Resolution
35th	Dec. 1857	John C. Breckinridge		Resolution
	Dec. 1858	John C. Breckinridge	✓	Resolution
36th	Dec. 1859	John C. Breckinridge	✓	Resolution
	Dec. 1860	John C. Breckinridge	✓	Resolution
37th	July 1861	Hannibal Hamlin	✓	Resolution
	Dec. 1861	Hannibal Hamlin	✓	Resolution
	Dec. 1862	Hannibal Hamlin		Resolution
38th	Dec. 1863	Hannibal Hamlin	✓	Resolution
	Dec. 1864	Hannibal Hamlin		Resolution

* No vice-presidential candidate received a majority of electoral votes in the 1836 election. The U.S. Senate elected Richard M. Johnson vice president on February 8, 1837, the only time since the adoption of the Twelfth Amendment that the Senate has exercised this power and chosen its own president (Hatfield 1997, 121, 127).

Note. This table reports the method used for naming the chairmen and basic membership of the standing committees. In many cases, the Senate used a different method for filling vacancies. This table does not include the special sessions of the Senate, which were usually very brief. To determine the method for committee assignments, we consulted the *Senate Journal*, the *Annals of Congress*, the *Register of Debates*, and the *Congressional Globe*. Since official sources do not specify the method of assignments in the 1810s and early 1820s, for these years we also consulted the *New York Evening Post*.

Senators often assigned this power to their presidents pro tempore in these years because the only alternative method—balloting—was time-consuming and produced outcomes that accorded with no one's preferences. In aggregating votes one committee position at a time, senators annually rediscovered the perverse problem of collective action, as they struggled to coordinate assignments for large numbers of senators and committees without consuming too much time on the floor. Each time the Senate turned to their presiding officer—in 1823, 1829, and 1837—they understood the collective action problem and expressed the hope that empowering the president pro tempore to name committees would solve this problem. Barbour, proposing the new method in 1823, suggested that the Senate "adopt the practice of the House of Representatives, and give the selection of its Standing Committees to the presiding officer" (*Annals of Cong.*, 18th Cong., 1st Sess., 26, as cited in Swift 1996, 134). Felix Grundy (D, Tenn.), who offered the resolution in December 1837, "explained his object to be to save time and trouble" (*Cong. Globe*, December 6, 1837, 9). Four years before, when partisan considerations led the Senate's anti-Jackson majority to debate a return to balloting, William R. King (Jacksonian, Ala.) reminded his colleagues that the decision to abandon balloting and transfer the power to the president pro tempore had been wise:

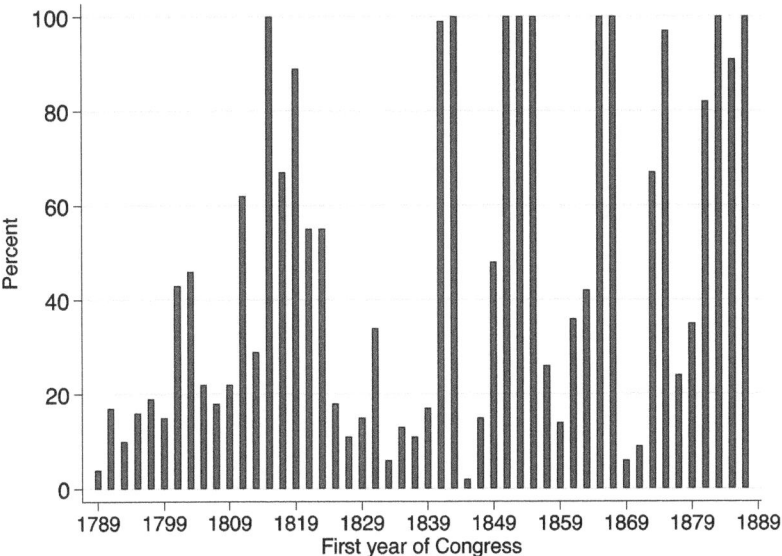

FIGURE 2.1 Terms of presidents pro tempore, as percent of all days in Congress

Note. This figure is based on the dates of service listed in Table A.3. In measuring the length of a president pro tempore's term, we count the total number of days that elapse between the beginning and end of each term, excluding recesses. This is similar to the method used by the *Congressional Directory* to measure the "length in days" of each session of Congress. The *Congressional Directory*, though, counts all elapsed days— including recesses. Consequently, we subtracted recesses from the total "length in days" reported in the *Congressional Directory*; in early Congresses for which recesses are not listed in the *Directory*, we subtracted Christmas recesses of at least four days.

They had placed the matter in the hands of an individual well calculated to fulfil the important duty which devolved upon him; one who knew the separate capabilities of each member—some gentlemen had talents for one description of business, others for another; one who would be able to parcel out the labor in a proper manner; one who was of, and amenable to, their own body; and one who had hitherto, in every respect, fulfilled his duties to their satisfaction. The matter is at present, he (Mr. K.) believed, settled in the manner most conducive to the general good; he saw no necessity for a change. By balloting for each member, four or five gentlemen might be chosen for the same committee. Arrangements might be made out of doors, and members might be influenced, for the moment, by popular individuals. (*Reg. of Debates*, December 9, 1833, 21)

Grundy, for reasons of partisanship as much as logic, agreed with King's assessment that the president pro tempore had successfully resolved this collective action problem for the Senate. "Since the alteration of the rule to its present form, Mr. G. had been sensible of no inconvenience," according to the *Register of Debates* (December 9, 1833, 21), "and he doubted whether there had been any sufficient to authorize a change, because it had been the instrument of harmony and despatch in their proceedings."

Three times, however, the Senate removed the power to make committee assignments from the presiding officer and returned it to the full Senate. For a Senate majority, the horrors of balloting were preferable to delegating this power to a presiding officer they had not chosen. The Senate's decision to resume balloting in 1826 reflected short-term considerations and the inability of a Senate majority to control its presiding officer. In that year, the problem was straightforward: the vice president sat in the chair, preventing a president pro tempore from exercising the power to name committees. The vice president was Calhoun, who was angered by the decision of the House of Representatives a year earlier to elect John Quincy Adams president, even though Andrew Jackson had received a plurality (though not a majority) of electoral and popular votes, and who believed that Adams had struck a "corrupt bargain" with Speaker of the House Henry Clay, whom Adams appointed as his secretary of state. "Calhoun, taking the Chair contrary to precedent on the opening day of the Nineteenth Congress, assumed this power," Haynes (1938, i: 274) explained, "and appointed the committees with such obvious bias that the session was only four months old when, with hardly a dissenting vote, the Senate took the appointment of committees away" from its presiding officer. "It has been charged upon him [Calhoun] that he took the chair ... with a view of appointing committees of the Senate, (more especially the committee on Foreign Relations) which might be hostile to the Secretary of State and to the President," according to the *Richmond Enquirer*, "and that he has spared no effort, which policy could supply, to get up the opposition."[13] The *Boston Statesman*, reporting on the decision to restore balloting, protested that this was not a repudiation of Calhoun but rather a decision to protect the chamber's prerogatives. "The appointing the committees of the Senate by the Senate, and not by its officer, is considered judicious for many reasons," the *Statesman* explained. "It is merely restoring a former usage."[14]

Seven years later, senators confronted a different situation—in this case, a vice president who would not come to the Senate chamber—but the same problem, a presiding officer hostile to the Senate majority. In December 1833, Hugh L. White (Jacksonian, Tenn.) resumed his chair as president pro tempore. Elected in the preceding Congress by a Jacksonian majority, White continued in his office at the opening of the 23rd Congress, in which the Senate was now controlled by an anti-Jackson majority. Because senators believed that the terms of presidents pro tempore could end only with the appearance of the vice president, anti-Jackson senators could not depose White until Vice President Martin Van Buren, ironically a Jacksonian Democrat, had arrived. But Van Buren remained in Albany (Niven 1983, 356). Consequently, anti-Jackson senators, who sought to place one of their own in the chair, vigorously attacked

---

[13] "From the Richmond Enquirer," *Eastern Argus* (Portland, Maine), Feb. 28, 1826, 2.
[14] "From the Boston Statesman," *United States Telegraph* (Washington, D.C.), Apr. 28, 1826, 3. See also Robinson 1954, 56–62.

Van Buren for not attending the Senate for the first two weeks of the session. They regarded Van Buren's absence as strategic. "It was generally supposed," the *Columbian Centinel* reported, "that the Vice President held back a few days, to secure the organization of the committees by the acting President, conformably to the views of the Administration."[15] Rather than permit the president pro tempore to name committees in Van Buren's absence—which, as Jacksonian senators correctly but disingenuously insisted, had been standard practice for the previous four sessions—the anti-Jackson majority returned to balloting in 1833. "The resolution had no reference to the present presiding officer," George Poindexter (Anti-Jackson, Miss.) argued. "A single consideration ought to govern the vote; the committees should represent the Senate. It was of great importance that their reports should express to the public the sense of the Senate on all important measures" (*Reg. of Debates*, December 10, 1833, 24). Observers understood the institutional and partisan stakes. "The Senate have resumed their legitimate right of appointing their own Committees, instead of allowing one Senator to do it," the *New-York Commercial Advertiser* reported. "The Albany Regency cannot now appoint the Chairman, and give a majority to every Committee in that body."[16]

A new alternative to balloting emerged in December 1845, when the Senate caucuses assumed full control of the standing committees. That month, senators refused to permit Democratic vice president George M. Dallas to appoint the committees, though they had allowed him to do so during the brief special session in March (McConachie 1898, 280–83, 330–31; Haynes 1938, i: 276; Merk 1967, 374–75). Dallas's decision to assume the chair in the opening days of the regular session, and thus to take responsibility for committee assignments, was clearly unsettling for a number of senators. For the last eight consecutive regular sessions, as Table 2.1 shows, the president pro tempore had named committees. (Indeed, with the ascension of John Tyler to the presidency in April 1841, the Senate had operated for four years with no vice president at all.) Only twice before, in the cases of Calhoun in 1825 and Johnson in 1837, had a vice president named committees in a regular session of the Senate, and senators did not regard either example as precedent. The decision of senators to take this power from Dallas came about "from no feelings of disrespect or unkindness," the *Daily Union* explained to its readers,

---

[15] "Committees in the Senate," *Columbian Centinel*, Dec. 25, 1833, 1. See also *Albany Argus*, Dec. 13, 1833, 2.

[16] "Correspondence of the Commercial Advertiser," *Commercial Advertiser* (New York, N.Y.), Dec. 14, 1833, 2. Behind the scenes, as Niven (1983, 356—59) shows, the battle to shape committee assignments in 1833 was made even more complex when Daniel Webster (Anti-Jackson, Mass.) approached an ally of Van Buren, suggesting that Webster would support committees with pro-Jackson majorities and opposed to the coalition led by Henry Clay (Anti-Jackson, Ky.) and John Calhoun (Nullifier, S.C.). But Van Buren rejected the proposal, believing it would undermine the integrity of the emerging Democratic party and his own leadership. See also Robinson 1954, 64–68.

"but because it was contrary to the universal rule of the Senate, with one or two brief exceptions, as understood from the debate, and inconsistent, in their view, with the responsibilities which of right attached to themselves."[17]

At a time, notably, when the two parties were closely balanced, four Democrats voted with the Whig minority to force the election of committees by ballot (Robinson 1954, 124–26; Hatfield 1997, 156). "The present case was different from that where the appointment of the standing committees is devolved on a President *pro tempore*, who is an officer selected from our own body, and responsible to the Senate," Willie Mangum (W, N.C.) asserted. "The Senate, by conferring this power upon an officer who is not responsible to the body for his acts, would be, on our part, an abdication of our legislative powers" (*Cong. Globe*, December 4, 1845, 19–20). Thomas Hart Benton (D, Mo.), one of the four Democrats who refused to allow the vice president to name committees, defended his decision as a matter of principle—or, in the language of the 1826 debate, which he quoted at length, "on the score of its abstract propriety" (*Cong. Globe*, December 4, 1845, 21). Reporting on the vote, the *American and Commercial Daily Advertiser*, a Baltimore newspaper, noted succinctly that, with this action regarding the appointment of standing committees, "the Senate has conferred its authority upon itself."[18] Abruptly, with that vote, the window to a new institutional world—with committee assignments coordinated in caucus—opened in the Senate. No longer would senators rely only on their presiding officer to bring order to their collective chaos.

Maintaining Order

While senators never seriously entertained the idea of granting agenda-setting authority to presiding officers, at times in the nineteenth century they confronted serious challenges to order and decorum on the floor and evolved rules intended to give the presiding officer responsibility for maintaining order and making parliamentary rulings (Haynes 1938, 212–16).[19] Early vice presidents and presidents pro tempore appeared quite willing to enforce the rules of the Senate, to call senators to order when they offered intemperate remarks, and, at times, to insist that debate be germane to the question pending before the

---

[17] "The Vice President—President of the Senate," *Daily Union* (Washington, D.C.), Dec. 9, 1845, 2.

[18] "Correspondence of the American," *American and Commercial Daily Advertiser* (Baltimore, Md.), Dec. 5, 1845, 2. Of course, not all observers understood the significance of what the Senate had done. The *Boston Courier* described the proceedings in Congress that day—specifically including the Senate vote denying the vice president the power to appoint committees—as having been "brief and of no great importance." See "Congress," *Boston Courier*, Dec. 8, 1845, 2.

[19] On the modern Senate practice on rulings of the chair, see Riddick 1949 and Bach 1991.

Senate. They did so under the 1789 Senate rules and general parliamentary law, encapsulated in Jefferson's *Manual*.[20]

In fact, the 1789 rules left some doubt as to whether the presiding officer should take the initiative to call a senator to order if the senator's remarks violated the Senate's rules. The ambiguity was exploited by Vice President John Calhoun in 1826, who presided during a tirade by John Randolph (Jacksonian, Va.) against President John Quincy Adams and Secretary of State Henry Clay. Calhoun, a political foe of the president and Clay, conveniently let Randolph proceed even after demands were heard that he be stopped. "It could not have escaped the recollection of our readers," the *Rhode Island Republican* wrote in the spring of 1826, "that ever since the latter part of December, John Randolph has been permitted by Mr. Calhoun, to abuse every member of the Administration, in the most vulgar and obscene language."[21] Sharp criticism of the vice president followed this incident, which led Calhoun to respond with a carefully worded statement in which he asserted that the chair may intervene only upon the demand of a senator (*Reg. of Debates*, April 15, 1826, 572–73; Kerr 1895, 21; Donnelly 1930, 20–21; Hatch 1934, 71–76; Beeman 1968, 421–25; Kravitz ca. 1971, v: 23–24; Lynch et al. 2018, 150; Jentleson 2021, 48–49). Calhoun's action, or inaction, and subsequent statement set a precedent that other presiding officers cited for decades.

Not all senators agreed with Calhoun's ruling. To the contrary, a lengthy debate over a rule to eliminate ambiguity about the duty of the presiding officer followed two years later. A proponent of the new rule, David Barton (Adams, Mo.), offered some historical perspective by contrasting Calhoun to John Gaillard (Republican/Crawford Republican/Jacksonian, S.C.), who had served as president pro tempore during most of the preceding decade. The reporter for the *Register of Debates* recorded Barton's comments:

[Gaillard] was placed in a situation that gave him decided advantage over the present presiding officer—a situation that gave particular weight and dignity to his decisions, and to the practice of the Senate under his long and benign administration. He presided in a time when the present rancor of party strife was unknown. He stood aloof, in that Chair, from the parties of the day. He was not looked to as the head of any great party in this nation, contending for rule; nor were his decisions subjected to the illiberal imputation of having any ulterior object in view. Drawing precedents, then, from those times ... he considered the law of the Senate clearly settled, that the Vice President possessed, and ought to have exercised, the power of restraining the wholly irrelevant latitude of debate of that period...

---

[20] The 1789 rules provided (Rule XVI) that "when a Member shall be called to order he shall sit down until the President shall have determined whether he is in order or not; and every question of order shall be decided by the President without debate; but if there be a doubt in his mind he may call the sense of the Senate."

[21] "The Vice-President's Apology," *Rhode Island Republican* (Newport, R.I.), Apr. 27, 1826, 2.

JOHN C. CALHOUN

OF SOUTH CAROLINA

VICE PRESIDENT OF THE UNITED STATES, AND, PRESIDENT
OF THE SENATE.

Engraved by J. B. Longacre   from a Painting by C. B. King

Vice President John C. Calhoun. In 1826 he refused to intervene during a tirade
launched by John Randolph (J, Va.) against the administration of John Quincy Adams,
establishing a precedent that it was not the role of the presiding officer to limit speech by
senators, even uncivil attacks.

The Miriam and Ira D. Wallach Division of Art, Prints and Photographs: Print Collection, New
York Public Library (EM1404)

[Gaillard] was in the constant practice of preserving order in the body, by calling back a rambling member to the subject before the Senate, when he had gone entirely from it, even in language of the most decent and orderly style ...

He [Barton] went on to instance some cases in which the present presiding officer had, as he thought, exercised the general power of preserving order in cases where the written rules of the Senate were silent. (*Reg. of Debates*, February 12, 1828, 305–6)

Most senators agreed with Barton on the question of calling a senator to order for uncivil language, but a few supporters of the new rule indicated that they had no intention of insisting that senators be held to a standard of relevancy. The new rule explicitly recognized the presiding officer's ability to call a senator to order for transgressing the rules of the Senate. It also clearly established the right of any senator to appeal the chair's ruling, unlike the previous rule, which allowed the presiding officer to let the Senate decide whether a senator was out of order.[22]

Opponents of the new rule insisted that the Senate should not hand power to the vice president. Thomas Hart Benton (Jacksonian, Mo.) argued that the vice president could not be trusted. It is not "safe to vest the power of restraining debates in an officer like him, not concerned in the debate, and not responsible to us for the exercise of his power," Benton stated. "He may abuse his power and we are without remedy" (*Reg. of Debates*, February 11, 1828, 282; see also Lynch et al. 2018, 150–51). Proponents argued that the provision guaranteeing to each senator the right to appeal the chair's ruling to the full Senate was adequate protection against abuse.

Although the Senate adopted the new rule, practice was still not settled. Unparliamentary language, nongermane remarks, and physical confrontations became an everyday occurrence in the late 1840s and 1850s in debates over slavery and states' rights (Beeman 1968, 428–31; Freeman 2018, 142–76). One episode in 1850 generated widespread attention. Henry Foote (D, Miss.) and Benton used offensive language to describe each other in a debate over California statehood (*Cong. Globe*, March 26, 1850, 602–4). Vice President Millard Fillmore subsequently warned the Senate that he would henceforth use his power to call a senator to order. In his warning, he emphasized the importance of rules to maintain order in a legislative chamber. "We all know that many little irregularities may be tolerated in a small body that would cause much disorder in a large one," Fillmore said. "The Senate has increased from twenty-six to sixty members. The natural tendency of the increase of members is, to relax the discipline—that when the strict observance of rules is most essential to the dignity and comfort of the body, it is the most difficult to enforce" (*Cong. Globe*, April 3, 1850, 632). No one challenged Fillmore's view, and no formal actions were taken. But

---

[22] The 1828 rule referred to "when a member shall be called to order *by the President or a Senator*" (emphasis added), thus explicitly recognizing two ways to call a senator to order. The new rule also made the presiding officer's decision "subject to appeal to the Senate."

Fillmore's promise proved vacuous. Two weeks later, Foote lashed into Benton again. Benton became so outraged that he rushed toward Foote down the center aisle. As Benton approached, Foote drew a pistol and was then restrained by colleagues (Smith 1958, 265–72; Byrd 1988, i: 195–96). The event attracted national attention, but a special committee absolved Foote of intent to assassinate Benton and managed only to recommend that senators not bring pistols into the Senate chamber.

The infamous caning of Charles Sumner (R, Mass.) by South Carolina representative Preston Brooks in 1856 stimulated a lengthy debate about the obligation of the chair to maintain order. Brooks had attacked Sumner in retaliation for Sumner's verbal criticism of Senator Andrew Butler (D, S.C.). In a fiery speech on the crisis in Kansas, Sumner had described Butler, an elderly relative of Brooks, as a modern Don Quixote. "Of course he has chosen a mistress to whom he has made his vows, and who, though ugly to others, is always lovely to him; though polluted in the sight of the world, is chaste in his sight," Sumner said of Butler. "I mean the harlot, Slavery" (Byrd 1988, i: 209; see also Freeman 2018, 208–64). Some senators and observers believed that the presiding officer's failure to call Sumner to order for unparliamentary language precipitated the brutal beating. Jesse Bright (D, Ind.), who as president pro tempore was in the chair, later noted that he was following Calhoun's precedent in not calling Sumner to order (*Cong. Globe*, June 26, 1856, 1483).

A committee investigating the episode recommended several rules changes, including a requirement that senators confine themselves to the subject under debate. That rule was rejected, but the Senate adopted a rule providing that, "if any member in speaking, or otherwise, transgress the rules of the Senate, the Presiding Officer shall, or any member may, call to order." The use of "shall" established the affirmative obligation of the chair to maintain order in debate; the phrase "or otherwise" extended the reach beyond the words spoken (*Cong. Globe*, June 26, 1856, 1477–78).[23]

In the 1856 debate, the principal opposition to the new rule came from senators who believed that proponents were overreacting to the caning and that the proposed power was already implied in parliamentary law. Advocates of the rule, on the other hand, insisted that senators could not be expected to call a colleague to order without an explicit rule. This debate was the last major controversy over the role of the presiding officer in enforcing decorum and relevancy. Although the Senate in 1856 had explicitly authorized its presiding officer to maintain order, it had decisively rejected a role for its presiding officer in maintaining the relevancy of debate. In the future, presiding officers varied in their aggressiveness in maintaining order. Experienced legislators in the late nineteenth century, such as Henry B. Anthony (R, R.I.), George F. Edmunds (R,

---

[23] The procedure for an appeal to the Senate was clarified in 1877 when the rule was modified to prohibit debate on a motion to allow a senator to proceed in order. Debate on such a motion would prevent the senator from continuing to address the Senate and undermine the point of appealing the decision of the chair.

Vt.), and John Sherman (R, Ohio), retained firm procedural control but understood the limits of their authority.

PARTY ORGANIZATION AND THE NEUTRALITY OF THE CHAIR, 1845–1914

The president pro tempore, once an obvious solution to the Senate's collective action problems, faced new competitors in the 1840s and 1850s. Short-term considerations—in 1826, in 1833, then finally in 1845—had caused senators to remove from their presiding officer the power to name the standing committees. In 1845, both parties turned to their caucuses to assemble committee lists. Once caucuses assumed this power—and began articulating new institutions, like committees on committees—they did not relinquish it. Similarly, by the 1850s, when senators had grown accustomed to unlimited debate on irrelevant subjects, they were no longer willing to return to their chair the authority to define relevancy. The diminution of the Senate's presiding officer came ultimately not from deficiencies in the position of president pro tempore but in the construction of alternative institutions and practices. As a result, the principal tasks of the presiding officer were reduced to presiding over the chamber and enforcing the Senate's rules, standing orders, and, eventually, unanimous consent agreements.

Scheduling and Recognition

In the 1870s and 1880s, the Senate's workload burgeoned. Since the party caucuses were still struggling to develop effective agenda-setting mechanisms and the presiding officer possessed no authority over the agenda, senators fended for themselves much of the time, as they attempted to gain consideration of measures put in their charge. Consequently, presiding officers were left helpless to deal with a backlogged calendar of measures waiting for floor action. In the second half of the nineteenth century, morning hour was filled with squabbles among members, often all of the majority party, seeking action on their bills. As the mandatory March 3rd adjournment date approached, conflict became particularly intense. As a general rule, vice presidents and presidents pro tempore presided over these turbulent proceedings in a neutral fashion.

To ease the burden on morning hour consideration of routine and sometimes not-so-routine legislation, the Senate adopted the so-called Anthony rule at the start of each Congress in the 1870s and early 1880s. Named after Henry B. Anthony (R, R.I.)—who authored the rule and served simultaneously as president pro tempore and Republican caucus chairman during the 1869–75 period—the rule provided that a senator could speak only once, and for only five minutes on any question, during the call of the calendar following routine morning business. In the early 1880s, the Senate incorporated the Anthony rule in its standing rules. Other rules were adopted in an attempt to handle the Senate's workload more efficiently.

In 1882, George Edmunds (R, Vt.) argued that the Senate was still unable to manage routine scheduling problems:

The business [of the Senate] has so increased and accumulated, with the increasing number of Senators as well, that it has become a matter of more labor, difficulty, and time, to take it month in and month out, to find out what bill we are willing to consider than to consider and dispose of it; and the thing goes just by a kind of sporadic impulse if I may so speak. A Senator today from Vermont gets up and appeals to the Senate out of consideration to him to let him call up a bill that is at the very bottom of the calendar, the last one reported. I say, "it will not take a minute; it is a hard case, poor man," or whatever it may be. That occupies on average ten minutes probably. Then another Senator, a Senator who is more modest than we are, who has had his constituent's bill reported four weeks before, is squeezed out. And so we are in a continuous struggle, of good temper and good nature generally, but a continual struggle that takes up time, to see what it is we will do rather than in spending our time doing it. (*Cong. Rec.*, January 27, 1883, 675)

Edmunds hoped, in vain, that the Senate would tighten its procedures to allow bills to be considered during morning hour in the order in which they were placed on the calendar.

Responding to the problem identified by Edmunds, presiding officers by the late 1880s maintained a list of senators who sought recognition during morning hour to move consideration of a bill. The president pro tempore seemed to be recognizing senators whose names appeared on his list over others seeking recognition from the floor. As John Ingalls (R, Kans.), the president pro tempore, explained in 1888:

The Chair has been subjected to great embarrassment by importunities, natural and reasonable, from members of the Senate for action upon bills in which they are concerned. The rules require the presiding officer to recognize the first Senator who rises in his place and addresses the Chair. When several rise simultaneously and address the Chair it is obviously impossible for that rule to be literally executed, and therefore, to avoid embarrassment, by the exercise of arbitrary authority and apparent partiality, the Chair has followed the practice of setting down upon a list alternately those who desire to be recognized, first upon one side of the Chamber and then upon the other, in the order in which they have applied, as being the only equitable and practicable method of escaping from the difficulties which the Chair experiences in consequence of the applications that are made for recognition. (*Cong. Rec.*, August 1, 1888, 7110)

In short, the Senate's rule, dating to 1806, requiring the presiding officer to call on the senator first seeking recognition proved inadequate. If the list was discontinued, one senator noted, a mad scramble for recognition would be the result. When a senator challenged the list, another senator noted that Ingalls's predecessors had followed the same procedure (*Cong. Rec.*, August 1, 1888, 7109–10). No one suggested another mechanism, and complaints by a senator that he had a right to be recognized—as no doubt he did according to a strict interpretation of the rule—went unanswered. The presiding officer's reliance on such a list appears to have persisted for decades. In the 1910s and 1920s, the chair maintained a list of senators seeking recognition when a measure was debated under a time-limit agreement (*Cong. Rec.*, March 4, 1917, 5012, and February 9, 1924, 2185). Not until the 1930s did floor leaders, a position unknown to the Senate before the 1890s and still developing in the first two decades of the twentieth century, gain the right of first recognition, which gave the majority party's leader an opportunity to set the agenda.

Beyond adopting the Anthony rule and allowing the presiding officer to rely on a list of senators to be recognized, senators in the late nineteenth century also more frequently employed other parliamentary devices—special orders, and, as we discuss below, unanimous consent agreements—to secure Senate action on bills, often quite important bills. A special order required a two-thirds majority, but if approved, the special order guaranteed that the bill would be taken up at a specified time or immediately after the Senate disposed of a pending bill. Routine unanimous consent requests were used to call up measures or ask that a measure be considered next in order. Individuals' repetitive and conflicting efforts to use these techniques, all without the coordination of floor leaders, further cluttered floor sessions and created animosities among members of the same party.

As the presiding officer attempted to establish some order on the floor in the 1880s and 1890s, the majority caucus was itself paying increased attention to scheduling priorities. Although most of the caucus's attention was initially devoted to major legislation, by the early 1890s, as we discuss later, steering committees had begun managing the floor agenda. These developments helped coordinate the efforts of members to gain Senate action on their bills and relieved some of the pressure on the presiding officer to manage the process of considering routine legislation. But they did not immediately reduce the use of special orders and certainly did not slow down unanimous consent requests, which became an everyday feature of floor activity in these years.

Unanimous Consent Agreements

The emergence of the modern responsibilities of the presiding officer is closely connected with the rise of unanimous consent agreements. Unanimous consent agreements (UCAs) are critical to managing the business of today's Senate. On a daily basis, the majority leader takes the lead in arranging agreements that expedite consideration of legislation by limiting or structuring debate and amending activity. Usually distinguished from routine motions that take the form of unanimous consent requests, unanimous consent agreements supplement or supplant the standing rules of the Senate to organize floor debate. The term "complex" has sometimes been applied to this more important class of unanimous consent agreements (Keith 1977; Smith and Flathman 1989).

UCAs did not exist in the early Senate. Though the Senate has always been less formal and more leisurely than the House in its handling of legislation, unanimous agreements to limit debate or amendments do not appear to have been utilized until 1846 (Keith 1977). In the late nineteenth century, UCAs became a standard feature of bill managers' strategies and raised significant questions about how the Senate governed itself that were not answered until senators amended Rule XII in 1914. The evolution in unanimous consent practices, largely untold in existing literature, is related closely to the authority of presiding officers and their relation to party leaders.

UCAs are not reliably indexed in any source. To reconstruct the emergence of UCAs in Senate procedure, therefore, we searched the *Globe* and the *Record* for UCAs associated with bills that were considered on the Senate floor for more than one day, as indicated in the bill index of the *Journal*. Consequently, we do not have a systematic count of all UCAs and miss many UCAs that concern floor action on bills considered on a single day.

The 1846 agreement appears to have happened by accident (*Cong. Globe*, April 13, 1846, 659). William Allen (D, Ohio) observed that the debate on the Oregon resolutions seemed to be winding down (after more than two months) and "that it would be an accommodation to many Senators to have an understanding as to the exact day" the Senate would vote on the resolutions. "He was desirous that a day should be determined on," the *Congressional Globe* reported, "inasmuch as some of the members of the body would be unavoidably absent, he understood, within a few days, and they would like to time their absence so that it should not fall on that day when the vote should be taken." The agreement was quite informal—merely to vote on the resolutions in three days. James T. Morehead (W, Ky.) noted that the chamber could not be sure that debate on amendments would end by then, but both Allen and Daniel Webster (W, Mass.) replied that they expected that debate would be short. Notably, Morehead said that he "had not the slightest objection to fixing upon some day for terminating the debate, provided it was not to be regarded as establishing a precedent," to which Webster offered assurance "that such was not the intention." On the appointed day, the debate lasted longer than some senators expected, but they brought the resolutions to a vote.

Despite the protestations that day, the precedent had been established. By 1870, UCAs were being used with some frequency. These early UCAs were, as they are today, time-limitation agreements that provided for the disposal of a measure by a specified time. The typical UCA provided for a vote on a bill by a certain time (usually four or five o'clock) and a certain day (usually a day or two in the future). By that time, the presiding officer, who was invisible in the process of reaching and implementing the 1846 agreement, usually repeated the agreement once offered so that senators could hear and understand it. Bill managers were generally responsible for drafting and negotiating UCAs. The *Congressional Record* is replete with long exchanges among senators about a bill manager's unanimous consent request. Confusion about the provisions of UCAs was common, with senators sometimes quoting the *Record* to prove a point. "So an hour and a half or two hours' discussion of the rules may not be amiss," Stephen White (D, Calif.) observed wryly on one such occasion.

"Their lucidity is daily becoming more apparent, and the remarkably clear statement of the position which we are in which has been had from a large number of Senators, no one of whom agreed with another, demonstrates that the American Republic can not exist without the present rules [Laughter]" (*Cong. Rec.*, January 25, 1895, 1344). The appropriate use of UCAs could cause contention, as senators sometimes complained that they were not present when unanimous consent was granted.

As UCAs became more common and as violations of agreements reached by unanimous consent occurred, the Senate found itself bound by an interpretation of the parliamentary status of UCAs that made them difficult to enforce. On Saturday, July 4, 1870, with many senators losing patience with their extended stay in Washington, the hour for a final vote on a naturalization bill under a UCA passed with opponents continuing to press amendments and debate the bill. Senators observed that the debate continued in violation of the UCA. John Sherman, in fact, complained that it was the first violation of a UCA in the history of the practice (*Cong. Globe*, July 4, 1870, 5152). When a point of order was raised by another senator, the president pro tempore, Henry Anthony, stated that the chair did not have the power to enforce the agreement. "The agreement under which the Senate came to an understanding to vote at five o'clock on Saturday was by unanimous consent," Anthony declared. "It was not an order entered on the Journal, but merely an understanding among Senators. The Chair has no power and no right to enforce an agreement of that kind" (*Cong. Globe*, July 4, 1870, 5150). Anthony's repeated rulings established a precedent that led to much confusion over the next four decades.

Anthony's interpretation appeared to be based on the casual nature of UCAs in the years before the Civil War, when UCAs were viewed as "gentlemen's agreements." The argument was based on two premises—that UCAs were not recognized in the Senate's rules and that the presiding officer had no authority except that granted explicitly by the rules. After Anthony left the Senate, Henry Cabot Lodge (R, Mass.) became the Senate's parliamentarian-in-residence and frequently articulated this rationale.

Presiding officers were not entirely consistent in their approach to UCAs in the late nineteenth century. From time to time, presiding officers suggested a UCA as a way out of a sticky scheduling problem. At other times, they restated UCAs and encouraged clarification and approval of unanimous consent requests (*Cong. Rec.*, 1880, 2268). Most presiding officers contributed to the implementation of UCAs by noting that the time had arrived to call up or vote on a measure subject to a UCA. But senators varied in their understanding of the role of the presiding officer. John Ingalls (R, Kans.), Ambrose Burnside (R, R.I.), and Thomas Ferry (R, Mich.), who had just served as president pro tempore for four years, had this exchange in 1880:

INGALLS. It has always been the case when that hour has been reached which has been agreed upon that the presiding officer rapped with his gavel upon the table and announced that the hour had arrived. He failed to do it in this case. I say that that agreement was abrogated by unanimous consent, and it is entirely competent now to make another agreement.

FERRY. I restate the fact that the Senator from Alabama was making a speech and had not concluded when the hour of four o'clock arrived. The Senate has always in such instances yielded to the condition of things and allowed the Senator to continue when objection was not made.

INGALLS. Never.

BURNSIDE. I do not think there ever has been a vote since I have been in the Senate that was taken at the hour it was agreed to be taken. (*Cong. Rec.*, 1880, 193)

Ingalls was probably right about some presiding officers, but Ferry and Burnside seem to have been right about the general practice. In fact, when limits on individual speeches became common features of UCAs in the 1880s, the presiding officer kept time.

While presiding officers routinely refused to enforce UCAs, some chose to go their own way, at least at times when it seemed convenient to do so. In 1888, Ingalls, then president pro tempore, interrupted a senator who exceeded the five-minute limit for a speech under a UCA and asked if there was objection to allowing the senator to continue (*Cong. Rec.*, 1888, 1848; see also *Cong. Rec.*, 1908, 3615). President pro tempore William Frye (R, Maine) once took the initiative to note that debate was not in order under a UCA and ruled on a point of order raised against amendments based on provisions of the same UCA (*Cong. Rec.*, 1900, 2448–49). And Vice Presidents Charles Fairbanks and James Sherman were not timid about enforcing UCAs at times (*Cong. Rec.*, 1908, 3602; *Cong. Rec.*, 1909, 549–50; *Cong. Rec.*, 1912, 10974; *Cong. Rec.*, 1913, 423–26).

Compliance with UCAs was usually good by the early years of the twentieth century, but critical features of modern floor practice were not yet in place. No formal majority leaders existed who could orchestrate agreements and oversee their implementation. The thesis that UCAs could not be modified, even by unanimous consent, made them inflexible tools for scheduling. Presiding officers enforced agreements sporadically, whether due to ignorance of precedent or the forbearance of senators. Not until 1914 did the Senate create a formal procedure for adopting an important class of UCAs and, also for the first time, grant enforcement authority to the presiding officer. Presiding officers began to exhibit consistency in their interpretation of the parliamentary status of UCAs and their power to implement them (see, for example, *Cong. Rec.*, March 1, 1916, 3347, and *Cong. Rec.*, April 8, 1916, 5717). Party leaders assumed control of the Senate floor in the 1910s, and the presiding officer's role as neutral arbiter was settled.

CONCLUSION

Contemporary observers tend to dismiss the Senate's presiding officer as a ceremonial figure, except when the body is otherwise deadlocked on a crucial vote and the vice president may cast the deciding vote. But, for the first decades of the chamber's history, senators regularly sought solutions to collective action problems by experimenting with enhanced authority for their presiding officer. Maintaining order on the floor and assigning senators to committees proved difficult at times before the Civil War, while managing the floor agenda and implementing unanimous consent agreements were vexing problems in the last decades of the century. In most cases, the arrangement of dual presiding officers—the vice president and the president pro tempore—reduced the viability of turning to a strong presiding officer for a solution. Vice presidents, who were not chosen by the Senate and were often political opponents of the Senate majority, proved untrustworthy; presidents pro tempore were only temporary officeholders. On matters concerning basic features of Senate floor procedure, such as maintaining order and enforcing unanimous consent agreements, the presiding officer was eventually granted clear authority. But the authority was nondiscretionary. And, on other matters, such as setting the agenda and making committee assignments, senators and their parties invented other means for managing collective action problems.

Senators proved remarkably tolerant of inconvenience and uncertainty, sometimes for decades, until a plainly unacceptable event generated a consensus for a new rule or practice. Particularly destructive behavior on the floor, perverse outcomes in committee assignment balloting, genuine confusion in setting the daily schedule, and eventually a truly convoluted interpretation of a unanimous consent agreement persuaded most senators of the need for a change in the inherited practice. A common response of senators was to propose a new rule or set of rules. In some cases, new rules were adopted; in other cases, rules were put off in hope that the events would not recur. But in all cases, senators initially turned to the presiding officer for a solution.

A natural inclination is to argue that the weakness of the Senate's presiding officers merely reflects the tradition of informal governance preferred by senators. A great deal of circumstantial evidence and senatorial commentary supports this interpretation. At least as important, though, is the fact that senators who were frustrated under informal practices or ambiguous rules found their efforts to change the rules easily blocked by others. Only when extraordinary events forced nearly all senators to recognize the severity of a festering collective action problem was a new rule tried.

By understanding more fully what did not happen in the Senate—the emergence of a powerful presiding officer—we can better appreciate those solutions to collective action that emerged in the nineteenth and twentieth centuries and persist to the present day. Senators of the nineteenth century saw nothing inevitable about the rise of party caucuses, scheduling routines, unanimous consent practices, or party leadership. These features of the modern Senate developed only after failed experiments with other approaches, often involving the chamber's presiding officer. Not until party leadership emerged—first in the caucus, then in the caucus committees, ultimately in floor leaders—could senators abandon their attempts to place critical powers in the hands of their presiding officer.

Print of an engraving showing Henry Clay in the Senate, 1850. Nine years before, in 1841, when Whigs gained control of the presidency and both houses of Congress, Clay and other Whig senators created the party caucus as a regular vehicle for conducting legislative business.

Library of Congress, Prints & Photographs Division, reproduction number LC-DIG-pga-05850 (digital file from original print)

3

Caucus, 1789–1879

In 1875, on the occasion of William Gladstone's decision to retire as leader of the Liberal party and the consequent struggle in London among those hoping to succeed him, the *New York Tribune* noted that no comparable battle loomed in the American Congress, where they "get on well enough without any leaders." In its editorial, the *Tribune* proceeded to satirize the pretensions of various Republican senators. "If Mr. Logan should some day decline to lead the Senate any longer, Mr. Morton would ask him how long he had been leading it, Mr. Conkling would observe that his standing at the White House was as good as any one's, and Mr. West would say that Pinchback [a Black person and prominent Louisiana Republican whose claim to a seat would eventually be rejected by the Senate] might as well wait awhile before aspiring so high." As the *Tribune* concluded, "If all these leaders should give their places up to their coachmen, it would make no difference whatever in the policy of their party."[1]

The verdict of their contemporaries—a verdict reaffirmed by Rothman (1966) almost a century later—was unmistakable: senators did their business with little semblance of organization or leadership. To be sure, senators met in party caucuses in this era, but these caucuses were informal, haphazard, and disorganized. Individualism reigned supreme; the Senate drifted without guidance or direction. Congress lacks "distinctly recognized leaders," the *New York Times* contended in 1878. "Business is left to the initiative of individuals or of numerous unconnected committees."[2] Not until the late 1890s, according to this account, when a small group of leaders accumulated significant powers, was the Senate truly disciplined. The first century of the

---

[1] "Mr. Gladstone's Abdication," *New York Tribune*, Jan. 18, 1875, 4.
[2] "Congressional Debates and Public Opinion," *New York Times*, Dec. 15, 1878, 6.

Senate, this narrative suggests, was characterized chiefly by disorder and individual initiative.

That account is incomplete and misleading. As we will elaborate, Senate caucuses were mature institutions by the late 1870s, and they had taken shape in four distinct eras of institutional innovation. First, beginning in 1796–1800, members of Congress turned to caucuses as vehicles to nominate presidential candidates. Second, in 1841–45, senators reinvented the caucus as a regular, ongoing institution to help steer legislative business, oversee the policy process, and make committee assignments. Third, in 1856–62, the newly established Republican party formalized caucus organization, creating the position of caucus chairman as well as establishing the Republican committee on committees and the Republican congressional campaign committee. Then, finally, in the 1870s, several events marked the maturation of caucus organization—the creation of a formal caucus room for the minority, the election of the first Democratic caucus chairman, the rebirth of the Democratic committee on committees, the decision of the Senate to assign a party secretary to each caucus (then called "assistant doorkeeper" and "acting assistant doorkeeper"), and the beginnings of caucus committees on the order of business.

The developments over these nine decades, culminating in the 1870s, laid the groundwork for the highly structured caucuses and steering committees that controlled the Senate at the turn of the twentieth century. The four eras of greatest institutional change—1796–1800, 1841–45, 1856–62, and 1871–79— align closely with the eras in the Senate's first 90 years when parties were at their most competitive and control of the Senate was most clearly at stake. Our general theory predicts that senators are likeliest to innovate when party competition is fiercest—and the evidence here is strongly consistent with that theory.

ENTREPRENEURS, FACTIONS, AND PARTY COMPETITION

The creation of Senate party caucuses took most of the nineteenth century. Innovations in one era set baselines for the next era. But the pace of innovation was not gradual. Rather, senators established and reconfigured their caucuses in four distinct bursts of activity. As Figure 1.1 shows, there were, in the first century of Senate history, just four periods when the two major parties were evenly matched: *1800–1802*, when the Federalists and Jeffersonian Republicans competed on equal terms in Senate elections; *1841–45*, when the Whig party controlled a closely divided Senate, its only time in the majority, and modern mass party competition emerged; *1857–61*, when Republicans first emerged as a party, then quickly became the Senate majority; and *1875–83*, when Senate Democrats, whose numbers had collapsed during the Civil War and Reconstruction, began again to compete for control of the Senate on even terms with Republicans. Each of these eras aligns closely with the moments when senators turned to the caucus in new ways and strengthened the capacity of its internal institutions.

When the first Senate convened on March 4, 1789, parties did not exist. Over the next decade, as senators came to identify with Alexander Hamilton on one side, or James Madison and Thomas Jefferson on the other, an inchoate party system emerged, and, with it, the possibility of Federalists and Republicans meeting separately in caucus. These were primitive parties, led by people who rejected the value of political parties and, especially on the Federalist side, eschewed efforts at mass organization. Federalists, led by Hamilton, valued deference, order, and a strong central government. In the late 1790s, they controlled both chambers of Congress. But, with Jefferson's election in 1800, Republicans gained control of the House and the Senate. Once Federalists lost their majorities in Congress, they never recovered as a national party. From 15 seats in the 34-person Senate that convened in 1801, Federalists fell to just 9 seats in 1803, then to 7 seats in 1805. Competition in the months surrounding the 1800 election had been fierce, but it proved brief. Republicans soon became hegemonic.

After years with no significant party competition, the dominant Republican party began to fragment. Following the 1824 election, when the House of Representatives selected John Quincy Adams as president even though Andrew Jackson had won a plurality of votes, party organizing intensified step by step. Factional and party activity grew intense, as sparring between Jacksonians and anti-Jackson senators began to evolve into an entirely new party system. Henry Clay, a close ally of Adams, served as secretary of state during the Adams administration, in 1825–29. The two were opposed by supporters of Andrew Jackson, led by Martin Van Buren, organizer of the Albany Regency and a senator from New York. Van Buren sat in the Senate between 1821 and 1828. The Senate was small at the time, with just 48 members, and senators knew one another very well. They worked from their desks in the cramped old Senate chamber and in a few nearby rooms, and most senators lived in nearby boardinghouses and entertained themselves in their messes, in the dancing halls, and at frequent dinner parties (Young 1966; Bogue and Marlaire 1975). During the Adams administration, Van Buren helped to mobilize opposition in the Senate—"working behind the scenes, as always; calling caucuses to legitimate their activities and speaking on the floor of the Senate against Adams as he deemed it necessary" (Silbey 2002, 52; see also Niven 1983, 156–64).

Jackson was elected president in 1828, and, over the next eight years, the outlines of a new party system began to coalesce. Jackson, Van Buren, and their allies created the Democratic party, and, by the mid-1830s Clay and Daniel Webster had emerged as leaders of the new Whig party (Silbey 2002, 95, 98). Conflict over several issues in the 1830s—the national bank, currency, an independent treasury, protective tariffs, internal improvements, and public lands—involved intense partisan divisions and orchestrated action by informal, ambitious Senate leaders. After his arrival in the Senate in November 1831, Clay became the recognized anti-Jackson leader whose influence animated the opposition (Carroll 1925; McConnell and Brownell 2019, 86–88). When Van Buren called the Senate "the headquarters of the opposition" (Silbey 2002, 89), he was referring to the considerable success of Clay, working with Webster and later John Calhoun, in mobilizing anti-Jackson forces. Clay pulled together a bicameral caucus on a tariff bill in 1832, although he rejected the idea of an opposition caucus meeting regularly (Remini 1991, 386–88). He also led the effort to censure Jackson over the removal of federal deposits from the Second Bank of the United States (Remini 1991, 421–58; Holt 1999, 26–27; MacNeil and Baker 2013, 61; McConnell and Brownell 2019, 88–89).

Formalizing the positions of Senate pages provided recognition to the growing divisions in the chamber. Various expense reports and the *Senate Journal* suggest that, by the mid-1820s, the Senate had begun to hire at least one boy for "attendance in Senate Room."[3] In the expense reports, these boys "were listed under messengers," Holt finds, "with the only distinction being that they were paid less than ordinary messengers."[4] Isaac Bassett, who was eleven years of age in December 1831, when he became a page, recalled later in his life that, with his appointment, he became one of just two pages in the Senate.[5] Since his father was "messenger in charge of the Senate Chamber," Bassett had been spending many days in the chamber. "Daniel Webster frequently took notice of him, and one day, patting him kindly on the head, said: 'My son, how would you like to be a page?'" Bassett recalled for a newspaper reporter. "The boy thought he would like it, and his father gave his consent."[6] To justify the appointment to his colleagues, Webster alluded to the divisions emerging in the Senate between Jacksonians and Anti-Jacksonians. "As there was only one page," according to an account decades later in the *Minneapolis Tribune*, Webster argued that "another be appointed, so that the Senators on each side of the chamber could have the services of one."[7] While the details of Bassett's account may have been apocryphal, his story long ago became part of Senate lore. The Senate adopted the title "page" for these young messengers in 1837 and set a minimum age of 13 for pages in 1854. The number of pages

---

[3] "Auditor's Report on the Account of Walter Lowrie," No. 50518, Aug. 1826, as shared by Daniel Holt of the Senate Historical Office.

[4] Daniel Holt to authors, email correspondence, Dec. 28, 2021. See also Gonzalez 2010.

[5] Bassett served for decades in the Senate as a page and in other posts: see, for example, Items 135a and 137a, Folder E, Box 14, Isaac Bassett Papers, National Archives. Bassett worked for a time without pay and began receiving pay in 1831. See also "Daniel Webster's Page," *Washington Post*, Feb. 25, 1878, 1; "Historical Chairs," *Minneapolis Tribune*, Sept. 17, 1878, 2; "An Historical Character," *Minneapolis Tribune*, Dec. 8, 1879, 2; "Congressional Proceedings," *Burlington (Vt.) Free Press and Times*, Dec. 9, 1881, 1; "Capt. Bassett's Snuff-Box," *Washington Post*, Mar. 20, 1882, 1; "Fifty-Six Years in the Senate: Doorkeeper Bassett Appointed as Page by Daniel Webster," *Washington Post*, Dec. 5, 1887, 2; *Cong. Rec.*, Sept. 8, 1980, 24534.

[6] "The Senators' Snuff-Boxes," *New York Times*, June 7, 1884, 3.

[7] "Civil Service in the Senate," *Minneapolis Tribune*, Aug. 12, 1876, 2. See also Remini 1997, 286–87.

grew over time—there were 14 by 1879—but the practice of giving the appointments to the two parties continued, with the majority party naming most of the pages, while assigning the duty of supervising the pages to the sergeant-at-arms.[8]

As political entrepreneurs, Clay, Van Buren, Webster, and Calhoun, all with strong presidential aspirations, were conspicuous in the Senate, indeed in national affairs generally. They were central to coalition building across sectional, social, and economic interests (Russo 1972; Remini 1997, 273–75, 356–87). Clay and Van Buren, in particular, coordinated issues personally and with lieutenants in Congress and in the states. Their influence was felt primarily through informal meetings of groups and factions and written correspondence. In this era, senators, like most politically engaged American men, abandoned the Jeffersonian era's strong anti-party philosophy and embraced a world in which competitive parties played accepted, even lauded, roles. The Panic of 1837 helped drive voter mobilization efforts, strengthened the Whigs as an opposition party, and sharpened differences between the parties as they sought to shape policy programs to win votes (Holt 1999, 60–88). With the congressional elections of 1838 and the presidential election of 1840, competitive two-party mass politics emerged on the world stage. Whigs gained control of the presidency and both chambers of Congress when the new government took office in March 1841.

After four years of Whig majorities, in 1841–45, Democrats enjoyed continuous control of the Senate from 1845 until 1861. Between the middle 1850s and early 1860s, politics were thrown into upheaval by the rapid mobilization of the Republican party as a fierce contender for power. In 1859, Democrats held 38 of the 66 Senate seats, but their number fell to just 15 in 1861, a consequence first of secession, then of civil war. Between 1863 and 1871, the number of Democrats ranged from 9 to 12, in a Senate of between 52 and 74 members. States left and then were readmitted to the Union, causing a radical shrinkage and expansion of the Senate. The resurgence of the Democratic party began slowly, in March 1871, when 17 Democrats took their seats in the Senate. In the next four Congresses, the Democratic caucus grew to 19, 28, 35, and then to a majority of 42 in 1879–81. The gains were due primarily to the reentry of southern states, the recreation of the party in that region, and the end of Reconstruction, although Democrats made gains in the West as well.

The struggle for Senate control was crucial to developments in the 1870s. Permanent steering committees and elected floor leaders still lay in the future, but the groundwork for Senate party organization was laid decisively by the 1870s. Both parties, majority and minority, now appointed committees on

---

[8] "An Historical Character," *Minneapolis Tribune*, Dec. 8, 1879, 2; "About Senate Pages: Historical Overview," www.senate.gov/about/officers-staff/pages/overview.htm (accessed February 9, 2025). In 1995, the Senate opened the Daniel Webster Senate Page Residence (Webster Hall) to provide better housing for pages.

committees, and both caucuses elected regular chairmen and appointed various ad hoc committees. The Senate gave formal recognition to the caucuses in awarding a room to the minority caucus, relying on caucus chairmen to enforce the agreement that resolved the 1876 election, removing the Senate's officers when Senate majorities shifted, and allowing the minority caucus to retain an officer. The restoration of two-party politics was sufficient to prompt both parties to consolidate a raft of new, lasting institutions. And the advances of the 1870s rested firmly on a foundation set during the three previous times that partisans had wrestled robustly for control of the chamber.

SENATE CAUCUSES BEFORE THE 1880S: EXISTING
SCHOLARSHIP

The origins of Senate caucus organization are a longstanding mystery. "It is difficult to tell just when party caucuses … on legislative measures came into use," Kerr (1895, 81) wrote in her study of the early Senate (see also Donnelly 1930, 38). Kravitz concurred, in his unpublished book manuscript on the history of the Senate. "Until at least the 1830's and perhaps as late as the mid-1840's—there is no certainty about the exact dates of the transformation, or even that there were exact dates—like-minded Senators caucused; that is, they met privately and more or less informally to discuss policies, legislation, and mutual political interests," Kravitz (ca. 1971, viii: 7) argued. "But there were no formal, continuing caucus organizations as we know them today." Rothman reached a similar conclusion, arguing that caucuses in the 1840s and early 1850s limited themselves to organizational matters, like assembling committee rosters and choosing Senate officers. "Colleagues at times consulted and voted together but did not create permanent institutional party structures," according to Rothman (1966, 14). "No caucus or informal committee determined general political policies, or designed specific measures, or enforced discipline, or looked after desired legislation. Senators performed their tasks as individuals rather than as Democrats or Whigs."[9]

Rothman argued that congressional caucuses went through two rapid transitions through the Civil War and Reconstruction. As hostilities approached and war broke out, according to Rothman, Senate party organizations gained unprecedented influence over both organizational and substantive matters. In the late 1850s, the Democratic caucus disciplined senators who deviated from majority policy regarding slavery. "The exigencies of the time brought a

---

[9] Indeed, so little has been known about the origins of Senate party caucuses that the Senate Historical Office reports that it was not until 1903 that the "Senate Democratic caucus decided it was time to get organized" and, according to this account, "for the first time in the Senate's history," elected a chairman and secretary and began to keep minutes. See "Senate Democratic Caucus Organized," Senate Historical Office, www.senate.gov/about/origins-foundations/ parties-leadership/democratic-caucus-organized.htm, accessed February 9, 2025.

similar discipline to the Republicans," Rothman contended, "and even issues peripheral to the Union effort were frequently decided by calls to solidarity" (Rothman 1966, 14–15). As evidence for the unprecedented strength of party caucuses in the 1850s and 1860s, Rothman cited three incidents: the 1858 decision of the Democratic caucus to strip Stephen Douglas (D, Ill.) of his chairmanship of the Committee on Territories and the strength of Republican support for a tariff bill and for the impeachment of Andrew Johnson.

By the late 1860s, however, according to Rothman, "members threw off discipline with a startling urgency" (Rothman 1966, 15). Through the 1870s and into the 1880s, both party caucuses were weak, decentralized, and lacking in meaningful positions of authority. "The weakness of party discipline reflected the lack of Senate leadership," Rothman (1966, 15) argued. No individual or faction was able to award committee assignments or party posts to gain special influence within either caucus, and most of the caucus's activity was devoted to distributing patronage among senators. Notably, Rothman emphasized that the weakness of the Republican caucus reflected not only the personality of its leaders, such as long-time caucus chairman Henry Anthony (R, R.I.), but the failure of the caucus to establish permanent organizational structures.

In support of this argument, Rothman drew contrasts between the divided Republican leadership of this era and the tightly knit group of senators who dominated the caucus in the late 1890s and 1900s. Although there was considerable evidence of caucus discipline in the 1870s—Rothman mentioned, for example, the decision to remove Charles Sumner (R, Mass.) from the chairmanship of the Foreign Relations Committee in 1871 as well as frequent criticisms made by senators and journalists of caucus discipline—Rothman rejected this as evidence of a strong or effective caucus. He emphasized instead a variety of other factors, including the fact that the Republican caucus chairman did not sit on the committee of committees (Rothman 1966, 16), the fact that the committee on committees did not use their positions "to reward friends and punish enemies" (Rothman 1966, 17), the fact that caucus decisions were not binding on the floor (Rothman 1966, 18), the fact that levels of party voting on the Senate floor were relatively low (Rothman 1966, 29), and the failure of efforts to limit debate in the Senate (Rothman 1966, 40).

By these criteria, though, the Republican caucuses of the 1890s and 1900s would also fail to qualify as disciplined. Even in the heyday of William Allison (R, Iowa) and Nelson Aldrich (R, R.I.) in the late 1890s and early 1900s, the caucus chairman never sat on the committee on committees, caucus decisions were never binding on the floor, and the right to filibuster continued unimpeded. Higher levels of party voting in 1897 than in 1872 probably reflected only a greater degree of preference homogeneity (Cooper and Brady 1981, but see Smith and Gamm 2001). And the committee on committees never disciplined members more than it did in the period 1866–72—neither in the 1850s nor the 1890s. Yet, for Rothman, the 1890s and 1900s represented the epitome of Senate party organization, while the 1870s and 1880s were an age of individualistic politics. The bases upon which Rothman distinguished the two eras relied heavily upon personality, in particular the small group of senators who dominated caucus leadership positions in the latter era, and the rhetoric in the 1890s that criticized this accumulation of party power.

Rothman appeared not to have investigated the possibility that the 1870s was an era of remarkable institutional innovation in Senate party organization—and the culmination of generations of work creating and articulating the powers of the party caucuses. He mentioned only one organizational innovation, the use of temporary committees on the order of business used by Republicans in 1874 and 1878 and by Democrats in 1879 (Rothman 1966, 30, 36–37; see also *History, Rules, and Precedents* 2022, 1, in which the Senate Republican conference mistakenly identifies the origins of its steering committee to 1874, almost certainly an inference from Rothman's work). And Rothman identifies this innovation only to emphasize the difficulties faced by the caucuses in setting an agenda. Thus he concluded that these years were a time of disorganization rather than an era of institution-building. "Existing positions seemed to carry little or no potentiality for power," Rothman (1966, 16) wrote. "The war years had inaugurated no permanent changes, and in this sense the Senate continued to resemble its predecessors, not its successors." Summarizing the argument, Rothman asserted, "In 1885 party could neither discipline its members nor drive malcontents from the ranks. With no leader to enforce regularity and no caucus to compel obedience, it still was unable to control the business of the Senate" (Rothman 1966, 42).

But Woodrow Wilson, writing in 1885, offered a contrary observation, challenging Rothman's account. "There is a certain well-known piece of congressional machinery long ago invented and applied for the special purpose of keeping both majority and minority compact. The legislative caucus has almost as important a part in our system as have the Standing Committees, and deserves as close study as they," Wilson (1885, 326–27) argued. "The caucus is the drilling-ground of the party. There its discipline is renewed and strengthened, its uniformity of step and gesture regained."

From his 1885 vantage, Wilson called for a "close study" of the rise of the caucus. Wilson (1885, 327–28) himself tentatively dated the origins of congressional caucuses to 1804–5, citing *Statesman's Manual*, which claimed that Jeffersonian Republicans were meeting in caucus during the 8th Congress to coordinate party business before it came to the floor. Other scholars also provide evidence that party members, in one or both chambers of Congress, relied on caucuses in the first years of the nineteenth century (Harlow 1917, 183–93; Luce 1922, 508–9; Berdahl 1949, 310). But only recently, with Jenkins and Stewart's (2013) study of the rise of party organization in the House of Representatives, have any scholars looked carefully and systematically at the origins of caucus organization in either chamber. No comparable study exists of Senate parties in the nineteenth century. As Jenkins and Stewart (2013, 310) write, "What remains to be done is a comprehensive accounting of the Senate's institutional development from the perspective of party leaders—from the founding to the present—with the idea of the organizational cartel in mind."

PARTIES AS CARTELS

The cartel metaphor was proposed by Cox and McCubbins (1993, 2005) to characterize the way members of House parties collaborate to control the factors that influence their reelection prospects. The principal factors are the composition of committees and, when in the majority, control of the legislation that is considered on the floor. In the modern era, majority parties have empowered standing committees to be gatekeepers—setting the policy agenda in a manner that serves the party's interests. Cox and McCubbins's 1993 book, *Legislative Leviathan*, emphasizes the control of the majority party over key organizational components of the House; their 2005 study, *Setting the Agenda*, focuses on the majority party's procedural advantages. Jenkins and Stewart (2013) demonstrate that the choice of House posts—speaker, printer, and committee positions—was brought within the majority party only after years of conflict and trial-and-error processes in the early and mid-nineteenth century. This cartel-like behavior did not become the norm until Republicans took control of the House in 1859. In this account, House parties necessarily became organizational cartels before procedural cartels, the latter taking hold only with the rulings and rules written by Speaker Thomas B. Reed in 1890 that broke minority efforts to obstruct House action (Binder 1997; Klotz 2022). When controlling institutional positions proved inadequate for the majority party, the party sought to gain greater advantage in parliamentary procedure. As Reed concluded, controlling legislative outcomes demanded that the party be both a procedural and an organizational cartel.

Extending the cartel metaphor to the Senate is not straightforward. The evolution of the filibuster limited the power of a Senate majority to impose rules that gave it a meaningful advantage in the legislative process. The ability of the minority to obstruct—and the tolerance of the majority party of the practice—has shaped party development throughout the history of the Senate. And, of course, there is no speaker of the Senate, no person with the power to name committees or set agendas whose appointment rests on a vote of the full chamber. Nevertheless, Senate parties organized, as well as they could, to control the factors that allowed them to enact or protect policy and win elections. Fights over the selection of a Senate printer often involved the same printers and newspapers competing for House business. After parties reemerged in the late 1820s and 1830s, decisions over Senate positions often generated conflict among majority senators.

Crucial institutional innovations—including regular caucus meetings, selection of caucus chairmen, and the appointment of caucus committees—were not automatic inventions. As we show, the creation of each institution occurred in meaningful sequence and at specific times, and identifying these developments is essential to understanding modern Senate parties. There was no point at which parties suddenly became procedural or organizational cartels. Rather, there was a series of accretions, forward and backward steps, representing organizational changes intended to influence the Senate's agenda or procedural choices. By the time robust two-party competition reemerged in the 1870s, many of these organizational practices were well accepted and readily continued from one Congress to the next.

PRESIDENTIAL NOMINATING CAUCUSES, 1796–1800

Party caucuses have existed since the first years of Congress, when Republicans and Federalists held at least some secret meetings to discuss legislative strategy (Ostrogorski 1899, 259–60; Ostrogroski 1902, ii: 13–15). But by far the most important caucuses in the early nineteenth century were presidential nominating caucuses. These were joint caucuses, including senators as well as House members, which convened every four years in the nation's capital to nominate the party's candidates for president and vice president. While there was an informal, inconclusive meeting of Republicans in 1796, only in 1800 did a disciplined caucus emerge (Ostrogorski 1899, 259–64; Ostrogorski 1902, 13–15; Donnelly 1930, 39; Cunningham 1957, 91, 162–66; Chambers 1963, 152; Cunningham 1963, 103; Cunningham 1965, 123–32; Morgan 1969, 185–87; Wilentz 2005, 73, 87).

Republicans and Federalists both met in 1800 to coordinate their presidential and vice-presidential slates. In subsequent years, the congressional caucus became synonymous with the Republican party, which used the caucus successfully between 1800 and 1816 to manage its nominations (Ostrogorski 1902, 13–19, 25–34; Brant 1953, 419–34; Cunningham 1963, 101–24, 302; Young 1966, 113–17; McCormick 1982, 5, 63–65, 70, 88–92, 96, 104–8, 116, 119, 132–34; Wilentz 2005, 115, 134–35, 139, 156–57, 178, 202, 246). Three presidents—Jefferson, Madison, and Monroe, all from Virginia—were effectively anointed through this system. Especially in the earlier years, when the Republican nominee for president was widely known, coordinating the choice of a vice-presidential nominee became the crucial business.

"There was never any doubt that Jefferson would be the party's candidate for President" in 1800, but the choice of Aaron Burr for vice president was less obvious, according to McCormick (1982, 64). "Meeting secretly at Maraché's boarding house in Philadelphia on May 11, Republican members of Congress, and other party leaders, agreed unanimously to endorse him as Jefferson's running mate." The Charleston (S.C.) *City Gazette* and *Niles' Weekly Register* each published detailed articles in the 1820s reviewing the history of the congressional nominating caucus. The *City Gazette* noted that "Maraché's boarding house" was generally known as "republican head-quarters," then listed all of the members of Congress who were supposed to have attended the 1800 caucus. "The venerable John Langdon (afterwards V.P.) was chosen chairman of the meeting, and presided as such," the *Gazette* noted. "In respect to the *presidency*, there was no difficulty—Mr. Jefferson was then, and from the time that Gen. Washington withdrew, had been the choice of the Republicans for that office."[10] The next caucus, in 1804, according to *Niles' Register*, "had respect only to the *vice presidency*—to supply the place of Mr. Burr, whom the former caucus had selected, he being now politically dead."[11] Both journals then chronicled the 1808 caucus, which selected Madison for president, and the caucuses of 1812 and 1816.

A desultory effort to organize a caucus in 1820 was quickly abandoned, as Monroe ran unopposed for his second term. "It was at this time so unnecessary, that the failure is a subject of almost universal congratulation," the *Richmond Enquirer* reported in April 1820. "What! can the people at no time whatever, not even at a moment when all faction is lulled, all opposition is put to sleep, be permitted to give their votes without the nomination of a Caucus at Washington?"[12] With the demise of the Federalist party, it had become increasingly difficult to explain the need for a nominating caucus. In 1824, as the Republican party splintered over its presidential nominee, the congressional caucus could no longer play its old, unifying role, and the system of nominations by members of Congress collapsed. "There are many Republicans who believe that a Caucus can only be justified when there is a contest between *two great political parties*," a contributor to the *National Intelligencer* wrote in 1824. "Thus, during the great struggle for power between the *Federalists* and the *Democrats*, it was often found necessary for *each party* to meet in caucus, and to select *the candidate of the party*. But, where all the candidates *are of the same party*, there can be no excuse for a caucus."[13]

There is no evidence that Senate business was conducted at any of these caucuses. Most of the people in the room were members of the House, and these caucuses were convened solely to select nominees for president and vice president. Even so, these caucuses regularly stirred up controversy. "If any thing will rouse the freemen of America, it must be the arrogance of a number of members of Congress to assemble as an *Electioneering Caucus*," one observer wrote in an 1803 pamphlet (Cunningham 1957, 166). "Under what authority did these men pretend to dictate their nomination? Did they receive six dollars a day for the double purpose of *caucussing* and *legislating?* Do we send members of Congress to *cabal* once in four years for President?" Controversial or not, these quadrennial presidential nominating caucuses

---

[10] "Communication, No. IV," *City Gazette* (Charleston, S.C.), July 1, 1824, 2.

[11] "The Sovereignty of the People—No. 5," *Niles' Weekly Register*, Oct. 2, 1824, 66, also 65–68. See also "Caucus History," *Niles' Weekly Register*, Dec. 20, 1823, 244–45; "Political History," *Niles' Weekly Register*, Dec. 27, 1823, 258–59; "End of the Caucus Project," *Niles' Weekly Register*, Jan. 17, 1824, 305–9; "The Caucus of Sixty-Six," *Niles' Weekly Register*, Feb. 28, 1824, 401–6; "Sovereignty of the People—No. 3," *Niles' Weekly Register*, Sept. 18, 1824, 33–39; "Sovereignty of the People—No. 4," *Niles' Weekly Register*, Sept. 25, 1824, 49–53.

[12] "The Caucus," *Richmond Enquirer*, Apr. 14, 1820, 3.

[13] "Reasons Against a Caucus," *National Intelligencer*, Feb. 16, 1824, 1. See also "The Caucus of Sixty-Six," *Niles' Weekly Register*, Feb. 28, 1824, 401–6.

established the precedent that members of Congress could segregate themselves along party lines to meet and conduct business out of the public eye.

ORIGINS OF THE SENATE PARTY CAUCUS, 1841–45

Senate caucuses of any sort were scarce before 1841, and the few caucuses that were called were used only sporadically for legislative purposes. Federalists and Republicans sometimes met in secret legislative caucuses between the late 1790s and mid-1810s, but, between the mid-1810s and 1840, even after the reemergence of organized parties, senators rarely looked to caucuses to set agendas, debate bills, or conduct other legislative business. Democrats, newly organized as a party, had begun holding occasional caucuses by the mid-1830s to select Senate officers and discuss at least some committee appointments. In December 1836, for example, they gathered to nominate a candidate for secretary of the Senate; Asbury Dickens, who was selected in caucus, won election on the Senate floor but only on the second ballot, which showed the possibilities (and limits) of caucus decision-making.[14] But, as late as 1840, the caucus had yet to emerge as a systematic institution for structuring and organizing Senate business. That changed decisively—and permanently—in the first weeks of 1841. After Whigs gained control of the Senate following the 1840 election, they remade the Senate for posterity, establishing the caucus as the primary mechanism for managing the chamber's business.[15] Then, within five years, in December 1845, the caucus assumed full responsibility for standing committee assignments. The initial impetus in 1841 had come from Henry Clay and his Whig colleagues, but, by the mid-1840s, both the Senate Democratic and Whig caucuses had laid the foundations of an organizational cartel.

To identify the origins of the legislative caucus in the Senate, we conducted a comprehensive examination of 27 newspapers for the period 1800–1860, of which 23 were published during the 1800–1845 period, using the database *America's Historical Newspapers*.[16] We ran an array of searches, all focused on finding

---

[14] "From Washington," *New York Herald*, Dec. 17, 1836, 2. See also "Intrigues of Party," *Alexandria Gazette*, Dec. 23, 1836, 2.

[15] Swift (1989, 1996) also considers 1841 to be the start of a new era in the Senate. As she shows, it marked a time when the Senate more frequently took the initiative in legislation, when it became more dependent on its committees as its workload increased, and when election-oriented parties emerged.

[16] The newspapers searched were: *Evening Star* (Washington, D.C.), *Times-Picayune* (New Orleans, La.), *Philadelphia Inquirer*, *Plain Dealer* (Cleveland, Ohio), *Augusta Chronicle* (Augusta, Ga.), *Boston Herald*, *Evening Post* (New York, N.Y.), *Alexandria Gazette*, *Daily National Intelligencer* (Washington, D.C.), *Boston Daily Advertiser*, *Commercial Advertiser* (New York, N.Y.), *New York Herald*, *City Gazette* (Charleston, S.C.), *Charleston Courier* (Charleston, S.C.), *North American* (Philadelphia, Pa.), *Albany Evening Journal*, *New-York Gazette*, *Boston Evening Transcript*, *Philadelphia Gazette*, *Connecticut Courant* (Hartford), *Columbian Centinel* (Boston, Mass.), *Cincinnati Daily Gazette*, *Cincinnati Commercial Tribune*, *Albany Argus*, *Aurora General Advertiser* (Philadelphia, Pa.), *Enquirer* (Richmond, Va.), and *Macon Telegraph* (Ga.).

stories including the words "caucus," "senate," and "congress" in close proximity to one another—with additional searches on the words "committee" and "order of business." Altogether, we identified 883 stories during this time period using some combination of these words, of which 340 stories related, in some fashion, to caucuses either in Congress generally or the Senate specifically. We also searched for every mention of the word "caucus" in the published debates of both the House and Senate, for the period 1800–1860, which yielded 364 distinct sets of remarks. In addition to our work with these two databases, we scrutinized other sources for any coverage of Senate caucus activity between the 1790s and 1860s.

Caucus Activity through 1840

Evidence of Senate caucus activity before 1841 is fragmentary: early caucuses to coordinate legislative priorities were informal, intermittent, secretive affairs. Most of the references we have found to Senate caucus activity is from the period between the late 1790s and mid-1810s, during the height of competition between Republicans and Federalists. Kravitz (ca. 1971, viii: 7–8; see also Maclay 1890; Swanstrom 1988, 229; McConnell and Brownell 2019, 124–25) identifies a small number of meetings held by Federalist senators in the 1790s. However, contemporary reports of these caucuses tended to be highly partisan and thus contested. "In the Summer session of 1798, when Federal thunder and violence were belched from the pestiferous lungs of more than one despotic minion, a caucus was held at the house of Mr. Bingham, in this city. It was composed of members of the Senate, and there were present seventeen members," a majority of the chamber, the Philadelphia *Aurora* reported. "Prior to deliberation on the measures of war, navy, army, democratic proscription, &c., it was proposed, and agreed to, that all the members present should solemnly pledge themselves to act firmly upon the measures to be agreed upon by the majority of the persons present at the caucus." In the winter of 1800, according to the *Aurora*, Federalist senators met in caucus again, this time to draft a bill. "We noticed a few days ago the caucuses (or secret consultations) held in the Senate Chamber," the *Aurora* stated. "The bill we this day present was discussed at the caucus on Wednesday evening last." On the basis of these accounts, William Duane, the Republican editor of the *Aurora*, informed his readers that Federalist senators were relying on "a secret self-appointed" caucus to discuss their agenda and frame legislation. But Duane's accusation was not uncontroverted. In March 1800, the Senate's Federalist majority adopted a formal resolution denouncing the *Aurora*'s report of caucusing as "false, defamatory, scandalous, and malicious assertions, and pretended information" (*Annals of Cong.*, March 20, 1800, 113–16).[17]

---

[17] See also "From the Gazette of the United States," *Commercial Advertiser* (New York, N.Y.), Oct. 16, 1801, 2; Swanstrom 1988, 307. In the House of Representatives, Albert Gallatin (R, Pa.) recalled that Republicans met in caucus just twice between 1795 and 1801, a time of great partisan conflict (Cunningham 1957, 82).

Caucus activity continued, in a scattered way, through the 1800s and as late
as 1815. In his daily summary of Senate business, William Plumer (F, N.H.)
identified just four instances of Republican senators meeting in caucus—in
October and December 1803, to consider whether to replace the secretary of
the Senate; in February 1804, to reach agreement on the substance of a bill
regarding the laws and government to be adopted for the Louisiana Territory;
and in December 1804, to nominate a governor for the Orleans Territory—and
no examples of Federalist Senate caucuses (Brown 1923, 28, 81–83, 141, 220,
597–98). We discover references to a caucus that was held in 1807 to discuss
"the first embargo" and to a Republican caucus in February 1809 to consider the
repeal of the Embargo Act and support for "the Non-Intercourse resolutions."[18]
The practice of caucusing had "begun about seven or eight years ago," and it was
still going on, the *Connecticut Courant* reported in 1811, though this assertion
was supported more by bluster than by evidence. "The important affairs of the
nation are pre-determined in secret conclave, and the votes on questions are fixt
before they are debated."[19] In 1815, House and Senate Republicans held "a
grand Caucus" to discuss the proposal to establish the Second Bank of the United
States. The caucus appointed a committee, composed of three senators and three
representatives, to formulate a plan. "Accordingly, on Friday night, the grand
caucus met again," the *New-York Gazette* reported in February 1815, "and the
committee appointed the previous evening, did then and there unfold a system of
a Bank that must be passed into a law."[20]

Drawing on diaries, personal papers, and congressional records,
Cunningham (1963, 99–100) concludes that party caucuses were "irregularly
employed" in 1801–9 and that, given the scarcity, vagueness, and secondhand
quality of surviving accounts, "it is impossible to establish the extent to which
the caucus was adopted as a method of party procedure" in either chamber.
"Much party business of which the historian will ever remain unaware,"
Cunningham (1963, 103) notes, "was undoubtedly transacted at the dinner
tables and in the private quarters of members." But, as Young (1966, 125)
writes, examining the period 1800–1828, "one searches the community record
in vain for evidence that common party affiliation was the basis of any associ-
ational activity whatever in the everyday life of Capitol Hill."

In our examination of congressional proceedings, newspapers, and
other sources, we locate no reference to any Senate caucus in the period

[18] "Congress: Debate on the Amendments to the Constitution," *Albany Argus*, Apr. 2, 1824, 2;
"From Washington, Feb. 14," *Philadelphia Gazette*, Feb. 17, 1809, 2. See also *Annals of Cong.*,
Feb. 7, 1809, 1419–21; Johnstone 1978, 123; Young 1966, 125–26.
[19] "Hartford, July 10," *Connecticut Courant* (Hartford), July 10, 1811, 3. See also "From the
Connecticut Courant," *Alexandria Gazette*, Oct. 18, 1811, 3.
[20] "Another Caucus Bank," *New-York Gazette*, Feb. 9, 1815, 2. See also *Register of Debates in
Congress*, Oct. 3, 1837, 482–83; "From the Federal Republican of Monday: Another Caucus
Bank," *Commercial Advertiser* (New York, N.Y.), Feb. 8, 1815, 3.

1816–31—apart from three stories in 1827 debating the veracity of accounts that Jacksonian senators had met in caucus that spring.[21] We find evidence of caucus meetings in the 1830s, but just a smattering: a joint caucus in 1832 of House and Senate National Republicans to discuss a tariff bill (Remini 1991, 386–88); a "full caucus" of Democrats in 1834 to discuss plans to publish extra copies of a report of the Committee on Post Offices and Post Roads; a Senate Democratic caucus in 1836 that resolved to limit debate on the question of Michigan statehood; and a Senate Democratic caucus in 1837 to discuss the sub-treasury bill, along with a caucus of Democrats from both chambers on the same subject.[22] As late as 1840, senators meeting in caucus appears still to have been an exceptional event. Kravitz (ca. 1971, viii: 10), in his comprehensive review of the literature, reaches a similar conclusion, writing, "Little was heard of the caucus during the Jackson and Van Buren administrations," between 1829 and 1841. Legislative caucuses were not unknown in the Senate in the first four decades of the nineteenth century, but, at best, they were held rarely and irregularly.

Emergence of the Legislative Business Caucus, 1841

As Whigs prepared to take control of the presidency, House, and Senate in the spring of 1841—all for the first time—Whig senators agreed on the urgency of enacting their program in order to address the economic crisis and demonstrate that they could follow through on their campaign promises to reverse a number of Democratic policies (Remini 1991, 567–84; Holt 1999, 126–31). With two national parties now competing on equal terms in national elections, the Whigs could launch their experiment in party government. They had an expansive agenda: repeal the sub-treasury system, create a new national bank, strengthen protective tariffs, establish national bankruptcy rules, and distribute federal land revenues to the states (*Cong. Globe*, June 7, 1841, 22; Smith 1858, 375–76; Peterson 1987, 303–4; Holt 1999, 126). Most Whigs looked to Capitol Hill, not to the White House, for leadership. "William Henry Harrison may have been elected president," Peterson (1987, 297) observed, "but Henry Clay was still the leader of the Whig party." The Whig party had emerged in the 1830s as a congressional counterpoint to the Jackson presidency, and, even with a Whig president taking office in March 1841, it was Clay who led the party. "All Whigs expected Congress to formulate Whig policies," Holt (1999, 126) argues, "and as the party's legislative leader, Clay

[21] "Signs of the Times," *Charleston (S.C.) Courier*, Mar. 20, 1827, 3; "Signs of the Times—Reviewed," *Daily National Intelligencer* (Washington, D.C.), Apr. 19, 1827, 3; "The National Intelligencer—Its 'Signs' and Its Fallacies," *Albany Argus*, July 13, 1827, 2.

[22] "From Washington," *Philadelphia Inquirer*, June 12, 1834, 2; "More Vandalism," *Connecticut Courant* (Hartford), Apr. 11, 1836, 2; "A Senatorial Caucus," *Alexandria Gazette*, Dec. 20, 1837, 2; "How to Manufacture Public Opinion," *Connecticut Courant*, Dec. 23, 1837, 3.

expected to get the main credit for the program that was passed." Determined to lead the Whigs nationally from his perch in the Senate, Clay took the initiative, mobilized other Whig senators, and began to lay the groundwork for a comprehensive legislative program (Silbey 1967, 50; Holt 1999, 125–26; Wilentz 2005, 523; MacNeil and Baker 2013, 63, 170–71; McConnell and Brownell 2019, 89).

On January 23, 1841, more than a month before the old session of Congress ended, the Whig senators met in caucus. "It was decided in Whig caucus, on Saturday evening, that a special session of Congress shall be held. The caucus was represented by the Whig members of the Senate only," the New York *Evening Post* reported, before offering sardonic commentary, using a common nickname for Clay. "What an impatient restless creature this 'Harry' is! He cannot wait a few brief days or months at most, for time in its ordinary channels to hand him into power!"[23] Nineteen Whig senators participated in the caucus, which was held in the Senate chamber. They concluded that they had to move swiftly to address the financial crisis and "save the country from the deep disgrace ... created by Mr. Van Buren's administration," according to the *New York Herald*. "It was therefore agreed to recommend to Gen. Harrison to call an EXTRA SESSION of Congress in the month of May, or as soon thereafter as practicable."[24] The recommendation was unprecedented. They "expect to rule the President Elect," the *Richmond Enquirer* contended. The Senate's Whigs sought "to preach up a plausible pretext for a called Session, to fasten on the country a Bank, and a Distribution of the Sales of the Public Lands, and an increased Tariff, before they can be 'palsied' by the will of Instructing Legislatures."[25] This agenda, the Raleigh *Standard* observed, is "to usher in Mr. *Clay's*—we beg pardon—Gen. *Harrison's* administration."[26]

Calling a caucus, let alone a caucus to discuss whether Congress should meet in a special session, given that this decision belonged only to the president, was still a novelty that winter. In its coverage, the *New York Herald* helpfully explained to its readers that a caucus was a "private meeting of the Whig Senators."[27] Even on the House floor, members debated the propriety of the Senate Whig caucus—with one Whig representative, Daniel Jenifer (W, Md.), "disclaiming any knowledge of such a caucus" and disingenuously challenging Democrats to prove it had even taken place (*Cong. Globe*, February 3, 1841,

---

[23] "Correspondence of the Evening Post, Washington City," *Evening Post* (New York, N.Y.), Jan. 27, 1841, 2. See also "From Our Correspondent," *Emporium and True American* (Trenton, N.J.), Feb. 5, 1841, 3; "Correspondence of the Evening Post," *Evening Post* (New York, N.Y.), Feb. 8, 1841, 2; "Extra Session," *Nashville Union*, Feb. 8, 1841, 2; "From Washington," *Albany Argus*, Feb. 12, 1841, 2.

[24] *New York Herald*, Jan. 29, 1841, as quoted in "Extra Session," *Nashville Union*, Feb. 8, 1841, 2.

[25] "Mr. Wise," *Richmond Enquirer*, Feb. 2, 1841, 3.

[26] "Extra Session of Congress," *The Standard* (Raleigh, N.C.), Feb. 10, 1841, 2.

[27] *New York Herald*, Jan. 29, 1841, as quoted in "Extra Session," *Nashville Union*, Feb. 8, 1841, 2.

appendix, 146). Clay strongly supported the call for a special session—indeed, it is likely he instigated the movement to call the Senate caucus—but William Henry Harrison, the newly elected president, initially ignored the caucus recommendation, only to relent when he discovered the government was facing a large deficit (Peterson 1987, 299–301; Remini 1991, 575–77; Holt 1999, 126–27; Brands 2018, 270–71).

By the time the new session convened in May, Harrison had died and John Tyler was in the White House. "Clay got to the capital a full week ahead of the scheduled opening of Congress. He needed to get right to work organizing the Whigs in both houses if he expected to get his program through the legislature and adjourn by August," according to Remini (1991, 582). "That meant regular caucus meetings, that meant providing an agenda at the very outset, and that meant asserting undisputed leadership of the party." Almost immediately, the Whig caucus fell into a routine.[28] "The Whig Senators met in the room of the Vice-President, one evening early in the extra session, and organized by the choice of the Hon. Nathan F. Dixon, of Rhode Island, chairman," Oliver Hampton Smith (W, Ind.) recalled later. "Mr. Dixon, as a presiding officer, at once adopted the idea, that each Senator was bound to keep himself in order, and if he did not, the dignity of the chair would not permit him to interfere. The debates, therefore, at times assumed a personal character not very becoming in brethren of the same political party." Smith, who served just one term in the Senate, published his reminiscences in the late 1850s. His memories of the Senate Whig caucuses of the 1841 special session filled an entire chapter. "Some of the finest speeches I have ever heard from Mr. Clay, Mr. Rives, Mr. Southard, Mr. Crittenden, Mr. Davis, Mr. Choate, Mr. Preston, Mr. Simmons, and many other Senators, I have heard in the Whig caucus," Smith (1858, 593) wrote. "Time rolled on, meeting after meeting was held, nightly; measure after measure, vote after vote resolved upon, and carried out in open session."

Frustrated by the Tyler administration's half-hearted proposal for a new national bank, which it had sent to Congress only under pressure, Whig senators, led by Clay, turned to their caucus in June 1841 to draft their own bank bill (Peterson 1987, 306; Remini 1991, 587–88). "The Senate Whig caucus, meeting in three-hour sessions for four or five consecutive nights, designed a substitute," which they reported to the full Senate, Holt (1999, 129) writes. But the substitute represented a rebuke to the president, an assertion by Clay and his colleagues in the Senate that they understood better than President Tyler what was needed to revive the economy and to enhance electoral prospects for Whigs.[29] They turned again to their caucus, meeting

---

[28] "From Our Correspondent," *Baltimore Sun*, June 3, 1841, 4; "Correspondence of the Tribune," *New York Tribune*, June 14, 1841, 2.

[29] *New York Herald*, June 19, 1841, as quoted in "Political Aspect at Washington—The 'Fiscal Bank,'" *Albany Argus*, June 25, 1841, 1; "Fiscal Agent—Difficulties in the Way of Its Passage—Gen. Harrison's Promises, &c.," *Weekly Herald* (New York, N.Y.), July 3, 1841, 339; "From Washington," *Evening Post* (New York, N.Y.), July 14, 1841, 2.

regularly to debate how to proceed. "There was a caucus, last night, and another this morning, but no definitive determination was arrived at," the *New York Herald* reported in mid-July.[30] A group of senators "argued both in the Whig caucus and on the Senate floor that Clay's measure was suicidal, for Tyler would veto it. Some kind of bank was better than no bank, they contended," according to Holt (1999, 132–33). "Late in July the Whig caucus finally agreed upon a concession that might carry enough Whig votes to pass the bill on the Senate floor."[31] The amended bill passed the Senate, then the House, only to be vetoed by the president (Smith 1858, 148–55; Peterson 1987, 306–8; Remini 1991, 589–91; Wilentz 2005, 524–25). Whig senators responded to the veto by calling more caucus meetings in an effort to reach a compromise with the president that would enable the chartering of a new bank.[32] But Tyler's veto of the second bank bill led only to a deepening chasm between congressional Whigs, for whom a strong national bank was an urgent priority, and President Tyler.

Following the second veto, every member of Tyler's cabinet, except Secretary of State Daniel Webster, resigned in protest—and Senate Whigs joined with House Whigs in an extraordinary joint caucus to issue a statement denouncing the president for his action, effectively excommunicating him (Smith 1858, 152–54, 377–78; Peterson 1987, 313; Holt 1999, 137; Howe 2007, 594; Brands 2018, 274–75). "The President, by the course he has adopted in respect to the application of the veto power to two successive bank charters, each of which there was just reason to believe would meet his approbation; by his withdrawal of confidence from his real friends in Congress and from the members of his Cabinet; by his bestowal of it upon others notwithstanding their notorious opposition to leading measures of his Administration," the joint Whig statement declared, "has voluntarily separated himself from those by whose exertions and suffrages he was elevated to that office through which he reached his present exalted station."[33] Referring to the driving force behind

---

[30] "Despatch of Business in the House—Bank Bill—Locofoco Folly—Herald Reports, &c.," *Weekly Herald* (New York, N.Y.), July 17, 1841, 361. See also "Correspondence of the Evening Post," *Evening Post* (New York, N.Y.), July 16, 1841, 2; "Congress—Extra Session," *Albany Argus*, July 20, 1841, 1.

[31] See also Remini 1991, 589.

[32] "Congress—Extra Session," *Albany Argus*, Aug. 24, 1841, 1; "Correspondence of the Courier," *Charleston Courier*, Sept. 1, 1841, 2; *Cong. Globe*, Sept. 2, 1841, appendix, 345–47; "Congress," *Albany Argus*, Sept. 3, 1841, 3; "Aspects at Washington," *Albany Argus*, Sept. 7, 1841, 2; "In Senate: The Fiscal Corporation Bill," *Daily National Intelligencer*, Sept. 25, 1841, 2.

[33] "Congressional Whig Meeting," *Richmond Whig*, Sept. 17, 1841, 2. See also "Correspondence of the Courier," *Charleston Courier*, Sept. 17, 1841, 2; "From Washington," *Weekly Herald* (New York, N.Y.), Sept. 18, 1841, 429; "The Whig Address—Its Character and Tendency— Names of the Whig Members of Congress Who Had Nothing To Do with It," *Weekly Herald* (New York, N.Y.), Sept. 25, 1841, 438.

this statement, whatever its ostensible authorship, the *New York Evening Post* summed things up for its readers: "It is all Clay."[34]

Whig senators caucused frequently throughout the special session, between May and September 1841. "Despite their disarray on the banking issue, the disciplined Whig majority wielded their control of committees and skillfully employed the caucus to push their other measures through on largely party-line votes, and they received Tyler's signature," Holt (1999, 135) notes. They looked to their caucus to set legislative strategy, to coordinate on a set of standing committee chairmen, and to debate provisions of the land distribution bill, the tariff bill, and the bankruptcy bill.[35] "As in the case of the National Bank, the [land distribution] bill seems to have passed in caucus, with an understanding, that no essential amendment should be allowed," the *Albany Argus* reported on August 17, 1841. "Such is the force of the caucus party drill over principle and the interests of the people."[36] Whig senators relied so thoroughly on their caucus during the special session that the Senate erupted in guffaws when on August 21 James Morehead (W, Ky.) abruptly called for an adjournment of the day's proceedings, with Whigs disagreeing on the Senate floor about an amendment to the tariff bill. As Morehead made the motion to adjourn, the *Congressional Globe* (August 21, 1841, 366) reported that the chamber responded with "much laughter, and cries of 'Oh, oh! another caucus necessary.'"

Even as Whig senators were inventing the caucus in 1841 to realize their expansive agenda, the minority Democrats were honing new tools of obstructionism. The filibuster—the weapon of an organized minority in the Senate— emerged in this same era, a Democratic barnacle clinging to the side of the majority Whig caucus. It was Clay, ironically, who had demonstrated how the Senate's lack of a rule limiting debate could be used to frustrate majority action. In 1837 Clay and his Whig colleagues had engaged in an extended debate in an effort to block the Democratic effort to expunge the censure of Andrew Jackson (Burdette 1940, 19–21; Remini 1991, 493–96; Binder and Smith 1997, 91; Koger 2010, 62–63). Then, in 1841, Democrats, building on this example, waged two historic filibusters—one in the spring "when the Whigs moved to fire Blair and Rives as Senate printers"[37] and select a Whig printer instead, and the other, much lengthier, which was orchestrated that summer to obstruct passage of the bank bill (Burdette 1940, 21–25; Binder and Smith 1997, 91;

---

[34] "Correspondence of the Evening Post," *Evening Post* (New York, N.Y.), Sept. 15, 1841, 2.

[35] "From Our Correspondent," *Baltimore Sun*, June 3, 1841, 4; "Congress—Extra Session," *Albany Argus*, Aug. 17, 1841, 2; *Cong. Globe*, Aug. 18, 1841, 347; "Congress," *Albany Argus*, Sept. 3, 1841, 3; "Aspects at Washington," *Albany Argus*, Sept. 7, 1841, 2; *Cong. Globe*, June 30, 1842, 702; *Cong. Globe*, June 30, 1842, appendix, 554; *Cong. Globe*, July 2, 1842, appendix, 593.

[36] "Congress—Extra Session," *Albany Argus*, Aug. 17, 1841, 2.

[37] Daniel Holt to authors, email correspondence, Aug. 23, 2023.

Wawro and Schickler 2006, 72–76; Koger 2010, 63; Madonna 2012, 133–41; Jentleson 2021, 50–53). In his memoir, Benton described the Democratic strategy, which was to introduce a steady stream of amendments and to hold the floor for lengthy debates (Benton 1856, 247–57). For Clay, those tactics proved maddening. "He was impatient to pass his bills, annoyed at the resistance they met, and dreadfully harassed by the species of warfare to which they were subjected; and for which he had no turn," Benton (1856, 249), who, as a Democratic senator was helping to lead the filibuster, recalled with evident satisfaction. "The Whigs unsuccessfully tried to amend Senate rules to limit debate," Holt (1999, 129) writes. "The all-important Whig caucus, which Willie P. Mangum of North Carolina chaired, agreed to vote down any Democratic amendments. And the Whig leadership kept the House and Senate sitting for seven or eight hours a day, six days a week, despite the suffocating summer heat and humidity." But it was minority obstructionism that prevailed—not this early effort to adopt majority cloture, even if in its early incarnation the filibuster succeeded only in delaying, not killing, legislative action (Peterson 1987, 304–5; Binder 1997, 178–81; Binder and Smith 1997, 74–75; Wawro and Schickler 2006, 72–76; Madonna 2012, 133–41). "We felt victorious in the midst of unbroken defeats," Benton (1856, 249) wrote, summing up the moment.

The party caucus—reinvented by Clay early in 1841 to organize Whig senators for the special session—had been transformed, over the course of a few short months, into the party's core institution for Senate governance. The caucus had managed a robust policy agenda, it had handled complex disagreements among senators, and it had become the primary vehicle for galvanizing congressional Whigs and strengthening Clay's presidential prospects as relations with President Tyler ruptured. "The Whig caucus gathered for a last time before its members went home at the end of the special session," Brands (2018, 294) wrote. Oliver Hampton Smith remembered that September evening vividly. "It was dark and rainy. The Whig Senators were there. Mr. Dixon took the chair early. Every thing around us looked like the weather and the night, dark and gloomy," according to Smith (1858, 593–94). "Our hopes had been blasted; President Tyler had deceived us; our triumphant victory had been turned into ashes in our mouths; we were about to part, with no cheering prospects." But then Clay stood up and began to speak, galvanizing his colleagues and reminding them, even in that doleful hour, that the Whigs were not bereft of leadership or faith in their future. "We, Senators, will soon pass away, but our principles will live while our glorious Union shall exist," Clay told his colleagues. Excoriating Tyler—"He will stand here, like Arnold in England, a monument of his own perfidy and disgrace."—Clay reminded the Senate Whig caucus that their party would survive this betrayal (Smith 1858, 594). "Justice will be done to the memory of those who have stood firm, as the friends of the people," Clay said resolutely. "My friends, we have done our duty. We have maintained the true policy of the Government." Dispirited and disheartened, but defiant and determined to gain vindication as his party's presidential nominee in the next election, Clay resigned from the Senate in the spring of 1842.

By then the caucusing habit was thoroughly ingrained in Senate life. Throughout the remainder of this Congress—during the second and third sessions in 1842–43, months after the first special session and after Clay had given up his seat—senators continued to look to their party caucus to help guide the chamber's affairs. In June 1842, James Buchanan (D, Pa.) chided his Whig colleagues for abruptly shifting their position on an amendment that had come to the Senate floor. "But whence this new light which has burst upon Senators? I do not positively know, but I shall hazard a conjecture with a great degree of confidence," Buchanan stated on the Senate floor (*Cong. Globe*, June 10, 1842, 609). "No power could have produced such an extraordinary and sudden conversion, except the power of a king who has reigned in these halls, with omnipotent sway, since the commencement of the late extra session: —I refer to king Caucus." Even as Buchanan singled out the Whig caucus, the Senate's Democrats had also begun to rely on their own caucus to set strategy, in an effort "to make the Administration odious by preventing all important action."[38] Still, with Whigs controlling both chambers, it was the Senate Whig caucus that appeared to command the entire Congress. As the New York *Evening Post* argued in June 1842, "The House, as usual, showed it cannot act independently upon its own judgment; but is governed by the Senate, and a Senate whig caucus."[39]

Committee Assignments, 1845

After four years of Whig control, Democrats in 1845 returned to the Senate majority—and, in that same year, the two caucuses assumed responsibility for committee assignments. The Senate had created its system of standing committees in December 1816 (Robinson 1954, 52–54; Gamm and Shepsle 1989, 53–57; Byrd 1991, 217–18), but, for the next three decades, senators had struggled to find a method of appointing committees that was efficient and insured a committee's accountability to the chamber. Elections, which took days, guaranteed that the floor controlled the committees, but at the cost of time and the ability to coordinate assignments. Appointment by the presiding officer, which solved the problems of coordination and efficiency, raised issues of accountability. Between 1816 and 1844, the Senate delegated committee-

---

[38] "Correspondence of the N.Y. Express," *Connecticut Courant* (Hartford), June 18, 1842, 2. See also *Cong. Globe*, Aug. 5, 1842, 849.

[39] "Two O'Clock," *Evening Post* (New York, N.Y.), June 18, 1842, 2. See also *Cong. Globe*, Mar. 17, 1842, 332; *Cong. Globe*, Mar. 18, 1842, appendix, 257; "Correspondence of the Evening Post," *Evening Post* (New York, N.Y.), June 23, 1842, 2; *Cong. Globe*, Aug. 2, 1842, 829.

assignment power to its presiding officer at three different times: 1823–25, 1829–32, and 1837–44. In other years, senators balloted. While it is likely, especially after the emergence of the Democratic and Whig parties in the mid-1830s, that party leaders played some role behind the scenes in identifying committee chairmen and prospective committee members (McConachie 1898, 277–81; Robinson 1954, 122–24)—whether by winnowing candidates to be considered on the floor or by offering suggestions to the presiding officer—there is no evidence of any reference to a party caucus in these years.

It was in December 1845, as we discussed in the previous chapter, that the Senate caucuses assumed the power to name members of the standing committees, ending the dominant roles that the chamber's presiding officer and the floor had long played. That a Senate party caucus would take on this new responsibility was hardly self-evident when the minority Whigs and four Democrats denied the vice president the power to appoint committees. Two days after senators had voted to coordinate committee assignments themselves, observers were dubious as to whether their resolve would hold. "I see no reason to believe that the caucus principle can be made to extend to the organization of the committees," a *Baltimore Sun* correspondent wrote on December 6, 1845. There was even speculation, according to this journalist, that the Senate would reconsider its decision to reject "appointment of the committees by the chair, that is, to sacrifice Senatorial independence upon the altar of party."[40]

The Senate Democratic caucus was riven by faction. Indeed, it was only because of the defection of four Democrats that senators were not relying on the vice president to make committee assignments. This new responsibility had been thrust onto an unwilling majority caucus. Perhaps Senate Whigs had hoped their vote would force a return to balloting on the floor, but Democrats must have realized that only caucus control could protect their party and personal interests on committees. For days, the majority Democrats struggled to coordinate their ballots. According to the Washington correspondent of the Philadelphia *North American*, William Allen (D, Ohio)—"the caucus manager and mouth-piece"—moved on December 8 for an abrupt, early adjournment of the Senate, to avoid beginning the process of balloting for committees, due to "the fact that several Democratic Senators were absent, and that a union between those who intended to secede from the caucus dictation, with the Whigs, would have defeated the whole organization which had been matured, and thinned down an efficient majority to a hopeless minority."[41]

The postponement was brief. On December 9–10, in accordance with decisions made in the Democratic caucus, and apparently concurred in by the Whig

---

[40] "The Senators of the democratic party … ," *Baltimore Sun*, Dec. 8, 1845, 4.
[41] "Washington Correspondence," *North American* (Philadelphia, Pa.), Dec. 10, 1845, 1. The motion appears to have been made by Ambrose Sevier (D, Ark.), not by Allen (*Cong. Globe*, Dec. 8, 1845, 25). See also McConachie 1898, 281–82.

caucus, the Senate balloted for all standing committee chairmen, then for the full membership of two committees, Foreign Relations and Finance (*Cong. Globe*, December 9, 1845, 31; *Cong. Globe*, December 10, 1845, 39; Robinson 1954, 126–30). But ratifying these decisions through the mechanism of balloting on the floor introduced its own complications, since the Democratic Senate caucus had not only agreed on the chairmen and the two committee memberships but had also ranked the members of each committee in a specific order. With balloting, those rankings had been scrambled. The problem emerged on December 10, as soon as the first of the committees, Foreign Relations, had been elected. Asked by Spencer Jarnagin (W, Tenn.) "how it was understood that the members of the committee would be arranged as to their order; whether in an arbitrary manner, or as their names stood on the ballot," Vice President George M. Dallas, a Democrat, explained "that they would be arranged according to the number of ballots which each Senator received" (*Cong. Globe*, December 10, 1845, 39). At that response, Ambrose Sevier (D, Ark.), speaking on behalf of the Democratic Senate caucus, protested. "Should that be the understanding, the members of the committee would occupy positions which were not contemplated by a majority of the Senate," Sevier declared (*Cong. Globe*, December 10, 1845, 39), "and, in the elections about to take place, it would be necessary to have two ballots," one to select the members of the committee, then another ballot to confirm the order in which those members were ranked.

On the spot, a second revolution was erupting! Senate Democrats were consolidating their organizational cartel. As senators that day debated parliamentary law and precedent, the same majority caucus that had just assumed the power to name Senate committees was realizing that it also possessed the right to rank its committee lists—and, at that moment of discovery, the Senate formally embraced the idea that committee rankings were, in fact, consequential. "Mr. Sevier said, in his experience it had always been the practice on the resignation or in the absence of the chairman of the committee, for the next member, in the order of the list, to take the chair. It was important, therefore, to know how they were placed," according to the *Congressional Globe* (December 10, 1845, 39). As a mark of respect for the minority party, Sevier said that "he would place every Senator, taken from the other side, the third on the list." John Berrien (W, Ga.), a Whig senator, shared Sevier's understanding. Observing from experience that committee rankings determined "succession" on Senate committees, Berrien described how that day's committee lists had been formulated. "He had understood (although he had arrived too late to be a personal participator in the arrangement) that a mutual conciliatory arrangement had been entered into by both sides of the Senate, with respect to the election of the committees," Berrien explained (*Cong. Globe*, December 10, 1845, 39), "as to the order of succession in which the members should stand." Sevier proceeded to offer a motion establishing a rank order for the members of the Committee on Foreign Relations, and the motion was adopted.

As the discussion wound down on December 10, the Senate then elected the members of the Finance Committee—and Sevier immediately followed that election with a motion, approved by the Senate, specifying the order in which those committee members were ranked. James Westcott (D, Fla.) was astonished by the whole proceeding. He insisted, for the record, that this was an innovation he could not countenance. "He had no idea that there was, or ought to be, any distinction of rank in the committees, or that anything like a law or right of primogeniture ought to be established here," Westcott said (*Cong. Globe*, December 10, 1845, 39). "He was opposed to everything of the kind. He was opposed to this infringement of the settled rule of our institutions." But Westcott was outvoted, as the Senate agreed that day to adopt the two committee lists arranged by the Democratic caucus and to endorse the understanding that there was significance to the ordering of the names on each list. On December 17, partly by ballot and partly by a comprehensive resolution prepared by the majority caucus—itself a new and lasting precedent—members of the Senate adopted full lists for the remaining committees, with senators ranked on each of these prearranged lists (*Cong. Globe*, December 17, 1845, 66; McConachie 1898, 282–83, 325–26; Robinson 1954, 129–30; Merk 1967, 375; Walton 1973, 45–47; Byrd 1991, 223–24).

The Whig claim that their earlier vote—as a minority party in the Senate, to take from the presiding officer the power to make committee assignments—had been based on principle rather than politics had some merit. "It had been infinitely better had the whigs assented, in the first place, to the appointment of the committees by the Vice President," the *New York Herald* observed before the final committee assignments were known. "Though, it is likely, he would have shown them no more favor upon No. 1, he would assuredly have given them some appointments as No. 2. Now there is scarcely a hope that even Webster, or Berrien, or Mangum, or Crittenden, or Corwin, or Dayton, or Johnson of Md., or Evans, or Archer, will be elevated to a higher order than No. 3."[42]

Freed of any pretense of impartiality, which might have constrained the vice president's assignments, the Democratic caucus made assignments and established committee rankings to cement their partisan advantage. The *Massachusetts Spy*, on December 17, reported that there would be just one Whig sitting on each of "the two most important Committees of the U.S. Senate," the five-member Finance Committee and the five-member Foreign Affairs Committee, and on both committees the Whig member was ranked third. And there were, of course, policy implications to these committee memberships. "*One* Whig each. The Foreign Affairs is a War Committee, strong enough; the Finance will stand three for smashing and tearing on the Tariff Question; one Whig opposed, and one Benton who will do as he has a mind to," the *Spy* wrote. "The Whigs are allowed to have the Chairman of *no*

---

[42] *New York Herald*, Dec. 12, 1845, 4.

Committee of any consequence."[43] The *New-York Commercial Advertiser* shared similar concerns: "These committees are now organized, and as a specimen of the fairness and magnanimity of the majority of the Senate we cite the fact, and call public attention to it, that Daniel Webster, one of the oldest members of the body, who has been for many years chairman of the committee on the judiciary, and chairman of the committee on finance—who has been Secretary of State, and is known to quite a number of people throughout the country as a man of industry and ability, possessing some acquaintance with public affairs, is on *one* committee, and at the very *tail* of that; at the very tail end of the committee on the judiciary!"[44]

Learning from its experience the year before, the Senate in December 1846 introduced new, more straightforward ways of assembling committees and gaining approval on the floor—developing a process where each party caucus drew up its own list of committee members, with the minority caucus being told in advance how many positions they had to fill on each committee; acknowledging on the floor that these lists existed; and adopting these lists as resolutions approved by unanimous consent. On December 14, 1846, after senators had selected six committee chairmen by balloting on the floor, John Davis (W, Mass.) interrupted to point out the absurdity of the proceeding and suggested an alternative method. "If any gentleman upon the other side of the Chamber had a list of the committees as they had been agreed upon by the majority, it might by common consent be read, and declared to be a list of the standing committees of the Senate," Davis suggested (*Cong. Globe*, December 14, 1846, 30), "which would be a great saving of time without altering the result which would be arrived at by the tedious process of balloting." Sevier confirmed that such a list existed—and that it was "a list of the committees which had been agreed upon, not only on his side of the chamber, but upon the other also" (*Cong. Globe*, December 14, 1846, 30). Willie P. Mangum (W, N.C.), presumptively acting on behalf of the Whig caucus, then offered a motion, which was approved, that the Senate adopt the list by unanimous consent. Every major committee was composed of five members, with the minority members ranked third and fifth on the list. "Three members on each committee had been selected on his side of the Senate," Sevier later recalled (*Cong. Globe*, December 14, 1847, 21). "The list had then been handed to the Senators on the other side, and they had filled it up."[45] The Senate now had perfected a process that empowered the two caucuses, working together, to manage committee assignments. While this process would face new challenges as the Senate soon welcomed members who identified with neither major party, the basic outlines of the process were in place in 1846.

---

[43] "The two most important Committees ... ," *Massachusetts Spy* (Worcester, Mass.), Dec. 17, 1845, 3.
[44] "The Standing Committees of the Senate," *New-York Commercial Advertiser*, Dec. 19, 1845, 2.
[45] See also McConachie 1898, 283–84; Robinson 1954, 130.

With the caucus now responsible for assembling committee lists, Democratic senators increased the coordination capacity of their caucus and invented a new institution—a committee on committees. In a dispatch dated December 9, 1847, the *New York Evening Post* reported that, after the Senate had adjourned for the day, "the democratic Senators met in caucus to select the chairmen of the several standing committees," but decided only that the matter should be "referred to a select committee," which would be charged with making a recommendation to the full caucus.[46] "Last evening there was a Caucus of the majority to make choice of Chairmen, &c.," the *Baltimore American and Commercial Daily Advertiser* wrote the next day in its own account of the caucus meeting. "Nothing, however, was done beyond the appointment of a Committee who will report the names of the most suitable persons to a second meeting."[47] On December 11, the committee made its report to the caucus, which then finalized its list of the chairmen and majority members of each standing committee.[48] The Senate Democratic caucus, which had assumed responsibility for committee assignments just two years earlier, was now delegating that work to its first committee on committees. Because of its ability to coordinate the caucus's decision and floor strategy, the committee on committees immediately became a powerful organ of the Democratic party. It was used continually from 1847 through 1859, then was dissolved, as the number of Democrats in the Senate plummeted during the Civil War.

Caucus Organization

The Senate party caucus was Clay's imperishable legacy. Democratic and Whig senators turned to the caucus to debate the annexation of Texas in 1845, the Oregon question in 1846, the declaration of war with Mexico in 1846, the Treaty of Guadalupe Hidalgo in 1848, the Compromise of 1850, and the Kansas-Nebraska Act of 1854.[49] When Joseph Underwood (W, Ky.) observed in February 1849 that he did "not know how to classify" John P. Hale (N.H.) —a Free Soil senator who was "somewhat repudiated by all classes in this

---

[46] "From the South," *New York Evening Post*, Dec. 11, 1847, 3.
[47] "Correspondence of the American," *Baltimore American and Commercial Daily Advertiser*, Dec. 11, 1847, 2.
[48] "By Magnetic Telegraph," *Baltimore Sun*, Dec. 13, 1847, 2; "Correspondence of the American," *Baltimore American and Commercial Daily Advertiser*, Dec. 13, 1847, 2.
[49] James G. Bennett, "Washington, Sunday, Feb. 16, 1845," *New York Herald*, Feb. 18, 1845, 4; "Washington, March 27, 1846," *Weekly Herald* (New York, N.Y.), Apr. 4, 1846, 106; *Cong. Globe*, Feb. 24, 1847, 501; "Correspondence of the Baltimore Sun," *Baltimore Sun*, Mar. 4, 1848, 4; "The Compromise," *Boston Evening Transcript*, July 24, 1850, 2; "Thirty-First Congress," *Alexandria Gazette*, July 25, 1850, 3; "Congressional," *Augusta Chronicle*, Feb. 9, 1854, 2.

Chamber"—Hale responded by celebrating his freedom from the two major parties. "If there be anything inconvenient to the Senator from Kentucky in the fact of having no distinctive mark, I think that inconvenience is counterbalanced by the advantage of being able to vote independent of caucus determination," Hale explained (*Cong. Globe*, February 27, 1849, 603). The caucus was now the forum for setting the Senate's order of business, for arranging the details of legislation, for appointing printers and Senate officers, for organizing committee assignments, for discussing day-to-day affairs, and for framing landmark legislation.

Senators also began using the caucus to punish recalcitrant senators. In December 1849—just four years after the Democratic caucus had begun appointing majority members to the standing committees—the caucus removed Thomas Hart Benton (D, Mo.) from the chairmanship of the Foreign Relations Committee because he had assumed a position on slavery that was unacceptable to most southerners. "Even Mr. Calhoun lent himself to caucus scheming," the *New York Tribune* reported, "and in violation of the uniform practice of his public career and of his long avowed principles, attended the caucus for the purpose of prostrating a rival."[50] Fascinated by the ability of secret party conclaves to reorganize the Senate's committees, one journalist referred in 1849 to "this caucus system of governing the Senate."[51]

In December 1858, the members of the Senate Democratic caucus disciplined Stephen Douglas (D, Ill.) as they had once disciplined Benton. "The action of the Senatorial caucus in removing Mr. Douglas from the Chairmanship of the Committee on the Territories has created the greatest excitement," the *Cincinnati Commercial* reported. "It is regarded as demonstrating the intention of the Democratic leaders to adhere to the extreme Pro-Slavery policy adopted at the last session—to reduce the Anti-Lecompton men to the position of a faction, and to drive them from the party."[52] The Cleveland *Plain Dealer* also condemned the action. "A gentleman who has served twelve years in that body

[50] "The Whig Caucus," *New York Tribune*, Dec. 20, 1849, 1. See also "From Washington," *North American* (Philadelphia, Pa.), Dec. 19, 1849, 2; "The Standing Committees of the Senate," *New York Evening Post*, Dec. 20, 1849, 2; "Correspondence of the Baltimore Sun," *Baltimore Sun*, Dec. 20, 1849, 4; "From Washington," *Louisville Courier*, Dec. 25, 1849, 2; "From Washington," *Louisville Courier*, Dec. 27, 1849, 2; "Benton, and His Prospects," *Richmond Enquirer*, Dec. 28, 1849, 1; Kravitz ca. 1971, viii: 13.

[51] "Postscript," *New York Evening Post*, Dec. 20, 1849, 3.

[52] "Washington News: Dispatches to the New York Tribune," *Cincinnati Commercial*, Dec. 13, 1858, 1. See also "Correspondence of the Baltimore Sun," *Baltimore Sun*, Dec. 10, 1858, 4; "The reporter of the Associated Press ... ," *New York Tribune*, Dec. 10, 1858, 4; "Correspondence of Commercial Advertiser," *Commercial Advertiser* (New York, N.Y.), Dec. 11, 1858, 2; "Telegraphic Despatches," *Alexandria Gazette*, Dec. 13, 1858, 2; "Letter from Washington," *Louisville Courier*, Dec. 18, 1858, 2; "Letter from Washington," *Daily Picayune* (New Orleans, La.), Dec. 18, 1858, 1; Robinson 1954, 199–203.

The new Senate chamber in 1859. The carpet is reported to have had a floral pattern with deep purple hues. At the start of that Congress, there were 66 senators in the chamber. By 1861, after the secession of southern states, just 50 senators remained.

The United States Senate in Session in Their New Chamber, by an unidentified artist after John McNevin, wood engraving published in *Harper's Weekly,* Dec. 31, 1859, Office of the Senate Curator, Accession No. 38.00001.001

with great credit to himself and high honor to the whole country," the *Plain Dealer* noted, "is sought to be degraded through the machinery of the caucus action of that body."[53] Or, as the *Louisville Courier* wrote, from an entirely different political perspective, "The Democratic members of the Senate held a sober, staid, dignified caucus to arrange their committees for the session ... After a small amount of talk in a quiet, sensible, Senatorial way, they concluded it would be mistaken policy to any longer consider Mr. Douglas as the exponent of the views of a majority of the Senate on Territorial questions."[54]

Although the Democratic caucus succeeded in rebuking and punishing two senators who had outraged the party's pro-slavery majority and challenged its electoral strategy, the caucus itself appears to have had no regular structure in

---

[53] "The Last Drive at Douglas," *Plain Dealer* (Cleveland, Ohio), Dec. 14, 1858, 2.
[54] "Letter from Washington," *Louisville Courier,* Dec. 17, 1858, 1.

this era. Most important, the caucus had no permanent chairman. At each meeting, members seem to have chosen someone to sit temporarily in the chair, with no expectation that this same person would hold the chair for more than a few meetings of a session.[55] Newspapers carefully chronicled caucus meetings, and we identified multiple reports of the caucuses that organized each Congress in this era, but there is no evidence of any permanent caucus chairmanship. In an unusually colorful account, the *New York Times* discussed how the Senate Democratic caucus selected its leaders in these years, including its chairmen and the members of its committee on committees. The account is shaped by the *Times*'s hostility to the set of southern senators who dominated the caucus, but the basic facts of caucus organization appear not to have been in dispute. "Much dissatisfaction exists, and is freely expressed here, as to the manner in which the Senate is managed by a few of its members, forming an inside organization within the Democratic Caucus. This little clique, controlled by Senator Slidell, representing the Secession element, is maintained in its ascendancy on the basis of hostility to Judge Douglas," the *New York Times* reported in December 1859. "Whenever a Democratic caucus is convened to select Standing Committees, or for any other important purpose, Mutual Admirationist Number One moves that his friend Mutual Admirationist Number Two be appointed Chairman. It would seem discourteous to contest this; and then Admirationist Number Two appoints a sub-Committee of his fellows: numbers One, Three, Four, Five and Six to report a 'programme of Committees' for the action of the Caucus."[56]

Lacking officers of any sort, the pre–Civil War Democratic caucus was a loosely organized institution, subject to the manipulation of small groups who gained temporary control of its agenda. In the mid-1850s, a time of great upheaval in the party system and within Democratic ranks, the Democratic caucus created two committees for a purpose other than to make committee assignments. The first, in December 1855, was charged with the task of deciding whether or not the party's senators should agree to a common set of principles.[57] The other, in July 1856, which we discuss in the next chapter, was created to propose an order of business. But both committees appear to have been short-lived affairs, with no evidence that either established any sort of precedent. The Senate Democratic caucus appointed a third committee in February 1860 to consider a resolution calling for the national party platform to support slavery in the western territories.[58] Despite the dramatic

---

[55] See, for example, Holt 1999, 128–29.

[56] "Cliqueism in the Senate," *New York Times*, Dec. 23, 1859, 1. See also "XXXIId Congress, First Session," *New York Times*, Apr. 23, 1852, 1.

[57] "The Senate Printer," *Washington Evening Star*, Dec. 13, 1855, 2.

[58] "From Washington," *New York Tribune*, Feb. 13, 1860, 5; "From Washington," *Chicago Tribune*, Feb. 17, 1860, 4; "The Duty of Congress in the Matter of Slavery in the Territories,"

humiliations of Benton and Douglas, no lasting institutional innovations had occurred since 1841–47, when the caucuses had assumed responsibility for legislative business as well as for committee assignments.

FORMALIZATION OF THE SENATE CAUCUS, 1856–62

With the demise of the Whigs and the organization of the new Republican party in the mid-1850s, a new period of institutional innovation dawned. Like the Democrats and Whigs before them, Republicans met regularly in caucus to plot legislative and electoral strategy. But, in a burst of innovation, Republican senators in 1856–62 created the position of permanent caucus chairman, established a committee on committees, and organized the congressional campaign committee, consolidating the place of the caucus as the center of Republican life in the Senate.

Caucus Chairmanship

The most important institutional innovation in this era was the establishment by the Republicans of a permanent caucus chairmanship. Republican senators had begun to meet in caucus by 1856, with John P. Hale (R, N.H.)—ironically, given his stance on the Senate floor a few years earlier—serving as their first caucus chairman.[59] As Table A.1 shows, Hale chaired the Republican caucus between 1857 and 1862, thus becoming the first person of any Senate party to preside on a regular basis over caucus meetings. While Hale was a well-regarded senator who had refused to caucus with either major party when he entered the Senate in 1847, instead helping to establish the anti-slavery Free Soil party, his duties as caucus chairman appear to have been minimal. Rather than assign him even the responsibility to call meetings, the caucus appointed William H. Seward (R, N.Y.), Benjamin Wade (R, Ohio), and Solomon Foot (R, Vt.) as a "committee to call future caucuses as desired."[60]

It was Hale's successor, Henry B. Anthony (R, R.I.), who placed the caucus chairmanship on a truly permanent basis. The start of Anthony's chairmanship was modest enough. Almost as an aside, the *Washington Evening Star* stated in a December 1862 story, "We learn that Senator Anthony presided in the recent sessions of the Republican party Caucus."[61] Anthony was not a prominent

---

Washington Evening Star, Feb. 17, 1860, 2; "At a caucus of the Democratic United States Senators ... ," *Louisville Courier*, Feb. 20, 1860, 2; "From Washington," *Chicago Tribune*, Feb. 25, 1860, 4.

[59] "Washington, July 5, 1856," *New York Herald*, July 8, 1856, 4.

[60] "Interesting from Washington: Organization of the Thirty-Fifth Congress," *New York Times*, Dec. 8, 1857, 1. See also *Cong. Globe*, Dec. 14, 1847, 21.

[61] "The Caucus Action," *Washington Evening Star*, Dec. 20, 1862, 2. See also MacNeil and Baker 2013, 173.

policy leader, and he was not unusually active on the floor. As Rothman (1966, 16) writes, Anthony was "personally popular with his colleagues—unfailingly sending each of them a turkey for Thanksgiving—but he enjoyed little authority." He was probably chosen on the basis of his knowledge of procedure and interest in organizational matters. Still, it appears that Anthony was self-conscious about the pathbreaking nature of his position. "Mr. Anthony, who has acted as chairman of the Senate caucus for the last seven years, to-day proposed to resign that position," the *New York Herald* reported in December 1869, "but his fellow members would not consent that he should do so."[62] Throughout his time as Republican caucus chairman, Anthony offered the resolution at the start of each session to appoint the standing committees, becoming the first person in Senate history to perform this function with regularity. Anthony's caucus chairmanship would continue without interruption for 22 years, until his death in September 1884—still by far the longest term of any caucus chairman in the Senate's history. Although Anthony himself was chosen in just his third year in the Senate, his long term in office would establish a seniority norm for the Republican caucus chairmanship that persisted into the 1920s.

Committee Assignments and the Republican Committee on Committees

In December 1859, Republican senators created their first committee on committees, and, building on a practice that had been emerging since the mid-1850s (Robinson 1954, 132–38), Democrats decisively confirmed a new norm for committee rosters by ranking every majority member ahead of every member of the minority party. The Democratic caucus completed work on Democratic committee assignments on December 17, when they turned the list over to the Republican caucus so it could identify names for the positions allocated to the minority. "The Republicans will confer upon them to-morrow," the *New York Tribune* reported, but "the present disposition is to return the list, and let the majority fill up to suit themselves."[63] Republican senators felt marginalized by the process, and they commented on the strong pro-southern bias in the Democratic assignments, observing that even northern Democrats had received "inferior" assignments. The *Vermont Watchman and State Journal* reached the same conclusion. "Every chairmanship, and the majority of every committee, is in the hands of Southern men, or of Northern Democrats with Southern principles, every one!" the *Watchman* wrote.[64] For Senate Democrats in 1859, the seniority rule was firmly in place—except, of course, for an apostate

[62] "Senatorial Caucus," *New York Herald*, Dec. 8, 1869, 5.

[63] "The Senate Committees," *New York Tribune*, Dec. 19, 1859, 5. See also McConachie 1898, 286–87.

[64] "From Washington," *Vermont Watchman and State Journal* (Montpelier, Vt.), Dec. 30, 1859, 2. See also McConachie 1898, 271–72.

like Douglas—and it was buttressed by an antipathy for the new Republican party. "The Democratic Rule of the Senate is that the Chairmanships shall result from promotion, original positions being graduated by seniority of service," according to the *New York Tribune*. "This process gives the heads to thirteen of the most important to the South—virtually the whole organization of the Senate."[65]

Senate Republicans met to discuss committee assignments and named three senators—Foot, James Dixon (R, Conn.), and Kinsley S. Bingham (R, Mich.)— as the party's first committee on committees, with Foot as the committee chairman. The *New York Tribune* noted that "the distribution of the Republican side of the Committees of the Senate was confided" to the three men.[66] On December 21, the full Senate approved the committee lists, with Republican senators voting uniformly against the resolution on the Senate floor.[67] Every major committee was composed of seven members, with five Democrats (or four Democrats and a senator from the Know-Nothing party) all ranked before two Republicans. The ranking convention introduced in the mid-1840s, when Democrats had reserved the third position on every committee for a Whig senator, had collapsed, along with the comity of the Senate, in the mid-1850s, when the Republican party, committed to stopping the expansion of slavery into the western territories, had supplanted the Whigs as the primary opposition party.[68] Senate Democrats could barely tolerate their Republican colleagues, and the committee lists of the mid- and late 1850s reflected that new Senate. Both institutions—the Republican committee on committees and the practice of arranging committee lists strictly by party—were firmly established by 1859, and both persist to this day.

Once in the majority, Senate Republicans occasionally used committee assignments to punish wayward senators, as Democrats had done in 1849 and 1858. Hale was removed from the chairmanship of the Committee on Naval Affairs in 1864 because of his inability to work with the secretary of the navy.[69] Three senators—Dixon, Edgar Cowan (R, Pa.), and James Doolittle (R, Wisc.)—were stripped of their committee chairmanships in 1866 because, according to the *New York Herald*, they "had betrayed the party and

---

[65] "The Senate Committees," *New York Tribune*, Dec. 19, 1859, 5.

[66] "The Senate Committees," *New York Tribune*, Dec. 22, 1859, 5. See also "From Washington," *Vermont Watchman and State Journal* (Montpelier, Vt.), Dec. 30, 1859, 2.

[67] "XXXVI. Congress—First Session," *Boston Courier*, Dec. 22, 1859, 3; *Cong. Globe*, Dec. 21, 1859, 198; "From Washington," *Vermont Watchman and State Journal* (Montpelier, Vt.), Dec. 30, 1859, 2.

[68] As late as December 1853, when there were six seats on most major Senate committees, Whigs were ranked fourth and sixth, with Democrats holding the first three spots along with the fifth spot, behind the top-ranked Whig. On five-seat committees that year, Whigs continued to hold the third and fifth seats. See *Cong. Globe*, Dec. 12, 1853, 27.

[69] "The Senate Naval Committee," *Washington Evening Star*, Dec. 7, 1864, 2. See also Robinson 1954, 203–8.

attempted to sell it out to Johnson."[70] And, following the 1872 election, in which several Republican senators endorsed the Liberal Republican ticket, three committee chairmen lost their positions.[71]

Sumner, in one of the most famous cases of stripping a post from a sitting committee chairman, was not reelected to his chairmanship of the Committee on Foreign Relations in March 1871. The precipitating issues were Sumner's opposition to President Grant's plan to annex Santo Domingo, Grant's dismissal of the minister to Great Britain, and negotiations with Britain on war claims and the status of Canada. Sumner's attacks on Grant were remarkably vicious and continued after the Senate had killed the Santo Domingo annexation treaty. In fact, Sumner toured the country giving speeches critical of the administration. After the secretary of state penned a disingenuous attack on the senator, Sumner refused to speak to the secretary even in a public venue. Several Republicans, including Roscoe Conkling (R, N.Y.), who believed that Sumner went beyond limits of acceptable behavior and who presumably wanted to maintain good relations with the Grant administration, voted to deny Sumner the chairmanship by a 26–21 vote in caucus.[72]

Rothman, in his discussion of the Sumner case, argued that committee posts were not a routine source of leverage that the Republican caucus used with its members. "Only the most bizarre and flagrant behavior," according to Rothman (1966, 24), "was ever called into question." These cases did more than cause turmoil within the caucus, we suggest: they undermined the party's public image and electoral prospects and necessitated that the party distance itself from the wayward senators. As was the case with Democratic senators in 1849 and 1858, policy differences were not sufficient to generate party retribution among Republicans in the 1860s and early 1870s. Overt activity with direct electoral consequences for the party, or its president, contributed to these caucus reprisals.

Congressional Campaign Committees

The electoral interests of the party were most obvious in the creation of the campaign committee, called the "congressional committee" during this period. While most scholars have concluded that Republican members of Congress did not create their first campaign committee until 1866, we have discovered that a joint House-Senate Republican congressional campaign committee was created in 1856—and reestablished every two years thereafter.[73] As a new party, eager

---

[70] "Senatorial Caucus," *New York Herald*, Dec. 6, 1866, 3. See also Robinson 1954, 298.

[71] "Deposition of the Liberal Chairmen and Members of Committees," *New York Herald*, Dec. 5, 1872, 7. See also Berdahl 1949, 314; Kravitz ca. 1971, viii: 15.

[72] "The Senate Committees," *New York Times*, Mar. 10, 1871, 1. See also Robinson 1954, 299–300; Kravitz ca. 1971, viii: 16–17.

[73] Fess (1910, 131) notes that an 1812 Republican congressional caucus, meeting to nominate James Madison for the presidency, also "took an important step in appointing a committee of

to compete with the long-established Democrats for control of Congress and the presidency, Republicans drew on the combined resources of House and Senate members. "A few days ago, the Congressional Executive Committee of the Republican party met at the rooms of the Republican Association of this city [Washington], to clear up matters and dissolve," the *Boston Traveler* reported in January 1857. "It appears that they have put into circulation above 4,000,000 documents, 'which is believed to be above three times the number ever distributed by any one party during a Presidential campaign.'"[74] Two years later, in 1858, according to the Washington *Evening Star*, "the country is being absolutely flooded" with circulars seeking people to assist in the work of the Republican congressional executive committee. "In the meanwhile," the *Star* asked, "what are the Democracy of Congress doing to counteract these really powerful efforts, even so early in advance, to affect the result of the next Presidential election adverse to the Democratic cause?"[75] While these early Republican campaign committees appear to have given considerable attention to the election of a president, it is notable that the campaign was created at two-year (rather than four-year) intervals and was composed entirely of sitting members of Congress.

In 1860, according to one of the committee's publications (Republican Executive Congressional Committee 1860), the committee was chaired by Senator Preston King (R, N.Y.), who also headed an executive committee of two other senators and six representatives (see also Muller 1957, 646–67; Abbott 1986, 87). The committee's primary responsibility was to publish and distribute several dozen speeches, originally delivered by senators and a few others, and various documents. The publications addressed both specific policy questions and general discussions of the positions of the two parties. The committee had a staff secretary and encouraged orders of the publications at modest prices. It raised funds "by voluntary contributions ... for circulating documents and necessary expenses," the *Chicago Tribune* reported,[76] and it also received financial support from the Republican National Committee (Muller 1957). King coordinated Republican strategy as best he could from

---

correspondence, which was the first congressional campaign committee of our history. It was made up of one member from each state, except Connecticut and Delaware. This step shows the beginnings of the party machinery which was soon to play an important part in elections." We have been unable to locate further evidence of the 1812 committee or of other congressional campaign committees between 1812 and 1856. Before congressional campaign committees were established, national campaign committees were created by the Democrats in 1848 and Whigs in 1852, which put most of their effort into assisting state committees (Sibley 1991, 52).

[74] "Letter from Washington," *Boston Traveler*, Jan. 2, 1857, 4.

[75] "Party Movements," *Evening Star* (Washington, D.C.), Mar. 20, 1858, 2.

[76] "From Washington," *Chicago Tribune*, Feb. 13, 1860, 4. See also "Republican Party Executive Committee," *Louisville Courier*, Feb. 13, 1860, 1; "Great Discovery: Secret Circular of the Black Republicans," *Chicago Tribune*, Mar. 17, 1860, 2; "The Two National Committees," *The Press* (Philadelphia, Pa.), Apr. 23, 1860, 2.

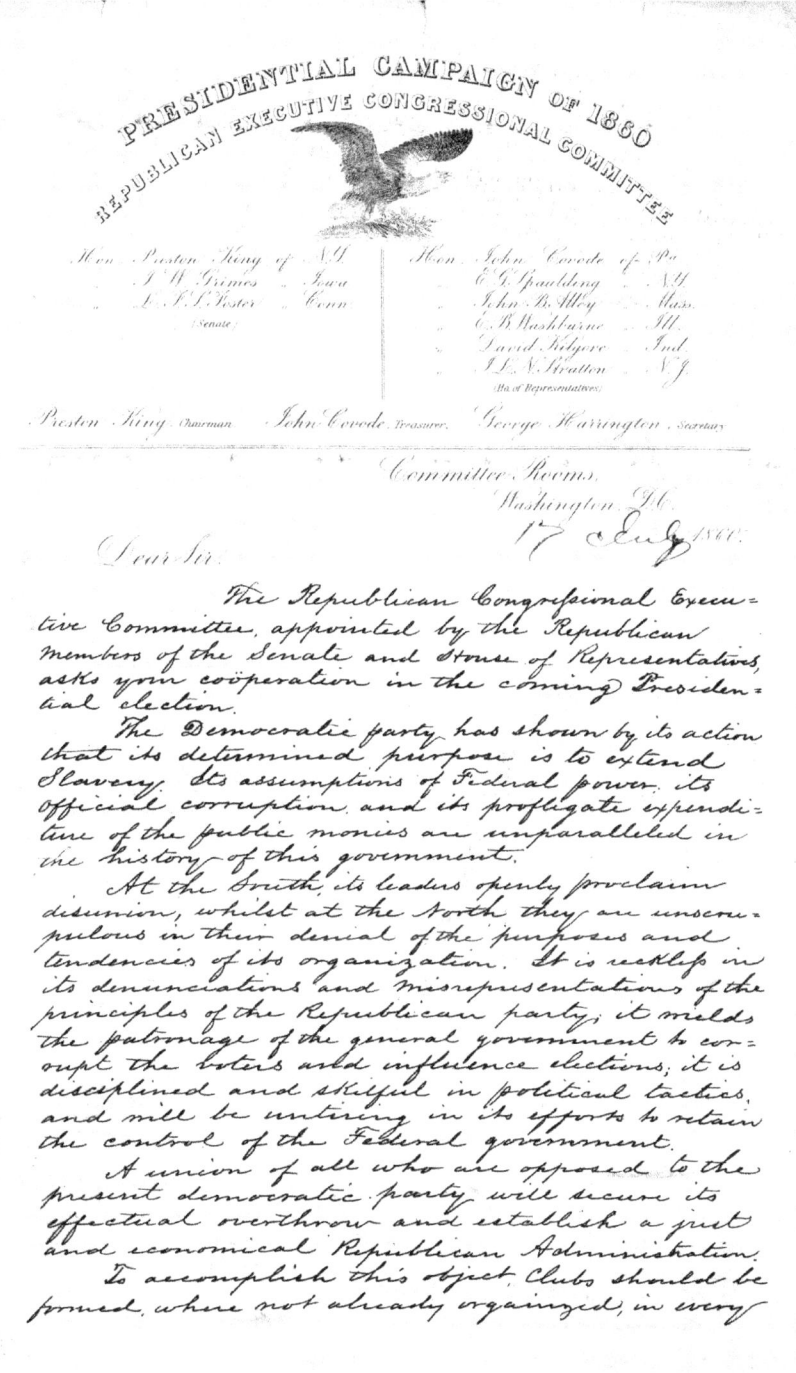

A letter from the Republican Executive Congressional Committee, July 17, 1860.
Library of Congress, Rare Book and Special Collections Division, Alfred Whital Stern Collection of Lincolniana, Portfolio 11, no. 30

Washington. He arranged for foreign language translations, encouraged Republicans in various states to pursue certain tactics, and arranged for speakers.

During the Civil War, the 1864 Republican (or Union) congressional committee was unusually active.[77] "The country will bear witness that the quantity of matter distributed by the committee was," according to a post-campaign assessment, "of an unusually high character, compared with that sent out by parties eight, or even four years ago."[78] The *Chicago Tribune* published an announcement in July 1864, on behalf of the Union Congressional Committee, urging the newspaper's readers to purchase and circulate the congressional committee's documents. In its announcement, the congressional committee listed 17 brief pamphlets for sale—available only for mass purchase of 100 pamphlets at a time—each of them a speech by a Republican leader. In September, the Union Congressional Executive Committee announced that it had just published another 15 pamphlets, all of them available for immediate purchase and distribution.[79] Demand for the pamphlets was enormous: according to the *New York Times*, "About 40,000 pamphlets are printed, folded, addressed and forwarded per diem."[80] The 1864 executive committee, chaired by Senator Edwin D. Morgan (R, N.Y.), was made up of three senators and four House members.[81] In addition to circulating pamphlets across the country, the committee also distributed absentee ballots to Union soldiers that fall.[82] The *Chicago Tribune* marveled at the success of the congressional committee. "The statement is going about in the newspapers that the Union Executive Congressional Committee distributed about four million documents during the last campaign. This must be an under-estimate, if circulars, hand-bills, newspapers, &c., are included," the *Tribune* noted at the end of the year. "Certainly no organization ever before sent out so many pages of matter in so short a time as was sent out by the committee during their ten weeks of active work."[83]

Most accounts of the origins of the congressional campaign committees emphasize the Union Republican congressional committee of 1866 (Macy

---

[77] For 1862, we have found only a single brief notice—signed by "E. S. Williams, Chairman of Republican Congressional Executive Committee"—calling on "every earnest supporter of the present Administration" to attend a local meeting: see "Political Notice," *Chicago Tribune*, Oct. 13, 1862, 4.

[78] "Campaign Work," *Chicago Tribune*, Dec. 15, 1864, 2.

[79] "Presidential Campaign of 1864: Union Congressional Executive Committee," *Chicago Tribune*, Sept. 7, 1864, 1.

[80] "The Union Congressional Committee," *New York Times*, Sept. 29, 1864, 8. See also "The Union Congressional Committee," *New York Times*, Oct. 29, 1864, 4.

[81] "Presidential Campaign of 1864: Union Congressional Executive Committee," *Chicago Tribune*, Sept. 7, 1864, 1.

[82] "The Union Congressional Committee," *New York Times*, Oct. 29, 1864, 4.

[83] "Campaign Work," *Chicago Tribune*, Dec. 15, 1864, 2.

1918, 87–91; Merriam and Gosnell 1929, 63; National Republican Congressional Committee 1966, 7–15; Bone 1968, 127–28; Kolodny 1998, 16–22; McConnell and Brownell 2019, 202). These accounts appear to rely on an early study of American parties in which it is erroneously claimed that the committee was invented that year (Woodburn 1903, 114). The 1866 committee, too, was a joint committee of House and Senate Republicans that focused its energies on House elections; senators, of course, were not subject to popular election. The 1866 elections were critical because of the sharp conflict between congressional Republicans and President Andrew Johnson over Reconstruction policies. Congressional Republicans sought to strengthen their numbers and to boost their cause in southern Reconstruction efforts. The Johnson administration controlled the Republican National Committee, so the separate Republican congressional committee was essential to assisting the campaigns of supportive congressional candidates. The congressional committee was active in 1867 and 1868 in Reconstruction efforts in southern states, where the committee sent a large field staff and pursued a variety of party building and voter registration activities.

The timing of this Republican institutional innovation is significant. The political conditions of 1856–60 and 1866 were very different. The Republicans of 1856–60 were working to establish themselves as a major party—to gain seats and attain majority status in both houses of Congress and to win the presidency. In 1866, in contrast, Republicans held more than three-fourths of the seats in both houses and were seeking to guarantee themselves a veto-proof Congress. While the committee's work in 1866, particularly in the South, may have represented a substantial expansion of party building, it took advantage of a decade-old organizational form that had been invented during an era of intense party competition.

The origins of the Democratic congressional campaign committee are obscure. Bone (1956, 117; 1968, 127–28) notes, without documentation, that congressional Democrats created a joint House-Senate campaign committee in 1866, while Kolodny (1998, 34) finds the first mention of the committee in an account of the 1868 campaign.[84] But we have discovered an 1860 committee. Titled the "National Democratic Campaign Committee," the 1860 committee was chaired by Representative Clement Vallandigham (D, Ohio) and included six other House members and one senator.[85] The next reference we can find is to a committee organized in February 1868.[86] The executive committee that year was chaired by a senator and had as members an additional senator, five

---

[84] The mid-twentieth-century manuals of the Democratic National Convention, written by Clarence Cannon, once House parliamentarian and later a member of the House, appear to be wrong. Cannon asserts that the Democratic national congressional committee was organized in 1882. See Cannon 1944, 9–10.
[85] "The Two National Committees," *The Press* (Philadelphia, Pa.), Apr. 23, 1860, 2.
[86] "Intelligence from Washington," *Richmond Whig*, Mar. 24, 1868, 1.

representatives, and, oddly, three prominent Democrats from the Washington, D.C., area who were not members of Congress. The number of Democrats in Congress was small going into the 1868 campaign—9 senators and 47 House members—so Democrats were seeking to reestablish their presence throughout the country. The Democrats appear to have used their committee as a distribution house and speakers bureau, following the Republican example.

Caucus Activity and Leadership in the 1860s

During the Civil War, and in its immediate aftermath, Republicans in the Senate regularly met in caucus, either on their own or in joint meetings with House Republicans (Krout 1928; Bogue 1989, 122–32; MacNeil and Baker 2013, 173–75). Benedict (1974, 25–26) notes that Senate Republicans tended to go into caucus whenever a majority coalition was not immediately available on the floor. For the period between December 1865 and July 1867, Benedict counted twenty caucus meetings mentioned in the newspapers. But congressional Republicans varied considerably in their judgments about the best policies to pursue regarding the war and Reconstruction. Consequently, even as Republican senators called these caucuses to coordinate legislative and electoral strategies, they often had trouble reaching agreement—and they lacked clear leadership. Roscoe Conkling (R, N.Y.) had arrived in the Senate, but he did not establish himself as the leading spoilsman until the 1870s. Wade, Sumner, and other Radicals were strong advocates for their wing of the party, but disagreement among them on tactics and substance sometimes limited their ability to shape policy (MacNeil and Baker 2013, 66–69). "The senatorial caucus is secret; it is confidential, if you please; it has no reporters present; it is not in the light of day," Sumner declared, with some frustration, on the Senate floor in December 1871, a few months after losing his committee chairmanship (*Cong. Globe*, December 18, 1871, 190). "Why, sir, to take the public business from this Chamber and carry it into such a caucus, is a defiance of reason and of the best principles of government."

Republicans struggled, during and after the war, to set an agenda for the Senate, a problem that would plague them until the 1890s. Many caucus sessions were devoted to sorting out the order of business, particularly during the short session between the November elections and the end of the Congress in March (Rothman 1966, 17–18; Kravitz ca. 1971, viii: 73–74). As often as not, nothing was resolved, and committee leaders relied on procedural tactics and appeals for majority support to gain timely consideration of their legislation on the floor. When the caucus was able to agree on priorities, it usually was very late in the short session, when passing appropriations bills had become an emergency. For the Senate Republicans of the 1860s, surely as motivated by policy as any congressional party, policy concerns were closely entwined with electoral calculations. While some senators believed that membership and participation in the caucus implied an obligation to abide by caucus decisions, others continued to insist on pursuing their own course on the floor.[87] "To run a party you must have a caucus. If some Senator does not vote for a resolution that some other Senator offers you are to call a caucus. If he votes against something that somebody else has offered, call a caucus and settle him by your caucus," John Logan (R, Ill.) said, with obvious sarcasm, in 1871 (*Cong. Globe*, December 18, 1871, 171). "It reminds me a good deal of school-boys playing marbles, and some chap in the crowd happens to strike what they call the 'middle man' a little more centrally than the rest, and they get together and read him out of the game, and take his marbles and play at the game themselves."

On a few occasions in the 1860s, the Republican caucus created ad hoc committees. In July 1862, a joint House-Senate committee of five senators and five representatives, most of them Radicals, wrote an impassioned defense of Republican policies and called for the enlistment of Black troops. A joint meeting of the full caucus, however, adopted a more moderate resolution, one that reflected a different view of the best electoral strategy for the party (Bogue 1989, 124–25). That December, Senate Republicans appointed a nine-member committee to notify President Lincoln that the caucus had lost confidence in Secretary of State William H. Seward and to call for his dismissal.[88] Then, in February 1863, a five-member committee was selected by Republican senators to set the order of business for the remainder of the session.[89] A joint caucus in July 1866 named an ad hoc committee of three senators and six representatives, chaired by Zachariah Chandler (R, Mich.), to discuss the question of adjourning the session (Krout 1928, 839–40). And the Senate Republican caucus organized another caucus committee in February 1867, composed of seven senators, to reconcile competing approaches to Reconstruction and make a recommendation to the full caucus (*Cong. Globe*, February 10, 1870, 1177–82).

RISE OF THE MODERN SENATE CAUCUS, 1871–79

Building on the precedents established in the 1860s—above all, the permanent caucus chairmanship, the committee on committees, and the congressional campaign committee, all rooted in the Republican caucus—senators in the 1870s embarked on a rapid series of institutional innovations. By the middle of the decade, Democrats, like Republicans, had created a permanent caucus

---

[87] "Washington," *New York Tribune*, Jan. 27, 1869, 1.

[88] "The Cabinet Crisis," *New York Times*, Dec. 22, 1862, 1; "The Late Cabinet Crisis: The Senatorial Caucus That Led to It," *Chicago Tribune*, Dec. 25, 1862, 2.

[89] "Republican Caucus," *New York Tribune*, Feb. 11, 1863, 4. Note that Bogue 1989 (124, 170 n.30) mistakenly states that the five-member committee was organized in February 1862, not 1863. We are grateful to Elizabeth Rybicki for locating the original citation in the *New York Tribune*.

chairmanship and restored their committee on committees. Both caucuses began regularly to utilize temporary committees to set agendas and manage legislation. And the two caucuses, until recently regarded as secret organizations, came to be accorded public recognition by the full Senate. "I suppose the democratic members, as the republican members have done a thousand times, meet in caucus and confer for the purpose of having concert of action," Benjamin Hill (D, Ga.) noted on the floor of the Senate in 1879. "That party does it every day; that party has done it during this session; that party has done it to a very memorable extent during the last ten or twelve years. All parties do that" (*Cong. Rec.*, April 18, 1879, 537). The caucus, which had often been a disorganized forum for intraparty discussion and intrigue, was by the late 1870s a well-structured institution that had the potential to coordinate the work of the Senate.

Caucus Chairmanship, Caucus Room, and the Committee on Committees

During the 1860s, Senate Democrats' small numbers and minority status minimized the need for elaborate party organization or formal meetings of the caucus. But in March 1871, as the number of Democrats increased from 12 to 17, the Republican caucus awarded the Democrats the chairmanship of the Committee on Private Land Claims. The action represented a sharp break with tradition. Although brief exceptions had occasionally been made, as a rule the majority party since the 1840s had claimed all committee chairmanships.

The decision to allow Democrats to name the chairman of the Committee on Private Land Claims—Garrett Davis (D, Ky.) received the appointment—had an immediate consequence. For the first time in the Senate's history, the minority caucus possessed a secure meeting room and a clerk. In the Senate of 1871, these were valuable resources. Contemporaries understood the significance of this action. "Last year, for the first time," the *New York Herald* reported in 1872, "an opposition Senator was appointed Chairman of a committee that he might have the use of a committee room for the conferences of his associates."[90] By December 1873, as Table A.2 shows, Democratic senators had elected John W. Stevenson (D, Ky.) as their first permanent caucus chairman, and the Private Land Claims committee room appears to have been the caucus's regular meeting place during Stevenson's tenure.[91]

In 1875, when the number of Democrats in the Senate had grown to 28, the Democratic caucus appointed a committee on committees—its first since before the Civil War—and Republicans awarded three committee chairmanships to

---

[90] "The Land Grab for Colleges in the Senate," *New York Herald*, Dec. 6, 1876, 3.
[91] See, for example, "The Senate Standing Committees," *Washington Evening Star*, Mar. 8, 1875, 1; "The Democratic Policy," *New York Times*, Dec. 8, 1875, 1. For more on Stevenson, see McConnell and Brownell 2019, 119–24.

Democrats. Now the minority party controlled Private Land Claims, Engrossed Bills, and Revolutionary Claims.[92] The Democratic caucus asked its committee on committees to meet with its Republican counterpart. "The object was to insist that in view of the increased representation of the democracy in the Senate they should be entitled to additional representation on important committees," the *Washington Evening Star* explained in March 1875.[93] In reporting the organization of this new committee, the *New York Times* also emphasized the viability of the Senate Democratic party. "The Democrats think their increased membership entitles them to more places on the committees," the *Times* stated, and they instructed their caucus committee "to submit a claim to that effect to the majority."[94]

Three institutions—a minority caucus room, the Democratic caucus chairmanship, and the Democratic committee on committees—had been established in rapid fashion between 1871 and 1875. The first two of these institutions had never previously existed, and the last of the institutions had been moribund since the 1850s. Once created (or recreated) in the 1870s, all three institutions proved permanent. When Stevenson left the Senate in 1877, the Democratic caucus elected his successor in regular fashion, having already grown accustomed to the institution of the chairmanship. "The Democrats of the Senate held a meeting to day," the *New York Times* reported in a small news item in March 1877, "and unanimously elected W. A. Wallace, of Pennsylvania, Chairman of the Senate Democratic caucus."[95] Seven years later, in December 1884, the Senate formally designated a "minority conference room" in the Capitol, converting for that use the room that had previously belonged to the Committee on Revolutionary Claims.[96]

When members of Congress struggled to develop a means for settling the electoral deadlock that resulted from the 1876 presidential election, the four caucus chairmen signed a public document binding their respective caucuses to respect the compromise. The document specified that the congressional members of the electoral commission would be composed of three Republican senators, two Democratic senators, three Democratic House members, and two Republican House members—and that these members would be selected (or, in case of death or incapacity, replaced) by their respective caucuses. The agreement itself, publicly recognizing the legitimacy of the party caucuses for settling one of the age's great crises, was an important landmark. Equally significant

---

[92] "The Republican Caucus," *New York Times*, Mar. 10, 1875, 1.
[93] "Senate Caucuses," *Washington Evening Star*, Mar. 6, 1875, 1. See also "The Democratic Caucus," *New York Times*, Mar. 7, 1875, 1; "Democratic Senators in Caucus," *New York Times*, Jan. 28, 1876, 1.
[94] "The Democratic Caucus," *New York Times*, Mar. 7, 1875, 1.
[95] "Notes from the Capital," *New York Times*, Mar. 6, 1877, 4.
[96] *Congressional Directory*, 48th Cong., 1st Sess., corrected to June 30, 1884; *Congressional Directory*, 48th Cong., 2nd Sess., corrected to Dec. 10, 1884.

was the understanding that four men, because of their selection as chairman of their respective caucuses, could bind their followers in the two chambers.[97] In 1879, the Democratic caucus, which had not possessed even a chairman at the start of the decade, now elected a caucus secretary as well.[98]

Drafting Committees and Committees on the Order of Business

Meanwhile, as Reconstruction ended and the Democrats regained their numbers in Congress in the middle 1870s, both caucuses relied increasingly on an array of ad hoc committees to set agendas, draft legislation, and manage electoral strategies. Senate Democrats appear to have named their first postwar ad hoc caucus committee in January 1876. Struggling to articulate a position on states' rights when white Democrats were "redeeming" southern governments, Democratic senators charged the committee with recommending a response to Republican demands for federal intervention. Most members of the caucus appear to have believed that adopting a militant, pro-Redemption position on the Senate floor—the approach favored by House Democrats—would jeopardize their party's prospects for picking up additional seats in the North. Creating the ad hoc committee was "an easy way of getting rid of the troublesome subject," the *New York Times* suggested. "A prominent Democratic Senator said to-day that they were not going to have any of the foolishness in the Senate that had been seen in the House, and would not give an opportunity for the opposition to lead off any of their indiscreet members into unguarded expressions upon which political capital could be manufactured."[99] Plainly, the electoral consequences of a divisive issue were involved in this party move; at the same caucus meeting, Democrats discussed plans to name members to a bicameral campaign committee. In their decision to create the ad hoc committee, Democrats were balancing an important policy goal of many members against the collective electoral interests of the party. Democratic senators named another ad hoc committee that March to consider a plan for the resumption of specie payments (*Cong. Record*, March 6, 1876, 1475).

Republicans named several order of business committees through the 1870s, all of them transitory and temporary. By the end of the decade, Democrats, like Republicans, began appointing their own committees on the order of business. The Democratic committee organized in March 1879, as the next chapter shows, proved anything but short-lived: it worked closely with its House counterpart over a period lasting several months and helped lay the

---

[97] "The Threatened Bolt," *New York Tribune*, Feb. 16, 1877, 1. In the absence of Anthony, who was ill, Aaron Cragin (R, N.H.) signed on behalf of the Republican Senate caucus.
[98] "Democratic Senate Caucus," *New York Tribune*, Mar. 17, 1879, 5.
[99] "Democratic Senators in Caucus," *New York Times*, Jan. 28, 1876, 1. See also "Congressional Topics," *New York Times*, Jan. 27, 1876, 1.

groundwork for the steering committees that would come to dominate the chamber later in the century.

"Assistant Doorkeepers"

In 1879, when Democrats gained control of the Senate for the first time in 20 years, they established a new precedent by replacing the Senate's secretary, clerk, and other officers, arguing that these officers and their patronage properly belonged to the majority party. Anthony, chairman of the Republican caucus, objected to the action. "This was the first time in the history of the Senate that such sweeping changes had been proposed," he argued. "Heretofore the principal offices of the Senate had been exempt from the reprisals of victorious partisans, and changes in the political character of the membership of the body wrought no material changes in its offices."[100] Notwithstanding these protestations, four years later, when Republicans were again a majority, they followed the Democratic example. Even as Democrats in 1879 extended the partisan principle to the Senate officers, they retained Isaac Bassett, then the assistant doorkeeper and a Republican, in his office (*Cong. Rec.*, April 24, 1879, 799–800; February 11, 1896, 1588). Bassett, who had worked in the Senate continuously since his first appointment as page when he was a young boy, had become the Republicans' chief floor staff assistant. The Democrats that year claimed for themselves the parallel post of "acting assistant doorkeeper," a position that had been around since the 1850s (*Journal of the Executive Proceedings of the Senate*, June 8, 1852, 396; *Cong. Globe*, March 24, 1869, 232), establishing the lasting precedent that each party could name a floor staff assistant.

In 1896, John Sherman (R, Ohio) and Arthur Pue Gorman (D, Md.), chairmen of the Republican and Democratic caucuses, offered resolutions on the floor of the Senate to transform these two appointed positions, nominally chosen since 1879 by the sergeant-at-arms, into elected positions. "The custom in the Senate ... has been that no matter which party controls the organization, on each side of the Chamber there shall be one officer satisfactory to the side. It is true that heretofore, since 1879, those offices have been filled by appointment and not by election, but I think myself that the better rule is to have both officers selected by a resolution," Gorman explained on the Senate floor in 1896 (*Cong. Rec.*, February 11, 1896, 1588). "The resolution offered by the Senator from Ohio [Sherman] is simply to fill the vacancy created by the death of Mr. Isaac Bassett. The other officer, Mr. [Bernard W.] Layton, is here by appointment. It is proposed simply to designate both by a resolution." Decades later, these two posts would become the majority and minority party secretaries.

---

[100] "The Senate Reorganized," *New York Times*, Mar. 25, 1879, 1.

CONCLUSION

The Senate caucus emerged as the fruit of party competition. The caucus traces its origins to the 1790s and early 1800s, when Federalists and Republicans engaged in battle for control of the national government. It was in those years that senators first met in caucuses, on a sporadic basis, to discuss legislative matters—and looked to congressional caucuses to nominate presidential and vice-presidential candidates. Only in 1841, though, spurred by Henry Clay and the sweeping Whig victory the preceding November, did the Senate caucus become a regular, routine vehicle for managing the chamber's business. Once established in 1841, the Senate caucus steadily accumulated powers, articulating new, permanent features over the next decades. The most important features in these years—the caucus chairmanship, the committee on committees, the congressional campaign committee, a minority caucus meeting room, and the forerunner of the party secretary—all developed at times of intense competition, in the mid- and late 1850s, then in the 1870s. The Senate caucus matured in spurts, but, through these spurts, it consolidated its role in the chamber's life.

Party competition defined these moments of institutional invention, but it was entrepreneurial senators who drove the changes in an effort to solve coordination problems and to address factional cleavages. Henry Clay was the signal entrepreneur of this era. Determined not to squander the opportunity presented by the Whig electoral victory in 1840 and committed to a vision that placed Congress, not the president, at the center of policy initiatives, Clay commanded the Senate through caucus meetings throughout the special session of 1841. It was through the Whig Senate caucus that year that he not only guided policy initiatives through both chambers of Congress but also laid the groundwork for the historic rupture between congressional Whigs and President Tyler. The Senate Whig caucuses of 1841 changed the course of the chamber's history. What had previously been used only on rare occasions to discuss legislative business became, abruptly, the core vehicle for steering the Senate. When Senate Democrats were back in the majority four years later, a small faction voted with the minority Whigs to prevent the presiding officer from naming committees, granting that power instead to the caucus. By December 1845 the institution Clay had created now managed legislation, helped set the chamber's agenda, and coordinated committee assignments.

Scholars of the House parties argue that antebellum developments in House parties represented a "cartelization" of the parties (Cox and McCubbins 1993; Jenkins and Stewart 2013). That is, party members agreed to behave like a cartel—to collectively control those factors that influence the success of its members. In the case of the House parties, this involved agreement among fellow partisans and factions to distribute important institutional positions within the chamber on the basis of decisions made within the party. For the majority party, this meant that members were obligated to support the election of the party's nominees for speaker, clerk, and printer on the chamber floor, a process that did not get fully settled until Republicans took over the House in 1859. This achievement transformed the parties into "organizational cartels." By the late nineteenth century, the majority party of the House took additional steps to control the floor agenda through the expansion of the powers of the speaker and the Committee on Rules, turning the party into a "procedural cartel."

The Senate, even more than the House, was the legislative home for emerging party leaders who were central to mobilizing mass parties and generating caucus activity inside Congress. Presidential ambitions, the jockeying of factions, and party competition were central to the emergence of Senate party caucuses and their efforts to control policy outcomes. The reach of leading senators even extended to the House. The campaign committees, designed to aid in the election of partisans to the House, were joint committees, exploiting the fundraising capability and personal prominence of senators. Senators also consulted with members of the House on the issues central to House parties as cartels—including the speakership, printers, and key committee assignments—as senators sought to shape the party's legislative and electoral effectiveness.

With the reemergence of Democrats as a viable Senate party in the 1870s, both Senate party caucuses became organizational cartels. However, if control of the floor agenda is the measure of an effective procedural cartel, majority parties of the Senate did not meet the standard. In the late nineteenth century, the minority party obstruction that motivated House majority party speakers to assert firm control over the floor agenda occurred in the Senate, too, but without a similarly effective response by the majority party. Filibusters stymied the majority in the Senate, even on some of the most important issues of the time, reflecting the powerful influence of inherited rules and practices that distinguished the two houses. By 1879, the Senate caucus was well-established, and, as we will show in the next two chapters, on the cusp of creating two new institutions, first a steering committee to manage the Senate's agenda, then a floor leader. Ultimately, neither institution provided the Senate majority with the ability to create a procedural cartel that matched that in the post-Reed House. But, by the early 1890s, just as the Reed rules were reshaping the House, both the steering committee and floor leadership would dramatically expand the capacity of the Senate caucus.

Four leading Republican senators at the home of Nelson W. Aldrich (R, R.I.) in 1903. From left to right, the "Senate Four" are Orville H. Platt (R, Conn.), John C. Spooner (R, Wisc.), William B. Allison (R, Iowa), and Aldrich.

U.S. Senate Historical Office

4

Steering Committee, 1856–1913

In his 1910 textbook on American government, Charles A. Beard noted that leadership of both the House and Senate had passed into the hands "of a few men whose long service, shrewdness in legislative management, and effective leadership have placed them in control of the speakership and the great committees" (Beard 1910, 268). Joe Cannon (R, Ill.), speaker of the House since 1903, had been facing regular criticism from Democrats and insurgent Republicans for using the speakership's great powers, including his influence over the Rules Committee, to suppress debate and manipulate the legislative agenda. But reformers condemned "Aldrichism"—referring to Nelson W. Aldrich (R, R.I.), a leading member of the Senate Republican steering committee—almost as regularly as they condemned "Cannonism." Writing in 1906, Charles W. Thompson observed that President Roosevelt had quickly come to appreciate that "a gentleman by the name of Aldrich was running the United States" (Thompson 1906, 25). Aldrich, of course, did not run the country on his own. "In the days of the Roman Empire it was customary for an emperor to associate with himself another emperor, both wearing the title of Augustus, and sometimes Rome had three or four emperors at once. Similarly the title of Augustus in the Senate is divided," Thompson (1906, 26) argued. "Associated with Mr. Aldrich [until Platt's death in 1905] were four other emperors, Messrs. Hale of Maine, Spooner of Wisconsin, Allison of Iowa and Platt of Connecticut." The *Cincinnati Enquirer* titled the group "the Executive Committee of the Board of Managers of the United States," calling them the "Real Rulers of the Nation."[1]

This was a novel view of Senate leadership. Until the middle 1890s, no serious observer suggested that the Senate was strongly led. James Bryce,

---

[1] "Real Rulers of the Nation," *Cincinnati Enquirer*, Feb. 20, 1903, 10.

writing in 1891 (i: 202), noted that "no senator can be said to have any authority beyond that of exceptional talent and experience." Woodrow Wilson was equally emphatic six years before in *Congressional Government*. "No one is *the* Senator. No one may speak for his party as well as for himself; no one exercises the special trust of acknowledged leadership," Wilson asserted in 1885 (213). "The Senate is merely a body of individual critics." The discovery of "Augustus" in the late 1890s and 1900s—the conclusion, as Wilson himself wrote in 1908 (107), that "the Senate submits to the guidance of a small group of senators"—represented an abrupt shift in the analysis of Senate organization.

If Wilson and Bryce could contend in the 1880s and early 1890s that the Senate lacked strong leaders, what changed—and when and why did this change occur? The primary tool of Senate leadership was the Republican steering committee. As we will show, this was an institution that emerged in 1879–83, assumed new strength and regularity in 1892–93, prospered for almost two more decades, and withered away quickly in 1911–13. Unlike the Senate's Democrats, who, as we will discuss in the next chapter, created the position of floor leader in the early 1890s, Republicans had no elected floor leader in these years. With the rise of the Republican steering committee, especially with its apotheosis from the winter of 1892–93 through 1911, control over the Senate's day-to-day business shifted from the full membership of the majority caucus to a handful of senators, led by Aldrich, William B. Allison (R, Iowa), and Eugene Hale (R, Maine). This small but powerful group of Republican senators shared control of the caucus, including the Republican steering committee and the Republican committee on committees. The Republican delay in creating the position of floor leader was due, probably, to their long years in the majority and the effectiveness of the Republican steering committee in directing the party's members in the Senate. Not until 1913, when Republicans were thrust into the minority for the first time in nearly two decades, did they identify one of their own to serve as floor leader.

In March 1910, just before Beard's book went to press, members of the House of Representatives rose in revolt, removing the speaker from the Rules Committee and seriously undermining the speaker's power. The House of Representatives, unlike the Senate, was an institution where a partisan majority could control their presiding officer, the floor, and the order of business. Battles over the agenda could be channeled into the Rules Committee, and struggles over leadership played out in the House chamber. As Beard argued (1910, 275 n.3), the Senate Republican steering committee "performs analogous functions to those performed by the committee on rules in the House." Woodrow Wilson, writing two years earlier, had reached the same conclusion. "The majority caucus [in the Senate] has ... its Steering Committee," Wilson (1908, 134) explained, "to which fall duties very like those of the Committee on Rules in the House." And McConachie, writing in 1898 (341), similarly described the steering committee as "a high governing body ... which corresponds to the

House Committee on Rules." The Rules Committee, which controlled the order of business in the House, had become a permanent standing committee, chaired by the speaker, in 1880; had reported its first special order in 1883; and had gained additional powers in the early 1890s as Speakers Thomas B. Reed (R, Maine) and Charles F. Crisp (D, Ga.) used the committee to fortify the majority's control of the chamber (Alexander 1916, 193–208; Luce 1922, 478–80; Robinson 1963, 58–59; Committee on Rules 1983, 4–5, 9, 55–79; Roberts 2010, 308–14). It was in these very years, as we lay out in this chapter, that the Senate Republican steering committee traces its own origins. Moving in parallel but using profoundly different tools—a standing committee in the House and a secretive committee of the Republican caucus in the Senate—the majority parties in both chambers established institutions to direct the course of legislative business.

The steering committee, like other major innovations in Senate leadership, arose and changed in response to competition between the two Senate parties. The timing is crucial: the creation and maturation of the steering committee did not occur in the late 1890s, when Republican hegemony and partisan polarization were at their peak, but rather in an era of intense competition for party control. The steering committee developed in two stages, in 1879–83 and in 1892–93, both times when the two Senate parties were closely matched. In March 1879, Democrats took control of the Senate for the first time in almost two decades. Two years later, when senators arrived for the 1881–83 session, the two major parties each controlled 37 seats. And in 1892–93, when the Republican and Democratic steering committees assumed their mature form, senators did not know at first which party would control the next Senate. The steering committees were organized for both electoral and legislative purposes—the events of 1892–93 were driven by a battle to control state legislatures, which had not yet chosen senators—and the electoral foundations of the newly strengthened steering committees echoed into future years.

BATTLING FOR CONTROL, 1877–95

Between 1877 and 1895, as Figure 4.1 shows, control of the Senate shifted four times. These years—bracketed on one side by secession, the Civil War, and Reconstruction, and on the other by the realignment of 1896—marked an era of fierce two-party competition. For the 18 years between 1861 and 1879, Republicans faced no serious challenge to their Senate majority. And for the 18 years between 1895 and 1913, they again faced no real threat from the Democratic party. But in 1879 Republicans lost their majority, and in 1881 the Senate was evenly divided. While Republicans controlled the chamber for the next decade, their majority in most sessions was small. Then, in the wake of the November 1892 state elections, they realized, along with their Democratic counterparts, that Democrats might be in a position to organize the next Senate. The battle for the Senate waged in the winter of 1892–93 ultimately

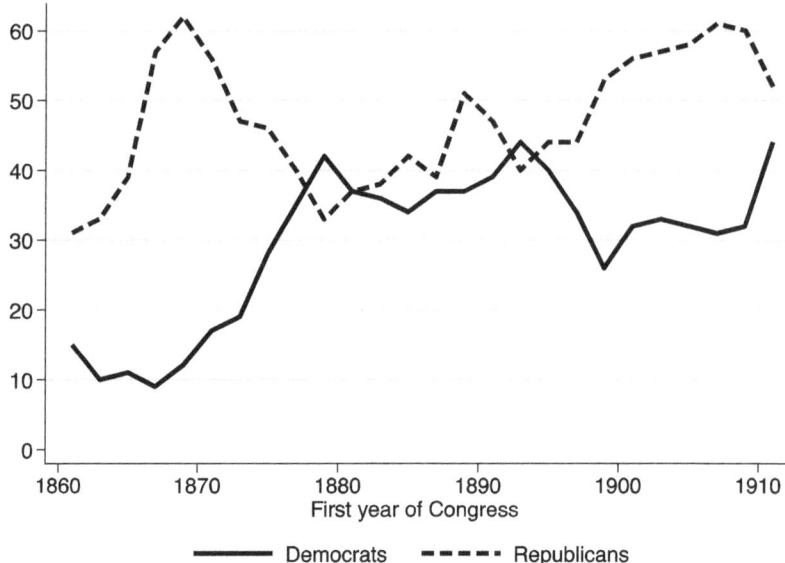

FIGURE 4.1 Size of parties, 1861–1913

yielded the Democratic Senate that was already foreshadowed in the November election results. Republicans regained their majority in the 1895 Senate. In an era of close competition, the Senates of 1879–83 and the winter battle of 1892–93 stood out as the two moments when the struggle to control the chamber was at its height.

The secession of southern states in 1860–61 had led to the demise of Democratic representation in the House and Senate. The Senate was a Republican preserve in the 1860s and 1870s. Reconstruction, tariff, and currency policies dominated the postwar Congresses, but the 1870s presented a cascading set of challenges to the majority Republicans. In 1872, dissident Republicans unhappy with the administration of Ulysses S. Grant—and also the domineering attitude of the party's majorities in the congressional caucuses—formed the Liberal Republican party to compete in the presidential contest. Crédit Mobilier, the Whiskey Ring, and other scandals subsequently rocked the Grant administration, and the "salary grab" fiasco undermined the image of congressional Republicans. The Granger revolt reflected deep discontent with a Republican party increasingly dominated by eastern elites, and public support for high tariffs waned. A financial panic in 1873 led to a severe economic recession, laying the groundwork for Democrats to win a House majority in the 1874 elections. Four years later, with the end of Reconstruction and the collapsing effort to protect the voting rights of Black men in the South, Democrats gained a majority of Senate seats for the first time in nearly two decades. The election of 1878—and the Democratic Senate that took office in 1879—began a period of intense competition for control of Congress. Republicans faced an external challenge from the Greenbacks, a largely agricultural movement that rejected the party's position on currency and successfully ran candidates for the House of Representatives. Internal divisions among Stalwarts, Half-Breeds, Mugwumps, and a variety of reformers over patronage, finance, and civil rights further complicated Republican party politics by the early 1880s.

Particularly noteworthy during this period was the "Great Senate Deadlock of 1881." The preceding two years of divided government, 1879–81, with small Democratic majorities in the House and Senate and a Republican president, had produced stalemate on nearly every key issue. The next Senate, convening in March 1881, was the first evenly split Senate in the history of the body and began with a lengthy deadlock over the organization of the chamber (McConachie 1898, 288–89; Hoar 1903, 2: 64–67). The outcome turned on William Mahone, a Virginian who had been elected as a Democrat but refused to caucus with his party. Mahone traded his support of the Republicans' committee list and Senate officer nominees for the chairmanship of the Agriculture Committee and control of patronage to his state. But Democrats, fearing the return of a southern seat to someone sympathetic to the Republican party, resisted coming to an agreement. Their resistance, enabled by absent Republican senators, generated a prolonged stalemate that lasted two months and 17 days. A compromise yielded adoption of the Republican committee list and the retention of the Democrats' Senate officers and patronage appointees.[2] The assassination of President James Garfield in September 1881 and promotion of Vice President Chester Arthur to the presidency resulted in the vice presidency being vacant for the remainder of the Congress, leaving the Senate with no way to break a tie vote. Still, the evenly divided Senate and Republican House were relatively productive in enacting legislation favored by Republicans, including immigration legislation, civil service reform, a rivers and harbors measure, and a tariff bill.

The drama of 1881–83, following the new Democratic majority in 1879, offered a vivid reminder to senators of the policy and electoral importance of majority party control. Being in the majority allowed senators to shape the chamber's committees, choose Senate officers, and make patronage appointments. These were important for their promotion of a party's legislative program and for the advantages they gave the members of a party in the electoral realm. The long battle for control of the Senate in 1877–95 put a premium on effective party organization, creating a historic hothouse for institutional

---

[2] Republicans lost the two New York senators over the president's unwillingness to adhere to patronage traditions, temporarily weakening the Republicans' bargaining position. See "End of the Extra Session," *New York Times*, May 21, 1881, 4; "Special Session of the Senate," *Washington Post*, May 21, 1881, 2; www.senate.gov/artandhistory/history/common/briefing/Senate_Deadlock_1881.htm (accessed March 2022); www.senate.gov/about/origins-foundations/parties-leadership/presidents-death-eases-senate-deadlock.htm (accessed February 2025).

innovation. Not only did Republicans create a steering committee that effectively managed the Senate for most of two decades, but Democrats devised the position of elected floor leader. In contrast, in the 18 years between 1895 and 1913, Republicans generally maintained cohesive majorities, until intraparty factionalism contributed to their unanticipated defeat in the 1912 elections (Brady, Brody, and Epstein 1989; Brady and Epstein 1997; Aldrich, Berger, and Rohde 2002). These conditions allowed both parties to settle into organizational and policymaking practices that remained largely stable until the final years of the period.

PERSONALITIES

The rise of the steering committee is one of the pivotal events in Senate history, but this story has never been told before. Since the 1890s, journalists and social scientists alike have stressed the personal nature of Aldrich, Hale, and Allison's power, arguing that they and their allies exercised influence because of their chairmanships of major standing committees and because of their individual abilities. To be sure, all three senators were entrepreneurial: they were institution builders who were critical to the creation of the Republican steering committee. But, while observers have noted that these senators used that committee as one of their instruments for controlling the chamber, few have regarded the steering committee itself as central to this era. Instead, most existing accounts personalize the period, writing about men rather than institutions, and studying the years when Aldrich and "The Big Five" reigned rather than the fuller period when the steering committee emerged as a keystone of Senate organization.

This century-old wisdom maintains that Aldrich's leadership was rooted neither in the rules of the Senate nor in any specific institutional position. In this regard, Aldrich's leadership was decisively different from that exercised by Cannon as speaker of the House. Leadership in the House of Representatives, Thompson noted in 1905, depended entirely upon institutional position; it was blind to ability and impervious to talent. The Republican leaders of the House were easily identified: the speaker, the floor leader, and the members of the Rules Committee. "If their official positions were taken away from them they would be bowled over immediately," according to Thompson. "In the Senate the leaders have risen to their places because they can lead, and have solidified that leadership by their strategic positions."[3] As Thompson (1906, 28–29) wrote one year later, "The House bosses are so by reason of their official position, and whether they are men of ability or not has nothing to do with the case ... But the Senate bosses are men of might." The work they did in guiding the Senate took place behind closed

---

[3] "'The Big Five' Who Run the U.S. Senate," *New York Times*, Mar. 19, 1905, SM6.

doors, over drinks or a poker game or at a summer home. "The public 'debates' to which the eager-eyed tourists listen so reverently are in the nature of a dramatic performance. They have nothing to do with the legislation to be enacted," Thompson (1906, 29–30) contended. "The legislation has been settled in the private debates."

Thompson identified "The Big Five" in his March 1905 article, noting that "the great debates of the Senate are held in whatever room Allison, Aldrich, Hale, Spooner, and Platt of Connecticut may be gathered to decide what shall be the policy of these United States on a given subject."[4] But Orville Platt (R, Conn.) was dead one month later, and Thompson (1906, 27) began referring instead to "the four bosses of the Senate." Phillips, also writing in 1906, constructed a different, and much longer, list of men who controlled the chamber. His rogues' gallery of the Republican "leaders of the Senate" featured Aldrich, Spooner, Allison, and Hale, but also Thomas C. Platt (R, N.Y.), Chauncey Depew (R, N.Y.), Stephen B. Elkins (R, W.Va.), Philander C. Knox (R, Pa.), Joseph Foraker (R, Ohio), Henry Cabot Lodge (R, Mass.), Winthrop Murray Crane (R, Mass.), Shelby Cullom (R, Ill.), John Kean (R, N.J.), Knute Nelson (R, Minn.), and William Frye (R, Maine).[5] "The leadership of the Senate is an intangible thing. It is here to-day in one man and there to-morrow in another," Ira E. Bennett wrote in his 1906 essay in the *Washington Post*. "The greater operations of the Senate are directed by a coterie of leaders, each contributing peculiar qualities lacking in his colleagues."[6] Some say four senators direct the Senate, "which is not true," according to Bennett, while others insist the number is six or thirteen. The *Washington Evening Star*, in a 1907 editorial, named five men, "each of whom is in a sense a leader" of the Senate Republicans: Allison, Aldrich, Spooner, Lodge, and Foraker.[7] Bennett himself identified an array of Republican leaders—Aldrich, Spooner, Allison, Hale, Lodge, Foraker, Crane, Knox, Elkins, Kean, Nelson, Cullom, Jonathan Dolliver (R, Iowa), Charles W. Fulton (R, Ore.), Moses Clapp (R, Minn.),

---

[4] "'The Big Five' Who Run the U.S. Senate," *New York Times*, Mar. 19, 1905, SM6.

[5] David Graham Phillips, "The Treason of the Senate: Fairbanks, Hale, and Frye," *Cosmopolitan Magazine*, vol. 42, no. 1 (Nov. 1906), 79, also 77–84. See also Phillips, "The Treason of the Senate," *Cosmopolitan Magazine*, vol. 40, no. 5 (Mar. 1906), 487–502; Phillips, "The Treason of the Senate: Aldrich, the Head of It All," *Cosmopolitan Magazine*, vol. 40, no. 6 (Apr. 1906), 628–38; Phillips, "The Treason of the Senate: Chief Spokesman of 'The Merger,'" *Cosmopolitan Magazine*, vol. 41, no. 2 (June 1906), 123–32; Phillips, "The Treason of the Senate: Confusing the People," *Cosmopolitan Magazine*, vol. 41, no. 4 (Aug. 1906), 368–77; Phillips, "The Treason of the Senate: The Rise of Foraker," *Cosmopolitan Magazine*, vol. 41, no. 5 (Sept. 1906), 525–35; Phillips, "The Treason of the Senate: Thrifty Patriot Allison," *Cosmopolitan Magazine*, vol. 41, no. 6 (Oct. 1906), 627–36.

[6] "Personality of Senators Who Lead in Railroad Rate Discussion," *Washington Post*, Mar. 18, 1906, M6.

[7] "The Senate and Leadership," *Washington Evening Star*, Feb. 16, 1907, 4.

and Jacob Gallinger (R, N.H.)—but emphasized that "it is impossible to make up a list of those who are always leaders and those who never are."[8] Gould (2005, 22–31), in his history of the Senate, refers to "The Four," but then identifies other senators closely connected with them (see also Stephenson 1930, 134–37; Fowler 1961, 200–201, 213–14, 224). For MacNeil and Baker (2013, 84–86, 176–77), it was the "Big Five" and the "Big Four." For Welch (1971, 200), it was the "Big Three." Republican leadership was personal, informal, unofficial. While Aldrich was the most influential senator in the group, he consistently acted in concert with others, each playing his own part.

The real source of these senators' influence, observers concluded, was their personal ability, buttressed by their chairmanships of major standing committees. "The two great committees of the Senate are Appropriations and Finance," Thompson wrote in 1905. "Of Appropriations Allison is the Chairman, and he and Hale control the committee ... Aldrich is Chairman of Finance, and associated with him on the committee are Allison, Platt, and Spooner; and these four men run that committee."[9] Writing in the early 1900s, Republican senator Albert J. Beveridge (R, Ind.) remarked that "the Senate was dominated by a 'marvelous combination,' composed of Aldrich as manager, Allison as 'conciliator and adjuster,' Spooner as floor leader and debater, and Platt as 'designer and builder'" (Bowers 1932, 138). In a profile titled "Nelson Wilmarth Aldrich, the Leader of the Senate," the *Washington Post* offered this assessment in December 1907. "Not Clay, nor Calhoun, nor Benton, nor Douglas, nor Fessenden, nor Conkling, ever exerted as great influence on Federal legislation as this man has for twenty years. Webster himself, with his gigantic mind and matchless eloquence, never was the force in the American Senate this man has been and is," the *Post* declared. "Aldrich does not convince, nor does he persuade—he dominates."[10] Contemporary observers and later scholars stressed that this influence could not be easily transferred to other senators. In April 1910, when Aldrich and Hale announced their intentions to retire from the Senate, the *Washington Evening Star*, speculating on who would succeed them as Senate leaders, considered the question without even mentioning the fact that Hale was chairman of the Senate's Republican caucus and steering committee. "These two senators occupy unique positions of power and influence," the *Evening Star* explained that spring, "the accretion of years of service and seniority on committees but primarily by virtue of their own great abilities and masterful characters."[11]

---

[8] "Personality of Senators Who Lead in Railroad Rate Discussion," *Washington Post*, Mar. 18, 1906, M6.
[9] "'The Big Five' Who Run the U.S. Senate," *New York Times*, Mar. 19, 1905, SM6.
[10] "Nelson Wilmarth Aldrich, the Leader of the Senate," *Washington Post*, Dec. 2, 1907, 5.
[11] "Two Senators Quit," *Washington Evening Star*, Apr. 19, 1910, 8.

Later scholars have shared this perspective. In his account of the reaction of conservative senators to the progressive insurgency, Hechler (1940) titles his chapter, simply, "On to Aldrich." Hechler (1940), Rienow and Rienow (1965), Holt (1967), Merrill and Merrill (1971), and Caro (2002) analyze Senate leadership in this era through the prism of personalities, with little reference to caucus organization. Indeed, the words "steering committee" or "Republican steering committee" appear in the indexes to none of these books—though the name "Aldrich, Nelson W." appears prominently in every index. "Because it was so apparent that the power of the Four transcended control by traditional Senate machinery, their colleagues and outsiders came to view them as more than just presiding chairmen of committees," Merrill and Merrill (1971, 19) explain. "The Four were chieftains of a vast but viable political superstructure which changed with the strength of each individual member as he grew older and with shifts in his political constituency."

Synthesizing generations of scholarship, Caro describes the Senate as a "dam," a chamber holding fast against the surging waters of progressive legislation. And, in Caro's telling, it was Aldrich above all who maintained that dam at the turn of the twentieth century. "Aldrich, it was said, had 'but to whisper in the committee rooms' to pass or kill a bill," Caro (2002, 31) contends. In 1909, "as a 'prairie fire' of indignation spread across an outraged nation, editorials denounced Aldrich as 'dictator,' 'despot,' 'tyrant,' but the Founding Fathers had armored the Senate against indignation, and Aldrich did not even attempt to conceal his contempt for the people," Caro (2002, 48) writes. "His only response was a sneer on the Senate floor. Certainly, the Republican platform had promised tariff 'revision,' he said, but 'where did we ever make the statement that we would revise the tariff *downward*?'"

TIMING

David J. Rothman, whose 1966 *Politics and Power* remains the seminal account of Senate leadership in the late nineteenth century, is the great exception to this narrative—emphasizing institutions rather than personalities and demonstrating the ways in which Aldrich and his allies exercised their power through the caucus and the Republican steering committee. He contrasts the Senate of the 1870s and early 1880s with the Aldrich-led Senate of 1897, describing at length the influence of caucus institutions and of the Senate's leading figures in those years. His interest, though, is not in excavating the origins of those institutions. Rothman refers to the development of the steering committees only in passing, and with scant supporting evidence. Yet his two statements regarding the establishment of the Republican steering committee— in which he indicates that it had come into regular existence in the middle 1880s and reached its most mature form in 1897 (Rothman 1966, 30, 48; see also Fowler 1961, 200)—have shaped all subsequent scholarship. These dates are embedded in Ripley (1969a, 1969b), Munk (1974), *Congressional Quarterly* (1976, 202), Keller (1977, 303–4), Byrd (1988), Brady, Brody, and Epstein (1989), and Schickler (2001, 53–59), all of whom draw directly on Rothman for their analysis.

But neither date is correct—and the consequences of this error in timing are vast for any explanation of party development. The nature of party competition in 1879–83 and 1892–93, when, as we will show, the steering committees first emerged and then consolidated their strength, was sharply different from that of the mid-1880s and 1897. In the mid-1880s and again in 1897, the Republican party controlled the Senate, albeit by small majorities. But that was not the case in 1879–83 and 1892–93: these were years when the Senate majority was actively contested, at times entirely in doubt, and when Democrats regained control of the Senate after many years of Republican rule.

The year 1897 looms especially large.[12] Rothman contends that Allison and Aldrich rose to power in 1897, when Allison succeeded John Sherman (R, Ohio) as chairman of the Republican caucus. Although Allison assumed the caucus chairmanship because of "calculations of seniority" rather than ambition, Rothman suggests that he quickly transformed the position into an instrument with which he and his allies could control the Senate. "When Allison chaired the Republican caucus, the faction that he and Aldrich dominated acceded to power. In the course of their rule, they established and clarified the authority that Senate party officers could wield," according to Rothman (1966, 44). "They institutionalized, once and for all, the prerogatives of power." As senior members of the Republican party, Allison chaired the Appropriations Committee and Aldrich chaired the Rules Committee; within two years, Aldrich assumed the chairmanship of the Finance Committee. But the committee chairmanships, like Allison's chairmanship of the caucus, reflected only their seniority within the party. Through the caucus, they and their allies also dominated the Republican committee on committees as well as the Republican steering committee. "Various members of the Allison-Aldrich circle intermittently occupied key Senate positions before 1897," Rothman (1966, 50) states, "but after Allison assumed power they monopolized party offices."

By this account, Allison and Aldrich's influence over the Senate was rooted in Allison's seat as caucus chairman, which he assumed in 1897 and which made him, according to Rothman, the ancestor of the modern floor leader.

---

[12] In focusing on 1897, Rothman might have been influenced by Stephenson (1930, 132–37), whose biography of Aldrich includes a chapter suggesting that Aldrich and his allies were at the peak of their power by 1897.

"Party leadership for the first time dominated the chamber's business, and the tactics of Allison, Aldrich, and Gorman were faithfully emulated by Lyndon Johnson," according to Rothman (1966, 72). "One of the first duties Allison faced in 1897 was to select the chairman and members of the Republican Steering Committee," Rothman (1966, 48) writes. "Previous caucus leaders had usually appointed other senators to head it; Allison, however, invariably chaired the committee himself." The year 1897 seemed, then, to be a historic turning point. "When choosing the remaining members, he [Allison] again regularized practices that predecessors had followed erratically," Rothman (1966, 48–49) claims. "Repeated service on the eleven-man committee was not exceptional before 1897, but most often a majority of the group was replaced at the start of each Congress. Allison, concentrating authority, habitually named the same senators to fill the places." In a footnote, Rothman (1966, 297 n.18) cites for support his finding that "Allison himself, Aldrich, Hale, and [Shelby] Cullom [R, Ill.] served on the committee from 1897 on."

Several scholars have acted on Rothman's history of the late nineteenth century, repeating his claim that centralized party leadership arose in 1897. Schickler (2001, 54) acknowledges that the significance of 1897 is not well-documented, observing, "Unfortunately, the evidence base on this change is relatively thin." But he and many other scholars nevertheless assume the accuracy of this date for their analyses, in part because the date quickly grew familiar through repetition. "Aldrich and Allison were at the center of a clique containing a number of other Republican senators," Ripley (1969b, 27; also Ripley 1969a, 21, 29–30) writes. "Gradually, two principal lieutenants emerged from this group: John Spooner of Wisconsin and Orville Platt of Connecticut. 'The Four' (Aldrich, Allison, Spooner, and Platt) dominated the work of the Senate from the mid-1890's until 1905." Merrill and Merrill (1971), noting that McKinley's inauguration as president restored Republican control of the national government, share Rothman's emphasis on 1897. Brady, Brody, and Epstein (1989), also citing Rothman (1966), introduce a theory of legislative leadership that assumes that a centralized Republican hierarchy came to dominate the Senate in the late 1890s. "The electoral realignment of 1894–96 yielded two homogeneous Senate parties," they write (Brady, Brody, and Epstein 1989, 207, also 209), creating the conditions necessary for Aldrich, Allison, and the Republican steering committee to assume power. Brady and Epstein (1997) extend this theory, relying again on Rothman's characterization of the late-nineteenth-century Senate. "In most accounts, 1897 was a crucial year in the Senate Four's rise to power because Allison became chairman of the GOP Caucus and Steering Committee," Schickler (2001, 54) observes. "The committee assignment process and other levers of Senate power were soon largely in the hands of Allison, Aldrich, and their allies." MacNeil and Baker (2013, 177) concur: "By 1897, they dominated the Senate as no other group of senators had ever done before."

A 1903 Clifford Berryman illustration depicting Nelson W. Aldrich's (R, R.I.) grip on
Senate Republicans.
Berryman Political Cartoon Collection, Office of the Senate Curator

Accepting Rothman's account, Robert C. Byrd (D, W.Va.) argues that the
consolidation of power by Aldrich and Allison in 1897 had lasting significance,
characterizing it as the birth of modern Senate leadership. "With Allison
chairing the caucus, the faction that he and Aldrich dominated came to power,"
Byrd writes in his official history of the Senate (Byrd 1988, 363; see also Baker
1988, 67; *History, Rules, and Precedents* 2022, 1). Echoing Rothman's language, Byrd contends not only that Allison and Aldrich in 1897 "established
and clarified the authority" of Senate party leaders but "institutionalized, once
and for all, the prerogatives of power" (Byrd 1988, 363). The precedents
established in the late 1890s proved lasting and permanent, according to

Byrd. Offering no new evidence and relying exclusively on Rothman's study of the pre-1901 Senate, Byrd repeats the argument that Aldrich and Allison set the pattern for contemporary Senate party leadership. "The Senate at the turn of the twentieth century seemed to have more in common with the institution that Presidents Eisenhower and Carter confronted than with that of the Jackson or Grant eras," Byrd suggests (Byrd 1988, 363, 362; see also Rothman 1966, 43). It was "newly organized and strong," decisively transformed into "what we might all recognize as the modern Senate."

Yet these oft-told stories are fundamentally flawed. Allison and Aldrich were not floor leaders in the modern sense; they exercised their leadership through the collective institution of the Republican steering committee. Only when this institution was cast aside in the 1910s did Republicans turn to floor leadership, an entirely different institution that traces its origins to events in the Democratic caucus unrelated to the steering committees. And it was the institution of floor leadership, not the steering committees, that proved to be the organizational foundation of the modern Senate.

To the extent that Aldrich and Allison exercised unusual power, their reign was nearly four years old by 1897. (Allison, as we will show, became chairman of the newly strengthened and reorganized Republican steering committee in 1893, a position he relinquished only with his death 15 years later. And, beginning in 1893, he, Aldrich, Hale, and Cullom all sat on the committee.) The focus on 1897, which coincides with a high point in the Republican party's homogeneity and strength, has misled scholars in their attempts to explain Aldrich and Allison's rise to command of the institution. "Even as late as the 54th Congress of 1895–97, the Senate Republican party had a substantial number of dissident members," Schickler (2001, 54) notes, in writing that the supposed institutional revolution of 1897 was due to the dramatic upsurge in Republican party homogeneity in that year's new Congress. "The Republican party that emerged from the 1896 election faced less internal division than had existed at any other time in the post–Civil War era," Schickler (2001, 54) continues. "Not coincidentally, in 1897 the Allison-Aldrich faction gained unmistakable control of the Senate GOP machinery and became the dominant force in Senate politics." The real drama, however, had occurred when those dissidents and the opposition Democrats were at their strongest, during the fiercely competitive Senates of 1879–83 and in the winter of 1892–93, times when Senate Republicans were unusually weak and divided.

In the remainder of this chapter, we defend the claim that the Republican steering committee emerged in two stages and that each of those stages was rooted in a deeply competitive Senate environment. The origin point of the Republican steering committee was in 1879–83, in a Senate balanced between the two major parties. For the next decade, Senate Republicans regularly created a committee on the order of business, sometimes termed a "steering committee," to help manage their legislative affairs. But there is little evidence to suggest that the committee in the 1880s or early 1890s enjoyed unusual power or was led by any particular set of senators. The mature, fully developed steering committees were created in 1892–93—with Aldrich and Allison assuming command of the Republican steering committee in December 1893—and these new steering committees, established by both Democrats and Republicans, represented a direct response to the November 1892 elections, the consequent struggle for control of the next Senate, and the determination by Republicans to develop a collective strategy to reclaim their lost majority. The institution of the Republican steering committee—more than the personal qualities of Aldrich or Allison or any other particular senator—defined Senate governance between 1893 and 1911. And the steering committees emerged out of the cauldron of party competition.

COMMITTEES ON THE ORDER OF BUSINESS, 1856–79

The post–Civil War Senate was a chaotic place. Senators would frequently use the floor to set the Senate's agenda, as senator after senator explained why one bill deserved precedence over another. Even senators in the same party, ostensibly sharing a similar set of policy goals, had no consistent institutional mechanism for resolving disagreements and establishing priorities. So they sometimes fought one another on the floor, in full view of their colleagues. On January 8, 1868, for example, John Sherman (R, Ohio), Lyman Trumbull (R, Ill.), and Oliver Morton (R, Ind.)—three Republicans—debated the next day's order of business. Sherman took the floor to suggest an agenda for the next day, Trumbull responded by asserting that the next day's business did not need to be decided in advance, Sherman replied that he believed setting the agenda in advance would be helpful, and then Morton entered the debate to state that he agreed with Sherman (*Cong. Globe*, January 8, 1868, 384). Such debates occurred regularly. As an exasperated Matthew Carpenter (R, Wisc.) explained on the Senate floor, on July 8, 1870: "The only apology that a new Senator can make for interfering in a debate about the order of business is this, that those Senators who have been here many years seem to have got so accustomed to devoting about half our time to a discussion of what we shall do the other half, that it produces no astonishment to them that two or three hours of every day are wasted in that way. To a new Senator it does seem very strange" (*Cong. Globe*, July 8, 1870, 5376). Carpenter suggested some mechanisms that the Senate could adopt to set an order of business. "I do not care what system is fixed upon myself," he explained to his colleagues. "Any, the most faulty that can be conceived of, if the Senate would adhere to it, would accomplish twice the business we accomplish now."

As the Senate's business grew, the order of business assumed increasing importance. A majority party that could bring discipline to the Senate agenda could ensure that the bills that its members favored gained priority over other bills. From the 1840s through the 1870s, senators relied on the caucus itself as the primary forum for resolving intraparty disputes over the content and scheduling of legislation, even as their attempts to manage the Senate's agenda continued to meet with controversy. Senate Republicans met in caucus through the Civil War and Reconstruction to coordinate their actions, many times meeting jointly with House Republicans. "In 1867 the Republican caucus attempted to designate the subject and order of Senate business," according to Rothman (1966, 17–18). "Antagonisms quickly mounted and debate soon broke out in open session. Massachusetts' fractious senator, Charles Sumner, refused to concede that a party gathering could limit the topics for consideration." But the practice was already growing less controversial. By the 1870s, Democrats and Republicans alike routinely met in caucus to consider the order of business.

Only once before the Civil War—in 1856—have we located a reference to a committee appointed by a Senate caucus and charged with the responsibility for setting an order of business. The committee, created by the Democratic caucus, existed for several weeks. "In the Senate a Committee of five Chairmen of principal Committees arrange the business of each day,—deciding what shall and what shall not be considered," the *New York Times* reported in July 1856. "This arrangement is the result of a caucus agreement by the majority, and is strictly adhered to."[13] On the floor of the Senate, John B. Weller (D, Calif.), a member of this committee and chairman of the Committee on Military Affairs, explained that this committee had been managing the Senate agenda for two weeks. He clarified that it was "a committee of six Senators having charge of the most important bills pending in the Senate, that they might go and assign particular days for the consideration of each" (*Cong. Globe*, July 23, 1856, 1719). The committee's responsibility, Weller explained, was to schedule legislation, but not to recommend any particular piece of legislation for passage. In assuming this power, the caucus was attempting to manage the chamber's business, since otherwise, in Weller's language, "it had become almost impossible to do anything here." Republicans protested vigorously. William Seward (R, N.Y.) condemned the interference of this "extra-judicial and irregular committee outside of the organization of the Senate." Lyman Trumbull (R, Ill.) also rose in protest at this process. "That majority of the Senate might as well expel the minority as to adopt it," Trumbull argued. "I wish it to go out and be understood, that all who do not cooperate in a particular class of political views ... are not only to be proscribed upon your committees, but the business is to be so arranged by a secret, unconstitutional, irresponsible caucus, hidden from public view, that others can bring no measure before the Senate for its consideration" (*Cong. Globe*, July 23, 1856, 1719–20).

To justify the creation of the 1856 committee, Weller reminded senators of the trouble that resulted when caucuses did not manage the order of business and the urgency of bringing the session to a close. With the upcoming election presumably in mind, Weller observed that "the majority of the Senate were

[13] "The Three Million Armament Bill in the Senate," *New York Times*, July 23, 1856, 1.

anxious to adjourn at a very early day" (*Cong. Globe*, July 23, 1856, 1720). Addressing Trumbull, he asked, "Did he never hear of a political caucus being held before? Is not the Senator well aware that that is the usual course of a majority?" Weller proceeded to explain what led the Senate Democratic caucus to act. "They saw that the business of the Senate was conducted in such a manner day after day, that it had become almost impossible to do anything here. We were discussing one day the Navy bill, the next day the Kansas question, and the next day Kansas in some other shape or form, and then Central American affairs and the Clayton-Bulwer treaty. We have had various bills discussed here day after day, and then postponed for weeks, in order to debate some new question," Weller recalled (*Cong. Globe*, July 23, 1856, 1720). "But I am falling into the habit of some much older Senators than myself in consuming time in discussing what you shall take up. As a general rule, we can pass half a dozen bills while we are discussing which one shall be taken up for consideration first."

Weller's arguments notwithstanding, the caucus committee of 1856 appears to have been sui generis. There is no evidence of another Democratic committee on the order of business through the 1850s, 1860s, and most of the 1870s. Senate Democrats appear not to have appointed their next committee on the order of business until 1878, followed by another committee in 1879, when they gained control of the Senate for the first time in 18 years.

Tables A.4 and A.5 (in the Appendix) identify every Senate committee on the order of business that we have located, from the origins of the Senate through 1913. Finding these committees and their memberships required scanning hundreds of different newspapers—and reading tens of thousands of stories on Senate organization. Until we had begun this project, scholarly knowledge of committees on the order of business (their usual name until the early 1890s) and steering committees (as they were more frequently called after the early 1890s) was scant. Even the best studies identify committees on the order of business only in anecdotal ways, the fullest accounts mentioning just a handful of committees. Tables A.4 and A.5 therefore represent the first comprehensive accounting of the origins and development of steering committees in the U.S. Senate, and the research we did in creating these tables forms the backbone of this chapter.

As these tables show, Republican senators began naming ad hoc committees to coordinate Senate business in the 1860s and 1870s. This generation of ad hoc committees was, until its final years, an entirely Republican institution, though the memory of the 1856 Democratic committee must still have been on the minds of many in the new majority party. (Trumbull, for example, who railed in July 1856 against the Democratic committee on the order of business, himself sat on the Republican committees in February 1863 and March 1869.) Republicans named at least nine committees on the order of business, in sporadic fashion, between 1863 and 1879, all when they were in the majority—one committee in 1863, another in 1869, four in 1872–74, and three in 1878–79.

The 1863 committee on the order of business was established to coordinate action within the sprawling Republican wartime caucus. "The Republican Senators held a caucus this morning, at which a Committee, consisting of Senators Fessenden, Trumbull, Wilson, Collamer, and Grimes, was appointed to determine the order of business and hours of adjournment," the *New York Tribune* stated in a special dispatch dated February 10, 1863, "and to secure the attendance of members of the majority during the rest of the session."[14] It seems likely that an additional purpose of this committee was to maintain the campaign against Secretary of State William H. Seward. "The republicans continue to caucus as to how Mr. Seward may be ousted from the Cabinet," the *New York Herald* reported the next day, noting that "the republican Senators at their last caucus initiated a plan by which their feelings in antagonism to Mr. Seward shall be formally presented to the President."[15] Four of the five members of the new committee had been on the caucus committee in December that had asked President Lincoln to remove Seward from the cabinet—including Jacob Collamer (R, Vt.), chairman of the December committee, and William P. Fessenden (R, Maine), who chaired the February 1863 committee.[16] On February 12, two days after the committee was named, the full Republican caucus met and "agreed upon the order of business for the remainder of the session,"[17] presumably after receiving a recommendation from its committee. While records of the committee are sparse, it appears to have continued to exist through the remainder of the session. Early in March, the *Chicago Tribune* reported that "the Committee of the Senate's Republican caucus" had met with Lincoln to share some of "Mr. Seward's dispatches which the President never saw," correspondence that the committee apparently hoped would undermine Seward's standing with the president.[18] While occasionally House and Senate Republicans would create joint committees to manage congressional business, especially on matters related to the war or Reconstruction, we have located no other instance of a Senate Republican committee on the order of business before 1869.

[14] "Republican Caucus," *New York Tribune*, Feb. 11, 1863, 4. See also "From Washington," *Chicago Tribune*, Feb. 11, 1863, 1. For this citation—indeed, for the discovery of this committee altogether—we are indebted to Elizabeth Rybicki. Although Bogue (1989, 124) refers to this committee and quotes directly from this newspaper story, in both his text and footnote he mistakenly places the committee (and newspaper citation) in 1862, rather than 1863.

[15] "News from Washington: Efforts of the Radicals to Get Rid of Mr. Seward," *New York Herald*, Feb. 12, 1863, 4. See also "Secretary Seward and the French Correspondence," *Cleveland Morning Leader*, Feb. 13, 1863, 1; "From Washington: The Radical Republicans After Seward," *Nashville Daily Union*, Feb. 14, 1863, 3; "The Secretary of State," *Weekly National Intelligencer*, Feb. 19, 1863, 1.

[16] "The Cabinet Crisis," *New York Times*, Dec. 22, 1862, 1; "The Late Cabinet Crisis: The Senatorial Caucus That Led to It," *Chicago Tribune*, Dec. 25, 1862, 2.

[17] "Senate Republican Caucus," *New York Times*, Feb. 13, 1863, 4.

[18] "From Washington," *Chicago Tribune*, Mar. 2, 1863, 1. See also "Secretary Seward's Private Confidential Dispatches," *New York Tribune*, Mar. 2, 1863, 1.

Every one of the eight Republican committees that we have located between 1869 and 1879 was a short-term enterprise, appointed by the caucus at one session, with instructions to report back immediately to the caucus with a recommendation regarding the order of business. Upon reporting back to the caucus, the committee was dissolved. Some of these committees existed for as little as two or three days, like the committees of March 1869 and December 1874. All existed a few days at most, with the longest-lasting of these committees, those of December 1878 and February 1879, functioning for nine days. Without exception, these committees were short-lived extensions of the Republican caucus, lacking any real autonomy.

The first of these committees was appointed by the Republican caucus on March 8, 1869, just as the session was beginning. It appears that the idea for appointing a committee emerged in the midst of the caucus meeting, as Republican senators struggled to agree on plans for the session. After discussing committee chairmanships, "the caucus took up the question of what business should be transacted at the present session, and also how long Congress should remain here," the *New York Herald* reported. "After a full discussion, the general tenor of which was that no legislation should be introduced except such as is absolutely necessary, a committee, composed of Senators Sherman, Trumbull, Edmunds, Stewart and Pool, was appointed to confer with a similar committee which it is expected will be appointed at a caucus of the republican members of the House to be held to-morrow."[19] Two days later, on March 10, the committee reported back to the Senate Republican caucus. "The Republican members of the Senate had a two hours' caucus to-day, to hear the report of the committee of five appointed on Monday, on subjects of legislation for this session," according to the *Cincinnati Daily Gazette*. After consulting with "leading men in both branches of Congress," the committee recommended that the Senate take action on a limited, specific set of bills.[20]

Three years elapsed before Republican senators appointed another committee. The decision to name a committee in 1872 emerged as caucus deliberations threatened to break down. "A Senate Republican caucus was called for this evening to arrange the order of business for the remainder of the session, and to facilitate the prospect of an early adjournment," the *Chicago Tribune* reported in April 1872. "There being considerable contrariety of opinion as to the manner in which the order should be arranged, although none as to bringing the session to a speedy close, a Committee of seven was appointed for the purpose of preparing an arrangement of the calendar ... When the report is finished, the caucus will be again convened for the purpose of passing upon it."[21] Five days after it had been charged, the committee completed its

[19] "Republican Senatorial Caucus," *New York Herald*, Mar. 9, 1869, 3.
[20] "Republican Caucus," *Cincinnati Daily Gazette*, Mar. 11, 1869, 3.
[21] "A Senate Republican Caucus," *Chicago Tribune*, Apr. 25, 1872, 2.

work and reported back to the caucus, which adopted the committee's recommendations.[22]

Each of the Republican committees in this era seems to have been appointed in ad hoc fashion, in response to some difficulty experienced in the caucus itself. At their caucus on December 8, 1874, the Republicans began to debate the order of business for the upcoming short session of Congress. "It was deemed important that some agreement should be made which would give each important subject a place for consideration and avoid waste of time in struggles for supremacy," the *New York Times* reported the following morning. To reach that agreement, senators decided to create a committee which would recommend an order of business to a later meeting of the caucus. But establishing that committee was hardly straightforward. "A motion was made to give this committee certain instructions," the *Times* explained. "This proposition gave rise to an animated discussion involving various topics, which continued for about two hours, when it was decided to leave the committee to prepare and report an order of business for the session without instructions."[23] As the *Chicago Tribune* observed, perhaps ironically, in its coverage of this 1874 meeting, "The purpose of these extended caucus debates is understood [to be] to save time in discussing the order of business in open Senate."[24]

More than four years later—and 16 years after they had appointed their first ad hoc committee—the Republican Senate caucus continued to rely on occasional, short-term committees. "The republican Senators met in caucus this a.m.," the *St. Albans Daily Messenger* reported on February 5, 1879, "and after having informally discussed the prominent measures which are to come up during the remainder of the session, chose a committee to decide the order in which they should be brought up for consideration, to facilitate pending measures and appropriations, and to avoid an extra session."[25] The caucus adopted the report eight days later, and the committee was dissolved.[26]

"THE EXPERIMENT," 1879–92

The blows to Republican hegemony came quickly in the latter half of the 1870s. First, in 1876, Samuel Tilden nearly wrested the presidency from Republican hands, winning the popular vote and losing the electoral vote only through political maneuvering. Second, in that same year, Democrats won a majority of

[22] "Work for the Senate Caucus," *New York Times*, Apr. 29, 1872, 1; "Order of Business in the Senate," *Louisville Courier Journal*, Apr. 30, 1872, 1.
[23] "The Caucus of the Republican Senators," *New York Times*, Dec. 9, 1874, 5.
[24] "Senatorial Conference," *Chicago Tribune*, Dec. 9, 1874, 1.
[25] "Caucus of Republican Senators," *St. Albans (Vt.) Daily Messenger*, Feb. 5, 1879, 1. See also "A Caucus of Republican Senators," *Washington Evening Star*, Feb. 5, 1879, 1.
[26] "Republican Senatorial Caucus," *Minneapolis Tribune*, Feb. 13, 1879, 1; "Washington," *St. Louis Post Dispatch*, Feb. 13, 1879, 4.

the House of Representatives, their first since before the Civil War. And, third, in 1878, the Senate too, a Republican stronghold since 1861, fell into Democratic hands. When the new Congress convened in March 1879, both chambers were controlled by Democratic caucuses. Two years later, state elections left the Senate deadlocked. The Senate that convened in 1881 was split evenly between both parties.

The 1879–83 period was a time of robust competition for control of the Senate, and both parties responded with new institutions—culminating, in 1882–83, with the creation of the first Republican steering committee. The 1882–83 committee was an institutional invention that traced its roots to two decades of Republican ad hoc committees and to a Democratic committee on the order of business that had flourished in 1879. But the Republican committee of 1882–83 stood apart from these predecessors. In establishing this committee, Republican senators understood that they were tinkering with the Senate, trying out something that, even at the time, they realized was wholly new. The invention succeeded. For the next decade—through 1892–93, when the steering committee took on new strength and responsibilities—the Senate Republican caucus appointed committees on the order of business with regularity.

A first shift had come when Democrats gained control of the Senate. In March 1879, they organized an order of business committee, which, unlike the Republican committees of the 1860s and 1870s, assumed an expansive, ongoing role—and also blurred boundaries between the two chambers. The 1879 Democratic committee remained in existence for an entire session, then into the start of another session. The committee emerged, it appears, almost as an accident. When the Senate Democratic caucus met on the afternoon of March 17, 1879, they began debating an order of business for the extra session. "After some discussion," the *Cincinnati Enquirer* reported, senators in caucus created a committee to confer with a House counterpart, "with instructions to report to the caucus to-morrow, or as soon thereafter as practicable."[27] Some senators protested, arguing that Senate Democrats should set their order of business independent of the preferences of their colleagues in the House. "Senator [James] Beck [D, Ky.] wanted the Senate to declare what would be its line of action in this regard without reference to the House, and offered a resolution declaring, in substance, that the legislative business of the Senate during the extra session should be confined to the passage of the two Appropriation bills which failed at the last session, and the repeal of the jurors' test oath, the Federal Election law, and the law authorizing the presence of troops at the polls," the *New York Times* reported. "This motion gave rise to considerable discussion, and it was finally referred to the above-named

---

[27] "Mr. Speaker," *Cincinnati Enquirer*, Mar. 18, 1879, 1. See also "Caucuses of Democratic Senators," *Washington Evening Star*, Mar. 17, 1879, 1.

committee."[28] Allen Thurman (D, Ohio) was named chair of the nine-member Senate caucus committee.

Democrats in the House of Representatives met in caucus three days later, on March 20, to settle on an order of business. The House caucus had been convened, Fernando Wood (D, N.Y.) observed, "to take into consideration the question of what legislation should be introduced and acted upon during the extra session," the *Washington Post* reported. "He reminded the caucus that for the first time in eighteen years the Democrats were in control of both houses of Congress, and the country naturally expected something from the party very different from the rule of Radicalism."[29] The debate that ensued among the House Democrats was lengthy and contentious. Apparently exasperated, they accepted the Senate's invitation and appointed their own committee on the order of business to confer with the Senate committee.[30]

On March 26, 1879, the Senate and House committees made a report to an extraordinary joint meeting of Senate and House Democrats that had been convened in the House chamber.[31] Notably, the Senate committee did not make independent recommendations. Members of both committees, according to the *Chicago Tribune*, "explained the character of the report and outlined the discussions which had taken place during the joint sessions of the two Committees."[32] James G. Blaine (R, Maine) expressed his astonishment on the Senate floor at what he understood to be occurring. "For the first time I think in the history of Congress, so far as I know anything of it, notification was served that debate in the Senate upon a proposition before it must wait until a caucus committee of the dominant party had come to some conclusion," he said (*Cong. Rec.*, March 27, 1879, 78). "We are waiting now for somebody unknown to the Constitution, unknown to the organization of both branches, to prepare legislation which is to be taken, swallowed whole, and which members on that side do not propose even to discuss until the edict of King Caucus has determined what shall be forced through both branches of Congress." This was, Blaine emphasized to his Senate colleagues, "a new departure in legislation; that a sort of committee of safety, for the meeting of

---

[28] "The Democratic Senators," *New York Times*, Mar. 18, 1879, 1. See also "Getting Ready to Begin," *Washington Post*, Mar. 18, 1879, 1; Rothman 1966, 36–37.

[29] "Laying Out the Work," *Washington Post*, Mar. 21, 1879, 1.

[30] "The Conference Committee," *Minneapolis Tribune*, Mar. 21, 1879, 1; "Laying Out the Work," *Washington Post*, Mar. 21, 1879, 1; "Details of the Democratic Caucus," *Baltimore Sun*, Mar. 21, 1879, 1; "Washington: A Dull Day in Both Houses of Congress," *Detroit Free Press*, Mar. 21, 1879, 2; "Democratic Conferences," *Baltimore Sun*, Mar. 22, 1879, 1.

[31] While congressional Republicans had held several joint caucuses during the Civil War and the first years of Reconstruction, we have not found evidence of any committees setting agendas for those caucuses. See also Bogue 1989, 124.

[32] "The Joint Caucus," *Chicago Daily Tribune*, Mar. 27, 1879, 1. See also "Washington: Plan of Operations Agreed Upon by the Democratic Caucus Yesterday," *Louisville Courier Journal*, Mar. 27, 1879, 4.

which both branches are adjourned at premature hours in an unprecedented manner, is in existence, preparing, devising, and directing the measures of both bodies—a sort of extra-legislative and extra-constitutional proceeding." Henry B. Anthony (R, R.I.)—after learning that Thurman had charge of pending business "as the chairman of a subcommittee of the joint committee of the democratic caucus"—introduced some levity into the day by asking "if it would be in order to refer this resolution to the democratic caucus, which seems to have charge of the matter" (*Cong. Rec.*, March 27, 1879, 77).

The Senate committee continued in existence for several more months, but functioned largely as the Senate half of a joint Democratic committee setting an order of business for both houses—except for matters (like patronage and officers) that concerned only the Senate.[33] "It was to secure a continued harmony of action between the Democrats of the two houses that the Joint Advisory Committee was originally appointed, and so many joint caucuses have since been held," the *New York Tribune* explained in June 1879, on the occasion of another joint Democratic caucus. "The Democratic party is nothing if it is not well disciplined. Its members grumble and indulge in profanity, and declare that they will smash things if they cannot have their own way; but when the caucus meets and a vote is taken everybody falls into line and the party comes up solid once more."[34] While Democrats made a show of valuing secrecy for their caucus deliberations—hiring "watchmen" and bolting doors, in response to concerns that journalists "had obtained their accurate reports of the proceedings of recent caucuses through key-holes, transoms, ventilation pipes and similar avenues of communication with the outer world"—they surely understood that the House chamber was a grand stage and that their own members were talking with newspaper reporters.[35] The twin 1879 committees represented a remarkable exercise in bicameral coordination, an exercise that appears to have been abandoned, along with the Senate committee itself, by the end of the year, just as the second of that Congress's three sessions was beginning.[36]

For the next two years, both parties reverted to old practices. The 1879 Democratic example—a Senate committee working jointly with a House committee to set an order of business, reporting regularly both to the

---

[33] *Cong. Record*, Apr. 18, 1879, 536–38; "Caucus Action on the Veto Message," *New York Times*, May 1, 1879, 1; "A Caucus in Deep Secrecy," *New York Tribune*, June 3, 1879, 1; "Democratic Council," *Chicago Daily Tribune*, June 17, 1879, 1; "Safety: What the Democrats Are Now Seeking Through Their Committee," *Chicago Daily Tribune*, June 25, 1879, 1; "A Bourbon Caucus," *New York Tribune*, June 26, 1879, 1; "An Unburdening of Minds," *New York Tribune*, June 26, 1879, 1; "The Senate Patronage," *Washington Evening Star*, Dec. 4, 1879, 1; "Returning Reason," *Chicago Daily Tribune*, Dec. 11, 1879, 2.

[34] "An Unburdening of Minds," *New York Tribune*, June 26, 1879, 1. See also "A Bourbon Caucus," *New York Tribune*, June 26, 1879, 1.

[35] "An Unburdening of Minds," *New York Tribune*, June 26, 1879, 1.

[36] We have found no references to this committee after December 1879.

Senate caucus and to merged caucus meetings held in the House chamber, gaining widespread press coverage, and with a chairman whose role was so public that he was known as the "czar of the caucus"[37]—proved a dead end. Republicans organized an ad hoc committee on the order of business in April 1881, which, like every other Republican committee that preceded it, dissolved within a few days' time. That October, both the Republican and Democratic Senate caucuses created committees to confer with each other on the organization of the new Congress, but each of those committees existed for just a few hours.

Then, in the first days of December 1882, Republican senators invented a new institution. It was the *Boston Herald* that uncovered the story; as far as we know, the account appears nowhere else. In a dispatch dated December 14, 1882, in a brief article on page four of the next morning's newspaper, the *Herald*'s Washington correspondent explained to readers why Senate Republicans had yet to meet in caucus, even though 10 days had passed since the start of the session. "The delay in holding the Republican senatorial caucus is explained by the fact, which your correspondent is allowed to make public to-night, that the Republicans of the Senate have been trying the experiment of intrusting the direction of business to a 'steering committee,'" the reporter wrote. "Some of the Republican senators are not very fond of caucuses, and there were some minor reasons why the caucus should not be held early in the session. So a committee, of which Allison of Iowa is chairman, and Morrill, Hawley, Sherman, Harrison, Logan, Ingalls and several others are members, was appointed to take the place, for a time, of the caucus."[38] Even though the full caucus itself had not met, this "steering committee" had drafted and approved amendments to the Pendleton civil service reform bill, amendments which had then been introduced on the floor of the Senate, and the committee had also been working closely with the Republican members of the Finance Committee.

Republican senators were self-conscious about the novelty of what they were doing in December 1882: they were engaged in an "experiment." And these senators had given their committee a distinct name—"steering committee," a term which was used that month, as far as we can tell, for the first time in history to refer to a Senate caucus committee. The institution they created that December has persisted, in at least some form, to the present day, and, beginning in the winter of 1892–93 and lasting into the early 1910s, it would be the

---

[37] "From Washington: The Situation in Congress," *Burlington Daily Free Press and Times*, June 3, 1879, 3.

[38] "Senate Republicans: Why They Have Not Yet Held a Party Caucus," *Boston Herald*, Dec. 15, 1882, 4. See also "Washington: The Senators Still Debating the Possibility of Civil-Service Reform," *Chicago Tribune*, Dec. 17, 1882, 17, which includes the subtitle "Talk of a Republican Steering Committee," but otherwise makes no reference to the committee in the article.

Boston Herald, 15 Dec. 1882

SENATE REPUBLICANS.

Why They Have Not Yet Held a Party Caucus.

[Special Dispatch to the Herald.]

WASHINGTON, D. C., Dec. 14, 1882. The delay in holding the Republican senatorial caucus is explained by the fact, which your correspondent is allowed to make public tonight, that the Republicans of the Senate have been trying the experiment of intrusting the direction of business to a "steering committee." Some of the Republican senators are not very fond of caucuses, and there were some minor reasons why the caucus should not be held early in the session. So a committee, of which Allison of Iowa is chairman, and Morrill, Hawley, Sherman, Harrison, Logan, Ingalls and several others are members, was appointed to take the place, for a time, of the caucus. Last week this committee appointed a sub-committee, consisting of Hawley, Harrison and Logan, to prepare amendments to the Pendleton civil service reform bill. This sub-committee reported to the full committee last Saturday night. Certain of the amendments were approved by the committee and have since been offered, one by one, in the Senate. They are the amendments which have already been commented upon. The "steering committee" has done nothing in regard to the tariff or internal revenue, except to approve in a general way the course of the finance committee. No official consultations have been held by the committee with Republicans of the House. The new arrangement does not seem to fill the bill, and a caucus will probably be called within a very few days to consider revenue questions. The chief advantage, of course, of the "steering committee," is its secrecy.

FIGURE 4.2 The Republican steering committee "experiment," 1882

leading organ of the Senate. Like the Democratic committee of 1879, this new committee would sit for months at a time. But otherwise the 1882–83 Republican committee represented a radical innovation: a Senate committee on the order of business that convened for long stretches of a Congress, reported exclusively to the Senate's Republicans, met in secret, attracted little notice in the press, often made decisions without regular consultations with its caucus, and, at least in its early years, assigned no fame to its leaders. "No official consultations have been held by the committee with Republicans of the House," the *Boston Herald* noted. "The chief advantage, of course, of the 'steering committee,' is its secrecy."[39]

The committee appears to have met regularly through the session, ending its work only when the Senate adjourned in March 1883. As December progressed, the committee continued to oversee action on the Pendleton bill, "canvassing the Republican side of the Senate" to set a date for a final vote, while also negotiating with the House on dates for a Christmas and New Year's recess.[40] By early February, with just weeks left in the Congress and the Senate already considering tariff and appropriations bills, the steering committee had asked the chairmen of standing committees for their remaining legislative priorities.[41] It drew on this information to make reports to the full caucus. "The Republicans of the Senate held another caucus this morning, to determine the order of business for the remainder of the session," the *Cincinnati Enquirer* reported later in February. "The committee appointed several weeks since made a report to the effect that they had considered the subject, and that in their opinion action should be taken at the present session upon the Shipping bill, the Dakota Division bill, the Pension bills and the Bankruptcy bill."[42] In the last days of the session, the committee was still active and looking ahead to the next Congress. "It is understood that what is known as the governing committee of the Senate republican caucus," the *Baltimore Sun* stated on February 28, "is opposed to any special session, and that the President has been advised to this effect."[43] Who led the Republican steering committee of 1882–83 is unclear— the original December account in the *Boston Herald* names William B. Allison (R, Iowa), while the *Baltimore Sun* account at the end of February names George Edmunds (R, Vt.)—but the few stories published in these months by

[39] "Senate Republicans: Why They Have Not Yet Held a Party Caucus," *Boston Herald*, Dec. 15, 1882, 4.

[40] "Prospects of Mr. Pendleton's Bill," *Memphis Public Ledger*, Dec. 26, 1882, 2, citing *Cincinnati Commercial*. See also "Christmas Holidays," *Boston Herald*, Dec. 20, 1882, 2.

[41] "Caucus of Republican Senators," *New York Tribune*, Feb. 7, 1883, 1; "Notes from Washington," *New York Times*, Feb. 11, 1883, 8.

[42] "King Caucus," *Cincinnati Enquirer*, Feb. 23, 1883, 1. See also "Washington: News Gathered about the Capital City," *Austin Daily Statesman*, Feb. 23, 1883, 1; "Business Before the Senate," *New York Times*, Feb. 23, 1883, 1.

[43] "News from Washington: The Senate Organization," *Baltimore Sun*, Feb. 28, 1883, 1.

informed journalists otherwise tell a consistent story of an experiment that would resonate through subsequent generations.

In two regards—length of term and frequency of appointment—the example set by the 1882–83 committee was felt immediately. Beginning that winter, Republican senators routinely appointed a committee on the order of business, and each committee met for weeks or even months. As we detail in the Appendix, in Table A.4, we have identified a Republican committee on the order of business every calendar year between 1882–83 and 1892–93, with the single exception of 1889. They were appointed in every regular session of Congress in this decade, except the 1888–89 short session, and, once appointed, the committee on the order of business continued its work until the session ended. And all of these were long-serving committees, a decisive break with Republican practice in the late 1860s and 1870s, when no committee had lasted more than nine days. Lengthy terms granted these committees some independence from the caucus. Unlike the short-term Republican committees before 1882–83, the new committees on the order of business met and deliberated on their own, without explicit direction from the caucus, and made reports on multiple occasions in a session.

In other ways, though, the Republican committees between 1882–83 and 1892–93 reverted to older practices. These committees remained fundamentally ad hoc institutions, with little continuity in composition or even in committee size. Nine members served on the committee in 1884–85, but just three in 1886. Eleven sat on the committee in 1888, and, of those 11, just three senators— Allison, Sherman, and Henry Teller (R, Colo.)—also served on the seven-member committee appointed in March 1890. Most senators who appear on the committee list in one year disappear in another year, and a committee's life rarely extended beyond a single session. These committees, too, remained closely tethered to the caucus. Only rarely did these committees set agendas or draft legislation on their own; almost always they reported to the caucus, and the caucus continued to drive policy and the order of business. Consequently, the name "steering committee" went largely unused in these years. Overwhelmingly, journalists (and, it appears, senators themselves) resumed the old practice and referred to these simply as "committees on the order of business" through the 1880s and into the early 1890s.

Democratic committees, too, built on the precedents from 1879–83 and, when they were appointed, tended to serve for long terms. In contrast to the Republican practice, though, Democratic committees on the order of business existed only sporadically. After the 1881 committee, as shown in the Appendix in Table A.5, we can find no Democratic committee appointed until 1886, and there were no committees in 1889 or 1890. Committee size fluctuated for Democrats as for Republicans, as did membership. Just one person, Daniel Voorhees (D, Ind.), sat both on the nine-person 1879 Democratic committee and the five-person 1881 committee, and there was no overlap at all between the 1881 committee and the three-person 1886 committee. Beginning in 1886, however, a core group of Democrats—Isham Harris (D, Tenn.) and Francis Cockrell (D, Mo.), soon to be joined by Arthur Pue Gorman (D, Md.)—served on nearly every committee. For Democrats, the caucus chairman emerged as the default chairman of the committee on the order of business. And, they, like Republicans, continued to appoint two caucus committees in this era—a committee on the order of business and a separate committee on committees.

Over the course of the 1880s and early 1890s, both caucuses came to rely on their committees on the order of business. But the effectiveness of these committees varied, their status remained uncertain, and the strength of the caucus itself was often more potential than actual. As the *New York Times* reported in February 1887, "Republican Senators made two more attempts to-day to agree in caucus upon what they should do for the rest of the session, and with the usual result—a wrangle and a flat failure." Sometime in the next week, the *Times* predicted, the senators would hear from their caucus committee, but the committee report would lead only to "another fruitless discussion" in the caucus.[44] A year later, in March 1888, the caucus again appointed a committee on the order of business, as it had been doing regularly since 1882–83. But then two full years passed—including an entire session and much of the next session—before Republican senators established, in March 1890, another committee on the order of business. "The Republican leaders in both the House and Senate are becoming alarmed at the outlook for the important legislation to which the party is committed. Almost four months of the session is gone and practically nothing has been done," the *Pittsburg Dispatch* reported in March 1890. "On Tuesday night a conference of Republicans was held at the house of Mr. Edmunds, where Senators gave free vent to their feelings on the situation, and protested that immediate steps should be taken looking to the disposal of some portion of the mass of important legislation piled up on the calendar and in the committees."[45] By the time the meeting had ended, Republican senators had appointed a committee on the order of business. This committee, though, was disbanded in May.

In the summer of 1890, as the battle over the Federal Elections Bill began to rage in the Senate—the same moment that Democrats turned to Gorman, their new caucus chairman, to lead them in the fight against the bill—Republicans named two caucus committees to galvanize their members and articulate strategy. The first of these committees was appointed in July and met for only a few weeks, while the second was appointed in August and continued to exist through the end of the following session, until March 1891. Both committees were led by George Frisbie Hoar (R, Mass.), who was the Senate manager for the Federal Elections Bill. Criticizing "caucus dictation" in Congress, the *New York Times* that summer reprinted an editorial from the *Philadelphia Ledger*

---

[44] "A Fruitless Caucus," *New York Times*, Feb. 6, 1887, 6.
[45] "The Leaders Alarmed," *Pittsburg Dispatch*, Mar. 21, 1890, 1.

condemning "the attempt at 'caucus' coercion by the domineering leaders of the dominant party."[46] However, the Republican caucus committees of 1890–91 succeeded only in demonstrating their continued weakness as agenda-setting institutions. A different mix of senators was named to each of the three committees in the 1890–91 session, but ultimately all this maneuvering failed to break the historic Democratic filibuster and save the Federal Elections Bill. The Republican committee on the order of business, now eight years old, proved feckless when the moment demanded collective Republican action.

ELECTION DISPUTES AND INSTITUTIONAL INVENTION,
1892–93

That memory surely lingered two years later, in the winter of 1892–93, when Republican and Democratic senators strengthened and reinvented their steering committees in a fierce clash to determine control of the Senate. From then through the remainder of their years in Congress, Aldrich, Allison, and Gorman routinely used steering committees to direct party policy and strategy. On the Democratic side, the steering committee was led by the floor leader, itself a newly created position. "By reason of his position as chairman of the 'steering committee,'" the *Washington Evening Star* argued in the summer of 1893, referring to Gorman, "he can with two of its members decide the course of the party in the Senate."[47] But, for Republicans, who lacked an elected floor leader until 1913, the steering committee emerged as the primary vehicle for a group of powerful senators to direct their caucus and to drive policy for the whole chamber. Just as the Republicans had experimented with a new form of the committee on the order of business in 1882–83, when the Senate was evenly divided, so they reconceived the committee when they were in the minority. Created at a time of vulnerability, the Republican steering committee would become identified with Republican hegemony later in the 1890s.

These new steering committees were the products of a particular crisis, established to address electoral challenges and legislative priorities. Their initial duties were focused on securing control of the Senate following the 1892 elections, which required intervening in state legislatures. Merging electoral responsibilities with the older work of the committees on the order of business, a wholly new type of committee emerged. By 1893–95, the two steering committees had effectively become standing committees of their respective caucuses, with lengthy terms and, especially for Republicans, a developing expectation that membership was a property right. At times, the steering committee came to eclipse even the caucus itself in assuming control of the day-to-day management of the Senate's business.

---

[46] "Legislation by Caucus," *New York Times*, Aug. 27, 1890, 4.
[47] "In the opinion of many … ," *Washington Evening Star*, Aug. 14, 1893, 4.

Since 1877, the two major parties had battled on relatively even terms for control of the Senate. In the 46th Congress (1879–81), Democrats had secured a majority, and in the next Congress (1881–83), the two major parties had each claimed 37 seats. But Republicans controlled the chamber for the full decade after 1883, thanks in part to the strategic admission of certain western states to the Union (Stewart and Weingast 1992). Democrats had regained control of the House of Representatives in 1891 in a landslide, following two years of Republican control, but the Senate that year remained a Republican redoubt. Although their majority was often small, Republicans in the fall of 1892 had controlled the Senate for five straight Congresses. That fall, as the election approached, there were 47 Republicans, 39 Democrats, and two Populists in the chamber.

The central contest in the fall of 1892 was the battle for the White House between an incumbent president and a former president, Benjamin Harrison and Grover Cleveland. In the excitement leading up to the election, few observers paid attention to the looming struggle for the Senate. But there was occasional comment. "The Presidential campaign has engrossed the popular attention so much that the fact has almost been lost sight of that there are twenty-nine United States Senators whose terms expire on the 4th of March next, and that the legislatures to be elected this fall in the various States will be called upon to elect the successors of twenty-three of this number," the *Washington Post* observed on November 3, 1892, five days before the election. "It is within the range of possibility that the Democrats will secure a small majority in the Senate of the Fifty-third Congress; or, at least, put the balance of power in the hands of the third party."[48] In an editorial on November 7, the *New York Times* outlined a scenario under which Republicans might lose their absolute majority in the Senate, with Populists and Democrats gaining critical seats.[49]

Election Day, however, proved to be much worse for Republicans than anyone had predicted. Republican majorities in several state legislatures disappeared, and Democrats made unanticipated gains. The implication was clear. At minimum, observers concluded that Republicans would no longer hold a majority of seats in the Senate when the new Congress convened in March 1893. Whether Democrats could form a majority alone—or whether Democrats outnumbered Republicans only with the addition of Populist senators—was the question that could not immediately be answered. "In the last weeks of the campaign the leading organs of the McKinley party sought to disturb what the New York *Tribune* called the 'overconfidence' of Republicans by warning them that the loss of the Presidency would carry with it the loss of the Senate, which had been regarded as an impregnable stronghold of

---

[48] "The Senate Also at Stake," *Washington Post*, Nov. 3, 1892, 2.
[49] "The Fifty-third Congress," *New York Times*, Nov. 7, 1892, 4.

McKinleyism. But they did not admit that the Senate could be lost before 1895, even if Mr. Cleveland should be elected in 1892," the *New York Times* wrote in an editorial the day after the election. "It now seems very probable that on March 4, 1893, there will be a working majority in the Senate opposed to McKinleyism."[50]

Uncertainty lingered, however, regarding the scale of Democratic advances. "The Democrats have gained the lead in the United States Senate, but have not secured a clear majority," the *New York Times* reported three days after the election.[51] With many legislatures divided among three parties, the fate of many Senate seats was still unknown.[52] By the end of November, rumors had begun to circulate—at least in the vicinity of Democratic newspapers—that Republicans had resolved to intervene in some doubtful states to prevent the election of Democrats to the Senate. "Reports are current that the Republicans are giving close attention to the Legislatures in which the parties are about evenly divided, and that an attempt will be made to purchase enough votes to insure the election of Republicans, and thereby maintain a Republican majority in the Senate," the *New York Times* reported on November 29, 1892. "The Republicans now count a plurality of eight over the Democrats in the Senate, and they propose to use every effort to prevent the election of four Democrats in place of four Republicans, and so preserve the Senate to themselves. The Legislatures of Montana, Wyoming, California, and Nebraska are the ones which Republicans expect to manipulate."[53]

Democratic leaders immediately began to mobilize, claiming that their actions were necessary to protect the Senate plurality (or even majority) that they had fairly won. At the end of November, Gorman, chairman of the Senate Democratic caucus, announced plans for a meeting with a group of national Democratic leaders to discuss strategy for the upcoming weeks and months. "The purpose of the conference is to lay out a policy for the legislative branch of the party this winter and to authorize a committee to look after Senatorial seats in States like Kansas, where combinations may have to be made with a third party," the *Washington Post* reported. "It is proposed to give thoughtful consideration to the policy the party should pursue in Congress this winter, so that nothing rash shall be done."[54]

[50] "The Senate and the House," *New York Times*, Nov. 9, 1892, 4. See also "A Shake-Up in the Senate," *Washington Post*, Nov. 10, 1892, 4; "The United States Senate," *New York Times*, Nov. 10, 1892, 1; "Senate to Be Democratic," *Washington Post*, Nov. 11, 1892, 4.
[51] "The United States Senate," *New York Times*, Nov. 11, 1892, 1.
[52] "The Wyoming Legislature," *New York Times*, Nov. 22, 1892, 1; "Montana Senatorial Aspirants," *New York Times*, Nov. 22, 1892, 2; "Gossip About the Senate," *Washington Post*, Nov. 23, 1892, 2; "California Senatorship," *New York Times*, Nov. 25, 1892, 3; "Casting Lots in Kansas," *Washington Post*, Nov. 26, 1892, 4; "Deciding Vote in the Senate," *Washington Post*, Dec. 1, 1892, 4.
[53] "No Conference After All," *New York Times*, Nov. 29, 1892, 2.
[54] "Conference of Party Men," *Washington Post*, Nov. 27, 1892, 1.

As senators returned to Washington in December for the lame-duck session of the 52nd Congress, politicians and journalists continued to speculate about the composition of the Senate that would be assembling on March 4. Many Republicans insisted that they hoped the Senate, like the House and the presidency, would be firmly in Democratic hands, so that Democrats would have full responsibility for the government. But stories continued to circulate that some Republican senators were refusing to concede seats in nominally Democratic states. "Some of the Democrats who have been watching for several days the dispatches from Wyoming and California are beginning to doubt the talk of Republicans about their delight at the Democratic control of both branches of Congress," the *New York Times* reported, "and to wonder whether the Republicans are not getting ready to steal the Senate next March by reversing the elections in States that have been reported as electing Democratic Legislatures."[55] Democratic confidence was shaken by news that the Wyoming legislature now appeared to be favoring a Republican senator.[56] News in early December from Montana, where Republican and Democratic legislators were apparently discussing a plan to elect a Republican senator, exacerbated Democratic fears that their control of the new Senate remained uncertain.[57] In a December 7 editorial, the *New York Times* condemned these Republican "schemes of fraud," observing that these reported machinations could result only in a Senate with no governing majority, placing the balance of power in the hands of three Populist senators.[58]

Democratic senators responded that same day, establishing a committee to intervene in doubtful states, with the goal of securing the election of Democrats to the Senate. "The Democrats here fear that the Republicans in those states where the Legislatures are close will resort to any means to elect senators," according to an account of the caucus meeting in the *Boston Herald*, "and propose to checkmate them if possible."[59] The caucus lasted two hours. "The election of Senators from the northwestern states—Montana and Wyoming— where the standing of the legislatures was in doubt was the principal topic under discussion," according to the *Washington Evening Star*. "It was determined to do all that could be done to aid in bringing about the choice of democratic Senators from those states, and Chairman Gorman was authorized to appoint a committee of three Senators to act in an advisory capacity to the legislatures of those states in the conduct of the contests and election of Senators."[60] In addition to Montana and Wyoming, Democratic senators were concerned about affairs in California, Kansas, Nebraska, and the

---

[55] "The Senate Organization," *New York Times*, Dec. 1, 1892, 5.
[56] "Democratic Control of the Senate," *New York Tribune*, Dec. 2, 1892, 3.
[57] "To Unseat Senator Power," *Washington Post*, Dec. 3, 1892, 1.
[58] "Trying to Steal More Senators," *New York Times*, Dec. 7, 1892, 4.
[59] "Democratic Conference," *Boston Herald*, Dec. 8, 1892, 2.
[60] "After the Senate," *Washington Evening Star*, Dec. 8, 1892, 3.

Dakotas.[61] The *Washington Post* suggested that the creation of such a committee, charged to interfere in state legislative politics, was an extraordinary event. "It is understood that a committee was appointed which will act as a law-advisory body to Democratic members of Western and Northwestern legislatures wherein the vote is close and the ways of the enemy are dark and the Senatorial succession trembles in the balance," the *Post* wrote. "It was not recalled that the annals of Senate caucuses furnished any precedent for the action, and it created much discussion."[62]

On December 9, two days after the committee was named, the three committee members—Gorman, Calvin Brice (D, Ohio), and John Carlisle (D, Ky.)—arrived in New York to confer with President-elect Cleveland and other Democratic leaders. "The Democrats of the Senate are very much concerned about publications which allege that there is an organized attempt to reverse the will of the people expressed at the last election," Gorman explained, in remarks quoted by the *San Francisco Chronicle*. "Hence our visit here is to confer with the campaign committee and take such measures as possible to prevent any such attempt that might be made."[63] According to both the *Washington Evening Star* and the *New York Tribune*, the committee was now known as the "steering committee" of the Senate Democratic caucus.[64] "Senators Gorman, Carlisle and Brice go to consult the head of the party in an official capacity, as representatives of the Democratic steering committee in the Senate," the *Boston Herald* stated, "to advise with him, partly as to the Democratic attitude toward legislation in the present Congress, but chiefly as to plans to be laid for circumventing the attempts of the Republicans to steal the doubtful Legislatures in the West."[65]

Legislative business was closely aligned to the work of securing Senate seats. While the members of the Democratic steering committee themselves opposed the anti-option bill pending in Congress, they understood that persuading Populist legislators in western states to vote for Democratic senators required that the three of them support the bill's passage. "Before Messrs. Brice, Gorman, and Carlisle make any progress in their deals to secure Senators," according to the *Chicago Tribune*, "they will have to give assurances that the Anti-Option bill will be passed."[66]

The *New York Tribune*, a Republican newspaper, assigned sinister motives to the Democratic steering committee. Members of the steering committee

---

[61] "The Control of the Senate in Doubt," *New York Tribune*, Dec. 9, 1892, 3; "An Accidental Meeting," *Washington Evening Star*, Dec. 10, 1892, 6.
[62] "To Watch Republicans," *Washington Post*, Dec. 8, 1892, 7.
[63] "Hill Will Be Absent," *San Francisco Chronicle*, Dec. 10, 1892, 2.
[64] "To Confer with Mr. Cleveland," *Washington Evening Star*, Dec. 9, 1892, 1; "Hatching the Conspiracy," *New York Tribune*, Dec. 10, 1892, 1.
[65] "Want to Talk with Cleveland," *Boston Herald*, Dec. 9, 1892, 5.
[66] "It Is Hard Sledding," *Chicago Tribune*, Dec. 13, 1892, 9.

"boldly announced that they meant to adopt all possible means to prevent the election of Republican Senators," the *Tribune* explained. "It is understood that corruption funds proportionate in size to the exigencies of the case will be sent out to the Democratic State chairmen and National committeemen of the States under the guise of counsel fees."[67] The *Tribune* rejected any possibility that Republican politicians had already begun to funnel money into these same doubtful states.[68] Of course, Democratic newspapers interpreted events in a different light. "The next Senate will represent the will of the people and not the questionable and designing methods of those politicians who have in the past made a specialty of throttling public opinion," the partisan *Washington Post* stated that month. "There has been organized a Senatorial committee, headed by Hon. Arthur Pue Gorman, of Maryland. Speaking for the Democracy, Senator Gorman gives every assurance that the rights of his party will be vigorously contended for, and that the Republican plot to reverse the will of the people will surely be thwarted."[69]

Republican senators—who at first criticized the Democratic steering committee and described its activities as "pernicious"[70]—responded by organizing their own emergency "steering committee." Western senators had addressed their colleagues in the Republican caucus, arguing that decisive action was necessary to save doubtful states for the Republican party.[71] "Unless there is a change in the programme, the Republican Senators will hold another caucus to-morrow morning to devise a scheme to aid Western Republicans in their efforts to capture the Legislatures of several States," the *New York Times* reported on December 15. "They take the ground that nothing should be surrendered that can be held. They want a 'steering' committee, and at the conference will do all in their power to have one appointed."[72] In a caucus held that day, Republican senators voted unanimously to establish the committee, authorizing Sherman, chairman of the caucus, to appoint the five members.[73] George Frisbie Hoar (R, Mass.) was named chairman of the committee. The other members were James McMillan (R, Mich.), William Chandler (R, N.H.), Henry Teller (R, Colo.), and John Mitchell (R, Ore.).[74] The Republican committee was created to save Senate seats and to organize the Senate's legislative agenda for maximum partisan advantage. "Notwithstanding the pretense of prominent Republicans that they were willing to give the Democrats 'full swing'

[67] "Hatching the Conspiracy," *New York Tribune*, Dec. 10, 1892, 1.
[68] "Lying from Force of Habit," *New York Tribune*, Dec. 10, 1892, 6.
[69] "The Senate Is Safe," *Washington Post*, Dec. 19, 1892, 4. See also "Trying to Steal Senators," *New York Times*, Dec. 11, 1892, 4.
[70] "Doubtful Senate Seats," *New York Times*, Dec. 16, 1892, 5.
[71] "Fighting for Their Seats," *Washington Post*, Dec. 14, 1892, 1.
[72] "They Want a 'Steering Committee,'" *New York Times*, Dec. 15, 1892, 5.
[73] "All Sections Now in Line," *Washington Post*, Dec. 16, 1892, 1.
[74] "'Tis Greek Meet Greek," *Washington Post*, Dec. 21, 1892, 1; "The Republican 'Steerers,'" *New York Times*, Dec. 21, 1892, 5.

after the 4th of March by conceding to them the control of the Senate, the present majority in that body is evidently intent upon retaining control if the thing can be compassed by stealing the Legislatures of certain close States beyond the Mississippi River," the *New York Times*, a Democratic newspaper, observed. "They will not give up their control of the Senate without a determined fight."[75]

Both the Republican and Democratic Senate committees went to work quickly. "The two special Steering Committees appointed by each party to look after their respective interests in the doubtful Senatorial States of Nebraska, Kansas, Wyoming and Montana, have all their machinery at work at the capitols of these States," the *Philadelphia Inquirer* noted in late December 1892.[76] Quickly, though, it grew apparent that Democrats would control the chamber when the new Congress gathered in March. "The Republican managers of the Steering Committee," according to the *Inquirer*, "are not as much encouraged now as they were ten days ago, and the indications are that they will not be able to secure a single Senator out of the five close contests."[77] Organized for electoral purposes, the Republican committee began planning to set an order of business for the lame-duck session. "The republican Senate caucus will not appoint a new 'steering committee,'" the *Washington Evening Star* predicted. "The present committee … will be continued in force, and will conduct all the business that would come within the province of a steering committee."[78]

CONSOLIDATION, 1893–95

For both Senate parties, the struggle to organize the 53rd Congress had spurred a series of new organizational initiatives. Between the November 1892 election and the end of the first session a year later, Democrats appointed five committees, one focused on the state elections and the others on legislative business. In March 1893, as the new Congress convened, Gorman named a seven-person committee "to formulate a plan of reorganization" for the Senate, with responsibility for making assignments to Senate committees. This committee included Gorman and Brice, two of the three people who had been named to the election "steering committee" in December. (The third person, Carlisle, had left the Senate to become secretary of the treasury.)[79] The Democratic committee on committees, which traced its origins to December 1847, was thus, unceremoniously and permanently, subsumed by the Democratic steering committee in the

[75] "Senators Intent on the 'Steal,'" *New York Times*, Dec. 16, 1892, 4; "Doubtful Senate Seats," *New York Times*, Dec. 16, 1892, 5.
[76] "Fighting for the Senate," *Philadelphia Inquirer*, Dec. 31, 1892, 1.
[77] "Fighting for the Senate," *Philadelphia Inquirer*, Dec. 31, 1892, 1.
[78] "The Republican Senate Steering Committee," *Washington Evening Star*, Dec. 29, 1892, 6.
[79] "Democrats in Caucus," *New York Times*, Mar. 8, 1893, 2.

spring of 1893. "The Democratic Senators will hold a caucus to-morrow to pass upon the work of Mr. Gorman's 'steering committee' in reorganizing the committees of the Senate," the *New York Tribune* reported. "It is likely that the lists as made up now will be accepted without much grumbling, for the 'steering committee' seems to have recognized fully the fact that there can be but one sound and impartial basis for the distribution of committee honors—namely, seniority of service."[80] In August, Democrats named another steering committee, this time "to shape and direct the course of the democrats during the coming struggle over the Sherman bill and free silver."[81]

The events that year permanently reconfigured the Senate Democratic caucus. A few weeks into the second session of the 53rd Congress, in February 1894, Gorman appointed his sixth steering committee since the election, but this committee, drawing on an array of forebears, proved lasting: its nine members served without interruption for almost two years—through two sessions and two recesses, to the very beginning of the next Congress. In November 1895, more than eight months after the last Congress had ended and just days before the start of the next Congress, the committee was still active. "The Democratic steering committee of the Senate held a meeting of three hours' duration on Wednesday last. The members who were present are very reticent as to what occurred, but it is known that a thorough canvass was made of the Democratic situation, with a view to deciding upon a line of policy in the next session," the *Washington Post* reported late that month. "It appeared from the discussion that the Democratic Senators are divided as to the policy to pursue, some advocating an active effort to retain Democratic control of the Senate, while others advise a surrender to the Republicans without a struggle. The steering committee finally concluded that it would be wise to wait."[82] Apart from its Republican counterpart, the 1894–95 Democratic committee in its longevity had no precedent in the annals of the Senate. The membership of this Democratic committee, itself little changed from the membership of the committees formed in March and August 1893, formed the core of later steering committees.

The new Republican steering committee also had multiple parents. After appointing the December committee to contest Senate seats, Sherman named two new caucus committees on January 5, 1893. "Initial steps were taken toward the beginning of a bitter fight for the control of the next Senate," the *Louisville Courier* reported. "If there has been any belief that the Republicans intended permitting the organization of the next Senate to go by default, that belief was shattered by the action taken to-day," when Sherman created a reconstituted committee on the electoral emergency alongside an

[80] "The Senate Chairmanships," *New York Tribune*, Mar. 14, 1893, 3.
[81] "The Situation in the Senate," *Baltimore Sun*, Aug. 12, 1893, 4.
[82] "The Senate Organization," *Washington Post*, Nov. 23, 1895, 3.

order of business committee.[83] The stand-alone elections committee was soon abandoned, as it became clear that Republicans had lost the Senate. The order of business committee lasted two months, and then it too was dissolved. But the urgency of that winter, as Republicans watched their Senate majority crumble, had laid the groundwork for lasting changes.

In the minority, committed to affecting political business and electing more Republicans to the Senate, Republicans organized a new steering committee on December 5, 1893, on the second day of the second session of the 53rd Congress. Republican senators, according to the *Washington Post*, were "preparing for a campaign of opposition."[84] They created the committee explicitly to strategize "for the coming campaigns in the various states" as well as to set policy for the Senate minority.[85] The Republican steering committee would have a broad set of responsibilities, reflecting the lessons of the previous year. "This committee will be charged, among other things, with looking after the political end of all legislation and lining up the party on all questions that require concerted action," the *Post* reported. "The committee will keep in touch with State politics and take care that the elections in such States as have United States Senators to elect are conducted under a proper Republican organization."[86] As the *Boston Herald* explained, "This committee will, it is said, also be charged with the duty of looking after the general welfare of the party; and its scope will be enlarged somewhat, after the fashion of the Democratic committee, which during the 52d Congress was said to have taken such an active part in various state campaigns where Legislatures were to be elected that would elect United States senators."[87] Without the ability to set the Senate's agenda, members of the Republican steering committee worked to frustrate Democratic goals and to lay the groundwork for a restoration of Republican power. This committee ultimately sat for two full years, even longer than the Democratic steering committee appointed by Gorman.

The Republican committee of 1893–95—taking inspiration from the emergency committees of 1892–93—was a landmark, the first in a continuous line of Republican steering committees that continued, with only incidental interruptions, for nearly two decades. The 1893–95 committee included senators who had sat on the Republican caucus's earlier committees on the order of business, but it acquired its decisive cast from Allison, who joined the committee as its chairman, and his close allies Aldrich and Hale. "One of the members said yesterday afternoon after the announcement of the choice of Mr. Sherman that he had shown great discretion in his selection" of members of the new steering committee, the *Washington Post* reported on December 6, 1893, "for the reason that he had named some of the most astute politicians in the

[83] "Stand Together," *Louisville Courier Journal*, Jan. 6, 1893, 1.
[84] "Will Fight Cleveland," *Washington Post*, Dec. 6, 1893, 7.
[85] "Senate Republicans," *Boston Herald*, Dec. 5, 1893, 2.
[86] "Will Fight Cleveland," *Washington Post*, Dec. 6, 1893, 7.
[87] "Senate Republicans," *Boston Herald*, Dec. 5, 1893, 2.

Senate."[88] More than three years before Allison became chairman of the caucus, he, Aldrich, and Hale now commanded the Republican steering committee. Allison would not relinquish the committee chairmanship until his death in August 1908, and Hale and Aldrich remained leaders of the Republican steering committee until they left the Senate in March 1911.

STEERING COMMITTEES IN THEIR HEYDAY, 1893–1913

Republican senators regained their majority in 1895. Between 1895 and 1911, an era when Republicans enjoyed uninterrupted control of the Senate, the steering committee, a device honed in the minority, became the vehicle by which the majority Republicans led the Senate. While both parties possessed steering committees in this era, the Democratic steering committee, the organ of a minority party that also possessed an elected floor leader, was in a weak position to shape the Senate's business; year after year, its overriding concern was to assign Democratic senators to committees. Even on those occasions when it waded into the policy arena, the Democratic committee did not forget that core mission. "The democratic steering committee, of which Senator Gorman is the chairman, has been in session half a dozen days," the *Washington Evening Star* reported in 1903, "and while the chief purpose of its meetings has been to arrange for the assignment of democratic senators to committees, it has discussed in an informal way the subject of the recognition of Panama, and the proposition of the government to negotiate another canal treaty."[89] It was the Republican steering committee, acting for a party lacking a designated majority leader and in a chamber without a strong rules committee, that provided collective leadership for the Senate. The turbulence of 1892–93 had brought forth a qualitatively new Senate institution. That institution remained robust until 1911, when Aldrich and Hale retired from the chamber, and persisted as the primary vehicle for Republican leadership, albeit in attenuated form, until 1913. On six distinct dimensions— nomenclature, independence, committee tenure, leadership, membership, and their electoral role—the steering committees of 1893–1913 stood apart from the committees that had existed in preceding decades, differing even from the committees of the 1880s and early 1890s.

Nomenclature. A first difference was simple nomenclature: the term "steering committee" stamped the new era. Senate Republicans might have continued to insist that the (official) name of their (unofficial) caucus committee was the Committee on the Order of Business (Rothman 1966, 48), but, in day-to-day parlance, few people minced words after 1892–93. Before that election battle, journalists and senators tended to refer to the Senate caucus committee as a "committee on the order of business," but that shifted in an instant. The term "steering committee," which had been used sparingly since its first

---

[88] "Will Fight Cleveland," *Washington Post*, Dec. 6, 1893, 7.
[89] "The Panama Canal," *Washington Evening Star*, Nov. 13, 1903, 2.

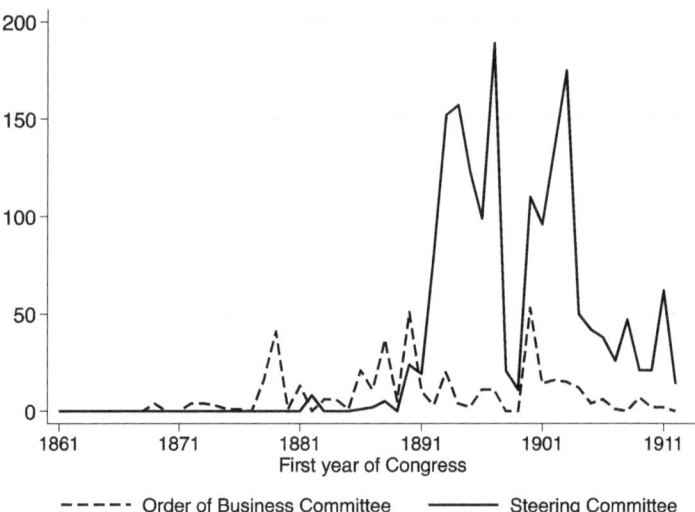

FIGURE 4.3 Number of references to caucus committees, by year, 1861–1913
Source: See discussion in text.

appearance with the Republican experiment of 1882–83, suddenly appeared everywhere in December 1892—and dominated nomenclature in subsequent years. Our evidence comes from the same newspaper database that we assembled to create Tables A.4 and A.5. From tens of thousands of news stories on the Senate, we identified every story that referred to a caucus committee on the order of business—whatever name the committee might have been given.[90] Figure 4.3 summarizes this raw count of news stories, distinguishing stories that refer to a "committee on the order of business" from those referring to a

[90] For this newspaper database, we conducted a comprehensive search of the following newspapers for the full period 1855–1913: *Atlanta Constitution, Baltimore Sun, Boston Globe, Boston Herald*, Chicago Tribune, Christian Science Monitor, Los Angeles Times, New York Times, New York Tribune, Philadelphia Inquirer*, Wall Street Journal, Washington Evening Star**, and *Washington Post*. All but three of these newspapers are available through ProQuest Historical Newspapers; the others, identified with asterisks, are in America's Historical Newspapers. Since many of these newspapers did not begin publication until well after 1855, and also because finding earlier stories about caucus committees proved much more difficult than finding later stories, we also conducted a comprehensive search of the following newspapers, all through ProQuest Historical Newspapers, for the period 1855–93: *Arizona Republican, Austin American Statesman, Cincinnati Enquirer, Detroit Free Press, Louisville Courier Journal, Minneapolis Star Tribune, Nashville Tennessean, San Francisco Chronicle, St. Louis Post Dispatch*, and *St. Petersburg Times*. For many years, we expanded the search much more broadly, including the full roster of newspapers in America's Historical Newspapers, the U.S. Northeast Collection in ProQuest Historical Newspapers, and Chronicling America: Historic American Newspapers. We conducted these expansive, in-depth searches for several different time periods, with special attention to earlier decades but also including later years where information was otherwise incomplete. Redd Brown, Hugh Curran, and Zach Lawlor did outstanding work searching these databases.

"steering committee." Between 1869 and 1889, we find just 16 news stories on the Senate using the term "steering committee," half of them from 1882–83, the year of the Republican "experiment." Newspaper reporters used the term more frequently in 1890 and 1891, with a total of 43 references over the two years. Then, following the November 1892 elections, the use of the term exploded in popularity. In December 1892 the term "steering committee" appeared in 79 stories—more in that single month than all earlier references combined. The term "steering committee" remained the dominant title in subsequent years, presumably a reflection of how much the committee's portfolio had grown in the aftermath of the 1892 elections. As Figure 4.3 shows, news coverage of this committee was sporadic, with extensive coverage in some years (such as 1892–97 and 1900–1903) and little coverage in other years (like 1898–99 and much of 1904–12), but we attribute the ebbs and flows in newspaper accounts to the relative success of committee members in keeping their work confidential. Members of the Republican steering committee often emphasized the need to maintain secrecy and privacy, and it appears that they succeeded at this more in some years than in others—including times, as in 1898–99 and 1904–11, when we have abundant evidence from other sources that the committee remained at its peak of influence.

Independence. Second, beginning in 1892–93 steering committees often assumed the power of coordinating the Senate's business without prior referrals to their caucuses, setting direction for their Senate colleagues and even determining when the full caucus would itself meet. Earlier committees, apart from the pioneering Republican committee of 1882–83, tended to be dutiful agents of their caucuses. They simply made reports, leaving decisions to the full caucus. In February 1879, for example, the *Washington Evening Star* reported that "the republican members of the Senate in caucus this a.m. adopted a report presented by the committee appointed to arrange the order of business for the remainder of the session."[91] More than a decade later, the basic practice had not changed. "A brief caucus of Republican Senators was held this morning," the *New York Times* reported in March 1890, "at which the order of business arranged by the committee appointed at the recent conference was approved."[92] But the steering committee gained a measure of independence after the 1892–93 transition. In May 1896, newspapers reported that the Republican steering committee was setting the order of business for the remainder of the session, without any indication that the committee was reporting to the caucus.[93] Indeed, the Senate Committee on Public Lands, seeking floor consideration for one of its bills, took

---

[91] "Order of Business in the Senate," *Washington Evening Star*, Feb. 13, 1879, 1.
[92] "A brief caucus ... ," *New York Times*, Mar. 27, 1890, 5.
[93] "Clearing Up the Decks," *Washington Post*, May 5, 1896, 4; "The End Is Drawing Near," *New York Times*, May 13, 1896, 2; "Capitol Chat," *Washington Post*, May 13, 1896, 6; "Programme for the Senate," *Washington Post*, May 14, 1896, 4; "Cannot Adjourn Yet," *New York Times*, May 14, 1896, 2; "Senator Dubois Objects," *Washington Post*, May 17, 1896, 5; "For an Order of Business," *Washington Post*, May 27, 1896, 4.

its case directly to the Republican steering committee.[94] McConachie, writing two years later, in 1898, described this institutional world. "Steering committees watch proceedings upon the Senate floor, call caucuses, and give the cues to action," according to McConachie (1898, 342). "On the 10th of March, 1897, the Republican Senators appeared in their seats promptly upon the opening of the Senate; each had received a note from the steering committee, bidding him to so order himself, though without any reason supplied." As the *Washington Post* explained in November 1900, anticipating the upcoming session of Congress, "Everything will depend upon the action of the steering committee, which arranges the programme of legislation in the Senate and which will be called upon early in the session to decide what measures shall receive consideration."[95] More than three years later, in January 1904, the *Boston Herald* reported that the Republican steering committee directs "what measures shall be brought up for consideration, as well as the action to be taken upon each bill or resolution," noting that it was the steering committee, and not the caucus, that met regularly to make these decisions.[96] The power of the steering committee was undiminished later in the decade. "President Roosevelt's legislative programme was punched full of holes yesterday by the Republican steering committee of the Senate," the *Washington Post* observed in April 1908. "The 'steering committee' is not that in name only; it is the body that actually steers things, does things, and decrees what shall not be done."[97]

Committee tenure. A third significant difference was the transformation of the steering committees, after 1892–93, into standing committees of the two caucuses. What were purely ad hoc committees in the 1860s and 1870s, meeting for just a few days, had become more established after the Democratic and Republican innovations of 1879–83. In the 1880s and early 1890s, as Tables A.4 and A.5 show, several committees met for weeks at a time. Senate Republicans, though not the minority Democrats, appointed a committee in almost every regular session in these years. But in the decade before 1892–93, just two committees stayed active for more than a single session. The committees in these years remained ad hoc committees, generally created only in the final weeks or months of a session to manage the chamber's business as time ran short. After 1892–93, however, steering committees served through entire Congresses. The appointment of the committee in the first session of each Congress became routine. "A caucus is to be held to-morrow to discuss the order of business and to appoint the usual Committee on Order of Business, which is better known as the Steering Committee," the *New York Times* wrote in February 1900. "The business of the Senate is arranged" by the Republican steering committee, the *Times* explained, "the majority usually accepting the

---

[94] "Clearing Up the Decks," *Washington Post*, May 5, 1896, 4.
[95] "Will Provoke a Fight," *Washington Post*, Nov. 24, 1900, 1.
[96] "Congress Controlled by a Few Men, Who Practically Rule the Country," *Boston Sunday Herald*, Jan. 17, 1904, 37.
[97] "Doom Roosevelt Plan," *Washington Post*, Apr. 22, 1908, 4.

order of business so arranged without question."⁹⁸ Organized in the first session of a Congress, Republican and Democratic steering committees in 1893–1911 tended to meet regularly through the remainder of Congress, often conducting business through recesses and sometimes continuing to exist through the special, organizing session of the next Congress. They were invisible in the Senate's rules, but otherwise the steering committees in this era had effectively achieved the stature of standing committees, in continuous existence for two-year periods. In July 1908 Smith D. Frye, writing in the *Los Angeles Times*, explained to the newspaper's readers that, "being a caucus matter, and not an official matter, the Congressional Directory has no official knowledge of the existence of that committee," but the Republican steering committee was "the most important committee of the United States Senate."⁹⁹

Leadership. Fourth, suggesting the new prominence of these committees in setting the Senate's agenda, the leadership of the committees was fused with the leadership of the party caucus. This had happened only rarely in 1879–92, when examples of caucus chairmen chairing the committees on the order of business were exceptional—George Pendleton (D, Ohio) in 1881, Beck in 1886, Edmunds in 1886 and 1890—but it became a firm rule in the aftermath of the reorganization of these committees in 1892–93. The shift on the Democratic side was immediate. Gorman, who chaired the Democratic caucus (and served as the Senate's first recognized floor leader) from 1890 until 1898, chaired every steering committee appointed in those years. His successor, James K. Jones (D, Ark.), chaired both the Democratic caucus and the steering committee in 1899–1903. Then Gorman, who returned as caucus chairman and floor leader in 1903, reclaimed his position as chairman of the Democratic steering committee, maintaining a precedent that ultimately continued until the late twentieth century. On the Republican side of the aisle, the shift occurred with a lag. Aldrich and his closest allies gained firm control of the Republican steering committee in 1893. When Sherman, the caucus chairman, appointed the Republican steering committee that December, he named Allison chairman and placed Aldrich and Hale second and third on the committee list.¹⁰⁰ Sherman named the same three men to the Republican steering committee every year until 1897, each time naming Allison as chairman of the steering committee. Then, in 1897, Allison assumed the caucus chairmanship. Allison, as caucus chairman, continued to chair the Republican steering committee until his death in 1908, when he was succeeded, both as caucus chairman and as head of the Republican steering committee, by Hale. "The conference of Senate Republicans today formally selected Senator Eugene Hale of Maine as the leader in that legislative body," the *Boston Herald* reported in December 1908, when Congress returned after its recess. "The caucus chairman is always chairman of the steering committee, which is the governing body of the Senate."¹⁰¹

⁹⁸ "Senate Order of Business," *New York Times*, Feb. 14, 1900, 5.
⁹⁹ Smith D. Frye, "'The Lucky Thirteen,'" *Los Angeles Times*, July 12, 1908, II: 11.
¹⁰⁰ "Will Fight Cleveland," *Washington Post*, Dec. 6, 1893, 7.
¹⁰¹ "Hale Chosen Leader," *Boston Herald*, Dec. 10, 1908, 1.

WILLIAM B. ALLISON.

William B. Allison (R, Iowa). He was named chair of the newly strengthened
Republican steering committee in 1893 and, by virtue of seniority, became chair of the
Senate Republican caucus in 1897. He held both posts until his death in 1908.

Library of Congress, Prints & Photographs Division, reproduction number LC-DIG-ppmsca-46429

Membership. A fifth shift took place with committee membership. Before the winter of 1892–93, there was little regularity in committee membership or even size. That changed decisively in 1893. Membership on the steering committees stabilized, with great continuity from year to year. Allison, Aldrich, and Hale appear to have served together on the Republican steering committee for 15 uninterrupted years, from 1893 until Allison's death, and Cullom served alongside them in nearly every session.[102] Beginning in 1900, perhaps as early as 1898, membership on the Republican steering committee became a property right for every senator on the committee. Nine members served on the committee in 1900: Allison, Hale, Aldrich, Cullom, Edward Wolcott (R, Colo.), William Sewell (R, N.J.), Spooner, George McBride (R, Ore.), and Mark Hanna (R, Ohio). Six of them—Allison, Hale, Aldrich, Cullom, Spooner, and Hanna—remained in the Senate when the next committee was appointed in February 1902, and all six held their seats on the new Republican steering committee. (Sewell had died in December 1901, and Wolcott and McBride failed to be reelected to the Senate.) Over time, the Republican steering committee "has been slowly but surely increasing its powers," the *Cincinnati Enquirer* observed in 1903. "The personnel may change, as political retirement or the dread reaper Death may cut a hole in the board," but otherwise senators kept their places.[103] From 1900 until 1911, property rights on the Republican steering committee were absolute; no senator lost his seat on the committee as long as he remained in the Senate.

While Republicans were perfecting this exercise in collective leadership, Democrats, as we discuss in the next chapter, had distilled their caucus's powers into the vessel of floor leadership. Each new Democratic leader, beginning with Gorman in the 1890s, looked to the committee as an advisory body for setting strategy, building coalitions, and making committee assignments. In 1907, when the Democratic caucus considered electing the steering committee rather than authorizing their caucus chairman, Charles Culberson (D, Tex.), to appoint its members, the *Washington Evening Star* noted that the steering committee constituted the foundation of party leadership. There is no justification for "making Mr. Culberson a nonentity as to the party's committee

---

[102] We make this claim with some uncertainty, given that, as shown in the Appendix, in Table A.4, Hale is not on the list of committee members in the spring of 1898, and we have located the names of just two committee members in 1898–99 (i.e., Allison and Cullom). But these are the two most poorly documented years in the 1892–1911 period. We located, for example, 200 news stories about steering committees and committees on the order of business from 1897, but just 21 from 1898 and 11 from 1899, and most of these refer to the Democratic committee. The historical record of the Republican steering committee for those two years is sparse and fragmentary: just four stories from 1898 and five stories from 1899 refer, even in passing, to the Republican committee, which leaves open the possibility that the membership list for spring 1898 is incomplete or even incorrect, given that this is a secondhand report of a secret proceeding.

[103] "Real Rulers of the Nation," *Cincinnati Enquirer*, Feb. 20, 1903, 10.

dispositions and steering program," the *Star* argued. "In the very nature of things he should have a large voice in choosing his lieutenants and directing the courses to be taken. Otherwise he might be, probably would be, reduced to the terms of a mere executor."[104] Democratic caucus chairmen had the right to reorganize the committee, but they rarely displaced anyone. Between 1895 and 1907, without exception, every returning senator retained his seat on the Democratic steering committee. And even Culberson and Thomas S. Martin (D, Va.), who thoroughly reconstituted the membership of the steering committee at the starts of their terms in 1907 and 1911, kept that membership intact for the duration of their tenures as leaders.

Electoral role. Finally, in the wake of the 1892–93 state elections, these new steering committees not only determined the order of business in the Senate but also actively monitored electoral politics. In combining electoral, legislative, and policy responsibilities, they served the multiple, interlocking needs of their Senate parties. The shift in nomenclature—the embrace of the name "steering committee"—suggested the more expansive responsibilities assumed in these years. While every committee on the order of business in the 1870s, 1880s, and early 1890s would have considered the implications of their work for their party's standing in elections, the steering committees of 1893–1911 made this concern explicit. The Republican committee of 1893–95 was a triumph in this regard: chaired by Allison, this committee attended both to legislative affairs in the Senate and elections in the states, leading Senate Republicans back to the majority in 1895. But the battle to hold that majority continued. With Republican control of the Senate tenuous, Hanna met with members of the steering committee in December 1896. "The gathering was held in Senator Aldrich's committee-room and around a well-filled lunch table the complexion of the next Senate was discussed," the *Washington Post* reported. "The first topic of consideration was the importance of securing this much-needed Republican majority. The Legislatures of four States—Washington, South Dakota, North Carolina, and Kentucky—were regarded as offering available working ground." After discussing the urgency of these electoral contests, members of the Republican steering committee turned to questions of impending legislation.[105] More than three years later, the Republican steering committee continued to link legislative action to electoral concerns. "The steering committee of the senate, of which Senator Hanna and Senator Aldrich are the dominating factors, propose to take charge of the work of arranging the party programme for the coming campaign. To this end a caucus has been determined upon," the *Atlanta Constitution* reported in March 1900. "The principal object of the proposed caucus ... is to round up the party in support of the Porto Rican bill and at the same time to instruct some of the

[104] "The Minority in Congress," *Washington Evening Star*, Dec. 4, 1907, 4.
[105] "Mr. Hanna's New Job," *Washington Post*, Dec. 10, 1896, 1.

unruly members in party discipline."[106] The *Los Angeles Times* described the work of the Republican steering committee in setting the Senate agenda in the spring of 1908, noting that Albert J. Beveridge (R, Ind.), a member of the committee, was keenly concerned about the electoral implications of inaction by the Senate majority. "Senator Beveridge declared that it would be bad politics for Congress to adjourn without passing some of the measures desired by the President, and that the 'do-nothing' policy would be heard of in the coming campaign," according to the *Los Angeles Times*. "He spoke of the difficulty Republican campaigners would have in answering the charge that the President's programme for beneficial legislation had been ignored by a Republican Congress."[107]

Then, on March 3, 1911, the reign of the Republican steering committee came to an end. With the Republican caucus increasingly riven by factionalism and progressives growing in numbers, Aldrich and Hale together retired from the Senate. They had made twin announcements on the night of April 18, 1910, explaining that they would not be seeking reelection. "This news comes as a political sensation in Washington," the *Boston Herald* reported the next morning. "The character of the Senate will change materially with the passing of the two present leaders. There will be different methods, perhaps different standards, in the transaction of public business in the Senate."[108] Aldrich and Hale were the last of the generation that had transformed the steering committee into the Senate's governing body in the early 1890s and maintained its strength over the succeeding two decades. From the historic steering committee of 1893–95, only Cullom remained, and Cullom, though senior and well-respected, never commanded the Senate like his old colleagues. "It is a vastly different Senate from that which helped frame the Payne-Aldrich tariff bill and which adjourned in the early spring," the *Washington Sunday Star* observed in May 1911.[109] Measured by its membership, its power and influence, even its longevity, the Republican steering committee struggled to sustain itself in 1911–13. A committee that had been defined by long tenure and stable memberships became, in 1911, a short-lived, ad hoc institution, much like the committees of the 1880s. Between 1911 and 1913, the Republican caucus named three different steering committees, each with a different chairman and each with a reconstituted membership.

ELEMENTS OF LEADERSHIP: REPUBLICANS, 1893–1913

Looking backward from the twenty-first century, the Republican steering committee was a curious institution, a bold experiment that ultimately collapsed.

---

[106] "Porto Rican Blunder Laid to Wrong Man," *Atlanta Constitution*, Mar. 7, 1900, 1.
[107] "Will Consider No New Bills," *Los Angeles Times*, Apr. 22, 1908, 14.
[108] "Hale Will Quit Senate Because of State Fight," *Boston Herald*, Apr. 19, 1910, 1, 2.
[109] "New Men in Command," *Washington Sunday Star*, May 21, 1911, 4:2.

It was instead elected floor leadership, a Democratic invention in those same years, that ultimately paved a path forward for Senate party organization. But hindsight can deceive. Political observers in the 1890s and 1900s all understood that Republicans had discovered a solution to a problem that had vexed the Senate for more than a century's time: how to lead a body filled with strong individuals, each possessing the power to slow the institution's business, and in a chamber lacking an effective presiding officer. The solution—a plural executive for a legislative body—was distinctive in American history. Its distinctiveness belied its strength. Next only to the president himself, and at times the speaker of the House, the members of the Senate Republican steering committee shaped the course of American national government between 1893 and 1911. Presidents as diverse as Grover Cleveland, William McKinley, Theodore Roosevelt, and William Howard Taft all understood that the steering committee ruled the Senate.

Of the five functions that would come to characterize Senate floor leadership by the middle of the twentieth century, two—*managing the caucus* and *building policy coalitions*—were mastered by the Republican steering committee of 1893–1911. Both functions are essential to the legislative process, and both are best done out of the public eye. Committee assignments were overseen by a separate Republican committee on committees, itself invariably named by the caucus chairman. But otherwise, as a body that worked in secrecy and derived its authority from the Republican caucus, the steering committee was designed to perform these two fundamental tasks. Even in the minority, in the summer of 1894, the Republican steering committee was assuming these functions. During the debate over the Wilson-Gorman tariff bill, the Republican steering committee met regularly to hone a party position on the tariff schedules. It considered the implications of "putting sugar on the free list," concluding that such a move "will receive the support of nearly the entire republican side."[110] The steering committee spoke for its caucus throughout these years, routinely setting agendas and building coalitions. When Allison died in 1908, the *Washington Evening Star* reflected on the power he had wielded. "As chairman of the steering committee he was permitted to select his own associates, and thus he became, in a peculiar sense, the arbiter of the fortunes of legislation in the Senate, for, as is generally known, this committee, although not recognized by law, practically determines what important bills shall be passed and what shall be either defeated or allowed to die," the *Evening Star* reported. "It was the steering committee, more than any other sub-organization of the Senate, which directed the legislation in connection with the Spanish-American war. Indeed, in latter years there has been little, if any, legislation of moment which has not had the sanction of this organization."[111]

[110] "Many Rumors: A Tariff Agreement May Be Reached Tomorrow," *Washington Evening Star*, Aug. 8, 1894, 2.
[111] "His Ability Recognized on Entrance to Congress," *Washington Evening Star*, Aug. 5, 1908, 4.

The three other elements of modern Senate leadership—*speaking on behalf of the party, serving as an intermediary with the president,* and *leading the party on the floor*—were not easily performed by the steering committee. On the contrary, the Republican steering committee, as a collective body whose proceedings were meant to be confidential, was a clumsy device for assuming these functions. Still, individual members of the steering committee could (and often did) perform these three functions. While there is no evidence that any particular senator was formally designated to perform these tasks, members of the steering committee often shared news with the press, worked closely with the president, and directly managed floor proceedings.

When newspaper reporters in this era sought information about congressional proceedings, they frequently turned to a member of the Republican steering committee. A seat on that body endowed a senator with authority. Aldrich—identified by the *Washington Evening Star* as a member "of the Senate finance committee and of the republican steering committee"—issued a lengthy statement to the press in January 1895 regarding the sugar tariff, "the ill effects of the general democratic policies," and consequent "retaliatory measures against American exports."[112] Throughout this era, Aldrich rarely agreed to be quoted on the record, "but the half-dozen reporters who dared approach Aldrich found him a wellspring of information on the Senate's business," Ritchie (1991b, 185–86) writes. "Correspondent Louis Coolidge labeled Aldrich among the Senate's best 'news-gatherers' because he seemed so much better informed than other senators about when things were likely to happen." In February 1899, a senator, identified simply as someone on the Republican steering committee, was quoted anonymously by the *Chicago Tribune* as saying that "an extra session seems almost inevitable."[113] A year later, in May 1900, the *New York Times* reported on plans for Congress to adjourn. "'Our programme is nearly complete,' said a Republican member of the Steering Committee to-night," according to the *Times*. "'We did lay out a bit more work than we have accomplished, but since we have a government for Porto Rico and one for Hawaii, and have adopted the gold standard and set the law in working order without trouble, we feel as if we had earned a rest, and the country will be thankful when we have gone home.'"[114] In March 1902, Hale—"a leading member of the Senate committee on appropriations, and also of the republican steering committee"—stated, presumably to a reporter, that he believed "Congress would be prepared to adjourn for the session by June 10."[115] Following the November 1910 elections, when Democrats gained 12 seats in the Senate and claimed control of the House, Hale, now chairman of the Republican steering committee, spoke at length to reporters about

[112] "Tariff and Finance," *Washington Evening Star*, Jan. 9, 1895, 3.
[113] "To Force Extra Session," *Chicago Tribune*, Feb. 23, 1899, 7.
[114] "Talk of Early Adjournment," *New York Times*, May 9, 1900, 6.
[115] "Adjournment by June 10," *Washington Evening Star*, Mar. 14, 1902, 10.

Republican plans for the lame-duck session and for the next Congress. "He fully expected to see the Republican party in Congress get together again and present a united front," according to the *Baltimore Sun*. "Mr. Hale declared he had little fear of any long continuance of Democratic ascendancy in politics. Republican policies, under President Taft's leadership, he said, would triumph again."[116]

Presidents in these years communicated regularly with leading senators, a group that overlapped considerably with the membership of the Republican steering committee. In March 1898, as war loomed with Spain, the full membership of the steering committee called at the White House to inform McKinley "that unless he took speedy action all hope of restraining the senate from adopting one of the numerous resolutions declaring war would be futile."[117] Through his years as president, McKinley consulted with many senators, and "Roosevelt was no less shrewd than McKinley in his appreciation of the necessity of working by and through the leaders of the Senate," according to Donnelly (1930, 168). "He assiduously cultivated the friendship of men like Aldrich, Allison, Hanna, Spooner, and Lodge, and censured Taft for his failure to do the same when he came to the presidency."[118] When he became president in the fall of 1901, Roosevelt reached out to several senators for advice on his first message to Congress (Fowler 1961, 261; Welch 1971, 293). "Hardly a week went by when Spooner was in Washington that he did not receive a note from the White House, inviting him to one of the famous 'stag dinners' or to stop in informally for a chat," Fowler (1961, 262) recounts. "'When you come here, *always* come straight into my room,' the President directed Spooner." In September 1902, at a meeting Roosevelt organized at Oyster Bay, he conferred with five members of the steering committee—Allison, Aldrich, Lodge, Spooner, and Hanna—in an effort "to hammer out some position on the tariff which would be acceptable to all of the conflicting regional and economic interests" (Fowler 1961, 264–65). Despite Roosevelt's criticism, Taft, too, reached out to leaders of the Senate for advice and counsel. Aldrich met with the president in March 1910, informing him that the Republican steering committee was committed to passing the railroad bill and that it intended to "hold it before the senate to the exclusion of any other business except appropriation measures until it is passed."[119]

For managing the floor, Republicans in these years relied heavily on Aldrich and Hale, as well as a raft of bill managers, but no one person held the position in any official capacity. Leadership was a collaborative effort. In a 1903 article, the *Cincinnati Enquirer* identified a group of six senators who controlled Senate

---

[116] "Hale Smiles at T. R.," *Baltimore Sun*, Nov. 30, 1910, 13.
[117] "Must Know by Monday," *Boston Globe*, Mar. 31, 1898, 2.
[118] Citing letter from Theodore Roosevelt to William Howard Taft, Mar. 13, 1903, as quoted in Bishop, *Roosevelt*, i: 237–38.
[119] "Another Blow at the Bill," *Boston Globe*, Mar. 10, 1910, 8.

action. Rather than voting down bills on the floor, the group "kills uncomfortable things by indirection where possible," according to the *Enquirer*. "Hence, if the statehood bill is permitted to come to a vote something else will come up . . . to stave off action on the measures that are troublesome."[120] More than anyone else, Aldrich led the Senate. "For cunning and adroitness the Democrats have no one in the Senate who can compare with Nelson W. Aldrich, of Rhode Island," the *Baltimore Sun* wrote in 1901. "He knows when to 'bluff,' when to bully, when to flatter and when to anger. The man who is lacking in alertness he bluffs, the timid man he bullies, the vain man he flatters and the man whose judgment is overturned when angry he torments and taunts until he loses his temper and is put at fault."[121] Thompson, chief Washington correspondent for the *New York Times*, offered a similar observation, writing in the spring of 1905, "A session of the Senate without Nelson W. Aldrich to run it is a thing almost unthinkable."[122] Less than a year later, though, Thompson revised his assessment, arguing that Hale now functioned as leader.[123] "This is not to intimate that Senator Aldrich has been unhorsed or driven from power," Thompson (1906, 38–39) emphasized. "He is the chess-player of the senate, the wire-puller, the manager of votes. But Hale has come to be the great force in arranging party policies." Others, while recognizing a constant flux of duties within the group of leading senators, still emphasized the role played by Aldrich. "In political generalship no other Senator pretends to rival him," Ira E. Bennett argued in March 1906.[124] "The leader, the boss of the Senate for the past twenty years has been—Aldrich!" David Graham Phillips thundered in April 1906.[125] But Aldrich, even at the peak of his influence, never chaired the caucus or the steering committee, and he was never elected by his peers to lead them on the floor. "Senator Aldrich, while most influential in committee work

[120] "Real Rulers of the Nation," *Cincinnati Enquirer*, Feb. 20, 1903, 10.

[121] "Aldrich as a Leader," *Baltimore Sun*, Dec. 29, 1901, 9. See also Coolidge 1901.

[122] "'The Big Five' Who Run the U.S. Senate," *New York Times*, Mar. 19, 1905, SM6. Charles Willis Thompson provided, in a series of newspaper articles and in his 1906 book, vivid portraits of congressional leaders in this era. The *New York Times* did not identify Thompson as the author of these articles. We attribute to him any articles that appear in the *New York Times* in this era that begin with the italicized words "Special to The New York Times" or some variant of that phrase (otherwise rare in news stories) and that duplicate passages in his 1906 book. For more on Thompson, see Ritchie 1991b.

[123] "Hale Senate Leader, Succeeding Aldrich," *New York Times*, Jan. 2, 1906, 6; "Hale, Senate Leader, a Warrior for Peace," *New York Times*, Jan. 8, 1906, 9.

[124] "Personality of Senators Who Lead in Railroad Rate Discussion," *Washington Post*, Mar. 18, 1906, M6. See also "Nelson Wilmarth Aldrich, the Leader of the Senate," *Washington Post*, Dec. 2, 1907, 5.

[125] David Graham Phillips, "The Treason of the Senate: Aldrich, the Head of It All," *Cosmopolitan Magazine*, vol. 40, no. 6 (Apr. 1906), 632, 628. See also Phillips, "The Treason of the Senate: Fairbanks, Hale, and Frye," *Cosmopolitan Magazine*, vol. 42, no. 1 (Nov. 1906), 78; Phillips, "The Treason of the Senate: Thrifty Patriot Allison," *Cosmopolitan Magazine*, vol. 41, no. 6 (Oct. 1906), 627, 630.

and in party conferences, has never been the leader of the majority in the sense that other senators of both parties have been," the *Boston Herald* observed in January 1906. "His lack of ability as a debater and of force as a speaker would have handicapped him for that post. For the last few years the Republicans have been directed by a coterie, or 'steering committee,' of strong men of varied gifts and long experience."[126]

CONCLUSION

The Republican steering committee was reimagined in 1892–93 by a party that was losing control of the chamber for the first time in a decade, an institution forged by the Senate's minority party. It was newly fortified in 1892–93 just as it had been created in 1882–83, by a Republican party no longer dominant in the Senate. Allison and Aldrich's reliance on the Republican steering committee is noteworthy. Rather than calling more caucus meetings or assuming floor leadership responsibilities when he became caucus chairman in March 1897, Allison continued to depend on this party committee. Allison, Aldrich, Hale, and their allies used the committee to manage the Senate's business. "Arranging the legislative schedule in detail week by week, the committee extended the party leaders' authority unimpaired from the caucus to the chamber," Rothman (1966, 58–59) argues. "Senators knew that they had to consult the committee before attempting to raise even minor matters."

The finding that steering committees—and the dominance of Aldrich and Allison in the Senate's affairs—date from the early 1880s and early 1890s, rather than 1897, presents an entirely new perspective on organizational change from the one that currently shapes all existing scholarship on Senate development. It roots institutional invention in moments when the parties were evenly balanced and fiercely contesting each other for leadership of the Senate, far from the highpoint of Republican hegemony. The Republican steering committee was not created for the purpose of establishing party government in the Senate. To the contrary, the new steering committees, those of 1879–83 as well as those of 1892–93, were created by senators of each party who consciously sought a way to balance competing considerations in a context in which the parties' policy and electoral interests were at stake. The greatest innovations, in 1882–83 and in 1892–95, came on the Republican side—the work of entrepreneurial senators who, finding themselves no longer in the majority, developed, with deliberateness and intention, a new institution to help lay the groundwork for a restoration of Republican power. While party homogeneity may have been crucial to the reign of the Republican steering committee in the late 1890s and early twentieth century, as Brady, Brody, and

---

[126] "The Senate Leadership," *Boston Herald*, Jan. 3, 1906, 6.

Epstein (1989) suggest, it cannot explain the emergence of the steering committee. It was party competition, factionalism, and electoral concerns that prompted Aldrich, Allison, and their allies to design this new institution. The homogeneous, dominant Senate Republican party of that era owed its governance structure to moments when its caucus was internally divided and struggling to control the chamber.

Eighteen years of Republican majorities made the steering committee central to the course of American national government at the turn of the twentieth century. And the persistence of those majorities helped strengthen the Republican steering committee: electoral success could readily be understood as evidence that the steering committee was doing its work well. The reign of the steering committee ended in 1911, when Aldrich and Hale both left the Senate—and a time when factionalism within the Republican party had nearly toppled the speaker of the House and brought new challenges to Senate governance. The steering committee continued as an institution attempting to guide Republicans for the next two years, but its residual value was eclipsed in 1913 when Republicans named their first elected floor leader.

The personal power of floor leaders in the 1910s made the collective management of steering committees anachronistic (Haynes 1938, 484–86). The drilling-ground of party leadership in the Senate, the caucus itself reached its apogee under John Kern (D, Ind.), who was elected Democratic leader in 1913—thereby becoming the Senate's first majority leader. Kern established agendas directly in caucus, rather than working through his steering committee (Oleszek 1991, 28–30). And Jacob Gallinger (R, N.H.), who assumed leadership of the minority Republican caucus in 1913, appears not even to have appointed a Republican steering committee.[127] When Republicans regained their majority in 1919, Henry Cabot Lodge (R, Mass.) "resuscitated" the steering committee but used it ineffectively (Widenor 1991, 53–54). In later years, when Democratic and Republican leaders expanded their role on the floor and assumed greater personal responsibility, they consulted less often with their caucuses. Having created the foundation for modern party leadership in the Senate, the steering committee and the caucus dwindled in significance as managers of the Senate's daily business.

Remarkably, though, the Republican leadership structure of the 1890s and 1900s is imprinted on the modern Senate. The essence of that governance structure was shared power. Republicans in the Senate did not entrust their leadership in this era to any single person. On the contrary, they created and relied on a large directorate to set their agendas, name their committees, manage the floor, and build policy coalitions. The preeminent institution in that era was the Republican steering committee, but this was a large body that

---

[127] "Gallinger Heads Party," *Washington Evening Star*, Mar. 5, 1913, 2.

governed alongside powerful committee chairs, a caucus chairman, and a committee on committees. Even as the steering committee withered away, the Republican party resisted centralizing power in a single leader. Deep into the twentieth century, Democrats invested their floor leader with the power to name committees, set agendas, and chair their caucus. But the Republican model of collective authority, honed in the late nineteenth century, has persisted into the twenty-first century—with separate senators serving, generation after generation, as floor leader, caucus chair, chair of the committee on committees, and chair of the modern-day policy committee. The Republican steering committee's heyday was brief, but its impact reverberates through the ages.

"A Promising Outlook for the New Year," political cartoon by Clifford Berryman, 1904. Arthur Pue Gorman (D, Md.), who had invented the position of elected Senate floor leader in 1890, then later left the Senate, was elected leader again by Senate Democrats upon his return in 1903. Here he is portrayed as the baby Moses, bringing "leadership" to the Democratic party.

Library of Congress, Prints and Photographs Division

5

Arthur Pue Gorman, the Federal Elections Bill, and the Invention of Elected Floor Leadership, 1890–1913

Senators gathered on Capitol Hill in the summer of 1906 to lay the cornerstone for a new office building. The structure, faced with granite, marble, and limestone, was designed to hold ninety-nine two-room office suites, along with some single-room offices, six committee rooms, and a dining room.[1] Its center-piece was the Caucus Room. When the Senate Office Building was completed, in March 1909, the *New York Times* described the structure as "a veritable palace" and declared that the Caucus Room was "the most beautiful" of the spaces in the building. "A caucus is not held more than once or twice in a session, as a rule," the *Times* explained, "so that this great marble room will be rather a show place than a real office."[2] But it was a "show place" that testified to the power of the two Senate caucuses and, in particular, to the dominance of the steering committee that led the Senate in the name of the Republican caucus. In those years, the control of the Senate by a small group of Republican men was the preeminent fact of Senate organization. But the age of the Republican steering committee proved ephemeral: in 1912, when senators met in the Caucus Room to conduct hearings on the sinking of the *Titanic*, Allison was dead, Aldrich and Hale had left the Senate, the chamber's Republican leadership was weak and fractured, and the steering committee was in decline.

Rising quietly in the background since 1890—predating even the ascendancy of the Republican steering committee, persisting throughout the entire period of Republican rule, yet barely noticed by contemporaries—was an entirely different institution. The Democrats possessed their own steering committee, but this committee, with the power to make all Democratic committee assignments and help shape the party's legislative strategy, answered to the direction of their

---

[1] "Corner Stone Laid for Senate's New Building," *Washington Post*, Aug. 1, 1906, 9.
[2] "The Senate's 'Office'—Cost, Five Millions," *New York Times*, Mar. 14, 1909, SM-9.

caucus chairman. In the minority, searching for a way to affect the Senate's affairs, the Democratic caucus had concentrated its leadership into a single person, whom they dubbed their floor leader.

Arthur Pue Gorman (D, Md.) was the first person elected in the Senate's history to serve as his party's leader on the floor. Chosen by his colleagues in 1889 as acting chairman of the Democratic caucus, when chairman James Beck (D, Ky.) had grown seriously ill, Gorman assumed the caucus chairmanship the next year upon Beck's death and quickly transformed the longstanding position of caucus chairman into a thoroughly new institution. The watershed moment came immediately, between the summer of 1890 and the following winter, when Gorman successfully led the effort to block passage of the Federal Elections Bill. Republican senators had routinely elected caucus chairmen since before the Civil War, and Democrats had done so since the 1870s. But, before Gorman, caucus chairmen had done little more than preside over party meetings; except on rare occasions, their position as caucus chairmen did not give them any special role on the Senate floor or in the public realm. Various senators had helped to direct the floor throughout the Senate's history, but the position of floor leader had been a temporary, shifting position that was never formally assigned to any senator. All that changed in 1890. Gorman's long chairmanship, which lasted until his resignation in 1898, redefined the position of Democratic caucus chairman. He and his successors became the Senate's first elected floor leaders.

By 1913, when John W. Kern (D, Ind.) became majority leader with his election as chairman of the Senate Democratic caucus, the institution of Democratic leader was already a generation old. While his position as majority leader and his relationship with President Woodrow Wilson allowed Kern to play a special role in the development of Senate party leadership, his election was just one of several events in the 1910s that signified the maturation of the Senate parties. The Republican caucus, which until 1913 had lacked an elected party leader in the Senate and instead relied on the collective leadership of the Republican steering committee, that year finally adopted the two-decade-old Democratic model and designated their caucus chairman as minority leader. At the same time, the two Senate parties formalized and expanded their leadership structures: the Democrats created the position of whip in 1913, the Republicans in 1915. There was no institutional continuity on the Republican side. The old hegemony of collective leadership, embodied in the Republican steering committee, had ended. In its place, both parties embraced the model created by Gorman in 1890 and sustained by the Democratic minority through their many years in the wilderness.

The battle over the Federal Elections Bill in 1890–91 was the crucible in which modern Senate leadership was forged. We begin this chapter by reviewing the stakes of this legislative battle, arguing that the collective party goals of achieving policy and winning elections were unusually stark for senators in both parties. To demonstrate the significance of Gorman's achievement—and to underline the extent to which the origins of this institution had been lost to scholars and other Senate observers—we next examine previous efforts to document the rise of floor leadership, then show, drawing on original sources from the late nineteenth and early twentieth centuries, that Gorman's tenure established an entirely new institution. After describing the pre-1890 caucus chairmanship, we discuss how Gorman became caucus chairman and created the position of floor leadership in the 1890s. We then introduce the early floor leaders who succeeded Gorman, the men elected to this position by the Democratic caucus between 1898, when Gorman stepped down, and 1913, when Kern became majority leader. Next we examine leadership in the Republican caucus in the same period, where, unlike on the Democratic side, elections for caucus chairmen remained perfunctory events, leadership remained disconnected from the caucus chairmanship, and elected leadership did not yet exist. In the last section of the chapter, we analyze the extent to which this first generation of Democratic floor leaders performed the functions identified with modern Senate leadership.

THE FEDERAL ELECTIONS BILL OF 1890–91

In his inaugural address as president, Benjamin Harrison called on Congress to pass a law guaranteeing the integrity of elections in every part of the Union. "The freedom of the ballot is a condition of our national life, and no power vested in Congress or in the Executive to secure or perpetuate it should remain unused upon occasion," he declared. "The people of all the Congressional districts have an equal interest that the election in each shall truly express the views and wishes of a majority of the qualified electors residing within it" (*Inaugural Addresses* 1965, 161). In the campaign just past, the Republican party had identified an elections bill as one of its top legislative priorities, charging in its platform that Democratic victories in recent years had been possible only because of the unconstitutional disenfranchisement of Black voters (Hoar 1903, 2:150; Valelly 2004, 246; Valelly 2007, 126; Valelly 2009, 126–27; Jenkins and Peck 2021, 246–48). The Federal Elections Bill provided that, where there were allegations of fraud in elections to the House of Representatives, federal circuit courts, rather than state or local officials, would monitor elections and certify the results (Hoar 1903, 2:153; Welch 1965, 514; Valelly 2007, 136–39).

The battle over the Federal Elections Bill was a landmark in congressional history. Voting rights for African-American men had been under siege in the South since the early 1870s, and the Federal Elections Bill was the last gasp for a generation of northern politicians who remembered the Civil War and were determined to address this wrong. Its defeat ended, for generations, the long federal battle to secure civil and political rights for African Americans in the South. Not until two-thirds of a century had passed would Congress again consider a law securing voting rights for all Americans regardless of race.

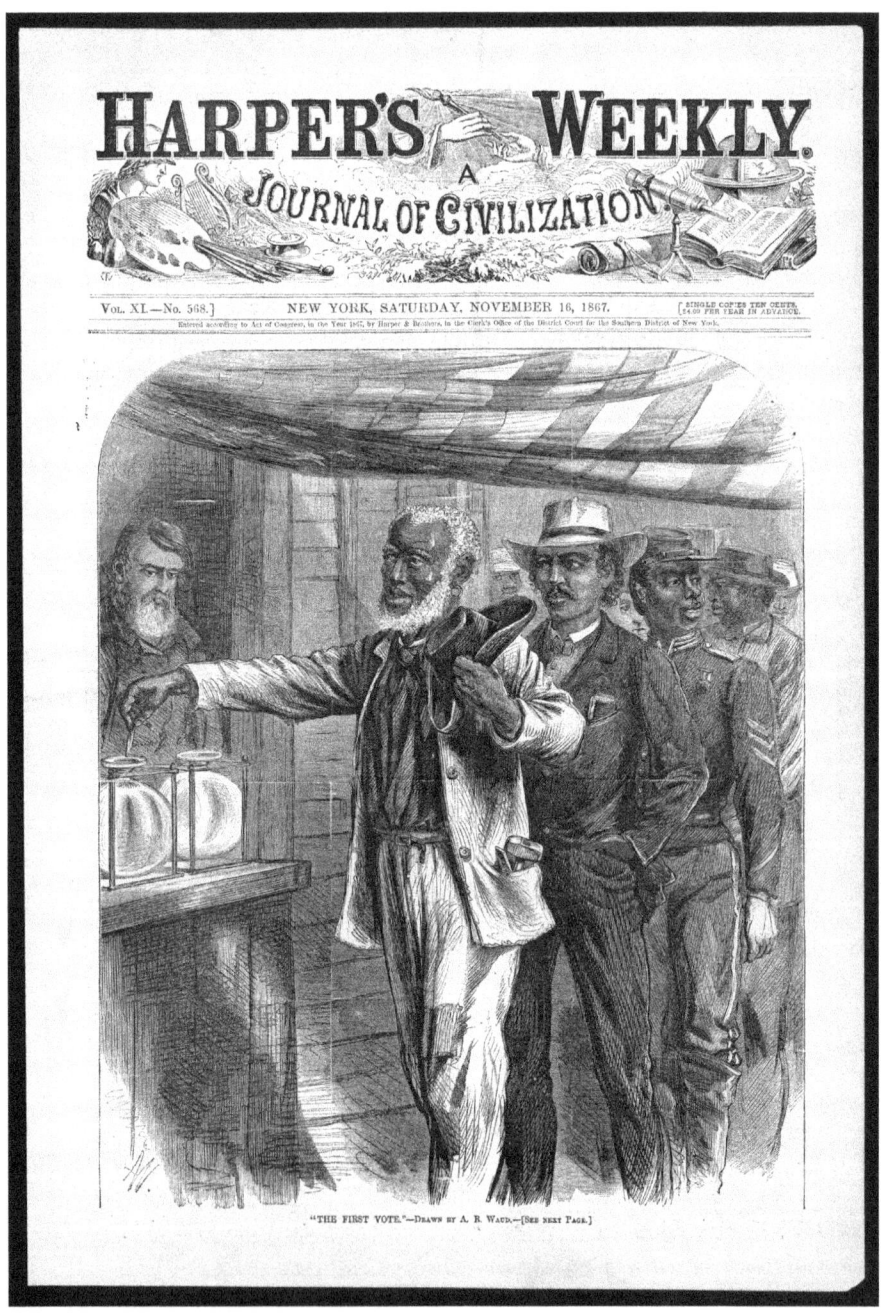

"The First Vote," from *Harper's Weekly*, Nov. 1867. Print shows Black men in a line to cast their votes.

The partisan implications of the Federal Elections Bill were as dramatic as its impact on policy. Probably no other bill coming close to passage in the hundred years between the Civil War and the Civil Rights Movement so concentrated the minds of legislators on the relationship between electoral success and policy achievements. Many Republicans, including George Frisbie Hoar (R, Mass.), who managed the bill in the Senate, supported passage of the Federal Elections Bill because of a principled commitment to the ideal of equal rights for African Americans (Welch 1965, 515–16, 522–23; Welch 1971, 146, 153–57; Socolofsky and Spetter 1987, 60–61; Valelly 2007, 129, 136–37; Jenkins and Peck 2021, 248). But all Republicans were concerned about their party's success in congressional and presidential elections, and they knew that passage of the bill would undermine the Democratic party in the South and restore a viable Republican presence to the region (Morgan 1963, 135; Welch 1965, 522; Valelly 2007, 139–44). Democrats, led by Gorman, scoffed at any suggestion that the bill's supporters were motivated by noble sentiments.[3] They regarded the Federal Elections Bill—in their language, the Force Bill—as a direct assault on the right of white southerners to manage their own region's affairs, an attack on the system of white supremacy, and a naked grab for power by the Republican party (Lambert 1953, 148; Welch 1965, 524–25; Welch 1971, 147–48; Socolofsky and Spetter 1987, 62; Dailey 2004, 257–58; Upchurch 2004, 127; Calhoun 2005, 91; Valelly 2007, 146).

The national parties were more closely balanced in this era than at any previous time in American history. Benjamin Harrison had won election to the presidency the preceding year despite losing the popular vote to Grover Cleveland, and the 1888 election was not exceptional: Samuel Tilden, the popular-vote winner in 1876, had been defeated by Rutherford Hayes, and only a few thousand votes separated the presidential candidates in 1880 and 1884. In the Senate, neither party had a majority in 1881–83, and Republicans held slim majorities for the next six years, until gaining a 14-seat advantage in 1889. Meanwhile, with a single two-year exception, Democrats had controlled the House of Representatives continuously since 1875. When Republicans won control of the House and the presidency in 1888, while holding the Senate, they were acutely aware of how rare unified government was in the late nineteenth century and of the remarkable partisan equipoise that characterized the time. A shift in a few seats in the House or of a handful of votes in a presidential

---

[3] Gorman's sordid record on race extended far beyond the Federal Elections Bill. The baseball league that Gorman started excluded Black players throughout his association with the game. Gorman also played a central role in the Maryland Democratic party, which turned to white nationalist themes to unseat Republicans in state government at the turn of the twentieth century. He was instrumental in authoring and campaigning for the "Poe suffrage amendment," a proposed amendment to Maryland's constitution that would have disenfranchised Black people by adding grandfather and "understanding" clauses. The amendment was approved by the Maryland legislature but defeated in a 1905 referendum. See "Senator Gorman Dead; Void Left in Party," *Baltimore Sun*, June 5, 1906, 1.

election, and the tide would turn again. The Federal Elections Bill was not only the culmination of the movement for human liberty that began with Emancipation. It was a historic legislative effort to restore a national Republican majority and hobble the Democratic party in national elections. The collective goals of congressional parties—legislative (passing or blocking legislation) and electoral (winning or maintaining majority party status)—were perhaps never more closely intertwined than they were in 1890.

Newly disciplined by the adoption of the Reed rules, the House of Representatives passed the Federal Elections Bill in July 1890, sending the measure to the Senate. Republicans in the Senate postponed consideration of the elections bill to focus their attention on tariff revision, their other major priority for the session. Hoar, who was managing the Federal Elections Bill, fought the postponement, but ultimately agreed after securing written support from all but one Republican in the Senate—a majority of the whole chamber— to take up the elections bill when Congress returned for its short session in December 1890 and to ensure that the bill was brought to a vote (Hoar 1903, 2: 155–56; Welch 1965, 517–18; Welch 1971, 153–54; Socolofsky and Spetter 1987, 63). With this agreement, Senate Republicans pledged to adopt rules to stop a filibuster, should that be necessary. The filibuster came, Aldrich led the Republican effort to change the rules to stop debate by majority vote, but the effort failed and the bill never came to a vote. Frustrated by the endless obstruction, only weakly committed to the Federal Elections Bill, and eager to gain support for the free coinage of silver, a small group of Silver Republicans twice voted with the Democrats in January 1891 to table the bill (Hoar 1903, 2: 156; Lambert 1953, 152–66; Welch 1971, 155–60; Socolofsky and Spetter 1987, 64–65; Upchurch 2004, 167–85; Calhoun 2005, 114–16; Wawro and Schickler 2006, 76–87). The Federal Elections Bill had expired, victim of an exhausted and divided Republican caucus.

The battle created the modern Congress. On four fronts, Congress was transformed in 1890–91. First, the majoritarian House emerged in this struggle: as Valelly (2009) convincingly demonstrates, Thomas Reed moved in January 1890 to end filibustering in the House because he understood that the Federal Elections Bill could pass the House only if the small Republican majority could stop obstruction. In advocating for the new rules, several Republicans in the House explained that "the point of the Reed Rules was to permit the enactment of the Federal Elections Bill" (Valelly 2009, 116; see also Schickler 2001, 27; Upchurch 2004, 66–84; Bateman, Katznelson, and Lapinski 2018, 199–200).[4] Second, a unified Senate minority used a filibuster to defeat a bill that was supported by the president and by majorities in both chambers of Congress (Valelly 2004, 121). That filibuster, engineered by Gorman, was one of the

---

[4] See also Frederic J. Haskin, "The American Congress: IX. The Force Bill and Cloture," *Washington Post*, Dec. 1, 1909, 4.

most dramatic and successful filibusters in the history of the Senate. With the failure of the Federal Elections Bill, the filibuster became a more visible weapon in the arsenal of the Senate. Third, simultaneous with the adoption of majority rule in the House, the Senate abandoned the effort to limit debate by majority vote. Faced with a historic filibuster, the Senate came closer than at any time before or since to enacting cloture by a simple majority. Aldrich fought for majority cloture and most senators had endorsed the idea in principle, but the elections bill was tabled and majority cloture died with it. Fourth, out of this struggle Gorman became his party's elected floor leader, navigating his party's dual policy and electoral concerns and, in the process, as we will show, creating the leadership position that would prove central to the Senate's future.

OBSCURE ORIGINS

Although scholars have long made assumptions about the nature of Senate floor leadership in the nineteenth and early twentieth centuries, Jones (1970, 40) conceded that any conclusions were tentative, since "no sources discuss the development of the floor leadership" in the Senate. Burnham (1959, 150 n.8) could find no "written evidence," so he cited instead, for his brief summary of the rise of Senate leadership, "personal conversations with a number of persons acquainted with several generations of congressional history." The origins of floor leadership are "exasperatingly obscure," Kravitz (ca. 1971, x: 2–3) observed. "We are not even certain just when the titles by which they were to become known and celebrated, 'majority leader,' 'minority leader,' or 'floor leader,' in the elected sense, first came into use or who first bore them."

Those who have studied the subject have confined their attention either to the rise of centralized, but informal, leadership in the Republican party in the 1890s or to the years following 1913, when John Kern became majority leader. No one has previously examined the transition from the 1890s to the 1910s or the rise of formal institutions in the Senate caucuses in that period. Indeed, until now scholars have not even known the identity of Senate Republican caucus chairmen before 1911 or Democratic chairmen before 1903—let alone the relationship of those unknown caucus chairmen to the rise of elected floor leadership.[5] "To seek the identity of early Senate caucus chairmen," Kravitz

---

[5] Munk (1970), Riddick (1971), and Kravitz (ca. 1971) all attempted to identify nineteenth- and early-twentieth-century caucus chairmen and all three scholars acknowledged that their lists were imperfect. Riddick (1971, 6) included four people on his list (John T. Morgan, Orville Platt, George F. Hoar, and Nelson W. Aldrich) who we now know never served in this capacity and omitted many other men who had been elected caucus chairmen. Kravitz (ca. 1971, x: 124–25) included, with question marks, Thomas A. Hendricks and John T. Morgan, neither of whom served as caucus chairman, and omitted three Democrats and two Republicans who did serve in this capacity. Munk (1970, 35), who provides a very thorough account of Kern's significance as Democratic leader, identifies seven men who "evidently served as caucus chairmen" in the 1870s, 1880s, and 1890s. Of the seven men she names, we now know that three (Allen G. Thurman,

(ca. 1971, 7) noted, "is to plunge into still another dark pool of Senate history." Barfield, who states that minority floor leadership existed in the Senate by the turn of the twentieth century, offers no account of the origins of the position. On the contrary, discussing Gorman's return to the Senate and reelection as Senate minority leader in 1903, Barfield seems baffled, unaware of Gorman's historic role. "For over a decade, Democratic solons had acted independently of each other. The position of minority leader held no prestige and no power," Barfield (1970, 314) contends. "The situation had reached such a state in 1903 that, when a battered and worn spoilsman from the 1880s and 1890s, Arthur Pue Gorman of Maryland, was surprisingly reelected to the Senate, he was immediately given the post."[6]

The most important account of the late-nineteenth-century Senate, Rothman's *Politics and Power* (1966), suspends discussion in 1901, when Republican control was at its peak. Rothman focuses on Aldrich, Allison, and their allies, examining the power they accumulated through their penetration of the chief offices of the Republican caucus, including the Republican steering committee, and their work as bill managers and committee chairmen. Democrats, according to Rothman, showed little aptitude or appetite for institutional innovation. They simply imitated the Republican model of collective leadership, while centralizing more power in Gorman than Republicans placed in any one senator. According to Rothman (1966, 61), "If Senate Democrats in some ways matched their rivals, Gorman was pleased." It was the Republican example, in Rothman's view, that laid the foundation for the development of the modern Senate. "Republicans, not Democrats, dominated the chamber and effected most of the changes of these years," Rothman (1966, 68) writes. "Realizing more fully the powers and potentialities of party unity and leadership, they transformed the character of the institution." Since he does not discuss the rise of floor leadership, Rothman, in his otherwise comprehensive account of the 1890s Senate, devotes most of his attention to the Republican narrative. Gorman becomes little more than a bit player. Cited by an array of subsequent scholars, Rothman's argument has long since become common knowledge (Kravitz ca. 1971, x: 11–24; Ripley 1969a, 1 n.1, 21; Ripley 1969b, 24–29; Jones 1970, 40; Munk 1970, 35–43; Merrill and Merrill 1971, 17–35; Peabody 1976, 327–29; Josephy 1979, 268–69; Nelson 1980, 6; Sundquist 1981, 165; Baker 1988, 67; Brady, Brody, and Epstein 1989, 208–9; Byrd 1991, 235; Brady and Epstein 1997, 34–35; Schickler 2001, 55; MacNeil and Baker 2013, 176–81). As a consequence, Gorman is chiefly remembered as the Democratic figure who spent his career in Aldrich's shadow, emulating on a smaller scale Aldrich's work with the Republican steering committee—a footnote to the era's main story.

Thomas F. Bayard, and Isham G. Harris) never served as caucus chairmen and a fourth (William Wallace) served as Democratic, not Republican, caucus chairman.
[6] See also Sarasohn 1989, 6.

Of the few scholars who have examined the subject closely, nearly all agree that the position of Senate floor leader emerged sometime between 1911 and 1925. Riddick (1971, 4), examining the exact language used by the Republican and Democratic caucuses when they gathered to elect caucus chairmen, reports that the practice of referring to caucus chairmen as "leaders" in caucus minutes began in the 1920s. Byrd (1991, 187–88), following Riddick's logic, asserts that Senate Democrats did not elect a floor leader until 1920 and that Senate Republicans elected their first floor leader in 1925.[7] Ripley (1969b, 26), Jones (1970, 40), *Congressional Quarterly* (1976, 221–22), Peabody (1976, 327–29), Baker and Davidson (1991, 4), and Oleszek (1991) emphasize the period in the 1910s when Thomas S. Martin (D, Va.) and John Kern served as Democratic leaders. They contend that Kern's election as floor leader in 1913 represented a sharp break with existing practice, but none of them examine Kern's predecessors in any detail. Ripley, offering no new evidence and citing only Rothman, contends that the practice of electing "a chairman of their caucus who was assumed to be the party's floor leader" was already well-established by the Republicans in the 1880s—but immediately concedes that this practice remained irregular until the 1910s and admits that "it was not always clear which men were floor leaders" (Ripley 1969b, 25, 26, also 28–29; Ripley 1969a, 4, 21). On the Democratic side, Gorman functioned as floor leader in the 1890s, Ripley notes, but he had no successors. After Gorman left the Senate in 1899, "no one took his place as *the* leader of the Democrats," according to Ripley (1969b, 29, 26). "The practice of electing a single Majority Leader or Minority Leader who would serve during an entire Congress and presumably would be reelected did not become established until the period between 1911 and 1913."

Only Kravitz and Munk hesitate to accept this consensus. While admitting that evidence was scant and fragmentary, Kravitz (ca. 1971, x: 5–6) suggests that Senate Democrats may have begun to regard their caucus chairman as their floor leader as early as 1907, possibly even by 1902. In a single paragraph of a manuscript that ran hundreds of pages, Kravitz notes that he had discovered references to three men—James K. Jones (D, Ark.), Joseph Blackburn (D, Ky.), and Charles Culberson (D, Tex.)—who appeared to have assumed the title of minority leader through their election to the caucus chairmanship. He had found just three sources, the minutes of a 1906 caucus meeting and brief accounts of two biographers, so Kravitz was reluctant to reach any conclusion. Still he was intrigued by these "shreds and tatters of evidence," clues to the origins of Senate floor leadership. Similarly, Munk (1970, 10, 93, 95, 116) observes that contemporary sources described Culberson, who was chosen in 1907, and his successors, Hernando Money (D, Miss.) and Thomas Martin, as

---

[7] See also *History, Rules, and Precedents* 2022, 1; "Majority and Minority Leaders," Senate Historical Office, www.senate.gov/artandhistory/history/common/briefing/Majority_Minority_Leaders.htm (website accessed Jan. 2021).

presumptive floor leaders because of their election as Democratic caucus chairmen. She adds, though, that she had found "no mention of such a position in the sizeable body of material written about Arthur P. Gorman of Maryland"— which she considers peculiar, since Culberson took office one year after Gorman's death, and she had found multiple references to Culberson as minority leader (Munk 1970, 12). For both Kravitz and Munk, however, these few clues pale next to Kern's 1913 ascension. "Kern's brief tenure," Kravitz writes (ca. 1971, x: 25), "was a landmark in the history of Senate leadership." As Munk asserts (1974, 28), "The pattern for the role of the modern leader began to solidify in 1913, when Wilson went to the White House and John W. Kern was elected floor leader in a Senate controlled by the Democrats."

Nomenclature in the party conference minutes—which is the source for the belief that floor leadership was not recognized until the 1920s—is misleading. The language used in caucus minutes to describe these positions was formal and brief, and that language lagged considerably behind the changed reality. Riddick (1971, 4) deems it a historic event that in January 1920 the Democratic caucus was called for the purpose of selecting a "leader," rather than simply a "caucus chairman." But there is no evidence in the minutes or in contemporary newspapers that these senators believed that they were doing anything innovative. There is no suggestion that they were creating a new position with that language, rather than bringing a long-familiar term into the formal language of the caucus. And there was little consistency even in the formal language. When Alben Barkley was elected the Senate Democratic leader in 1937, the official minutes state that he was nominated to be "Leader of the Senate" but that he was only elected to the position of "*Conference Chairman*" (Ritchie 1998a, 354; italics in original). This language is nearly indistinguishable from that used in 1906, when Joseph Blackburn was elected to the position of "Chairman of the Conference" and when the official caucus minutes explain that, by this election, the Democratic senators had selected Blackburn to serve as "their chosen official leader in the great forum of the Senate of the United States" (Ritchie 1998a, 9). Whatever the language of these minutes, certainly no one doubts that Barkley was elected both conference chairman and floor leader for the Senate's Democrats in 1937. Neither, we contend, should anyone doubt that Blackburn—like Gorman before him—was also elected to serve in both capacities more than three decades earlier. Senate floor leadership grew directly out of the caucus chairmanship, as students of Congress have long surmised, but the transition took place in 1890–91, a full generation before scholars have realized.

CAUCUS CHAIRMEN BEFORE 1890

Until the 1890s, the caucus chairmanship was a largely ceremonial and ministerial position. This was especially true for Senate Republicans, who controlled the chamber during the Civil War and most of the years that followed.

Although many distinguished and influential men served as Republican caucus chairmen, those qualities were not the basis for their selection. Rather, Republicans selected their caucus chairmen according to a seniority rule, and the position carried with it little authority. "Nothing in the congressional sources or in newspaper comment of the time suggests that the Republican caucus chairman in the Senate was a figure of great power," Bogue (1981, 76) writes. "When the senators assembled [in December 1862], after notification by the door keeper, to hold the famous caucus meeting in which they initiated their open war on Seward, Anthony was forced to inquire what the subject of discussion was to be—hardly the act of a real mover and shaker." According to Rothman (1966, 16), Henry B. Anthony (R, R.I.), chairman of the Senate Republican caucus between 1862 and 1884, named the members of the Republican committee on committees, but did not sit on the committee himself or attempt to influence the committee in any way. His successors hewed to that precedent: Republican caucus chairmen never sat on their party's committee on committees and, despite their seniority, often found themselves at odds with their own appointees. John Sherman (R, Ohio), who succeeded Anthony as caucus chairman, was unable even to secure his own committee preferences. In March 1885, on the day that new committee assignments were announced, Sherman rose on the floor of the Senate to declare— "in tones," according to the *New York Times*, "in which anger was scarcely suppressed"[8]—that he refused to accept reappointment to the Finance Committee. The *New York Times* and the *Washington Post* reported that Sherman's anger resulted both from the ideological composition of the committee and the committee on committees' decision not to offer him the chairmanship. Sherman's position as chairman of his party's caucus appears to have mattered little in the battle to shape committees. "Neither the caucus nor the caucus committee," the *Post* stated, "seems to have seen its way clear to make the change desired by the Senator from Ohio."[9]

For Republicans and Democrats alike, the selection of a caucus chairman was entirely an internal party matter, with no obvious consequence for policy leadership or floor management. Little attention was given to the event, which helps explain the difficulty scholars have had in tracking past caucus chairmen and the development of party leadership. Many newspapers, like the official records of the Senate, ignored caucus elections altogether. When nineteenth-century newspapers did report the election of a new caucus chairman, the account was always brief, an incidental detail in the larger story of the opening business of Congress. The selection of James Beck (D, Ky.) in March 1885 as Democratic caucus chairman was typical: the *Washington Evening Star* devoted three sentences to the meeting at which he was elected, with a single

[8] "Mr. Sherman Declines to Serve," *New York Times*, Mar. 14, 1885, 1.
[9] "The Republican Senate Caucus," *Washington Post*, Mar. 12, 1885, 1.

sentence taking note of his election; the *Chicago Tribune* devoted four sentences to the meeting, with again just one sentence on the election of Beck; the *Hartford Courant* printed those identical four sentences, as did the *Atlanta Constitution*, the *New York Times*, the *New York Herald*, and many other newspapers across the nation. In its entirety, this news story—the fullest account we have found of the election of one Democratic caucus chairman that year and the retirement of another—read:

> There were short Senatorial caucuses of both parties after the adjournment of the session. The democrats effected an organization by selecting Mr. Beck as chairman and Mr. Kenna as secretary. The chairman was authorized to appoint a committee of nine to arrange the minority membership of committees. A resolution was adopted thanking Senators Pendleton and Jonas for their courtesy and efficiency in the discharge of their duties as chairman and secretary respectively of the democratic caucus.[10]

The account four years earlier was even pithier. As Figure 5.1 shows, the full report of the *New York Times* in March 1881 of the election of a new Democratic caucus chairman and the end of his predecessor's service was this: "Mr. Pendleton was elected Chairman of the caucus, in place of Mr. Wallace, whose Senatorial term expired yesterday."[11]

When William A. Wallace (D, Pa.) had lost his seat in the Senate, thus forcing the vacancy in the caucus chairmanship in 1881, few paid any attention. The *Macon Weekly Telegraph*, which did take note, emphasized that the main order of business of Democratic senators was to attend to the office of the president pro tempore. "It was agreed that a caucus meeting be held before the 4th of March to select a candidate," the *Telegraph* reported, "and also to elect a successor to Senator Wallace, the present chairman of caucus meetings."[12] While senators usually described the person as "caucus chairman" or "chairman of the caucus," the *Telegraph* communicated through its language the circumscribed nature of the position, implying that his only role was to preside over meetings. In an age when newspapers devoted many column inches each day to the affairs of Congress, the organizing meetings of caucuses were buried in a terse paragraph, in small print, beneath detailed accounts of the opening business of each session and the arrival of new members. Personal papers and biographies offer no more information: Gorman's sole biographer notes only

---

[10] "Senatorial Caucuses," *New York Herald*, Mar. 6, 1885, 4. See also "Senatorial Caucuses," *Washington Evening Star*, Mar. 5, 1885, 1; "Both Parties Hold a Caucus," *Chicago Tribune*, Mar. 6, 1885, 1; "Senate Caucuses," *Hartford Courant*, Mar. 6, 1885, 3; "Senatorial Caucuses," *Atlanta Constitution*, Mar. 6, 1885, 1; "Notes from Washington," *New York Times*, Mar. 6, 1885, 3.

[11] "Opening the New Senate," *New York Times*, Mar. 6, 1881, 1.

[12] "Democratic Caucus," *Macon Telegraph and Messenger*, Feb. 27, 1881, 1.

New York Times, 6 Mar. 1877

NOTES FROM THE CAPITAL.

WASHINGTON, March 5.—The Supreme Cour·
of the United States to-day adjourned till Monday
next.

The Democrats of the Senate held a meeting to
day, and unanimously elected Senator W. A. Wal·
lace, of Pennsylvania, Chairman of the Senate Dem
ocratic caucus.

Benjamin F. Bristow is almost certain to be ap·
pointed to the Supreme Court to fill the vacancy
caused by Judge Davis' resignation.

New York Times, 6 Mar. 1881

wise created. The caucus decided to retain the present officers of the Senate.
Mr. Pendleton was elected Chairman of
the caucus, in place of Mr. Wallace, whose Senatorial term expired yesterday. There was much talk at to-day's

New York Times, 6 Mar. 1885

SENATORIAL CAUCUSES.]

There were short senatorial caucusses of
both parties after the adjournment of the
session to day. The democrats effected an
organization by selecting Mr. Beck as chairman and Mr. Kenna as secretary. The chairman was authorized to appoint a committee
of nine to arrange the minority membership
of the committees. A resolution was adopted
thanking Senators Pendleton and Jonas for
their courtesy and efficiency in the discharge
of their duties as chairman and secretary
respectively of the democratic caucus.

FIGURE 5.1 News coverage of pre-1889 elections of Democratic caucus chairmen

that "Gorman was elevated to the chairmanship of the Democratic minority conference or 'caucus,'" giving the incorrect date of December 1889 for the event (Lambert 1953, 146). Beck, who preceded Gorman in the chair, lacks even a published biography.[13] Decade after decade, from before the Civil War into the 1890s, there is no evidence of any excitement of a pending election or subsequent interest in who was selected to chair the caucus. Elections appear to have been uncontroversial, unanimous, and little-noticed. They were, it seems, perfunctory affairs. The most important business of the caucus in the first

---

[13] For an excellent brief sketch on Beck, see McConnell and Brownell 2019, 127–33.

weeks of a Congress was to assign members to committees and to select the party's candidates for president pro tempore and other Senate offices.

In selecting their caucus chairmen, Republicans adhered closely to a seniority rule. The first two chairmen of the Republican caucus, John P. Hale (R, N.H.) and Henry B. Anthony (R, R.I.), were chosen within their first years of coming to the Senate, when the Republican party itself was in its youth. Hale was in his second term, and Anthony was just three years into his first term when he was elected chairman of the Republican caucus. But Anthony's colleagues were evidently pleased by his management of caucus meetings. "Mr. Anthony, who has acted as chairman of the Senate caucus for the last seven years, to-day proposed to resign that position," the *New York Herald* reported in December 1869, "but his fellow members would not consent that he should do so."[14] Eight years later, the *New York Tribune* noted that Anthony "has for many years been the chairman of all party gatherings in the Senate."[15] Editor and owner of a Providence newspaper, Anthony came to the Senate in 1859 at the age of 44. By the time of his death in 1884, he had served 25 continuous years in the Senate, nearly all of them as chairman of his party's caucus. Though Anthony himself had been elected to the caucus chairmanship midway through his first term as senator, he unwittingly established the seniority rule simply by growing old in the office. "He is the oldest Senator in consecutive service," the *New York Times* reported in 1883. "There is no man in the United States Senate now who was a member of it when Henry B. Anthony took the oath of office, March 4, 1859."[16] John Sherman (R, Ohio), who became caucus chairman in 1884 after Anthony's death, had entered the Senate two years after Anthony, though he had not served continuously.[17] George Edmunds (R, Vt.), ranking next to Sherman in earliest date of service and ranking first in continuous service, succeeded to the caucus chairmanship in 1885, when Sherman was elected president pro tempore. And Sherman himself was reelected caucus chairman in 1891, when Edmunds resigned from the Senate.

As Table 5.1 shows, Democrats did not pay heed to seniority. Rather, they elected junior, or relatively junior, members to their caucus chairmanship in this era (Rothman 1966, 62–63; Munk 1970, 70–71). John W. Stevenson (D, Ky., 1873–77), Wallace (1877–81), and George Pendleton (D, Ohio, 1881–85) all assumed their chairmanships in their first (and only) terms in the Senate. Beck was elected caucus chairman in March 1885, at the beginning of his ninth year in the Senate. The election of newer members to the caucus chairmanship may have reflected a belief among Democrats that this was a low-status position, but the decision rule itself—or lack of decision rule—meant that a

---

[14] "Senatorial Caucus," *New York Herald*, Dec. 8, 1869, 5.
[15] "The Republican Caucus," *New York Tribune*, Nov. 19, 1877, 1.
[16] "Senator Anthony," *New York Times*, Oct. 30, 1883, 2.
[17] In 1877–81, Sherman was secretary of the treasury.

TABLE 5.1 *Years of prior service of caucus chairmen*

Chairmen of the Senate Republican caucus, from origins to 1929

Caucus Chairmen	Election as Caucus Chairman	Years since Freshman	Years in Senate	Consecutive Years
John P. Hale (N.H.)	*Dec. 1857*	10	8	2
Henry B. Anthony (R.I.)	Dec. 1862	3	3	3
John Sherman (Ohio)	Dec. 1884	23	19	3
George Edmunds (Vt.)	Dec. 1885	19	19	19
John Sherman (Ohio)	Dec. 1891	30	26	10
William Boyd Allison (Iowa)	Mar. 1897	24	24	24
Eugene Hale (Maine)	Dec. 1908	27	27	27
Shelby Cullom (Ill.)	Apr. 1911	28	28	28
Jacob Gallinger (N.H.)	Mar. 1913	22	22	22
Henry Cabot Lodge (Mass.)	Aug. 1918	25	25	25
Charles Curtis (Kans.)	Nov. 1924	17	15	9
James Watson (Ind.)	Mar. 1929	12	12	12

Chairmen of the Senate Democratic caucus, from origins to 1929

Caucus Chairmen	Election as Caucus Chairman	Years since Freshman	Years in Senate	Consecutive Years
John W. Stevenson (Ky.)	*Dec. 1873*	2	2	2
William A. Wallace (Pa.)	Mar. 1877	2	2	2
George Pendleton (Ohio)	Mar. 1881	2	2	2
James Beck (Ky.)	Mar. 1885	8	8	8
Arthur Pue Gorman (Md.)	May 1890	9	9	9
David Turpie (Ind.)	Apr. 1898	35	12	11
James K. Jones (Ark.)	Dec. 1899	14	14	14
Arthur Pue Gorman (Md.)	Mar. 1903	22	18	0
Joseph Blackburn (Ky.)	June 1906	21	17	5
Charles Culberson (Tex.)	Dec. 1907	8	8	8
Hernando Money (Miss.)	Dec. 1909	12	12	12
Thomas S. Martin (Va.)	Apr. 1911	16	16	16
John Kern (Ind.)	Mar. 1913	2	2	2
Thomas S. Martin (Va.)	Mar. 1917	22	22	22
Oscar Underwood (Ala.)	Apr. 1920	5	5	5
Joseph Robinson (Ark.)	Dec. 1923	10	10	10

Democratic caucus might elevate a senator to the caucus chairmanship on the basis of ability and capacity for leadership. Beck, for example, was well-regarded by other senators. "He is by far the best posted man on the tariff and kindred subjects on the Democratic side of the chamber," the *New York Times* reported in 1888.[18] When Gorman became acting caucus chairman, in March 1889, he was already a national figure in the Democratic party; he had served in the Senate for eight years and was a few days short of his fiftieth birthday.

The potential for leadership was beginning to stir in the caucus chairmanship before Gorman assumed the position. While Republicans never permitted their caucus chairman even to sit on their committee on committees, Democrats routinely invested in their caucus chairman the power of chairing the Democratic committee on committees.[19] Stevenson, Wallace, Pendleton, and Beck all served as chairmen of their party's committee on committees during their terms as caucus chairmen. As a consequence, Democratic senators grew accustomed to their caucus chairman taking the lead in solving one of their caucus's central coordination problems. While he was not generally visible as a leader on the floor or in the public realm, the Democratic caucus chairman by the mid-1880s had the potential to play a central role in managing the caucus's affairs.

Beck's brief caucus chairmanship, in particular, established a new model for his colleagues. For three years, from his election as caucus chairman in March 1885 until he grew ill in the summer of 1888, Beck exerted great influence in debates on tariff and monetary policy. As the ranking Democrat on Appropriations and the only Democratic senator sitting on both the Appropriations and Finance committees—his service on both committees predating his election as caucus chairman—Beck was uniquely positioned to guide party policy in these realms.[20] The confluence of his position as caucus chairman with his expertise and his committee assignments proved fortuitous. As the *New York Times* explained in 1888, "Senator Beck of Kentucky is the leading authority on the Democratic side on all subjects relating to the tariff and finance, and as he is the Chairman of the Democratic Caucus Committee his

---

[18] "At the National Capital," *New York Times*, Sept. 12, 1888, 5. See also "Honors to the Dead," *Washington Post*, May 5, 1890, 1.

[19] While we can reconstruct only some chairmanships of the committee on committees, we know from newspaper accounts that Stevenson chaired this committee in Mar. 1875, Wallace in Mar. 1879, Pendleton in Mar. 1881, Beck in Dec. 1889, and Gorman in Mar. 1889 and Dec. 1891. Only in Dec. 1875 and in Dec. 1883 do we find someone chairing the committee on committees who was not the caucus chairman (or acting caucus chairman).

[20] "Committees of the Senate," *New York Tribune*, Dec. 11, 1883, 2; "The Committees Fixed," *Washington Post*, Dec. 11, 1887, 5. See also "Senator Beck Dead," *Washington Post*, May 4, 1890, 1; McConnell and Brownell 2019, 129–30.

opinions have naturally great weight with his associates."[21] Neither Beck's predecessors as Democratic caucus chairmen nor his contemporaries on the Republican side could be as effective as Beck in offering leadership to his party on the major issues coming before the Senate. Although this leadership was confined to financial issues, Beck used the caucus chairmanship as a source of strength. He named the party's committee on committees at the start of each session, he called caucus meetings to coordinate party policy on legislation, and he led the party on the floor at various times. In the process, he began to enhance the value of the caucus chairmanship.

Had Beck's health not deteriorated, his leadership on financial matters might have changed expectations for the role of caucus chairman. But the caucus chairmanship—and the separate work of party leadership—languished after Beck fell ill. Suffering from "heart trouble," "nervous exhaustion and indigestion," and "nervous prostration," Beck was absent from the Senate most days from the summer of 1888 until his death in May 1890.[22] Even at the times when he was present in the Capitol, he was too weak to lead the Democrats on the floor. "In all matters relating to the finances of the country, Mr. Beck was the leader of the Democratic Party in the Senate," the *New York Times* stated in its front-page obituary in May 1890. "The sickness which prevented him from taking part in the tariff debate in the last Congress was a great blow to his associates, who had relied upon him to head their assaults upon the Finance Committee's bill, and in all the pending agitation of the silver question and other financial matters his absence has been sorely felt."[23] Attending the Senate only rarely in his final two years, Beck was absent not only on the floor but also from most caucus meetings. Still, it was in the minority caucus room where Beck's influence lingered. "It was here that Senator Beck presided most actively over the Senatorial destinies of his party—here that he was the leading Democratic Senator in the advocacy of the measures in which he so firmly believed," the *Washington Post* explained. "Long after his voice ceased to ring through the Senate chamber, because of his failing strength, he continued prominent in the councils of his party, and did his work in this caucus room."[24] Although many newspapers published lengthy encomiums to Beck at the time of his death, none raised the question of who would succeed Beck as chairman

---

[21] "The Senate Tariff Bill," *New York Times*, Sept. 1, 1888, 1. See also *Landmark* (Statesville, N.C.), Dec. 18, 1885, 1.

[22] "Senator Beck of Kentucky may not be seen again ... ," *New York Times*, Sept. 12, 1888, 5; "Senator Beck's Poor Health," *New York Tribune*, Dec. 7, 1888, 2; "Senator Beck Dead," *Washington Post*, May 4, 1890, 1. See also "Purely Partisan Talk," *New York Times*, Dec. 5, 1888, 1; "Arrangement of the Senate Committees—Mr. Beck's Warm Welcome," *New York Sun*, Mar. 12, 1889, 1; "Senator Beck Is Dead," *New York Times*, May 4, 1890, 1.

[23] "Senator Beck Is Dead," *New York Times*, May 4, 1890, 1. See also "No Holiday for Senators," *New York Times*, Dec. 19, 1888, 2.

[24] "Honors to the Dead," *Washington Post*, May 5, 1890, 1.

of the Senate Democratic caucus—and none presumed that this chairman would be responsible for leading his colleagues on the floor. The position of caucus chairman, even on the Democratic side, still attracted scant attention.

Despite Beck's example, in neither party did the caucus chairman enjoy special status in the late 1880s as his party's designated leader in the Senate. There is no evidence, whether in newspapers or firsthand accounts or biographies, that senators expected their caucus chairmen, more than other prominent senators, to lead them on the floor. For Republicans throughout this era and for Democrats until Beck's tenure, this was a simple ministerial position, with responsibility for running meetings and appointing internal caucus committees. While we have collected abundant qualitative evidence on this score, a simple quantitative analysis buttresses the point. Table 5.2 summarizes the results of a search of news stories and editorials in seven newspapers, identifying every story where a caucus chairman is identified as his party's leader in the Senate.[25] Between 1857 and 1889, the year Gorman was elected acting caucus chairman, we find no instance of any caucus chairman being described as his party's Senate leader in 23 of the 27 chairman-Congress dyads. The exceptions—five news stories over a 32-year period—were truly rare. Notably, four of the five exceptions were on the Democratic side, and three of them were references to Beck. Given that we are examining a list that includes many of the most senior and talented members of the chamber, the virtual absence of news accounts identifying them as their party's Senate leader is striking. In the 1860s, 1870s, and 1880s, the caucus chairman of each party was, at best, one among a group of senators who helped manage his party's affairs in the Senate, spoke to reporters on behalf of his party, and met with the president. Caucus chairmen generally offered routine resolutions in the first days of a Congress, as representatives of their party, but, before Beck, there is no evidence that they assumed any responsibility for managing business. They named caucus committees but struggled to influence the decisions of those committees or of their party colleagues.

---

[25] We performed this analysis using ProQuest Historical Newspapers, searching the following newspapers: *Atlanta Constitution, Boston Globe, Chicago Tribune, Los Angeles Times, New York Times, New York Tribune,* and *Washington Post.* To identify a universe of relevant news stories, we searched these seven newspapers for the last name of the caucus chairman within 10 words of either "Republican leader" or "Democratic leader." We also searched for the name of the caucus chairman within 10 words of the word "leader" and within four words of either "minority," "majority," "floor," or "party on the floor." In all cases, we limited our search to instances where the name of the caucus chairman appeared within 400 words of the word "Senate." Once we had collected this full set of stories, we read each story carefully to locate the relevant terms and to determine whether the caucus chairman was, in fact, identified as the leader of his party in the Senate. The numbers in Table 5.2 reflect the total number of stories where caucus chairmen are identified in this fashion. This analysis was done by Ben Swanger.

TABLE 5.2 *Caucus chairmen, with number of times identified in news accounts as leaders of their party in the Senate*

Congress	Republican		Democrat	
35th (1857–59)	Hale	0		
36th (1859–61)	Hale	0		
37th (1861–63)	Hale	0		
	Anthony	0		
38th (1863–65)	Anthony	0		
39th (1865–67)	Anthony	0		
40th (1867–69)	Anthony	0		
41st (1869–71)	Anthony	0		
42nd (1871–73)	Anthony	0		
43rd (1873–75)	Anthony	0	Stevenson	0
44th (1875–77)	Anthony	0	Stevenson	0
45th (1877–79)	Anthony	0	Wallace	0
46th (1879–81)	Anthony	0	Wallace	0
47th (1881–83)	Anthony	0	Pendleton	0
48th (1883–85)	Anthony	0	Pendleton	1
	Sherman	0		
49th (1885–87)	Sherman	1	Beck	2
	Edmunds	0		
50th (1887–89)	Edmunds	0	Beck	1
51st (1889–91)	Edmunds	0	Beck	0
			Gorman	4
52nd (1891–93)	Edmunds	0	Gorman	2
	Sherman	0		
53rd (1893–95)	Sherman	1	Gorman	15
54th (1895–97)	Sherman	1	Gorman	6
55th (1897–99)	Allison	0	Gorman	7
			Turpie	0
56th (1899–1901)	Allison	0	Jones	20
57th (1901–3)	Allison	1	Jones	22
58th (1903–5)	Allison	0	Gorman	30
59th (1905–7)	Allison	2	Gorman	14
			Blackburn	16
60th (1907–9)	Allison	1	Culberson	54
	Hale	1		
61st (1909–11)	Hale	9	Culberson	34
			Money	30
62nd (1911–13)	Cullom	0	Martin	102
63rd (1913–15)	Gallinger	71	Kern	175

Note: The numbers in this table are gleaned from a set of searches, conducted in March 2014, of the ProQuest Historical Newspapers database. Numbers reported in this table include stories in any of the following newspapers: *Atlanta Constitution, Boston Globe, Chicago Tribune, Los Angeles Times, New York Times, New York Tribune,* and *Washington Post.* We searched for stories where the caucus chairman's name appeared within 10 words of "Republican leader," "Democratic leader," "minority leader," "majority leader," "leader of the minority," "leader of the majority," "floor leader," or other combinations of those terms, then we read the news story to see if the term was used to refer to the senator named. A news story is counted for this table only if the senator is identified as his party's leader in the Senate.

ARTHUR PUE GORMAN AND THE CREATION OF FLOOR
LEADERSHIP, 1890–98

For Democrats, that changed permanently in the 1890s, as Gorman built on
Beck's tentative foundation to erect a wholly new institution. The battle over
the Federal Elections Bill reconfigured expectations for the role of the
Democratic caucus chairman. Yet Gorman is the forgotten man of Congress.
His lasting monument, the creation of a new structure of Senate leadership as
consequential as Reed's simultaneous refashioning of the House speakership,
was forgotten even as it happened. Contemporaries understood that Gorman
had become the Senate Democratic leader in 1890–91, but they lacked the
hindsight to appreciate the lasting significance of that event, and subsequent
scholarship has been entirely silent. In contrast, Reed's ascension in the
House—and his rapid moves to consolidate power in the majority and, through
it, the speakership—galvanized the nation. Although it is only recently that
scholars have understood the relationship of the Federal Elections Bill to the
Reed rules, the revolution in House procedure is a watershed in any study of
Congress. Similarly, the dramatic events in the Senate in 1890–91—the
extended filibuster and the failure of Republican efforts to adopt majority
cloture—are reviewed in every major examination of Senate procedure. But
Gorman is generally absent from these analyses. A Democrat in a Republican
Senate, a floor leader in the age of the Republican steering committee, his role in
legislative development is easily overlooked. Scholars looking for the origins of
Senate party leadership locate it in the 1910s or 1920s or simply concede that it
is shrouded in the mists of time. Some have suggested that it grew out of the
Republican steering committee but without identifying evidence of any linkage.
We have found no previous study that identifies Gorman as the person who
created the position, none that shows that what Gorman created has been in
continuous existence from 1890 to the present day, and none that locates this
institution in the same pitched battle that yielded the Reed rules and
strengthened the filibuster.

   Gorman first came to Congress as a boy. Born in 1839, he was the eldest of
five children. Since formal schools did not exist near their Maryland farm, his
parents hired a tutor in 1850. When the tutor left at the end of the year,
Gorman's father consulted two Maryland congressmen for advice on how best
to continue his eldest son's education, and they arranged for the boy to serve as
a page in the U.S. Senate. Just 11 years old, Arthur Pue Gorman moved to
Washington (Lambert 1953, 4–6). He came of age in the Senate, working there
for the next 16 years—first as a page, then as messenger in the Senate post
office, then as assistant postmaster, then as Senate postmaster (Lambert 1953,
6–7; see also Poore 1886, ii: 508; Upchurch 2004, 126). Gorman watched
firsthand as senators debated the Kansas-Nebraska Act, the Lecompton
Constitution, the Homestead Act, and the great issues of the Civil War, and
he became friends with Andrew Johnson (D, Tenn.), who served as senator

between 1857 and 1862. Although legend links Gorman with Stephen Douglas (D, Ill.), with some even suggesting that Gorman traveled with Douglas through Illinois in 1858 for the seven debates with Abraham Lincoln, there is little evidence to support the story. Rather, it was Andrew Johnson who emerged as Gorman's great mentor in these years (Poore 1886, ii: 508; Lambert 1953, 6–13). But Johnson's patronage had a cost. In 1866, as animosity grew between President Johnson and the Republican Senate majority, culminating in the passage of the Civil Rights Act of 1866 over Johnson's veto, Gorman was dismissed as Senate postmaster. Gorman, now 27 years old, returned to Maryland in 1866 as a collector of internal revenue (Lambert 1953, 11–13).

But he was no dull civil servant. In his time in Washington, Gorman had not only come to know Congress but had also emerged as a leader of the nascent sport of baseball. The game was in its formative stages in the late 1850s, when Gorman joined other government employees for games on the Capitol grounds or in the area—then known as the "President's Grounds" or the "White Lot" and now known as the Ellipse—that lay south of the White House, near the unfinished Washington Monument (McKenna n.d.). These informal games became more structured in 1859, when Gorman helped organize the Nationals, which represented Washington in the newly formed National Association of Base Ball Players; he soon became captain of the team and president of the organization "as well as its dashing shortstop" (Thorn 2011, 136; also McKenna n.d.). Johnson, as president, took a personal interest in the Nationals. Not only did Johnson watch games himself but he allowed federal employees to take time out of their days to attend the games (McKenna n.d.). In the summer of 1865, when the Nationals hosted visiting teams from Brooklyn and Philadelphia, Johnson authorized the games to be played on the President's Grounds, with paid seating for five thousand, and he hosted Gorman and the Nationals in the White House at the conclusion of the tournament (McKenna n.d.; Thorn 2011, 136). In 1866–67, as he left the Nationals and settled in Maryland, Gorman served as president of the National Association of Base Ball Players, the first national organization of baseball clubs (Lambert 1953, 13; Goldstein 1989, 73; Kirsch 1989, 210–13; Upchurch 2004, 126; McKenna n.d.). Gorman never lost interest in baseball— in the spring of 1905, one year before he died, Gorman would be named to the Mills Commission, which had been given the sacred task of determining baseball's true origins (Thorn 2011, 6, 136; McKenna n.d.)—but his active participation in the game ended in the middle 1860s, when he began focusing his attention on Maryland politics.

Gorman owed his appointment as collector of internal revenue to Johnson, but, once in Maryland, Gorman looked to state politics to advance his career. Between 1869, when Gorman, a conservative Democrat, lost his post as collector after the election of a Republican president, and 1881, when Gorman returned to Washington as U.S. Senator, he was a member of the Maryland state legislature. He served three terms in the house of delegates, including one as speaker, then three terms in the Maryland state senate (*Biographical Directory* 2021; Lambert 1953, 15, 23–24, 34, 40–41). In these 12 years, Gorman created a powerful political machine, taking command of the state's politics. William Pinckney Whyte, elected governor in 1871, named Gorman president of the Chesapeake and Ohio Canal, providing Gorman a base for distributing patronage and building support in western Maryland (Lambert 1953, 23, 35–36). By 1875, when Whyte left for Washington as the state's junior senator, Gorman, working closely with Isaac Freeman Rasin, assumed responsibility for managing the state's Democratic organization in Whyte's absence (Lambert 1953, 29–30, 37). Quickly, Gorman and Rasin consolidated their control of the machine, coordinating elections for the governorship and the state legislature, while ensuring that other political figures in the state could not threaten their control. By 1880 Gorman's triumph was complete. His organization—the "Old Guard"—had come together to support Gorman's election to the Senate. On the very night in Baltimore that Whyte announced his candidacy for reelection, Democratic legislators were meeting informally in Annapolis to pledge their support to Gorman (Lambert 1953, 46–47). Two weeks later, the state legislature ratified this decision, selecting Gorman as senator on January 20, 1880.

Over the next decade, even as he worked assiduously to maintain control of the Maryland Democratic machine, Gorman gained respect as a senator and prominence in national politics. He was selected in March 1884 to chair the Democratic congressional campaign committee, then, in July, following the national convention in Chicago, Gorman was named chairman of the national committee, with responsibility for conducting the campaign not only for Congress but for electing Grover Cleveland to the presidency (Poore 1886, ii: 508–9; Nevins 1932, 160; Lambert 1953, 95–104; Welch 1988, 35). Until the 1884 campaign, Gorman was little-known outside the state of Maryland: in his first three years in the Senate, he had delivered just one major speech (Lambert 1953, 83, 86). But, with his successful management of the Cleveland campaign—the first Democratic presidential victory since before the Civil War—Gorman strengthened his position in Maryland while ascending to the front ranks of Democratic leaders in Washington. "He is rather an under-sized, squarely built man, with jet-black hair, a Roman nose, a clean-shaven face, very dark blue eyes, and a decisive manner," Poore (1886, ii: 508–9) observed. "He is noted for his fidelity to his friends, and at the same time he often forgives those who have shamefully treated him, but who come to ask favors of him." Gorman obtained a seat on the Appropriations Committee in 1885, and he was one of two Democrats named that year to the five-member select committee investigating abuses by railroads, whose work led to the passage of the Interstate Commerce Act of 1887 and the creation of the Interstate Commerce Commission (Lambert 1953, 128–31). He sided forcefully with the Cleveland administration when it set limits to silver deposits after the Treasury Department reported a large surplus (Lambert 1953, 131–32).

Gorman then worked at Cleveland's behest, with minimal success and some frustration (since Cleveland himself had ignited discussion of dramatic reductions in tariff rates), to moderate language in the 1888 party platform favoring free trade (Nevins 1932, 400–401; Lambert 1953, 140–42). Despite winning more popular votes that November than Benjamin Harrison, Cleveland lost the election, and the following spring Republicans controlled the presidency and had firm majorities in both houses of Congress for the first time in 14 years.

On March 7, 1889, Senate Democrats elected Gorman to be their acting caucus chairman. James Beck, who had been caucus chairman since 1885, was reelected that day, but he was in poor health and unable to appear in the Senate with any frequency.[26] Isham Harris (D, Tenn.) had been serving as acting caucus chairman since Beck had fallen ill, and he chaired the meeting at which Gorman was elected.[27] While several newspapers took note of Gorman's election, only a handful of reporters speculated about the reasons why the caucus had chosen Gorman over Harris. None indicated that there had been any active contest between the two men for the position. According to the *St. Louis Post-Dispatch*, Harris had alienated his colleagues by not consulting with them on a proposed order of business.[28] The *Washington Post* suggested that senators were endorsing Gorman's conservative position on the tariff. Concerned about aggravating divisions within the party, Gorman had opposed the efforts of many Democrats to seek deep tariff reductions, which had been initiated by Cleveland in December 1887 and then had become a prominent

[26] "A Democratic Caucus," *Washington Evening Star*, Mar. 7, 1889, 1. See also "That Tariff Bill," *Atlanta Constitution*, Sept. 12, 1888, 1; "Senator Beck's Health," *Washington Post*, Dec. 7, 1888, 2; "The First Prizes Drawn: Three Diplomats Who Are Chosen to Go Abroad," *New York Times*, Mar. 12, 1889, 1; "Senator Beck in His Seat," *Washington Post*, Mar. 12, 1889, 7; "General Washington News," *Chicago Daily Tribune*, Apr. 4, 1890, 9; "Capital Chat," *Washington Post*, Apr. 4, 1890, 4. See also Kravitz ca. 1971, x: 22.

[27] Beck had become very ill by early September 1888. Later that month, describing the work of the Senate Finance Committee on a tariff bill, the *Boston Herald* reported that "Senator Harris, in the absence of Mr. Beck, will have to prepare the minority report." While this account refers to the Finance Committee rather than the Democratic caucus, this is the earliest reference we find to Harris acting on Beck's behalf. Perhaps it was their joint membership on the Finance Committee that led to Harris assuming a similar role in the caucus. See "Senate Tariff Bill Ready," *Boston Herald*, Sept. 25, 1888, 1; see also "Illness of Mr. Beck," *Louisville Courier Journal*, Sept. 12, 1888, 5; "That Tariff Bill," *Atlanta Constitution*, Sept. 12, 1888, 1; "At the National Capital," *New York Times*, Sept. 12, 1888, 5; "Senator Beck," *Louisville Courier Journal*, Sept. 16, 1888, 2; "Senator Beck Returns to Washington," *New York Tribune*, Oct. 7, 1888, 1; "Senator Beck's Health," *Washington Post*, Dec. 7, 1888, 2; "Senator Beck Improving," *Rochester Democrat and Chronicle*, Dec. 12, 1888, 1; "Let Him Come to Atlanta," *Atlanta Constitution*, Dec. 16, 1888, 23; "Senator Beck in the South," *Washington Post*, Dec. 27, 1888, 4; "Senator Beck in Cuba," *Washington Post*, Jan. 24, 1889, 2; "Senator Beck has arrived at Tampa, Fla., on his return from Cuba … ," *Louisville Courier Journal*, Feb. 4, 1889, 2; "Senate Caucus," *Boston Herald*, Mar. 11, 1889, 1.

[28] "Democratic Senators' Combine," *St. Louis Post-Dispatch*, May 10, 1890, 1.

issue in the disappointing 1888 campaign (Lambert 1953, 137–44). "Senator Harris was one of the Democratic Senators who, in his advice to the President and in the National Convention, favored an advanced and aggressive position on the tariff question, while Senator Gorman has at all times been extremely conservative in his tariff ideas and was opposed to making an issue in the tariff at the last campaign," the *Washington Post* noted in its story announcing Gorman's election as acting caucus chairman. "'It looks,' said an old observer of Democratic policy, 'as if the Democratic party was gradually coming back to its old moorings.'"[29] But the *Baltimore Sun* rejected this analysis, arguing that there was no evidence that policy considerations contributed to Gorman's election as acting caucus chairman.[30] Still, given the sweeping Democratic electoral defeat and the bold agenda of the Republican party, it seems unlikely that Gorman was chosen at random. Harrison had been inaugurated as president three days earlier, Republicans now controlled both chambers of Congress, and it was becoming clear that Beck's illness was serious. Democratic senators were surely keen to identify someone who had the skills and experience to lead them in the months ahead, and, for the minority, the caucus chairmanship was the only prize available. Following Beck's death, Gorman was elected chairman of the caucus on May 12, 1890.[31]

Two months later, the Senate girded for war. "We are on the eve of one of the greatest political battles ever fought in Congress," Gorman asserted in July 1890, "and it is difficult to predict what the outcome will be."[32] By a nearly straight party vote, with just two Republicans joining a united Democratic caucus in opposition, the House of Representatives had passed the Federal Elections Bill and sent the bill to the Senate (Lambert 1953, 149; Welch 1971, 147; Socolofsky and Spetter 1987, 62; Binder 1997, 186; Upchurch 2004, 105–7; Calhoun 2005, 91; Valelly 2007, 126–27, 137; Koger 2010, 74; Bateman, Katznelson, and Lapinski 2018, 199–200; Jenkins and Peck 2021, 252).[33] Gorman emerged immediately as the senator who

---

[29] "The Senate Committees," *Washington Post*, Mar. 8, 1889, 6. See also "It is an interesting fact … ," *New York Sun*, Mar. 12, 1889, 4; "To Scholars and to Quacks," *Chicago Daily Inter Ocean*, May 14, 1890, 4.

[30] "Caucus of Democratic Senators," *Baltimore Sun*, Mar. 8, 1889, 1. See also "Senate Caucus," *Boston Herald*, Mar. 11, 1889, 1; "Political Drift," *Galveston Daily News*, Mar. 13, 1889, 4; "Senator Gorman was on the 7th instant … ," *Montgomery County Sentinel (Rockville, Md.)*, Mar. 15, 1889, 2.

[31] "Democratic Senators' Combine," *St. Louis Post-Dispatch*, May 10, 1890, 1; "Democratic Caucus," *Raleigh News and Observer*, May 13, 1890, 1; "Mr. Gorman Made Chairman of the Senate Caucus," *Baltimore Sun*, May 13, 1890, 1; "News of the Day," *Philadelphia Inquirer*, May 13, 1890, 1.

[32] "From Washington: The Eve of a Great Political Battle in the Senate," *Baltimore Sun*, July 11, 1890, 1.

[33] "Passes the House," *Chicago Daily Tribune*, July 3, 1890, 1; "Under the Lash," *Boston Globe*, July 3, 1890, 6; "Dictator Reed Obeyed," *New York Times*, July 3, 1890, 1.

would lead the fight against the bill (Welch 1971, 147–48; Socolofsky and Spetter 1987, 62–63; Upchurch 2004, 106, 126–27; MacNeil and Baker 2013, 176). There appears to have been a widespread sense that no Democrat understood better than Gorman the linkages between legislative action and electoral success, as demonstrated both by his successful management of the 1884 campaign and his effort to tamp down disagreements over the tariff during the last election. Perhaps this is why his colleagues had named him caucus chairman; certainly, this is why they looked to him to lead them on the floor. The *Louisville Courier Journal* reported in July that Democratic senators had chosen Gorman "to lead the fight against the infamous Federal election bill" because he was regarded by many people as "the best politician in the Democratic party." As the *Courier Journal* noted, "He made no mistake in 1884, and he won."[34] That same month, the *Augusta Chronicle* referred to "the courage and the knowledge of practical affairs" that Gorman had demonstrated in explaining his selection "to lead the fight in the Senate against the Lodge bayonet bill." According to the *Chronicle*, "His wisdom was demonstrated by the unfortunate defeat of our party in the Presidential election. Tariff revision and reduction were rightful issues, but in his judgment the fight should have been made after and not before the Presidential contest."[35] The *Daily Inter Ocean*, published in Chicago, predicted that Gorman's name would be remembered alongside that of Reed if the Senate minority blocked the Republican program. "Minority rule is a very different thing from majority rule," the *Inter Ocean* argued. "Should this Congress adjourn with the tariff and election bills passed by the House and tied up in the Senate, one of the inevitable results would be to throw all other political names in the shade except Thomas B. Reed and Arthur P. Gorman. Each party would have a popular leader. The Democrats would look upon Gorman as their Wellington for the Republican Napoleon, and the Republicans of the country would say that if there had only been a Reed in the Senate the enemy would not have snatched victory from defeat."[36]

Republican leaders that summer had competing priorities and limited time. They decided first to take up the tariff bill, then to consider the elections bill when Congress returned for its short session in December (Hoar 1903, 2:

[34] "O. O. Stealey's Washington Special to the Courier-Journal," as reprinted in "Senator Arthur P. Gorman," *Washington Post*, July 18, 1890, 4. See also "Political Drift," *Galveston Daily News*, Mar. 13, 1889, 4.

[35] "Augusta (Ga.) Chronicle," as reprinted in "A Call for Gorman," *Washington Post*, July 20, 1890, 4. See also "Sick of Their Dirty Job," *Macon (Ga.) Telegraph*, July 12, 1890, 2.

[36] "Gorman and Reed," *Daily Inter Ocean*, July 14, 1890, 4. See also "How Gorman Has Grown," *Macon (Ga.) Telegraph*, August 9, 1890, 6.

155–56; Lambert 1953, 149–50; Morgan 1963, 141–42; Welch 1965, 514–18; Welch 1971, 152–55; Socolofsky and Spetter 1987, 63; Upchurch 2004, 106–7; Calhoun 2005, 102–4; Wawro and Schickler 2006, 77, 147; Valelly 2009, 136–37; Bateman, Katznelson, and Lapinski 2018, 200–201; Jenkins and Peck 2021, 253–54). Republican candidates in the 1888 campaign had promised to maintain and strengthen an array of protective tariffs, and they enshrined this commitment in the McKinley Tariff Bill. Aldrich, managing the bill for the Republican majority, consulted with Gorman on questions of scheduling. In July 1890, when asked by Aldrich if Senate Democrats would "give the tariff bill a chance before the force bill came up," Gorman indicated that Democrats planned to debate the tariff bill extensively, delaying final action.[37] Gorman's policy, according to the *Macon Telegraph*, "is simply stout resistance to everything that may help the force bill through."[38] Keeping his eye on the battle looming ahead, Gorman used the debate on the tariff bill as a dress rehearsal. He was convinced that an embrace of free-trade principles had divided his party and cost them the last presidential election, but Gorman equally opposed the high tariffs embodied in the McKinley bill and wholeheartedly led his colleagues in opposition. "He sits in his seat with his calm, imperturbable face, and gives his orders like a general on the battle-field," the *Daily Inter Ocean* wrote, describing Gorman's leadership on the Senate floor that summer. "He directs the forces of the opposition. The Democratic speakers report to him before they take the floor, as if to receive orders, and they go to him after they have taken their seats, as if for his approval."[39] The Democrats were not engaged in a probing examination of the bill, according to the *Inter Ocean*. "They do not state facts. And they apparently do not care whether they do or not," the newspaper observed. "They simply talk."[40] Gorman mobilized his colleagues in opposition to the bill, organizing this filibuster, while ultimately allowing the bill to come to a vote. The Senate passed the tariff bill on September 30, then Congress adjourned the next day.[41]

---

[37] "Sick of Their Dirty Job," *Macon (Ga.) Telegraph*, July 12, 1890, 2. See also "The Vote on the Tariff Bill," *Washington Post*, Aug. 25, 1890, 4; "Will the Democrats Consent?" *New York Times*, Aug. 25, 1890, 4.

[38] "Sick of Their Dirty Job," *Macon (Ga.) Telegraph*, July 12, 1890, 2.

[39] "National Capital Topics," *Chicago Daily Inter Ocean*, July 31, 1890.

[40] "National Capital Topics," *Chicago Daily Inter Ocean*, July 31, 1890. See also "National Election Bill," *Chicago Daily Inter Ocean*, Aug. 11, 1890, 8; "The Vote on the Tariff Bill," *Washington Post*, Aug. 25, 1890, 4; "Will the Democrats Consent?" *New York Times*, Aug. 25, 1890, 4.

[41] "Tariff Goes," *Boston Globe*, Oct. 1, 1890, 4; "Work of Congress: The Tariff Debate Comes to an End," *Los Angeles Times*, Oct. 1, 1890, 4; "Approval of the Tariff," *Washington Post*, Oct. 2, 1890, 1; "Congress Adjourns," *Atlanta Constitution*, Oct. 2, 1890, 9; "Congress Ends Its Work," *New York Times*, Oct. 2, 1890, 1.

SENATE SCREECHING.
UNCLE SAM—"For goodness' sake cease this noise, and act instead of talking—or go home !"

"Senate Screeching," cover of *Judge*, Sept. 1890. The caption reads: "Uncle Sam—'For goodness' sake cease this noise, and act instead of talking—or go home!'" In the summer of 1890 Gorman led Senate Democrats in a filibuster of the McKinley Tariff Bill, a prelude to the historic filibuster later that year that blocked passage of the Federal Elections Bill.

Judge magazine cover, Sept. 6, 1890

In December, the Senate took up the Federal Elections Bill, a majority having pledged their support not only to the bill but to ensuring that the bill came to a vote. Time was running out fast. The November elections, widely perceived as a referendum on Reed's leadership of the House and the McKinley Tariff Bill, had been a rout; Democrats would hold 238 seats in the next House, compared to just 86 Republican seats. It would be the largest majority enjoyed by either party since the 1860s, and Republicans were dispirited. Political observers believed that the Senate would, of necessity, enact a cloture rule, just as the House had ended dilatory tactics and embraced majority rule earlier that same year. From the start, however, Gorman understood that a pivotal group of Republicans, though weakly committed to the elections bill, cared more about passing a new currency bill in the remaining three months of the lame-duck Congress. This was Gorman's audience: the more successful he was in extending debate and delaying a vote on the elections bill, the more eager Silver Republicans would become to strike a separate deal with him. Barely a week into the debate on the Federal Elections Bill, Gorman's strategy was in place. "He has worked skillfully upon the fears of the Republican Senators who are anxious to secure further silver legislation. He has told them: 'I will consent to this or that in the way of financial legislation if you will kill the Election bill,'" the *Chicago Daily Tribune* noted in mid-December. "The Republicans have a strong and positive majority in the Senate, and yet the country is treated from day to day to the humiliating spectacle of a constant conference between some of the Republican financiers and Senator Gorman."[42] Gorman's interest in silver was entirely strategic. As he later told an audience in Elkton, Maryland, he would have supported "the free coinage of lead to preserve the liberties of the American people" (Lambert 1953, 159).

The debate—a filibuster in everything but name—lasted over a month. The Democrats were firmly united behind Gorman. When, two days before Christmas, Aldrich presented a cloture resolution, "the Democratic Senators presented an undisturbed front," the *Washington Post* reported. "Senator Gorman, the leader of that side, did not move a muscle of his face, and, while all the Democrats paid strict attention, no one indicated by word or look or smile his personal feeling. When it is remembered that the resolution threatened at least an overthrow of all Senatorial precedent it is not hard to see why the occasion became for the moment something impressive."[43] With short breaks for Christmas and New Year's, the debate continued unabated (Burdette 1940, 53; Lambert 1953, 152–59; Welch 1965, 518–19; Welch 1971, 155–57; Upchurch 2004, 129–56; Bateman, Katznelson, and Lapinski 2018, 204). Then, on January 5, 1891, William M. Stewart (R, Nev.) startled his Republican colleagues by offering a motion that the Senate lay the elections

[42] T. C. Crawford, "Gorman as a Dictator," *Chicago Daily Tribune*, Dec. 12, 1890, 9. See also "Seeking a Compromise," *Washington Post*, Dec. 14, 1890, 1.
[43] "The Cloture Rule Is In," *Washington Post*, Dec. 24, 1890, 1.

bill on the table and take up currency legislation.[44] Hoar, as bill manager, objected. "But Senator Gorman instantly interrupted with the point of order that the question was not debatable," according to the *Washington Post*. "Mr. Gorman's words cut the air like a knife, so cool and emphatic were they."[45] Silver Republicans voted with the Senate's Democrats to support the motion, and consideration of the Federal Elections Bill was suspended (Burdette 1940, 53; Lambert 1953, 159; Fowler 1961, 156; Welch 1965, 519–20; Welch 1971, 157–58; Socolofsky and Spetter 1987, 64; Binder 1997, 187; Calhoun 2005, 114–15; Wawro and Schickler 2006, 78; Valelly 2009, 137; Koger 2010, 74; Bateman, Katznelson, and Lapinski 2018, 204–5; Jenkins and Peck 2021, 254). But the silver bill was quickly passed, and, on January 14, an evenly divided Senate, with the vice president casting the tie-breaking vote, took up the elections bill again (Burdette 1940, 54; Lambert 1953, 159–60; Koger 2010, 74; Jenkins and Peck 2021, 255).[46] Led by Gorman, Democrats resumed their filibuster, refusing to surrender even as the majority Republicans insisted on keeping the Senate in constant session through the night of January 16–17.[47] "From 3 o'clock yesterday morning until the first streaks of daylight began to pierce the muggy curtain of a dense fog and heavy rain, the only business transacted by the Senate was the calling of the roll at regular intervals," the *Washington Post* reported. "Senator Gorman, moving here and there like a perturbed spirit, did not miss a roll-call."[48] As Democrats continued their relentless filibuster, Republican leaders, led by Aldrich, mounted plans to pass a cloture resolution to end the debate and force a vote (Haynes 1938, i: 397; Burdette 1940, 55–57; Lambert 1953, 160–64; Welch 1965, 520–21; Welch 1971, 158–59; Byrd 1991, 104; Binder 1997, 187; Binder and Smith 1997, 138; Schickler 2001, 40; Upchurch 2004, 160–65; Wawro and Schickler 2006, 3–4, 77–82; Binder, Madonna, and Smith 2007, 730, 734; Valelly 2007, 145; Valelly 2009, 137–38; Koger 2010, 74; Bateman, Katznelson, and Lapinski 2018, 205–6; Jentleson 2021, 61–62; Jenkins and Peck 2021, 255).[49] Standing alongside those Republican senators was Vice President Levi Morton, who was

---

[44] "From Washington: A Probably Fatal Blow to the Vicious Force Bill," *Baltimore Sun*, Jan. 6, 1891, 1; "Force Bill Laid Aside," *Washington Post*, Jan. 6, 1891, 1. Two weeks earlier, Stewart had become the first Senate Republican to speak against the elections bill: see "Mr. Stewart Revolts," *Washington Post*, Dec. 20, 1890, 1. See also "A Republican Caucus," *Washington Post*, Dec. 31, 1890, 1.

[45] "Force Bill Laid Aside," *Washington Post*, Jan. 6, 1891, 1.

[46] "A Free Coinage Bill," *Washington Post*, Jan. 15, 1891, 1.

[47] "A Drawn Battle," *Atlanta Constitution*, Jan. 18, 1891, 15; "After Thirty Hours," *Washington Post*, Jan. 18, 1891, 1.

[48] "After Thirty Hours," *Washington Post*, Jan. 18, 1891, 1.

[49] "Will Mr. Morton Do It," *Washington Post*, Jan. 19, 1891, 1; "By Aid of the Chair," *Washington Post*, Jan. 23, 1891, 2; "To Close the Debate," *Washington Post*, Jan. 26, 1891, 1; Frederic J. Haskin, "The American Congress: IX. The Force Bill and Cloture," *Washington Post*, Dec. 1, 1909, 4.

expected to make rulings from the chair in support of majority cloture.[50] Gorman, meanwhile, was working to build a coalition to stop the bill altogether. On January 26, even as most observers were predicting that Republicans would succeed in bringing majority rule to the Senate, Gorman's work came to fruition. Edward O. Wolcott (R, Colo.) introduced a motion that the Senate immediately take up an apportionment bill, and, the alliance of Democrats and Silver Republicans still intact, the motion passed by one vote, 35 to 34 (Hoar 1903, 2: 156; Burdette 1940, 57; Lambert 1953, 164–65; Fowler 1961, 156–57; Welch 1965, 521–22; Welch 1971, 159; Socolofsky and Spetter 1987, 64–65; Byrd 1991, 104–5; Binder 1997, 187; Upchurch 2004, 165; Calhoun 2005, 115–16; Wawro and Schickler 2006, 4, 82; Valelly 2007, 126–27, 145; Koger 2010, 74; Bateman, Katznelson, and Lapinski 2018, 206; Jenkins and Peck 2021, 255).[51] The Federal Elections Bill was dead, entombed alongside the movement for cloture.

Had the Republicans succeeded that winter, they would have laid the foundation for majority rule in the Senate. "If this effort had been successful, the Senate would now proceed under rules practically the same as those obtaining in the House," Frederic Haskin, who would soon become president of the National Press Club, wrote in 1909.[52] Unlimited debate in the Senate might well have become a historical curiosity, much like the dilatory tactics that paralyzed procedure in the House in the years before the adoption of the Reed rules. After all, it had been the House—and not the Senate—where obstructionism and "filibusters" had threatened to overwhelm the chamber in the late 1880s and where minority rights had been in the ascendancy.[53] "Till

---

[50] "By Aid of the Chair," *Washington Post*, Jan. 23, 1891, 2.

[51] "Black Eye to Cloture," *Washington Post*, Jan. 27, 1891, 1; "May It Rest in Peace," *Washington Post*, Jan. 27, 1891, 4; "A Constitutional Gossip," *Atlanta Constitution*, Jan. 28, 1891, 4; Frederic J. Haskin, "The American Congress: IX. The Force Bill and Cloture," *Washington Post*, Dec. 1, 1909, 4.

[52] Frederic J. Haskin, "The American Congress: IX. The Force Bill and Cloture," *Washington Post*, Dec. 1, 1909, 4.

[53] "The Filibuster's Advantage," *Chicago Tribune*, Jan. 1, 1889, 18; "Sherman's Bill to Prevent Election Frauds—Those Alleged Alaskan Infamies Fail to Materialize—The House Still in the Hands of Political Filibusters," *Los Angeles Times*, Jan. 9, 1889, 4; "Jedge Waxem a Filibuster," *Washington Post*, Jan. 12, 1889, 6; "Mr. Springer's Victory," *Washington Post*, Jan. 22, 1889, 2; "Filibustering Run Mad," *New York Times*, Feb. 14, 1889, 4; "Fiftieth Congress," *Los Angeles Times*, Feb. 19, 1889, 4; "Cabinet Fixtures," *Atlanta Constitution*, Feb. 20, 1889, 1; "A Majority of Three," *Washington Post*, Feb. 22, 1889, 2; "The Tariff Bill," *Atlanta Constitution*, Feb. 24, 1889, 11; "Men Who Quit Congress," *Washington Post*, Feb. 25, 1889, 6; "A Sunday Session," *Los Angeles Times*, Mar. 4, 1889, 4; "Mr. Springer Appears in the Role of a Filibuster," *Atlanta Constitution*, Mar. 4, 1889, 1; "Safety in the Rules," *Atlanta Constitution*, Mar. 5, 1889, 6; "Methods that Must Go: The Odious Rules of the House of Representatives," *Washington Post*, Apr. 29, 1889, 6; "A Big Fight over the House Rules," *Chicago Tribune*, June 24, 1889, 4; Henry Loomis Nelson, "The Speaker's Power," *Atlantic Monthly*, July 1889, 64–73; "Mr. Blaine on Majority Rule in Congress," *Chicago Tribune*, July 9, 1889, 4; "It is a Trifle Slim," *Washington Post*, Sept. 8, 1889, 9; Thomas B. Reed,

recently," James Bryce wrote in 1891 (i: 100), "systematic obstruction, or, as it is called in America, 'filibustering,' familiar to the House, was almost unknown in the calmer air of the Senate." In the winter of 1890–91, with Reed's revolution only months old, a similar revolution in the Senate had seemed likely, the denouement of that season's great drama. "Legislative filibustering and time-killing and attempts on the part of minorities to override majorities have never been popular in this country and never will be," the *Chicago Tribune* declared on January 24, 1891. "The people are on Speaker Reed's side in his contest with the would-be bulldozers and they will be with the Republican Senators in their present battle for the rights of the majority."[54] The *Atlanta Constitution* in 1889 had described the stakes in the struggle over the elections bill: "Should the republicans of the next house succeed in changing the rules so as to render the democratic minority helpless the south will be at their mercy."[55] With those very rules changes now enacted in the House, the Democratic minority in the Senate took center stage in the bicameral drama. Stopping the Federal Elections Bill required perfecting dilatory tactics in the Senate, and the filibuster of 1890–91 proved a landmark. Binder and Smith (1997, 134) argue that the elections bill was "perhaps the best known of the measures killed by filibuster before the adoption of Rule 22." This filibuster "shook not only the Senate but also the country," Burdette (1940, 52, 57) contends. "Filibustering against the Federal Elections Bill had supplied the most remarkable spectacle of obstruction then known to the Senate, and the country was amazed."

Scholars still debate why Senate Republicans failed to adopt majority cloture and secure the bill's passage. Binder (1997, 186–88), Binder and Smith (1997, 75), and Binder, Madonna, and Smith (2007, 732), pointing to votes that suggested that a majority supported the bill, emphasize the role of inherited rules, in particular the lack of a previous question motion in the Senate. Had Republicans imposed majority cloture, Binder, Madonna, and Smith (2007, 734) contend, Democrats could have thrown the chamber into "chaos in response at a time when so much vital legislation was still pending." Wawro and Schickler (2006, 76–87), in contrast, argue that the vice president's support provided a strategy for rules reform that did not require a previous question motion. The strategy collapsed, they contend, because a majority of senators did not support the Federal Elections Bill wholeheartedly; had the policy majority existed, a procedural majority would also have existed to limit debate. Agreeing with this analysis, Koger (2010, 74) argues that the 1890–91 battle demonstrates that "closure reform is *possible*" and that the result was a

---

"Obstruction in the National House," *North American Review*, Oct. 1889, 421–28; "Let the Majority Rule," *New York Times*, Oct. 12, 1889, 4; "Randall Has a Policy," *Chicago Tribune*, Oct. 28, 1889, 2; Roger Q. Mills, "Republican Tactics in the House," *North American Review*, Dec. 1889, 665–72; Lodge 1893, 525–26.

[54] "The Senate Getting Down to Business," *Chicago Tribune*, Jan. 24, 1891, 4.

[55] "Safety in the Rules," *Atlanta Constitution*, Mar. 5, 1889, 6.

consequence of "asymmetrical intensity," where Democrats proved more tenacious in their efforts to defeat the elections bill than Republicans in their attempts to pass the bill. "Aldrich's bid to change the rules to pave the way for passage of the Elections Bill was, in the end, not doomed by the ability of the minority to obstruct the change," according to Wawro and Schickler (2006, 86). "Instead, it faltered because Aldrich and Hoar lacked the support of a Senate majority to pass the bill itself."

While this accurately describes the state of affairs in January 1891, when the bill was laid aside, it does not explain why the majority had come apart by then. Even Wawro and Schickler (2006, 76), whose account focuses on the final weeks of debate, note that "the bill may well have passed in summer 1890, when a slim majority of members apparently were willing to vote for the bill." But the long, excruciating delay destroyed support for the bill, and the delay was no act of nature. It was instead a carefully calculated design. Gorman used time as his most powerful ally: building a coalition with Silver Republicans, encouraging Republicans to push the debate into a time-limited short session of Congress, and allowing concerns to build among Republicans chastened by the disastrous election results in November 1890. Explaining the failure of the bill, Cullom (1911, 255), a leading Republican senator, recalled that "the opposition to it was so bitter and strong and so skilfully managed by the late Senator Gorman on the part of the minority, and it stood for so long a time in the way of other legislation, that one afternoon Senator Wolcott arose in his seat and, very much to the astonishment of every one, moved to lay it aside and take up some other bill. The motion carried, and that was the last we heard of the Force Bill." Gorman understood, too, that rules reform in the House, coupled with House passage of the elections bill, had abruptly made the Senate the last redoubt for minority obstructionism. "It will not do for the republicans to protest against any tactics the democratic minority may employ," Gorman explained, "for the arbitrary rulings of Speaker Reed, at the dictation of his party's caucus, have established precedents which estop them from complaining."[56] The final margin could not have been closer. In a city where Republicans ostensibly controlled the presidency, the Supreme Court, and both houses of Congress, probably the vote of just one senator blocked passage of "both the Elections Bill and sweeping change in Senate rules," Valelly (2009, 138) emphasizes, along with "the simultaneous institution of both the Aldrich Rules and the Reed Rules."

It was Gorman's great triumph, from beginning to end. Democratic newspapers throughout the country—above all, of course, in the South—praised his achievement. "Among those entitled to the unbounded gratitude of the American people for the preservation of their institutions from this deadly

---

[56] "From Washington: The Eve of a Great Political Battle in the Senate," *Baltimore Sun*, July 11, 1890, 1.

assault stands easily first Arthur P. Gorman," a correspondent to the *Baltimore Sun* declared. "But to affirm that Senator Gorman was pre-eminently the leader is to cast no reflection upon his associates or to detract in the least from the honor which belongs to each of them. He was their leader because they made him so, and it is to their peculiar credit that they did. In all the long and heroic struggle they did nothing wiser than this."[57] In the estimation of the *Denton (Md.) Journal*, Gorman, "who led the minority in this determined fight, will always be reckoned as one of the shrewdest parliamentarians of modern times."[58] Three weeks after the defeat of the elections bill, the *Dallas Morning News* published a lengthy biography of Gorman, knowing that "the public would be naturally anxious" to know more about the person who led the battle against the bill and had emerged from the fight as "the Democratic Leader in the Senate."[59] Yet, remarkably, Gorman now goes unmentioned in most scholarly accounts. Even as they document the corrosive effect of the filibuster on the Senate majority in 1890–91 and the efforts of Republican leaders to secure the elections bill's passage, Haynes (1938), Burdette (1940), Byrd (1991), Binder (1997), Binder and Smith (1997), Schickler (2001), Wawro and Schickler (2006), Binder, Madonna, and Smith (2007), Valelly (2009), Koger (2010), and Jentleson (2021) never cite Gorman by name. It is a glaring omission. More than any other person, Gorman elevated the filibuster to its place as the distinguishing feature of the U.S. Senate, he ended the movement for majority cloture, and, in the process, he invented the position of elected floor leader.

Gorman was at his best leading in opposition. In 1893–95, when Cleveland was back in the White House and Democrats controlled both chambers, Gorman was anything but the president's lieutenant. Intent on uniting his fractured caucus, Gorman worked to cobble together compromises on currency and tariff legislation that conflicted with the president's positions. Gorman— who had managed Cleveland's first presidential campaign in 1884 and represented Cleveland in trying to moderate language on the tariff in the 1888 Democratic platform—focused on the need to write bills that could secure support in the Senate, which Cleveland saw as a betrayal of party principles and sound policy. As a consequence, after Gorman had led a united caucus to defeat the Federal Elections Bill in 1890–91, Senate Democrats splintered and Gorman looked inept as their leader. In his capacity as caucus chairman and floor leader, Gorman was responsible for trying to keep his party together, working with the president, and speaking for the party on the Senate floor. But his differences

---

[57] "Mr. Gorman's Leadership," *Baltimore Sun*, Jan. 31, 1891, Supplement 2. See also "A Constitutional Gossip," *Atlanta Constitution*, Jan. 28, 1891, 4.

[58] "Senator Gorman," *Denton (Md.) Journal*, Feb. 7, 1891, 2.

[59] "Arthur Pue Gorman: Sketch of the Democratic Leader in the Senate," *Dallas Morning News*, Feb. 18, 1891, 4. See also "Senator Gorman: One of the Great Lights of Democracy," *Atlanta Constitution*, Feb. 22, 1891, 7.

with a president of his own party and serious factionalism within his party on economic issues were developments that he could not overcome. That these policy fights took such a toll on him reflected how he and others had come to view his duties as Senate Democratic leader.

The breach between Gorman and the president began early in the new administration. Cleveland called Congress into special session in the summer of 1893 in response to the financial panic and economic depression that had begun earlier that year. The president, convinced that the rapid depletion of the nation's gold supply was contributing to the crisis, called for the repeal of the Sherman Silver Purchase Act (Nevins 1932, 523–28, 533–36; Lambert 1953, 183–87; Hollingsworth 1963, 11; Welch 1988, 115–19; Bateman, Katznelson, and Lapinski 2018, 138). After the House voted for repeal, the debate shifted to the Senate, where opponents of the gold standard refused to support the president's call to end the policy of bimetallism. "This is Mr. Gorman's opportunity," the *Baltimore Sun* declared. "The senior Senator from Maryland, as chairman of the democratic caucus of the Senate, and, therefore, as leader of the majority of that body, is in a position to place himself at the head of the substantial interests of the country by falling in line with the President's policy of an unconditional repeal of the Sherman act."[60] For Cleveland, compromise was out of the question: in his view, only an immediate, unconditional end to silver purchases could save the gold reserve and restore economic stability (Nevins 1932, 545–46; Lambert 1953, 187–99; Hollingsworth 1963, 14–16; Welch 1988, 122–23). He had little patience for senators, whether fellow Democrats from the agrarian South or Republicans from silver-producing states in the West, who believed that the movement for silver repeal helped only the financial and manufacturing interests of the Northeast and Midwest. As Cleveland watched in a rage, opponents of repeal launched a filibuster that delayed action through the summer and into the fall (Nevins 1932, 542–43; Burdette 1940, 58–68; Lambert 1953, 187–99; Wawro and Schickler 2006, 48–50, 183). Gorman began work on a compromise bill, looking for some way to hold his caucus together, but Cleveland continued to stand firm (Lambert 1953, 189–99; Hollingsworth 1963, 16–17; Welch 1988, 123; Wawro and Schickler 2006, 49). Gorman's efforts at compromise fell apart, and the Senate finally took up Cleveland's demand for unconditional repeal. The bill passed with substantial Republican support. Democratic senators were evenly divided, with 22 for repeal and 22 opposed (Lambert 1953, 197–99). Although Gorman voted for repeal, he and Cleveland had found themselves sharply at odds. The Democratic president—using the powers of patronage, agenda setting, and the veto—had secured his legislative objective, while the Democratic "leader of the majority" of the Senate could not prevent his caucus from fracturing.

---

[60] "Senator Gorman," *Baltimore Sun*, Aug. 11, 1893, 1. See also "A Word to Mr. Gorman," *New York Times*, Aug. 14, 1893, 4.

Any chance for cooperation between Cleveland and Gorman ended decisively with the next great legislative battle, over the tariff. Reductions in duties was a Democratic policy objective that would require strict party unity, given the continuing commitment of Republicans to protectionism. In working with William L. Wilson (D, W.Va.) to craft the House bill, Cleveland knew that many Democrats rejected an explicit embrace of free-trade principles. The Wilson bill, endorsed by Cleveland, was therefore "a modest effort at tariff revision" (Welch 1988, 132; also Nevins 1932, 564–65). It ended tariffs on many raw materials—coal, iron ore, wool, lumber, copper, and sugar—but left intact most remaining tariffs, yielding a slight reduction in the general tariff level. Once the bill passed the House, it went to the Senate, where Democrats held a narrow majority. Without Republican support, Gorman understood that he could spare few Democratic defections. But Democratic senators, holding a three-day-long caucus, swiftly lined up against specific provisions in the bill, demanding amendments to protect home-state industries: sugar in Louisiana, iron ore and coal in Alabama and West Virginia, fruit in California, shirt collars and cuffs in New York, and leather in New Jersey (Nevins 1932, 572–73; Lambert 1953, 205–7; Welch 1988, 133–34; Wawro and Schickler 2006, 150). Recognizing that the Wilson bill had no chance of passage in the Senate, Gorman directed a caucus subcommittee to amend the bill, with the goal of securing sufficient votes for passage.

The Senate bill, now called the Wilson-Gorman tariff, bore little resemblance to the bill that had passed the House with Cleveland's support. The Wilson-Gorman tariff left only wool and copper on the free list, raised tariffs on many items, and set new duties on other products. In all, the Senate had added over six hundred amendments to the House version of the bill (Nevins 1932, 573–74; Lambert 1953, 213–24; Hollingsworth 1963, 20; Welch 1988, 133–34). The bill passed the Senate on a party-line vote, but it was hardly tariff reform. After bitter wrangling between the branches, as House Democrats regarded the bill as little better than Republican tariff measures, the House acceded to the Senate amendments (Nevins 1932, 578–84; Lambert 1953, 237; Welch 1988, 134–37; Bateman, Katznelson, and Lapinski 2018, 121). Cleveland, who let the bill become law without his signature, condemned the work of Senate Democrats. The promise of tariff reform had been so closely identified with the Democratic party, the president declared, that "our abandonment of the cause … means party perfidy and party dishonor" (Nevins 1932, 581; Lambert 1953, 227–28; Hollingsworth 1963, 20; Welch 1988, 136, 205–6; Wawro and Schickler 2006, 151). Gorman, stunned at the president's attack, rose in the Senate to respond. Stating that the president had been fully informed and agreed to the necessity of making these changes to secure Democratic votes and the bill's passage, Gorman accused Cleveland of dishonesty and deceit (Nevins 1932, 581–82; Lambert 1953, 228–37; MacNeil and Baker 2013, 79, 176). As a reporter for the *Lowell (Mass.) Daily Sun* observed, "The president was assailed with keenness and vigor by the leader of his party on the floor of the Senate."[61] In the summer of 1894, the rupture between them was complete.

Gorman returned to the minority the next year, when Republicans regained control of the Senate, and he remained floor leader until 1898, when he resigned the position. Still, the filibuster he led against the Federal Elections Bill in 1890–91 was the defining event of his leadership. While many other senators in the nineteenth century had managed their party's affairs for a particular bill or over some short period of time, in that battle Gorman had fused his new responsibility as minority leader with his formal position as caucus chairman, creating a new institution. That institution, once created, has been in permanent existence ever since. Every one of Gorman's successors as caucus chairman has been simultaneously elected to lead Senate Democrats on the floor. They were expected, as we show later in this chapter, to perform many of the tasks required of modern Senate leaders. While the first generation of floor leaders consistently fell short of expectations—indeed, even Gorman himself could never replicate his great achievement of 1890–91—senators and journalists agreed that Senate Democrats were electing their leader each time they cast ballots for a caucus chairman.

Reflecting on Gorman's years as floor leader, observers viewed his achievement through the prism of his early success in defeating the Federal Elections Bill. "In the days when the republicans shoved the 'force bill' to the front to cover up the tracks of the other iniquities they were perpetrating as the agents of the protected classes and of the gold owners, Gorman was a tower of strength to the south," the *Atlanta Constitution* wrote in 1897, in an extensive biography.[62] A correspondent to the *Dallas Morning News* also summed up Gorman's legacy, at the time in 1897 when Maryland's voters had placed the state's legislature in the hands of his enemies. "In the great force bill fight . . . the conduct of the fight against it was placed wholly in his hands. And he whipped it when the chances of its defeat were of the most remote kind," W.G.S. wrote in the *Dallas Morning News*. "The future looks gloomy for the old war horse and leader. He fell the victim, not of his own indiscretion, but to changes in policies of the party, to his disposition to harmonize the elements in his party when there was no such thing as harmony."[63] When he died in 1906, his leadership of Senate Democrats against the Federal Elections Bill was remembered clearly. "Senator Gorman was a big man in every sense—clear-headed, dispassionate, wise, indomitable, calm. He was easily the leader of his party on the floor," the *Washington Post* wrote in its editorial. "His part in the defeat of the 'Force Bill,' some twenty-odd years ago, won him imperishable renown."[64] As the *Chicago Daily Tribune* recalled, "Gorman was unique in that he was

[61] "Gorman: Opens upon Cleveland in the Senate," *Lowell (Mass.) Daily Sun*, July 24, 1894, 7.
[62] "Senator Gorman a Smooth Politician," *Atlanta Constitution*, Aug. 9, 1897, 1.
[63] W.G.S., "Defeat of Senator Gorman," *Dallas Morning News*, Nov. 22, 1897, 4.
[64] "Arthur Pue Gorman," *Washington Post*, June 5, 1906, 6.

able to handle a minority so skillfully as to defeat the will of the majority. He beat the force bill by sheer political cunning. His party was in a minority, but he was clever enough to see that the force bill . . . could be made odious even to the north with proper effort."[65] Years later, observers still marveled at the electoral consequences of Gorman's achievement. According to the *Los Angeles Times*, "It resulted in giving the Democrats an issue which united the party and paved the way to Democratic success in the next election for President."[66]

DEMOCRATIC CAUCUS CHAIRMEN AND FLOOR LEADERS, 1898–1913

When Gorman announced, in April 1898, that he was stepping down as caucus chairman, newspapers treated his decision as a major story. The coverage was without precedent. Caucus chairmen in both parties had come and gone unnoticed for many decades—and elections for chairmen of the Republican caucus would excite little interest for decades more—but in 1898–99 the retirement of one Democratic caucus chairman and the selection of another was now a matter of great interest. The *New York Times*, the *Washington Post*, the *Washington Evening Star*, the *Boston Globe*, the *Boston Daily Advertiser*, the *Charlotte (N.C.) Observer*, and the *Los Angeles Times* all ran articles covering the event, each newspaper printing some version of the same basic text.[67] "Mr. Gorman Resigns—Gives Up the Chairmanship of the Democratic Caucus of the Senate—Senator Cockrell in Tears," the *Baltimore Sun* reported, in a story that ran 11 paragraphs.[68] The *New York Times* devoted seven paragraphs to the story; the *Boston Globe*, four paragraphs; the *Washington Evening Star*, 10 paragraphs; the *Washington Post*, 10 paragraphs; the *Boston Daily Advertiser*, nine paragraphs; the *Charlotte Observer*, seven paragraphs. Figure 5.2 reproduces the *Washington Post*'s account.

These stories reported how Gorman explained his decision to resign his leadership position, and they speculated on the reasons for his decision. "Mr. Gorman, in tendering his resignation, stated that he had desired to withdraw from the position last fall, and that he had been dissuaded by some of his fellow-Senators, but that he had since given the matter careful attention, and

---

[65] "Gorman's Death Democracy's Loss," *Chicago Daily Tribune*, June 5, 1906, 6.

[66] "Leader Gorman," *Los Angeles Times*, Mar. 8, 1903, 1.

[67] "Turpie Succeeds Gorman," *New York Times*, Apr. 30, 1898, 2; "Mr. Gorman Retires," *Washington Post*, Apr. 30, 1898, 4; "Democratic Senators Caucus," *Washington Evening Star*, Apr. 30, 1898, 8; "Gorman Succeeded by Turpie," *Boston Globe*, Apr. 30, 1898, 7; "Senator Gorman," *Boston Daily Advertiser*, Apr. 30, 1898, 1; "Senator Gorman Resigns," *Charlotte (N.C.) Observer*, Apr. 30, 1898, 4; "Chairman Gorman Resigns," *Los Angeles Times*, Apr. 30, 1898, 3.

[68] "Mr. Gorman Resigns," *Baltimore Sun*, Apr. 30, 1898, 6.

Washington Post, 30 Apr. 1898

MR. GORMAN RETIRES

He Is No Longer Chairman of Democratic Caucus.

SENATOR TURPIE HIS SUCCESSOR

The Scene at the Caucus Yesterday When Mr. Gorman Tendered His Resignation Was Affecting--The War Revenue Bill Discussed and Serious Objection Made to Railroading It Through the Senate--Reasons Given for Change of Leadership.

Senator Gorman, who, for many years has been Chairman of the Democratic caucus of the Senate, resigned the position yesterday, and Senator Turpie, of Indiana, was chosen as his successor. The change was made in a Democratic caucus held this afternoon, and the scene was an affecting one. Several speeches were made, eulogizing Mr. Gorman in high terms and expressing deep regret that he should insist upon retiring. Senator Cockrell, who has been Mr. Gorman's principal adviser for many years, broke down and shed tears over the occurrence. Speeches were made by Senator Jones, of Arkansas; White, and others, all referring to Mr. Gorman's long and glorious recognized services to the party. Mr. Gorman, in tendering his resignation, stated that he had desired to withdraw from the position last fall, and that he had been dissuaded by some of his fellow-Senators, but that he had since given the matter careful attention, and was fully persuaded that it was the proper course for him to pursue. He said that he had reached the conclusion only after mature consideration, and while he appreciated to the utmost the trust that had been reposed in him, he could not see his way clear to longer hold the office. The following resolution, offered by Senator Cockrell, was adopted by a rising and unanimous vote:

"Resolved, That the thanks of the Democratic Senate in conference assembled."

Atlanta Constitution, 17 Nov. 1899

BACON AS LEADER OF THE DEMOCRATS

Georgian Suggested As the Successor of Gorman.

KANSAN SAYS HE IS THE MAN

Senator from Sunflower State Speaks Highly of Empire State Senator.

DECLARES HE IS THE ABLEST LEADER

FIGURE 5.2 News coverage following Gorman's resignation in 1898

was fully persuaded that it was the proper course for him to pursue," according to the *Washington Post*. "He said that he had reached the conclusion only after mature consideration, and while he appreciated to the utmost the trust that had been reposed in him, he could not see his way clear to longer hold the office."[69] Some observers speculated that Gorman resigned the caucus chairmanship because he was denied a particular committee assignment, but that seems unlikely, given that his term as a senator was drawing to a close: the Maryland legislature, controlled by Republicans, had already selected a new senator to take Gorman's seat when his term ended in March 1899 (Lambert 1953, 263–65). Moreover, Gorman himself chaired his party's steering committee, which made committee assignments. A likelier reason for Gorman's resignation was his support for issuing bonds to raise revenue for the Spanish-American War, a minority position within his party (Lambert 1953, 268). This policy dispute, the *Washington Post* contended, was "the real reason of Senator Gorman's withdrawal."[70] After nine years as his party's leader, with no prospect of serving beyond the end of the current Congress, Gorman was probably predisposed to curtail his activities in the Senate. Demoralized by events in Maryland, Gorman must have had little enthusiasm for several more months of leading his fractured caucus on Capitol Hill, especially when he found himself at odds with most of his colleagues on how best to fund the war. As the *Charlotte Observer* bluntly concluded, "The truth of the business is that his counsels and leadership are no longer wanted, and he knows it."[71]

David Turpie (D, Ind.) was elected caucus chairman in April 1898 upon Gorman's resignation, but this was a stopgap. Turpie appears to have been chosen simply to fill out the remainder of Gorman's term. He was elected at the same meeting at which Gorman announced his resignation, and there is no evidence of any discussion. Unlike every preceding Democratic caucus chairman, none of whom had any claim to seniority, Turpie had first sat in the Senate during the Civil War. While respected by his colleagues, Turpie lacked the vigor and temperament to be an effective leader. "Of late years he has failed in health," the *Washington Post* reported upon the Senate's adjournment in March 1899, "and was not in his seat yesterday when the session came to a close, being ill at his home in Indianapolis."[72] He was "almost a recluse," according to the profile, though widely admired as someone with a sharp mind and a peerless command of ancient and modern literature. Turpie served as caucus chairman for the remaining 10 weeks of the long session, from his election on April 29, 1898, to the end of the session on July 8. By the time Congress reconvened for its short session in December, Turpie knew that he would not be returning to the Senate after the session and his term ended, the

---

[69] "Mr. Gorman Retires," *Washington Post*, Apr. 30, 1898, 4.
[70] "Mr. Gorman Retires," *Washington Post*, Apr. 30, 1898, 4. See also "Gorman No Longer Chairman," *Kansas City Star*, Apr. 30, 1898, 10.
[71] "The Plans of the Chairmen for Fusion," *Charlotte (N.C.) Observer*, May 1, 1898, 4.
[72] "Retire to Private Life," *Washington Post*, Mar. 5, 1899, 22. See also Chilton 1908, 31–36.

Republicans having gained control that fall of the Indiana legislature, and he was frequently incapacitated by sickness.[73]

Gorman remained at the forefront of senators' minds in the final weeks of the session. It had been months since he had resigned as caucus chairman and party leader, yet Washington observers wondered who would succeed him as Senate minority leader. In the first days of February 1899—a month before the end of the session and 10 months before the next Congress would convene—two different newspapers ran stories about Gorman and the future of Democratic leadership in the Senate. "During the fight on the pending treaty in the Senate the democrats have been looking over their senatorial timber for a recognized leader after March. Senator Gorman, of Maryland, has for a number of years been the pilot of the senatorial democracy in matters of national legislation, as well as general party politics," the *Baltimore Sun* reported. "So many prominent democrats retire from the Senate with Senator Gorman that it is difficult to find a successor who possesses the qualities of leadership for which the Senator from Maryland is noted."[74] That same week the *Washington Post* stated that "with the departure of Senator Gorman from the Senate the Democrats in that body lose their recognized and respected leader."[75] Later that month, the Philadelphia *North American* noted, "With the retirement of Gorman, there is considerable discussion in political circles as to who will have the honor of leading the Democratic minority in the next Senate."[76] Newspaper coverage, as suggested by the images in Figure 5.2, was extensive. Surveying the field of possible Democratic Senate leaders that fall, William Harris (Populist, Kans.) reflected on Gorman's example. "There is no one to take Gorman's place," Harris said, according to the *Atlanta Constitution*. "I don't know who will be Senator Gorman's successor."[77]

Several senators emerged as potential candidates to be the next Democratic floor leader. James K. Jones (D, Ark.), who had served in the Senate since 1885, was mentioned frequently in newspaper accounts. Chairman of the Democratic National Committee, Jones was an expert on finance and tariff matters and well-versed in parliamentary strategy, but he could be "cold" and "distant" in his interactions with others.[78] Still, one of his colleagues, writing a decade later, remembered Jones as "a man of large executive ability," someone with the capacity "to address himself to the individual men composing the Senate, to go to one to-day, to another to-morrow, to another the day after, and so

---

[73] "There Will Be Senate Changes," *Atlanta Constitution*, Nov. 9, 1898, 4; "Retire to Private Life," *Washington Post*, Mar. 5, 1899, 22; "Statesmen Ill from Grip," *New York Times*, Jan. 3, 1899, 3.

[74] "Will Succeed Mr. Gorman," *Baltimore Sun*, Feb. 2, 1899, 1.

[75] "Capitol Chat," *Washington Post*, Feb. 9, 1899, 6.

[76] "Gorman and Mills Soon to Be Memories," *North American*, Feb. 27, 1899, 5.

[77] "Bacon as Leader of the Democrats," *Atlanta Constitution*, Nov. 17, 1899, 1.

[78] "Senator J. K. Jones," *Arkansas Democrat*, Mar. 15, 1899, 2. See also "Will Succeed Mr. Gorman," *Baltimore Sun*, Feb. 2, 1899, 1; "Capitol Chat," *Washington Post*, Feb. 9, 1899, 6.

continually trying to find a common ground upon which all could meet" (Chilton 1908, 57). Another candidate for leadership was Francis Cockrell (D, Mo.), an ally of Gorman who had served in the Senate since 1875 and built a reputation as "the guardian of the national treasury."[79] But both Jones and Cockrell seemed to lack the qualities that Gorman exemplified. As Harris stated in the *Atlanta Constitution*, "Neither of them will supply Gorman's alertness, astuteness and resourcefulness."[80] Harris, along with others, viewed Augustus Bacon (D, Ga.) more favorably, as someone with the energy and determination to lead the caucus in the years ahead. The Philadelphia *North American* listed George Vest (D, Mo.), John T. Morgan (D, Ala.), and John W. Daniel (D, Va.) as other men who could provide leadership in the wake of Gorman's retirement. But this newspaper, too, was hesitant in making predictions as it surveyed the field. "It seems to be pretty generally accepted that the Democratic party will be at a disadvantage in the new Senate in the matter of an able and strong man on the floor to shape its course," the *North American* wrote. "Senator Jones, of Arkansas, hardly fills the bill. Senator Cockrell is almost too old, and Senator Vest's health is so poor that he cannot be counted on for very much aggressive and active work. Senator Morgan is easily the best equipped man on the Democratic side of the chamber, but his health will hardly permit him to become the leader of his party."[81]

Although there was some lingering ambiguity that year regarding the responsibility of the caucus chairman to serve as the party's leader on the floor—with some insisting that Democratic leadership was not necessarily vested in the caucus chairman[82]—Gorman's example was too powerful to dismiss. "From the time Senator Gorman went out of the Senate, Senator Jones held the chairmanship of the so-called Minority Conference in that body," Newberry (1913, 117) wrote. "This carried with it the position of floor leader." As Table A.2 shows, James K. Jones was elected the new caucus chairman in December 1899 and, with his election, other senators quickly came to regard him as the minority leader and to evaluate his effectiveness by that standard. The account of Jones's election was brief, but the language used by the *Washington Post* indicated that expectations for the position had shifted decisively. "The Democrats recognized the leadership of Senator Jones, of Arkansas, by making him their caucus chairman," the *Post* reported in December 1899.[83] It is the earliest election account we have uncovered stating that "leadership" was now the basis for selecting a Senate caucus chairman.

---

[79] "Will Succeed Mr. Gorman," *Baltimore Sun*, Feb. 2, 1899, 1. See also "Mr. Gorman Retires," *Washington Post*, Apr. 30, 1898, 4.

[80] "Bacon as Leader of the Democrats," *Atlanta Constitution*, Nov. 17, 1899, 1. See also "Capitol Chat," *Washington Post*, Feb. 9, 1899, 6.

[81] "Gorman and Mills Soon to Be Memories," *North American*, Feb. 27, 1899, 5.

[82] "Gorman and Mills Soon to Be Memories," *North American*, Feb. 27, 1899, 5.

[83] "Both Parties in Caucus," *Washington Post*, Dec. 6, 1899, 4.

Over the next few months, observers routinely identified Jones as "the Democratic leader," "the leader of the Democratic side," or "the leader of the minority in the Senate."[84]

As Democratic caucus chairman, Jones was measured by his ability to lead his party on the floor, and he fell short. Where Gorman established the precedent that Democrats would look to their caucus chairman as their floor leader, Jones demonstrated that fecklessness as a leader would cause many observers to contend that Senate Democrats needed a new caucus chairman. "Dissatisfaction with the leadership of Jones has become general on the Democratic side," the *Kansas City Star* reported in March 1901. "The reorganization of the Democratic steering committee is under consideration with a view to substituting some other senator for Senator Jones as chairman and leader of the party on the floor of the Senate."[85] The criticism of Jones—and the drumbeat of calls to elect some other senator to lead the caucus—began early in 1901 and continued through the year. The *Atlanta Constitution* stated in March that Augustus Bacon was denying reports "that he is seeking to replace Senator Jones, of Arkansas, as leader of the democratic minority in the senate." According to the newspaper, Bacon believed that such a contest "might do more harm than good," since any effort to defeat Jones could rupture the party.[86] A week later, however, the *Constitution* published a story suggesting that many senators continued to hope that Bacon would challenge Jones for the leadership post. "Strong pressure is being brought to bear upon Senator Bacon to accept the chairmanship of the democratic steering committee of the senate, which carries with it the minority leadership," the *Constitution* wrote. "There is a great deal of dissatisfaction with Jones's leadership."[87] That fall, the *Baltimore Sun* reported that concerns remained, even if it now seemed likely that no one would stand to oppose Jones's reelection. "Toward the close of the last Congress considerable grumbling was heard within the ranks of the minority, and there was some talk of deposing Senator Jones and electing a new chairman of the Democratic caucus," the *Sun* reported in November 1901. "A contest with this in view might have been begun but for the fact that those opposed to Senator Jones could not agree upon anyone whom they regarded as

[84] "Twice Called Traitor," *Washington Post*, Feb. 1, 1900, 1; "Mr. Aldrich's Clever Move," *Washington Post*, Feb. 7, 1900, 4; "Free Silver Knocked Out," *Los Angeles Times*, Feb. 16, 1900, 1; "Senate Passes Currency Bill," *New York Times*, Feb. 16, 1900, 1; "For National Defense," *Washington Post*, Mar. 10, 1900, 1; "Harmony Not in Sight," *Washington Post*, Mar. 16, 1900, 4; "No Extra Star for Miles," *Washington Post*, Apr. 28, 1900, 4; "Congress to Adjourn in June," *Washington Post*, May 3, 1900, 3.

[85] "They Doubt Senator Jones," *Kansas City Star*, Mar. 8, 1901, 2. See also "To Depose Jones," *Dallas Morning News*, Mar. 9, 1901, 1; "Want a New Leader," *Boston Herald*, Mar. 8, 1901, 2; "Democratic Leadership," *Boston Herald*, Mar. 9, 1901, 14.

[86] "Senator Bacon to Make No Fight for Leadership," *Atlanta Constitution*, Mar. 1, 1901, 1.

[87] "Bacon Suggested for Leadership," *Atlanta Constitution*, Mar. 10, 1901, 2.

entitled to be his successor."[88] Although Jones indicated at the December caucus meeting that some senators might wish to nominate a new leader, the Senate Democrats "unanimously" reelected him.[89]

One month later, in January 1902, the Maryland legislature returned Gorman to the Senate for the term beginning in 1903 (Lambert 1953, 291; Gould 2005, 28). Democrats had won control of the state legislature, and he was the unanimous choice of his party's caucus in Annapolis.[90] "Ever since the overthrow in 1895 of the organization he had absolutely controlled for years," the *New York Times* reported in January 1902, "ex-Senator Gorman has been quietly planning and working to restore his party to power in Maryland, and secure his return to the Senate."[91] Then, in March, Jones was defeated in Arkansas's Democratic primary for election to another term in the Senate.[92] "He succeeded Arthur P. Gorman as the leader of the minority in the Senate," the *Washington Post* observed. "Singular as it may seem, Gorman will return to the Senate on the same day that Mr. Jones leaves it."[93] Senators began looking ahead to the next Congress and considering anew the question of Democratic Senate leadership. The *Baltimore Sun* noted in April 1902 that it was generally assumed that Gorman would be elected to his old position of "leadership of the Democratic side in the Senate" when he returned to Washington.[94] But even Gorman faced opposition. A few younger members of the Democratic caucus expressed reservations, insisting that they would support his election only if he committed himself to naming two younger Democrats to the party's steering committee. "A movement is on foot among the older Democrats of the Senate to establish Senator A. P. Gorman at once in the leadership of the minority," the *Baltimore Sun* reported in March 1903. "It has developed, however, that there will be opposition on the part of the younger element which has

---

[88] "No One Yet to Lead," *Baltimore Sun*, Nov. 24, 1901, 9.
[89] "Democratic Senators," *Washington Evening Star*, Dec. 12, 1901, 17.
[90] "Gorman Wins in Maryland," *New York Times*, Nov. 7, 1901, 2; "To Re-Elect Mr. Gorman," *New York Times*, Nov. 10, 1901, 3; "Arthur Pue Gorman," *Washington Post*, Nov. 17, 1901, 18; "Changes in the Senate," *Washington Post*, Nov. 19, 1901, 6; "Pledge Support to Gorman," *New York Times*, Dec. 31, 1901, 1; "First Session Brief," *Washington Post*, Jan. 2, 1902, 4; "Gorman Sure of the Toga," *Atlanta Constitution*, Jan. 2, 1902, 2; "Gorman Gets All," *Washington Post*, Jan. 9, 1902, 3; "Gorman on the Scene," *Washington Post*, Jan. 14, 1902, 3; "Gorman Sure of Election," *New York Times*, Jan. 14, 1902, 3; "Mr. Gorman Chosen," *Washington Post*, Jan. 15, 1902, 1; "Gorman Easily Elected," *New York Times*, Jan. 15, 1902, 3.
[91] "Gorman Easily Elected," *New York Times*, Jan. 15, 1902, 3.
[92] "Jones' Fate in Balance," *Atlanta Constitution*, Mar. 29, 1902, 3; "Senate to Loose [sic] James K. Jones," *Chicago Tribune*, Mar. 30, 1902, 2; "Clarke Takes Toga from Senator Jones," *Atlanta Constitution*, Mar. 30, 1902, 3; "Defeat of Senator Jones," *Atlanta Constitution*, Mar. 31, 1902, 4.
[93] Amos J. Cummings, "James K.'s Last Swim," *Washington Post*, Apr. 20, 1902, 15.
[94] "Must Start Anew," *Baltimore Sun*, Apr. 17, 1902, 2.

dominated during the last two years."[95] After Gorman agreed to expand the size of the steering committee, the opposition evaporated.[96] The *Washington Evening Star* reported that Gorman was elected "by common consent and without the suggestion of rivalry."[97]

Coverage of the 1903 caucus meeting and Gorman's election was extensive, appearing prominently in both national and regional newspapers. Almost always, these accounts identified the dual nature of the post.[98] The *New York Times* emphasized that, with his election as Democratic caucus chairman, Gorman became the "parliamentary leader" of Senate Democrats.[99] The *Chicago Tribune* explicitly noted that Gorman had been elected minority leader when he was elected caucus chairman. "Senator Gorman today was chosen formally leader of the democratic party in the senate," the *Tribune* explained to its readers. "He becomes chairman of the caucus committee, which carries with it the position of chairman of the caucus and chairman of the steering committee, as well as floor leader of the party."[100] The *Baltimore Sun* declared that Gorman's election to the position of caucus chairman "carries with it the leadership of the minority."[101] The *Wilkes-Barre Times* explained to its readers that Gorman was elected to the position of "chairman of caucus and leader in the minority on the floor of the Senate."[102] The *Charlotte Observer* wrote simply, "He was this morning selected as the Democratic leader in the Senate."[103]

In December 1905, when Gorman was reelected— as "chairman of the caucus and leader of his party on the floor," in the words of the *Baltimore Sun*; "minority leader of the Senate," in the words of the *Washington Post*[104]— several of his colleagues had begun asking whether he should continue in the post. Suffering from declining health and unable to hold his fragmented caucus together, Gorman seemed to be failing in the leadership role to which he had been elected—the role that he himself had invented. "The wreck of Gorman as a political leader has been in process since he re-entered the Senate two years

[95] "Some Opposition to Gorman," *Baltimore Sun*, Mar. 6, 1903, 1. See also Acheson 1932, 159–60.
[96] "Gorman Chosen Leader," *Baltimore Sun*, Mar. 7, 1903, 1.
[97] "Democratic Caucus," *Washington Evening Star*, Mar. 6, 1903, 1.
[98] "Gorman the Senate Leader," *Kansas City Star*, Mar. 6, 1903, 1; "Democratic Caucus," *Washington Evening Star*, Mar. 6, 1903, 1; "Gorman Leader," *Aberdeen Daily News*, Mar. 7, 1903, 1; "Gorman at Helm for Democrats," *Philadelphia Inquirer*, Mar. 7, 1903, 7; "Gorman for Leader," *Washington Post*, Mar. 7, 1903, 4; "Leader Gorman," *Los Angeles Times*, Mar. 8, 1903, 1.
[99] "Gorman Chosen Leader," *New York Times*, Mar. 7, 1903, 9.
[100] "Gorman to Lead Party in Nation," *Chicago Tribune*, Mar. 7, 1903, 1.
[101] "Gorman Chosen Leader," *Baltimore Sun*, Mar. 7, 1903, 1.
[102] "Gorman Democratic Leader for Senate," *Wilkes-Barre Times*, Mar. 6, 1903, 8.
[103] "Gorman Selected as Leader," *Charlotte (N.C.) Observer*, Mar. 7, 1903, 1.
[104] "Gorman Still Leader," *Baltimore Sun*, Dec. 9, 1905, 2; "Gorman Again Chosen as the Minority Leader," *Washington Post*, Dec. 9, 1905, 4.

ago and was hoisted immediately and with acclaim to the leadership," the *New York Times* observed.[105] As Joseph Bailey (D, Tex.) took on day-to-day leadership responsibilities on the floor, Charles Willis Thompson, correspondent for the *New York Times*, observed growing "Democratic restlessness, which began back in the days of the leadership of James K. Jones."[106] But this was a restlessness that had an obvious institutional resolution. "Bailey is unmistakably at the front now," Thompson wrote in January 1906, "and will undoubtedly become the titular leader immediately upon Gorman's retirement."[107] Indeed, on the very day that Thompson's story appeared, at a time when Gorman was weak but still quite alive, Bailey issued a statement denying any interest in becoming caucus chairman should Gorman "relinquish the leadership."[108] It was an astonishing, even presumptuous, statement, covered by newspapers that were themselves engaged in feverish discussion of when Gorman would step down as minority leader and enable his colleagues to elect Bailey as successor.

As the *Washington Evening Star* recognized in June 1906, upon Gorman's death, the big question in Congress was this: "Who will succeed Mr. Gorman as minority leader in the Senate?"[109] Within days of Gorman's death, when Democratic senators met to elect Blackburn (rather than the controversial Bailey) as their new caucus chairman, they unanimously adopted a resolution declaring that Blackburn, by this election, was now "their chosen official leader in the great forum of the Senate of the United States."[110] Bailey continued to play a prominent role on the floor of the Senate (Barfield 1970, 318–19; Sarasohn 1989, 6), but observers understood that the role of Democratic leader

---

[105] "Gorman Left Behind in Rush of Politics," *New York Times*, Nov. 20, 1905, 9.

[106] "Gorman to Quit Lead of Senate Minority," *New York Times*, Dec. 23, 1905, 4. See also Acheson 1932, 173, 186; "Gorman Still Leader," *Baltimore Sun*, Dec. 9, 1905, 2; "Gorman Again Chosen as the Minority Leader," *Washington Post*, Dec. 9, 1905, 4.

[107] "Hale Senate Leader, Succeeding Aldrich," *New York Times*, Jan. 2, 1906. See also "Gorman Still Leader," *Baltimore Sun*, Dec. 9, 1905, 2; "2 Leaders for Democrats," *New York Times*, Dec. 9, 1905, 6; "Gorman to Quit Lead of Senate Minority," *New York Times*, Dec. 23, 1905, 4; "Bailey Will Not Be Leader," *New York Times*, Jan. 3, 1906, 1; "No Leadership for Joe Bailey," *Atlanta Constitution*, Jan. 3, 1906, 11; "Hale, Senate Leader, a Warrior for Peace," *New York Times*, Jan. 8, 1906, 9; "Spar for Points," *Washington Post*, Feb. 16, 1906, 4; "No Amendments to Hepburn Bill," *Washington Post*, Feb. 24, 1906, 1; "Democrats to Confer," *Washington Post*, Mar. 13, 1906, 4; "Personality of Senators Who Lead in Railroad Rate Discussion," *Washington Post*, Mar. 18, 1906, M6; "Speaks on Rate Bill," *Washington Post*, Mar. 20, 1906, 4.

[108] "Bailey Will Not Be Leader," *New York Times*, Jan. 3, 1906, 1. See also "No Leadership for Joe Bailey," *Atlanta Constitution*, Jan. 3, 1906, 11; "Topics of the Times," *New York Times*, Jan. 4, 1906, 10; "Hale, Senate Leader, a Warrior for Peace," *New York Times*, Jan. 8, 1906, 9.

[109] "The Senate's Minority Leadership," *Washington Evening Star*, June 7, 1906, 4.

[110] "Blackburn's Election," *Washington Evening Star*, June 9, 1906, 5. See also Ritchie 1998a, 9; McConnell and Brownell 2019, 143.

was assigned by election, even if the Democratic floor leaders of that decade were distinguished more for their deficiencies than their achievements. Blackburn himself had been chosen to fill the position until his retirement from the Senate in the next year and to avoid, for a few months, conflict within the caucus over the choice of a new floor leader.[111] "Mr. Blackburn, who succeeded to the post of leadership, was but a stop-gap," the *Washington Evening Star* explained. "The prize was of the consolation order, and was thrown to him because of his age and his defeat at home. Had there been the need of a strong man just then he, of course, would not have been chosen."[112]

The looming leadership contest was a constant topic of conversation in the Senate Democratic cloakroom in the first two months of 1907, and discussion and speculation continued through the lengthy recess that spring, summer, and fall.[113] As the *Chicago Tribune* observed in February, Blackburn "retires from the senate next month, and then there will be a battle royal."[114] Joseph Bailey (D, Tex.), Augustus Bacon (D, Ga.), Charles Culberson (D, Tex.), Thomas Martin (D, Va.), William Stone (D, Mo.), John W. Daniel (D, Va.), Furnifold Simmons (D, N.C.), Lee Overman (D, N.C.), and Murphy Foster (D, La.) were all regarded as serious candidates for the minority leadership. "It is not an easy matter to find a man who will combine good qualities of leadership on the floor of the Senate with ability to preserve Democratic harmony," the *New York Times* observed. "The job is not going begging. There are aspirants in plenty, though it is not generally considered a position for which a Senator comes out boldly and announces himself a candidate."[115] In December 1907, Culberson was elected "minority leader of the Senate" by the Democratic caucus.[116]

[111] "Blackburn to Lead Minority," *Washington Evening Star*, June 8, 1906, 1; "The Two Texas Stars Rivals in the Senate," Columbia (S.C.) *State*, June 12, 1906, 6.

[112] "Culberson of Texas," *Washington Evening Star*, Nov. 6, 1907, 4. See also "Democrats at Sea without a Pilot," *Chicago Tribune*, Feb. 19, 1907, 1; "The Senate's Minority Leadership," *Washington Evening Star*, May 3, 1907, 4; McConnell and Brownell 2019, 142–44.

[113] "Senate Democrats Look for a Leader," *New York Times*, Jan. 30, 1907, 4. See also "Bailey is an Embarrassment," *Kansas City Star*, Jan. 26, 1907, 7; "May Ask Vindication," *Dallas Morning News*, Jan. 27, 1907, 1; "The Senate's Minority Leader," *Washington Evening Star*, Jan. 27, 1907, 20; "Senate Minority," *Washington Sunday Star*, Feb. 3, 1907, 2; "Democrats Can't Agree," *Washington Post*, Feb. 14, 1907, 4; "Democrats at Sea without a Pilot," *Chicago Tribune*, Feb. 19, 1907, 1; "Bailey May Be Made Leader in the Senate," *Lexington Herald*, Mar. 4, 1907, 1; "Texan is Chosen," *Dallas Morning News*, May 1, 1907, 1; "The Senate's Minority Leadership," *Washington Evening Star*, May 3, 1907, 4; "Culberson Liked," *Dallas Morning News*, May 5, 1907, 2; "Lane Marking Time," *Dallas Morning News*, July 28, 1907, 29; "Culberson in Favor," *Dallas Morning News*, Sept. 20, 1907, 6; "Culberson of Texas," *Washington Evening Star*, Nov. 6, 1907, 4; "Speaking of Culberson," *Dallas Morning News*, Nov. 7, 1907, 2; "Heard on a Street Car," *Macon Daily Telegraph*, Nov. 11, 1907, 4.

[114] "Democrats at Sea without a Pilot," *Chicago Tribune*, Feb. 19, 1907, 1.

[115] "Senate Democrats Look for a Leader," *New York Times*, Jan. 30, 1907, 4.

[116] "Culberson Is Elected," *Washington Post*, Dec. 4, 1907, 4.

Culberson was reelected caucus chairman and Democratic leader in March 1909 but resigned his position that December because of illness.[117] For his successor, the Democrats avoided a contest by selecting Hernando Money (D, Miss.). In electing Money as their leader, the Democrats were paying tribute to another colleague in poor health, who had already announced his intention to retire from the Senate in 1911. They made this decision, it appears, in order to avoid dividing the caucus. "The Democratic members of the Senate having become sadly divided over the question of the minority leadership, decided in effect to postpone the selection of a leader for another 16 months by persuading Senator Money to accept the leadership," the *Dallas Morning News* explained. "This will throw the selection of the party's leader to March, 1911, when Senator Money retires from the Senate."[118]

The new Congress convened in April 1911, called into extraordinary session by William Howard Taft. Democrats had made large gains in both chambers, taking control of the House of Representatives for the first time since 1895 and capturing 12 new seats in the Senate.[119] Just eight seats separated the Republican majority and Democratic minority, the smallest margin between the two Senate parties since 1897. Champ Clark was now speaker of the House, replacing Joseph Cannon, who had been humbled by the historic revolt in the preceding Congress. Many senators identified as insurgents or progressives, and long-time conservative leaders in both the Republican and Democratic caucuses struggled to accommodate the insurgency. In the Republican Senate caucus, insurgents, organized as a bloc of 12 members, insisted on one-quarter of the seats on major committees as well as substantial representation on the steering committee and committee on committees, and the caucus majority acceded to this demand.[120]

---

[117] "Senate Revolt Ends," *New York Tribune*, Mar. 6, 1909, 2; "Culberson Will Continue as Leader," *Dallas Morning News*, Mar. 6, 1909, 1; "Culberson Will Resign," *Los Angeles Times*, Dec. 5, 1909, 14; "Culberson Quits Post of Leader," *Atlanta Constitution*, Dec. 5, 1909, D7; "Culberson to Quit," *New York Tribune*, Dec. 5, 1909, 5; "Culberson Gives up Senate Leadership," *New York Times*, Dec. 5, 1909, 12; "Culberson Resigns Chair," *Washington Post*, Dec. 5, 1909, 1; "Due to Ill Health," *Washington Sunday Star*, Dec. 5, 1909, 2; "Culberson Resigns as Minority Leader," *Fort Worth Star-Telegram*, Dec. 5, 1909, 1; "The Senate Minority," *Washington Evening Star*, Dec. 6, 1909, 6.

[118] "Mr. Money as Compromise," *Dallas Morning News*, Dec. 10, 1909, 1. See also "Election Is Deferred: Choice of Minority Leader in the Senate," *Washington Evening Star*, Dec. 6, 1909, 2; "No Minority Leader Yet," *New York Tribune*, Dec. 7, 1909, 2; "Money the Captain," *New York Tribune*, Dec. 10, 1909, 3; "Money Chosen Party Leader," *Atlanta Constitution*, Dec. 10, 1909, 6; "Senator H. D. Money Minority Leader," *Macon Daily Telegraph*, Dec. 10, 1909, 1; "Senator A. D. Money New Minority Leader," *Macon Daily Telegraph*, Dec. 15, 1909, 1.

[119] "Congress Opens; Clark Speaker," *New York Times*, Apr. 5, 1911, 1.

[120] "Mann Made Leader of House Minority," *New York Times*, Apr. 4, 1911, 1; "Congress Opens; Clark Speaker," *New York Times*, Apr. 5, 1911, 1; "Insurgent Senators Win," *New York Times*, Apr. 5, 1911, 2; "Senate Dozen Win," *Washington Post*, Apr. 5, 1911, 1; "New

Erupting on the Democratic side of the chamber in 1911 was the first open leadership contest in Senate history. Progressives, following the lead of three-time presidential candidate William Jennings Bryan, mounted a campaign to elect one of their own as the new minority leader (Reeves 1960, 357–58; Barfield 1965, 289–93; Strother 1966, 31; Haughton 1973, 29–33; Holt 1975, 5–6; Sarasohn 1989, 101). The campaign lasted for a month, from the start of March through the first week of April. Bailey, widely regarded since the mid-1900s as the most effective Democrat on the floor of the Senate, had failed to secure election in 1907 as his party's minority leader, due in part to charges of corruption growing out of work he had done for an oil company that had violated antitrust law.[121] Bypassing Bailey again in the spring of 1911, regular Democrats gave their support to Thomas Martin, a Virginia senator in his third term.[122] Progressives rejected Martin and considered as alternatives Culberson, Stone, Thomas Gore (D, Okla.), Francis Newlands (D, Nev.), John Sharp Williams (D, Miss.), and, finally, Benjamin Shively (D, Ind.). In an effort to prevent an open contest, Democratic senators did not call an organizational caucus at the opening of the session, as was the usual practice. According to the *Washington Post*, "It was manifest that an effort was being made to harmonize the conflicting differences, if possible, and to elect a chairman unanimously."[123]

Senate Meets," *Washington Post*, Apr. 5, 1911, 4; "Fair Share Granted," *Washington Evening Star*, Apr. 5, 1911, 10.

[121] "The Two Texas Stars Rivals in the Senate," Columbia (S.C.) *State*, June 12, 1906, 6; "The Senate's Minority Leader," *Washington Evening Star*, Jan. 27, 1907, 20; "May Ask Vindication," *Dallas Morning News*, Jan. 27, 1907, 1; "Senate Democrats Look for a Leader," *New York Times*, Jan. 30, 1907, 4; "Senate Minority," *Washington Sunday Star*, Feb. 3, 1907, 2; "Democrats at Sea without a Pilot," *Chicago Tribune*, Feb. 19, 1907, 1; "Bailey May Be Made Leader in the Senate," *Lexington Herald*, Mar. 4, 1907, 1.

[122] "Looking for a New Leader," Biloxi (Miss.) *Daily Herald*, Mar. 7, 1911, 1; "Senator Bailey's Resignation," Columbia (S.C.) *State*, Mar. 7, 1911, 4; "Party Leadership Is Now Discussed," *Columbus (Ga.) Enquirer*, Mar. 11, 1911, 6; "Senate Dozen Win," *Washington Post*, Apr. 5, 1911, 1; "New Senate Meets," *Washington Post*, Apr. 5, 1911, 4; "Bryan Foe to Martin," *Washington Post*, Apr. 6, 1911, 4; "Senate Democrats Appear Divided," *Dallas Morning News*, Apr. 6, 1911, 6; "Martin's Defeat Urged by Bryan," *Atlanta Constitution*, Apr. 6, 1911, 6; "Martin's Chances Are Growing Less," *Atlanta Constitution*, Apr. 7, 1911, 7; "Martin for Senate Leader," *New York Times*, Apr. 7, 1911, 1; "Democrats in Senate in Hot Fight," *Bellingham (Wash.) Herald*, Apr. 7, 1911, 10; "Martin's Opponents Promise Contest," *Dallas Morning News*, Apr. 7, 1911, 6; "Senate Has a Contest, Too," *Kansas City Star*, Apr. 7, 1911, 6; "Virginia Senator to Be Democratic Leader in Senate," *Fort Worth Star-Telegram*, Apr. 7, 1911, 1; "May Be Explosion in Senate Caucus," Columbia (S.C.) *State*, Apr. 7, 1911, 1; "Defeat for Bryan in Senate Caucus," *New York Times*, Apr. 8, 1911, 1.

[123] "Senate Dozen Win," *Washington Post*, Apr. 5, 1911, 1.

Thomas S. Martin (D, Va.), on right, with Frank Putnam Flint (R, Calif.). In April 1911 Martin won the first open contest in Senate history to become Democratic floor leader, defeating Benjamin Shively (D, Ind.) by a vote of 21–16 in the caucus.

Library of Congress, Prints & Photographs Division, photograph by Harris & Ewing, reproduction number LC-DIG-hec-01071

But unanimity could not be secured. Bryan himself came to Washington to galvanize progressives against Martin's election as floor leader.[124] "A bomb is expected to explode when the senate Democratic caucus [meets] to select a minority leader tomorrow," the Columbia (S.C.) *State* wrote, describing the tense atmosphere on Capitol Hill on April 6. "In the senate chamber proper, in the lobbies of the capitol and in the offices of the various senators, little else was discussed today. Those who are opposed to Senator Martin say that by voting for him Democratic senators can give the nearest possible indorsement to the Payne-Aldrich tariff."[125] When the vote came, Martin defeated Shively on a roll call, 21 votes to 16.[126] "If there ever was a time when the party needed harmonious action it was now," Augustus Bacon said after the vote, in remarks paraphrased in the *Post*. "For the first time during the sixteen years of his service, he said, a ballot had been taken for the election of a chairman of the caucus. He hoped it would be the last time, and at that sentiment there was a general shaking of heads in approval. Hitherto such action has been unanimous and by common consent."[127] The *New York Times* described the vote as a "direct slap at the efforts of William Jennings Bryan to organize the Senate minority on a radical basis," and Bryan was, indeed, enraged by the caucus's action.[128] Two weeks later Bryan excoriated Martin—and the Senate Democrats who had elected him—in an editorial titled "Mr. Martin, Leader (?)" that dominated the front page of his weekly newspaper, *The Commoner*. "Mr. Martin's record is just about as bad as it could be and his selection not only stifles the party but brings odium upon those who are responsible for his elevation," Bryan contended in the editorial. "Martinism will become as obnoxious to the democrats as Aldrichism did to the republicans; the sooner we get rid of it the better for the party, and the country."[129] Bryan expressed the hope that the voters of Virginia would possess the wisdom not to return Martin to the Senate and the confidence that "if Virginia fails to do this the next senate is likely to retire him from leadership."[130]

---

[124] "Bryan Foe to Martin," *Washington Post*, Apr. 6, 1911, 4.
[125] "May Be Explosion in Senate Caucus," Columbia (S.C.) *State*, Apr. 7, 1911, 1.
[126] "Virginia Senator Made Minority Leader," *Bellingham (Wash.) Herald*, Apr. 7, 1911, 7; "Martin Made Leader," *Washington Post*, Apr. 8, 1911, 1; "Defeat for Bryan in Senate Caucus," *New York Times*, Apr. 8, 1911, 1; "Senator Martin Named," *Charlotte (N.C.) Observer*, Apr. 8, 1911, 1; "Martin, Leader of Democrats," *Columbus (Ga.) Enquirer*, Apr. 8, 1911, 1; "Bryanism Divides Senate Democrats," *Philadelphia Inquirer*, Apr. 8, 1911, 7; "Congress Is Waiting," *Washington Post*, Apr. 10, 1911, 5; "The Office Not as Big as It Sounds," *Macon Daily Telegraph*, Apr. 19, 1911, 4.
[127] "Martin Made Leader," *Washington Post*, Apr. 8, 1911, 1.
[128] "Defeat for Bryan in Senate Caucus," *New York Times*, Apr. 8, 1911, 1.
[129] "Mr. Martin, Leader (?)," *The Commoner*, Apr. 21, 1911, 1. See also "Bryan Attacks Senator Martin," *Grand Forks (N.Dak.) Herald*, Apr. 22, 1911, 6; "Leader Martin and Mr. Bryan," *Macon Daily Telegraph*, Apr. 30, 1911, 4.
[130] "Mr. Martin, Leader (?)," *The Commoner*, Apr. 21, 1911, 1. See also "Virginia Vote 85,000," *Washington Post*, Sept. 9, 1911, 5; "Senator Martin's Victory," *New York Times*, Sept. 15, 1911, 8; "Martin and Swanson Elected," *Washington Post*, Jan. 25, 1912, 3.

Martin kept his Senate seat in 1913, but, as Bryan had predicted, Martin lost his position as leader. Senate Democrats had gained seven seats in the new Congress, and most of the caucus now sympathized with progressive policies. For the first time since 1895—midway through Gorman's initial tenure as leader—Democrats controlled the Senate. With Woodrow Wilson's election, the government was unified under Democratic leadership. At last, after almost a generation laboring in the minority, Democrats in the Senate prepared to elect a majority leader and to reorganize the chamber's committees, with many arguing for an end to the seniority system that favored long-time conservative members.[131] "The progressive and reactionary Democrats of the United States senate are engaged in a struggle for control of that body which is exciting extreme bitterness," the *Chicago Tribune* reported in December 1912, three months before the new Senate would convene. "The two factions have lined up over the question of the continuance of Senator Martin of Virginia ... as the leader of the Democrats in the senate."[132] John W. Kern (D, Ind.), who had run for vice president alongside Bryan in 1908, emerged as the candidate for progressives seeking to end Martin's leadership.[133] Kern had so far served just two years in the Senate. He enjoyed the vigorous support not only of Bryan but apparently of Wilson, who was eager to have a reliable ally in the Senate to manage his agenda (Bowers 1918, 289; Reeves 1960, 359–60; Strother 1966, 40–42; Munk 1974, 28; Holt 1975, 7–18; Nelson 1980, 43–44; Oleszek 1991, 19–20; Gould 2005, 56–58). Regular Democrats rallied behind Martin, but they lacked the votes to retain him as leader.[134] In late February 1913, "in the interest of party harmony," Martin withdrew his name as a candidate for reelection, ensuring the unanimous election of Kern the following

---

[131] "Great Struggle Is Forecast in Senate," *Dallas Morning News*, Nov. 10, 1912, 6; "Democratic Fight in Senate Expected," *New York Times*, Nov. 11, 1912, 5; "Mr. Gorman and Mr. Martin," *Washington Evening Star*, Nov. 12, 1912, 6; "Curb on Senators," *Washington Post*, Nov. 29, 1912, 1; "Seek Senate Caucus Control," *Dallas Morning News*, Dec. 11, 1912, 2; "Progressives to Rule," *New York Times*, Dec. 18, 1912, 6; "The Senate Democrats," *Washington Evening Star*, Dec. 20, 1912, 6; "Democrats Confer on Senate Tangle," *Philadelphia Inquirer*, Dec. 21, 1912, 5; "End Seniority Rule," *Washington Post*, Dec. 29, 1912, 4; "Seniority Rule to Be Abolished," *Atlanta Constitution*, Dec. 30, 1912, 2; "Wilson Men Plan U.S. Senate Fight," *New York Times*, Dec. 31, 1912, 4; "Defend Seniority Rule," *Washington Post*, Dec. 31, 1912, 4; "Resembles War on Cannon," *Washington Post*, Jan. 1, 1913, 3; "Plan to Take Lead," *Washington Evening Star*, Jan. 8, 1913, 9.

[132] "Democrats Split on Senate Rule," *Chicago Tribune*, Dec. 10, 1912, 1.

[133] "30 to Vote for Kern," *Washington Post*, Feb. 23, 1913, 4; "Kern as Caucus Head," *Washington Post*, Feb. 24, 1913, 3; "Kern to Succeed Senator Martin as Party Leader," *Atlanta Constitution*, Feb. 24, 1913, 3; "Hope to Oust Martin," *New York Times*, Feb. 27, 1913, 5; "Rough Sledding Ahead for Martin," *Charlotte (N.C.) Observer*, Feb. 27, 1913, 3; "Kern Opposition Diminishes," *Dallas Morning News*, Feb. 28, 1913, 10.

[134] "Democrats Split on Senate Rule," *Chicago Tribune*, Dec. 10, 1912, 1; "Democrats Confer on Senate Tangle," *Philadelphia Inquirer*, Dec. 21, 1912, 5; "Martin Drops Out," *Washington Evening Star*, Feb. 28, 1913, 2; "Radicals Control Senate," *New York Times*, Mar. 6, 1913, 2.

week.[135] Elected by a Democratic party that now controlled the Senate, Kern was the first senator widely known as "majority leader" and the first to hold the position in the majority since Gorman, who had invented it two decades earlier.

REPUBLICAN CAUCUS CHAIRMEN, 1890–1913

Republicans—along with most observers of the Senate—paid little attention in these years to the revolution taking place on the Democratic side of the aisle. For nearly the whole of this period, the Senate was a Republican stronghold, and Republican leadership was collective, embodied in their most powerful committee chairmen and distilled in the Republican steering committee. Republican caucus chairmen continued to be chosen according to seniority, and they held no special responsibility for leading their party. What was true of both parties until the early 1890s remained true of the Republican party until the 1910s: the caucus chairmanship was a largely ceremonial and ministerial position. The great exception, beginning in 1897, was the caucus chairman's role in serving also as chairman of the Republican steering committee, but even there he was often overshadowed by other senators.

Only the most senior members of the party were eligible to be caucus chairmen (Haynes 1938, i: 480). William B. Allison (R, Iowa), beginning his fifth consecutive term in the Senate, was the second-ranking member of his party when, in 1897, he succeeded Sherman to become caucus chairman; Justin Morrill (R, Vt.), the only member with greater seniority, was, at the age of 86, the oldest person ever to have sat in the Senate.[136] Eugene Hale (R, Maine), who succeeded Allison in 1908, was the most senior member of the chamber, having served continuously since 1881. Shelby Cullom (R, Ill.) in 1911, Jacob Gallinger (R, N.H.) in 1913, and Henry Cabot Lodge (R, Mass.) in 1918 all assumed their positions as Republican caucus chairmen on the basis of seniority. "Senator [William] Frye [R, Maine] declined to be chairman of the caucus, because of his infirmity," the *Washington Post* reported in April 1911.

---

[135] "Martin Drops Out," *Washington Evening Star*, Feb. 28, 1913, 2. See also "Leadership in Senate Has Not Been Settled," *Macon Daily Telegraph*, Mar. 1, 1913, 10; "Wilson Men to Run Senate," *New York Times*, Mar. 1, 1913, 7; "Martin Gives up Rule," *Washington Post*, Mar. 1, 1913, 4; "Martin Will Retire as Senate's Leader," Columbia (S.C.) *State*, Mar. 1, 1913, 1; "Martin Calls Senate Caucus for March 5," *Washington Evening Star*, Mar. 1, 1913, 1; "Caucus for Both Houses," *Chicago Tribune*, Mar. 5, 1913, 5; "Kern Is Chosen as Leader at Caucus of Senate," *Bellingham (Wash.) Herald*, Mar. 5, 1913, 1; "Senator Martin's Opportunity," Columbia (S.C.) *State*, Mar. 5, 1913, 4; "John W. Kern Named to Head Senate Caucus," *Christian Science Monitor*, Mar. 5, 1913, 8; "Kern Named to Head Democrats in Senate," *Washington Evening Star*, Mar. 5, 1913, 2; "Kern Is Leader of Democrats," *Los Angeles Times*, Mar. 6, 1913, I:7; "Senator Kern Named to Succeed Martin," *Atlanta Constitution*, Mar. 6, 1913, 2; "Radicals Control Senate," *New York Times*, Mar. 6, 1913, 2; "President's Nominations Confirmed by the Senate," *Wall Street Journal*, Mar. 6, 1913, 3.

[136] "Personal," *New York Times*, Feb. 26, 1897, 6.

"Seniority, that inflexible rule of the Senate, never violated, passed responsibility to Mr. Cullom. He accepted it, and was declared chairman."[137] Cullom, in his fifth term and ranking only behind Frye in seniority, was 81 years old when he was elected. Gallinger, 75, was in his fourth term and ranked first in seniority. With Gallinger's death in 1918, Lodge became the most senior member of the Senate and ascended to the leadership position.[138] Not until 1924, when Charles Curtis (R, Kans.) was elected caucus chairman, was a Republican leader chosen without regard to seniority.

Since the Republican caucus chairmanship was not itself a source of power in the Senate, elections remained perfunctory affairs. In February 1897, the *New York Times* published an article titled "Organizing the Senate," reviewing the changes in Senate offices and committees that were likely to take place when the new Senate convened in special session on March 4.[139] In this account, the *Times* not only discussed the composition of major committees but the position of president pro tempore and even sergeant-at-arms, with the *Times* assuring its curious readers that the incumbent sergeant-at-arms, Richard J. Bright ("a man and officer satisfactory to all parties under the circumstances"), would probably retain his position. Newly elected president William McKinley had asked John Sherman to serve as secretary of state, which left open the chairmanship of the Committee on Foreign Relations and a seat on the Finance Committee. As part of its exhaustive analysis of committee chairmanships and memberships, the *Times* speculated as to who would fill these vacancies left by Sherman. The whole story filled nine, very dense, paragraphs, yet there was no mention of the Republican caucus chairmanship, which Sherman was vacating along with his committee assignments. The *New York Times* took no notice of this position. It would be just a year before Gorman's resignation as Democratic caucus chairman, which by then carried with it the responsibility of party leadership. Yet the contrast in coverage, and presumably interest, could not have been more stark: newspapers across the country published lengthy stories about Gorman's decision to step down in 1898 and the resulting void in Democratic Senate leadership, but none of them regarded as newsworthy Sherman's resignation as Republican caucus chairman. The Republican caucus met on the afternoon of March 6, 1897, and elected Allison its new caucus chairman. The *Washington Post* dedicated eight paragraphs to business conducted at the caucus meeting—and half of one sentence to Allison's election.[140]

---

[137] "Senate Dozen Win," *Washington Post*, Apr. 5, 1911, 1.
[138] "Lodge to Succeed to Leadership," *New York Times*, Aug. 18, 1918, 19; "Republicans Name Lodge as Leader," *Washington Evening Star*, Aug. 24, 1918, 1.
[139] "Organizing the Senate," *New York Times*, Feb. 22, 1897, 2.
[140] "Only Talk in Caucus," *Washington Post*, Mar. 7, 1897, 5. See also "The Senate Organization," *New York Times*, Mar. 7, 1897, 3.

Allison, still caucus chairman, died in 1908. After Hale, his successor as caucus chairman, left the Senate in the spring of 1911, no one emerged to lead the Senate Republicans. There was no senator in the Republican ranks who could duplicate the work of Aldrich, Allison, Hale, and Spooner in building coalitions and in managing the work of their party—whether through the Republican steering committee or as an informal floor leader. As the *Washington Evening Star* observed, "They will sadly lack a fighting captain."[141] More fundamentally, there was no mechanism in existence for selecting that person. Twenty years after Gorman had masterfully fused the positions of caucus chairman and Democratic leader—and at precisely the moment when divisions between progressive and regular Democrats had erupted in a battle for the position of Senate minority leader that was fierce enough to bring William Jennings Bryan to the Capitol—Senate Republicans still relied in 1911 on informal, haphazard methods for coordinating leadership. "After the retirement of the giants will come a 'show down,' it is said; let those who can lead prove their ability," the *Star* reported after Aldrich and Hale had announced their plans to leave the Senate.[142]

Even at this late date, the Republican caucus chairman remained an honorary position, awarded on the basis of seniority, with mainly ministerial duties. Nearly every newspaper in the country covered the dramatic struggle in April 1911, which resulted in Martin's election as Democratic leader and caucus chairman by a 21–16 vote. But the parallel accounts of Cullom's election as Republican caucus chairman that same week were brief and perfunctory.[143] The relationship between insurgents and conservative Republicans had grown tense by 1911, but, in contrast to the case on the Democratic side, there is no indication that any Republican senators saw the caucus chairmanship as a prize to which anyone assigned value. The fight in the Republican caucus was over the distribution of committee assignments. Cullom's election as caucus chairman attracted no special interest, and for the two years that he served there is no evidence that any observers characterized him as his party's leader. "The question is often asked, 'Who has succeeded Aldrich as leader of the Senate?' No one," Cullom himself contended (1911, 425–26). "Leaders are born, not made. Leadership is not a matter of selection, but of fitness."

---

[141] "Leaders in Senate," *Washington Evening Star*, Nov. 20, 1910, 1.

[142] "New Senate Power," *Washington Evening Star*, Apr. 19, 1910, 1. See also "The Senate Leadership," *Washington Post*, July 13, 1910, 6; "The Senate," *Washington Evening Star*, Oct. 24, 1910, 7.

[143] "Congress Opens; Clark Speaker," *New York Times*, Apr. 5, 1911, 1; "Insurgent Senators Win," *New York Times*, Apr. 5, 1911, 2; "Senate Dozen Win," *Washington Post*, Apr. 5, 1911, 1; "Fair Share Granted," *Washington Evening Star*, Apr. 5, 1911, 10.

ELEMENTS OF LEADERSHIP: DEMOCRATS, 1890–1913

From the origins of the Senate in 1789, there have been a multitude of senators who have functioned as bill managers—like Hoar in the 1890–91 effort by Republicans to pass the Federal Elections Bill—and some who have served as unofficial floor leaders, coordinating work for their party across multiple bills. "The practice of floor management of legislation by committee chairmen," according to Peabody (1976, 326), "is as old as the Senate itself." Thompson (1906), the *New York Times* correspondent who wrote extensively on Congress in the mid-1900s, examined the ways in which Aldrich and Hale served, in colloquial terms, as Republican floor leaders in that era and how Bailey assumed that role on the Democratic side, as the party's formal leaders were failing to fulfill their responsibilities. Scholars have identified other senators who functioned, at one time or another, as their party's manager on the floor (McConachie 1898, 339; Kravitz ca. 1971, x: 6–25; Ripley 1969b, 24–29; Munk 1970, 29–52; Riddick 1971, 1–3; Byrd 1991, 186–87). What changed in 1890–91 was that this role became an elected, ongoing institution of the Senate. Gorman and his successors were now accountable, as leaders, to their party colleagues. Journalists and senators referred to Gorman not only as Democratic caucus chairman but also as his party's designated leader in the Senate, and, when he stepped down, his colleagues immediately began to consider the selection of a successor. This shift is visible in Table 5.2, which identifies references to each caucus chairman as his party's leader in the Senate, with stories drawn from seven major newspapers. On the Republican side, apart from a burst of stories referring to Hale as leader, there is no significant number of references until 1913–15, when Gallinger assumes the position. The pattern on the Democratic side is much different. There are multiple references to Gorman as leader throughout the 1890s—the 15 stories referring to Gorman as leader in 1893–95 is three times the number of all references, for both parties, before 1889—and the number increases when Jones succeeds Gorman as floor leader and caucus chairman. References again rise sharply with Culberson in 1907–9, then with Martin in 1911–13, and with Kern in 1913–15. This was an entirely Democratic phenomenon before 1913: there were six times as many references to Martin as the Senate Democratic leader (102) in a single Congress (1911–13) than to every Republican caucus chairman in the period 1857–1913.

In a 1907 editorial, the *Washington Evening Star* described the responsibilities of the Senate minority leader. "He should be a thorough parliamentarian, a tactician of a high order, a clever and a ready debater, and an excellent judge of men," the *Star*'s editors contended. "He should know the qualities and possibilities of every man under him, and be able to command his whole force at a moment's notice. He must also have decision, and always know what is going on in his own, and, if possible, in the other fellow's, camp."[144] Modern Senate leaders, as we have discussed earlier in this book, have a multitude of responsibilities: organizing their caucuses, managing floor business, setting policy, interacting with the president, and acting as their party's spokesperson. Gorman and those who succeeded him as floor leader in the period 1890–1913 understood their job as embracing four of those five responsibilities, all except the role of liaison with the president. Building on the ministerial role of caucus chairmen who had served before them, the new floor leaders organized their caucuses, staffed caucus committees, and played the leading role in making committee assignments. Members also looked to their leaders on the floor, and they expected their leaders to coordinate policy for their party. They began, too, to see their leaders function as spokespersons. But, in this era, there was little evidence that leaders communicated regularly with the president. The ideal leader, in short, was Gorman circa 1890–91, guiding a unified caucus, articulating and pursuing a clear set of policy goals, and formulating a strategy that reflected a command of Senate procedure and an understanding of the chamber's cleavages. It was leadership defined through command of the caucus, the floor, and policy, as well as a willingness to communicate.

This early generation of floor leaders rarely performed these tasks well. Indeed, some of the best evidence that the position of party leader was established in the 1890s is found in the complaints of senators and contemporary observers that Gorman's successors in the 1900s and early 1910s were not leading their party effectively and that, consequently, they should be replaced by new leaders. "Mr. Gorman's service set the pegs pretty high. He had spent so much time in politics, and knew the Senate so thoroughly, he met the matter of his party's responsibility there with unusual success," the *Washington Evening Star* reflected one year after his death. "Caucuses, conferences, feints, and both frontal and flank attacks, were in his line. He grew to be an expert, and able to read with ease a parliamentary situation by the back."[145] In criticizing Jones in November 1901, Democratic senators emphasized Jones's failings both in setting policy for his party and leading them on the floor. "The difficulties which Senator J. K. Jones has encountered as a floor manager of the Senate and a leader of party policy arise chiefly from his temperament, which leads him to be misunderstood," the *Baltimore Sun* claimed. "His failure to inquire into the views of his colleagues to the extent that is expected of a leader has been interpreted by some as evidence of an arrogant assumption of superiority and a purpose to rely upon his own unaided judgment. This has embarrassed his leadership and resulted in lack of harmony in action."[146] Four years later, in evaluating Gorman's second term as leader, the *New York Times* observed that he was failing in his responsibility to unify his party behind a set of policy

---

[144] "The Senate's Minority Leadership," *Washington Evening Star*, May 3, 1907, 4.
[145] "The Senate's Minority Leadership," *Washington Evening Star*, May 3, 1907, 4.
[146] "No One Yet to Lead," *Baltimore Sun*, Nov. 24, 1901, 9.

objectives and to get his colleagues to work together on the floor. "There is a general feeling that the Senate minority ought to be strengthened," the *Times* reported in December 1905. "Never in recent years has it been effective for anything, as it always has been divided."[147] As the *New York Times* observed in January 1907, discussing successors to Blackburn as leader, "It is not an easy matter to find a man who will combine good qualities of leadership on the floor of the Senate with ability to preserve Democratic harmony."[148]

Throughout this era, practice consistently lagged expectations. Democrats between 1890 and 1913 were much more successful at establishing a position and endowing it with clear responsibilities than they were in finding someone who could execute this new job well. Floor leadership remained a relatively primitive institution in these first two decades, and Democratic floor leaders in these years were an easily forgettable set of skippers. Even so, looking at each of the five elements of floor leadership, we see that many aspects of the modern role were established in these years. Observers articulated what was expected of the Democratic floor leader, though they struggled to find someone who possessed these qualities.

Caucus organizer. First and fundamentally, the Democratic leaders were responsible for managing their caucus and their party. Senate leadership grew directly out of the Democratic caucus chairmanship, and, with the reestablishment of Democratic caucus organization in the 1870s, the Democratic caucus chairman had quickly assumed the role of managing the caucus's affairs. Stevenson, Wallace, Pendleton, and Beck—Gorman's predecessors as Democratic caucus chairmen in the 1870s and 1880s—called meetings of their caucus, chaired those meetings, formally notified their Republican counterparts of certain caucus decisions, named caucus committees, and often chaired those same committees. In contrast to Republican organization, where the powers of caucus chairmen remained largely ministerial, the Democratic caucus fused its most powerful offices in one person: the Democratic caucus chairman usually served as chairman of the Democratic committee on committees and, after the committee was reorganized in 1892–93, he served, without exception, as chairman of the Democratic steering committee. In that capacity, the Democratic caucus chairman not only led the effort to direct the Senate party's policy and strategy but also oversaw all of his party's committee assignments.

"The minority chief, a much more powerful personage in the Senate than in the House, has his room in a secluded part of the so-called attic story," McConachie wrote in 1898 (340). "Here he presides at councils which plan the battle in the Senate. He appoints the caucus committees, including that one which slates his party's membership of the Senate's legislative committees, and which is known as the committee on committees. Often the caucus assigns to

[147] "Gorman to Quit Lead of Senate Minority," *New York Times*, Dec. 23, 1905, 4.
[148] "Senate Democrats Look for a Leader," *New York Times*, Jan. 30, 1907, 4.

him powers plenipotentiary for negotiations with the enemy's caucus chairman." In all these ways, the Democratic caucus chairman functioned as the head of his party's caucus organization. These powers were in full flower in 1898, at the end of Gorman's tenure (Rothman 1966, 63; Munk 1970, 43), but they were rooted in the work of his predecessors, as we discussed in earlier chapters. When the Senate Democratic caucus in February 1876 created "a committee of four" to confer with their House counterparts on the composition of the upcoming campaign committee, Stevenson, chairman of the caucus, served as chairman of the Senate group.[149] Three years later, when Democrats gained their first Senate majority in 18 years, Wallace, as caucus chairman, was responsible for convening caucus meetings, for communicating with the House Democratic caucus regarding a decision made in the Senate caucus, and for notifying the Senate Republican caucus of the need to fill some committee vacancies.[150] Pendleton and Beck performed similar organizational duties during their terms as caucus chairmen.[151]

Caucus management was the foundation of Gorman's power, and he expanded his responsibilities in 1892–93, with the reorganization of the Democratic steering committee. Combining the powers of the earlier committee on committees with those of a policy committee, the Democratic steering committee served as the caucus's all-purpose executive committee. Gorman— and each of his successors as caucus chairmen—named the membership of the Democratic steering committee and served as its chairman. Gorman was "indefatigable in his attentions to particular Senators—to all the Democratic Senators—and employed ... the ingratiating influence of hospitality, favoring Senators in regard to Committees, helping them concerning pet measures—and the other expedients of constant personal interest in the affairs of the men with whom he had to deal," Chilton (1908, 74) recollected. "On account of his long service in the Senate, his occupancy of the place as Chairman of the Democratic Caucus, and member of the Committee of Rules he had opportunity to employ individual methods which were not enjoyed by any other Senator on the Democratic side." In April 1894, the *Los Angeles Times* described a "conference" where Gorman alone represented the majority Senate Democrats in a meeting with several Republicans, "known as the steering committee of that party," including Aldrich, Allison, and Hale, to reach agreement on how to proceed with the tariff bill.[152] It was a remarkable moment, putting on vivid

---

[149] "Senatorial Democratic Caucus," *Macon Weekly Telegraph*, Feb. 8, 1876, 8.

[150] "The Oppressive Republican Legislation," *Baltimore Sun*, Feb. 15, 1879, 1; "Senate Democratic Caucus," *Baltimore Sun*, Mar. 17, 1879, 1; "Caucus of Democratic Senators," *Washington Evening Star*, Dec. 2, 1879, 1.

[151] "The Dog in the Manger," *Summit County (Akron, Ohio) Beacon*, May 18, 1881, 2; "The Senatorial Contest," *Philadelphia Inquirer*, Oct. 6, 1881, 1; "The Presidency of the Senate," *Baltimore Sun*, Dec. 5, 1885, 4.

[152] "Lots of Time," *Los Angeles Times*, Apr. 25, 1894, 1. See also "Mills Stands by the Tariff Bill," *Philadelphia Inquirer*, Apr. 25, 1894, 1.

display the competing institutions of Senate leadership that had just then emerged—a single floor leader in one party, a collective steering committee in the other.

Jones, who struggled throughout his caucus chairmanship to unite his caucus and to offer effective leadership, demonstrated his weakness in this realm also. Announcing without consultation the appointment of Henry Teller (D, Colo.) to fill a vacancy on the steering committee, Jones quickly discovered that Teller preferred that someone else, Fred Dubois (D, Idaho), take his spot. Flummoxed, Jones relented, but insisted that he retained the power of making the appointment. "Senator Jones proceeded to inform his colleagues that they were treading on delicate ground when they questioned his authority to appoint whom he pleased to the steering committee," the *Los Angeles Times* reported in 1901. "He wanted it known that the position of chairman carried with it the power and privilege to fill all vacancies without let or hindrance from any source. However, after he cooled off a bit, he declared he was glad Dubois has been selected by him as a member of the steering committee."[153] Gorman, returning as caucus chairman two years later, disappointed younger members of his caucus, especially western progressives, when he filled vacancies on the Democratic steering committee. But the challenge to his appointments collapsed when Gorman threatened to resign as chairman (Lambert 1963, 108).[154] Controlling the steering committee, Gorman showed no reluctance to reward himself with choice committee assignments. "As Chairman of the Democratic steering committee he has abundant chance to get what he wanted by manipulation of the fifty-four vacancies that the Democrats had to fill," the *New York Times* observed, leading many senators "to discuss what was not infrequently called Mr. Gorman's committee hunger."[155] When Culberson assumed the caucus chairmanship, in December 1907, a dissident senator offered a resolution for the caucus to elect the membership of the steering committee. But the resolution was defeated, and instead the caucus adopted a resolution offered by James Taliaferro (D, Fla.), authorizing Culberson to appoint the committee's membership. According to the *Dallas Morning News*, Taliaferro "expressed the opinion that the appointment of the steering committee was properly a prerogative of the chairman of the caucus, and he thought that to deprive him of that privilege would be a disparagement of him."[156]

In 1909, with Money, and in 1911, with Martin, this precedent remained intact. When Money was elected caucus chairman, the *New York Tribune* noted simply that "in a few days a steering committee will be appointed."[157]

[153] "Democratic Rumpus," *Los Angeles Times*, Dec. 11, 1901, 2.
[154] "Gorman Chosen Leader," *New York Times*, Mar. 7, 1903, 9; "Gorman's Lot Hard," *Biloxi (Miss.) Daily Herald*, Mar. 11, 1903, 6.
[155] "Democracy's New Leader," *New York Times*, Nov. 30, 1903, 7.
[156] "Texan Is Elected," *Dallas Morning News*, Dec. 4, 1907, 1.
[157] "Money the Captain," *New York Tribune*, Dec. 10, 1909, 3.

And Martin, the new caucus chairman in April 1911, thoroughly reorganized the Democratic steering committee. Just days after taking office, he removed four sitting senators from the nine-member committee; with Money having left the Senate, Martin appointed five new senators to the steering committee.[158] The *Baltimore Sun* and *New York Times* reported that progressive Democrats were satisfied with their representation on this committee, while the *Washington Post* reported that progressives "made no secret last evening over their disappointment."[159] Five members of the committee were counted among "the newer element" in the caucus, though just two of them had voted for Shively, the candidate of the progressive Democrats, in the recent contest between him and Martin.[160] No one, however, disputed Martin's right to reorganize the Democratic steering committee—or his place as its chairman. "As minority leader," the *Baltimore Sun* explained, Martin "must necessarily be the chairman of the committee."[161] Immediately, Martin went to work making assignments to the Senate's standing committees. "The making up of the Senate committees is not an easy job," he wrote to a Virginia newspaper publisher (Holt 1975, 7). "That matter is requiring a great deal of my time."

Floor manager. With the reorganization of the Democratic steering committee in 1892–93, Gorman strengthened the existing role of the caucus chairman as organizer of his party's affairs. But, more than anyone else in the Senate's history, he invented the second set of responsibilities assumed by modern leaders: leading his party on the floor of the Senate. Prior to Gorman among Senate Democrats, and continuing a generation longer for Senate Republicans, caucus chairmen did their work behind closed doors. It was Gorman's innovation to bring party leadership to the floor. There is no evidence that Democratic caucus chairmen had this responsibility before Gorman. Even Beck, who immediately preceded Gorman in his chair, made no pretense at floor management. Beck was a master of financial legislation, who made his presence known not through his coordination of floor activity or even the ability to respond rapidly to opponents' arguments and tactics but through his carefully constructed remarks. "He is a man full of resources but not a ready debater; his speeches gain when read in print," the *Raleigh Register* reported in 1885. "In delivery Beck is singularly awkward. His heavy, muscular body sways to and fro, while his arms, from the elbow down, keep up a pump-handle movement which makes the Senator frequently appear as if he were engaged in an exercise to aid digestion rather than enforce

---

[158] "Favors Low Tariff Senators," *New York Times*, Apr. 12, 1911, 2.
[159] "Will Steer Minority," *Washington Post*, Apr. 12, 1911, 2. See also "Martin's List Favored," *Baltimore Sun*, Apr. 12, 1911, 2; "Favors Low Tariff Senators," *New York Times*, Apr. 12, 1911, 2.
[160] "Martin's List Favored," *Baltimore Sun*, Apr. 12, 1911, 2.
[161] "Martin's List Favored," *Baltimore Sun*, Apr. 12, 1911, 2.

argument."[162] Gorman, in contrast, announced that he "had had the honor of being selected as Chairman of the caucus of the Democratic Party to determine what measures should be considered," the *New York Times* reported, "and he had faithfully endeavored to carry out the programme—which was, first, the Nicaraguan Canal bill; second, any financial measures reported from the Finance Committee; third, the Bankruptcy bill—with the appropriation bill always and above everything, and then the bills to admit two new states."[163] Gorman possessed "absolute control of the Democratic side of the Senate," the *Boston Herald* reported in 1894. "Such legislation as he approves will be passed at this session by the Senate and none other."[164] As the *Baltimore Sun* noted on the occasion of Gorman's retirement in 1898, he "has for a number of years been the pilot of the senatorial democracy in matters of national legislation, as well as general party politics."[165]

During the battle over the Federal Elections Bill, Gorman was regularly on the Senate floor—managing the filibuster, probing for weaknesses in the Republican coalition, and employing parliamentary maneuvers to obstruct passage of the bill. "Senator Gorman outgeneraled the republicans again today," the *Atlanta Constitution* stated, in the final days of debate over the bill, "and poor old Granny Hoar and his gang of partisans have not been able to tell all day whether they were afloat or sinking."[166] His leadership was active and in public view. Gorman first demonstrated his abilities as floor leader in the debate over the McKinley Tariff Bill in the summer of 1890. It was Gorman whom Aldrich approached that summer to discuss scheduling, and it was Gorman who committed his caucus to an extended debate over the tariff bill.[167] On the floor of the House of Representatives, discussing the tariff bill in September 1890, Rep. Nelson Dingley, Jr. (R, Maine) referred to Gorman as the person in the Senate "who acted as the Democratic leader" and who, in that capacity, spoke for his caucus (*Cong. Rec.*, 1890, 10631, as cited in McConnell and Brownell 2019, 146). As the *Daily Inter Ocean* stated, Gorman directed and coordinated the remarks given by other Democrats and oversaw the party's legislative strategy.[168] That December, as debate began on the elections bill, Gorman led the minority on the floor. Even Republicans sought out Gorman that December "to obtain his permission or approval as to what can or cannot be done," according to the *Chicago Daily Tribune*. "At present he is the

[162] "Democratic Senate Leader," *Raleigh (N.C.) Register*, Dec. 9, 1885, 2. See also "Washington Letter," *Trenton (N.J.) Times*, May 9, 1890, 3.
[163] "Railroads and Pooling," *New York Times*, Feb. 24, 1895, 3.
[164] "Senator Gorman the Boss," *Boston Herald*, Dec. 8, 1894, 3.
[165] "Will Succeed Mr. Gorman," *Baltimore Sun*, Feb. 2, 1899, 1.
[166] "Gorman's Hand," *Atlanta Constitution*, Jan. 22, 1891, 1.
[167] "Sick of Their Dirty Job," *Macon (Ga.) Telegraph*, July 12, 1890, 2; "The Vote on the Tariff Bill," *Washington Post*, Aug. 25, 1890, 4; "Will the Democrats Consent?" *New York Times*, Aug. 25, 1890, 4.
[168] "National Capital Topics," *Chicago Daily Inter Ocean*, July 31, 1890, 9.

dictator of the Senate."[169] He nurtured alliances with Silver Republicans and he attended to proceedings on the floor. On January 5, 1891, when Stewart, a Silver Republican, offered his resolution to table the elections bill so that the Senate could consider a currency bill, Gorman's handiwork was evident. Earlier that day, "Senator Gorman was observed moving about on the democratic side talking earnestly but briefly with his associates," then he offered a point of order at a crucial moment to avoid a delay in voting on Stewart's resolution. After senators voted to lay the elections bill on the table, "all eyes were turned upon Senator Gorman," the *Baltimore Sun* stated. "On every hand Senator Gorman's management was commended in the highest terms."[170]

When, at month's end, the Senate ended all consideration of the bill, many observers attributed the outcome to Gorman's management of the floor. "The peculiarity of Gorman's work is that he accomplishes all he aims to do with such marvelous celerity and in absolute silence," the *Atlanta Constitution* noted. "He gives his lieutenants their instructions in the briefest terms, and, like all great men of action, he has a simply miraculous capacity for selecting fit instruments."[171] Charles J. Faulkner (D, W.Va.), who worked closely with Gorman in the effort to stop the elections bill, offered this characterization of Gorman as floor leader: "sleepless in his activity, watching intelligently every movement of his opponents, never suffering a surprise, ever ready to conform his lines of defense to those of attack, cool, collected, and brave under the varying phases of the contest, and, above all, a natural leader of men."[172] Two years later, in October 1893, the *Knoxville Journal* discussed Gorman's leadership as the Senate debated repeal of the Sherman Silver Purchase Act. "He is the acknowledged and undisputed leader in that body, now that the Democrats are in power there," the *Journal* reflected, "and he has been ever since his signal success as manager of the antiforce bill fight 2-1/2 years ago."[173] When he left the Senate in 1899, the *Washington Post* featured this fight in Gorman's biographical profile. "The defeat of partisan legislation aimed against the South, accomplished through the masterful leadership of Senator Gorman, must ever stand as the great result of the most memorable political battles ever fought in the halls of Congress," the *Post* stated. "For three long months Mr. Gorman parried the thrusts of the Republican opposition, outwitted all their maneuvers, utilized every known parliamentary tactic, and finally came out victorious."[174]

---

[169] "Gorman as a Dictator," *Chicago Tribune*, Dec. 12, 1890, 9.
[170] "From Washington: A Probably Fatal Blow to the Vicious Force Bill," *Baltimore Sun*, Jan. 6, 1891, 1.
[171] "A Constitutional Gossip," *Atlanta Constitution*, Jan. 28, 1891, 4.
[172] "Gorman for President," *Washington Post*, July 19, 1891, 5.
[173] "A Significant Wink," *Knoxville (Tenn.) Journal*, Oct. 10, 1893, 2. See also "The Senate Chairmanships," *New York Tribune*, Mar. 14, 1893, 3; "The Situation in the Senate," *Baltimore Sun*, Aug. 12, 1893, 4.
[174] "Retire to Private Life," *Washington Post*, Mar. 5, 1899, 22.

Gorman's strengths as a floor leader were manifest in 1890–91 and established new expectations for Senate leadership, but it was a standard that neither he nor his successors over the next two decades could meet consistently. Democratic caucus chairmen were now responsible for leading their party on the floor of the Senate, but, more often than not, they did not perform this task well. Leading the majority, in debates over silver purchase repeal and the tariff, Gorman struggled to control the floor in 1893–94 and to broker compromises satisfactory both to his restive caucus and to President Cleveland. Jones, who served as minority leader between 1899 and 1903, was frequently criticized for his inability to manage Democratic business on the floor. He was often not in the Senate at all. Because of Jones's absence in February 1900, the *Washington Post* reported, Aldrich could place a financial bill at the top of the Senate's agenda and, without opposition, secure an agreement for a vote.[175] When Jones was on the floor, attempting to broker agreements with Republicans or oppose their initiatives, he often failed first to consult his caucus, with embarrassing results.[176] "Jones presided over their caucus and bore the name of leader; but every senator was his own captain," Thompson (1906, 109) observed. Consequently, most Democrats celebrated when Jones was defeated for reelection to the Senate and Gorman prepared to return.[177] "No one who knows him doubts Senator Gorman's political astuteness. It is almost a byword," the *Chicago Tribune* reported in March 1903, when Senate Democrats elected Gorman as their floor leader and caucus chairman. "During the four years he has been out of the senate the democratic party in the upper house of congress has been decidedly out at the elbows. It has commanded the respect of no one, has lacked cohesiveness, has run after all sorts of follies, and has been exploited by little men."[178] But Gorman inherited a Democratic party riven by factions and reduced in size, and his old methods of leadership—brokering agreements, making deals, and fighting every initiative of the Republican president Theodore Roosevelt—proved ineffective. "From the day Gorman took the leadership his fame began to crumble. There is nothing left of it now," Thompson (1906, 110, 111) wrote. "The age has passed by and left him." Gorman's health failing, Bailey took on the day-to-day management of the floor.[179]

After Gorman's death in 1906, Democrats continued to look to their caucus chairman to lead them on the floor, and they faced fresh disappointments.

[175] "Mr. Aldrich's Clever Move," *Washington Post*, Feb. 7, 1900, 4.
[176] "Harmony Not in Sight," *Washington Post*, Mar. 16, 1900, 4; "Bacon Suggested for Leadership," *Atlanta Constitution*, Mar. 10, 1901, 2.
[177] "Jones Wouldn't Be Missed," *New York Times*, Mar. 31, 1902, 1.
[178] "Gorman to Lead Party in Nation," *Chicago Tribune*, Mar. 7, 1903, 1.
[179] "Gorman to Quit Lead of Senate Minority," *New York Times*, Dec. 23, 1905, 4; "A Senate Leader," *Grand Forks (N.Dak.) Herald*, Jan. 18, 1906, 3; "Democrats to Confer," *Washington Post*, Mar. 13, 1906, 4; "Gorman Dies Suddenly; Was Seemingly Better," *New York Times*, June 5, 1906, 9.

Blackburn, chosen in 1906 as a caretaker to fill the position until the new Congress assembled the following year, displayed brief flashes of leadership during his tenure. As debate was concluding regarding the Brownsville resolutions in January 1907, "Mr. Blackburn, minority leader in the Senate, yesterday proved his right to that title," the *Washington Post* declared. "Mr. Blackburn offered an amendment that threw the Republicans into confusion. It was a veritable parliamentary bomb, hurled with unerring aim."[180] But, for Blackburn, moments such as this were rare. In 1908 Culberson, in his role as "the minority floor leader in the Senate," informed Republican leaders that his colleagues would allow a vote on the ship subsidy bill but insist on "full discussion" before agreeing to a vote on a currency bill.[181] And, according to Madden (1929, 182), he led the Senate fight against the Payne-Aldrich tariff legislation. However, as was the case with his predecessors, Culberson fulfilled his floor responsibilities only fitfully. "Senators say that the minority leader must possess oratorical ability and parliamentary skill as prerequisites," the *Washington Evening Star* explained in 1909. "The minority leader must also have a physique to stand intense physical strain. He must be in attendance upon the sessions of the Senate almost continuously, and constantly on the alert."[182] Culberson struggled with ill health, and Bailey, as before, regularly stepped in to play this crucial role for the Senate minority. Money, too, failed to meet expectations. "The Democratic minority in the senate is disappointed in their leader. He's too peaceful-like," the *Wilkes-Barre Times* reported in May 1910. "Money leaves the senate in March and he says he is glad of it, as are many of the minority who thought they were going to have a real leader at last."[183]

By 1911, cynicism ruled the day. Senate Democrats had been designating their leader for two decades, their leader was responsible for floor management, yet this responsibility was honored much more in the breach than in the execution. "The only thing clearly established concerning the post of Democratic leader in the Senate as at present constituted seems to be that he doesn't lead. Money didn't, nor did Culberson before him," the *Macon Telegraph* (quoting *Harper's Weekly*) stated in April 1911, a few days after Martin's election to the post. "We fancy that if things were different, and the leadership carried with it any considerable amount of real authority, Mr. Martin would hardly have got it."[184] Martin was active on the floor, even vocal at times (Barfield 1965, 293; Holt 1975, 7). He was "a fighter," according to the *Washington Post*. "When he rises to take a fall out of the Republicans he goes right at the point without circumlocution. 'He barks at

---

[180] "G.O.P. in Turmoil," *Washington Post*, Jan. 18, 1907, 1.
[181] "Near an Agreement on Currency Bill," *New York Times*, May 27, 1908, 1. See also "Ship Subsidy May Reach Vote in Senate," *Philadelphia Inquirer*, Feb. 29, 1908, 6.
[182] "Due to Ill Health," *Washington Evening Star*, Dec. 5, 1909, 2.
[183] "In the Public Eye," *Wilkes-Barre Times*, May 26, 1910, 10.
[184] "The Office Not as Big as It Sounds," *Macon (Ga.) Telegraph*, Apr. 19, 1911, 4.

'em,' remarked a listener in the galleries the other day when Senator Martin was speaking on the proposition to force a report from the finance committee upon the wool bill."[185] Martin built a coalition between Democrats and insurgent Republicans to fight the Canadian reciprocity bill, he offered resolutions, he spoke on the floor on behalf of his caucus, he worked with Republicans to set dates for adjournment, and he tried to corral senators for crucial votes.[186] Still, Martin, like his predecessors, endured frequent criticism for his leadership, much of it coming from progressive Democrats who criticized his conservative policy goals. In January 1913, as Woodrow Wilson prepared to assume the presidency, he met with several congressional Democrats, but pointedly did not seek a meeting with Martin (Reeves 1960, 360; Holt 1975, 13). "While he has conferred with the official party leaders in the House, he has not consulted with the official leader in the Senate, Mr. Martin of Virginia," the *New York Times* noted. "Mr. Martin is a conservative of so deep a stripe that he is usually referred to not as a conservative, but as a 'reactionary,' or a 'stand-patter.'"[187] Two months later, John Kern, with progressive support, would supplant Martin as the Senate's Democratic leader.

Policy leader. At the head of a resurgent majority executing Wilson's program, Kern led a caucus that was unusually unified and disciplined. Party unity—"harmony," as it was frequently called—had become the responsibility of Democratic leaders beginning with Gorman. This had not been a concern of earlier caucus chairmen, whose responsibilities were centered in caucus organization. Yet no leader before 1913, not even Gorman himself, could recapture the extraordinary solidity of purpose that characterized the Democratic minority in its fight to defeat the Federal Elections Bill of 1890–91. Achieving that harmony became the goal of every Democratic leader between 1891 and 1913, but all of them fell short of expectations. Rather than viewing ideological homogeneity within the caucus as the foundation of strong leadership, senators looked to their leaders to impose an artificial unity when preferences were divergent and then faulted those leaders when they failed at the task.

As early as December 1890, months after assuming the caucus chairmanship outright in the midst of the elections bill battle, Gorman had already gained a reputation for uniting his party. "The Democrats in the Senate are much more compactly organized than the Republicans," the *Chicago Tribune* wrote. "They have also there a leader whom they obey without hesitation. This leader

---

[185] "Sidelights on Washington," *Washington Post*, July 9, 1911, E4.
[186] "Lorimer Case Again Brought up in Senate," *Duluth News Tribune*, May 24, 1911, 1; "Senate Votes for Reopening Lorimer Case," *Chicago Daily Tribune*, June 2, 1911, 1; "Insurgents Tricky," *Philadelphia Inquirer*, June 19, 1911, 16; "Democratic Leaders Sore over Absence of Mr. Smith," *Atlanta Constitution*, Aug. 2, 1911, 16; "Veto Will Be Signal for End," *Bellingham (Wash.) Herald*, Aug. 7, 1911, 4; "Rush Bribery Case into the Senate," *New York Times*, Aug. 27, 1912, 6.
[187] "Wilson Welcomes Only Progressives," *New York Times*, Jan. 2, 1913, 5.

is Senator Gorman."[188] At times, as leader, Gorman functioned as whip, sending notices to Democratic senators reminding them to be present on the Senate floor throughout the 1894 debate on tariff legislation.[189] Horace Chilton (D, Tex.), writing a few years later, described one of Gorman's strengths as a leader. "Gorman rarely ever announced a position until after he had conferred with his Democratic associates sufficiently to know that the view he espoused, was endorsed to the extent that it would command a large support," Chilton (1908, 67) recalled. "In other words Gorman took no chances on standing alone or with two or three, on a roll-call. He always made sure that his views expressed met sufficient approval among the other Senators, to make his announcement a view more or less representative or authoritative." As a consequence, Chilton (1908, 68) observed, "Gorman was rated nearly always as a leader, because his opinion seemed to always meet response, when in truth his opinion was not simply his, but a composite which he had gathered from consultation." Gorman was "the recognized leader" of Senate Democrats, the *Atlanta Constitution* explained in 1895, and he "possesses the confidence of a larger number of senators than any other man in the chamber."[190]

James K. Jones did not enjoy comparable success. His critics argued in 1901 that he was failing to unite Senate Democrats, that he made commitments to Republican leaders without first consulting with his own party.[191] They described him as aloof and out of touch with other senators. "His sensitiveness, not so much for himself as for other persons, almost disqualifies him as a director and leader in such a body as the Senate," according to the *Baltimore Sun*. "In his intercourse with men he expresses his own views frankly, but, though he desires advice and suggestion and respects the opinions of others, he is supersensitive about asking another what he thinks, feeling that to do so might appear as an assumption of right to know."[192] Reluctant to count votes or gather opinions, Jones had little success in organizing Senate Democrats for action. "For four years," the *Chicago Record-Herald* observed in 1903, "the democrats in congress have been without a leader who could command a loyal and undivided party following."[193]

Many hoped for change with Gorman's return to the Senate. "With Arthur Pue Gorman as the recognized leader of the Democrats in the Senate, the Republican majority, for the first time in four years, may be compelled to face a resolute and determined opposition," the *Dallas Morning News* predicted in March 1903. "The Democrats have had no effective leader in the Senate since

---

[188] "Gorman as a Dictator," *Chicago Tribune*, Dec. 12, 1890, 9.
[189] "Amendments in Order To-Day," *New York Times*, Apr. 25, 1894, 2. See also "The Republican Sugar Trust Alliance with Gorman," *New York Times*, Dec. 12, 1894, 4.
[190] "After the Battle," *Atlanta Constitution*, Jan. 16, 1895, 1.
[191] "Bacon Suggested for Leadership," *Atlanta Constitution*, Mar. 10, 1901, 2.
[192] "No One Yet to Lead," *Baltimore Sun*, Nov. 24, 1901, 1.
[193] Editorial in the *Chicago Record-Herald*, as cited in "Gorman's Leadership," *Grand Forks (N.Dak.) Herald*, Mar. 10, 1903, 2.

Mr. Gorman retired."[194] Welcoming Gorman back to Senate leadership in 1903, the *Los Angeles Times* emphasized Gorman's ability to keep "the Democrats in the Senate compact, aggressive and effective, whether in the minority or in majority."[195] Yet harmony remained elusive. On the question of the Panama Canal, Democratic senators splintered and divided, and Gorman was held responsible for the fracturing.[196] Divisions within their ranks were great enough that Democrats voted to create the binding caucus in December 1903, with Senate Democrats pledging to support on the floor any policy decision made by a two-thirds vote in caucus (Lambert 1963, 105–8; Rothman 1966, 68–69; Kravitz ca. 1971, viii: 24, 63–64; *Congressional Quarterly* 1976, 203–4; Ritchie 1998a, 3–5; Gould 2005, 28–29; McConnell and Brownell 2019, 142).[197] But this rule was quickly forgotten, and Gorman was held accountable for the continued failure of his colleagues to work together. "His leadership in the Senate has been full of mistakes," the *Philadelphia Inquirer* argued in April 1904. "He has floundered around for issues and has been unable to unite his party on any of his propositions."[198] As the *New York Times* reported in December 1905, "The party in the Senate has been chaotic under his leadership."[199]

With Gorman's death, observers again expressed faith that new leadership would bring unity to Senate Democrats. But, before 1913, no leader was wholly successful. Frustrated by their small numbers and riven by growing divisions between progressives and conservatives, the Senate's Democrats proved difficult to lead. Blackburn showed little skill in managing the floor, but had been chosen as leader, the *New York Times* asserted, "because he not only preserves his own temper but is eminently adapted for the preservation of other men's tempers."[200] Culberson, succeeding Blackburn as minority leader, promised the steering committee in 1908 to "prod the Democratic Senators to closer attention to business."[201] At least one reporter, writing for the *Dallas Morning News* in March 1909, believed that he had made real progress, writing that "under Senator Culberson's leadership the Democrats of the Senate acted with much concert and coherence of action."[202] But Culberson, suffering from illness, stepped down from his post later that year, and a "sadly divided" caucus elected Money, who had already announced his retirement, to fill out

[194] "Gorman Is Strong," *Dallas Morning News*, Mar. 15, 1903, 5.
[195] "Leader Gorman," *Los Angeles Times*, Mar. 8, 1903, 1.
[196] "Democracy's New Leader," *New York Times*, Nov. 30, 1903, 7; "The Senate's Minority Leadership," *Washington Evening Star*, June 7, 1906, 4.
[197] "Gorman Tired of Leadership," *Atlanta Constitution*, Dec. 13, 1903, 3.
[198] "Hard Sledding for Gorman," *Philadelphia Inquirer*, Apr. 1, 1904, 8.
[199] "Gorman to Quit Lead of Senate Minority," *New York Times*, Dec. 23, 1905, 4. See also "Gorman Left Behind in Rush of Politics," *New York Times*, Nov. 20, 1905, 9.
[200] "Senate Democrats Look for a Leader," *New York Times*, Jan. 30, 1907, 4. See also "Democrats at Sea without a Pilot," *Chicago Daily Tribune*, Feb. 19, 1907, 1.
[201] "Prod Democratic Senators," *New York Times*, Mar. 15, 1908, 8.
[202] "Culberson Will Continue as Leader," *Dallas Morning News*, Mar. 6, 1909, 1.

the term.[203] Martin, elected minority leader in 1911, was embattled throughout his two years as caucus chairman. Actively opposed by progressive Democrats, Martin narrowly won election in 1911 and then stepped down in 1913 rather than be defeated. Given the heterogeneity of Senate Democrats, Martin was weakly positioned to offer strong policy leadership.

Presidential liaison. Gorman followed his predecessors in organizing his caucus, and he forged new ground in floor management and policy leadership, but there is little evidence that he or his pre-1913 successors had any special role in interacting with the president. This element of modern leadership emerged only with Kern and Wilson in 1913, as we discuss in the next chapter. This was a function, perhaps, of circumstance and personalities. The period 1890–1913 was a Republican era: with a single two-year exception, Republicans had control of the Senate, and Grover Cleveland was the only Democratic president in these years, serving between 1893 and 1897. Republican presidents consulted with Aldrich, Allison, Hale, Lodge, and other leading Republican senators, and, when they reached out to Democrats, they spoke not just to the minority leader but to others in the party. Cleveland, meanwhile, who came to office with a Democratic Senate majority, had previously enjoyed a constructive relationship with Gorman, extending back to Gorman's management of the 1884 presidential campaign (Poore 1886, ii: 508–9; Nevins 1932, 160, 195–96). But their alliance, already fraying when Cleveland began his second term, came apart quickly.

Within weeks of taking office, Cleveland had established a hostile relationship with the Senate's Democratic floor leader, who was viewed as a contender for the presidency and competitor to Cleveland. "It is said that Senator Gorman is not at all familiar at the White House," the *Idaho Daily Statesman* reported in April 1893. "The president is credited with a purpose to assist those who would break up the senator's machine in Maryland, and a sort of armed neutrality exists between them."[204] As debate began that summer on silver purchase repeal, their relationship worsened. "There is more or less distrust and antagonism on both sides," the *Knoxville Journal* reported in September 1893.[205] It was Sherman, a Republican senator, who spoke for Cleveland on the Senate floor and helped manage the president's fight for full repeal (Nevins 1932, 544–45).[206] Any remaining comity was destroyed in 1894, when Cleveland publicly accused Gorman and his colleagues of "party perfidy" in the congressional struggle over tariff revision. "Perhaps no more remarkable scene was ever witnessed in the United States Senate than that which occurred today for two and a half hours. Senator Gorman, the Democratic political leader on the floor, delivered his speech against the President in defense of the Senate tariff bill," the *Los Angeles Times* asserted in July 1894. "His personal attack upon the President was full of sensational

[203] "Mr. Money as Compromise," *Dallas Morning News*, Dec. 10, 1909, 1.
[204] "It is said that Senator Gorman ... ," *Idaho Daily Statesman*, Apr. 11, 1893, 4.
[205] "The Battle Raging," *Knoxville (Tenn.) Journal*, Sept. 22, 1893, 2.
[206] "Repeal Bill Passed," *Decatur (Ill.) Daily Republican*, Oct. 31, 1893, 1.

characteristics."[207] For the remainder of Cleveland's time in office, the relationship between him and Gorman, leader of the Senate Democrats, was barely civil. "In those closing days of the Cleveland Administration, it was very seldom that a Democratic Senator was seen at the White House," Cullom (1911, 269) wrote. "The President became completely estranged from the members of his party in both House and Senate, but it seemed to bother him little."

There were times, of course, that the Senate's Democratic leaders visited the president. While the leader was occasionally singled out for these visits, more often the president reached out to a range of senators. Thus, in March 1898, President William McKinley summoned "Gorman as leader of Democratic senators" to the White House to discuss the looming conflict with Spain.[208] Jones called on President Theodore Roosevelt in the fall of 1902. He told reporters that his main purpose in visiting the White House was to pay his respects to the president but "admitted having talked politics" as well.[209] In a visit to McKinley the previous year, reported by the *Washington Post*, Jones was one of eight different senators calling that day, and there is no indication that he had any special stature as Senate minority leader.[210] Gorman, when he returned as leader, and Blackburn and Culberson, who succeeded Gorman, met with Roosevelt rarely, if at all.[211] Similarly, there is little evidence of consultation between Taft and Money. And, in 1912, when Martin called on Taft at the White House, he was there as an advocate for his Virginia constituents, not as minority leader. The *Washington Post*, in its account, noted that Martin had come to the White House to seek the president's support for funding a road from Washington, D.C., to Mount Vernon. Martin was joined in his White House visit not by any senators but instead by a Virginia representative.[212]

Party spokesperson. Finally, beginning with Gorman, Democratic leaders started to function as spokespersons for their party. When the press sought senators who could speak on behalf of their caucus, they frequently interviewed the Democratic leader. This was a new role with Gorman: caucus chairmen before 1890 were not seen as party spokespersons, and Republican caucus chairmen remained in the background through these years. But, between 1890 and 1913, Democratic leaders frequently represented Senate Democrats in their public remarks—identifying policy priorities, legislative strategy, plans for filibusters, criticisms of the president, and projected dates for adjournment. This role was still developing in this era: there were few extensive interviews, and quoted remarks were usually no more than a sentence or two. But, in this realm too, we find the origins of modern Senate leadership.

---

[207] "Broken Faith," *Los Angeles Times*, July 24, 1894, 1.
[208] "M'Kinley Sees Crisis at Hand," *Atlanta Constitution*, Mar. 23, 1898, 1.
[209] "President Moves In," *Washington Post*, Oct. 31, 1902, 4.
[210] "President Gone West," *Washington Post*, Mar. 15, 1901, 3.
[211] We have not yet found any record of a meeting between the president and any of these senators. While we suspect that a more exhaustive search might yield evidence of at least some meetings, we are confident that these meetings were not regular occurrences.
[212] "For Mt. Vernon Road," *Washington Post*, Nov. 15, 1912, 4.

Arthur Pue Gorman late in life. Leading the filibuster against the Federal Elections Bill in 1890–91, Gorman offered "the most remarkable spectacle of obstruction then known to the Senate," in the words of Franklin Burdette. In that battle Gorman created the position of Senate floor leader, serving in that position in 1890–98 and 1903–6.

The Miriam and Ira D. Wallach Division of Art, Prints and Photographs: Photography Collection, New York Public Library (Spalding 9-22)

Gorman spoke on behalf of Senate Democrats when, in the summer of 1890, he announced that no date had yet been set for a vote on the McKinley Tariff Bill, prelude to the debate over the Federal Elections Bill.[213] Later that year, in an interview, Gorman declared that Senate Democrats "would fight every inch of the ground" if Republicans persisted in their efforts to pass the elections bill, "and the measure would be defeated unless Reed's methods were adopted by Vice President Morton and the Republican majority."[214] It was Gorman in 1894 who launched the blistering attack on Cleveland, after the president had sharply criticized the Senate's Democrats for their work on the Wilson-Gorman Tariff Bill. The *Atlanta Constitution*, in a January 1896 news story, referred to Gorman as the "leader and spokesman" of Senate Democrats. Upon relinquishing control of the Senate to Republicans in 1895, Gorman, speaking for his caucus, "gave formal warning that the party holding the committees would be held responsible for all legislation."[215] Chilton viewed Gorman's relationship with the press as a central feature of his leadership. Gorman was "in close touch with the newspaper correspondents—especially the representatives of the Washington papers. His influence was very strong with those papers. And through his connection with the press representatives and his constant cultivation of that craft, he had at hand instrumentalities of information and methods of impressing his views which were beyond the reach of other Senators," Chilton (1908, 77–78) wrote. "Every morning the Senators from every State would peruse the Washington Post, the great capital daily—every evening they would glance at the Star or Times. And things that Gorman thought made an imperceptible headway as if they were the things that impressed disinterested observers."

As the "Democratic leader of the Senate," Jones regularly issued statements to the press in 1900—on the Boer War, on the Hay-Pauncefote Treaty, on the army reorganization bill.[216] "Senator Jones, of Arkansas, the leader of the minority in the Senate, stated very emphatically to The Post yesterday that the Democrats would prevent the passage of the army bill," the *Washington Post* reported. "In fact, Senator Jones characterized it bluntly as 'rascality.'"[217] Two years later, in a front-page analysis of the upcoming congressional agenda, the *Atlanta Constitution* interviewed Jones, identifying him as "democratic leader in the senate," who said that he expected that the tariff, trusts, and appropriations would dominate the session.[218] Gorman, returning to the

[213] "Program for the Tariff Bill," *Columbus (Ga.) Daily Enquirer*, Aug. 24, 1890, 1.
[214] "That Way Madness Lies," *New York Times*, Nov. 27, 1890, 4.
[215] "All in the Family," *Atlanta Constitution*, Jan. 12, 1896, 13.
[216] "What Think Americans?" *Biloxi (Miss.) Daily Herald*, Feb. 16, 1900, 1. See also "For National Defense," *Washington Post*, Mar. 10, 1900, 1; "No Extra Star for Miles," *Washington Post*, Apr. 28, 1900, 4.
[217] "No Extra Star for Miles," *Washington Post*, Apr. 28, 1900, 4.
[218] "Side Stepping the Programme of the G.O.P.," *Atlanta Constitution*, Dec. 1, 1902, 1.

Senate, and Blackburn appeared less frequently in the press than Jones. But Culberson was often quoted. In 1908 Culberson, in his capacity as "Democratic leader," protested proposed increases in railroad rates and, on another occasion, promised that no effort would be made to block a vote on the ship subsidy bill.[219] He issued a statement in 1909 regarding the tariff bill, pledging that "the democrats will debate the conference report thoroughly, but will not filibuster against its adoption."[220] Earlier that same year, following a four-hour caucus meeting, Culberson released a statement summarizing the meeting's outcome and expressing his colleagues' support for an income tax amendment.[221] Money, identified as "the titular leader of the Democratic minority of the Senate," spoke on a range of issues in a November 1910 interview with the *Dallas Morning News*.[222] Money told the *News* that he expected Ohio governor Judson Harmon to be the Democrats' presidential candidate in 1912 (with Woodrow Wilson as his running mate) and that the Democrats should make tariff revision their first priority in the new Congress. "The Democrats had been given a mandate by the people of the country to relieve them of some of the burdens imposed by the schedules of the Payne-Aldrich bill," Money stated in the interview, "and the party must obey that mandate at the earliest possible moment."[223]

More than any of his predecessors, Martin began to stake out the role of party spokesperson as a responsibility of the floor leader. Speaking in the summer of 1911, he outlined his party's agenda for the next session. "With half a dozen issues to choose from, Senator Martin of Virginia, minority leader of the Senate, is confident that the next session will be taken up chiefly with tariff matters," the *New York Times* reported. "Mr. Martin did not make any predictions for harmonious co-operation next session between the insurgents and the Democrats."[224] Tariff revision was on Martin's mind when he was interviewed that summer, telling a reporter that "so far as the Democrats are concerned the situation is up in the air."[225] He later made a statement to another reporter predicting a date for adjournment.[226] When, in November 1912, President-elect Wilson indicated that he would welcome an extra session of Congress, Martin emphatically endorsed the suggestion. "Among those who pronouncedly advocated an early session plan was Senator Martin of Virginia, who is the caucus leader of the party in the

---

[219] "Rate Increase Being Fought," *Atlanta Constitution*, May 8, 1908, 3; "Ship Subsidy May Reach Vote in Senate," *Philadelphia Inquirer*, Feb. 29, 1908, 6.

[220] "Senate to Vote on Conference Report Last of the Week," *Macon (Ga.) Daily Telegraph*, Aug. 2, 1909, 1.

[221] "Democrats for an Income Tax," *Grand Forks (N.Dak.) Herald*, Apr. 15, 1909, 1.

[222] "'Harmon and Wilson for 1912 Ticket,'" *Dallas Morning News*, Nov. 15, 1910, 1.

[223] "'Harmon and Wilson for 1912 Ticket,'" *Dallas Morning News*, Nov. 15, 1910, 1.

[224] "Tariff Coming Up Again," *New York Times*, Aug. 27, 1911, 12.

[225] "Democrats in Air on Wool Question," *Philadelphia Inquirer*, July 25, 1911, 14.

[226] "Veto Will Be Signal for End," *Bellingham (Wash.) Herald*, Aug. 7, 1911, 4.

Senate," the *Los Angeles Times* reported. "'I can see no reason why the performance of the promises of the Democratic party should be delayed nine months,' said Senator Martin. 'If the legislation promised is wise and of such a nature as to promote the welfare of the people of the country, the sooner it is enacted the better.'"[227] Martin, as leader, understood his role in speaking for his caucus. When Kern became leader in 1913, he inherited an office with an array of responsibilities—caucus organizer, floor manager, policy leader, and party spokesperson—and he would quickly add presidential liaison to that list. Gorman's status as institutional inventor had receded into history, most of his successors had proved to be weak and ineffective floor leaders, yet, as Kern became majority leader, the office Gorman created had endured. Now, with Kern and the next generation of leaders, the office would grow dramatically in importance.

CONCLUSION

The institution of floor leadership is the cornerstone of the contemporary Senate. Between 1913 and 1924, as we show in the next chapter, senators in both parties refined the position, adapted it for majority as well as minority rule, endowed it with expanded responsibilities, introduced whips to assist leaders in the chamber, and established powerful norms allowing leaders to direct the work of their parties on the floor. Republicans in this new era finally abandoned their seniority rule for selecting caucus chairmen and floor leaders. And, in both parties, leadership elections were now actively contested. The Senate Republican steering committee—which was the dominant institution in the chamber in the 1890s and 1900s and the instrument of majority rule—became a shell of its former self. The majority leader and minority leader rose in its place, bearers of an institutional tradition that originated in 1890–91 and persisted, for more than two decades, as the obscure curiosity of the Democratic minority.

Modern Senate leadership emerged in the midst of the Democratic battle to blockade passage of the Federal Elections Bill. Convinced that their survival as a competitive national party was at stake, convinced too that the steady destruction of voting and civil rights for African Americans in the South would be reversed, Democrats rose up in 1890–91 to fight the legislation. The passage of the Reed rules in the House suddenly ended the principal congressional arena for dilatory tactics and minority obstructionism. All eyes then shifted to the Senate, where Democrats turned to their caucus chairman, Arthur Pue Gorman, to lead their fierce and furiously united minority, and he obliged. In inventing this new position, Gorman was reconciling the collective goals of his party—

---

[227] "Early Session Likely," *Los Angeles Times*, Nov. 14, 1912, 17.

pursuing a legislative agenda that was consistent with furthering his party's electoral success—and he performed his job brilliantly.

Notably, this innovation came from the minority party, from the Democrats. That was probably no accident. Although the Democratic party traced its origins to the 1820s, it was, in many ways, the new party in Congress in the 1870s. As a congressional force, the Democratic party had been decimated by secession and the Civil War, and Senate Democrats in the mid-1870s were forced to rebuild their party apparatus from scratch; with the 1850s now the distant past, prewar precedents were irrelevant. Being in the minority, and having languished in the minority for most of the previous three decades, made it likelier that Democrats were willing to innovate, and the need to assert their strength may have led Democrats to seek more effective leadership. The absence of Democratic committee chairmen was a by-product of minority status and also contributed to Gorman's emergence as floor leader. On the Republican side, several strong committee chairmen existed, exercising power not only in their own realms but collectively through the Republican steering committee. In a world dominated by Aldrich, Allison, Hale, Platt, and Spooner and with regular Republican majorities, it is difficult to imagine how Senate Republicans would have permitted the emergence of a floor leader with responsibilities that challenged the individual jurisdictions of powerful committee chairmen. Gorman, in contrast, did not have to contend with others controlling institutional resources. Moreover, the typical task of a majority—to enact new legislation—required cooperative effort by many members of the leading party. The minority's task, often reduced to the simpler goal of blocking action, was in clear view in the Federal Elections Bill struggle. A single party leader, who in the 1890s might have struggled to build a governing coalition, could succeed in organizing opposition to a majority initiative. Gorman's personality and political position were crucial to his success. Within the regionally divided Democratic caucus, he transformed the caucus chairmanship into a position of floor leadership, showing the value of unified action and the virtue of finding allies on the other side of the aisle. His subsequent difficulties as leader—and those of his successors in the 1900s and early 1910s—came from leading a caucus that fractured quickly after the battle of 1890–91. Senate Democrats now had their floor leader, but his ability to manage the caucus was undermined by divisions roiling the caucus.

The fact that Democrats did not choose their caucus chairmen according to seniority facilitated the transformation of this institution into a position of floor leadership. Republicans had enjoyed the extended service of Henry Anthony as their caucus chairman in the two decades following the Civil War, which resulted, by the end of his very long term, in a Republican expectation that their most senior member sit in the chair. Anthony pursued only ministerial functions and did not become a particularly influential senator even after years of service in the post. The experience under Anthony appears to have persuaded his colleagues that senior status and a ministerial role had virtues. In contrast, electoral defeats and illness required Democrats to replace their caucus chairmen every four or five years, replacements were from the ranks of junior senators, and expectations for the role of caucus chairman remained in flux. Because Democrats elected relatively younger members to the caucus chairmanship, they could potentially select members on the basis of talent, and the caucus chairmen themselves had room to experiment with the position. Beck, who assumed the caucus chairmanship in 1885 and was well-regarded on financial matters, demonstrated the value of a caucus chairman who could provide leadership to his caucus on major policy matters.

Culminating with Beck's tenure, Democratic caucus chairmen before Gorman had set precedents on which Gorman could build. Since the reestablishment of Democratic caucus committees in the 1870s, the Democratic caucus chairman had generally chaired the party's committee on committees. That was never the case on the Republican side: from the creation of the Republican committee on committees in 1859 into the 1890s, the caucus chairman never coordinated his party's committee assignments. What was common practice before the 1890s became a firm rule with the establishment of permanent steering committees in 1892–93 and the rise of floor leadership on the Democratic side. Democrats centralized leadership in one person, who served as caucus chairman, floor leader, and chairman of the steering committee, and they assigned to the steering committee the power to make committee assignments. Republicans, who made their caucus chairman the head of their steering committee in the 1890s, otherwise fragmented power, with the caucus chairman sharing leadership responsibilities with a separate chairman of the committee on committees as well as the chairmen of the various Senate committees.

The ease with which the leading Republicans collaborated, reducing the need for a single floor leader, may have limited the need to identify a formal leader as the Democrats did. In contrast to the argument that party homogeneity on policy matters centralizes power in a single leader, the cohesiveness of Senate Republicans may have facilitated the collective leadership of like-minded senior senators. The heyday of the Republican steering committee occurred when the party had a sizable majority, so some inefficiency in central leadership was tolerable during the late 1890s and early 1900s. Not until 1913, when the Republicans found themselves in the minority and their old leaders had died or left the Senate, did they follow the Democratic example and identify a formal floor leader. Then both parties, along parallel paths, reconfigured this institution into its modern form.

John W. Kern (D, Ind.), the first senator to be called majority leader. An ally of Woodrow Wilson, he served as Senate Democratic leader in 1913–17.

6

Leaders and Whips, 1913–1924

John W. Kern (D, Ind.), known as "Old Whiskers" for his neatly trimmed, moon-shaped beard, was the Senate's first elected majority leader.[1] His election as Democratic caucus chairman in March 1913 was treated, both by his party colleagues and the press, as the election of a majority leader and an important boost for the interests of progressives—even as it was also understood that the election of a Democratic floor leader was now well-established practice, dating back to the early days of Gorman. The caucus's vote, the *New York Times* observed, "makes Mr. Kern the Democratic floor leader in the Senate."[2] As the *Wall Street Journal* noted in its matter-of-fact way: "Senator Kern of Indiana was elected caucus chairman by the Democratic Senators. This carries with it the title of majority leader."[3] The *Los Angeles Times* headline succinctly summarized the situation—"Kern is Leader of Democrats: Indiana Senator to Direct Policy from Floor."[4] Newspaper accounts thereafter are replete with references to Kern as "majority leader," "Democratic leader," and "floor leader." With Kern in office, we find what appears to be the first instance that the position of "majority leader" is recognized by the Senate's official reporter

---

[1] Arthur Pue Gorman had served eight years as leader, 1890–98, two of them in the majority, but these were years when the position was still in its earliest development, and few observers described Gorman as "majority leader" during that two-year period. With Kern, the attribution by his contemporaries seems to have been universal.

[2] "Radicals Control Senate," *New York Times*, Mar. 6, 1913, 2.

[3] "President's Nominations Confirmed by the Senate," *Wall Street Journal*, Mar. 6, 1913, 3. The *Washington Post* simply referred to Kern, and to Martin, his predecessor, as "leader of the Democrats" in reporting Kern's succession to the post: "Martin Gives Up Rule," *Washington Post*, Mar. 1, 1913, 4.

[4] "Kern is Leader of Democrats: Indiana Senator to Direct Policy from Floor," *Los Angeles Times*, Mar. 6, 1913, I:7.

(*Cong. Rec.*, 1915, 3266) and the first time the position, "Senate majority leader," is mentioned on the House floor (*Cong. Rec.*, 1914, 225).[5]

On the Republican side of the Senate, there had been no elected floor leader before 1913—no expectation that party management was a duty that belonged to the caucus chairman. Upon Allison's death in 1908, Hale had become chairman not only of the Republican caucus but of the Appropriations Committee, which for both him and Allison was a sturdier foundation for leadership than the caucus chairmanship. But Hale and Aldrich's power had diminished by then. Caught in pincers, losing their long-time colleagues on the one side—with Platt's death in 1905, Spooner's resignation from the Senate in 1907, and Allison's death in 1908—and the rise of Insurgency on the other, Aldrich, Hale, and their allies were under siege.[6] An era had ended, a realization that grew sharper after the revolt in March 1910 against House Speaker Joseph Cannon, who, like Aldrich, had personified the conservative leadership against which progressives were railing. "The very night of the overthrow of Speaker Cannon and his removal from the House Committee on Rules," according to the *New York Times*, "the insurgents set up the cry of 'on to Aldrich.'"[7]

In April 1910, within a month of the House revolt, both Aldrich and Hale, whose current terms were to end the following spring, announced that they would not seek reelection to the Senate. "The retirement of Aldrich now means the final breaking up of the Old Guard," the *Times* argued. "The time-tried and fire-tested organization will go to smash. There is no successor in sight, and the leadership will pass to new and untried hands."[8] Observers speculated about the future of Republican leadership, but the discussion was not about the caucus chairmanship or even the chairmanship of the Republican steering committee, both of which Hale held. Rather, it centered on Aldrich, his personal qualities and his long service as chairman of the Finance Committee. "The brief list of his official positions," the *Times* noted, "makes it plain that Mr. Aldrich's power in the Senate is unofficial."[9] Indeed, the *Washington Evening Star* felt compelled to explain to its readers that the question of

---

[5] See McConnell and Brownell 2019, 154.

[6] "Radicalism Gains in the Senate," *New York Times*, Aug. 6, 1908, 2; "Aldrich Weary of Senate," *New York Times*, Nov. 2, 1908, 1; "Radicalism in Senate," *New York Tribune*, Dec. 12, 1908, 2; "Revolt in Senate," *Baltimore Sun*, Feb. 12, 1909, 1; "No Senate Insurrection," *New York Times*, Mar. 15, 1909, 2; "Senate Conciliatory," *New York Times*, Mar. 16, 1909, 2.

[7] "Aldrich to Retire at End of His Term," *New York Times*, Apr. 16, 1910, 1.

[8] "Aldrich to Retire at End of His Term," *New York Times*, Apr. 16, 1910, 2, also 1. See also "Aldrich to Give Up Because Plans Fail," *New York Times*, Apr. 17, 1910, 3; "New Senate Power," *Washington Evening Star*, Apr. 19, 1910, 1; "Two Senators Quit," *Washington Evening Star*, Apr. 19, 1910, 8; "Aldrich and Hale," *Washington Evening Star*, Apr. 19, 1910, 6; "Passing of the 'Big Five' Who Ruled the Senate," *New York Times*, Apr. 24, 1910, SM3; "The Senate Leadership," *Washington Post*, July 13, 1910, 6.

[9] "Aldrich to Retire at End of His Term," *New York Times*, Apr. 16, 1910, 2.

leadership was now thoroughly unsettled, noting that "there is no rule or precedent under which the mantle of leadership goes with the chairmanship of the finance committee."[10] Insurgent senators, identifying party leadership with conservative policymaking, looked hopefully to a future with no strong Senate leaders. When one insurgent was asked "upon whom he thought the mantle of leadership would fall he replied: 'We are going to take it over to the Smithsonian Institution and keep it as a relic of an obsolete system.'"[11] Shelby Cullom (R, Ill.) assumed the chairmanship of the Republican caucus and the Republican steering committee in 1911, but only by virtue of seniority. No senator, certainly not Cullom, assumed Aldrich's or Hale's mantle as an informal floor leader that year. Responding to the question of who had replaced Aldrich as the Republican leader of the Senate, Cullom (1911, 425) was emphatic in the summer of 1911: "No one."

Only in 1913, plunged into the minority for the first time in almost two decades, did Senate Republicans adopt the longstanding Democratic model and, in electing their caucus chairman, designate a floor leader. With his election as caucus chairman, Jacob Gallinger (R., N.H.), the most senior member of his party, assumed responsibility for managing the affairs of the minority on the floor of the Senate. In its account of the election, the *New York Times* stated that Senate Republicans had selected Gallinger "as their floor leader"[12]—using a title that had long ago become routine in the election of Democratic caucus chairmen, but that was a radical innovation in reference to the election of a Republican caucus chairman—and Gallinger was consistently referred to as the Senate Republican leader throughout his five-year term.[13] Upon Gallinger's death in August 1918, as Table A.1 shows, Henry Cabot Lodge (R, Mass.), now the most senior member of his party, was elected to succeed him as Republican caucus chairman and floor leader.

[10] "Two Senators Quit," *Washington Evening Star*, Apr. 19, 1910, 8.

[11] "Insurgents Wary of Aldrich Move," *New York Times*, Apr. 20, 1910, 1.

[12] "Radicals Control Senate," *New York Times*, Mar. 6, 1913, 2. See also "Kern Is Chosen as Leader at Caucus of Senate," *Bellingham (Wash.) Herald*, Mar. 5, 1913, 1; "Kern Is Leader of Democrats," *Los Angeles Times*, Mar. 6, 1913, I:7.

[13] For examples, see "Immunity for Labor," *New York Times*, May 7, 1913, 4; "Senate Tariff Debate Gets Well Under Way," *Dallas Morning News*, July 19, 1913, 3; "'No Recess Plan' Approved," *New York Times*, Aug. 15, 1913, 3; "Hitchcock Rebels; Fights Caucus Rule," *New York Times*, Aug. 30, 1913, 3; "Pass Tariff Bill in Senate, 44 to 37," *Washington Post*, Sept. 10, 1913, 1; "Primary Plan Wins Praise for Wilson," *New York Times*, Dec. 3, 1913, 2; "Closing Struggle over Canal Tolls to Stir Congress," *Atlanta Constitution*, Mar. 30, 1914, 1; "End of Congress in September Seen," *Christian Science Monitor*, July 29, 1914, 1; "Long Night Sessions To Stop Filibuster," *Atlanta Constitution*, Jan. 27, 1915, 2; "Partisanism and Defense," *Chicago Tribune*, Dec. 10, 1915, 6; "Senator Gallinger Is 79," *Washington Post*, Mar. 29, 1916, 2; "Long Session of Congress Nearing," *Christian Science Monitor*, Nov. 17, 1917, 11; "Dean of Senators, J. H. Gallinger, Dies," *New York Times*, Aug. 18, 1918, 19; "The Senate Minority," *Washington Evening Star*, Aug. 19, 1918, 6.

During the 1913–24 period, the responsibilities of floor leaders crystallized, and both parties created new leadership positions. The Democratic and Republican whip positions date to 1913 and 1915, and the two senatorial campaign committees also emerged in the mid-1910s. These innovations were driven by the struggle to pass legislation with sometimes-small majorities and serious factionalism, intense competition for majority control of the Senate, and the ratification of the Seventeenth Amendment providing for popular election of senators (Brown 1922, 273–82; Rogers 1922). Leaders of each party struggled to keep their parties working as a team to win legislative battles and still meet the expectations of the factions that put them in office. They responded with organizational innovations that, depending on the circumstances, concentrated, shared, or distributed power within their parties and, particularly for the majority party, for the Senate.

THE PARTISAN CONTEXT

Party competition and factionalism, particularly among Republicans, was intense through the 1910s and into the 1920s. Republicans had dominated the Senate during the previous half-century. In the 26 Congresses between 1861 and 1913, with three exceptions, Republicans had been in the majority, including the 18 consecutive years between 1895 and 1913. Then, in the 1910 elections, Democrats won a net of twelve additional seats and, in the 1912 elections, an additional seven to gain a majority in the Senate convening in March 1913 (Figure 6.1). With Woodrow Wilson in the White House and a majority in the House of Representatives, Democrats had unified control of the national government for the first time since 1895.

Over the three Congresses of the mid-1910s, Senate Democrats had 6-, 16-, and 12-seat advantages over the Republicans. Their hold on a majority of votes was particularly tenuous in the first of those Congresses, the 63rd Congress (1913–15), which was devoted to Wilson's large domestic legislative agenda. Wilson's agenda included reduced tariffs, the Federal Reserve system, the Federal Trade Commission, the Department of Labor, antitrust legislation, and eventually legislation on child labor and an eight-hour workday. For the most part, these issues divided senators along party lines. Democrats lost their Senate majority to the Republicans in the 1918 elections, the midterm elections of Wilson's second term, which produced a narrow two-seat advantage for the Republicans just as World War I was ending. That outcome would prove vital to the successful Republican effort to block Wilson's League of Nations plan, but the tiny majority and factionalism proved to be a serious challenge for Republican leader Lodge on domestic issues. Republican Warren Harding won the presidency in 1920 and Senate Republicans expanded their Senate majority to 59–37, which fell back to 53–42, with one Farmer-Laborite from Minnesota, after the 1922 elections.

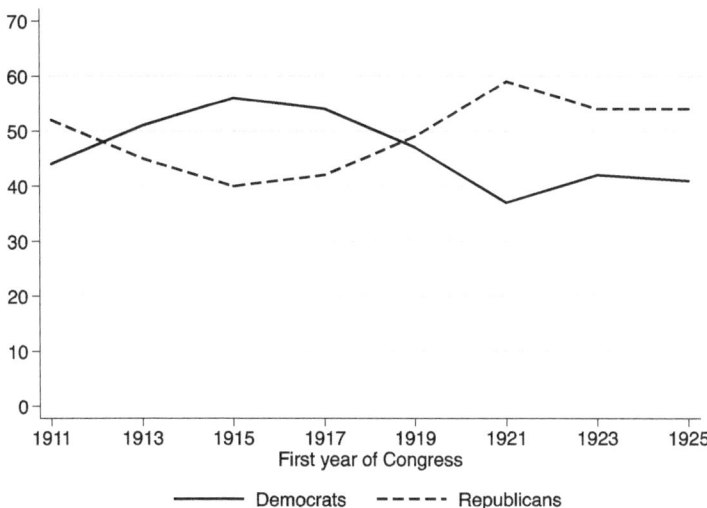

FIGURE 6.1 Size of parties, 1911–25

The Republican majorities of the late 1910s and early 1920s were accompanied by the reemergence of the division between progressives and more traditional partisans in both parties, but the political consequences were greater for Republicans. The pro-business and largely eastern "Old Guard"—which supported small government, low income taxes, minimum regulation, and high tariffs—was challenged by progressives, led by Robert La Follette (R, Wisc.), and other senators from agricultural states (Rogers 1920, 1922; Bradley 1925). Following the war, high production levels and the collapse of foreign markets reduced prices, depressing the farm economy when much of urban America was thriving. This happened at a time when farmers were well organized in the American Farm Bureau Federation and other groups (Hansen 1991) and generated considerable pressure on legislators from farm states to address problems in the farm economy. Farm-state senators, allying themselves with older progressives, formed the Farm Bloc (Rogers 1922, 48; Donnelly 1930, 144–51). Working closely with the Federation leadership, the Farm Bloc met regularly, interviewed cabinet members and outside experts, and devised legislation collectively (Bradley 1925). Senators in the bloc could control Senate outcomes if they could coordinate effectively, and Republican leaders struggled to overcome Democratic and Farm Bloc opposition on many issues.[14]

---

[14] The La Follettes became the leaders of progressives. The elder La Follette ran as the Progressive party candidate for president in 1924. He carried only Wisconsin and 17 percent of the national vote. Senate Republicans then excluded him from their conference, and he died in late 1925. His son, Robert La Follette, Jr., running as a Republican, replaced him in the Senate and ran for the regular term in 1928 as a Republican. In 1934 and 1940, the younger La Follette ran successfully

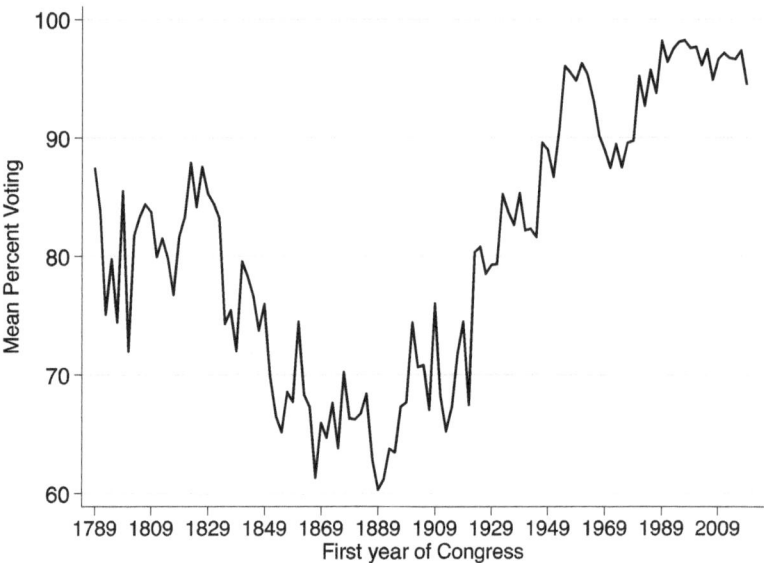

FIGURE 6.2   Mean percent of senators voting on roll-call votes, by Congress, 1789–2020
Source: voteview.com

Senators' uneven attendance, common in that era, made small majorities troublesome for both parties. In the five Congresses before Kern's Democratic majority took over in 1913, a mean of 68.9 percent of senators voted on roll-call votes—a number that dipped to about 66 percent for Kern in the 63rd Congress of 1913–15.[15] Attendance was a little better during the war years but fell again in 1921–23. While Republicans enjoyed a sizable majority in that Congress, the Farm Bloc's emergence meant that attendance could still mean the difference between winning and losing. The pattern has not received much attention from scholars, but we speculate that travel times, particularly from midwestern and western states, senators' often-poor health, and even distractions in Washington contributed to the low levels of attendance in the nineteenth and early twentieth centuries. Figure 6.2 shows how serious the problem could be in Kern's time, a problem that plagued the House, too.[16]

for reelection under the Progressive label. The Wisconsin Progressive party dissolved during World War II, in large part because of its association with isolationism, and La Follette was narrowly defeated in the 1946 Republican primary by Joseph McCarthy (Johnson 1964; Thelen 1976; Weisberger 1994).
[15] Roll-call data from voteview.com.
[16] The pattern for the House of Representatives is very similar, which likely reflects the fact that senators and representatives faced the same distance and transportation challenges.

THE LEADERS

These challenges—control of the Senate, winning legislative battles with factionalism and majorities of modest size, and even attendance—motivated organizational moves in both parties. With Kern as the first recognized majority leader and Gallinger as the first recognized Republican leader, we examine their roles and describe the other new features of party organization in the 1910s and early 1920s.

The Democrats. By most accounts, Kern did not actively seek the floor leadership post, but, when notified by leading Senate progressives that he was their choice, was happy to have his name put forward. Two years earlier, Kern had been among the Democrats who had worked with William Jennings Bryan in the attempt to elect Benjamin Shively (D, Ind.), a progressive Democrat, rather than Thomas Martin (D, Va.), as minority leader. After he had defeated Shively for the post and side-stepped an effort to formally change the composition of the party's steering committee, Martin made Shively vice chairman of the committee, which made standing committee assignments, and named Kern to the committee. Kern remained an active strategist among Senate progressives, served as the party's platform chairman in 1912, and made many speeches on behalf of Woodrow Wilson's presidential candidacy. Following Wilson's victory and the new Senate majority, progressive Democrats initiated a post-election effort to limit the power of senior, conservative Democrats on the steering committee as well as the ability of conservatives to determine committee assignments that could be important to Wilson's program (Grantham 1958, 231, 234–35, 239–41). They quickly coalesced around Kern for the position of Senate Democratic leader, and Wilson endorsed the idea (Haughton 1973, 121–26; Olezsek 1991). Martin withdrew from the contest, and, in March 1913, as the new Congress convened, Kern was elected without opposition.

Soon after Kern's election, Democrats created the post of whip (Bowers 1918, 350–53; Munk 1970; Oleszek 1985, 5; Dole 1989, 183–84; Byrd 1991, 196–98; Gould 2005, 59; MacNeil and Baker 2013, 181–82). In early May 1913, Kern called a caucus meeting to address the attendance problem, which, with the Democrats' narrow majority, was delaying action on Wilson's nominations. Democrats had been embarrassed by their failure to muster a majority on the first day of the month and by Republicans' absence and unwillingness to answer to their names during a quorum call. In an effort to correct the situation, the caucus first adopted a resolution asking all caucus members to be present unless the leader consented to their absence and, that not being sufficient, then asked caucus members to drop or avoid all pairs with Republicans in executive sessions (Ritchie 1998a, 76–78).[17] Apparently, these steps were still inadequate, so, within a month, Sen. William Stone (D, Mo.)

---

[17] Pairing is an informal practice that allows a senator to agree not to vote while a senator who would vote the opposite way is absent. The practice allows both senators to register their votes without affecting the outcome. It also may make it more difficult to muster a quorum.

The natty J. Hamilton Lewis (D, Ill.) at the Capitol, 1914. One year earlier he had become the first senator elected to the position of whip.

Library of Congress, Prints & Photographs Division, photograph by Harris & Ewing, reproduction number LC-DIG-hec-04366

suggested creating a "whip" position and proposed that J. Hamilton Lewis (D, Ill.) be appointed to the post (Ritchie 1998a, 79). The *Atlanta Constitution* reported that Lewis was elected "Democratic floor manager and assistant to Majority Leader Kern," although the caucus minutes use only the term "whip."[18] The *New York Times* provided more detail. "As a further precaution against a snap division in the Senate by which the Democrats might find themselves in the minority, the caucus elected Senator J. Hamilton Lewis of Illinois today to serve as 'whip,' although designated as assistant to Majority Leader Kern in the capacity of floor leader. Mr. Lewis's chief duty will be to see that Democrats are present or paired at every roll call," the *Times* reported. "The appointment of an assistant to Senator Kern, though brought about in a way to avoid wounding the majority leader's pride, is in fact partly explained by general dissatisfaction with Mr. Kern's leadership."[19]

Kern's immediate task as majority leader was the enactment of Wilson's legislative proposals, as his party's progressive majority expected. This entailed his engagement with most of the functions of a modern majority leader: managing party activities, overseeing the floor agenda, building majorities, and coordinating with the president. Kern performed these functions in consultation with leading progressive Democrats and his steering committee. But Kern did not take an exceptionally visible role on the floor, although he was quoted in the newspapers as a spokesperson for his party.

Kern served just four years as leader: he was defeated for reelection to the Senate in 1916 by Harry S. New (R, Ind.). With no controversy, Martin, who was approaching 70 and near the end of his fourth term in the Senate, was unanimously elected to replace Kern in March 1917. He had proven to be loyal to his party and the president, and he appeared to be without an opponent in his bid to get reelected from Virginia in 1918. Perhaps more important, war with Germany was on the horizon, and the Senate was in the midst of a pitched battle over Wilson's war-related measures, including the armed-ship bill that was killed by filibuster, and cloture reform, which Martin supported. Democrats were in no mood for an intraparty fight.[20]

---

[18] "J. Ham Lewis Named Whip of the Senate," *Atlanta Constitution*, May 29, 1913, 1; "Keeps Senators Here," *Washington Post*, May 29, 1913, 4.

[19] "Democrats Agree to Lobby Inquiry," *New York Times*, May 29, 1913, 1. Democrats also considered pushing for a new Senate rule that would grant the presiding officer the power to count senators present but not answering to their names toward meeting the quorum requirement of a majority of senators duly chosen and sworn. They did bar the use of pairs on their side for executive sessions in which presidential nominations were considered, thereby requiring conference members to be present to go on the record on nominations and assisting the party in producing a quorum. See "Congressional Notes," *Washington Post*, May 15, 1913, 4; "Test in the Caucus," *Washington Post*, May 19, 1913, 3; "To Force Confirmation," *Baltimore Sun*, May 20, 1913, 2.

[20] Martin was elected with token opposition from Thomas Walsh (D, Mont.), who was a strong Wilson supporter and played a prominent role in getting Democrats elected in western states.

Martin did not serve long. Senate Democrats lost their majority in the 1918 elections. As minority leader, Martin fell ill in mid-1919 and died in November. Gilbert Hitchcock (D, Nebr.), elected the conference vice chairman in 1917, served as acting leader and also ranking member of the Committee on Foreign Relations in the fall of 1919 when the Treaty of Versailles was before the Senate.[21] Hitchcock failed to gain Senate ratification of the treaty,[22] an outcome that made some of his colleagues less than keen to see him elected conference chairman and leader. A months-long deadlock in support for Hitchcock and his competitor, Oscar Underwood (D, Ala.), was broken in the spring of 1920 by Carter Glass (D, Va.), who had left Wilson's cabinet and been appointed to the Senate to replace Martin, and Hoke Smith (D, Ga.), who changed his neutral position to favor Underwood. Hitchcock withdrew from consideration, and Underwood took the post.[23]

Underwood had served in the Senate only since 1915. However, he had considerable leadership experience and a national reputation by virtue of having served as House minority whip, House majority leader, and House Ways and Means Committee chairman, and for authoring the Underwood Tariff Act of 1913, a major Wilson administration measure. Despite his initial eagerness to be elected leader, he did not enjoy serving as leader of the minority party and served only until 1923, in the middle of his second Senate term, when he chose not to be considered again for party leader. At the time he announced his decision to step down in late 1922, he indicated that his health made it difficult for him to continue. He was struggling to perform "the full task required of a party leader, calling for practically constant attendance at Senate sessions," as one newspaper reported his close friends to say.[24] He did not seek reelection to the Senate in 1926 in the face of active opposition from the Ku Klux Klan, prohibitionists, and others in Alabama.

When Underwood declared his intention to step down as leader, Joe Robinson (D, Ark.) was among the most popular and prominent Democrats in the country. Elected to the Senate in 1913 by the Arkansas legislature after serving in the U.S. House for a decade and as governor for only days, Robinson proved to be a team player, articulately supported Wilson's domestic program and war efforts, and was rewarded by being named chairman of the Democrats' national convention in 1920. In the 1924 campaign season, with his own

---

[21] Hitchcock became Foreign Relations chairman in mid-1918 following the death of William Stone (D, Mo.).

[22] These included divisions among Democrats on key provisions, strong opposition from the majority Republicans, and President Wilson's physical condition and political tactics following his stroke in early October.

[23] Underwood may have challenged Hitchcock's tactics on the peace treaty to gain ground against Hitchcock in the race for minority leader (Johnson 1980, 270–71). See "Senate Row Holds Glass," *Los Angeles Times*, Jan. 24, 1920, I:3. On the end of the contest, see "Expect Underwood to Lead Senate Democrats," *New York Times*, Apr. 23, 1920, 17; "Hitchcock Quits Leadership Fight," *New York Times*, Apr. 24, 1924, 1.

[24] "Underwood Renounces Leadership in Senate," *New York Times*, Nov. 8, 1922, 5.

reelection not in doubt, he was one of the most in-demand speakers for the presidential ticket and other Democrats.

Although Robinson was well known, the leading candidate to replace Underwood was initially Furnifold Simmons (D, N.C.), a conservative who was a former chairman of the Finance Committee and who, having been in the Senate for 21 years, was the most senior Senate Democrat. Robinson waged a far more aggressive campaign for the post than Simmons, and the contrast bolstered his promise to turn Underwood's moribund caucus into a "fighting force" (Bacon 1991, 68–71). Oratorical skill, mastery of parliamentary procedure, a knack for wheeling and dealing, relative youth (Simmons was 70, Robinson was 50), and, most conspicuously, sheer effort worked to his advantage (Weller 1998, 96–97). After seven or eight weeks of effort, Robinson became the frontrunner and Simmons dropped out of the race (Ritchie 1998a, 306).[25] In electing Robinson over Simmons, the minority Democrats responded to Republican rule by choosing the more aggressive leader, someone who shared a commitment to Wilsonian progressivism, could work with Democrats of most ideological stripes, had a combative style, and seemed tireless. They had chosen a leader to lead.

The Republicans. In gaining election as Republican conference chairman in March 1913, Gallinger was immediately recognized as the "Republican leader," "floor leader," and "minority leader."[26] Gallinger served until his death in August 1918, when Lodge was elected conference chairman on the basis of seniority—and his election, the *Washington Evening Star* noted, "means that Senator Lodge is the republican leader of the Senate, succeeding the late Senator Gallinger of New Hampshire in that office."[27] Lodge's reelection as leader in 1919, following the Republican successes in the 1918 elections, made him the first Republican majority leader. The term "majority leader" was

---

[25] "Start Leadership Fight," *New York Times*, Dec. 6, 1922, 2; "Leadership in Next Congress Clarifying," *Washington Post*, Jan. 18, 1923, 4; "Robinson Will Lead Senate Democrats," *New York Times*, Feb. 9, 1923, 3. Bacon (1991, 72) reports that Robinson was "elevated" to his position on March 4, 1923. In fact, the Democrats waited until the regular session in December 1923 that was convened by Underwood, who was officially caucus chairman until that meeting. Robinson was nominated by Simmons (Ritchie 1998a, 305–7).

[26] "Radicals Control Senate," *New York Times*, Mar. 6, 1913, 2; "Gallinger Will Run," *Washington Post*, May 21, 1914, 3; "La Follette Tilts with Gallinger," *New York Times*, Aug. 28, 1913, 5; "Outwitted by Gallinger," *New York Times*, July 10, 1914, 2.

[27] "Republicans Name Lodge as Leader," *Washington Evening Star*, Aug. 24, 1918, 1. At the time of Gallinger's death in August 1918, the *Boston Daily Globe* reported that Lodge had been serving as "vice chairman" of the Republican conference. This may have been an informal designation provided by Gallinger. There is no mention in the conference minutes of a vice chairmanship assigned to Lodge or any other senator until 1921. See "Dean of Senators, J. H. Gallinger, Dies," *New York Times*, Aug. 18, 1918, 19; "Gallinger's Death Makes Lodge Minority Leader," *Boston Globe*, Aug. 18, 1918, 6; "J. H. Gallinger Dead," *Washington Post*, Aug. 18, 1918, 4; "Senate Leader of Minority Party," *Christian Science Monitor*, Aug. 20, 1918, 6; "Urge Suffrage Vote," *Washington Post*, Aug. 25, 1918, 2; "Lodge Republican Leader in the Senate," *Boston Globe*, Aug. 25, 1918, 7.

applied to Lodge as soon as the Republicans took majority control in 1919, just as it had been to Kern six years before.[28] Lodge served as Republican leader until his death in November 1924.

For almost the whole of this era, from 1915 until his election to succeed Lodge as floor leader in 1924, Charles Curtis (R, Kans.) was the central player in the emergence of secondary leadership posts for Senate Republicans. Two years after Democrats had created the position of whip, Republicans in December 1915 established a parallel post (Wolff and Ritchie 1999, 46, 47). Initially, the Republican whip's position was added to the title of secretary, and James Wadsworth (R, N.Y.), who had served as speaker of the New York state assembly but was new to the U.S. Senate, was elected to the combined position of "secretary and whip." But that merged position lasted just one week, after which Republicans split the jobs and elected Curtis as whip.

The creation of separate positions allowed the party to accommodate two rising stars, to address factional interests, and to bring younger members into party leadership. Having just lost four more Senate seats, the Republicans needed to rally the party and manage attendance on the floor. Curtis, a Kansan, had better relations with western Republicans than Wadsworth, a New Yorker, while still being a "standpatter" associated with regular Republicans.[29] It is likely that a whip-like role had already existed informally: even as the Republican caucus was creating the new post for Wadsworth, the *New York Times* noted that Curtis is "one of the trusted whips of the Old Guard and he will probably resume his old duties."[30] Curtis had served for 14 years in the House (1893–1907) and six years in the Senate (1907–13) before losing his first reelection effort and then regaining his seat in 1915. Perhaps the rapid reorganization of the whip position that December reflected a desire by Curtis to gain official recognition for a role he had already performed—and to hold the title that had existed now for two years on the Democratic side. Curtis kept his position as whip until 1924, when he became conference chairman and floor leader, and Wadsworth remained conference secretary until 1927, when he left the Senate.

Under Lodge's wing, Curtis acquired a remarkable array of committee and party positions. In 1921 Curtis was made "vice chairman and whip" (Wolff and Ritchie 1999, 113), which signified that he was Lodge's chief lieutenant or "right-hand" man, as the *Post* described it.[31] He was also a member of the Appropriations, Finance, and Rules committees, and he sat on the committee on committees. It also seemed likely that Curtis would be elected president pro

---

[28] "Proceedings of Congress and Committees in Brief," *Washington Post*, May 20, 1919, 6; "Proceedings of Congress and Committees in Brief," *Washington Post*, May 21, 1919, 6.

[29] "Senate Installs Clarke," *New York Times*, Dec. 7, 1915, 3.

[30] "Senate Installs Clarke," *New York Times*, Dec. 7, 1915, 3.

[31] "Curtis Aid to Lodge: Elected by Senate Republicans Vice Chairman of Caucus," *Washington Post*, Jan. 22, 1921, 1.

tempore in the near future. By that year, some western Republicans expressed concern that Curtis was acquiring too many positions of power and suggested that another senator from their region, presumably a progressive or Farm Bloc senator, be given his Finance seat.[32] Curtis had already chaired a conference meeting in Lodge's absence before his appointment as conference vice chairman (Wolff and Ritchie 1999, 105), and his new title seemed to clarify who would preside over the conference in Lodge's absence in the future, which was of concern because of Lodge's unstable health.[33]

But precedents were still being established in 1921. A somewhat chaotic situation that autumn illustrates how much the Republicans, like the Democrats, had come to depend on a floor leader to guide party affairs. Lodge was appointed to the U.S. delegation to the armament conference and was expected to be away from the Senate for at least a few weeks starting in late November, which stirred his party colleagues to seek an acting floor leader to take his place. To make matters more complicated, the party's conservatives were experiencing attendance problems on the Senate floor, which, along with the defections of progressive Republicans, had recently contributed to losing key votes on an important tax bill. Some of the regulars blamed Lodge and ineffective senior committee leaders and so hoped that Lodge's temporary replacement might be more effective. They advocated for James Watson (R, Ind.), who was still in his first term in the Senate but was a protégé of the conservative House speaker Joseph Cannon, had served as Republican whip in the House, and was closely associated with Lodge (Watson 1936, 92–103, 190, 213).[34] However, apparently without additional action or deliberation by the conference, and, we assume, reflecting Lodge's wishes, Curtis became acting chairman and floor leader for the nearly three months that Lodge was absent from Washington. The episode reflected widespread recognition in the Republican Senate conference of the central importance of having an experienced floor leader. It also proved to be a step toward setting aside seniority as the rule for choosing a conference chairman.

Curtis's promotion to leader following Lodge's death in 1924 was the first time a Republican leader or conference chairman was not selected on the basis of seniority. There was a contest—the first ever on the Republican side—but only barely so (Garraty 1953, 423). The most senior Republican, Francis Warren (R, Wyo.), who had been in the Senate since 1895 and was over 80 years old, chose not to seek the post at a time when his colleagues clearly wanted Curtis to take over. Wadsworth was considered Curtis's primary

---

[32] "Want Finance Post," *Washington Post*, Oct. 22, 1921, 1. A few Republicans suggested creating two vice chairmen so that each major faction could be represented. See "Rail Bill Hopes Fade," *Washington Post*, Oct. 21, 1921, 1.

[33] "Want Finance Post," *Washington Post*, Oct. 22, 1921, 1.

[34] "Watson May Be G.O.P. Choice to Succeed Lodge," *Chicago Daily Tribune*, Sept. 15, 1921, 7; "Senate Leadership to Pass from Lodge to Watson," *Boston Daily Globe*, Sept. 18, 1921, 58.

competitor for the position, but he withdrew from the race before the conference met (Wolff and Ritchie 1999, 154). Senators George Moses (R, N.H.),
James Watson (R, Ind.), and David Reed (R, Pa.), each of whom was in his first
or second term, were mentioned as potential candidates for the post at the
time.[35] Watson was elected vice chairman, and the conference, at Curtis's
request, reserved for Curtis the authority to name a separate whip (Wolff and
Ritchie 1999, 154). Curtis appointed Wesley Jones (R, Wash.). Jones was a
senior, regular Republican, but, unlike Wadsworth and Watson, he had a
record of trying to bridge the differences between regulars and progressives.[36]
The party's whip post remained appointive until 1944, when the Republicans
codified their rules and made it elective.

MANAGING THE PARTY

Kern, Gallinger, and the leaders who followed them took charge of intraparty
organizational affairs during this period. They did so by calling and chairing
caucus meetings[37] and chairing the parties' steering committees.[38] While these
were inherited roles of the caucus chairman in both parties, they became more
important when the conference chairmen, as floor leaders, took the lead in
implementing party strategies on the floor. The net effect of the developments of
the 1910s and early 1920s was to place the floor leader in a central place to
address intraparty conflicts and set party strategy.

---

[35] "Successor to Senate Chief," *Boston Daily Globe*, Nov. 10, 1924, 1A; "Wadsworth or Curtis for
Senate Leader," *New York Times*, Nov. 10, 1924, 2; "Senators in Race for Two Offices," *New
York Times*, Nov. 17, 1924, 3; "Curtis of Kansas Gets Lodge's Job as Floor Leader," *Atlanta
Constitution*, Nov. 25, 1924, 1.

[36] "Radicals, Read Out by G.O.P., to Fight Program of Party," *Washington Post*, Nov. 29,
1924, 1.

[37] The Democrats used the terms "caucus" and "conference" somewhat interchangeably. The
Democratic minutes indicate the use of the term "conference" in 1903, long before the
Republicans used the term officially in 1913 (Ritchie 1998a, 1), but there are numerous
references to the "caucus," "caucus chairman," and similar terms during the first decade of
the twentieth century. Senate Republicans called their party organization a "caucus" through
their meeting on Jan. 28, 1913, but, according to their minutes, called the organization the
"conference" on Feb. 6, 1913 (Wolff and Ritchie 1999, 29, 30). We have found no explanation
for the change in newspapers or other sources. A reasonable hypothesis is that the term "caucus"
had gained a strongly negative connotation, largely because of caucus activity in the House, and
the Senate Republicans chose to distinguish themselves by changing the name of their organization, as the House parties soon would. At the time of the change, Senate Republicans were
struggling with Democrats who, meeting in caucus, were deciding to block presidential nominations as the Congress and the Taft administration were coming to a close.

[38] On patronage in the Senate, see Kimmitt 2001, 138–39. Also see https://www.senate.gov/about/
resources/pdf/st-claire-darrell-full-transcript-with-index.pdf (accessed July 2024).

A Contrast in Inherited Practices and Intraparty Politics

Differences in party factionalism led the two parties to diverge in how they handled committee assignments and other challenges that they had to manage. For the majority party Democrats of 1913–19, whose president dominated their legislative agenda, progressive Democrats controlled party affairs with relatively little difficulty. In contrast, Gallinger took over in 1913 as Republican caucus chairman under difficult circumstances—with his party in the minority for the first time since 1895, without control of the White House for the first time since 1897, with the conservative Senate leaders of the previous generation gone, with intense intraparty factionalism between insurgents and regular Republicans, and with leadership assigned by seniority rather than aptitude. On the other side of the Capitol, House Republicans had experienced the revolt of progressive Republicans against the conservative House speaker, Joe Cannon, in 1909–10, then lost their majority to the Democrats in the 1910 elections. The deep division among Republicans generated the presidential candidacy of Theodore Roosevelt in 1912, who challenged the reelection of William Howard Taft and helped Democrat Woodrow Wilson win the White House in an electoral vote landslide.

In the minority, Gallinger played a limited role and proved to be a transitional figure. Due to the inherited organization of the Republican caucus, Gallinger was less central to his party's affairs than was Kern, or Kern's predecessors, for the Democrats. Since the days of Allison, the Republicans had looked to their caucus chairman to chair the Republican steering committee, but, unlike the situation for the Democratic leader, other senators had chaired the committee on committees. Senate Republicans maintained this distribution of authority under Gallinger—though, lacking responsibility to set the floor agenda, they went without a regular steering committee during these years in the minority. Gallinger was about to turn 76 years old when he was elected leader, and there was speculation that he would not run for reelection to his Senate seat in 1914, which would be his first popular election.[39] He successfully ran for reelection but died four years later. The challenges for Republicans during these years included establishing peace among Republicans and keeping up with the Democrats in their aggressive innovations in campaign preparations as the Seventeenth Amendment took effect, neither of which was easy for Gallinger. He was squarely associated with party conservatives and he had not faced serious opposition in the New Hampshire legislature for his election to the Senate through four terms.

---

[39] "Gallinger to Quit Senate," *Washington Post*, Nov. 28, 1912, 3.

Jacob H. Gallinger (R, N.H.), the first Republican floor leader. He became caucus chairman and floor leader in March 1913, when Senate Republicans became the minority for the first time in 18 years. In those years the Senate Republican caucus still assigned leadership on the basis of seniority.

Library of Congress, Prints & Photographs Division, photograph by Harris & Ewing, reproduction number LC-DIG-hec-03930

To a significant degree, Gallinger relied on Lodge to assist with party management duties (Groves 2012, 121). Thirteen years younger than Gallinger, Lodge was next in line for the conference chairmanship based on seniority. Lodge was viewed by many as the leader of party regulars and made most of the organizational motions within the conference (Wolff and Ritchie 1999). He was appointed by Gallinger to chair the committee on committees in 1913 and again in 1915—unusual, since this position had seldom been given to the heir apparent to the conference chairman. In 1915, the Republican Senate conference explicitly authorized Gallinger and Lodge to consult with Democratic leaders on the organization of the Senate and "to take such action in regard thereto on the floor of the Senate as might be rendered necessary" (Wolff and Ritchie 1999, 46). And, on policy and party strategy, Lodge, the leading Republican on foreign affairs, was the central figure in his caucus as Europe erupted in war and the United States was drawn into the conflict. By February 1917, when Gallinger became ill and did not return to the Senate for a few weeks, Lodge, rather than the conference secretary or whip, assumed responsibility as the acting conference chairman and performed the regular duties of the chairman, including the appointment of a committee on committees and a committee to develop a new cloture rule (Wolff and Ritchie 1999, 64, 67, 69).[40]

Committee Assignments

Kern quickly took charge of the Democrats' committee assignments. After the 1912 elections, progressive Democrats had organized an effort to depose Martin and ensure that progressives controlled the major committees. By the time they settled on Kern as their choice for leader, they had developed plans to reform committee assignment practices to take control away from Democratic conservatives who, by virtue of their seniority, would move into important chairmanships and dominate top committees. Kern, once elected, appointed a steering committee stacked with progressives, but he personally performed the balancing act of asserting progressive control of key committees while accommodating the seniority and requests of as many of his colleagues as possible. He introduced several reform resolutions, but only one, providing that a majority of Democrats on a standing committee may call a meeting and may select subcommittees and conferees, was adopted. The Kern-led steering committee proposed and made assignments to a new standing committee, Banking and Currency, to take over jurisdiction of a large category of legislation important to progressives, thereby reducing the jurisdiction under the control

---

[40] In February 1917, Gallinger is reported to have been ill with the grippe, or flu, a serious condition for someone of his age. He died in August 1918, apparently from arteriosclerosis. See "Senator Gallinger Ill," *Boston Daily Globe*, Feb. 25, 1917, 8; "Rush Congress Plans," *Washington Post*, Mar. 23, 1917, 1; Kelly and Burrage 1920, 419.

of Furnifold Simmons (D, N.C.), the conservative chairman of the Finance Committee (Bowers 1918, 289–93). With the experience of the Republican Senate during the previous two decades in mind, along with persistent criticism of how decisions had been made by the Democratic steering committee in those years, the steering committee's report to the caucus explained that "we propose that this great body shall be Democratic not only in name, but in practical reality, and that the charge so often made that it is controlled by a few men through committee reorganization and otherwise shall no longer have any basis in fact" (Ritchie 1998a, 61).[41]

In the years after the progressive rebellion of the 1910s, Democrats reverted to their old pattern of entrusting committee assignments to the party leader, and Martin and Underwood relied on seniority. During this era, the last time the steering committee's list was presented to the full Democratic conference for approval was in 1919. Thereafter, under Underwood in the early 1920s and continuing into the 1940s, the caucus adopted a motion creating a steering committee and giving it, as the 1921 motion reads, "authority to assign representatives on the several committees of the Senate from time to time and make selections to fill vacancies that might occur" or similar phrasing (Ritchie 1998a, 303–4, 307, 312, 328, 332, 341, 350, 365, 385, 402). Comprised of the leader, whip, vice chairman, and several senators appointed by the leader, the Democratic steering committee kept party leaders in firm control of the committee assignment process.

On the Republican side of the Senate, Gallinger, like his predecessors as conference chairman, appointed the committee on committees, including its chairman, but did not sit on the committee himself (Wolff and Ritchie 1999, 35–36). With Republicans in the minority from 1913 to 1919, committee assignments generated little or no discussion in the full conference; they were handed the leftovers and did not expect to have much voice in writing legislation in committee. There were a handful of exceptions—such as the desire of an anti-war, progressive senator for a Foreign Relations assignment in 1915—but generally there was little conflict, and conflicts were readily settled in favor of regulars.[42] This was still an era in which the Senate had more committees than majority party members, so Republicans received about 20 minor committee chairmanships, primarily on committees that never met, which gave about half of the Republicans additional office space and staff.

Replacing Gallinger in the summer of 1918, Lodge wanted more assertive and conservative committees, but he found himself in a tangle of factional fights over committee assignments. Later that year, after it became clear that

---

[41] Olezsek (1991, 21) attributes this statement directly to Kern, citing the *Washington Post*, Mar. 16, 1913, 6, which does appear to quote Kern. The conference minutes report the same statement word-for-word as the report of the steering committee.

[42] "Senate Lists Made Up," *Washington Post*, Dec. 12, 1915, 5; "Congress Will Wait," *Washington Post*, Dec. 13, 1915, 2.

Republicans would have a new majority in the next Congress, progressive Republicans began agitating for reforms to spread important chairmanships and committee assignments to more senators, including themselves (Rogers 1920; Nelson 1980, 33). To stem the revolt, which could cost the party its 49–47 majority if progressives bolted the party, Lodge named a party committee to "harmonize" the proposals of progressive George Norris (R, Nebr.) with the concerns of the regulars. Lodge went along with the resulting resolution that called for a change in Senate rules to limit senators to two of the nine most important committees and to bar a chairman (or ranking member) of one of those committees from serving on a conference committee associated with one of the other eight committees (Wolff and Ritchie 1999, 87–89).

But that did not resolve the matter. When a special session convened in May 1919, progressive Republicans opposed the appointment of Boies Penrose (R, Pa.) as chairman of the Finance Committee and of Francis Warren (R, Wyo.) as chairman of Appropriations, both of whom were the most senior Republicans on their committees. Penrose was the boss of the Pennsylvania Republican organization and a senator closely associated with high-tariff policies and conservative views on wartime taxation; Warren was nearly 75, the Senate's last Civil War veteran, and a strong conservative. Lodge and Curtis negotiated a truce on committee assignments by putting off the issue until after the Senate was organized, with Lodge appointing a committee on committees that included two progressives. The committee on committees recommended the selection of Penrose and Warren, and only Penrose was challenged in conference. Five senators voted against Penrose, but several progressives chose to protest by not attending the meeting. Perhaps most remarkable, Lodge called an extra and public session of the conference so that progressives could openly explain their opposition to Penrose and Warren. The crisis passed as the Senate moved into the debate on the League of Nations.[43]

Intraparty conflict over committee chairmanships and assignments continued through the 1920s. Lodge's task was made more difficult in 1921 when the Senate eliminated 42 committees, most of which never met, and limited the size of some of the most powerful committees.[44] This left fewer key positions to distribute and intensified conflict over those that remained. In late 1923, with

---

[43] During the public conference, eight progressives voted against Penrose. A transcript of the public conference is printed with the conference minutes (Wolff and Ritchie 1999, 99–104). See also "Progressives Will Oppose Penrose," *New York Times*, May 11, 1919, 13; "Warren and Penrose to Head Big Committees," *St. Louis Post-Dispatch*, May 26, 1919, 3; "Progressives End Their Senate Fight," *New York Times*, May 27, 1919, 17; "Penrose Is Chairman," *Washington Post*, May 27, 1919, 1.

[44] Nearly all committees that never or seldom met were eliminated, and the Senate restored full jurisdiction to the Appropriations Committee. The remaining chairmen benefited from more office space and staff, and some other committees gained additional jurisdiction: *Cong. Rec.*, May 27, 1920, 7715–16. After the cuts were made, only Lodge and Wadsworth had important chairmanships among Republicans from northeastern states (Brown 1922, 278).

La Follette and progressives holding the balance of power between regular Republicans and the Democrats, control of the Committee on Interstate Commerce, with its jurisdiction over railroads, flared into open controversy. Progressive Republicans wanted Iowa's Albert Cummins to relinquish the committee chairmanship to La Follette, next in line by virtue of seniority. Cummins refused, and progressive Republicans and Democrats forced a floor vote on the Interstate Commerce chairmanship, with Democrats voting for their ranking member, Ellison Smith (D, S.C.), and progressive Republicans voting for La Follette and later James Couzens (R, Mich.), denying Cummins the required majority. After 32 ballots and the passage of a month, most progressive Republicans shifted their votes to Smith, and he was elected.[45] While Lodge had kept the regulars together behind Cummins, his influence with the progressives proved limited. Success in navigating intraparty divisions, one of Lodge's central challenges, proved elusive. It was a perverse outcome—a Republican Senate electing a conservative Democrat to chair a major committee, in response to progressive dissatisfaction—but, for Lodge and other regular Republicans, the greater evil would have been to reward the progressives for opposing the party conference on the floor and accepting a compromise Republican as committee chairman. The episode intensified the rift between progressives and regular Republicans and was an important step toward La Follette's decision to run for president against Calvin Coolidge in 1924.[46]

Campaign Committees

The transition from the selection of senators by state legislatures to direct popular election of senators came to a close with Robinson's selection for a vacant Senate seat by the Arkansas legislature in 1913 (Schiller and Stewart 2014). Senate parties and leaders had long worried about the partisan composition of their institution and had worked to raise money, provide campaign literature, and organize stump speakers, but they did not have campaign committees devoted solely to persuading legislatures to elect partisans to the Senate. Congressional campaign committees traced their origins to the 1850s

---

[45] "Radicals to Fight to Control Congress," *New York Times*, Nov. 19, 1923, 1; "Lodge and Smoot Lay Out Campaign," *Boston Daily Globe*, Nov. 24, 1923, 5; "Cummins to Drop One Senate Post," *New York Times*, Nov. 25, 1923, 4; "Progressives Offer a Deal to Cummins," *New York Times*, Nov. 27, 1923, 4; "Cummins Refuses to Quit Senate Post; Deadlock Impends," *New York Times*, Nov. 28, 1923, 1; "Cummins to Allow Senate to Decide if He Retains 2 Posts," *Washington Post*, Nov. 28, 1923, 1; "Senate Factions in Truce," *New York Times*, Dec. 1, 1923, 2; "Radical Senators Force a Deadlock," *New York Times*, Dec. 11, 1923, 1; "Insurgents Hold Up Cummins' Election," *Washington Post*, Dec. 11, 1923, 11; "Senate Fight to Go Over for Holidays," *Washington Post*, Dec. 20, 1923, 2; "Senate Still Deadlocked," *New York Times*, Jan. 8, 1924, 22; "Smith Is Elected Over Cummins and Senate Tie-Up Ends," *Washington Post*, Jan. 10, 1924, 1.
[46] "Smith's Election," *Atlanta Constitution*, Jan. 11, 1924, 6.

and 1860s, and senators benefited to a limited degree from their participation in the congressional campaign committees, which for both parties were joint House-Senate committees. Beginning in the 1890s, the Senate's Democratic and Republican steering committees had begun monitoring and intervening in elections. But it was only in 1916 that each party established a senatorial campaign committee, three years after the adoption of the Seventeenth Amendment and in the midst of intense party competition for control of the Senate. As these new, independent campaign committees developed, the Senate's floor leaders by the 1920s had taken charge of appointing the members and chairmen.

The Democrats. In 1913, soon after his election, Wilson pushed congressional Democrats to get an early start on developing campaign strategies for the 1914 midterm elections. This included more coordination between the Democratic congressional campaign committee and the Democratic National Committee, as well as increased resources for the national committee. With the advent of direct Senate elections, Democratic senators pressed for more representation on the joint campaign committee.[47] Kern appointed five Democratic senators to confer with the congressional campaign committee about expanding Senate representation. Senate representation on the congressional committee appears to have increased from nine to 21, along with a member of the House from each state, as had been the practice.[48] The committee was chaired by Frank Doremus (D, Mich.), a member of the House of Representatives, who appointed two House members and two senators as an executive committee charged with coordinating activities with the national committee.[49]

Two years later, in 1916, a third of the Senate was again up for popular election, with many progressive Democrats finishing their first terms. It was a presidential election year, and the Democratic National Committee was firmly under Wilson's control. Discussions about coordinating the national committee and Senate efforts took place, yielding the origins of a distinct Senate Democratic campaign organization. According to the *New York Times* in early July 1916, "Senator [Willard] Saulsbury [Jr.] of Delaware was selected tentatively to take charge of that feature [the Senate] of the campaign, and it was said tonight that he might be made head of a bureau under Mr. McCormick [chairman of the Democratic National Committee] rather than Chairman of a Senatorial Committee, independent of the National Committee."[50] The

---

[47] "Keeps Senators Here," *Washington Post*, May 29, 1913, 4; "More Senators To Be Put on Congressional Committee," *Minneapolis Morning Tribune*, May 20, 1913, 4.

[48] "Democrats Defer to Wilson's Wishes," *New York Times*, May 10, 1913, 4; "Democratic Joint Plans," *New York Times*, May 18, 1913, 13; "Approved by Wilson," *Washington Post*, May 20, 1913, 4.

[49] "Scully's Ability Recognized," *Daily Home News* (New Brunswick, N.J.), Aug. 19, 1913, 6.

[50] "Democrats Devise New Plan to Hold Control in Senate," *New York Times*, July 6, 1916, 1.

Washington Post indicated that the chairman of the national committee was expected to name other senators and referred to Saulsbury as the "chairman of the special senatorial bureau."[51] The *Boston Globe* reported in early August that "Senator Walsh of Montana, who will be Western manager of the Democratic National campaign; Senator Saulsbury of Delaware and Senator Stone of Missouri have been designated as a special committee to direct the Democratic Senatorial campaign."[52] The same day, the *Chicago Daily Tribune* noted that "Senator Thomas J. Walsh of Montana and Senator Willard Saulsbury of Delaware will arrive tomorrow. They with Senator Stone of Missouri compose the senate campaign committee to try to keep the upper house Democratic."[53] While the Saulsbury "committee" appears to have been a bureau of the national committee, it represented the first clearly designated senatorial campaign committee for the Democrats. It was headquartered in Chicago that year because of the large number of midwestern and western Senate races.[54] The Democratic caucus minutes do not mention a campaign committee during the summer of 1916, which suggests that the caucus did not vote to approve this arrangement.[55]

For the next two election cycles, Senate Democrats followed the 1916 precedent. The Senate was the center of attention in the 1918 election campaign because of the implications of Senate control for treaties that would follow the war. As the elections drew close in 1918, newspapers made several references to Senator Peter Gerry (D, R.I.) as "chairman of the Democratic Senatorial Committee," suggesting an independent Senate campaign committee, but not indicating how Gerry had been chosen.[56] In 1920, after Ohio Governor James Cox was nominated the Democratic candidate for president, the *Washington Post* reported that "Senator Peter G. Gerry, of Rhode Island, has been selected by Gov. Cox to head the all-important senatorial campaign

[51] "Plans to Hold Senate," *Washington Post*, July 6, 1916, 2; "Opens Senate Campaign," *Washington Post*, Aug. 13, 1916, A9.

[52] "To Aid Democratic Senators," *Boston Daily Globe*, Aug. 6, 1916, 8.

[53] "Nutshell Politics," *Chicago Daily Tribune*, Aug. 6, 1916, 7. Also see "Plan Campaign for Senate," *New York Times*, Aug. 6, 1916, 5; "Democrats See Senate Control After Election," *Chicago Daily Tribune*, Aug. 13, 1916, 8; "Democrats Will Control Senate and Gain 4 Seats, Says Saulsbury," *Washington Post*, Aug. 13, 1916, A4.

[54] "G.O.P. Majority in Lower House; May Get Senate," *Chicago Daily Tribune*, Nov. 8, 1916, 4.

[55] Previous research on the history of the Senate Democrats did not uncover this transitional process (Kolodny 1998, 70–75).

[56] "Line Up for Congress," *Washington Post*, Oct. 21, 1918, 5; "Wilson Appeals to Nation," *New York Times*, Oct. 26, 1918, 1; "Democrats to Shut Off Debate," *New York Times*, Oct. 30, 1918, 5; "Wilson Appeal Is Boomerang," *Chicago Daily Tribune*, Oct. 31, 1918, 5; "Republicans Take a Hopeful View," *New York Times*, Oct. 31, 1918, 6; "Democrat Campaign Expenses $395,459," *San Francisco Chronicle*, Oct. 29, 1918, 8; "Democratic Fund Reported $412,138," *New York Times*, Oct. 29, 1918, 22; "Charges Big Fund to Block Wilson," *New York Times*, Oct. 28, 1918, 1; "Armour Gave $5,000 to Republican Fund," *New York Times*, Oct. 30, 1918, 11.

committee."[57] Then, a week later, according to the *Post*, the chairman of the national committee announced that Senator Thomas Walsh (D, Mont.) would replace Gerry as "chairman of the Democratic senatorial committee."[58] If the *Washington Post*'s accounts are accurate, they would be consistent with the continued treatment of the senatorial committee as a unit of the national committee as late as 1920, reflecting close coordination between the presidential candidate and the senatorial effort.

With a Republican in the White House for the midterm elections of 1922, the Democratic Senate caucus—and its leader—assumed responsibility for the campaign committee. Minority Leader Underwood, according to the *Washington Post*, appointed a Democratic senatorial committee that year, with David Walsh (D, Mass.) as chairman. In announcing the committee, Underwood explained that "the selection of this committee was made after a conference with all the Democratic candidates for election and with the unanimous consent of the Democratic steering committee of the Senate."[59] Thereafter, the chairmanship and composition of the campaign committee was left for Senate Democrats to determine themselves and the committee was staffed by the Senate party secretary, a staff post, who operated under the direction of the leader.[60] It appears that the conference chairman—the Democratic floor leader—appointed the campaign committee chairman and membership from 1922 onward, although the caucus minutes in these years do not mention an announcement from the leader as they do for other party committees.

The Republicans. Republicans emerged from the 1912 elections a battered and divided party, with many of them in two years facing direct election for the first time. Watching the early efforts of President Wilson to build a stronger campaign organization for Democrats under the national committee, Senate Republicans moved quickly to expand senatorial representation on their own party's congressional committee. In May 1913, Senate Republicans authorized Gallinger to appoint five senators to consult with House leaders on increasing the number of senators on the Republican congressional campaign committee. Gallinger's appointment of progressives and regulars was notable (Wolff and Ritchie 1999, 42).[61] "It was the prevailing opinion of the senators' conference

---

[57] "Cox His Own Leader," *Washington Post*, July 30, 1920, 1.
[58] "50,000 To Hear Cox," *Washington Post*, Aug. 7, 1920, 1.
[59] "Walsh Will Head Senate Campaign," *Washington Post*, Sept. 8, 1922, 2.
[60] "Jones Succeeds Walsh," *New York Times*, July 22, 1924, 3; "Democratic Senate Majority This Year Predicted by Jones," *Washington Post*, July 22, 1924, 4; "Democratic Committee Named," *Washington Post*, Jan. 18, 1926, 2; "Day in Congress," *Washington Post*, May 4, 1928, 4; "Swanson Will Head Senatorial Campaign," *New York Times*, Aug. 11, 1932, 4; "Lewis Named Head of Senate Group," *New York Times*, Feb. 8, 1934, 13; "Guffey Heads Campaign," *New York Times*, Oct. 22, 1935, 15.
[61] "Drop G.O.P. Feuds," *Washington Post*, May 23, 1913, 1; "Republicans Consider Reorganization Plans," *Minneapolis Tribune*, May 23, 1913, 1.

that the congressional campaign committee should be organized at once with representation from the senate as well as from the house, following the suggestion from President Wilson and adopted by the Democrats," the *Minneapolis Tribune* reported that May, "that headquarters should be established, a publicity campaign inaugurated, and a definite campaign policy outlined as early as possible."[62] A joint conference of Republican senators and representatives, co-chaired by Gallinger, was held in August.[63] At its first meeting, held that month, the newly organized Republican campaign committee promised to give special attention to the Senate races.[64]

In the next election cycle, in March 1916, congressional Republicans initially held a joint conference to organize their campaign efforts.[65] But that summer, Republicans took the initiative in creating a Senate-only campaign committee, appointed by the floor leader, who selected senators from the two major factions to the committee. In July 1916, the day after Saulsbury was named to head the Democrats' efforts under the auspices of the Democratic National Committee, Republican leader Gallinger appointed a committee of five as a "special committee" on the senatorial campaign. Gallinger did this without specific authorization from the conference. The special committee was headed by John Weeks (R, Mass.), and the other members were prominent and mostly junior Republicans—Reed Smoot (R, Utah), who was in his third term; Curtis, in his second term; and first-term senators Thomas Sterling (R, S.Dak.) and Wadsworth. It was expected to coordinate its work with the national committee and the presidential campaign.[66] Notably, unlike the Democrats' version that year, which was a subunit of the national committee and was named by the national committee chairman, the Republican senatorial campaign committee of 1916 was named by the Senate floor leader and conference chairman. By the time Lodge was elected to replace Gallinger in the summer of 1918, the Senate Republican conference had already established its campaign committee that year, apparently with Gallinger as committee chairman. Following his death, the conference elected Smoot as campaign chairman and Curtis as the secretary of the campaign committee.[67] Even as Republicans established an

[62] "Republicans Consider Reorganization Plans," *Minneapolis Tribune*, May 23, 1913, 1.

[63] "Caucus Names Committee," *New York Tribune*, Aug. 27, 1913, 4.

[64] "Woods New Head of Campaign Committee," *New York Tribune*, Aug. 30, 1913, 4.

[65] "Plan G.O.P. Campaign," *Washington Post*, Mar. 10, 1916, 11.

[66] "Named to Win Senate," *Washington Post*, July 7, 1916, 2; "Hughes Plans Trip with Eye to Moose," *New York Times*, July 18, 1916, 6; "Hughes Will Assist Congress Campaign," *New York Times*, July 19, 1916, 5; "Moose and G.O.P. Meet in Council to Hear Hughes," *New York Times*, July 21, 1915, 1; "To Make Fight to Carry Maine," *Hartford Courant*, July 21, 1916, 20.

[67] "Proceeding of Congress and Committees in Brief," *Washington Post*, Sept. 22, 1918, E4; "Wilson Appeals to Nation," *New York Times*, Oct. 26, 1918, 1.

independent campaign committee in the 1910s, they relied on the Republican National Committee to raise and distribute money for campaigns.[68]

The 1920 election cycle proved pivotal. Miles Poindexter (R, Wash.), a progressive and leading opponent to the League of Nations, announced his candidacy for president in October 1919 with some hope of attracting support from both progressives and regulars. He was never a major factor in the race for the nomination—it went to Senator Warren Harding (R, Ohio)—but in June 1920 Poindexter was named chairman of the Republican senatorial committee, with Joseph Frelinghuysen (R, N.J.) as secretary.[69] Senators raised concerns about the Senate efforts being swallowed up by the presidential campaign and the national committee, but Poindexter made a special effort to describe the autonomy of the senatorial effort. "This campaign will be conducted entirely under the control of the Republican Senatorial Committee of the Senate," Poindexter said in a statement. "It will not in any way be amalgamated with the National Committee, although it will work in entire harmony and cooperation with that committee."[70] In the early fall, Poindexter indicated that the committee hoped to raise $200,000 to be spent in 20 states, which is the first campaign season in which a large fund for the Senate committee is mentioned that is independent of the national committee.[71] Kolodny (1998, 68–73), who otherwise writes little about the origins of the two senatorial campaign committees, describes, in detail, the activities of the 1922 Republican committee, which raised a substantial amount of money, assisted candidates, and distributed two publications. By the early 1920s, the Republican senatorial committee was, in every regard, organizationally independent of the national committee. It was a creature of the Republican senatorial conference—its members and chairman named by the Republican leader, as the December 1927 conference minutes noted, "following the general custom for many years" (Wolff and Ritchie 1999, 191).[72]

LEADING ON THE FLOOR

The term "floor leader" is used only once in the Democratic conference minutes in the 1903–64 period—in a 1959 list of leaders—but the term had already

---

[68] "Republicans Face a Hard Task in Naming a Party Chairman," *New York Times*, June 3, 1934, XX7; "Lenroot's Attack Centres on Wilson," *New York Times*, Mar. 29, 1918, 9; "Hays Gets Illinois SOS," *New York Times*, July 29, 1918, 9.

[69] "Harding Aids Fight for Senate Control," *New York Times*, June 24, 1920, 3. The Republican conference minutes do not mention Poindexter's appointment.

[70] "Fight for Control of Next Senate," *New York Times*, July 14, 1920, 3; "Harding Preparing to Leave Washington," *St. Louis Post-Dispatch*, July 1, 1920, 13.

[71] "Senate Committee Decides on Widest Inquiry on Funds," *New York Times*, Sept. 3, 1920, 1.

[72] The method of appointment is not mentioned in the newspapers, conference minutes, or other sources of the early 1920s, but we do know that Gallinger appointed the committee in 1916 and, it appears, before his death in 1918, and the 1927 reference in the Republican conference minutes strongly suggests that this was a routine practice in the early and mid-1920s.

been in regular usage for two decades, by senators and journalists, when Kern was elected conference chairman and floor leader in 1913. With his election, Kern immediately assumed responsibility for managing the Senate floor. He negotiated the schedule with his party colleagues, made motions to consider important bills, and worked with the president to arrange the Senate schedule to ensure consideration of priority and time-sensitive legislation. On the Republican side, the term "floor leader" first appears in the conference minutes in 1925, when Curtis was nominated and elected to be "Chairman of the Republican Conference and Floor Leader" (Wolff and Ritchie 1999, 168), though Gallinger, Lodge, and Curtis himself—who became conference chairman and leader in November 1924, upon Lodge's death—had served in this position in the years since 1913.

Floor Management as a Full-Time Activity

In the 1910s—first with Kern, then with Martin and Lodge—Senate majority leaders assumed personal responsibility for scheduling and floor management. One objective measure of this shift is the frequency with which leaders addressed the Senate. In Figure 6.3, we report the number of pages in the *Congressional Record* that are listed in the *Record*'s index for remarks made on the Senate floor by the majority leader. For comparison, we show the mean

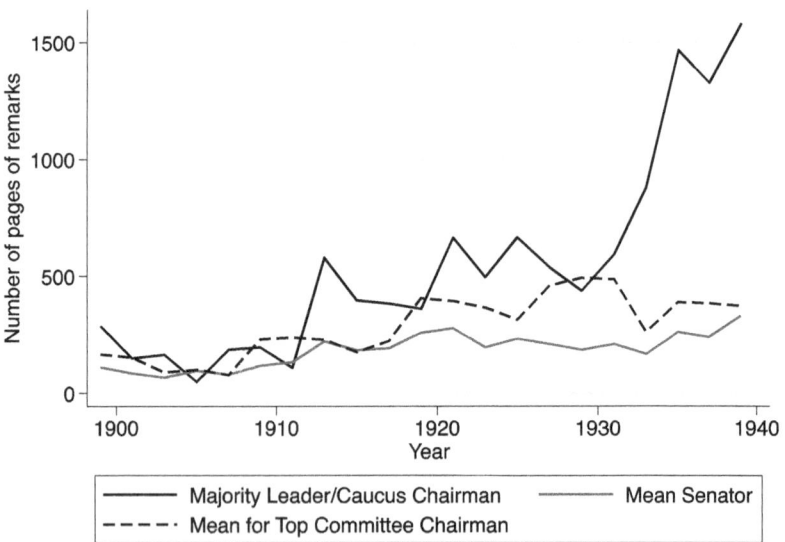

FIGURE 6.3 Number of pages for floor remarks listed in the index of the *Congressional Record*, for majority leader, top committee chairs, and all senators, by Congress, 1899–1940

Source: *Congressional Record* Index.

for four top committee chairs (Appropriations, Armed Services, Finance, and Foreign Relations, or their predecessors) and the mean for all senators. As the figure shows, the majority party's caucus chairmen between 1900 and 1913—all of them Republican and thus in a caucus that did not yet expect its caucus chairman to serve as leader—played no special role on the floor. The transformation in 1913 was dramatic and about much more than nomenclature. Not only was Kern the first senator elected by his caucus to be majority leader and Gallinger the first Republican leader in the Senate, but these men, and their successors, assumed new floor responsibilities along with their titles. It was an altogether new feature of Senate party organization.

The Democrats. As majority leaders, both Kern and Martin were the central players in party discussions of the floor agenda. They took command of the schedule and the motions required to implement it—negotiating and offering unanimous consent agreements, which are used to schedule and expedite Senate action on legislation, amendments, and nominations; announcing the unavoidable absences of colleagues; moving the Senate in and out of executive session; and revising the daily agenda to work around minority obstruction. On occasion, a whip, bill manager, or another senator would handle routine floor activity, but responsibility rested with the party leader. The steering committee and caucus met frequently under Kern, providing guidance about legislative priorities.[73] On the Senate floor, Kern was ever-present, but he tended to remain in the background and seldom spoke (Bowers 1918, 361–62; Gould 2005, 53–71). During Kern's four years as leader, President Wilson used a heavy hand with Senate Democrats to help set the schedule of business, meeting or corresponding frequently with Kern and even with the steering committee a few times. After taking over for Kern, Martin continued to be responsive to Wilson, while relying on the steering committee and on discussions with committee leaders for setting the floor agenda.[74] Unlike Kern, neither Martin nor Underwood relied much on the caucus for guidance, and Underwood, in the minority, had little role in scheduling.

Kern's role was evident to everyone. It was Kern who received a petition in 1915 from 41 fellow Democrats who wanted the creation of a special caucus committee to formulate a cloture rule. Frustrated with Republican obstructionism, all but 11 Senate Democrats, 10 of them southerners, favored a cloture rule but were blocked by a Rules Committee majority that opposed a new rule.

---

[73] "Swift Progress on Revision Bill," *Atlanta Constitution*, June 13, 1913, 14; "Wilson Prodding Senate: Sends for Steering Committee to Urge Haste on Currency," *New York Times*, Sept. 10, 1913, 8; "Senate to Tackle Three Money Bills," *New York Times*, Nov. 21, 1913, 13; "May Adjourn July 1," *Washington Post*, May 5, 1914, 1; "Senate Will Speed Up," *Washington Post*, Dec. 13, 1914, 8; "Busy Week in the Senate," *Washington Post*, July 17, 1916, 2; "Strive to Push Bills," *Washington Post*, Jan. 22, 1917, 2.

[74] "War Resolution Put Off in Both Houses Until Tomorrow," *St. Louis Post-Dispatch*, Apr. 3, 1917, 1; "Wilson Favors House Food Bill," *Boston Globe*, July 14, 1917, 1.

Kern appointed a committee of five, including himself, with the objective of gaining Senate approval early in the next Congress.[75] The fight over adopting a cloture rule, which was added to Rule XXII, came to a head in 1916 when measures important to Wilson—most immediately a bill to allow merchant ships to be armed—were killed or delayed for a considerable time by filibusters (Binder and Smith 1997). Championed by Senators Robert Owen (D, Okla.) and Hoke Smith (D, Ga.), a resolution to create a cloture motion requiring a two-thirds majority was reported unanimously by the Committee on Rules in May 1916.[76] Kern and the Democrats, much to the regret of many of them, did not act on it. The limited opposition from Democrats, along with the Republicans, made action on the resulting proposal impossible before Kern was defeated for reelection from Indiana in late 1916.

The issue remained alive as Martin took over from Kern. When the next Congress convened in a special session in the spring of 1917 to deal with matters left unaddressed by the 64th Congress, cloture was the first issue on the table. Owen and Martin revived the proposal in conference, they consulted with Republicans, and the two conferences authorized the appointment of committees to work out final language for a rule. Martin appointed the Democratic committee, and Lodge, the acting Republican conference chair, appointed his party's committee (Ritchie 1998a, 259–61; Wolff and Ritchie 1999, 69). Martin persuaded colleagues, like Owen, who wanted simple-majority cloture to accept the two-thirds threshold and, when the reform resolution came to the floor, he persuaded a party colleague to withdraw an amendment. The resolution was adopted with only three senators voting against it.[77]

Hitchcock, serving both as acting leader after Martin died and as Foreign Relations chairman, was the central Senate Democrat in discussions regarding the peace treaty in 1919 and 1920. Underwood was responsible for few innovations in party operations, though, as minority leader, he responded to scheduling proposals and other unanimous consent requests from the majority side. But Underwood's greatest legacy was in the Senate seating chart. In 1921, when the front and center desk on the Democratic side of the Senate floor was vacated after the death of a senator, Underwood took it. At the time, having

---

[75] "Cloture Is Asked by 41: Democrats Petition Kern for Revision of Senate Rules; Leader Selects Committee," *Washington Post*, Mar. 3, 1915, 2.
[76] "Cloture Rule Approved: Senate Committee Agrees on a Modified Form, Designed to Hasten Legislation and is Backed by Administration Leaders," *Washington Post*, May 7, 1916, A4.
[77] *Cong. Rec.*, Mar. 8, 1917, 19–45; "Republicans May Revive Filibuster: Senate Minority Not Ready to Abandon Fight for an Extra Session, Plan Afoot for Cloture," *New York Times*, Feb. 26, 1917, 1; "Cloture Rule for Senate," *Washington Post*, Feb. 27, 1917, 2; "Thirty-Three Senators Give Pledge to Mend Rules to Halt Filibustering," *New York Times*, Mar. 5, 1917, 1; "Left Without Power to Arm Ships, President Urges Senate to Change Rules to Permit Action," *Washington Post*, Mar. 5, 1917, 1; "Parties Acting Together: Tentative Agreement on Cloture by Committees from Both Caucuses," *New York Times*, Mar. 7, 1917, 1; "Unlimited Debate Rule, Over a Century Olde, Abandoned by Senate," *St. Louis Post-Dispatch*, Mar. 9, 1917, 2.

arrived in the Senate only six years earlier, he had previously had a seat in the last row.[78] Oddly, when Underwood stepped down as floor leader in 1923, he did not relinquish his seat. Robinson retained his own third-row desk until Underwood retired from the Senate in early 1927. When the next Congress convened in December 1927, Robinson took the front and center seat on the Democratic side of the chamber, as have all subsequent Democratic leaders.[79]

The Republicans. By the time Republicans lost their majority status in 1913, their steering committee had fallen into irrelevance and disuse (Wolff and Ritchie 1999, 2). In the lame-duck session of the 62nd Congress, after the 1912 elections yielded a Democratic president and Democrats looked likely to win a Senate majority, the Republicans authorized the caucus chairman to appoint a separate committee on legislation to set legislative priorities for the remainder of the Congress while some Senate seats were yet to be filled.[80] The committee reported directly to the conference, which adopted its recommendations (Wolff and Ritchie 1999, 31–32). In the next three Congresses, the Republicans were in the minority and did not appoint a regular steering committee at all (Munk 1970).

Minority Leader Gallinger was often on the floor questioning Democratic bill managers, overseeing the routine call of the calendar, and making speeches that attracted press attention. As the 1913 tariff bill was about to be debated on the floor, the Republican conference agreed that Gallinger would be "the recognized leader of the Republicans in all tariff matters" (Wolff and Ritchie 1999, 43), although not all Republicans were happy with his performance.[81] It is not clear why this step was considered useful, but it made Gallinger's role explicit for floor action that might have been led by a Republican with more

---

[78] Seating charts are available in the *Congressional Directory* and are reproduced at www.senate .gov/artandhistory/art/special/Desks/earlychambermaps.cfm. The chart for 1935 places McNary next to Underwood—apparently not centered because of the shortage of Republicans.

[79] In the 69th Congress (1925–27), Robinson and Underwood were ranked 11th and 13th in seniority among Senate Democrats, yet Underwood retained his front and center seat without holding a leadership position: see www.senate.gov/artandhistory/history/resources/pdf/chronlist .pdf. The Senate Historical Office reports that Robinson was the first leader to take the front and center seat, doing so in 1927 after Underwood retired and gave up that seat. That report neglects to note that Underwood took the seat in 1921 as leader and simply did not give it up between 1923, when he left the leadership post, and March 1927, when he retired from the Senate: see www.senate.gov/artandhistory/history/minute/Republican_Leader_Front_and_Center.htm.
Lodge, the Republican majority leader, continued to operate from the second row on his side of the center aisle. Senators Curtis, Watson, and McNary, Lodge's successors as Republican floor leader, also operated from their regularly assigned desks. The chamber maps in the *Congressional Directory* indicate that McNary had moved to the center front of the chamber by 1935, although some reports place the date in 1937 (Munk 1970, 35).

[80] "To Fight on for Jobs," *Washington Post*, Feb. 7, 1913, 4; "Republican Plan to Revive Party," *Chicago Daily Tribune*, Feb. 8, 1913, 4.

[81] "Begin Tariff Debate Today; Gallinger Chosen Floor Leader by Republican Senators," *Boston Daily Globe*, July 19, 1913, 14; "Tariff Bill Faces Republican Fight: Senate Minority Decides to Quit Passive Resistance and Oppose Radical Rate Changes," *New York Times*, July 31, 1913, 5.

seniority on the Finance Committee.[82] While Gallinger deferred to committee leaders to manage most bills, he was, despite his age, active on the floor until he became ill in 1918, occasionally offering amendments that represented a collective party response to Democratic proposals.

His successor, Lodge, was ever-present on the floor in 1919–21. As majority leader, Lodge assumed responsibility for routine motions, such as the motions to recess or adjourn the Senate at the end of daily sessions. Following the suggestion of House Majority Leader Frank Mondell (R, Wyo.) in late 1918, and before the Senate Republicans assumed majority control of their chamber, Lodge had appointed a group to meet jointly with the House Republican steering committee. Then, in 1919, as leader of a new Senate majority party, Lodge tried to rejuvenate collective party organs—the conference and the steering committee—to generate concerted party action on a postwar agenda. Lodge successfully fought the Wilson administration's legislative proposals, using the steering committee to manage the flow of legislation and construct compromises within the party. In fact, his use of the steering committee stimulated sharp criticism from Democrats, who argued that important policy decisions were being made behind closed doors in Republican steering committee meetings (Garraty 1953, 355; Rogers 1921, 71).[83] He appointed the conservative Porter McCumber (R, N.Dak.) chairman of the steering committee in 1919 and then made himself chairman in 1921—the last time a Republican caucus chairman or floor leader held this position.[84] He also named La Follette and Joseph France (R, Md.) to the steering committee to represent progressive views.

By the time the next Congress convened and Republican Warren Harding was in the White House, Lodge's control over the Senate agenda was slipping. While Lodge benefited from the informal practice of easily gaining recognition from the presiding officer to make motions that set the floor agenda (McConnell and Brownell 2019, 157–58; Page 1922, 23), the deepening factional divide within the party limited the value of party meetings and undermined Lodge's ability to win votes on key motions. The steering committee met infrequently, the joint committee even more rarely. At times, progressive or Farm Bloc obstruction blocked Harding administration legislation and even forced floor consideration of legislation that the steering committee preferred to delay or kill.[85] "At present the Republican leaders in the Senate cannot control.

---

[82] "Guns on the Tariff," *Washington Post*, July 19, 1913, 1. For more background on Gallinger's floor activities during the 1913 tariff debate, see "Expects Long Tariff Fight," *Washington Post*, May 6, 1913, 4; "Immunity for Labor Approved by Senate," *New York Times*, May 8, 1913, 1; "Ask Facts on Lobby," *Washington Post*, May 28, 1913, 4; "Senators in a Tilt on Wilson's Lobby," *New York Times*, June 14, 1913, 5; "Guns on the Tariff," *Washington Post*, July 19, 1913, 1; "Wins on Free Sugar," *Washington Post*, Aug. 20, 1913, 1.

[83] *Cong. Rec.*, May 20, 1920, 7921.

[84] "Knit Congress Force," *Washington Post*, Mar. 20, 1921, 1.

[85] "Recess Effort Is Defeated," *Los Angeles Times*, July 29, 1921, I:9.

They are controled by the group which is insisting upon legislation intended to benefit the farmer," the *New York Times* reported in late 1921. "The Senate Steering Committee has not functioned for some time. The group seems to have put that time-honored party machinery out of business."[86] Informal discussions between Lodge, President Harding, committee chairmen, and other leaders more frequently shaped attempts to structure the Senate agenda than meetings of the steering committee or conference (Brown 1922, 252–72; Widenor 1991, 53; Wolff and Ritchie 1999, 94).[87] The situation did not improve for the remainder of Lodge's life and tenure. His writing projects and declining health kept him off the floor much of the time in 1923 and 1924, and Curtis substituted for him frequently.[88]

Unanimous Consent Agreements

By the turn of the twentieth century, agreements that provided for a vote on a bill and pending amendments at a certain time were a regular part of floor management practice, dating back to the 1840s. Senators in the late nineteenth century submitted unanimous consent requests in writing to the desk, where they were often read by the secretary at the request of the presiding officer. Unanimous consent agreements (UCAs) that were intended to govern the conduct of business on subsequent days were printed on the title page of the daily *Calendar of Business* as long as they were operative. And the secretary appears to have reworded numerous agreements so that they would conform to what had become the "usual form," as some senators noted on the floor. These innovations occurred without any official recognition of the UCAs in the standing rules of the Senate. Responsibility for negotiating UCAs rested with bill managers—typically committee chairmen—and orchestrating agreements and managing several bills proved difficult and consumed considerable time on the floor in the absence of recognized floor leaders.

How to enforce unanimous consent agreements and whether an agreement could be revised at a later date complicated the use of UCAs in the first years of the twentieth century (Roberts and Smith 2007). At that time, a UCA could not be enforced by the Senate's presiding officer because it was considered to be an informal agreement among senators, a "gentlemen's agreement." The argument was based on two premises—that UCAs were not recognized in the Senate's rules and that the presiding officer had no authority except that granted explicitly by the rules or an order of the Senate. Further complicating the use of

---

[86] "Congress in Grip of Farmers' Group," *New York Times*, Oct. 3, 1921, 8.
[87] "Tariff Fight Line-Up," *Washington Post*, July 6, 1921, 1; "Oppose Funding Plan," *Washington Post*, Sept. 27, 1921, 1.
[88] "The Senate Leader," *Atlanta Constitution*, Nov. 28, 1924, 8.

UCAs after the turn of the century was the thesis that UCAs could not be modified, even by unanimous consent. Lodge made this argument in 1907 (*Cong. Rec.*, January 10, 1907, 878–79) and consistently maintained the position (*Cong. Rec.*, January 10, 1913, 1389–90), along with the view that the presiding officer could not enforce UCAs. Lodge's theory was that a UCA, as a gentlemen's agreement, created an obligation that could not be violated by senators who happened to be on the floor at some later time. Lodge argued, as senators had for decades, that modifications in UCAs, even by unanimous consent, would eventually undermine confidence in UCAs. Although presiding officers were not consistent on this matter, the Lodge thesis was the prevailing interpretation during the first decade of the twentieth century.

Arguments about UCAs came to a head in January 1913, when the Republicans still held a majority (*Cong. Rec.*, January 10–11, 1913, 1324–29, 1354–56, 1388–95). After having failed in previous days to gain unanimous consent for a vote on a prohibition bill, Newell Sanders (R, Tenn.) asked for unanimous consent once again and, probably much to his surprise, received it. A moment later Smoot inquired, "Was there a unanimous consent agreement just entered?" When the presiding officer indicated that there was, Smoot immediately asked that it be reconsidered, to which the presiding officer responded that "it is beyond the power of the Senate to change or interfere with a unanimous consent agreement after it is made." Several senators insisted that they had not heard the request and that previous practice in such cases was to have the request submitted to the Senate again. Others, including Lodge, had to confess that a UCA must be observed. The next day, Smoot suggested that the request be resubmitted to the Senate, but President Pro Tempore Augustus Bacon (D, Ga.) indicated that he had no power to rule on the matter and referred the issue to the full Senate. A large majority voted to have Sanders's request resubmitted, which it was, and Smoot promptly objected to the request. Gallinger then restated the request—with a different date for action on the measure—and it was accepted.

In the next session, with the Democrats in the majority, a committee recommended the adoption of a new rule, an additional paragraph for Rule XII. The rule provided that "no request by a Senator for unanimous consent for the taking of a final vote on a specified date upon the passage of a bill or joint resolution shall be submitted to the Senate for agreement thereto until, upon a roll call ordered for the purpose by the presiding officer, it shall be disclosed that a quorum of the Senate is present; and when unanimous consent is thus given, the same shall operate as the order of the Senate, but any unanimous consent may be revoked by another unanimous consent granted in the prescribed manner" (*Cong. Rec.*, January 16, 1914, 1756). The requirement for a quorum call was not controversial. Even the provision for UCAs to be considered orders of the Senate, enabling the presiding officer to enforce them, received little discussion. Lodge and Smoot complained about the ability to modify UCAs by unanimous consent but appeared to accept the logic once the rule was amended to require one day's notice of a request to modify a UCA providing for a final vote.[89] A bipartisan majority supported the proposal, as amended (*Cong. Rec.*, January 16, 1914, 1756–59).

Within a few years, floor leaders assumed primary responsibility for negotiating UCAs and managing their approval on the floor. Lodge and Curtis were actively engaged in the process (*Cong. Rec.*, July 20, 1921, 4115, and August 1, 1921, 4480). With the new rule, the majority leader had a more useful tool for arranging the business of the Senate. The presiding officer could enforce an agreement, and the majority leader could seek to change agreed-upon plans with another unanimous consent request. In time, a large body of precedent accumulated in support of the proposition that presiding officers were obligated to take the initiative in enforcing the provisions of UCAs (see Riddick 1992, 1311–69). Enforcement by the presiding officer made the details of UCAs more important, which made the involvement of the floor leader to protect the interests of the party essential.

SERVING AS INTERMEDIARY WITH THE PRESIDENT

The expectation that the Senate leader of the president's party works closely with the White House was quickly established with Kern and President Wilson in 1913, then reinforced by Lodge, with Presidents Harding and Coolidge, in the 1920s. Both leaders assumed responsibility for explaining the situation in the Senate to the president and reported on their consultations with the president to their party colleagues, but the nature of the relationship turned on the president's assertiveness and on the personalities of the two primary actors. Kern consulted with Wilson even on the organization of the Senate (Haughton 1973, 138–41) and appears to have taken more direction from Wilson on Senate affairs than Wilson took from Kern. Harding, in contrast, relied heavily on Lodge's understanding of Senate politics. Presidents, of course, had other conduits to the Senate, particularly if, like Harding, they had served in the Senate themselves. The relationship between presidents and opposition party leaders, sometimes called out-party leaders, varied widely.

Wilson entered office in 1913 with a large legislative agenda, which he labeled the New Freedom, and envisioned a new arrangement between the

---

[89] Later rulings would allow the one-day notice requirement to be waived by unanimous consent (Riddick 1992, 1354).

White House and the Capitol, with the president leading and guiding congressional action. Kern served as the president's primary contact in the Senate. He met frequently with the president, received letters from the president, and reported the president's views to his party colleagues. Wilson also was consulting party leaders of the House of Representatives, but the Wilson-Kern relationship was especially consequential because the Senate represented a more serious challenge to enacting the president's domestic legislative program (Munk 1970, 1974; Oleszek 1991, 24–26). At Wilson's request, Kern made many visits to the White House that were kept secret and out of the newspapers (Bowers 1918, 363). Still, it appears that Munk (1970, 1974) overstated Wilson's contribution to the creation of modern floor leadership. Wilson certainly wanted a lieutenant in the Senate and relied on Kern, but Wilson shared a need with Senate progressives for a leader to organize the party and schedule the Senate to enact the progressive program. Wilson did not manufacture the floor leadership role for the Senate Democrats; it already existed. Wilson did not choose Kern; he found him an excellent choice. Wilson did not empower Kern to lead his party; he exploited Kern's role as majority leader and trusted progressive to enact a large legislative program that they both endorsed.

Less appreciated than Kern's role is the fact that Martin, Hitchcock, and Underwood continued the practice of having the Democratic floor leader serve as the chief intermediary between the Senate party and the president after Kern left the Senate in early 1917. Martin is particularly noteworthy—he was a conservative Democrat and he had been deposed by Kern and the progressives in 1913—yet he readily adapted to leading Wilson's Senate party.[90] In fact, in 1917 Martin seems to have been instrumental in reinvigorating Wilson's relations with other Senate Democrats at a time when many of them were growing weary of Wilson's assertiveness.[91] Even after the Republicans assumed majority control of the Senate in March 1919, Martin continued to be a regular consultant with the president until Martin was hospitalized in Charlottesville in early June of that year. Hitchcock, who became acting leader after Martin fell ill, had been a strong critic of the

[90] There are many examples of Martin visiting the White House or expressing the president's views in the Senate. For example, see "Embargo Power Given to Wilson: Drastic Provision Restored by Senate," *Atlanta Constitution*, May 8, 1917, 3; "Senate Assails Administration," *Boston Globe*, May 17, 1917, 1; "Puts Food Bill First," *Washington Post*, June 16, 1917, 2; "President Wants Simpler Food Bill," *New York Times*, July 13, 1917, 3. There were a small number of exceptions to Martin's support for Wilson's legislative requests, such as Martin's opposition to a bill to grant Wilson broad powers to reorganize executive departments during the war: see "Wilson Bill to Enlarge Power Facing Defeat," *Chicago Tribune*, Feb. 8, 1918, 5.

[91] "Wilson Visits Capitol," *Washington Post*, June 5, 1917, 3; "President Urges Senate to Speed," *New York Times*, June 5, 1917, 2.

Wilson administration's war effort before he assumed the leadership position. Nevertheless, he led the fight for the president's peace plan in 1919 and 1920, even as Wilson was recovering from a stroke and often unavailable. It was a difficult time for Hitchcock: Wilson was in his last year as president, the peace treaty was about to be killed by the Republican majority, and little other legislation was going to be pursued by congressional Republicans until after the 1920 presidential election.

The out-party Republicans were sensitive in these years about Wilson's relations with Congress. Wilson pressed Democrats to act on his agenda, which they did, with Republicans having little direct contact with the president. Wilson and Lodge's personal dislike for each other ran deep. Lodge was a good friend of Theodore Roosevelt, who lost to Wilson in the 1912 presidential contest, and he was a conservative who opposed Wilson's domestic agenda and foreign policy. Lodge is reported to have told Roosevelt before the outbreak of war that "I never expected to hate anyone in politics with the hatred I feel toward Wilson" (Berg 2013, 612). Needless to say, Wilson and Lodge did not consult with each other.

As leader of the minority Democrats, Underwood had complicated relationships with Wilson and Harding. By the time Underwood was elected leader in April 1920, Wilson was in his last year in the White House. Wilson's health was slowly recovering, but his relationships on Capitol Hill had deteriorated from his first years as president. Underwood supported Wilson on most matters, but he went his own way on more issues and had a business-like relationship with Wilson (Johnson 1980, 294–309). With the Republican president Harding, in contrast, Underwood's relations were personally warmer and somewhat controversial. Harding appointed Underwood to be one of four American delegates to the International Conference on the Limitation of Armaments. Underwood's support for the subsequent treaties, which were signed in February 1922, appeared to reflect a friendship with Harding that was a concern among some of his Democratic colleagues (Johnson 1980, 312–23). As soon as the arms conference ended, Underwood returned to the Capitol and asked for a caucus meeting on the question of his leadership.[92] While overt opposition to Underwood did not materialize and the meeting never happened, it was plain that many Democrats were unsatisfied with his commitment to his fellow partisans.

---

[92] "Underwood Faces Revolt in Party," *New York Times*, Dec. 15, 1921, 3; "Democrats Quit Cold," *Los Angeles Times*, Dec. 16, 1921, I:1. At least some resentment about Underwood's service on the delegation appears to have lingered: see "Democrats Decline Debt Board Service," *New York Times*, Mar. 5, 1923, 3. Underwood's relations with Harding were strong enough for Harding to write about nominating him to the Supreme Court, but it may have been that Underwood's presidential ambitions made some of his colleagues suspicious of his motives in playing such a prominent role in foreign policy (Johnson 1980, 323, 334–35).

From left to right, William Borah (R, Idaho), Henry Cabot Lodge (R, Mass.), and Reed
Smoot (R, Utah), posing after leaving the White House in 1924. Lodge died later that
year, having served 6 years as Republican floor leader.
Library of Congress, National Photo Company Collection, reproduction number LC-USZ62-96150

Lodge, leading the Republican majority in the 1920s, was the chief intermediary between his conference and Republican presidents Harding and
Coolidge. These presidents had other close political friends in the Senate, but they
consulted regularly with the floor leader, as was often reported in the press.
Harding promised to be more deferential to Congress and less "dictatorial" than
Wilson (Rogers 1922). In the view of a Lodge biographer, Harding promised a
new partnership in which the senator would take the lead and the president would
be as pliable as he had been in the Senate (Widenor 1991, 50–51). Harding was
deferential, but, while still in his first year in office, he openly expressed his
disappointment with the legislative priorities of congressional Republicans and
said so in a message to Congress.[93] By the end of 1921, Lodge was losing his grip
on the Senate because of the crystallization of the Farm Bloc and its demands for
legislation that neither he nor Harding could endorse.

BUILDING COALITIONS

Who took responsibility for building coalitions to pass, defeat, or amend
legislation was still unsettled in the 1910s. For decades, both parties had used

[93] "Laggard Congress Disturbs Harding," *New York Times*, July 9, 1921, 3.

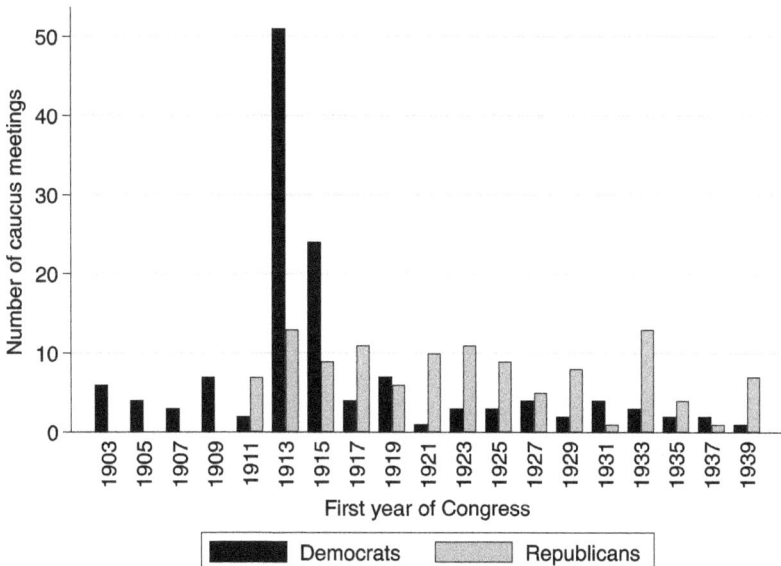

FIGURE 6.4 Number of caucus meetings, by Congress, for Democrats (1903–64) and Republicans (1911–64)

Source: Party minutes (Ritchie 1998a, Wolff and Ritchie 1999). Democratic minutes are available 1903–64; Republican minutes are available 1911–64.

caucus meetings to rally support, but the Senate was small enough for nearly any senator to take the initiative. Among the Democrats, Gorman and his successors as minority leaders played a leading role in the 1890s and 1900s, but the task was often assumed instead by ranking Democrats on committees. On the Republican side of the Senate, this work was shouldered by Aldrich and other Republican committee chairs, often working through the Republican steering committee. The emergence of two recognized floor leaders in 1913 began, however, to clarify lines of responsibility. More and more, in the 1910s and early 1920s, senators turned to their leader as chief strategist, head counter, and dealmaker, particularly on measures considered crucial to the party's legislative and electoral success. Gorman's role on the Federal Elections Bill two decades earlier set a pattern that Kern adopted in shepherding Wilson's New Freedom program, an example soon followed by Republican leaders.

The Democrats. Kern operated through caucus meetings to encourage attendance and rally support for legislation far more than any leader before or after him. Figure 6.4 reports the number of caucus meetings, starting with the first Congress for which the minutes are available for each party and extending through 1940.[94] The Democrats' 75 meetings in the 1913–17 period—on average, at least one meeting per week that the Senate was in

[94] The published minutes do not include any reference to meetings for which minutes were not found. At least a few such meetings are mentioned in newspapers or other sources. After World

session—far exceeded the number held by either party at any other time in the first decades of the twentieth century. Republicans at the time accused the Democrats of governing by caucus rather than by open debate on the Senate floor (Oleszek 1991, 28). But progressive Democrats contrasted the extended deliberations within their caucus to having no meaningful debates at all (Bowers 1918, 373). Kern's use of party meetings reflected a conspicuous rejection of the Republican model that, for two decades, had centralized policymaking in an interlocking directorate of a few committee chairmen, coordinated by the steering committee. It was an attempt to create a more democratic process, where legislation was shaped by the full majority party caucus.

Although the sessions were held behind closed doors, the press and party minutes provide a comprehensive account of the business conducted in these meetings. Kern chaired the caucus meetings and guided the discussion, but there is no indication that he used a heavy hand in doing so. Legislation was explained and debated, often for days, amendments to bills considered and approved, directions to committees given, motions to have the Senate take up certain measures considered, and strategy discussed. Democratic senators cast dozens of votes on substantive policy alternatives, often with proxies cast for absent senators, and Kern adopted the policy of publicly disclosing the vote outcomes. The caucus often requested that Kern, a committee chairman, or a bill manager act on a measure.

The use of binding votes added to the notoriety of the Kern-era caucus. In 1903, upon the return of Gorman as minority leader, Senate Democrats had approved a rule that required Democrats to support the party policy position when the position was endorsed by at least two-thirds of the caucus. The rule remained in place in 1913 when, with their narrow majority, Democratic senators invoked it for several legislative initiatives, including bills on tariff reform, war revenue, ship purchase, and child labor (Ritchie 1998a, 167, 179, 190, 210, 229). While the rule was invoked with genuine expectation of party discipline, senators violated it without serious repercussions. In 1916, Underwood worked conspicuously to amend the war revenue bill on the floor, despite the caucus having made it a "party measure." He disapproved of the cotton tax, dye tariff, and creation of a tariff commission, but, though he had mixed success effecting changes, he voted for the bill in the end (Johnson 1980, 252–53).[95] Sometimes, Kern chose not to ask for a binding vote when he feared exacerbating factional differences.[96]

War II, parties started meeting under the auspices of units such as the policy committees, which makes a comparison of Congresses across a longer period of time less useful.

[95] "Pass Revenue Bill Striking at Allies," *Washington Post*, Sept. 6, 1916, 1.

[96] "Change Money Bill on Vanderlip Lines," *New York Times*, Nov. 7, 1913, 2.

Kern's successors used the caucus far less frequently than he did. In 1917–19, in a Congress consumed by war-related legislation that was readily supported by most senators, the caucus under Martin met just five times— three organizational meetings, a long day in early 1917 to discuss the cloture rule, and a fifth meeting, in the winter of 1919, concerning the dire need to pass appropriations bills in a timely way. There is no record of any meeting of the Senate Democratic caucus in the whole of 1918. Martin relied heavily on committee chairmen, informal meetings with groups of colleagues, and frequent meetings at the White House to set a direction for the party. In the next Congress, with Republicans now in the majority, the emergence of the Farm Bloc kept Republicans from passing most of their domestic legislation, leaving little for Underwood and the Democrats to do. Underwood used the steering committee to proclaim Democratic positions on some issues and, on a few occasions, consulted with House Democratic leaders about the party response to President Harding's program.[97] He took a personal position on some major issues without serious regard to the balance of views in his caucus (Johnson 1980, 338–39), perhaps more interested in positioning himself for his unsuccessful presidential effort than in leading Senate Democrats (Murray 1976).

The Republicans. The first major policy issue for the Wilson administration was reform of the Republican-era tariff, and Minority Leader Gallinger led the effort against the bill. There was some discussion of binding party members to vote against the Democratic bill, but the conference rejected the idea. Unlike the Democratic senators, Republicans did not meet in conference to discuss the bill while it was on the floor, instead explicitly leaving the management of the issue to Gallinger—which was notable, given that Penrose, a regular Republican and long-time ally of Aldrich, served as the ranking minority member of the Finance Committee (Brown 1922, 261, 263). A year later, late in 1914, Gallinger led the successful filibuster against Wilson's ship purchase bill, which would have authorized the federal government to buy and operate merchant ships during the European war. It was opposed by Republicans who did not want the government to own merchant ships and argued that buying German ships would show favoritism in the European conflict (Schriftgiesser 1944, 267).[98] Although Gallinger's primary role was to oppose initiatives sought by Wilson and the Senate Democratic majority, he frequently authored proposals on issues of the day and made speeches on topics outside of the jurisdiction of his committee assignments.[99]

---

[97] "Open Fight on Tariff," *Los Angeles Times*, Dec. 21, 1920, I:1; "Tariff Fight Line-Up," *Washington Post*, July 6, 1921, 1.

[98] "Outwitted by Gallinger," *New York Times*, July 10, 1914, 2.

[99] For example, see "Stands by Open Door: Gallinger Offers Resolution on Chinese Emergency," *Washington Post*, Aug. 22, 1914, 3; "Would Retaliate on Foreign Ships: Gallinger for Barring All Subsidized Craft from Canal if Tolls Repeal Passes," *New York Times*, Apr. 26, 1914, 13; Wolff and Ritchie 1999, 63.

Lodge ascended to the leadership post after Gallinger's death in 1918 because of his seniority, but he was a formidable legislator and probably could have defeated any serious challenger. Not only did Lodge possess policy expertise, particularly in foreign affairs, but he was a considerable intellect, held a secure grasp on parliamentary procedure, and was held in respect, though not love, by his colleagues. The outcome of the 1918 elections, yielding a Republican majority for the first time in six years, laid the groundwork for Lodge's successful fight against the League of Nations. As majority leader and chairman of the Committee on Foreign Relations, he sought to manage the party's public image on the issue while shaping the membership of the committee to control Senate action on the treaty. He managed floor action with remarkable effectiveness: Lodge crafted an approach that demanded strong reservations that Wilson and most Democrats rejected, while retaining the support both of "irreconcilables" (opposed to a League of any kind) and the mild reservationists among Republicans (Holt 1933; Schriftgiesser 1944, 349; Garraty 1953; Widenor 1980). Lodge was responsible for keeping his fractious party coalition together on the issue, a task that he chose to pursue through personal interactions rather than large-scale meetings. Remarkably, as far as we can determine, the Senate Republican conference never met to discuss the League issue.

The Republican conference did meet on other issues in the late 1910s and early 1920s—meat-packer regulation, the economic situation, appropriations bills—but, on domestic matters, the rift between regulars, progressives, and the Farm Bloc left Lodge in a weakened position by the end of his first Congress as majority leader.[100] Insurgents sometimes stayed away from conference meetings, often demanded action on their legislation, and frequently joined with Democrats to force action on their bills. But Lodge, with the assistance of Curtis, continued to lead efforts to pass administration legislation favored by their party majority even when there was little hope of success (Widenor 1991, 56; Ripley 1969a, 100).

SPEAKING FOR THE SENATE PARTY

Reporters have covered Congress from its earliest days. Throughout the nineteenth century and well into the twentieth century, newspapers throughout the country, in big cities and in the smallest towns, devoted extensive coverage to congressional proceedings. The Senate began designating special seating for reporters in 1841 and formally established the Senate press gallery in 1877. In the late nineteenth century, reporters—many of whom had other jobs, including work as congressional clerks, to make adequate incomes—were ubiquitous when Congress was in session. Close and lasting relationships

---

[100] "Republicans Pave Way for a Recess," *New York Times*, May 23, 1920, 21; "Republicans in Split," *Washington Post*, May 23, 1920, 1.

between legislators and journalists were common, but few senators put in the effort or had the skill to acquire good press coverage.

When Kern and Gallinger became leaders in 1913, the Capitol Hill press corps was large, competitive, increasingly non-partisan and professional, better paid, no longer dependent on patronage, oriented more to mass circulation papers and news syndicates, and filled with talented journalists (Ritchie 1991b, 73–112, 171–72, 181–82). Newspapers routinely mentioned floor leaders and whips, often in reference to floor statements, meetings with the president, comments about the Senate schedule, or other activities associated with their official duties. Press accounts reflected the desire to report on important developments and to quote authoritative senators, which led reporters and editors to give disproportionate attention to floor leaders.

On occasion, Kern, Martin, and Underwood would offer floor remarks, grant interviews, or issue statements for the purpose of articulating a party view on a matter and getting quoted in the newspapers. In the late spring of 1917, for example, Martin vigorously responded to criticism that the Senate was slow in acting on war preparation legislation.[101] Nevertheless, these Democratic leaders lacked a modern communication strategy. They had no press secretaries. Unlike their contemporaries in the White House, who, beginning with Taft and Wilson, had begun holding press conferences (Ritchie 1991b, 204, 221), Senate Democratic leaders do not appear to have held any press briefings through the early 1920s, even though Washington correspondents spent more time on Capitol Hill than at the Executive Mansion.[102]

Service as a party spokesman was a modest role for Republican Senate leaders in this period, too. In the 1910s and early 1920s, Republican and Democratic majority leaders alike were speaking much more on the floor than had the Republican caucus chairmen of preceding decades, as Figure 6.3 shows. But, as was the case with the Democrats, there is no evidence of Republican leaders holding press conferences or hiring staff to manage relations with reporters. Still, Gallinger, like Kern, did recognize that leadership required speaking explicitly on behalf of his party. Once the conference voted to put Gallinger in charge of the tariff debate in 1913, for example, he assumed the lead in making the Republican case to the public.[103] In 1916 and again 1918, the conference approved a statement on a party position and resolved that Gallinger issue the statement to the press; the press reported the statement as if it came from Gallinger alone (Wolff and Ritchie 1999, 60, 62, 76).[104] Gallinger

[101] "Martin Defends Zeal of Congress," *New York Times*, May 26, 1917, 4; "Great Record of Achievement," *Washington Post*, May 27, 1917, 6.
[102] For a listing of presidential press conferences, starting with Coolidge, see Gerhard Peters, "Presidential News Conferences," at www.presidency.ucsb.edu/data/newsconferences.php.
[103] "Pig Iron Tariff Spat," *Washington Post*, Aug. 5, 1913, 3.
[104] "G.O.P. Behind Wilson," *Washington Post*, Feb. 10, 1918, 2; "Republicans Take No Party Action," *New York Times*, Feb. 10, 1918, 1.

also frequently responded to major presidential addresses or statements by Democratic leaders, usually by making a lengthy prepared statement on the floor that was given prominent coverage in the press.[105] Lodge, too, routinely made public statements—on the war, on the League of Nations, on domestic issues, on the death of President Harding.[106] Notably, Gallinger and Lodge, like their Democratic counterparts, were regularly identified as Senate floor leaders in relation to their statements.

CONCLUSION

As the Senate's first elected majority leader and first Republican floor leader, Kern and Gallinger assumed the full range of modern functions in 1913. They had precedents to build on, of course—more than 20 years of Senate floor leaders on the Democratic side, along with examples from the House, the presidency, and state legislatures—but, still, it is remarkable how quickly the role of floor leader matured in the 1910s and early 1920s. Equally important, the work of the floor leader was buttressed in these years by wholly new positions, including party whips and campaign committees. Each party's collective legislative and electoral interests, and individual senators' legislative and electoral interests, were implicated in the allocation of committee assignments, the floor agenda, relations with the president, building coalitions and managing factions, and public images of the parties. So leaders, once established, were expected to facilitate the achievement of their party colleagues' goals.

Responding to the expectations of his colleagues that he work closely with Wilson, and to Wilson's own demands, Kern structured committees in 1913 to promote quick action on his party's progressive and activist agenda, while minimizing violations of seniority to avoid unnecessarily alienating conservative colleagues. His small majority and the habits of his colleagues led him almost immediately to struggle to muster floor majorities. That led Kern to support the binding caucus rule, to rely on caucus meetings for building coalitions, to insist on attendance, and, at the behest of other senators, to acquire, in the new whip position, an ally to assist him in these efforts. As minority leader, Gallinger assumed new responsibilities on the Republican side of the Senate. Lodge, the first Republican majority leader, naturally took on the functions of leadership—communicating regularly with the Republican presidents, making

[105] "Senator Gallinger Sees One Repudiation of Principles after Another," *Washington Post*, Mar. 31, 1914, 2; "Fears Attack on U.S.," *Washington Post*, Mar. 31, 1914, 3.
[106] "Senate Commends Wilson's Answer," *Atlanta Constitution*, Oct. 15, 1918, 1; "Calls Peace League Peril to Real Peace," *Chicago Daily Tribune*, Dec. 22, 1918, 1; "Senators Score Wilson's Plan about Colonies," *Atlanta Constitution*, Feb. 1, 1919, 1; "Lodge Condemns League Covenant," *Boston Globe*, May 20, 1919, 1; "Senate Majority Reach Agreement on Reservations," *New York Times*, Oct. 20, 1919, 1; "Governors of Coal States Agree to Harding's Plan for Protection of Miners," *Ithaca (N.Y.) Journal-News*, July 19, 1922, 1; "Country First with Harding, Says Lodge," *New York Tribune*, Aug. 4, 1923, 3.

statements to the press, working with Curtis to manage the floor, forging a strong coalition to counter Wilson's advocacy of the League of Nations, and struggling with internal dissension on domestic issues.

Procedural developments in the 1910s enhanced the importance of floor leadership. The adoption of a formal rule that made unanimous consent agreements orders of the Senate rendered the supervision of floor activity more important for both parties. The possibility of cloture created more circumstances under which coalitions for or against cloture had to be constructed. These tasks reinforced the need for sustained floor leadership in the two parties and made a return to a world without a responsible floor leader unimaginable by the late 1910s. By the time Robinson and Curtis became Senate leaders in 1923 and 1924, the value and recognized roles of party leaders were firmly established.

Senate floor leaders Charles Curtis (R, Kans.) and Joseph T. Robinson (D, Ark.),
walking together on Dec. 8, 1925.

Library of Congress, Prints & Photographs Division, reproduction number LC-DIG-npcc-27323

7

Divergent Paths and the Consolidation of Leadership Structures, 1923–1944

Joe Robinson (D, Ark.) and Charles Curtis (R, Kans.) became leaders of their parties in 1923 and 1924 with most of the leadership tools enjoyed by modern Senate leaders. These included whips, floor staff, the 1914 rule on unanimous consent agreements (Rule XII), the 1917 rule on cloture (Rule XXII), and the chairmanships of their respective conferences. Underwood in 1921, followed by Robinson in 1927, established the precedent for the Democratic leader to take the seat front and center on the Senate floor, and, in the mid-1930s, Republican leaders took the companion seat on their side of the center aisle. The right of first recognition, which modern leaders consider to be their most important parliamentary advantage, was not officially asserted until a few weeks after Robinson's death in 1937, but Robinson, ever-present on the Senate floor, had no problems gaining recognition to move his legislative agenda forward.

For Senate Democrats, this was the age of Robinson and Alben Barkley (D, Ky.). Robinson, elected leader in late 1923, served until he died of a massive heart attack in the summer of 1937. Barkley took over from Robinson and served as leader until he was sworn in as vice president in January 1949. When Robinson became leader, he inherited a position that was by then well-established. Between 1923 and the mid-1940s, Robinson and Barkley confronted a wide range of political circumstances—an initial period of Republican dominance, then a few years of intense partisan competition, followed by a long stretch of commanding Democratic majorities—but both successfully managed party affairs and the Senate floor, even if organizational changes under their leadership were modest. Like their predecessors and successors, they chaired the Democratic steering committee, which gave them responsibility not just for the order of business but also for committee assignments. A separate policy committee was created by Robinson in 1931 as part of a joint policy committee with House Democrats (Humbert 1932), but, during this era and in the decades thereafter, the Senate Democrats' policy committee seldom played a role independent of the floor leaders who chaired it.

For Senate Republicans, in contrast, the period was defined by the atrophying of their party structure in the 1930s, when at one point they held just 16 seats in a 96-person Senate, and the thorough reinvention of their organization in 1944. Charles McNary (R, Ore.), Republican leader from 1933 until his death in 1944, followed his predecessors and his Democratic counterparts in concentrating the Republican leadership positions in his person. But, under McNary, with his caucus gutted by New Deal-era elections, this concentration was coupled with a simplified party organization. The Republican leadership structure by the late 1930s had been reduced to McNary and a few, informally appointed, lieutenants. With McNary's final illness and death in 1944, the Senate Republican conference embraced a new organizational structure, dividing the positions of caucus chairman, floor leader, and chairman of the steering committee between three different senators. They recreated secondary leadership posts and party committees. For the first time in either party, formal job descriptions were adopted in codified rules. This differentiation of roles was led by Robert Taft (R, Ohio) and his allies to reassert conservative control over the affairs of the party conference, as they began to imagine the possibility of regaining majority control of the Senate—with the innovations thus tied both to party competition and to intraparty factionalism. The rules adopted in 1944 continue to set the framework for Senate Republican party organization today.

THE PARTISAN CONTEXT

Senate Republicans had a clear edge over Democrats in the mid-1920s, as Figure 7.1 shows, but they continued to suffer internal divisions. The 1924 elections left regular Senate Republicans feeling vindicated. They had struggled with obstructionism at the hands of progressives and Democrats as well as the split that year caused by Robert La Follette's presidential campaign under the Progressive party label. But, with Coolidge's decisive victory in the three-candidate presidential race and Republicans gaining one seat in the Senate and 22 in the House, regular Republicans claimed a mandate for Coolidge's conservative policy agenda. Intraparty factionalism, however, persisted. The most prominent legislation involving the Farm Bloc was the McNary-Haugen farm relief legislation.[1] The bill, authored by the Oregon senator and an Iowa representative, sought to raise the prices of farm products through a system of government purchases and fees. Conservatives opposed the legislation as an unwarranted and expensive intrusion of government in the economy and successfully managed to delay Senate votes on the bill until 1927, when a

---

[1] L. C. Speers, "Farm Bill Veto Opens the 1928 Battle," *New York Times*, Mar. 6, 1927, XX1.

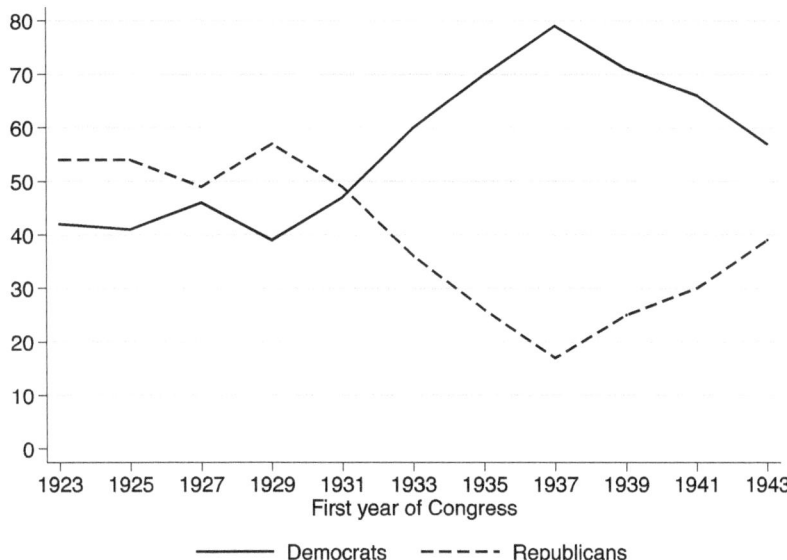

FIGURE 7.1 Size of parties, 1923–44

handful of Republicans and Farmer-Laborite Henrik Shipstead (Minn.) demanded votes on three measures, including the farm bill, as a condition for staying in the Republican conference (Wolff and Ritchie 1999, 192–96). Coolidge vetoed the legislation in 1927 and then again in 1928.

Republicans held their majorities in the Senate between 1927 and 1933, but, for four of those six years, their control was by the slimmest margins—by two seats in the 70th Congress (1927–29), with one seat held by Shipstead and another vacant at the start of the session, and by just one seat in the 72nd Congress (1931–33). While they had a large majority at the start of President Herbert Hoover's administration in 1929–31, these small margins, coupled with internal party divisions, limited the ability of Republican senators to support legislation advocated by Coolidge and Hoover in the final two years of each president's term in the White House. Attendance, however, as measured by votes on the floor, improved markedly in these years, as Figure 7.2 showed, rising to over 80 percent in the 70th Congress. The close division on many issues, advances in transportation, and more effective whips may have improved attendance, particularly on key votes.

Democrats won a large majority in the 1932 elections, with 59 Democrats, 36 Republicans, and one Farmer-Laborite in the new Senate. Franklin D. Roosevelt, the newly elected Democratic president, called a special session of Congress to move on his New Deal legislation. In this and succeeding sessions, much of Roosevelt's legislative program was enacted, sometimes after the president exploited patronage and other executive favors to attract support

(Herring 1934). The 1934 and 1936 elections yielded even larger Democratic majorities—69 and 76 seats—by any measure the largest for a Senate party since Reconstruction. As long as the Democrats remained unified, they could easily muster the majorities required to pass legislation. From the party's peak in the 75th Congress (1937–39), when Democrats controlled 76 seats and Republicans 16 seats, the Democrats lost seats in the next three elections. By 1943 they held 57 seats, with Republicans at 38 seats, placing the two dozen southern Democrats in a potentially pivotal position to determine legislative outcomes.

Southern opposition to elements of the New Deal program, particularly on labor, social welfare, regulatory, and spending matters, began to surface in the Senate in the mid-1930s and transformed legislative coalitions. Resistance from white southerners was enough to force amendments to some New Deal legislation even in Roosevelt's first years, often to discriminate against Black people (Katznelson 2013). Over time, southern Democrats became increasingly unreliable supporters of the president, and political observers by 1937 began to distinguish between an "administration bloc" and the southern Democrats. In these same years, the Republican Senate caucus grew more conservative, reducing the influence of progressives and making the party more unified in its opposition. By the end of World War II, as Republican factionalism abated, the rift within the Democratic party grew. On many important issues, a "conservative coalition" of Republicans and southern Democrats formed a working majority (Patterson 1967), creating ongoing challenges for Senate Democratic leaders.

THE LEADERS AND FACTIONS

Innovation in Senate party organization is a function of party size and party cohesiveness—both driven by electoral competition. It is weak majority parties, whether measured by size or cohesion, that more frequently seek to alter parliamentary rules in their efforts to win floor votes (Binder 1996). In the Senate, however, the ability of a large minority to block action, even after the introduction of cloture in 1917, limits the ability of the majority party to modify the rules, at least by the usual means of passing a resolution to change the standing rules of the chamber. Moreover, intraparty factionalism poses its own challenges to the leaders of each party, as senators within the party compete over strategy, policy, committee positions, and career advancement. Organizational innovation, therefore, provides a path for Senate parties to improve their capacity to compete on the floor and in elections, address factional conflicts, and accommodate ambitious senators.

The Democrats. Robinson served as Democratic leader from December 1923 until his death in July 1937, first as minority leader, then, starting in 1933, as majority leader during the New Deal Congresses. He played a critical role in ushering New Deal legislation through the Senate. The 1936 election was the high point of Democratic dominance: Roosevelt carried every state in the presidential election, except Vermont and Maine, and Democrats gained commanding majorities in the House and Senate. But, by the time of Robinson's unexpected death, southern Democrats were asserting their opposition to the president's court-packing plan and had begun to oppose important initiatives of the administration. Roosevelt unveiled his plan to add seats to the Supreme Court early in 1937, after the conservative majority on the court had struck down as unconstitutional some New Deal initiatives. Majority Leader Robinson had fought hard to secure the votes for the court-packing initiative, and his death dealt a severe blow to the effort. Republicans held few seats in the Senate, but their hopes rose with this evidence of Roosevelt's vulnerability and growing acrimony in Democratic ranks.

Barkley, who was in his second Senate term and serving as caucus vice chairman and assistant floor leader when Robinson died, succeeded Robinson by winning the post by one vote over Mississippi's Pat Harrison, the chairman of the Committee on Finance. The battle between New Dealers and conservatives played a significant role in the contest. The day after Robinson's death, President Roosevelt had written a letter to Barkley to offer his condolences and to express his concern for the fate of the judicial reform legislation. The text of the letter, which began with the salutation, "My Dear Alben," was quickly exploited by Barkley's opponents to make it appear that Barkley was the president's favorite, contributing to Barkley's early reputation for being a mere errand boy of the White House (Barkley 1954, 155).[2] Barkley struggled with eroding party numbers and the liberal-conservative divide within his party throughout his service as leader. His intelligence, erudition, storytelling ability, and dedication won over most of his colleagues as time passed, and his success in moving beyond a difficult start was reflected in Harry Truman's decision in 1948 to make Barkley his running mate.

Barkley's years as majority leader were marked by the mobilization of southern conservatives in his party and his modest efforts to keep them in check. Southerners blocked action on anti-lynching measures in late 1937 and early 1938. By the end of 1937, southerners had started to oppose outright the Roosevelt administration's wage, housing, and farm measures to address the recession.[3] Thereafter, the coalition of southern Democrats with Republicans was a regular problem, with Barkley and the administration on the losing end of several important legislative battles. Barkley favored New Dealers in making appointments to the existing steering and policy committees, but stalemate between the factions and the growing power of southern conservatives, whose seniority granted them several committee chairmanships, left the party

[2] The letter is available in the archives of the American Presidency Project at www.presidency.ucsb .edu/documents/letter-the-court-reform-recommendation (accessed March 2025).
[3] Turner Catledge, "F.D.R. Program Stalled in the Special Session," *New York Times*, Dec. 12, 1937, 82; Robert C. Albright, "Bitterness of Row Over Anti-Lynching Bill Threatens Sectional Split," *Washington Post*, Jan. 23, 1938, B4.

apparatus unchanged during Barkley's tenure.[4] As leader, Barkley used the conference only for organizational meetings and avoided policy discussions that would expose divisions within the party.

For Robinson's years as majority leader and the first years of Barkley's term, J. Hamilton Lewis (D, Ill.) served as Democratic whip. Lewis was a remarkable figure and a bridge between generations, having been the Democrats' first whip in 1913–19, under Kern and Martin, during the single term he served in the Senate in the 1910s. Lewis returned to the Senate in 1931 and was elected whip in 1933, when he turned 70. In December 1938, Lewis asked the party to elect Sherman Minton (D, Ind.) as assistant whip (Ritchie 1998a, 355). Minton was a loyal and articulate New Dealer who, in leading investigations of lobbying and concentration in the newspaper business and proposing Supreme Court reform, had won the amity of President Roosevelt (Gugin and St. Clair 1997, 87–122). Lewis died the following spring, and Minton was elected whip without opposition. Factionalism, however, was on everyone's mind: a reporter asked southerners if they would object to Minton's promotion, and they indicated that they would not.[5] Minton served as whip until 1941, when he lost his Senate seat, and he was succeeded as whip by Lister Hill (D, Ala.), a southerner, but one who was more supportive of administration than most of his southern colleagues.

The Republicans. Charles Curtis became Republican leader in November 1924, following Lodge's death. It was a natural transition for Curtis: he had been serving as whip since 1915 and vice chairman of the conference since 1921, and he had served as acting floor leader and conference chairman in Lodge's absence. In the wake of the 1924 elections, Curtis made an effort to consolidate the power of the regulars. In addition to naming Wesley Jones (R, Wash.) as his whip, Curtis recognized the importance of his competitors for majority leader by appointing James Wadsworth (R, N.Y.) as chairman of the steering committee and James Watson (R, Ind.) as vice chairman of the Republican conference as well as chairman of the committee on committees; Wadsworth also kept his post as conference secretary. The arrangement, which put leading party regulars in charge of all party functions, lasted for only one Congress. After Wadsworth was defeated for reelection in 1926, the conference elected Frederick Hale (R, Maine) as its secretary, and Curtis appointed Frederic Sackett (R, Ky.), a fellow regular who had been in the Senate for only two years and would likely take guidance from Curtis, to the chairmanship of the steering committee (Wolff and Ritchie 1999, 190). Curtis also named Simeon Fess (R, Ohio), also a party regular, as "assistant whip" (Wolff and Ritchie 1999, 191).

---

[4] "Barkley Fortifies New Deal Rule Over Senate Order of Business," *New York Times*, Jan. 7, 1939, 1.

[5] "On Capitol Hill: Minton Scheduled to Succeed Lewis as Senate Whip," *Washington Post*, Apr. 15, 1939, 2; "On Capitol Hill: Minton Succeeds J. Ham Lewis as Democratic Whip in Senate," *Washington Post*, Apr. 20, 1939, 2; "Senator Minton Chosen to be Democratic Whip," *New York Times*, Apr. 20, 1939, 13.

Charles Curtis (R, Kans.). From 1915 until his election to succeed Henry Cabot Lodge as floor leader in 1924, Curtis was central to the development of leadership positions within the Senate Republican caucus. He served as majority leader from 1924 until 1929, when he became vice president.

Library of Congress, Prints & Photographs Division, reproduction number LC-DIG-ggbain-06129

Two years later, after Curtis won the vice presidency as Herbert Hoover's running mate, Watson and Jones announced their candidacies for Senate Republican floor leader. Charles McNary (R, Ore.), a Farm Bloc progressive with good relations across the party, was actively discussed as a possible candidate for the post but did not run. Instead, McNary intervened and persuaded Jones to become the conference's vice chairman and assistant floor leader (Neal 1991, 61, 64, 103, 121–23), which cleared the way for Watson to become Senate Republican leader in March 1929.[6] Watson promoted Fess from assistant whip to whip. Hoover then made the conservative Fess chairman of the Republican National Committee for the 1930–32 election cycle, strengthening the tie between the conservative president and his party's Senate leadership.[7]

Watson served as majority leader for 1929–33, the four years of the Hoover presidency. It was a tumultuous four years, a time when a coalition of Democrats and Farm Bloc Republicans produced a bipartisan majority for

---

[6] "Jones Leaves Senate Post for Watson," *Hartford Courant*, Dec. 16, 1928, A3; "From a Senator's Diary," *Washington Post*, Mar. 3, 1929, M11.

[7] "Selection of Fess Taken to Forecast Hoover '32 Policies," *New York Times*, July 27, 1930, 1.

several important measures (Donnelly 1930, 144–51; Watson 1936, 264–65). Hoover called a special session in 1929 to consider tariff legislation, which divided progressive and Farm Bloc Republicans from the regulars.[8] A new faction, the Young Guard, emerged in the tariff debate. These recently elected senators, mainly from industrial states and generally supportive of Hoover, advocated a compromise on tariffs and suggested that Watson be replaced with McNary to get the party conference working more effectively. Not much came of the Young Guard's efforts—though McNary became conference vice chairman and assistant Republican leader, as Jones assumed the chairmanship of Appropriations.[9] "McNary's appointment will go far toward healing the breach between the Progressives and the regulars," the *Washington Post* averred. "He is not a Progressive, but then he is what they call agricultural-minded and the greatest little fixer in the Senate."[10] The 1930 elections made matters worse for Watson. Republicans lost their 56–39–1 seat advantage in the Senate, controlling just 48 seats in the aftermath of the election, alongside 47 Democrats and one Farmer-Labor senator. The outcome again spurred talk of replacing Watson with McNary. But Hoover's opposition to the progressive McNary, along with concerns about the effect of dumping Watson on Watson's reelection chances in 1932, allowed Watson to remain leader for two more years (Neal 1985, 127).

The 14-year span of Republican control of the Senate ended in 1933. In the 1932 elections, three years into the Great Depression, Republicans lost 12 seats (including Watson's seat in Indiana) and their majority. McNary was elected floor leader without opposition. His conference was a shadow of its old self: in the 96-seat Senate, Republicans held 36, 25, 16, 23, and 28 seats over the five full Congresses he served as floor leader. Like Curtis and Watson, McNary was well prepared for the job. A senator since 1917, McNary had quickly developed good relations with both progressives, with whom he was associated, and regulars. He was also an original member of the Farm Bloc. Lodge had appointed McNary to the committee on committees in 1919 to serve as a bridge between the wings of the party—and McNary kept his seat on the committee until 1933, serving as chairman for the last four years.[11] McNary became chairman of the Appropriations Committee in late 1929 and conference vice chairman in 1930 (Neal 1991, 104, 124; Wolff and Ritchie 1999, 224).[12] In 1933, when McNary was elected as conference chairman and minority leader, Fess assumed the

---

[8] "Coalition Fighting Move to Kill Tariff," *New York Times*, Oct. 30, 1929, 1; "Watson Quits as Tariff Ship Drifts on Rocks," *Chicago Daily Tribune*, Oct. 30, 1929, 5.

[9] "Senate Winds Up Farm Tariff Items," *New York Times*, Nov. 17, 1929, 1.

[10] "Healing Split in G.O.P. Goal of Old Guard," *Washington Post*, Nov. 30, 1929, 1.

[11] "M'Nary Accepts Lodge's Offer: Progressive Gets Place on the Committee on Committees," *Washington Post*, May 21, 1919, 5.

[12] McNary's biographer incorrectly reports that Jones was whip and McNary replaced him as whip (Neal 1985, 124). Jones had been whip, as appointed by Curtis, during the 1924–29 period; he was elected vice chairman in 1929, and Fess was appointed whip by Watson (Wolff and Ritchie 1999, 124).

position of "vice chairman and assistant floor leader," and Felix Hebert (R, R.I.) succeeded Fess as whip (Wolff and Ritchie 1999, 243).

Somewhat famously, McNary, who supported much of the New Deal legislative program in the 1933–34 Congress, sat out the 1934 and 1936 election campaigns. This was highly unusual, but McNary judged that his own political interests and those of his Senate party colleagues were best served by downplaying their differences with President Roosevelt. As he anticipated, these elections did not go well for Republicans, particularly for Republicans associated with the conservative policies of the 1920s. McNary did not attend the national convention in 1936 and remained silent on the candidacy of Alf Landon, the Republican presidential candidate. Indeed, he did not even seek or receive the endorsement of Oregon Republicans for his own reelection that year (Neal 1985, 110–12, 146–47).

Fess and Hebert, both strong opponents of the New Deal, lost their seats in the Democratic landslide in 1934. As the new Congress approached, at least some Republicans considered merging the posts of conference vice chairman and whip into a single position, with Arthur Vandenberg (R, Mich.)—respected for his parliamentary expertise, though somewhat controversial for his support of much of the New Deal program—promoted as a likely candidate.[13] But McNary saw no need for second-tier leaders in a depleted conference and probably wanted to avoid unnecessary conflict over the posts.[14] When the conference convened in early January 1935, it adopted a motion "that no Assistant Leader or Whip be elected but that the Chairman be authorized to appoint senators from time to time to assist him in taking charge of the interests of the minority" (Wolff and Ritchie 1999, 284). With Republicans showing no chance of regaining a majority soon, the party apparatus collapsed to McNary, a few senators he asked to assist him on occasion, and conference meetings.[15]

Leaders as Vice Presidents. Remarkably, three Senate party leaders of this period ran for vice president—Curtis in 1928 and McNary in 1940 for the Republicans, and Robinson in 1928 for the Democrats. In each case, the Senate leader was the choice of the presidential candidate. The story is different for each of the three, but a common thread is that these senators had become recognized political leaders for the party, their Senate leadership experience was taken as evidence that they could take over the presidency if called to do so, and

---

[13] "Meet the Senator," *Atlanta Constitution*, Jan. 5, 1935, 2.
[14] "President Calls Congress Chiefs to Chart Course," *Washington Post*, Jan. 2, 1935, 1.
[15] McNary used Vandenberg and others as informally appointed assistants during the mid- and late 1930s, although none of this was mentioned in the party minutes; Vandenberg is mentioned in one newspaper account as chairing an informal steering committee. In 1939, McNary appears to have named Warren Austin (R, Vt.) as his whip or assistant leader (Darilek 1976, 19, 61). See "Brief Session of New Congress Hoped For," *Los Angeles Times*, Dec. 30, 1934, A4; "Republicans Face Neutrality Test," *New York Times*, July 18, 1939, 1; "Senators Get Down to Plain Talking," *Christian Science Monitor*, Oct. 10, 1939, 2; "Pepper Urges Sale of Our War Planes," *New York Times*, May 22, 1940, 10.

they would represent a faction or region important to the presidential ticket. The conservative Curtis had run against Herbert Hoover, whose connection to the progressive Theodore Roosevelt was remembered. Robinson, of Arkansas, made some effort to gain the Democratic nomination for president in 1924, but was picked by New York governor Alfred E. Smith in 1928 after Robinson challenged a southern colleague's anti-Catholic speeches and was backed by his party conference. McNary was a western and progressive Republican on the 1940 ticket with the corporate president and attorney Wendell Willkie, who was then living in New York. In 1948, we also note, Barkley (D, Ky.), who became leader in 1937, was named to the ticket by Harry Truman. Barkley did not offer much regional balance to the Missourian Truman, but he had stronger relations with southerners than Truman yet could support Truman's pro–civil rights stance.

MANAGING THE PARTY

Floor leadership had become a full-time job by the mid-1920s. In both parties, leaders were responsible for refereeing factional disputes, chairing conference meetings, orchestrating committee assignments, working with the president, mustering majorities, and, of course, managing the floor. Like their Democratic counterparts, Republican leaders Gallinger, Lodge, and Curtis served as committee chairmen or ranking minority members when their seniority called for it; Lodge, most prominently, chaired Foreign Relations while serving as majority leader, leading the fight against the League of Nations in his dual role. Watson, the new Republican majority leader in 1929, was the first leader to give up a chairmanship due to him on the basis of seniority in order to commit himself fully to party leadership (Wolff and Ritchie 1999, 212).[16] Four years later, in 1933, when Democratic leader Robinson was moving from minority leader to majority leader, he was next in line to chair the Committee on Rules but turned down the position. According to the *New York Times*, "Senator Robinson said he would be fully occupied with his floor duties and the chairmanships of the two powerful groups, the Democratic steering committee and the Democratic policy committee."[17] Robinson envisioned his role as party leader to involve such a large commitment of time and effort that a standing committee chair-

---

[16] As newspaper accounts, conference minutes, and Watson's memoir (Watson 1936, 274) indicate, Watson served as chairman through the short session of 1928–29, during which he managed important legislation as committee chairman and floor leader. His replacement as committee chairman was named in April 1929 (Watson 1936, 274; Wolff and Ritchie 1999, 212). See also "Couzens and Moses Move Up in Senate," *Boston Globe*, Apr. 23, 1929, 19; "Senate Completes New Organization," *Washington Post*, Apr. 23, 1929, 4.

[17] "Congress Leaders to Speed Bank Aid," *New York Times*, Mar. 7, 1933, 1.

manship, even one with as modest a workload in the Senate as Rules, would be unmanageable.[18]

Committee Assignments

Like his immediate predecessors, Robinson managed intraparty affairs personally. The Democratic leader continued not only to appoint the steering committee, which made committee assignments, but to chair the committee, and the steering committee sent its list directly to the Senate without conference approval. In 1923, as one of his first innovations in office, Robinson implemented a policy that was favored by progressive senators in the party: no Democratic senator could be ranking minority member on more than one important committee, which forced a handful of senior Democrats to accept lower seniority rankings or switch committees (Bacon 1991, 73). A decade later, once in the majority after the 1932 elections, Robinson continued to observe the norm of giving a chairmanship to the senator with the longest continuous service on a committee, but he appointed new senators and awarded transfers by stacking important committees with colleagues he could trust to support him and the Roosevelt administration (Weller 1998, 136). Barkley, too, respected the seniority system for committee chairmanships, which enabled Democrats in the late 1930s and 1940s to avoid the intraparty fights over committee seats that had wracked the Republican caucus in the 1920s. Still, Barkley and the New Deal liberals exploited their numerical advantage over southern and conservative senators to control the steering committee and committee assignments, even as they generally accommodated most of their colleagues' requests.[19]

The Republicans were a different story. Curtis, when he became leader in November 1924, was instantly confronted with the La Follette problem. La Follette, who had just lost the presidential election as the candidate of the Progressive party, and three other Republican senators who endorsed him, were still members of the Republican conference. As acting chairman, Curtis had invited the progressives to the first conference meeting after the election, though only one of them, Edwin Ladd (R, N.Dak.), attended.[20] At that meeting, despite Curtis's hope to reduce tensions, leading conservative Reed Smoot (R, Utah) moved that the four not be invited to future conferences and not be allowed to fill Republican vacancies on standing committees. Progressive

---

[18] Kolodny 1998; "Walsh to Lead Democrat Party in Senate Fights," *Atlanta Constitution*, Sept. 8, 1922, 7; "Democrats Pick Walsh," *New York Times*, Sept. 8, 1922, 13.

[19] "Barkley Fortifies New Deal Rule over Senate Order of Business: He Adds Three Stanch Administration Supporters to Party's Steering Committee," *New York Times*, Jan. 7, 1939, 1.

[20] As in late 1921, Curtis served as acting leader immediately following Lodge's death by virtue of being vice chairman of the caucus. He was elected chairman (and majority leader) within the month.

senators in attendance objected strongly to the resolution, but it was adopted on a voice vote. A stronger resolution that would have immediately stripped the four progressive senators of their committee assignments was rejected (Wolff and Ritchie 1999, 154–55). While Curtis stated that he approved of the action, it was clear that he had little influence with most of the regulars on this issue.[21] By December 1925, La Follette had died, replaced in the Senate by his 30-year-old son. Curtis, making a conspicuous move for peace in the party, welcomed "Young Bob" La Follette to the conference meeting, and Watson, chairman of the committee on committees, invited La Follette to request committee assignments. Deadlocked at first, given La Follette's embrace of his father's legacy, the committee agreed, with some reluctance, to assign him to committees. There is no report of Curtis intervening with members of the committee on committees, but the outcome reflected his desire to avoid retribution and welcome the new Wisconsin senator into the party.[22]

Maintaining party harmony required renewed effort by Curtis following the 1926 elections, which produced a 48–46–1 split among Republicans, Democrats, and Shipstead, the Farmer-Labor senator who caucused with Republicans. This division placed the progressive Republicans in a position where they could join with the Democrats to organize the Senate and its committees in December 1927. To maintain control of the Senate, the Republicans needed the support of Shipstead as well as Lynn Frazier (R, N.Dak.), the only remaining La Follette supporter punished in 1924. Curtis acted quickly in the aftermath of the 1926 elections, inviting Frazier to attend conference meetings and successfully urging the committee on committees to restore Frazier's place and seniority on all committees.[23] In addition to restoring Frazier's committee rights, as Curtis requested, the committee on

---

[21] "Senators May Bar La Follette from Republican Caucus," *Washington Post*, Nov. 20, 1924, 1; "Proposes to Ban House Insurgents," *New York Times*, Nov. 21, 1924, 3; "Republicans Call Bolters to Caucus," *New York Times*, Nov. 22, 1924, 17; "Curtis Will Use Goad on Senate to Oust Bombast," *Atlanta Constitution*, Nov. 26, 1924, 1; "Republicans Still Lack Solidarity," *New York Times*, Nov. 26, 1924, 21; "Senate Insurgents Won't Be Disciplined," *New York Times*, Nov. 27, 1924, 23; "Ousting of Radical Senators by G.O.P. Finds Little Favor," *Washington Post*, Nov. 27, 1924, 1; "Republicans Oust Insurgent Group from Party Council," *New York Times*, Nov. 28, 1924, 1; "Radicals Read Out by G.O.P.," *Washington Post*, Nov. 28, 1924, 1.

[22] The committee on committees continued to refuse to assign the other two progressives who had supported the La Follette presidential candidacy: "Overtures Made to La Follette," *Atlanta Constitution*, Dec. 2, 1925, 1; "Republicans Offer Peace to Radicals," *New York Times*, Dec. 2, 1925, 27; "House Radicals Bolt Longworth on Congress' Eve," *New York Times*, Dec. 7, 1925, 1; "Party Split Wide Over La Follette," *New York Times*, Dec. 10, 1925, 10; "La Follette Gets Place in Ranks of Republicans," *Atlanta Constitution*, Dec. 15, 1925, 1; "La Follette Given Republican Status by G.O.P. Senators," *Washington Post*, Dec. 15, 1925, 1; "La Follette Curt to Republicans," *New York Times*, Dec. 16, 1925, 2.

[23] "Reinstating of Frazier Considered," *Los Angeles Times*, Nov. 19, 1926, 2; "Frazier Restored to Republican Fold," *New York Times*, Dec. 12, 1926, 7.

committees gave the Judiciary Committee chairmanship, which had become vacant, to George Norris (R, Nebr.), perhaps the most prominent progressive in the Senate at that time (Wolff and Ritchie 1999, 184–85).[24] But insurgent Republicans still threatened to join with the Democrats to organize the Senate in December 1927. Although Republicans denied that an explicit deal had been made, progressives received not only a commitment by the full conference to bring progressive legislative priorities to a vote in the new Congress but also several important committee assignments (Wolff and Ritchie 1999, 194–96). These assignments, combined with the seats held by Democrats, gave progressive Republicans the ability to block the flow of regular Republicans' legislation to the floor.[25]

Senate Republicans substantially increased their majority in the 1928 elections, with Hoover's landslide win for the presidency. After the elections, at least a few regulars discussed taking away important committee assignments from insurgents who supported the Democratic ticket, but the outgoing leader, Curtis, and the new leader, Watson, did not want to disturb the peace by entertaining proposals to punish the insurgents, and the conference heeded their advice. Expanded Republican contingents on committees made it easier to accommodate senators' requests, including young La Follette's request for a Finance assignment, and, following seniority, La Follette and other progressives obtained chairmanships. Even Norris, who had supported Democratic presidential candidate Al Smith, retained the Judiciary chairmanship. Underlying the conciliatory mood in early 1929 was the belief of some insurgents that Hoover would be a more progressive president than his two predecessors.[26]

Intraparty harmony was short-lived, creating an immediate challenge for Watson, now Senate majority leader. Hoover's tariff bill, pending on the Senate floor in October 1929 when the stock market crashed, sharply divided conservative, pro-tariff Republicans from progressive, pro-agriculture, anti-tariff Republicans. Regular Republicans attacked others in their party with unusually sharp language—with George Moses (R, N.H.), president pro tempore and campaign committee chairman, characterizing western senators and progressives as "sons of the wild jackass," David Reed (R, Pa.) calling them "far more

---

[24] "Frazier Invited Back into Party," *Atlanta Constitution*, Nov. 20, 1926, 8; "Frazier is Invited by G.O.P Senators to Reenter Fold," *Washington Post*, Dec. 12, 1926, M6; "Majority Senators Advance 'Rebels,'" *New York Times*, Dec. 15, 1926, 2.

[25] "Democrats Decide to Shun a Chance to Organize the Senate," *New York Times*, Nov. 29, 1927, 1; "Insurgent Senators Set Forth Demands," *Boston Daily Globe*, Dec. 2, 1927, 27; "Senate Insurgents Obtain More Posts," *New York Times*, Dec. 11, 1927, 5; "G.O.P. Irregulars in Senate Get High Committee Places," *Washington Post*, Dec. 11, 1927, 5; "Insurgents Amass Committee Power," *New York Times*, Dec. 13, 1927, 3; "Senate Insurgents Deny Making Trade," *New York Times*, Dec. 14, 1927, 21.

[26] "G.O.P. Plans to Crush Radical Power in Senate," *Chicago Daily Tribune*, Nov. 9, 1928, 6; "Senate Completes New Organization," *Washington Post*, Apr. 23, 1929, 4; "Progressives Will Aid Hoover in Senate," *Boston Globe*, Nov. 14, 1928, 9.

dangerous to our economic security than all the communists combined," and Fess, the majority whip, terming them "pseudo-Republicans."[27] Progressive and younger Republicans mobilized in response. Young Guard senators were concerned that regulars like Watson, Moses, and Finance chairman Smoot were hurting the party. They wanted to bridge divisions within the party over the tariff bill before the 1930 elections.[28] Watson conceded to the Young Guard on the substance of the tariff bill, and McNary, now assistant leader and chairman of the committee on committees, shared Watson's commitment to empower progressives and members of the Young Guard. They gave members of the Young Guard favorable treatment on various committees, sparing the conference a serious showdown.[29]

The 1930 elections left Republicans in control of the Senate by a single vote, and Democrats on the verge of a House majority. In November 1931, as the first session of the next Congress approached, Republican progressives fought to deny Moses's election as president pro tempore, in large part because of the vituperative comments he had made two years earlier. Regulars responded with a new tack—threatening, should Moses be dethroned, to vote for Democrats to chair some committees in order to deny chairmanships to the progressive Republicans. Borah, the progressive chair of Foreign Relations, worked with Watson to avoid a showdown, but they failed, and progressives voted against Moses. In January 1932, after 25 ballots were unable to produce a majority for either Moses or the Democratic nominee and a backlog of other business had been created, the Senate voted to take up another matter, and Moses retained his position. Progressive Republicans continued to hold a large number of committee chairmanships.[30]

---

[27] "Tariff Groups Disorganized," *Minneapolis Star*, Nov. 1, 1929, 2; "Reed Attacks Tariff Foes," *Pittsburgh Press*, Nov. 1, 1929, 59; "Fiery Western Solons Bitterly Assail East," *Atlanta Constitution*, Nov. 9, 1929, 6; "Western Senators Vent Rage at Moses for 'Jackass' Slur," *New York Times*, Nov. 9, 1929, 1; "Moses Stands by Derogation of Irregulars," *Washington Post*, Nov. 9, 1929, 1; "Western Independent Senators Discuss Bolt from Republican Party," *Hartford Courant*, Nov. 10, 1929, 1; "The Listening Post," *Washington Post*, Nov. 10, 1929, M3; "Will Refuse Any Moses Fund Money," *Boston Globe*, Nov. 11, 1929, 15; "Efforts to Silence Moses Indicated," *Boston Globe*, Nov. 12, 1929, 6.

[28] "Young Guards of G.O.P. Ask Moses to Keep 'Hands Off,'" *Washington Post*, Nov. 17, 1929, M1; "'Young Guard' Keeps Up Hot Tariff Pace," *Boston Globe*, Nov. 17, 1929, A2; "'Young Guard' Gets Series of Rebuffs," *Washington Post*, Nov. 19, 1929, 1; "Polling of Senate Cheers Insurgents," *New York Times*, Nov. 29, 1929, 1.

[29] "Healing Split in G.O.P. Goal of Old Guard," *Washington Post*, Nov. 30, 1929, 1; "Party Shift Seen as Jones Resigns," *Washington Post*, Dec. 1, 1929, M2; "Factions Compete for Senate Posts," *Boston Globe*, Dec. 15, 1929, A11; "G.O.P. Young Guard Wins Senate Battle on Committee Jobs," *Washington Post*, Jan. 9, 1930, 1; "Rebels Upset Plan for G.O.P. Harmony," *Washington Post*, Jan. 11, 1930, 1; "Old Line Republicans Lose Senate Control to West and Young Guard Coalition," *Atlanta Constitution*, Jan. 12, 1930, 12A; "The Young Guard Takes Command," *Washington Post*, Jan. 19, 1930, 61.

[30] "Insurgents Shake Control of Senate," *New York Times*, Nov. 22, 1931, 24; "Senate Fight Opens Way for Democrats," *New York Times*, Nov. 29, 1931, 1; "Senate Groups Name

Dealing with rebels did not end with the election disaster of 1932. Four Republican senators supported Roosevelt for president and, predictably, faced demands from regulars that they be denied conference membership. There was some seriousness to the threat—the case was made by Reed, an Old Guard senator who chaired the committee on committees—but McNary, about to be elected floor leader, opposed any disciplinary action, saying that "all Republicans look alike to me" (Neal 1985, 135). After a conference discussion made clear that most members were going to follow McNary's lead, Reed dropped the idea.[31] Even as his conference dwindled in size, committee assignments continued to be a headache for McNary. In 1943, in the middle of World War II, a prewar isolationist, James Davis (R, Pa.), sought a Foreign Relations Committee appointment, as did Warren Austin (R, Vt.), a supporter of the war and assistant minority leader. Austin's support of the Roosevelt administration's war policy led some Republicans to grumble about assigning him to the committee, but others came to his defense. McNary defused the issue by keeping Austin off Foreign Relations but in the leadership and putting Davis on the committee.[32]

Campaign Committees

Senatorial campaign committees, created by both parties in 1916, had quickly become organs of the Senate conferences. By the early 1920s, as newspaper accounts attest, the two committees were appointed, directed, and staffed by the Senate floor leaders. For Democrats, the first mention of the campaign committee in the conference minutes occurred in 1925 when, following a discussion of the campaign situation, Minority Leader Robinson stated that "undoubtedly the chairman of the Senate campaign committee would take all necessary steps to put the party in proper shape for the coming election" (Ritchie 1998a, 313). Twice over the next decade, a motion to thank the campaign committee is noted in the Democratic minutes (Ritchie 1998a, 320, 355). On the Republican side of the aisle, the first reference to the campaign committee in the party minutes came in December 1927, when the minutes note that Curtis named the committee "following the general custom for many years" (Wolff and Ritchie 1999, 191). In subsequent election years, the floor leader formally announced his appointment of the committee and chairman to the Republican conference (Wolff and Ritchie 1999, 191, 215, 238, 271,

---

Leaders; Fights Impend," *Washington Post*, Dec. 5, 1931, 1; "Senate in Recess on Moses Impasse," *Washington Post*, Dec. 11, 1931, 2; "Moses Keeps Chair as Vote Is Dropped," *New York Times*, Jan. 7, 1932, 8.

[31] "Reed to Ask Party to Drop Bolters," *New York Times*, Feb. 25, 1933, 6; "Norris Leads Move for Biparty Union of 'Progressives,'" *New York Times*, Feb. 26, 1933, 1; "Senate G.O.P. Fails to Oust Four Bolters," *Washington Post*, Mar. 8, 1933, 1.

[32] "Davis Named to Important Senate Post," *Washington Post*, Jan. 9, 1943, B7.

305).[33] In handing this responsibility to its floor leader, the party added to the leader's duties for organizing the party's legislative and electoral affairs.[34]

For Senate Republicans in the difficult years following the 1932 elections, McNary was careful to have both conservative and progressive factions represented on the committee. In January 1934, he appointed Daniel Hastings (R, Del.)—"more conservative than some of the other members of the committee," the *New York Times* observed, but "a prominent figure among the 'Young Turks' in the Senate who revolted against conservative leadership a few years ago"—to chair the campaign committee, which was made up of six westerners and only three easterners.[35] Looking to the 1934 elections, McNary called on his conference to rise above factionalism and to work together to elect Republicans to the Senate, declaring that "there will be no discrimination with respect to the definition of the word Republicanism."[36] Still, he could not prevent members of the campaign committee from almost immediately disagreeing about their rhetorical response to the New Deal program.[37] The campaign committee's activities that year appear to have been modest; it received little attention in the press, and few records remain (Kolodny 1998, 72–73).

Two years later, in 1936, McNary appointed John Townsend (R, Del.) to replace Hastings as chairman of the Republican campaign committee—and Townsend, remarkably, kept the position, first as a senator, then as a former senator, through the 1948 elections cycle.[38] Townsend's long tenure as committee chairman reflected his success in recruiting and supporting candidates and the close working relationship between him and the Republican floor leader. Even after Senate Republicans turned again to a sitting senator to serve as campaign chairman after the 1948 elections, Townsend remained involved with the committee for another two decades (Kolodny 1998, 73–74).

---

[33] According to a note attached to the Republican conference minutes in late 1927, Charles Curtis, chair of the conference, named the committee "following the general custom for many years" (Wolff and Ritchie 1999, 191).

[34] In 1931, for example, following the Republican losses in the 1930 elections, the national committee chairman, Senator Fess, was criticized for his uncompromising and highly visible pro-Prohibition stance, which was deemed by some Republicans as increasingly out-of-step with Republican and public opinion. Watson, then majority leader, intervened by asking that the postmaster general be allowed to take over for Fess. Ultimately, Watson and Fess agreed that a new national committee chairman would be named at the summer convention. See "Party's Wets Demand Fess Resign Chair," *Washington Post*, Nov. 19, 1931, 1; "Opponents of Fess Are in Stalemate," *Washington Post*, Nov. 20, 1931, 3; "Fess Row Settled," *Washington Post*, Nov. 22, 1931, M3.

[35] "Republicans Pick Campaign Chiefs," *New York Times*, Jan. 2, 1934, 10. See also "McNary Calls G.O.P. Forces to 1934 Battle," *Washington Post*, Jan. 2, 1934, 1.

[36] "Republicans Pick Campaign Chiefs," *New York Times*, Jan. 2, 1934, 10.

[37] "G.O.P. Senators Appoint Campaign Committee," *Boston Globe*, Jan. 2, 1934, 13; "McNary Calls G.O.P. Forces to 1934 Battle," *Washington Post*, Jan. 2, 1934, 1.

[38] See, for example, "Townsend to Remain Senate G.O.P. Campaign Chairman," *Washington Post*, Dec. 21, 1939, 15.

A Robinson loyalist, "Colonel" Edwin Halsey handled Democratic campaign committee duties for 16 years. Halsey did this work in his capacity as the chief aide to Democratic leaders Robinson and Barkley. With his staff, Halsey provided basic research support to the campaign committee chairman and other Democratic senators, including voting records and copies of floor speeches. During this period, campaign fundraising continued to be handled by the national committees, and most of the national party funding for Senate races was funneled through state party chairmen, an arrangement that helped to disguise the sources of funding (Kolodny 1998, 74–75). Committee members often traveled to speak on behalf of their colleagues and worked with the national committee to raise campaign funds.

Party Secretaries

Halsey's service to the Democratic conference had begun in the 1910s. When Kern became floor leader, he had moved Halsey, then a staff member in the press gallery, to the floor to manage Democratic pages and otherwise assist Democratic senators. Over time, Halsey acquired the trust of Democratic senators and became an important part of the floor leader's operations. Halsey helped Democratic leaders count votes, arrange pairs, manage the activities of pages in the Democratic cloakroom, communicate with senators, keep records, and support the campaign committee (Farley 1948, 81–82). Robinson gladly continued Halsey as his floor aide and, in 1925, named Leslie Biffle to be an assistant to Halsey (Ritchie 1998a, 315). In 1929, when a separate appropriations item was provided for floor staff, Halsey's position gained new recognition. Initially "chief of the pages," then "acting assistant doorkeeper," Halsey in 1929 became "secretary for the minority" or, more informally, "party secretary" (Ritchie 1998a, 278, 332).[39] When Democrats gained their majority in 1933, they elected Halsey to be secretary of the Senate, and Biffle became party secretary (Ritchie 1998a, 340). Biffle succeeded Halsey as secretary of the Senate in 1945.

Floor staff for the Republicans developed in parallel to the floor staff for the Democrats, with both parties using funding for Senate offices to support party operations. Carl Loeffler, who arrived in the Senate as a page, served as the Republicans' chief floor staff member beginning in 1910, under the title of "acting assistant doorkeeper" when the party was in the minority and "assistant doorkeeper" when the party was in the majority, until 1928, when the

---

[39] "Honored by Senators," *Washington Post*, Oct. 25, 1913, 12; "G.O.P. Caucuses Postpone Controversial Matters," *Washington Post*, Dec. 6, 1925, 1. The Republicans also had a chief page and assistant doorkeeper assigned to them. Also see the Senate Historical Office biographical stories on Halsey and Biffle: www.senate.gov/about/officers-staff/secretary-of-the-senate/SOS-Edwin-Halsey.htm; www.senate.gov/about/officers-staff/secretary-of-the-senate/SOS-Leslie-Biffle.htm (both sites accessed March 2025).

Senate authorized the post "assistant sergeant at arms." In 1929, Loeffler's title changed to "secretary for the majority." Loeffler remained party secretary through the 1930s and 1940s until the new Republican majority in 1947 made him secretary of the Senate (Munk 1970, 9–10).

MANAGING THE FLOOR

The clear expectation by the mid-1920s was that the conference chairman was the floor leader and would be the chief strategist and spokesperson for the party on the floor. This did not mean that the leader managed all bills; this was left for committee leaders much of the time. It did not mean that other senators did not make speeches representing party views or get quoted in the press; leaders seldom elbowed their colleagues aside. But it did mean that, if events on the floor were not going well for the party, the leader was blamed and expected to take corrective action. Leaders understood this, anticipated problems, and provided direction to Senate party floor activity.

Agenda Setting and Floor Leadership

Curtis, encouraged by the Republican party's successes in the 1924 elections, promised to reinvigorate party organs and develop more of a team spirit, looking to the steering committee to set the agenda and coordinate Republican priorities with President Coolidge. He committed himself to more conference meetings and weekly meetings of the steering committee, while expressing his hope for greater efficiency in the legislative process and less speechmaking.[40] They did not chair the Republican steering committee themselves—as former caucus chairmen from Allison to Lodge had done—but Curtis and Watson met with the steering committee, as well as other party colleagues and committee chairmen, to set the floor agenda and coordinate party strategy.[41] In fact, as the party minutes show, the conference regularly discussed and approved steering committee reports on the floor agenda through the remainder of the decade. Curtis was a strong, effective floor manager, while Watson frequently left daily floor duties to McNary (Neal 1985, 124–25).

In 1933, then in the minority, McNary renamed the steering committee when he appointed a seven-member "Committee on Legislation," keeping Vandenberg as the committee's chairman (Wolff and Ritchie 1999, 242–43).[42] But there are no references to the work of the committee in the

---

[40] "Curtis Will Use Goad on Senate to Oust Bombast," *Atlanta Constitution*, Nov. 26, 1924, 1; "The Senate Leader," *Atlanta Constitution*, Nov. 28, 1924, 8; "Curtis of Kansas Is Senate Leader," *Hartford Courant*, Nov. 29, 1924, 1; "Radicals, Read Out by G.O.P., to Fight Program of Party," *Washington Post*, Nov. 29, 1924, 1.

[41] Arthur W. Macmahon, "American Government and Politics," *American Political Science Review* 20:3 (Aug. 1926), 604–22; Arthur W. Macmahon, "American Government and Politics," *American Political Science Review* 21:2 (May 1927), 297–317.

[42] "Brief Session of New Congress Hoped For," *Los Angeles Times*, Dec. 30, 1934, A4.

conference minutes or the press. With McNary, Vandenberg, and many other Republicans supporting much of the Roosevelt administration's program in 1933 and 1934, the committee may not have had much reason to meet. McNary did not appoint the committee in the next Congress (Wolff and Ritchie 1999, 289), and the Republican steering committee was not revived until after McNary's death in 1944.

Democratic leader Robinson, like his contemporary Curtis, assumed personal responsibility for policing the floor. While he could not schedule legislation as minority leader, between 1923 and 1933, Robinson looked for opportunities to shape the floor agenda, particularly when progressive senators were pursuing farm and railroad legislation, and he used the Democratic steering committee to help him get backing for his strategies.[43] Kern, Martin, and Underwood had assumed responsibility for covering the floor, but Robinson was considerably more vigilant. Being on the floor placed him in the center of the flow of information, gave him opportunities to offer policy alternatives and to challenge the majority party, and allowed him to join with insurgent Republicans to block Republican measures and, occasionally, pass Democratic and progressive measures.

He was ever-present as majority leader—a fully modern floor leader. "Robinson believed he was the sole guardian of Democratic interests on the Senate floor," biographer Donald Bacon (1991, 74) wrote. "His daily practice, from which he rarely varied, was to remain on the floor from the morning hour to the closing gavel." Robinson let committee chairmen manage bills unless there was reason to take over himself, which he did with no apparent resistance from his caucus (Weller 1998, 145, 147, 152). He took personal charge of the first wave of New Deal legislation and, near the end of his life, handled the Supreme Court expansion bill when the Judiciary chairman opposed it. And Robinson consulted closely with Republican leader McNary, who supported much of the New Deal legislation, in his regular effort to avoid minority objections.

Barkley, too, committed himself to a nearly full-time presence on the floor while the Senate was in session. In an effort to depersonalize party operations, he organized committee chairmen into an advisory council on the floor agenda.[44] While he could have turned to the steering committee for that traditional function, Barkley viewed the committee chairmen, who had more control over the flow of legislation to the floor and often served as bill managers, as the more useful group. Over time, though, Barkley faced increasing pressure to rely on the steering committee. Disagreements among Democratic senators, whose majority had shrunk in size for three successive elections, culminated in a 1943 vote proposing that vacancies on the steering committee be filled by vote of the caucus rather than appointment by the leader. After Barkley threatened to resign should the proposal be approved, the resolution

---

[43] "Farm Legislation Worries Congress," *New York Times*, May 30, 1924, 3.
[44] For example, see "Democrats Meet to Push Senate Action: Barkley Hopes Session Today Will End 'Dilatory Tactics,'" *Washington Post*, Feb. 24, 1939, 2.

was defeated, 33–20.[45] The *Chicago Daily Tribune* reported that "the effort to reduce Barkley's powers as majority leader was regarded as an attack upon the White House leadership, for which he has been a loyal spokesman."[46] The conference, including Barkley, subsequently agreed to a resolution offered by Walter George (D, Ga.) expressing "the sense of the Democratic Conference that during the war period, it is desirable that the Steering Committee be called at convenient intervals to counsel together with respect to questions of major policy and legislation"—a resolution that served as a "declaration of independence" from the administration (Ritchie 1998a, 366).[47] There is no evidence that Barkley used the steering committee much more after that episode (Barkley 1954, 174–75; Davis 1979, 131; Ritchie 1998a, 365–66).

The Right of First Recognition

The most important power of the majority leader, the right of first recognition, was not officially acknowledged in the Senate until 1937. The ability to be recognized before other senators gives the majority leader an opportunity to set the agenda and propound unanimous consent agreements before another senator can do so. By the early 1920s, some reports suggest that it was common practice to recognize the majority and minority leaders before turning to other senators. Writing in 1922, William Tyler Page, clerk of the House of Representatives, noted that the two Senate floor leaders "are parliamentary and political mouthpieces, and are usually accorded prior recognition by the Chair" (Page 1922, 23; McConnell and Brownell 2019, 157–62). A review of the *Congressional Record* in these years suggests that the majority leader usually had little problem gaining recognition to address the Senate or make a motion. Nevertheless, in a fairly thorough Ph.D. dissertation on Senate leadership written in 1930, there is no mention of a practice or right of first recognition (Donnelly 1930, 23). John Nance Garner—who, as vice president, was presiding over the Senate—explained, in response to a controversy over recognition in May 1933, that he was obligated to recognize a senator in charge of legislation before recognizing other senators (MacNeil and Baker 2013, 198–99; *Cong. Rec.*, 1933, 4149). Notably, however, he made this statement in reference to Carter Glass (D, Va.), who was managing a landmark banking bill; there is no evidence that Robinson, the majority leader, was even present that day.

Recognition of a floor leader became an issue for Barkley on August 11, 1937, three weeks after he had been elected to replace Robinson as floor leader. Just after the Senate completed action on a bill, Robert Wagner (D, N.Y.) was

---

[45] "Barkley Retains Appointive Power," *New York Times*, Jan. 8, 1943, 10.
[46] "Rename Barkley as Democrats Split on Policy," *Chicago Daily Tribune*, Jan. 8, 1943, 9.
[47] "Democrats Quarrel while GOP Laughs," *Washington Post*, Jan. 24, 1943, B2; "GOP Senators Re-Elect M'Nary as Their Leader," *St. Louis Post-Dispatch*, Jan. 8, 1943, 7A; "Leadership Upheld: Barkley Wins Caucus Fight After Threatening to Resign," *Washington Post*, Jan. 8, 1943, 1.

recognized and made a motion to proceed to the consideration of an anti-lynching bill. Barkley intervened to say that he had arranged for other measures to be considered that day, outlining his order of business and the specific senators who were to speak on each bill. Vice President Garner acknowledged that he was familiar with Barkley's agenda, but that neither of the senators identified by Barkley was on the floor when Wagner sought recognition. Garner cited his responsibility, under Senate Rule XIX, to recognize the first senator seeking recognition. "The Chair wants not only the Senator from Kentucky [Barkley] but the entire membership of the Senate to understand that it is the duty of the Chair ... to recognize the Senator who is addressing the Chair," Garner explained (*Cong. Rec.*, August 11, 1937, 8694). "When three Senators are on their feet demanding recognition, the Chair has the privilege of choosing the one to recognize; but when only one Senator is standing and demanding recognition, the Chair has no choice." Wagner agreed with Garner's understanding of the rules, insisting that he had the right to be recognized. Barkley tried to adjourn the Senate, but the motion to adjourn was defeated. The Republican leader, McNary, then moved to recess, and the motion succeeded, a serious embarrassment to Barkley.

Alben Barkley (D, Ky.) with Vice President John Nance Garner, just after Barkley was elected majority leader in July 1937.

Library of Congress, Prints & Photographs Division, photograph by Harris & Ewing, reproduction number LC-DIG-hec-23065

Over the next two days Barkley and Garner consulted and reached a new understanding. They agreed that the two of them would discuss Barkley's floor agenda before the start of each session so that the vice president knew Barkley's plans and could look to the majority leader to be recognized (Libbey 2016, 191, 235). Then Garner explicitly laid out the right of first recognition to the Senate on August 13, 1937 (*Cong. Rec.*, August 13, 1937, 8840). "The Chair recognized the Senator from Kentucky because he is the leader on the Democratic side of the Chamber," Garner explained. "He would recognize the Senator from Vermont [Mr. Austin], acting Republican leader, in the same way." Pressed by La Follette, who did not challenge the practice of first recognizing the majority leader but insisted that the majority leader did not have the right to "[farm] out the floor" to another senator when others were seeking recognition in their own right, Garner then clarified his understanding of the right of first recognition. While the majority leader "cannot farm out his time," Garner explained, the leader had the right to suggest who should be recognized if there were multiple senators seeking recognition, and the presiding officer would follow the leader's suggestion (*Cong. Rec.*, August 13, 1937, 8839–40). A few months later, Garner reiterated his policy that when one of the two floor leaders is seeking recognition at the same time as other senators, the majority leader and then the minority leader would be given priority recognition (Riddick 1992, 1094; *Cong. Rec.*, February 21, 1938, 2202). This was an unusual source of precedent. It was not a ruling or Senate vote in response to a formal point of order. In fact, Barkley, who later served as vice president himself, would observe that "the rules don't require it, but it is a moral obligation and the custom of the chair to recognize a majority leader because he is the leader of the Senate and he maps the program."[48]

How much Garner's 1937 explanation changed preexisting Senate procedure is not entirely clear. While the right of first recognition was now firmly settled as a cornerstone of Senate floor leadership, majority leaders before Barkley do not seem to have had much difficulty seeking recognition. In everyday practice, senators in the 1910s, 1920s, and 1930s did not often attempt to get the jump on the floor leaders, and the presiding officer looked to recognize the majority leader or bill manager before another senator. Barkley, in fact, later noted that "all during Garner's eight years, he did that with Joe Robinson in the first place and with me."[49]

---

[48] Alben W. Barkley Oral History Project, University of Kentucky Libraries, July 22, 1953, BARK007. Even before this episode, there was a well-established precedent that the presiding officer's recognition of a senator could not be appealed or be subject to a point of order. Thus Rule XIX and the earlier precedent clearly implied that, if several senators were simultaneously seeking recognition, the presiding officer could use his discretion to recognize party leaders before other senators.

[49] Alben W. Barkley Oral History Project, University of Kentucky Libraries, July 22, 1953, BARK007.

SERVING AS INTERMEDIARY WITH THE PRESIDENT

Floor leaders are, first and foremost, elected leaders of their Senate parties. To serve the interests of their party colleagues, in-party leaders engage with the president to coordinate White House and legislative party strategies. Common policy and electoral interests usually make this a collaborative process, and the frequency of the interaction often spawns or reinforces personal friendships that both the president and in-party congressional leader value. By the mid-1920s, the Senate leader of the president's party was established as the conference's chief liaison with the White House. Often, because of the president's importance to the party, this entailed seeking to influence the president's strategy and then persuading congressional colleagues to support it. For the in-party leader, these roles reflected expectations of the president as well as senators, but expectations were not nearly so clear for the opposition leader. The result was far greater variation in the relationship between the opposition leader and the president, ranging from Robinson's dogged opposition to the programs of the Republican presidents of the 1920s to McNary's quiet support for Roosevelt's early New Deal program in the 1930s.

When Curtis took over for Lodge in late 1924, Coolidge had been president for over a year. The relationship between the two men was already strained as a result of the handiwork of William Butler (R, Mass.), who replaced Lodge in the Senate. Coolidge had made Butler chairman of the Republican National Committee and his 1924 presidential campaign manager. As Curtis knew, Butler had blocked Curtis from being nominated for the vice presidency at that year's convention. Curtis returned the favor by advocating the use of seniority as a rule for making appointments to top committees, including the seat on the Committee on Foreign Relations that Lodge had long held and Butler sought (Munk 1974). While Curtis had a somewhat cool relationship with Coolidge, he faithfully represented his colleagues at White House meetings and championed the cause of regular Republicans that both he and Coolidge supported. In 1928, when Curtis was elected vice president, both he and President-elect Hoover supported Watson as the Senate's new majority leader, and Watson enjoyed a close working relationship with them (Watson 1936, 262).[50] In fact, Hoover had a private telephone line installed in Watson's home "so that we might talk to each other freely without any interference day or night" (Watson 1936, 276).

When Joe Robinson was elected Democratic leader in 1923, he was known as a loyal partisan and proved to be a sharp and frequent critic of Presidents Coolidge and Hoover. Before becoming party leader, he had played a significant role in drawing attention to the Teapot Dome scandal in the Harding administration and was a vocal opponent to the Four-Power Pact that Underwood had helped to negotiate. As leader, Robinson took strong and visible positions against most major Republican initiatives of the 1920s, in line with the views of most of his party colleagues. Still, he was subjected to some unfriendly commentary by

---

[50] "Coolidge, Curtis and Butler in Conference," *Boston Daily Globe*, July 23, 1925, A14.

Democratic senators for his friendship with Coolidge and later for serving on the U.S. delegation to the London Naval Conference during the Hoover administration (Bacon 1991, 74; Weller 1998, 127–30). As minority leader, Robinson was also criticized for making early commitments to Hoover on unemployment and drought-relief legislation following the crash of 1929 without adequate consultation with his party. But this rapprochement did not last long. Robinson became a severe critic of the president during the last three years of Hoover's term (Weller 1998, 131–32).

Majority Leader Robinson was the champion of the Roosevelt administration in the Senate, as both the president and his Senate colleagues expected. Following the model set by Kern, Martin, and Underwood with President Wilson—and by Lodge, Curtis, and Watson with the Republican presidents of the 1920s and early 1930s—Robinson was at the center of communication between Roosevelt and Senate Democrats. He reported to the president on the situation in the Senate and reviewed the president's wishes with his Senate colleagues on a frequent basis. In his final years, though, in 1936 and 1937, Robinson experienced tension as he mediated between his conference and Roosevelt. By then, southern Democrats and even Robinson himself began differing with Roosevelt about the necessity of retaining some early New Deal policies. Robinson's efforts to navigate intraparty differences on bills to deal with strikes and to charge states for relief programs began to undermine his relationship with the White House (Bacon 1991). The tension was coming to a head over the president's court plan just when Robinson died.

Barkley met regularly with the president throughout his service as leader.[51] One episode in those years offered a fine illustration of the leader's dueling obligations to his Senate party and to the president. Contrary to Barkley's recommendation, Roosevelt vetoed a tax bill in early 1944 for failing to generate enough revenue for the war. Roosevelt's veto message used sharp language that angered Barkley, who addressed the veto from the floor in strong terms. The president responded with an apologetic letter that was hand-delivered to Barkley later in the day. Nevertheless, Barkley resigned the next day as majority leader in protest, then, as he surely had expected, was promptly reelected in a rare meeting of the party conference.[52] Both Barkley and Roosevelt, who had a close relationship, appear to have had lingering resentments over this episode, which may have contributed to the president's decision to choose Truman over Barkley as his running mate later that year (Barkley 1954, 169–82). Barkley would become Truman's running mate four years later.

McNary's term as Republican leader ran for nearly the entirety of the Roosevelt presidency (Neal 1985, 141–70). McNary became Senate minority

---

[51] Weekly meetings while Congress is in session was not always the practice. In 1937, for example, President Roosevelt started weekly meetings during a special session called to act on administration proposals to address the recession: "Senate Speeds Housing Bill to Repair Record," *Washington Post*, Dec. 20, 1937, 1, 4.

[52] C. P. Trussell, "Moves for Unity: Senate Leader Writes President of His Hopes of Future Accord," *New York Times*, Feb. 25, 1944, 1.

Minority Leader Charles McNary (R, Ore.), left, with Arthur Vandenberg (R, Mich.), Warren Austin (R, Vt.), and Robert Taft (R, Ohio) in 1940. Austin was minority whip at the time and served as acting minority leader for a few months while McNary was his party's candidate for vice president. Taft and Vandenberg were unsuccessful candidates for the Republican nomination for president that year.

Library of Congress, Prints & Photographs Division, photograph by Harris & Ewing, reproduction number LC-DIG-hec-27906

leader in March 1933, when Roosevelt was inaugurated president, and McNary served his colleagues until his death early in 1944, just one year before Roosevelt's own death. During those 11 years, McNary consulted with the president on numerous occasions.[53] Roosevelt, who had not known McNary personally until 1933 but knew his politics, moved quickly to secure his support—calling McNary to the President's Room in the Capitol immediately following his inaugural address—and McNary joined Roosevelt in calling for bold policy responses to the deepening depression. Progressives comprised about a third of the Senate Republican conference and, like McNary, supported the initial features of Roosevelt's New Deal program.[54] McNary's relationship

[53] "Roosevelt to Push Vote on Waterway," *New York Times*, Feb. 24, 1934, 16; "Between You and Me," *Washington Post*, Jan. 17, 1935, 2; "Robinson Chided by President on Delay in Senate," *Chicago Daily Tribune*, May 1, 1935, 5.

[54] "McNary Urges Passive G.O.P. in Congress," *Washington Post*, Dec. 31, 1933, 3.

with the president was an issue for some within his party at times, as when he was the only Republican invited to a dinner with the British prime minister early in the administration.[55] Even when he opposed the president on a St. Lawrence Seaway treaty, reciprocal trade, a veterans bill, and a few other issues, a *Chicago Tribune* reporter observed that he was "under suspicion of dealing tenderly with the administration."[56] McNary broke with Roosevelt on some matters but seldom took a leading role in opposition until 1937, when the president's court-packing plan galvanized Republicans and motivated McNary to orchestrate his party's efforts. In subsequent years, he frequently collaborated with conservative Democrats to oppose administration legislation.

BUILDING MAJORITY COALITIONS

By the mid-1920s, finding a majority, or even a supermajority, to support or oppose legislation was a shared responsibility of floor leaders, committee chairmen, bill sponsors, and, often, the president and the president's legislative aides. Floor leaders were central to any effort that involved important party or presidential interests. Coalition-building—specifically, Gorman's determined work, and that of his caucus, to defeat the Federal Elections Bill—had been central to the creation of elected floor leadership in the early 1890s. It had defined Kern's role as the first majority leader in 1913, as he coordinated action to implement Wilson's legislative program. And it remained a core responsibility of floor leaders in the 1920s, 1930s, and 1940s.

Soon after his election as majority leader, Curtis faced an effort by Democrats and some Republicans to override Coolidge's veto of a popular bill to provide a wage increase for postal workers. "The leadership not only of the President, but of Senator Curtis . . . , the new majority leader of the Senate, was at stake in the contest today," the *Chicago Daily Tribune* noted after the veto was narrowly upheld. "Senator Curtis won his first fight, but by such a squeak that he was visibly trembling in his chair as the roll was called."[57] Recognizing deep factional divisions within the party, Republican leaders conspicuously avoided taking binding votes in their conference throughout this period. In 1925, shortly after an attorney general nominee was rejected, the conference adopted a resolution offered by Wesley Jones, the majority whip, "to make clear and beyond question the long-settled policy of Republicans that our conferences are not caucuses or of binding effect upon those participating therein but are meetings solely for the purpose of exchanging views to promote harmony and united action so far as possible." Every Republican senator, the resolution affirmed, "shall be entirely free to act upon any matter considered by the conference as his judgment may dictate" (Wolff and Ritchie 1999, 174).

---

[55] "Hits Roosevelt's Dinners," *New York Times*, Apr. 25, 1933, 3.
[56] "G.O.P. Leaders' Hopes Revive as Tide Turns," *Chicago Daily Tribune*, Apr. 9, 1934, 1.
[57] "Coolidge Victor by a Single Vote on Postal Wage," *Chicago Daily Tribune*, Jan. 7, 1925, 3.

Offered after insurgents had been punished on committee assignments for their support for La Follette's presidential candidacy in 1924, the resolution reflected the strength of the radical faction and the desire of Curtis and other senior Republicans to keep the party from fracturing further.[58]

Curtis experienced uneven success during the next four years, and Watson, who faced an aggressive insurgent faction, struggled even more in his tenure. "Watson has been leading the vain fight of the Republican regulars against the Democratic-Insurgent coalition in the tariff fight," the *Los Angeles Times* wrote in late 1929, when Watson's health failed him. "The strain sapped his energy to such an extent that at last he came to share the physicians' alarm and concluded to take a vacation."[59] The newspaper went on to report that regulars were not sure who would take Watson's place as leader while he recovered, suggesting the importance of the floor leader's role in building coalitions. A few weeks later, the *Washington Post* reported that "Senator Watson has again assumed active leadership of the Republican forces in the Senate and it is reported that he is in a conciliatory mood" on the tariff issue.[60] As Donnelly (1930, 75–76) reflected, completing his dissertation in 1930, "The job of being floor leader is as big as the man who holds it. It stretches to accommodate the Lodges and shrinks to fit the Watsons." Donnelly (1930, 76) continued, with Watson's experience fresh in his mind: "The floor leader may be the leader of the Senate or the collie for the flock who merely yaps at those who dare to wander."

Robinson was a proactive leader in building coalitions and setting direction for Senate Democrats. In the minority, Robinson's strategies were heavily influenced by the deep divisions within the Republican conference. In the 70th Congress (1927–29) and 72nd Congress (1931–33), slim Republican majorities gave Robinson's Democrats and insurgent Republicans a floor majority on important legislation that often allowed them to block action by regular Republicans and the president. In other Congresses as minority leader, Robinson could occasionally find the six or seven Republicans required to prevent a Republican majority from materializing (Weller 1998, 103–25). As majority leader beginning in 1933, Robinson, with the support of his caucus, established a policy committee that would design legislation under his chairmanship (Ritchie 1998a, 341). With the chairmen of the major committees—Appropriations, Finance, Foreign Relations, Interstate Commerce—named to the new policy committee, along with other members who were trusted supporters of the administration, the policy committee had the appearance of a Senate cabinet (Robertson 1994; Weller 1998, 136). The committee considered scheduling and substantive policy issues that previously were in the jurisdiction of the steering committee. However, with large

---

[58] "Republicans Yield on Senate Radicals," *New York Times*, Mar. 13, 1925, 2; "Insurgents Keep Their Patronage," *Boston Globe*, Mar. 13, 1925, 16.
[59] "Watson Leaves Senate to Rest," *Los Angeles Times*, Oct. 30, 1929, 4.
[60] "A Compromise," *Washington Post*, Dec. 2, 1929, 6.

Democratic majorities and fully drafted bills from the White House, the policy committee had less to do than Robinson may have intended.[61]

Robinson, in the majority, also asked in 1933 for a new binding caucus rule. His motion allowed a simple majority to bind all party members to support a measure, in contrast to the two-thirds majority required in the 1903 and 1913 versions. Robinson's motion, which was debated and apparently modified after considerable discussion, was approved. "That until further ordered the Chairman is authorized to convene Democratic Senators in Caucus for the purpose of considering any measure recommended by the President; and that all Democratic Senators shall be bound by the vote of the majority of the Caucus," the caucus resolved in 1933; "Provided that any Senator may be excused from voting for any such measure upon his express statement to the Caucus that said measure is contrary to his conscientious judgment or that said measure is in violation of pledges made to his constituents as a candidate" (Ritchie 1998a, 341). While much was made of the new rule in the newspapers, the provisions for conscientious objector status and constituent pledges gutted the effect of the rule, and it was never used.[62] Robinson could count on winning majorities in the Senate until 1936, when conservative Democrats began actively to oppose some of the administration's legislation (Katznelson 2005). Robinson's most prominent losses as majority leader were on the ratification of the treaty on the World Court and on the expansion of the Supreme Court (Weller 1998). In both cases, Robinson was severely constrained in his ability to find compromises and salvage a favorable outcome.

Barkley's role as Democratic floor leader, until Roosevelt's death in 1945, was predominantly to schedule action on and solicit support for administration legislation. This task was more challenging than it had been for Robinson. With the emergence of southern Democrats as an organized bloc and their frequent alliance with Republicans, Barkley struggled to build coalitions to support legislative priorities, invoke cloture on civil rights and other matters, and carry votes on the floor. Barkley frequently proposed compromise language and often served as a bridge between competing factions and the White House.[63]

Republican Leader McNary was the chief architect of Republican strategy in the Senate in the Roosevelt years. He rarely opposed New Deal legislation in Roosevelt's first term, but that began to change in the summer of 1937. On Roosevelt's court-packing plan, McNary urged his party colleagues to

---

[61] "Congress Convenes Today; Roosevelt Plans to Read Brief Message in Person," *New York Times*, Jan. 3, 1934, 1; "Liquor Tax First Issue," *Los Angeles Times*, Jan. 3, 1934, 4. One report indicates that the two committees met jointly at least once to consider matters that might have been discussed in a meeting of the full caucus: see "Democrats to Let Cutting Take Seat," *New York Times*, Jan. 1, 1935, 13.

[62] "Democrats Vote for Strict Rule," *Boston Globe*, Mar. 7, 1933, 2; "Congress Leaders to Speed Bank Aid," *New York Times*, Mar. 7, 1933, 1.

[63] For examples on civil rights legislation, see Jenkins and Peck (2013); on water legislation, see Shanley (1988).

minimize their public statements about the plan and let conservative Democrats, who were critical of the plan, take the lead in blocking the scheme. While former president Hoover did not cooperate, congressional Republicans succeeded in lying low, allowing Democrats to kill the plan after Robinson's death. Soon after, some conservative Democrats and Republicans sought a more formal statement of an anti–New Deal manifesto, an effort, ultimately unsuccessful, that McNary refused to join. In the late 1930s and 1940s, though, McNary regularly combined efforts with conservative Democrats on behalf of his party to oppose and sometimes amend or repeal New Deal legislation (Neal 1991, 112–18; Patterson 1967, 106–7, 206–10).

PARTY SPOKESPERSON

Reporters quoted regularly from floor remarks and looked to leaders for comment. Robinson set a new standard for interacting with reporters and being quoted in newspapers, often from his voluminous floor statements, which he certainly expected to be mentioned in the press. After the stock market crash, between 1929 and 1933, the frequency of Robinson newspaper mentions nearly doubled over the average for the previous few years. The high number of Robinson mentions continued into the Roosevelt administration, even with the aggressive public relations efforts of the White House. On the Republican side, even Curtis, who took pride in being silent or brief on the floor, was far more visible than Republican caucus chairmen, except Lodge, had been before him. Watson, days before the 1932 election and seeing trouble on the horizon, delivered a fear-mongering radio address to the country asking listeners to return Republicans to office.[64] The election over, Watson then issued an awkward statement that congressional Republicans accepted the offer of leading Democrats to work cooperatively to address the economic crisis.[65]

The floor leader's formal press conference may have originated, at Robinson's direction, in the spring of 1933, although previously leaders often talked with reporters, sometimes in informal sessions.[66] In December 1935, Arthur Krock, writing for the *New York Times*, explained "press conference etiquette on Capitol Hill." It was a regular affair when Congress met, hosted jointly by the Democratic leaders of the two chambers. "After the Speaker and the Senate majority leader have arrived for the session, they receive the press

---

[64] "Watson Sees Chaos if Democrats Win," *Boston Globe*, Nov. 1, 1930, 12.

[65] "Offer of Democratic Aid in Ending Slump Accepted," *New York Times*, Nov. 10, 1930, 1.

[66] "A Washington Daybook," *Daily Home News* (New Brunswick, N.J.), July 7, 1933, 2. This is the earliest mention of a formal press conference held by a Senate leader that we have discovered. Other sessions with reporters are noted occasionally in newspaper accounts and surely happened far more frequently. For example, the *Boston Globe* noted in 1929 that Robinson had "dropped into the Senate press gallery and gave reporters a chance to question him on politics and business": see "Raskob Commends Business Parlays," *Boston Globe*, Dec. 5, 1929, 15.

Majority Leader Joe Robinson (D, Ark.) at a press conference in 1937.
Library of Congress, Prints & Photographs Division, photograph by Harris & Ewing, reproduction number LC-DIG-hec-21930

daily at a stated hour," Krock explained. "Most of the time they have really nothing to impart."[67] In the late 1930s and 1940s, Barkley retained the practice of holding press conferences. Barkley, notably, was the first majority party leader to fully exploit radio, and he took this role seriously. A well-liked orator and storyteller and the keynote speaker at the 1932 and 1936 national conventions, Barkley frequently made national radio broadcasts to give a congressional perspective in support of the president's program. Like Roosevelt, Barkley found radio to be a useful way to reach the public without dependence on newspapers, which were largely owned by Republicans (Libbey 2016, 174; Ritchie 1991).

McNary never was particularly vocal on the floor or aggressive in seeking press coverage, but he did seek to influence his party's public image (Neal 1985, 169). During the first years of the New Deal, he believed that the program's

---

[67] Arthur Krock, "In the Nation: Explaining How Adjournment Prophecies Develop," *New York Times*, Dec. 25, 1935, 26. See also "Senate Majority Leader Holds Press Conference," *Boston Globe*, Jan. 5, 1937, 8; "Reelection Poser Dodged by Barkley," *Washington Post*, Feb. 23, 1944, 2; "The Political Arena: Barkley Says Willkie Can't Withstand Pressure of Groups Supporting Him," *Washington Post*, Oct. 23, 1940, 8.

popularity required that Republicans keep their criticism and visibility to a minimum. But that changed. "By the summer of 1935, McNary felt it was time to become more assertive in his role as party spokesman," Neal (1985, 149) writes. "He publicly suggested that FDR give the country a breathing spell and focus his energies on existing programs instead of seeking more. 'The emotionalism, which always accompanies a political upheaval, had subsided,' McNary declared." Nevertheless, McNary's deliberate strategy on the court-packing issue and other legislative matters was to have the party, including himself, maintain a low profile while conservative Democrats took the lead in criticizing administration proposals. Republicans elected in the late 1930s and early 1940s were not satisfied with his efforts to counter President Roosevelt's relations with the press and public, but they could not effect meaningful change in McNary's behavior.

THE 1944 REORGANIZATION OF THE REPUBLICAN CONFERENCE

McNary had surgery for a brain tumor in early November 1943 and did not return to the Senate before he died in February 1944. That January, with McNary absent, Robert Taft (R, Ohio) proposed creating a committee that would examine ways to strengthen Senate Republican party organization. Elected to the Senate six years before, Taft led conservative Republicans, who were relatively young, dissatisfied with McNary's one-man governance, and frustrated with McNary's tolerance of New Deal programs and internationalism. Taft by 1944 had already become the leading Senate Republican conservative and, as the son of President William Howard Taft, had a national reputation. He openly wanted to bend the party in a conservative direction and, conspicuously to others, sought to lead conservative forces in the country as he entertained running for president (Drury 1963, 10; Merry 1991, 170–72). Senate Republicans, looking to the end of World War II and eager to return to majority status, embraced the Taft plan. Wallace White (R, Maine), who was acting leader in McNary's place, said, "We are getting ready to take control of the Senate" after the 1944 elections, in describing the purpose of the reorganization effort.[68] Taft reported that his goal was to create a "united front" for the party "whenever a matter involving party questions arises."[69] The *New York Times*, in a headline, proclaimed that Taft was going to use the committee "To Fix Republican Appeal."[70]

[68] "Senate Republicans Back McNary as Chief; Vote Study on Strengthening Party Position," *New York Times*, Jan. 21, 1944, 11. According to this story, the Republicans would need to gain 11 more seats to win control.

[69] "Conference of GOP Chooses Senate Steering Committee," *Washington Post*, Mar. 16, 1944, 1.

[70] "To Fix Republican Appeal: Party to Define in the Senate Its Stand on '44 Issues," *New York Times*, Mar. 19, 1944, 31; "Republicans Plan to Speed Congress: Party Chiefs, Expecting

In March 1944, soon after McNary died, Taft proposed, and the Republican conference adopted, party rules that recreated leadership posts and committees. The rules provided for separate senators to hold the positions of floor leader and conference chairman (Wolff and Ritchie 1999, 345, 353, 357)—and the conference reestablished the Republican steering committee, which had been defunct for nearly a decade's time, naming Taft its chairman.[71] The conference elected White its acting floor leader and Vandenberg, who had been conference vice chairman, acting chairman for the remainder of the Congress. Taft used the steering committee as the forum for defining a large legislative program on postwar policy for the party. A reading of the conference minutes and news accounts for 1944 shows that Taft was already effectively setting the agenda for discussions of policy and politics in the party conference, often by bringing steering committee resolutions to conference meetings (Patterson 1972, 267; Wolff and Ritchie 1999, 340–76). Journalist William White later asserted that Taft drew on his position as steering committee chairman to make himself the "party's intellectual and practical head" (White 1954, 57). Indeed, Taft became a powerful force in the party while spurning the floor leadership post until 1953, the year he died.

The 1944 Taft rules transformed the Senate Republican party's organization and promoted Taft's political career. At the start of the next Congress, the conference elected White floor leader and Vandenberg conference chairman (Wolff and Ritchie 1999, 386), and Taft retained the chairmanship of the steering committee. White had offered to step aside if either Taft or Vandenberg wanted the job, but, according to the Associated Press, both Taft and Vandenberg indicated that they preferred to avoid the tedious tasks of floor management.[72] The separation of the posts of floor leader, conference chair, and steering committee chair has been maintained ever since by the Senate Republican conference, in contrast to Senate Democrats, where floor leadership and the conference chairmanship—and, through the 1990s, the chairmanships of party committees—have been fused in the same person since the days of Gorman.

For three decades, from 1913 until 1944, Republicans had followed the Democratic model of centralizing leadership in a single person, with every Republican caucus chairman in this era serving simultaneously as floor leader. In reinventing their organization in 1944 at a time that Taft, the rising force in their party, chose not to become floor leader, Republicans forged a new pattern, choosing separate senators for leader and as chairs of most party committees, a pattern that is retained to this day. But, of course, this model was less novel than it must have seemed to the Senate of 1944. It echoed, on paper if not in the

Control, Evolve Plans to End Many Outmoded Procedures," *New York Times*, Mar. 20, 1944, 11.
[71] "Name Taft as Head of Steering Group," *New York Times*, Mar. 16, 1944, 36.
[72] "Looking Ahead in Washington," *St. Louis Post-Dispatch*, Dec. 17, 1944, 20.

actual allocation of powers, the old Republican model of collective governance that characterized the Republican steering committee at the turn of the last century.

CONCLUSION

While the way in which some functions are performed continued to evolve, the basic responsibilities of today's Senate leader differ little from those assumed by Curtis and Robinson in the 1920s. Curtis moved seamlessly from his job as whip and conference vice chairman into floor leadership and orchestrated the appointment of a leadership team dominated by his faction of Republican regulars. In the majority after the 1932 elections, Robinson more fully centralized collective party functions in his leadership. Constantly on the Senate floor, he coordinated all aspects of party strategy, took over bill management responsibilities whenever it was best for his party, and invented a policy committee to coordinate the work of the major committees. Although Barkley proved to be effective in exploiting the advent of national radio networks, Robinson vigorously managed relations with the press also.

Party competition drove many of the innovations in this period. Robinson's invention of a policy committee in 1933, upon the election of a new Democratic majority, reflected his interest in uniting the party to act on a wave of legislation. The committee did not prove to be very significant, largely because the Roosevelt administration quickly filled Congress's agenda with New Deal legislation. With dominant control of the Senate through the remainder of the period, Democrats considered no significant organizational changes.

Republicans, in contrast, illustrate that party development is driven also by political forces beyond party competition. In the 1920s, the Senate party suffered deep factional fights that threatened their majority control of the Senate. Floor leaders were central to resolving these conflicts and they played a significant role in creating and discarding leadership posts in the process. McNary's depleted party of the 1930s left little need for secondary leadership positions. He appointed informal assistants, but only in 1944 did Republicans reimagine their party organization. This happened after the party seemed within reach of majority status, McNary had fallen ill, conservative Republicans had replenished their numbers, and a senator with presidential ambitions, Robert Taft of Ohio, championed the interests of that faction, authoring a new organizational plan for the party and assuming a prominent leadership role within it.

Senate Majority Leader Alben Barkley (D, Ky.) shown in a 1946 illustration trying to whip the Senate into getting its work done. Democrats lost their congressional majorities in the 1946 elections.

Berryman Political Cartoon Collection, Office of the Senate Curator

8

Party Infrastructure, 1945–1980

The "era of committee chairmen" and the "textbook Congress" are the most common labels applied by political scientists to the mid-twentieth-century Congress (Davidson and Oleszek 1977; Shepsle 1989). Donald Matthews, in his *U.S. Senators & Their World* (1960), described senators as adhering to traditional folkways, which included deference to committee leaders and reciprocity across committees. These characterizations reflected the committee-oriented legislative process of those decades, one in which party leaders and organizations played a secondary role in determining policy outcomes. Elected party leaders were viewed as servants who performed important coordination and ministerial duties, but they were not the chief policymakers or strategists of their chambers. In most circumstances, that was left to committee chairmen.[1]

Contributing to this view of the Senate were studies of Senate party leadership during the period. Drawing upon his detailed examination of the 81st Congress (1949–50) and observations of the Senate through the 1950s, David Truman emphasized that the Senate's small size and individualism constrained party leadership resources, which, he argued, were restricted to the "personal and interstitial" (Truman 1959, 96). In Truman's view, the leadership role was limited and unsettled: "The function of the group [party] does not require standardized performance of the role as a condition of tenure, and ineffective performance may produce no compensating behavior elsewhere in the party" (Truman 1959, 117). In 1976, at the end of Mike Mansfield's 16-year leadership of the Senate Democrats, Charles Jones asserted that "strong substance-oriented policy leadership by party leaders is neither possible nor desirable in the United States Senate" (1976, 19–20). Senate party leaders had little formal

---

[1] For background on Senate party leaders in this period, see Bailey 1988; Bone 1956; Huitt 1961; Jones 1976; Oleszek 1971; Peabody 1981; Ripley 1969a, 1969b, 1976; Sinclair 2012; Smith 1993; Smith and Flathman 1989; Stewart 1971.

power and few resources, and their activities were limited to managing floor proceedings.

But these interpretations of leadership are incomplete. Senate parties by 1945 were already quite different than they had been before the advent of floor leadership posts just a few decades earlier. In fact, the conclusions of Truman and Jones belie their own accounts of the importance of leaders in negotiating among party factions, collecting and dispersing information, resolving conflicts over floor scheduling and strategy, and coordinating Senate activity with the House and the president, even in an era in which the substance of legislation was usually written in committee rooms. These leadership activities were seldom grounded in formal powers, but, as we have detailed in previous chapters, were settled in the expectations of their party colleagues. By the time political scientists Truman and Jones were on the scene, there were unwritten, but well-established, job descriptions for floor leaders.

In this chapter, we lay out the foundational developments that occurred in the late 1940s and early 1950s and then again in the 1970s. The first era was a period of intense inter-party and factional competition, which, along with personal ambition, motivated lasting innovations of party organization and the capacity of party leaders. The second era, the late 1970s, was a time of growing factionalism in the Republican conference, as insurgent conservatives, chafing after two decades in the minority, began challenging the party's long-standing leadership. There was much less innovation in the Mansfield years, from 1961 to 1977, when Democratic control of the Senate went unchallenged, and the party's leaders worked hard to suppress factional and ideological divides. What we discover in this era is abundant evidence of institutional change—many ways in which party leadership was consolidated and strengthened—in an era long described as static and assumed to be centered not on party organization but on committees.

PARTY COMPETITION, FACTIONALISM, AND INDIVIDUALISM

After more than a decade of unchallenged Democratic hegemony, Republicans began competing actively for control of the Senate in the mid-1940s, as New Deal Democrats came up for reelection for the first or second time and the public expressed frustration with wartime regulations (Ritchie 1991a, 142). Republicans gained a majority of seats in the 1946 midterm elections, erasing a 57–38 Democratic majority and transforming it into a 51–45 Republican majority (see Figure 8.1). For the next six election cycles, control of the Senate was always in doubt. Neither party had as many as 55 seats between 1947 and 1959, and in four consecutive Congresses just one or two seats divided the Senate majority from the minority. Republicans held majorities in both chambers in 1947–49 and 1953–55.

That competitive era ended abruptly with the 1958 midterm elections: the 49–47 Democratic majority of the old Congress gave way to a new Democratic

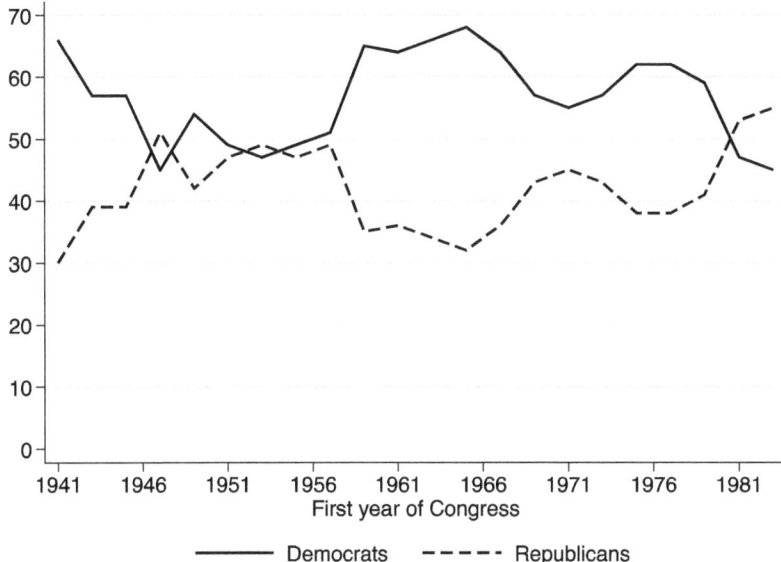

FIGURE 8.1 Size of parties, 1941–83

majority of 65–35. Over the next two decades, from 1959 until the 1980 elections, Democrats were in firm control of both chambers. In these years, Senate Democrats averaged 61 seats—a number large enough that they had little reason to worry about losing their Senate majority in any election. Democrats, and even Republicans, could fashion individualized legislative agendas and styles without much affecting their party's collective electoral interests. Indeed, the period is known for rising individualism among senators, who increasingly exploited the new technologies of mass media and transportation to cultivate national audiences (Rohde, Ornstein, and Peabody 1985; Sinclair 1989; Smith 1989).

The long tenure of activist Democratic presidents Roosevelt and Truman from 1933 through 1953 allowed Democratic leaders and committee chairs to rely on the White House to set policy priorities. Republicans, in contrast, grew impatient with their minority, out-party status and eventually took the lead in elaborating mechanisms for the Senate party to develop policy proposals. Later, in the 1960s and 1970s, Republicans' position as a minority party encouraged further expansion of their organizational capacity that the Democrats were slow to match.

Factions

Factionalism was central to developments in both parties. Before and during the war, the conservative coalition of Republicans and conservative Democrats had weakened or eliminated several New Deal programs. In the years after 1945, as President Harry Truman and liberal Democrats refocused on civil rights, labor, and other domestic issues, factional divisions among Democrats intensified. The Republican resurgence in 1947–59 came at the expense of northern, liberal Democrats, who found themselves at a disadvantage in intraparty leadership contests and representation on party committees; the seats of southern Democrats remained safe. When the liberal Democratic leader Scott Lucas (D, Ill.) lost his Illinois seat to Everett Dirksen (R, Ill.) in 1950, Richard Russell (D, Ga.) and other southerners joined with westerners to support Ernest McFarland (D, Ariz.) to replace Lucas as party leader. Two years later, after McFarland lost his own seat, southerners and westerners rallied behind Lyndon B. Johnson (D, Tex.), who served as leader for the rest of the decade (Caro 2002; McMillan 2004). After the 1958 elections, liberals gained better representation in leadership posts and party committees, but the liberal-conservative divide continued to be a central issue for the party and its leaders through the 1970s.

On the Republican side, the number of progressive senators declined in the 1940s, and traditional conservatives, led by Robert Taft (R, Ohio), gained the upper hand in party affairs.[2] The most visible intraparty divide concerned the role of the United States in world affairs. The internationalist wing associated with Arthur Vandenberg (R, Mich.) shared with most Democrats the view that the United States must take a leading role in world affairs, while the Taftites, as they came to be called, retained the pre-war isolationist tendencies of midwestern and western Republicans. The Taft wing also was more conservative on domestic issues, although Republican views on domestic issues were more homogeneous than on foreign affairs. In the 1950s, the intensification of the Cold War, the exploitation of national security issues by the Democrats, and the election of Dwight Eisenhower, an internationalist, as president resolved this intraparty division in foreign affairs in favor of the internationalists (White 1954; Rovere 1956, 101–2).

Although the cross-party conservative coalition persisted throughout this era, the greater representation of liberal Democrats after the 1958 elections and the emergence of moderate Republicans in the Northeast and Midwest in the 1960s created a liberal majority on many issues. Conservatives consequently turned to the filibuster to block civil rights measures and thereafter to block a wide range of liberal legislation. Until 1975, when the threshold for cloture was reduced from a two-thirds majority of senators voting to a three-fifths majority of all senators, filibuster reform created its own factional challenges for Democratic leaders, frequently pitting liberal Democrats against conservative Democrats (and minority Republicans).

---

[2] For a careful analysis of Senate Republican policy outlook at mid-century, see Malsberger 1987.

In the 1970s, a newer brand of conservative Republican arrived in the Senate, introducing fresh divisions into party ranks and spurring the development of new party organs. The religious right emerged as a force in Republican politics in the early 1970s, playing an important role in the election of Jesse Helms (R, N.C.) and James McClure (R, Idaho) to the Senate in 1972. McClure eventually ran for and won the Republican conference chairmanship in 1980. Helms and McClure were joined by Paul Laxalt (R, Nev.), elected in 1974, Orrin Hatch (R, Utah) and Malcolm Wallop (R, Wyo.), both elected in 1976, and Thad Cochran (R, Miss.), elected in 1978, all of whom replaced moderate or conservative Democrats and expanded the conservative wing of the Senate Republican conference. Meeting together nearly weekly, these new conservatives intensified pressure on the Senate party to adopt aggressive, uncompromising legislative strategies in confronting majority Democrats.

An important theme of scholarship on congressional parties is that intense intraparty factionalism is associated with weak party leaders and strong standing committees (Smith and Deering 1990, 171–73; Aldrich, Berger, and Rohde 2002). As we see in this chapter, that pattern does not fit the Senate as well as it does the House. That perspective, known as conditional party government, is rooted in observations of the House of Representatives, where the assertiveness of speakers appears to be correlated with the polarization of the parties. Our observation of the Senate is that weak leaders are only loosely associated with factionalized parties. For example, Democratic leaders Joe Robinson and Lyndon Johnson were remarkably assertive leaders, but Robinson, for the first two New Deal Congresses of the 1930s, led a unified party conference, and Johnson, who is commonly viewed as one of the most influential leaders in Senate history and someone who made lasting changes to party organization, served as leader at a time in which factionalism among Democrats was unusually deep.

Individualism

While ideological factions shaped party development in the postwar decades, this era was also a time of rising individualism. In the 1960s and 1970s, senators exploited technological developments in mass communications and transportation and the rising number of organized interests with representation in Washington to begin running campaigns that were more candidate-centered and less party-based. They used innovative tools to build national constituencies, acquire visibility beyond the Senate, and champion new causes. For this work, senators developed larger personal staffs, including press secretaries, speechwriters, and policy specialists, and, in the 1970s, acquired the support of the new Congressional Budget Office, an enlarged Congressional Research Service, and the growing community of think tanks. Senators by the 1970s were less constrained by clubby Senate norms (Ornstein, Peabody, and Rohde 1977).

They grew less dependent on committee staff for advice and legislative drafting—and more independent in forging a place in national politics.[3] Individualism, often layered with factionalism, greatly increased the burden of managing floor activity shouldered by the leader. Senators authored more legislation, offered more floor amendments, and more fully exploited their parliamentary rights, which pushed increasing numbers of issues onto the laps of the floor leaders (Smith 1989). At the same time, senators made more commitments for personal appearances elsewhere in Washington and around the country, which complicated the scheduling challenges that floor leaders were forced to address. Perhaps most conspicuous, senators more frequently exploited the practice of holds to block or delay action on bills, often at the request of lobbyists, and more frequently turned to filibusters—actual and threatened—as a strategy to extract concessions or demonstrate fealty to out-side constituencies, a development that has been called the "trivialization of the filibuster" (Binder and Smith 1997). For majority party leaders, obstructionism became a frequent and serious problem in the 1970s.

ORGANIZING THE SENATE PARTY

Both Senate parties elaborated their party organizations over the course of the 1945–80 period. Innovations were led by the minority party and justified as a means for making the party more competitive, although factional and personal considerations were also significant motivations at the same time. The long-term trend in both parties had three features: more full-conference meetings for discussion, more reliance on the floor leader to set party strategy, and a deepening leadership ladder.

The frequency of party meetings was exceptionally low as the New Deal Congresses ended and war legislation came to dominate the Senate's agenda. During the late 1930s and early 1940s, organizational matters were handled by leaders without discussion in party conferences. Leaders appointed their parties' steering committees (and, for Republicans, the committee on commit-tees), which met to make committee assignments but otherwise seldom con-vened. Standing committee assignments were decided under the direction of the leader by the party committees and sent to the floor without reconsideration by the parent conferences. Leaders also continued to appoint their campaign committees, which were staffed by Senate employees under the direction of floor leaders. The Democratic conference averaged just one meeting per year in the 1937–44 period. The Republican conference met infrequently, too, until 1944, after McNary had fallen ill and the Republicans, led by Taft, set out to reinvent their party's organization (Ritchie 1998a, 355).

---

[3] Commentaries on Senate individualism are numerous. Fenno 1989; Ornstein, Peabody, and Rhode 1977; Sinclair 1989; and Smith 1989 provide background. Also see Tom Wicker, "Winds of Change in the Senate," *New York Times Magazine*, Sept. 12, 1965, 52.

The Republicans

With McNary's illness and the growing hope that they might again compete for control of the chamber, Senate Republicans separated the posts of floor leader, conference chair, and steering committee chair. The outcome, as Taft intended, was to turn the steering committee—soon renamed the policy committee, with himself and the whip as members—into an engine for generating policy proposals that reflected the views of the conservative majority of the party. Taft's expressed purpose was to make the party more competitive by articulating a conservative alternative to the proposals of President Roosevelt and the Democrats, which, many observers noticed, also would benefit Taft's aspirations as a presidential candidate. Taft, elected in 1938, led conservative Republicans, who were relatively young, dissatisfied with McNary's one-man governance, and particularly frustrated with McNary's tolerance of New Deal programs and internationalism (Drury 1963, 10; Merry 1991, 170–72).[4]

Taft used the policy committee as a means for shaping party strategy without personally assuming the chores of the floor leader. He chaired the committee from 1944 until he became floor leader in 1953, when the Republicans regained majority status. In the majority in 1947–49, the policy committee frequently recommended a floor schedule and legislative agenda, which were typically accepted by the conference. To consider and approve Taft's plans, the Republican conference and policy committee met far more frequently than they had under McNary. In the 1944–53 period, the conference met 94 times, more than once a month when Congress was in session, far more than the total of 18 meetings held in the previous eight years (Wolff and Ritchie 1999, vi–viii). The motivations of party competition, factional interests, and personal ambition contributed to this surge in party activity.

Collective action in response to party competition had become a central issue for the Republicans even before they assumed the majority. Although conference meetings had already become more common by 1947, the 16 freshman Republicans signed a letter to the conference chair early that year about the lack of conference meetings. They observed that the new Republican majority was suffering internal divisions that were benefiting President Truman and the Democrats and argued that intraparty divisions might be avoided if Republicans shared information and built consensus in weekly conference meetings. Taft and conference chair Eugene Millikin (R, Colo.), a Taft conservative, disagreed with these critics, with Taft emphasizing that consensus could not always be expected and that rapid action by the policy committee was required to deal with evolving circumstances. Nevertheless, two freshmen were put on the policy committee as non-voting members, and Millikin called more

---

[4] For a brief history of policy committees in all four congressional parties in the mid-twentieth century, see Connelly 1991.

conference meetings over the 1947–50 period than the conference had had in any four years since the 1910s (Patterson 1972, 339; Wolff and Ritchie 1999, 492–95).[5] The strategy-setting role of Taft's policy committee did not survive him, largely because the ambitions of his handpicked successors, William Knowland (R, Calif.) and Everett Dirksen, took them and the conference in different directions. As the new floor leader at the start of the 1953 session, Taft nominated Knowland for policy committee chair and informally designated Dirksen to be "assistant majority leader," a slap at the elected whip, the more moderate Leverett Saltonstall (R, Mass.).[6] A few months later, Taft's illness led him to name Knowland acting floor leader, without sanction by the party conference, and Knowland was elected leader after Taft's death on July 31 (White 1954, 258–61). Instantly, there was interest in expanding the membership of the policy committee to more party and committee leaders and even to add a seat for a freshman senator. No action was taken immediately, but the expression of dissatisfaction with the Taft regime was firmly registered (Wolff and Ritchie 1999, 726).

After the Republicans lost their majority in the 1954 elections, and with Taft gone, the policy committee's role changed. Conservatives, led by freshman Barry Goldwater (R, Ariz.)—who as a group were disgruntled with Eisenhower, upset by the election results, and distrustful of Knowland—asked for more conference meetings to keep senators better informed on administration plans and to improve party unity (Wolff and Ritchie 1999, 754–55). A week after this request, Millikin gained conference approval to place on the policy committee all elected conference officers and all 17 Republicans seeking reelection in 1956. The prestige of the policy committee that Taft had created and led was now being exploited to add to the résumé of conference members up for election. Of course, floor scheduling was now the responsibility of the Democrats and, with a Republican in the White House, Styles Bridges (R, N.H.), who chaired the policy committee between 1955 and 1961, would

---

[5] "Republicans Strive for New Unity; Intensive Talks Marking Week-End," *New York Times*, Mar. 9, 1947, 1; "Sen. Bushfield Tells Colleagues GOP May Face Sad Awakening," *Washington Post*, Mar. 8, 1947, 1; "GOP 'Freshmen' Win Policy Group Link," *New York Times*, Mar. 11, 1947, 30; "Future of the GOP is Being Planned in Capital Talks," *New York Times*, Dec. 9, 1948, 1; "Looking to the Future," *Boston Daily Globe*, Dec. 10, 1948, 30; "Taft Declines Back Seat Role on G.O.P. Stand," *Chicago Daily Tribune*, Dec. 19, 1948, 9; "'Revolt' in G.O.P. Fades; Taft to Retain His Post," *Chicago Daily Tribune*, Dec. 21, 1948, 10; "The Eighty-first," *New York Times*, Jan. 2, 1949, E1; "Senator Reelected Head of Party's Policy Committee: Taft Beats GOP Insurgents," *Washington Post*, Jan. 4, 1949, 1.

[6] "Taft Talks Way Back to the Top," *Washington Post*, Dec. 22, 1952, 29; see also Wolff and Ritchie 1999, 697–98. In contrast, when Democratic leader Lucas was hospitalized in 1949, the whip, Francis Myers (D, Pa.), took over as acting floor leader. See "Lucas in Hospital from Overwork as Majority Leader," *Chicago Daily Tribune*, Apr. 27, 1949, 1.

not be using the committee to define Republican policy positions as Taft had done during the Truman administration (Bone 1956, 343).

The Taft-designed policy-generating policy committee effectively disappeared in 1957 (Jewell 1962, 92–93). It officially reverted to a smaller size with all elected leaders as ex officio members, but by that time all Republicans, not just the committee's members, were invited to its weekly sessions (Wolff and Ritchie 1999, 787–88), which began in early 1956 under Knowland and Bridges.[7] The initial rationale for this arrangement was to allow all Republicans to hear their leaders' review of their weekly meeting with President Eisenhower. When Knowland left the Senate in 1958 to run for governor of California, Dirksen successfully maneuvered among Republican factions to defeat a liberal challenger and replaced Knowland as minority leader (MacNeil 1970, 129–31, 160–61; Hulsey 2000, 110–15). A close associate of Bridges and eager to demonstrate that he would be different from Taft, Dirksen had a strong hand in the transition to using policy committee luncheons as a forum of discussion (MacNeil 1970, 185). He preferred the freedom to speak for the party and devise party strategy without an independent policy committee passing resolutions or dictating floor tactics. The policy luncheons became a lasting fixture for the Republicans and served as a substitute for conference meetings as a location for discussing party strategy.

After Dirksen's death in 1969, his successor, Hugh Scott (R, Pa.), who had been whip but was a moderate Republican somewhat out of tune with the conservative majority in his conference, attempted a "shared leadership" approach (Hildenbrand 1985, 92–93). In practice, this meant little change in the use of the conference or policy committee, but it did entail improving the quality of the discussion that took place at policy luncheons, consulting more frequently with the floor leader and other elected leaders, sharing floor duties with the party whip, and adding assistant or regional whips (Oleszek 1985).[8] Scott's successor, Howard Baker (R, Tenn.), elected Republican leader in late 1976, accepted that model, which created a more corporate, collegial leadership with some factional diversity.[9] Under Baker in the late 1970s, party task

---

[7] Robert C. Albright, "Minority 47 Summoned to Weekly Discussions," *Washington Post*, Jan. 11, 1956, 1.

[8] "Senate Support for Nixon Drops Under Scott Leadership," *CQ Weekly Report*, Feb. 6, 1970, 350.

[9] By the time Scott was minority leader, the policy committee chairmanship was considered a position of lesser importance. John W. Finney, the experienced *New York Times* Senate reporter, described the post as having "little influence" in explaining how Howard Baker might challenge John Tower and Robert Taft, Jr., for the chairmanship in 1972. See John W. Finney, "5 GOP Senators Eye '76 Nomination," *New York Times*, Dec. 17, 1972, 60. The position was viewed as desirable primarily because the chair was included in leadership meetings, press conferences, and other events, and was often included in meetings with the president of his party. The position helped generate press mentions and consideration for a higher leadership post. For example, see "'76 Race and New Senate Chiefs," *New York Times*, Mar. 27, 1976, 11.

forces became a feature of the minority Republicans' party activity (Annis 1995, 103–4).[10] A task force appointed by the leader on a major issue provided a means to involve legislators who were not members of the standing committee of jurisdiction to contribute to the party effort to design policy and strategy. By appointing task forces, Baker encouraged consensus-building within the party and satisfied demands of factions and individual senators for a voice in setting party strategy without regard for standing committee assignments.

The Democrats

In contrast to their practice of the late 1930s and early 1940s, Democrats of the 1947–52 period convened their conference more than once a month while Congress was in session (Ritchie 1998a, ix–x). Democratic leader Alben Barkley, under pressure from liberals after the party's loss of majority control in the 1946 elections, initiated conference discussions of pending legislation and urged his party to rally behind alternatives to legislation proposed by the majority Republicans. In the minority and without control of standing committees, Democrats knew that conference meetings could do minimal harm to the independence of committee leaders, and Barkley's move met with no resistance (Ritchie 1998a, 387–412).

Barkley's successor, liberal Scott Lucas (D, Ill.), lived up to his promise to call even more conference meetings during his years as leader, 1949–50 (Ritchie 1998a, 422), but Ernest McFarland (D, Ariz.), who succeeded Lucas as leader, reduced the number of conference meetings during the next two years (Ritchie 1998a, ix–x) and generally made them social occasions over dinner (McFarland 1979, 127). Both Lucas and McFarland looked to the policy committee and to the chairmen of the standing committees on scheduling matters. The policy committee membership was comprised of the elected leaders (leader, whip, conference secretary) and six others appointed by the leader who customarily served on the committee for the remainder of their Senate careers (Huitt 1961, 341–42). Lucas and McFarland usually convened the policy committee as a weekly Tuesday luncheon while the Senate was in session (McFarland 1979, 127; Jewell 1962, 97; Democratic Policy Committee 2007, 2; Deason 2019, 199, 208).[11] The difference between Lucas and McFarland in the frequency of conference meetings was due, almost certainly, to Lucas's responsiveness to the

---

[10] House Democrats are sometimes given too much credit for inventing party task forces when the idea was catching on in both Senate parties at the same time. On Speaker O'Neill's use of task forces, see Sinclair 1983. On earlier uses of task forces by House Minority Leader Gerald Ford, see Don Oberdorfer, "He Wants to be Speaker of the House," *New York Times Magazine*, Apr. 30, 1967, 34–52, and "Republican Conference Chief Target of Purge," *Los Angeles Times*, Dec. 10, 1970, A4. See also Richard L. Lyons, "Senators Reject Attempt to Scuttle Gas Compromise," *Washington Post*, Sept. 20, 1978, A1.

[11] The minutes of the Senate Democratic policy committee in 1949 and 1950 are available in the Scott Wike Lucas Papers, Abraham Lincoln Presidential Library, Springfield, Ill.

liberal wing of the party and McFarland's reliance on the southern and western conservatives who had promoted his candidacy for leader over the liberal Joseph O'Mahoney (D, Wyo.).[12] Liberals wanted a more active conference that would advocate their policy initiatives during these years. Conservatives, in contrast, wanted to avoid open conflict over civil rights and labor issues that divided the party and to instead rely on the standing committees where their seniority gave them greater control over action on legislation.

Lyndon Johnson replaced McFarland as leader in 1953, following McFarland's failed reelection bid in Arizona and the loss of the Democrats' majority in the 1952 elections. Even as minority leader, Johnson, like McFarland backed primarily by conservatives, saw danger in having factional differences aired in conference meetings. Thus he called conference meetings only for organizational purposes (Huitt 1961, 341; Stewart 1971, 63; Ritchie 1998a). Even more than McFarland, Johnson preferred to discover and manage intraparty divisions himself. He only rarely used the policy committee to endorse a policy position; rather, he used its meetings to gauge opinion, check his own judgments about the floor agenda and party strategy, and socialize (Shaffer 1980, 72). The committee had regular meetings while the Senate was in session, but Johnson, not the policy committee, set priorities (Bone 1956; Huitt 1961, 342; Reedy 1986, 12; Caro 2002, 508–12). The committee did not meet when Johnson was ill and away from the Senate (Bone 1956, 344; Stewart 1971, 63; Baker 2009, 38). Bobby Baker, Johnson's party secretary, explained that, "you know, we had a luncheon once a week. But it was just a place to go have a couple of toddies and brag on people about what a good job they're doing. The policy committee didn't make a lot of difference" (Baker 2009, 38).

After the 1958 elections, which increased the number of liberals in the Senate caucus, Johnson faced demands for filibuster reform, civil rights legislation, and a stronger voice for younger and more liberal senators in party affairs. Some of these new senators sought to increase the size and expand the functions of the policy committee, which had become very senior and disproportionately conservative, but their motion was defeated in conference (Jewell 1962, 104; Caro 2002, 1017). Johnson, in compensation, invited the members of the legislative review committee (also known as the "calendar committee") to sit with the policy committee when it met. The calendar committee had been created to monitor action on the minor bills placed on the consent calendar and gave junior Democrats a small role on the floor (Bone 1956, 349). By asking its members to attend policy committee meetings without giving them formal

---

[12] McFarland announced his intention to have committee chairmen meet collectively "as a policy group" shortly after his election as leader: "Senate Leader Picks His Key Committees," *New York Times*, Jan. 5, 1951, 11. A *Washington Post* story in early 1951, in McFarland's second week as Democratic leader, described a McFarland meeting with all committee chairmen as "unusual": "Acheson, GOP Chiefs Spar on How to Confer," *Washington Post*, Jan. 11, 1951, 1; see also "Acheson is Willing to Talk with Taft," *New York Times*, Jan. 11, 1951, 1.

membership, Johnson changed the political complexion of the meetings without reducing the leader's ability to name policy committee members or risking that an unfriendly voting majority would emerge (Huitt 1961, 341–42; Stewart 1971).

After replacing Johnson in 1961, Mike Mansfield (D, Mont.) held many more conference meetings than Johnson had—22 meetings in the 1961–64 period (Ritchie 1998a, 577–655; see also Ritchie 1998b). But he used the policy committee for true consultation and to create consensus on legislative priorities. In response to demands from liberals, Mansfield expanded the size of the policy committee, agreed to have his appointments to the committee subject to conference approval, and then made the committee more representative of the conference, in part by giving legislative review committee members voting rights (Stewart 1971, 79–82; Valeo 1985, 411; Ferris 2004, 65). On floor scheduling, Mansfield reviewed his plans with the policy committee every two weeks and sought consensus, but, as with previous Democratic leaders, it was accepted that final scheduling decisions rested with him (Ripley 1969a, 97; Ferris 2004, 16).[13] Once Richard Nixon became president in 1969, and with growing concern over the war in Vietnam, Mansfield asked that the conference allow the policy committee to "delineate Democratic positions" on significant issues, which the conference did unanimously. He then had the policy committee meet more frequently, initiated more discussions of major legislation, and urged the committee to endorse policy resolutions, which it did on 15 issues in 1969 and 1970 alone (Kravitz ca. 1971, 96; Valeo 1985, 516; Oberdorfer 2003, 173, 405), many of which received considerable attention in the press.

Robert Byrd (D, W.Va.) took over as floor leader as Democrat Jimmy Carter became president and wanted a tidy but collective process for setting legislative priorities for floor action. He called few meetings of the conference and relied on the policy committee to discuss the schedule. He instituted regular luncheons with committee chairs and had them meet with the policy committee on occasion, which created meetings that involved the attendance of over half of the Democrats (Scott and Wyatt 2019, 85).[14] While in the majority, Byrd deferred to formal and traditional venues—standing committees and the party policy committee—for policy and strategy. Byrd and the Senate Democrats did not follow the Republicans under Baker in creating party task forces on major issues until after they lost their majority in the 1980 elections, when the need for more effective party action was demanded (Oleszek 1985, 7).[15]

---

[13] The legislative review committee fell into disuse for its original purpose of reviewing minor bills; its members continued to sit with the policy committee (Ripley 1969a, 97).

[14] John H. Averill, "Antiquated Procedures Get Streamlined: Byrd Gets High Marks as Senate Leader," *Los Angeles Times*, June 2, 1977, C1; Alice Bonner, "Anti-Bias Measure for Senate Killed," *Washington Post*, Sept. 22, 1978, A2.

[15] Richard E. Cohen, "Minority Status Seems to Have Enhanced Byrd's Position Among Fellow Democrats," *National Journal*, May 7, 1983, 958–60.

Their caucus riven by factionalism throughout the postwar era, especially by divisions between southern conservatives and liberals from other parts of the country, Democratic leaders were always cautious about convening meetings that would expose divisions within the party and consequently expanded participation no more than seemed necessary to meet demands for more collective discussion of party strategies and policy positions. Mansfield—first as an opponent of Vietnam policy and then as the Democratic Senate leader serving with Republican presidents Nixon and Gerald Ford—was the exception when he used the policy committee and conference to endorse alternatives to the president's program and policies. While the 1970s ended with more venues for consultation under Byrd, he did not move to regular full-conference meetings until after the Democrats lost their Senate majority.

Committee Assignments

By the mid-1940s, both parties had well-established formal procedures for making committee assignments, but factional interests made committee assignments a source of tension in both parties. Senators sought assignments based on a variety of factors—including personal interests, fundraising potential, constituency interests, and visibility—and the tendency to observe seniority or even privilege powerful members often disadvantaged one faction and necessarily disadvantaged junior senators. These intraparty conflicts came to a head in both parties in the late 1940s and 1950s and produced alterations in norms about how assignments were allocated.

On the Republican side, the domination of the Taft wing left moderate Republicans complaining about committee assignments. For a time, Taft was both the policy committee chairman and a member of the committee on committees, which gave Taft and his conservative allies the ability to arrange committee assignments to control Republican committee action. In 1949, after Taft was unsuccessfully challenged for the policy committee chairmanship by the more moderate Henry Cabot Lodge, Jr. (R, Mass.), Taft gave up his seat on the committee on committees, but his influence with conservative Republicans who dominated the committee remained. Two years later, first-term senator Joseph McCarthy (R, Wisc.) offered a motion to give every Republican a major committee assignment before anyone took two. But the motion was defeated 29–10 after many senior Republicans realized that they might have to give up seats on committees where they had accumulated considerable seniority.[16]

For Democrats, conflict over committee assignments pitted liberals against southern conservatives, who controlled most of the Senate's committees. The 1946 elections cost the Democrats their Senate majority and decimated the ranks of liberals from the industrial North and Mountain West. It took years

---

[16] "Tobey Designated to Key Senate Post," *New York Times*, Jan. 12, 1951, 11.

for northern and western liberals to recover lost seats and, in the meantime, conservatives asserted themselves in electing McFarland and Johnson as leaders. McFarland added conservatives to the steering committee, which led to liberal protests about the composition of the committee and the committee assignments liberals were given.[17] When Johnson became leader in 1953, after Democrats had again lost their majority, liberal anger continued to fester, while the whole caucus grew anxious about how to regain control of the Senate. Offering a variation of what McCarthy had recently proposed for Republicans, Johnson made a multifaceted argument for a new approach to committee assignments: northern liberals needed better committee assignments to be reelected, southerners needed the liberals elected to put the party in the majority and regain their committee chairmanships, some of the new Democrats had talents that should be exploited on important committees, the party needed more effective teamwork, and Republicans were about to use various committees to reverse policies important to the party and individual senators.

Employing this logic, Johnson persuaded the senior conservatives who dominated the steering committee to accept his recommendation that all Democrats, even new senators, be given an assignment to at least one major committee— Appropriations, Armed Services, Finance, or Foreign Relations.[18] The new approach, soon called the "Johnson rule," worked to Johnson's personal advantage. By reducing the role of seniority in making assignments, he was creating more discretion for himself, which he could use to both keep peace in the party and reward friends. In the majority again in 1955, Johnson could alter the size of committees and create new seats on committees, which gave him even more flexibility to arrange committee assignments to suit his needs. To do this work, he kept steering committee meetings to a minimum and instead checked in with its members individually to gain their approval of his assignment recommendations, thereby avoiding the more uncertain outcomes of a committee discussion.[19]

Democrats under Mansfield and Byrd continued to follow the Johnson rule and show some flexibility with the seniority system, but Mansfield and Byrd did not seek to manipulate assignments for political purposes as Johnson did. Mansfield, however, did make a set of adjustments in response to demands from liberals. In 1962, after threatening to resign if the policy and steering committees were made elective, Mansfield accepted a proposal to give the conference power to approve of his appointments to those committees and to

---

[17] "M'Farland Foes Reap Their 'Dues' on Committees," *Chicago Daily Tribune*, Jan. 6, 1951, B4.
[18] "Freshmen Democrats Get Top Assignments," *Washington Post*, Jan. 13, 1953, 2; "Effective Opposition: Senator Johnson Displays Skill," *Washington Post*, Jan. 17, 1953, 9; "Party Also Assigns Every Freshman Senator a Place on Major Group," *Washington Post*, Jan. 11, 1955, 1. See also Caro 2003, 493–504, 565.
[19] "Leaders Face Test in Congress," *Washington Post*, Jan. 2, 1955, E5.

require the committees to be representative of the party's factions.[20] Mansfield had added liberal members to the steering committee (Rohde, Ornstein, and Peabody 1985, 163–65), but, in 1970, liberal senators, led by Fred Harris (D, N.Mex.), again agitated for an additional seat on the steering committee, better representation for liberals on key committees, monthly open meetings of the conference, and a caucus vote on committee chairs at the start of each Congress.[21] Without the adoption of a new party rule, Mansfield responded by offering the names of committee chairs for conference approval in 1971 (Kravitz ca. 1971, 97; Oberdorfer 2003, 405–6).[22] The result was a more open process in which the steering committee exercised some discretion but generally tried to meet the assignment requests of incoming senators. For the majority party Democrats during these decades, the ease of adjusting committee sizes to accommodate requests for assignments facilitated the process. In fact, the number of seats on standing committees increased by over 40 percent during this period (Smith and Deering 1990, 63).

Few changes in Republican committee assignment practices were adopted in the 1960s and 1970s. Dirksen observed his own version of the "Johnson rule" to give each freshman a prime committee assignment, even giving up his own assignment to accommodate the wishes of colleagues (Kravitz ca. 1971, 101, 103). But minority status limited their power to set the number of committee seats assigned to them, and adherence to seniority in making assignments left little influence to be exercised by party leaders (Smith and Deering 1990, 71–72).

MANAGING THE FLOOR

The imprint of Robert Taft, Lyndon B. Johnson, and Robert Byrd, and the nature of inter-party and factional competition in which they operated, is evident in floor operations today. By the late 1930s, Senate leaders had a fully acknowledged right of first recognition, offices near the Senate chamber, a desk front and center on the Senate floor, and floor aides. Managing the floor in the postwar years became a team effort directed by the leader, backed by professional staff and often assisted by the whip and his staff. With the exception of Taft's role in the 1940s and early 1950s, floor leaders were in charge. Most of these leaders were willing to spend hours on the floor each day the Senate was in session to personally oversee floor activity. The burden of keeping floor

---

[20] Tom Wicker, "Senate Democrats End Johnson Policy on Committee Seats," *New York Times*, Jan. 5, 1962, 28.

[21] Warren Weaver, "Liberal Democrats Press Senate Seniority Reform," *New York Times*, Dec. 1, 1970, 38.

[22] Moderate Republicans and outside reformers also advocated seniority reform, with Charles Mathias (R, Md.) holding an informal hearing with Harris to publicize their cause: see John W. Finney, "Liberals Stumble a Bit at Start of 92d Congress," *New York Times*, Jan. 24, 1971, E2.

Throughout the 1940s, steel bracing supported the weight of the Senate chamber's ceiling and roof, which were at risk of collapse. The Senate chamber was thoroughly renovated in 1949-50, including the replacement of the ornate glass-and-iron ceiling with a sleek oval design.

Architect of the Capitol

proceedings moving fell to the leader of the majority party, and the minority leader had the responsibility of protecting his party's interests as the majority leader offered motions to set the agenda. A persistent challenge for nearly every majority leader was scheduling and getting senators to the floor.[23] Leaders consulted with their party colleagues regularly but became very dependent on skilled staff who provided a range of floor and cloakroom services.

Three themes emerge about changes in the management of the floor in the 1945–80 period. First, the staff support in service of the leader's duties as floor manager expanded. Second, much of the innovation occurred in the electorally turbulent years of the late 1940s and early 1950s, a period of both tight party competition for control of the Senate and sensitivity to factional divisions within each party, with additional innovation in the late 1970s, a time of increased intraparty conflict, especially among Republicans. Third, senatorial entrepreneurs, looking to advance their own careers by exploiting opportunities created by acquiring leadership positions, produced lasting changes in how their parties pursued and staffed floor management activities.

---

[23] "Senate Absentee Practice Assailed by McFarland," *Washington Post*, July 3, 1951, 11; "Democrats Seek Speed on Tax Bill," *Washington Post*, Sept. 19, 1951, 2.

Staffing

The organizational capacity of Senate parties grew progressively, starting in the period of keen competition for party control of the Senate in the late 1940s and early 1950s. This was especially evident with Republicans under Taft's policy committee chairmanship and short service as majority leader. The separation of the floor leader and policy committee chair in the 1944 rules created a lasting organizational shift in which ambitious policy committee chairs, often as part of their campaigns for the job, promised to provide more services to meet party and individual needs. After the mid-1950s, as the long-term minority party without control of standing committee staff, Republican leaders kept demanding and often received incremental increases in policy committee and conference staff funding (Robinson 1976; Malbin 1980, 11–12). While both parties received the same appropriations in this era to support party staff, it was only in 1977 that the Senate adopted a formula guaranteeing the minority one-third of funding for staff on standing committees.

In the 1940s and 1950s, the floor staff operations, which operated from the cloakrooms, expanded and became more professional, with the most significant changes occurring with a shift in leadership or a new party majority. The party secretaries—who by the late 1930s each had an assistant and a team of specialized pages—acquired an additional clerk after the Republicans gained a Senate majority in the 1946 elections. In 1953, just after regaining a new majority, the Republicans added a full-time cloakroom assistant who took over some tasks performed by pages. Each time funding was added for Republican staff, the Democrats gained funding too, as had been the pattern for party staff in legislative appropriations bills since the 1920s.

As they still do, each party secretary had a seat on the Senate floor next to the door to the party's cloakroom.[24] The secretaries were, and have been, all-purpose political aides. They assisted with communication with other senators and personal and committee staff, kept track of senators' whereabouts and encouraged attendance, conducted vote counts, were active in campaign fund-raising (serving as treasurer of campaign committees at times), wrote speeches, assisted with committee assignments, and organized and joined in foreign travel. Most of them, starting with Leslie Biffle for Democratic leaders Robinson and Barkley and Carl Loeffler for Republican leaders McNary and Wallace White (R, Maine), served for many years and had close personal relationships with many senators, performing roles that might have been performed more by the whip and his staff but were assumed instead by people under the control of the floor leaders (Truman 1959, 117). Several of the party secretaries were eventually elected secretary of the Senate (Leslie Biffle, Felton

---

[24] The *Congressional Directory* lists all staff members in these offices, shows their offices, and provides maps of floor seating arrangements.

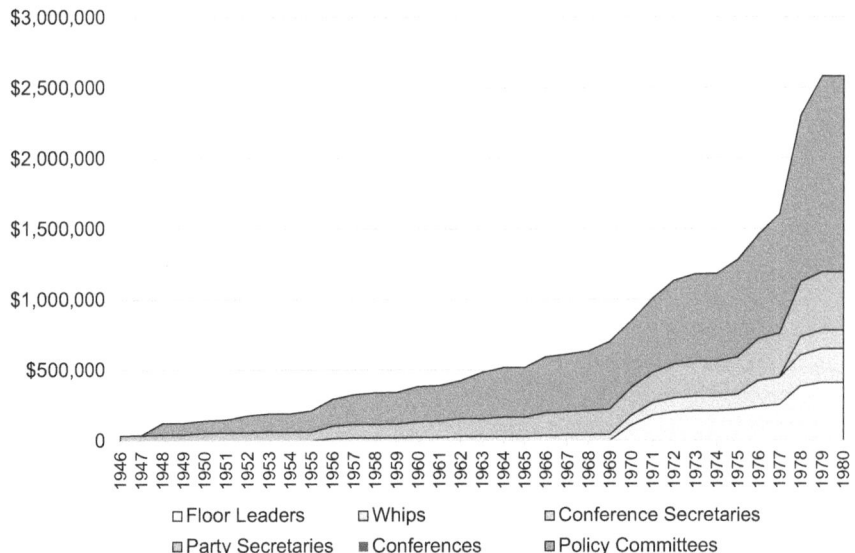

FIGURE 8.2 Appropriations for Senate parties (parties combined), 1947–80
Source: Enacted appropriations bills. Not adjusted for inflation.

Johnston, Francis Valeo, all Democrats, and Mark Trice on the Republican side) and then, in an era of small staffs in leaders' offices, continued to be leadership advisers.[25] Still, this small staff, skilled as they were, left the floor leaders dependent on the White House for legislative guidance and even the text of speeches (Ritchie 1991, 137).

The emergence of party staff is illustrated in Figure 8.2, which shows dollars authorized through annual spending bills for party-related staff through fiscal year 1980. Since the parties were given equal appropriations funding, we report total spending by office. Figure 8.3 illustrates the expansion by showing the number of people on party staffs.[26] Taft (in the early 1950s) and Johnson (in the middle and late 1950s) put their party staffs on an upward trend. Mansfield, in contrast, did not spend all of the funds appropriated for party staff, so actual outlays for staff were generally much smaller for Democrats than Republicans in the 1960s and early 1970s. In the 1970s, Mansfield folded the conference staff into the policy committee staff but made little change in the overall size of Democratic party staffing (Valeo 1985, 632). Campaign committee staff

---

[25] For example, in 1951 Biffle, then secretary of the Senate, and Felton M. Johnston, secretary for the majority, attended a meeting of the Democratic policy committee and President Truman: John D. Morris, "Democratic Chiefs Talk with Truman," *New York Times*, Jan. 28, 1951, 27.
[26] We show the growth in the number of staff based on the listings in the *Congressional Directory*.

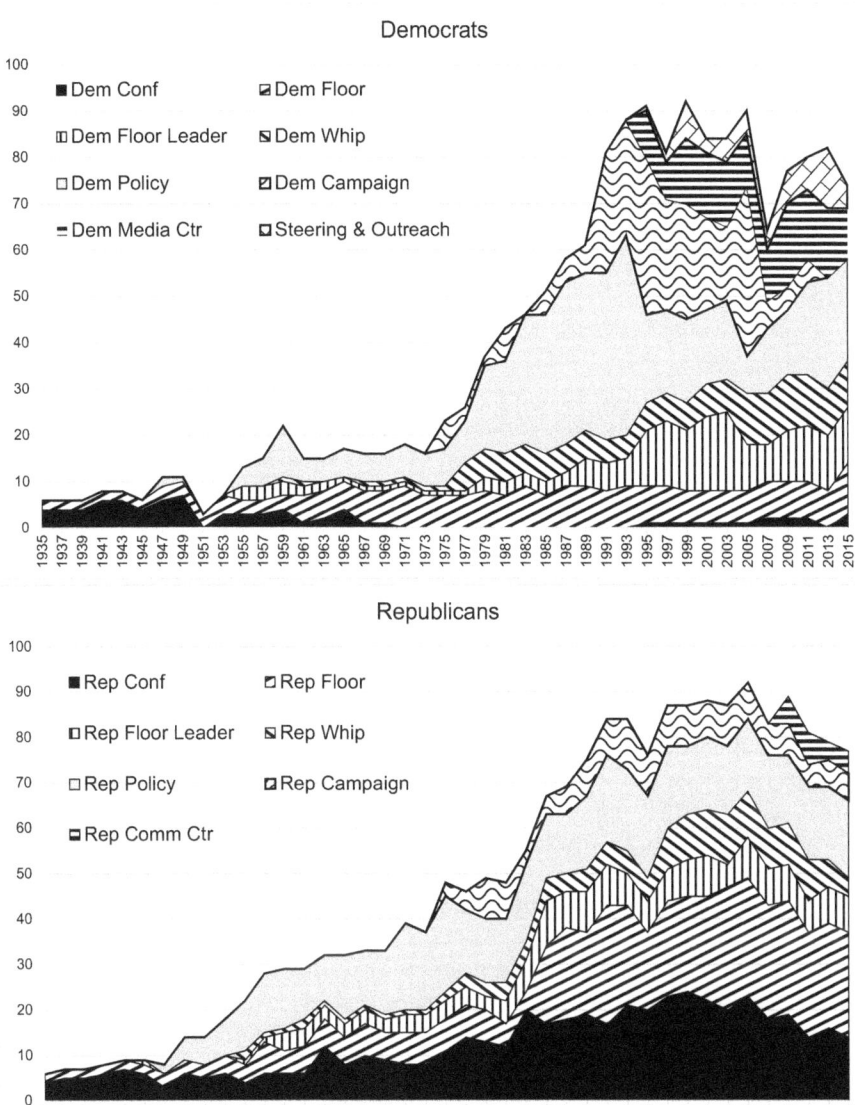

FIGURE 8.3 Number of party-based staff, Democrats and Republicans, 1935–2015

emerged as a separately funded appropriations item in 1975 following campaign finance law reform. In the late 1970s, Democratic leader Byrd boosted
the size of the policy committee staff, where he put staff used for scheduling,
research, and public relations (Sinclair 1990, 128), and Alan Cranston (D,
Calif.) expanded the whip staff.[27] Throughout these years, the great majority
of Democratic staff were assigned either to the policy committee or to the floor.
Most Republican staffers were assigned to the policy committee or the conference, perhaps reflecting Taft's lingering influence as well as the party's post-
1955 minority status, with smaller numbers assigned to the floor, the floor
leader, and the whip.

While Mansfield did little to expand party staff in the 1960s, the small staff
made a significant mark during the Nixon administration in assisting Mansfield
with resolutions on the Vietnam War. This was noticed by John Tower (R,
Tex.), the Republican policy committee chair who was first elected to the post
in 1973 and who initially retained the staff he inherited. After the Democrats
won the White House in the 1976 election, Tower, who had aspirations for a
higher leadership post or even a presidential run, moved to reconstruct the
committee staff to enable Senate Republicans to propose alternative policies.[28]
Spencer Rich, the experienced *Washington Post* reporter, observed that "at the
same time Tower will gain a higher profile in the GOP leadership."[29] With the
help of his new staff, Tower took the lead in devising Republican alternatives
on several issues and acquired considerable press attention for some of them.[30]
He was subsequently named chair of the platform committee for the
1980 Republican national convention.

The 1979 contests for Republican leadership posts reflected the party's
growing factional divide. Moderate Bob Packwood (R, Ore.) defeated James
McClure (R, Idaho), a leading conservative, for conference chair. Packwood
insisted on an independent staff to support the conference, not wanting to share
staff with the conservative Tower, and Howard Baker, the floor leader, supported the move (Annis 1995, 102–3). Even before Packwood took over the
conference staff, Republicans had begun to place public relations services in the
conference staff, including photographers and electronic media technicians,
leaving policy research for the policy committee staff. Packwood further
enlarged the staff by expanding press relations, election-related assistance,
and videotaping and distribution services. Remarkably, Baker kept the leader's

---

[27] Spencer Rich, "Disparate Byrd-Cranston Senate Team Pulls Together," *Washington Post*,
Apr. 17, 1977, 13.

[28] Michael J. Malbin, "The Senate Republican Leaders—Life Without a President," *National
Journal*, May 21, 1977, 780.

[29] Spencer Rich, "New Staff, Mission for GOP Policy Unit," *Washington Post*, Jan. 1, 1977, A4.

[30] For example, see "Tax on Gasoline Omitted in Senate GOP Energy Plan," *Los Angeles Times*,
May 13, 1977, B5; "38 GOP Senators Decry Carter's Foreign Policy," *Washington Post*, May 4,
1978, A1.

staff at the same size as Scott's, due largely to the parallel appropriations for the majority and minority leader offices.

On the Democratic side, Byrd found himself under pressure to improve the performance of Senate Democrats after the losses in the 1978 elections and the anticipation of even more difficulty in the 1980 elections. With President Carter increasingly unpopular, 24 Senate Democrats, including five freshmen, were facing elections in 1980 and Democrats were well aware of the improvements and reorientation of the Republican policy committee staff under Tower. By early 1979, Byrd had doubled the size of the policy committee staff.[31] Even so, his staff lagged far behind the combined staff of the Republican conference and policy committee in size and range of services provided.

These developments in party staffing in the late 1970s reflected increased factionalism in the Republican caucus, with the rise of a new generation of conservatives but also a changing political and media landscape. Leaders long had staff with press skills, but most of the public relations efforts of mid-twentieth-century leaders involved personal contact with Capitol Hill reporters. The party staffs of the 1970s, with the minority Republicans leading the way, developed a wide range of services for the parties and senators. Older activities—tracking bills, maintaining voting records, providing summaries of legislation, staffing the floor—were expanded to include policy and political research and, to a lesser extent, press and media relations.

Taft and Floor Management

Following McNary's death in 1944, the Republican conference made Wallace White, who had been conference secretary and stood in for McNary during his illness, its floor leader. But Taft became the center of efforts to set strategy for his party conference. In adopting the Taft plan, Republicans reduced the leader's independence and made the steering committee the place at which party policy and political strategy would be proposed.[32] Taft became steering committee chairman and immediately began using the committee as the forum for proposing a large legislative program on postwar policy. Taft arranged for conference chairman Vandenberg to hire George H. E. Smith, who had been at Yale and had coauthored four books on the New Deal with historian and political scientist Charles Beard, to staff the steering committee (Patterson 1972, 267; Wolff and Ritchie 1999, 366).[33] The 1946 elections brought a

---

[31] *Congressional Directory* listings.
[32] "Name Taft as Head of Steering Group," *New York Times*, Mar. 16, 1944, 36.
[33] "Republicans Map Senate Programs," *New York Times*, Apr. 22, 1944, 26. The Beard-Smith collaboration concluded with their book, *The Old Deal and the New* (New York: Macmillan, 1940), which provides a crisp history of New Deal programs and questions the internationalism of the Roosevelt administration, the effectiveness of the New Deal in changing the American economy, and the implications of rising budget deficits.

Republican majority to the Senate, allowing Taft to dominate floor scheduling through his control of the steering committee—renamed the policy committee in 1947 (Wolff and Ritchie 1999, 434)—without holding the office of floor leader. White, the majority leader, deferred to Taft and the committee, even to the point of looking back to Taft on the Senate floor for signals on what moves to make (White 1954, 57–60).

When the party returned to majority status in 1953, Taft became floor leader and used the committee to endorse his agenda decisions. Taft, who had avoided becoming his party's floor leader because he disliked the chores of managing floor activity, surprised many observers when he showed a commitment to floor activity as majority leader (Ripley 1969b, 129). He was assisted by Dirksen, whom he had named "assistant majority leader," a position not recognized in the party rules.[34] The move put Dirksen on the floor with some frequency as a substitute for Taft and helped position Dirksen to be elected whip and floor leader in the next few years.

Under Taft, George Smith became a central figure in scripting Republican floor activity. When the Republicans hired Smith in 1944, no funds had yet been appropriated for the steering committee, and Smith was placed under the conference chairman. When funds were made available two years later, Smith continued to be the leading Republican staff professional and was made director of both the conference and the policy committee staffs (Patterson 1972, 348–49). Smith retired from this position in 1949 (Wolff and Ritchie 1999, 598), but, remarkably, the practice of having a single staff director continued until the late 1970s. Smith remained on the policy committee staff through 1960, and the committee continued to house staff important to the floor operations. By the 1970s, this involved three or four professionals whose work complemented and reinforced the work of the party secretary and his staff.

After Republicans lost their majority in the 1954 elections, their floor leaders took the lead in devising floor tactics, looked to their whips to help cover routine floor activity, and used the party secretaries as their chief floor aides. Knowland was inconsistent in his attentiveness to the floor. In fact, Dirksen, as whip, became acting floor leader for most purposes when Knowland spent time in California running for governor in 1957 and 1958 (MacNeil 1970, 148). Minority leaders Dirksen and Scott were on the floor much of the time, but both were happy to have whips, especially Thomas Kuchel (R, Calif.) and Robert Griffin (R, Mich.), handle routine business and to rely upon staff—party secretaries Mark Trice and William Hildenbrand—to manage the calendar and consult with the Democratic leadership on scheduling, holds, and unanimous consent requests. Baker was more involved on the floor than Dirksen or Scott, but he continued to rely on Hildenbrand to work with Majority Leader Byrd and his office (Hildenbrand 1985, 309).

---

[34] "Taft Talks Way Back to the Top," *Washington Post*, Dec. 22, 1952, 29.

Johnson and Floor Management

Lyndon B. Johnson was at least as ambitious as Taft—and even more innovative than Taft in his use of staff. Johnson had been a favorite of President Roosevelt and moved aggressively to gain his appointment as whip in 1951 after serving just two years in the Senate. He viewed himself, and was viewed by Richard Russell (D, Ga.) and other southerners, as a future presidential candidate. At the time of his election as whip, Democrats had just lost five Senate seats, leaving Democrats only a 49–47 edge over the Republicans and making them anxious about losing the Senate majority once again in the next elections. Johnson quickly exploited Majority Leader McFarland's lack of assertiveness to establish himself as a key player in managing the floor and getting Democrats to the floor for votes (Truman 1959, 303–4; Caro 2002, 388–97; McMillan 2004, 221). With the support of Bobby Baker, who was the cloakroom assistant at the time, Johnson became involved in communicating the floor schedule to senators, checking with committees on the flow of legislation to the floor, identifying floor amendments that were expected, arranging pairs, counting votes, and, whenever he could, substituting for McFarland on the floor. Working in Johnson's favor was the argument that, in light of the election results, the Democrats needed to be more effective in managing the Senate and enacting a popular program.

The 1952 elections brought Eisenhower to the White House and a Republican majority to the Senate. McFarland failed to get reelected, and Johnson easily won the minority leader's post. Democrats were in a panic (Caro 2002, 520), and Johnson exploited the opportunity to build a larger staff to support his activities. Felton Johnston remained party secretary, and Bobby Baker was promoted to assistant secretary. The new leader made Walter Jenkins, his long-time aide, director of the conference staff, and then he hired Yale-trained Securities and Exchange Commission lawyer George Siegel, Washington reporter George Reedy, and former McFarland aide Roland Bibolet for the policy committee. He brought in a Dallas public relations man, Booth Mooney, to the leader's office as his speechwriter (Mooney 1956; Caro 2002, 521).[35] The legislative and political capabilities of this small staff exceeded those of any previous floor leader's operation and more than matched Taft's set-up in the Republican policy committee.[36] With the Democrats in the minority and Eisenhower in the White House, leading Democrats on the committees had little to lose as Johnson built a leader-centered information network, put real policy expertise at his immediate disposal, added to his ability to manage work on the floor and with party

---

[35] *Congressional Directory* 1953, 1954.
[36] White reports that Taft did not hire or use a speechwriter (White 1954, 205).

colleagues, and became a spokesman for the party on and off the floor (Reedy 1986, 111–12; Caro 2002, 508).

Johnson's skills at personal persuasion were considerable, but his staff support was central to his success as floor leader (Reedy 1986, 133). By the time Democrats regained their majority after the 1954 elections, Johnson had changed expectations about the relationship between the floor leader and committees and was getting credit for enhancing the party's political profile. He made aggressive use of unanimous consent agreements to lend order to Senate proceedings and speed action (Evans and Novak 1966; Smith and Flathman 1989; Caro 2002). Under his leadership, committee staff reported weekly to the policy committee staff, which maintained a status report on legislation (Ferris 2004, 21), and Johnson initiated meetings between himself, the policy committee staff, and committee staff directors (Caro 2002, 513). He used regular meetings of the policy committee to discuss the floor agenda, but he used the committee to learn of and steer around potential problems rather than as a decision-making body.

Lyndon B. Johnson did not fly solo. His effort was backed by staff assistants who tracked committee activity, catalogued demands for speaking and amending activity, and scripted floor activity, which made his use of unanimous consent agreements to organize floor action more effective (Jewell 1962, 83). "Over the years of the Johnson leadership, reams of newspaper copy speculated on the LBJ magic. Very little of the speculation was valid. Stories were written on 'arm twisting' and 'log rolling' but the reality eluded the scribes. What was really happening was a tremendous effort that involved constant work with not only the committee but the committee staffs," George Reedy wrote, reflecting on Johnson's early success as Democratic leader. "Our staff—the Senate Democratic Policy Committee—worked with all of them and often could tell Johnson what would be in legislative committee reports before they were even put on paper. Johnson personally built up relations with staff members and kept a constant check on the attitudes of key senators on bills that would come before them. It was delicate work as senators are always supersensitive about their prerogatives and could be offended easily by 'interference' in their domains" (Reedy 1986, 133).

The Johnson model of melding staff from the party secretary's office, the policy committee, and the conference continued under Mansfield and Byrd (Valeo 1985; Kimmit 2001; Ferris 2004). Initially, Mansfield kept Bobby Baker as party secretary and relied on his assistance for everyday floor proceedings. But, after a scandal involving bribery, sexual favors, and government contracts forced Baker to leave in 1963, Mansfield replaced him first with Francis Valeo and, after Valeo was made secretary of the Senate in 1965, with Stanley Kimmit. Neither Valeo nor Kimmit had Baker's political skills or close relations with senators. Charles Ferris filled the gap in his capacity as director of the policy committee staff. Ferris became Mansfield's chief advisor on the floor and he maintained close ties with most liberals (Ferris 2004, 23, 104–5).

Kimmit focused on the mechanics of floor and cloakroom operations, handled committee assignments with the steering committee, and generally kept up with conservatives, while Valeo served as a speechwriter and foreign policy advisor (Kimmit 2001, 59; Ferris 2004, 13). Under Byrd, the same general pattern was followed, with his policy committee staff director, Patrick Griffin, managing the floor agenda and covering the floor on a full-time basis (Williams 2009), while the party secretary focused on the administrative side of floor activity. For both Mansfield and Byrd, the policy committee staff continued the Johnson-era practice of tracking legislation through committees and keeping the leader and his top staff informed of developments (Peabody 1981).

Byrd and Floor Management

Byrd was more entrepreneurial than is often appreciated. Mansfield was a passive leader, spending a minimum of time on the floor and preferring to have committee chairs and self-motivated Democrats take the lead on issues and acquire recognition in the media (Stewart 1971, 76). During his first six years as majority leader, Mansfield gladly turned over routine floor supervision to assistant whips (Peabody 1976, 331–32), whom he appointed, as well as to bill managers and staff. After Robert Byrd was elected conference secretary in late 1966, Byrd began to master parliamentary procedure, spent considerable time on the floor, performed many favors in protecting senators' interests in floor proceedings, and quickly became indispensable to Mansfield and his party colleagues for assistance with their floor activities (Shaffer 1980, 173–75; Scott and Wyatt 2019, 79–80).[37]

Byrd's voluntary floor management activities came not purely out of generosity toward Mansfield or love of parliamentary procedure. Byrd was ambitious, seeing himself as a future whip and majority leader and even thinking that he would be a presidential candidate someday (Corbin 2012, 152–53, 160–61). And senators' expectations had evolved since the 1950s. They were more individualistic, increasingly engaged in activities that took them away from the Capitol and Washington, while also seeking to offer more floor amendments and expecting the Senate's schedule to accommodate their personal needs (Ornstein, Peabody, and Rohde 1977). Byrd's creativity and hard work kept the Senate functioning, and appreciation for his efforts was reflected in his successful challenge to Whip Edward Kennedy (D, Mass.) after the 1970 elections. As whip in 1971–77, Byrd innovated in structuring floor debate and

---

[37] Robert Albright, "Hard Worker in Ascendancy," *Washington Post*, Oct. 4, 1967, A1; Roland Evans and Robert Novak, "West Virginia's Robert Byrd Viewed as Newest Power in the Senate," *Washington Post*, Dec. 21, 1967, A21; Adam Yarmolinsky, "Who Is Senator Byrd?" *New York Times*, Jan. 30, 1971, 27; Clayton Fritchey, "Byrd: Senate's New Dynamo," *Chicago Tribune*, June 5, 1973, 18; Sanford J. Ungar, "The Man Who Runs the Senate," *The Atlantic*, Sept. 1975; Spencer Rich, "Byrd Reshapes His Image," *Washington Post*, Dec. 15, 1974, A1.

amending activity through unanimous consent agreements, moved the Senate to reduce the time for roll-call votes from 20 to 15 minutes, and invented the "tracking" of legislation in order to have both fast- and slow-moving legislation on the floor (Kravitz ca. 1971, 97; Smith and Flathman 1989).[38] Byrd also created "whip notices," daily updates on the floor schedule, a practice quickly adopted by his Republican counterpart (Byrd 1988, 203–4).

Once he became leader in 1977, Byrd was as assertive as Johnson in his efforts to manage the floor. Confronted with colleagues who were more difficult to manage than Johnson experienced, Byrd held late-night sessions when the Senate did not meet his expectations in more regular hours and tried to reduce uncertainty on the floor through more aggressive and creative uses of unanimous consent agreements. He drew the reprobation of Republicans by setting new precedents to limit obstruction in post-cloture debate and to bring up executive business. He took the lead in changing the 100-hour limit on post-cloture debate to 30 hours. These moves created a "Byrd Senate," as a former Senate parliamentarian called it, one that dealt with assertive senators and more partisan obstructionism by trying to respect the principle of supermajority cloture while limiting the places in the process at which filibusters could occur (Dove 2008, 36; Smith 2014, 129–41).

The Whips

For both parties, whips of the late 1960s and 1970s were expected to help the floor leader monitor floor activity, including being available for many hours to represent the party on the floor. In addition, whips in these years helped expand floor-related leadership services and added staff that contributed to their parties' ability to plan and implement legislative strategies. Their innovations aided rank-and-file colleagues whose schedules for activities on and off Capitol Hill were becoming more difficult to synchronize with floor activity.

For Republicans, Robert Griffin (R, Mich.) served as whip in 1969–77, overlapping with Byrd's years as whip on the Democratic side. Following Byrd's lead, Griffin started weekly whip notices that reviewed the floor schedule and indicated when votes were likely, a practice that was facilitated by the majority party's floor staff (Hildenbrand 1985, 105; Oleszek 1985).[39] Griffin occasionally provided "whip counts" before key votes on the floor, and he took the lead in organizing meetings for small groups of senators with diverse views.

---

[38] An experiment with 15-minute votes started in July 1971 (*Cong. Rec.*, July 22, 1971, 26783, and Jan. 26, 1973, 2300) and was extended subsequently. Since then, the voting period has been frequently extended to accommodate tardy senators and often has been the subject of complaints about failing to adhere to the time limit.

[39] The *Post* reported that Baker's candidacy was advocated by Republicans who were "convinced the party needs a new, articulate Senate spokesman with a new face and a new image": Spencer Rich, "Baker Upsets Griffin; Byrd Majority Leader," *Washington Post*, Jan. 5, 1977, A1, A8.

With the approval of Republican leader Scott, he added regional whips in 1970, who assisted in covering the floor when Scott and Griffin could not (Oleszek 1985). In 1977, when Scott left the Senate, Griffin lost to Baker in the contest for the new Republican leader; Ted Stevens (R, Alaska) was elected whip in his place. Even more than Griffin, Stevens aggressively sought to involve more senators in managing the floor, in part by making all first-year senators assistant whips. These activities were facilitated by a small but vital increase in the whip's staff from one person in the Dirksen era to three or four with Stevens in the late 1970s.

Democratic whips also assisted floor leaders with intraparty affairs (Oleszek 1985). Edward Kennedy (D, Mass.), who served as whip from 1969 until 1971, when he was replaced by Byrd, initiated meetings with senators and staff to discuss policy options and legislative strategy. Alan Cranston (D, Calif.), a strong liberal with presidential aspirations, became whip when Byrd became floor leader in 1977. With Byrd's approval, Cranston expanded the whip staff from one to six and eventually increased the number of deputy whips from four to 12. Cranston, who was gregarious and trusted by liberals, played an important role in keeping liberals connected to Byrd and as intermediary with the Carter White House. He held weekly meetings with his deputies, developed a computerized whip notice system, and worked to coordinate committee and floor activity. Perhaps most notable, Cranston assisted Byrd and bill managers by asserting a role as the chief head counter for his party, a role he had pursued informally for some time.[40]

CAMPAIGN COMMITTEES

For decades, the campaign committee operations had focused on providing print material from the *Congressional Record* and other sources, literature on the party record, and speakers for campaign events. By the early 1950s, both committees had expanded to providing other basic services, including cartoonists and the production of images of candidates for use in local newspapers and advertising. More important, the committees served as pass-through organizations for campaign contributions: funds from donors went to the Senate campaign committees and then to state parties for the purpose of supporting specific candidates, which disguised the original source of the funds and appeared to stay within the constraints of campaign finance laws. These limited activities required only a small staff. Over the next two decades, the campaign committees expanded their services to include raising independent funds to support Senate campaigns, and they became more focused on fundraising in the post-1974 campaign finance regime. Senate floor leaders continued to

---

[40] John H. Averill, "Cranston a Natural as Majority Whip," *Los Angeles Times*, Jan. 5, 1977, 17.

appoint campaign committees and their chairmen, as they had been doing for several decades (Kolodny 1998, 68–80).[41]

In the late 1970s, the minority Republicans leaped ahead of the more complacent Democrats in the organization of their campaign committee, with Republicans benefiting too from the rise of corporate political action committees (Sabato 1985). The modest Democratic losses in 1978—three Senate and 14 House seats—were readily rationalized as a reaction to the first two years of the Carter administration. It would take the surprise of losing majority status in the 1980 elections to motivate a significant upgrade of the Democrats' campaign committee operations. In the 1980 elections, the Democrats suffered a shocking loss, leaving them with only 47 seats in the Senate. They lost 12 of the 24 seats they were defending, with three incumbents defeated in primaries and another nine losing in the general election.

The Democrats

The Democratic senatorial campaign committee (DSCC) was only partly a Senate organization and showed little significant development in the 1940s, 1950s, and 1960s. While its membership was appointed by the party leader, the committee's budget for staff came from the Democratic National Committee (DNC). In 1950, the DSCC had just four full-time staff members and one part-time staff member. In response to efforts by Earle Clements (D, Ky.), funding from the DNC allowed the DSCC to hire a few year-round staff members following the 1952 elections (Kolodny 1998, 80, 83). Clements, a Johnson loyalist, was elected party whip in 1953 but was asked by Johnson to continue as campaign chairman. Under Clements and Johnson, the DSCC gained more independence from the DNC. The DSCC began to raise money for its activities separately from the DNC and to provide some assistance to newly elected senators as they were setting up their offices. Johnson used campaign funds as a source of influence with his colleagues, but Mansfield abandoned the practice, insisting that all Democrats running for reelection receive equal allocations (Valeo 1999, 86–87). Through the 1960s, the staff operation remained small, typically fewer than six people, although its fundraising efforts expanded to well over a half million dollars per cycle, some of which was used to support television and radio advertising by the party's candidates (Kolodny 1998, 80, 83, 85, 96).

With the expansion of costly television advertising in Senate campaigns in the 1960s and the advent of new campaign finance regulations in the early 1970s, the political environment of the campaign committee changed rapidly. Candidates needed more money, but fundraising became more regulated. Most

[41] For the Republicans, the conference rule provided for confirmation by the conference. In just one year, 1956, the Republican conference entertained a nomination and unanimously "elected" its campaign chairman (Wolff and Ritchie 1999, 781).

important was the 1974 enactment of spending limits and enforcement through the newly created Federal Election Commission. More sophisticated fundraising efforts, including legal and accounting services, were required, and the old pass-through functions of the campaign committees were undermined by new limits on party contributions to candidates. Most important, the authorization of political action committees created an opening for the congressional campaign committees to raise money in new ways.

Mansfield appointed Edmund Muskie (D, Maine) as DSCC chair for the 1968 election cycle, motivated at least in part by the electoral losses in the 1966 elections. Muskie hired Frank (Nordy) Hoffman to run the staff and modernize its operations. Hoffman had been the legislative director for the steelworkers union for two decades. Over the course of four election cycles, he and his new staff were proactive in connecting candidates to a new generation of political consultants, fundraisers, and pollsters; updating training efforts for candidates and their staff; commissioning a few polls; and, without adding much to the committee's own funds, providing some funding to challengers of Republican incumbents and to candidates in close races (Menefee-Libey 1989, 133–49).

The DSCC then atrophied under Byrd in the late 1970s. Hoffman and others left the staff when Mansfield retired, and Byrd largely neglected the committee. The staff did not recover its size during those cycles, and its services to campaigns were modest, although it raised more funds for candidates, targeted close races, and reached the maximum allowed for direct contributions to 25 candidates. One persuasive analysis attributes the stagnant DSCC operation to Byrd's preference to avoid the development of a sizable, off-campus, and somewhat independent party staff (Menefee-Libey 1989, 222–41). Byrd may also have taken for granted his party's majority status, which, on the eve of the 1980 elections, it had maintained without interruption since 1955.

The Republicans

For Republicans, John Townsend (R, Del.) was first appointed campaign committee chairman in 1936 and continued in that role until 1949, even though his service as a senator ended midway through that tenure. Townsend's success in organizing Republican efforts and his strong connections to fellow bankers and business leaders across the country made him the ideal campaign committee chairman. His success in steadily increasing the Republican numbers in the Senate, culminating in their winning a majority in the 1946 elections, encouraged his former colleagues to keep him involved. In 1949, following the loss of nine Republicans in the 1948 elections, the conference appointed a senator, Owen Brewster (R, Maine), as chairman and made Townsend "co-chairman" (Wolff and Ritchie 1999, 593). Over the next few cycles, the committee improved its press and radio operations, began sponsoring films on the work of Republicans in Congress, and made its staff a full-time, year-round operation. Remarkably, Townsend continued to serve the committee, sometimes as finance chairman or executive director, through the 1960s. Subsequent chairs usually followed the pattern established by the Democrats of serving for two election cycles when they were not up for reelection themselves (Kolodny 1998, 73–74; Wolff and Ritchie 1999, 659, 661).

The national Republican senatorial committee (NRSC) of the late 1940s and 1950s benefited from its ability to raise its own funds and from its association with Taft's policy committee. About a half million dollars were raised by the committee to cover staff costs and other expenses. The permanent and much larger policy committee staff greatly expanded the research, including opposition research, that could be provided to Republican candidates. The campaign committee staff performed all of the functions performed by its Democratic counterpart, but, with more funding and personnel, could pursue its activities on a larger scale. During the 1952 and 1954 cycles, Everett Dirksen (R, Ill.) expanded the quantity and quality of election services provided to campaigns. Dirksen was appointed whip in 1956, and his successors as campaign chair for the next four cycles, Barry Goldwater (R, Ariz.) and Andrew Schoeppel (R, Kans.), maintained the range of activities established by Dirksen (Kolodny 1998, 85–90).

It was not until the late 1970s, after the experience of the 1974 and 1976 election cycles, that the minority Republicans made substantial adjustments to the new campaign finance environment. The House Republicans took the lead in the 1978 election cycle by raising enough money to allow the NRSC to borrow from them and then erase a debt, build a staff that was four times the size of the DSCC staff, and invest in a direct mail campaign to raise more of its own funds. The NRSC chairman, Bob Packwood (R, Ore.), also exploited an interpretation of the law that allowed the Senate campaign committee to be the agent for state parties and the national committee and thereby coordinate overall party spending for Senate campaigns. Not only did the NRSC outspend the DSCC on staff and direct funds to candidates, but its coordinated spending surpassed the Democrats' effort by a ten-to-one margin. Like the Democrats, the Senate Republican campaign committee joined the House committee to move out of congressional offices and into new office space close to the Capitol. By 1980, the NRSC had created a permanent operation with substantial continuity in staff (Menefee–Libey 1989, 222–41; Kolodny 1998, 135–39).[42]

INTERMEDIARY WITH THE PRESIDENT

Service as intermediary with the president was a role that elected party leaders, particularly the floor leaders, continued throughout this period (Truman 1959,

[42] Richard Cohen, "Are the Senate's Liberal Democrats Becoming an Endangered Species?" *National Journal*, July 14, 1979, 1152–55.

302–3). All floor leaders of the president's party tried to serve their party colleagues by synchronizing the policy positions and public messages of the Senate party and the White House. The weekly meetings between the president and his party's congressional leaders that Barkley had established were continued by all subsequent presidents and leaders (Sorensen 1965, 355; Munk 1970, 258; Carter 1982, 71; Collier 1994; Deason 2019, 175). Many of these regular meetings, usually held over breakfast, were primarily social, but they kept lines of communication open and often included discussion of pending business in Congress. Every leader of the president's party, without exception, reported an obligation to give the president an honest assessment of the reception of the administration's proposals in the Senate and to give advice that the president might not want to hear.

Developments in the White House affected communication between the president and congressional leaders. During the Truman and Eisenhower years, these developments included a greater formalization of the annual process of developing a legislative program for the administration (Neustadt 1955) and the expansion of congressional liaison staff (Collier 1994). With a sizable liaison staff, the White House staff presence on Capitol Hill was nearly continuous, which reduced some of the president's dependence on leaders to report on developments there. It allowed more legislators to be approached by representatives of the president and enabled the White House to organize visits from senators well beyond the leaders in a strategic fashion. Some presidents, Eisenhower most notably, also scheduled meetings with opposition party leaders on a fairly regular basis.

While there were important and somewhat idiosyncratic differences among Senate leaders in their relations with presidents, Ripley (1969a) demonstrates how, in the first two-thirds of the twentieth century, the relationship was largely determined by common partisan interests but could be shaped by strategic choices made by both the president and congressional leaders. With a reasonably assertive president, a cooperative relationship was most likely between a president and his own party leaders in Congress. The relationship with opposition party leaders was more varied, ranging from generally oppositional to a more mixed relationship that involved some cooperative efforts. For example, Democrat Lyndon Johnson found that supporting Republican president Dwight Eisenhower on foreign policy promoted the interests of his party, exploited divisions among Republicans, and enhanced his own presidential prospects. At the same time, Republican William Knowland's differences with Eisenhower on foreign policy may have been genuine, but they improved his standing with Taft Republicans, whose support he sought for his prospective candidacies for governor and president. On a couple of occasions, Knowland left the majority leader's front-and-center seat and used a desk farther back to symbolize that he was not acting as majority leader in opposing the president's position (Kravitz ca. 1971, 100).

Richard Russell (D, Ga.), Majority Leader Lyndon B. Johnson (D, Tex.), and Minority
Leader William Knowland (R, Calif.) discuss the Civil Rights Bill, July 1957. Note the
photographer in the foreground.
LBJ Library photo by the *New York Times*

   While the 1944 Barkley-Roosevelt episode—Barkley's resignation and
reelection—was not repeated, differences over important policies occurred with
consequences for the president-leader relationship. Knowland actively opposed
Eisenhower on national security and foreign policy, along with a few domestic
issues, and eventually developed a cool relationship with the White House
(Truman 1959, 306; Jewell 1962, 64; Montgomery and Johnson 1998,
114–23, 136–38, 166–80). Eisenhower was pleased when Dirksen took over
informally for Knowland and then was elected leader when Knowland left the
Senate in 1958 (Greenstein 1982, 79). On the other hand, possible public breaks
between the president and his party's Senate leader were often submerged.
Mansfield, quite notably, opposed Johnson's Vietnam War policies but kept
his views private between himself and the president while Johnson was in office.
   Nevertheless, the relationship with the president was very important for
Senate leaders of the president's party. Taft, for example, sought the floor
leadership post only after his party won the White House in 1952. Taft wanted
direct and regular access to the president and wanted to control the flow of
information between the White House and Senate Republicans, which the floor

leadership post would provide and the policy committee chairmanship might not (White 1954, 215; Jewell 1962, 91; Patterson 1972, 370).[43] Taft and his successors knew from experience that the president's standing with the public would allow the president to set the policy agenda for his party, and, most of the time, their Senate colleagues would expect them to support the president. The *New York Times* columnist Arthur Krock observed at the time Taft was elected leader that, "as majority leader, Taft will have an implied obligation he otherwise would not have to represent the president at the Capitol."[44] Leaders of the president's party also understood that the established pattern of regular meetings with the president would give them an opportunity to shape administration proposals.

But cooperation and opposition hardly do justice to the range of relationships. Thus Lucas had a cooperative but one-way relationship with President Truman. "Every Monday morning, the limousine brought him [Lucas] to the White House, where he, along with Assistant Leader Francis Myers of Pennsylvania and House Democratic leaders, received from Truman a list of legislation that the President wanted passed," Caro (2002, 361) wrote. "Then the car returned him to Capitol Hill, where the southerners, who chaired the committees that would handle the legislation, let him know—quietly, courteously but firmly—that it would not be passed." Truman and Lucas even had a direct phone line between their offices (Huitt 1961; McMillan 2004, 201). This one-way relationship, with the leader serving as the president's Senate messenger, did not last. McFarland, Lucas's successor, usually insisted on personal meetings with the president and did not use the phone line often. Most subsequent presidents recognized that they benefited from a more meaningful exchange of views with their parties' congressional leaders (Truman 1959, 295–303).

The one leader of the president's party who had a somewhat icy relationship with his president was Robert Byrd, who became majority leader when Jimmy Carter entered the White House in 1977. Carter, in Byrd's view, did not consult adequately with Congress in designing important policy proposals, vacillated on important issues, had an ineffective congressional liaison team, and failed to understand the give-and-take bargaining and personal relationships that were required to be effective on Capitol Hill (Corbin 2012, 171–73). Byrd also emphasized his loyalty to the Senate and his Senate party and frequently instructed the White House on how to deal with his colleagues. Nevertheless, Byrd proved to be essential to the success of many of Carter's legislative efforts and, with few exceptions, backed the president's agenda. Carter, with the assistance of Walter Mondale, who had served in the Senate from 1964 until his election as vice president in 1976, made adjustments.

The opposition party's leaders' relations with the president have varied more widely. Johnson developed a good working relationship with Eisenhower and leveraged divisions among Republicans on foreign policy to shore up the

---

[43] "Taft Faces Brushoff in Senate," *Boston Globe*, Dec. 4, 1952, 1; "Taft as Senate Leader Prevents a Schism Now," *New York Times*, Dec. 21, 1952, E3.

[44] "Taft as Senate Leader Prevents a Schism Now," *New York Times*, Dec. 21, 1952, E3.

Democrats' image (Riedel 1969, 160). The strongest relationship between a president and a Senate leader of the opposite party appears to have been President Johnson's relationship with Dirksen, the Republican leader. The two men spent the 1950s in the Senate together, served simultaneously as floor leaders during the last two Congresses of the Eisenhower administration, shared a professional, pragmatic outlook on their role as party leaders, and had become good friends by the time Johnson left the Senate for the White House. They had an unusually large number of private conversations that proved critical on civil rights, the Vietnam War, and other issues (MacNeil 1970; Hulsey 2000).

POLICY LEADERS

Two generalizations about the Senate's policymaking process during much of this period are undoubtedly true but are not the full story. First, presidents took the lead in setting the legislative agenda in this period.[45] Second, for most major measures, as we have noted, committee chairmen were responsible for ushering legislation through committee and managing bills on the Senate floor.[46] While true, these generalizations may produce the false impression that leaders, particularly majority leaders, performed merely ministerial duties on the floor. Their choices in setting the floor agenda, their influence on the president's strategies, their assistance to presidents and chairmen in finding votes, and, on occasion, their effort to find and offer key compromises to win on the floor add up to far more than a ministerial function. In fact, leaders were engaged in most important policy battles, even if they did not assume solo responsibility to lead efforts to construct coalitions. Some episodes are famous, as when Dirksen, as minority leader, held sessions in his office to draft voting rights legislation in 1965. Also in that room were Majority Leader Mansfield, a bipartisan set of senators, and administration representatives (Shaffer 1980, 101–2).

Systematic investigation of the role of floor leaders in writing legislation and building coalitions is not easy. Finding public statements is relatively easy, but oral histories, personal papers, journalistic accounts, biographies, and other secondary sources usually provide inadequate detail on leaders' activities on most issues, even for major legislation. Serving as a coalition leader, of course, is a task that can be shared and often is not conspicuous on the floor. Moreover, it is not possible to separate rounding up votes from service as manager of the floor agenda, as an intermediary with the president, as a spokesman for the party, or even as a manager of the party organization. For the modern leader, these are threads of one cloth.

We know the extremes in approach—Democratic leaders Johnson and Mansfield. As Stewart (1971) described so effectively, Johnson's proactive,

---

[45] See, for example, Bond and Fleisher 1990.   [46] McFarland 1979, 128.

Majority Leader Mike Mansfield (D, Mont.) and Minority Leader Everett Dirksen (R, Ill.) prepare for the Senate's consideration of the 1964 Civil Rights Bill, which they knew would require a lengthy and contentious debate.

U.S. Senate Historical Office

controlling approach during the Eisenhower years eventually engendered some resentment, particularly from liberals who considered Johnson too willing to avoid issues that divided the party (Huitt 1961). Mansfield's laissez-faire approach yielded some criticism that the party was less cohesive and effective than it could have been, also from liberals who believed that more loyalty from conservatives could have been acquired with more assertive leadership.

In this period, most leaders operated somewhere between these extremes by taking an active role in overseeing the policy leadership and coalition-building efforts of committee leaders and bill managers and stepping in whenever they were needed. Political circumstances—most important, the sizes of the parties, the strategies of factions, and the party of the president—greatly influenced the assertiveness of leaders (Huitt 1961). Democratic leader McFarland, often considered a weak leader (Truman 1959, 303–5), struggled with a slim 49–47 seat advantage after his party lost five seats in the 1950 elections, had to manage a party split nearly evenly between northern liberals and southern conservatives, and was not going to get much help from the unpopular and somewhat unsympathetic president of his own party. McFarland chose a defensive posture to avoid legislative losses for his party and president, which left him looking less capable than his successor, Johnson, who, as minority leader and working with a Republican president, could more selectively and less conspicuously pick issues on which to assert himself and build a reputation for success (McMillan 2004, 202–3).

Minority leaders exhibited wide variation in their assertiveness in building coalitions in opposition to majority party proposals. Intraparty divisions on many issues limited minority leaders' assertiveness and effectiveness, just as for majority leaders. After Taft, Republican minority leaders used weekly luncheons to encourage party unity on many issues. If their party controlled the White House, they generally advocated for the president's program, but even then the record is uneven. Dirksen was the most assertive of minority leaders in the mid-twentieth century while working with presidents of the opposite party, but Dirksen sometimes found that his colleagues were willing to move without his leadership, as when conservatives decided to filibuster the Fortas Supreme Court nomination in late 1968 after Dirksen had agreed to a deal with President Johnson to allow the nomination to be considered (Shaffer 1980, 79–94).

Some perspective on leaders' coalition-building activity can be gained from a sampling of journalistic coverage of Senate legislative activity. We construct our count from *CQ Almanac*, an annual publication of Congressional Quarterly that summarized legislative activity on dozens of issues. We tallied the number of stories mentioning actions taken by a floor leader, providing the counts in the two panels of Figure 8.4. The *CQ Almanac* count covers over 250 legislative measures in its two reports for a typical Congress. Majority leaders, all Democrats after 1955, appear in perhaps 10 or 20 stories per Congress— considerably fewer than 10 percent of the total stories, but still a much larger number than that for minority leaders. Johnson, by this measure, was mentioned no more frequently than Barkley, Lucas, or Mansfield. Only Dirksen

Democratic leaders

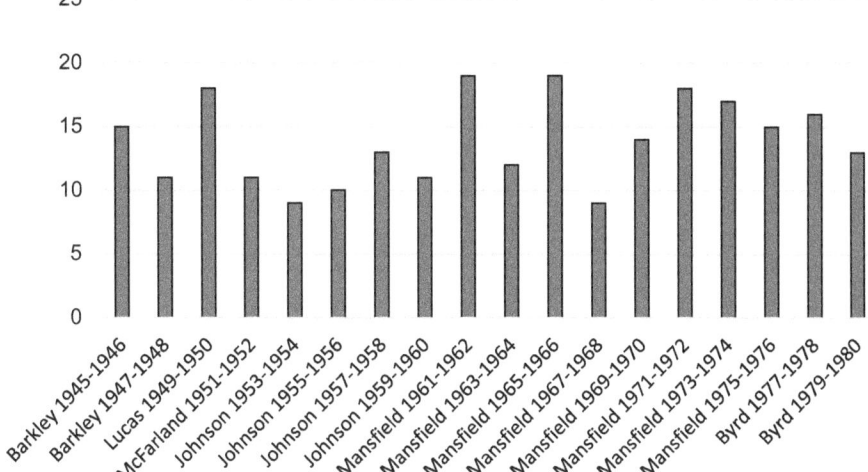

Republican leaders

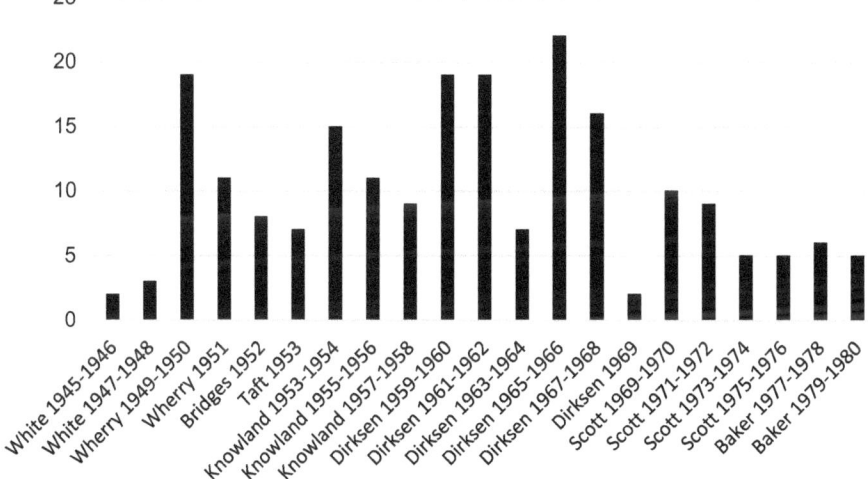

FIGURE 8.4 Frequency of *CQ Almanac* issue stories mentioning floor leader with a meaningful policymaking or strategy role, 1945–80

Source: *CQ Almanac*. Each cell is the number of issues for which the leader is mentioned in a meaningful policy or political role: "led" effort, offered compromise, offered amendment, or set strategy.

stands out among Republicans. Overall, for the broad coverage of *CQ Almanac*, the floor leaders are major players in only a few of the most important issues during this period. But these stories usually overlook the central role of majority leaders in managing floor activity, which can appear routine while having strategic significance.

LEADERS, CIVIL RIGHTS, AND FILIBUSTER REFORM

Every majority leader since Robinson has voluntarily or involuntarily been placed in the middle of a debate over reform of Rule XXII, the 1917 rule governing cloture to end filibusters.[47] Majority leaders, mostly Democrats, have struggled to manage diverse views about reducing the threshold for cloture. The issue became more intense as the New Deal faded and the conservative coalition of Republicans and southern Democrats rose in the late 1930s. Liberal Democrats became strongly interested in reform in the early 1940s after years of failure to get votes on anti-lynching and anti-poll tax bills. It appeared to some of them that southerners were siding with the Republicans on economic matters in exchange for Republican support in their efforts to filibuster civil rights measures. By the end of World War II, civil rights legislation advocates had grown severely frustrated with their inability to gain consideration and a vote on their proposals. President Harry Truman made civil rights a top priority and encouraged reform, which had support from most northern Democrats and many Republicans by 1948.

For Democratic floor leaders, civil rights legislation and filibuster reform meant managing a conflict that was perceived as central to the party's legislative and electoral viability. Under Barkley during the Roosevelt years, the issue of filibuster reform was side-stepped, but in the late 1940s the issue broke into the open after Truman replaced Roosevelt in the White House and then made civil rights a top priority. Barkley was elected vice president and Lucas replaced Barkley as leader. Lucas, like Truman, favored simple-majority cloture but was unable to gain enough support from Republicans to counter the opposition from southern Democrats. He was able, as Republicans wanted, to extend the cloture procedure to motions as well as measures. However, the conservative coalition changed the rule from a two-thirds majority of senators present and voting to two-thirds of all senators (a "constitutional majority") and exempted proposals to change the Senate rules from cloture. Lucas's successor, McFarland, accepted that arrangement as Truman's legislative agenda had little chance of enactment anyway. Johnson, taking over from McFarland in 1953, faced continual demands for reform from liberals and negotiated a modest change in 1959 that lasted until 1975. The reform extended cloture to a change in the rules and returned the threshold from a two-thirds constitutional majority to two-thirds of senators present and voting. Lucas and Johnson took different positions on reform, but both were central to working out an agreement that allowed the party to get past the issue, at least temporarily.[48]

---

[47] For background on filibuster reform during this period, see Smith 2014, 51–76, 92–99, 108–112.

[48] The roles of Johnson and Mansfield have been described in many sources. Lucas's role in filibuster reform was covered at length in the newspapers. See, for example, Robert C. Albright's reporting for the *Post*: "Democrat Liberal Wing Splits on Anti-Filibuster Procedure," *Washington Post*, Feb. 17, 1949, 3; "Drive to Curb Debate in Senate Runs Head-On Into Southern Opposition," *Washington Post*, Mar. 1, 1949, 1; "Implied Guarantee Against

After Mansfield replaced Johnson in 1961, filibuster reform was pushed by Democratic liberals at the start of every Congress until a reform package was adopted in 1975. Mansfield favored modest changes to Rule XXII, but he opposed simple-majority cloture, for which many liberals advocated, and objected to efforts to establish a precedent that a Senate majority could take up rules changes at the start of every Congress. While he accommodated liberals' requests for time to debate the issue in most Congresses, he did not take a leading role. Only in 1975, when it appeared that liberal Democrats, with a cooperative Republican vice president, could force a change in the rule by a simple-majority vote, did Mansfield step in to get agreement on a compromise—a three-fifths majority of senators "duly chosen and sworn" for most legislation, with no alteration to the threshold for changes to Senate rules.

For Republican leaders, in the minority for all but two Congresses, filibuster reform often presented an opportunity to foment trouble for the Democrats. At times in the 1940s and 1950s, some Republicans supported reform as a means for acting on civil rights legislation they favored; for others, supporting reform was strategic, a way to deepen divisions among Democrats. In 1953, Taft supported the proposal to shift the two-thirds constitutional majority to a two-thirds present and voting majority, but he put little effort into acting on the proposal. In general, Republican leaders were outsiders to the fights over filibuster reform that were driven by Democrats.

PARTY SPOKESPERSON

Political news spread from newspapers and radio to television in this era, an evolution in mass communications that was exploited by presidents but very little by congressional party leaders. In the 1940s and 1950s, leaders routinely interacted with Capitol Hill reporters. Starting with Barkley, majority leaders conducted a brief press conference each day before the Senate went into session (McMillan 2004, 206), a practice observed by all majority leaders until Byrd. On most days, these were held on the Senate floor at the leader's desk (Reidel 1969, 150, 163) and came to be known as "dugout" sessions—often called dugout chatter—by the time Johnson was majority leader.[49] In the late 1940s, many senators, including leaders, broadcast weekly radio programs from Washington to their home states, and leaders were occasional guests on national radio programs like *Meet the Press*. A few times, congressional leaders

---

Majority Cloture Reported; Truman Contacted," *Washington Post*, Mar. 13, 1949, M1; "New Combination Claims It Can Beat Leadership in Showdown," *Washington Post*, Mar. 16, 1949, 1.

[49] Warren Weaver, Jr., "Dugout Chatter, a Senate Tradition," *New York Times*, Jan. 27, 1982, A20. Weaver reports that the name may have originated with a United Press International reporter who drew a parallel to the "interview show that preceded radio broadcasts of Washington Senators baseball games in the 1950s."

participated in national radio broadcasts of their own.[50] They certainly did not exploit radio as a way of reaching voters the way Presidents Roosevelt and Truman did.[51]

Leaders were aware of the implications of Senate activity for the electoral success of their parties, but they did not place public relations high on their list of responsibilities, and remarkably little is reported about their public relations efforts by close observers and biographers. In fact, McFarland (1979, 109–41) did not mention the press in his autobiography's chapter "The Job of the Majority Leader in the U.S. Senate," while giving substantial attention to all other functions of the modern leader. Nevertheless, floor leaders in the late 1940s and early 1950s, including Lucas, McFarland, and Kenneth Wherry (R, Nebr.), were occasional sources for commentary on important legislative developments and were quoted frequently, but certainly not daily, in the press.

In the 1950s, attitudes toward the media began to change. Republican leaders White and Wherry were both overshadowed by Taft, who reporters recognized as the most influential Senate Republican. Taft, ironically, is reported to have been indifferent to reporters, but, before he was leader, he used the policy committee's pronouncements on important issues as opportunities to acquire some press attention. Knowland could be hostile to reporters but managed to get quoted frequently. In contrast, Dirksen, before and after his election as leader, courted reporters and, as leader, immediately started press conferences after the weekly policy committee luncheons (MacNeil 1970, 169–70). This was largely a personal effort. Dirksen wrote his own speeches, appeared before cameras daily, and generated his own quotable comments (Hulsey 2000, 161, 208; Ferris 2004, 47).

Johnson worked hard to develop useful relationships with reporters as whip, minority leader, and majority leader. He followed the Taft model in one respect: he and his staff would prepare a policy statement, have it endorsed by the policy committee, and then appear before reporters to read the statement

---

[50] Robert F. Whitney, "Lucas Threatens to Hold Congress Till Thanksgiving," *New York Times*, Aug. 22, 1949, 1; Coleman B. Jones, "Lucas Talks of Holding Congress Till November," *Washington Post*, Aug. 22, 1949, 1; "Democrats Mapping Radio Barrage of Oratory," *Boston Globe*, Dec. 19, 1949, 1; "GOP Drive Started over Radio Networks," *New York Times*, Dec. 24, 1949, 26.

[51] In the 1940s, members of Congress debated whether live radio broadcasts of floor sessions should be permitted and even funded by Congress, but neither house adopted the idea. Legislators feared that broadcasting would encourage grandstanding, an argument that would be repeated about televising floor sessions in the 1970s and 1980s. In 1945, a weekly half-hour program, "Congress on the Air," was broadcast on Sunday evenings. The program usually involved two senators and two representatives, balanced by party, addressing an important issue. The first live coverage of committee hearings occurred in 1947 on NBC. See "Congress on the Air," *Washington Post*, Mar. 24, 1947, 6. In the Senate, the radio gallery and facilities were approved in 1939 (Ritchie 1992, 217), opened in 1940, and expanded over the next decade. Television was added in the late 1940s (*Cong. Rec.*, Feb. 16, 1950, 1834). Individual senators, including Scott Lucas, began weekly programs for their home stations in these years. Transcripts are available in some personal paper collections, including the Lucas papers.

and answer questions (for example, see Caro 2002, 523). In general, Johnson was more attentive to press relations than his predecessors and worked hard at times to grab headlines. He hired an experienced reporter to his staff and established a process to keep himself informed of all significant developments in committee rooms.

But the television era was dawning (Roper 1983), and Republicans, led by Everett Dirksen, were the first to appreciate its significance. Beginning in January 1961, Dirksen and his House counterpart, Charles Halleck, appeared before cameras in the old Senate chamber after holding their weekly Thursday morning meeting together. Quickly dubbed the "Ev and Charlie Show" by the press, the effort was so valuable to the party that the Republican National Committee began to pay a publicist to serve as a producer for the program.[52] The show was an immediate success, but it drew complaints from moderate Republicans about the strongly conservative arguments advocated in the program, and the weak 1962 midterm elections led to the expression of more concerns about how Dirksen and Halleck represented their party in the media.[53] Nevertheless, the "Ev and Charlie Show" continued—becoming the "Ev and Jerry Show" after Gerald Ford defeated Halleck as House Republican leader in 1965 (Peabody 1966; MacNeil 1970, 187–89). Still, despite the production's popularity, Dirksen understood that it was not truly competitive with the White House in attracting television coverage.[54]

Mansfield, the Democratic leader from 1961 until 1977, was another story. While he talked with reporters, held dugout sessions, and made appearances on news programs, Mansfield put little effort into developing relationships with reporters or fashioning quotable comments. To the contrary, his one-word yes-or-no responses made him a quite difficult interview subject for either newspaper reporters or television hosts. He did not hire a press secretary, although a policy committee aide evolved into an informal press liaison (Valeo 1999, 21–22; Ferris 2004, 54). After Byrd became whip in 1971, Mansfield would often make a brief appearance at the dugout sessions and then leave Byrd to answer questions by himself (Kimmit 2001, 78).

As whip, Byrd received unanimous consent to allow each floor leader to be recognized for three minutes following the approval of the *Journal* at the beginning of each daily session (*Cong. Rec.*, 1971, 1073). The idea appears to have originated with senators who proposed ways to make floor activity more efficient (Kravitz ca. 1971, 97-98). No explanation was given by Byrd,

---

[52] Robert C. Albright, "TV Stars of GOP Plan Long Run; Some See 'Ev and Charlie Show' as Miscast," *Washington Post*, Mar. 15, 1961, A2; "Concession Is Won by GOP Liberals," *New York Times*, Apr. 19, 1961, 20.

[53] Robert C. Albright, "GOP Prods Policy Unit in 'Ev-Charlie' Backlash," *Washington Post*, Apr. 23, 1961, A23.

[54] Russell Baker, "'Ev and Charlie,' or a GOP Lament: Dirksen and Halleck Lag in Communications Fight," *New York Times*, Mar. 16, 1962, 15; "Republican Scores 'Ev-Charlie Show,'" *New York Times*, Nov. 15, 1962, 20; Cabell Phillips, "'Image' Problem Plaguing G.O.P.," *New York Times*, Mar. 4, 1963, 7.

but he surely believed that the leaders should be guaranteed an opportunity to address issues of their choice on a daily basis. In 1975 and thereafter, Byrd extended "leader time" to 10 minutes per leader (*Cong. Rec.*, 1975, 15; *Cong. Rec.*, 1977, 22). Floor leaders embraced leader time to address issues of the day, and their comments frequently were reported in the press, but, at least before the advent of televised floor sessions, it did not add much to the coverage that leaders received in the press.

Taking over as leader in 1977, Byrd seemed to have more appreciation for the media than Mansfield, but he had only a little more skill in dealing with reporters and television. He focused on legislative matters, substituted Saturday morning sessions with reporters for the daily dugout chatter (Paone n.d., 21; Scott and Wyatt 2019, 86), and generally did not assume a major role in representing the party to the media. His ineffectiveness on television played a role in a challenge to his reelection as floor leader in 1984 and sped his retirement from the post after the 1988 elections.[55]

Republican leader Howard Baker, Dirksen's son-in-law, was the first floor leader chosen with television skills in mind when he was elected in 1977. The ambitious Baker lost to Scott in contests for floor leader in 1969 and 1971 and was contemplating a future run for the presidency when Scott's retirement created an opportunity for Baker to run for floor leader. He had gained national visibility as a member of the Watergate committee in 1973–74, had been on short lists for the vice presidency several times, and had been seen as a presidential prospect for some time (and, in fact, ran in 1980). Elected in a contest with Griffin by a 19–18 vote, Baker was seen as the "cheerleader with dimples," a dynamic personality suited for television, in contrast to Griffin, the "diligent secretary of the Glee Club" known for his parliamentary skills (Annis 1995, 85–103). Many of his colleagues were looking for a new party image after falling to 38 seats after the 1974 elections and not improving in 1976.[56]

Studies of press and television coverage of senators during the 1950s, 1960s, and 1970s demonstrate that floor leaders were consistently among the top 10 senators in terms of the frequency of coverage (Wilhoit and Sherrill 1968; Weaver and Wilhoit 1974, 1980; Foote and Weber 1984). Coverage of senators in national news outlets was spread across much of the Senate, but over a third of the coverage focused on 10 senators (Hess 1986, 132–34). In fact, despite the wide variation in floor leaders' approaches to managing

---

[55] Hedrik Smith, "For Democrats, the Medium's a Mess," *New York Times*, Dec. 10, 1984, B10; Jonathan Fuerbringer, "Byrd: No More Mr. Quiet Guy," *New York Times*, May 9, 1985, B16.
[56] On Baker's election as leader, see Jon Margolis, "After Years of Struggle, Baker Wins a Big One," *Chicago Tribune*, Jan. 5, 1977, 2; Spencer Rich, "Baker Upsets Griffin; Byrd Majority Leader," *Washington Post*, Jan. 5, 1977, A1; James P. Gannon, "Senate Republicans Tap Baker in Surprise; While Democrats Elect Byrd as Forecast," *Wall Street Journal*, Jan. 5, 1977, 3. On the presidential contest, see David S. Broder, "The Pros and Cons of a Political Pro," *Washington Post*, Oct. 31, 1979, A21.

Democrats

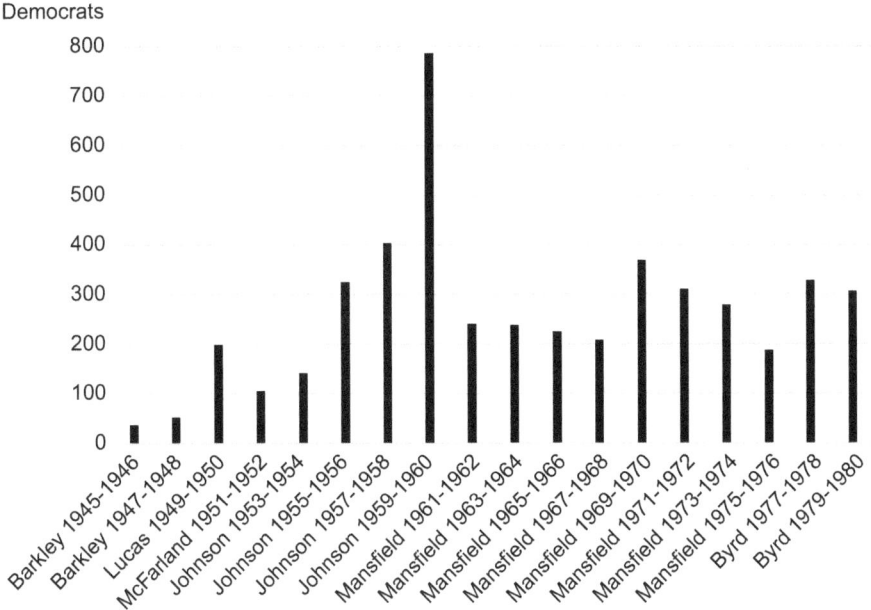

Republicans

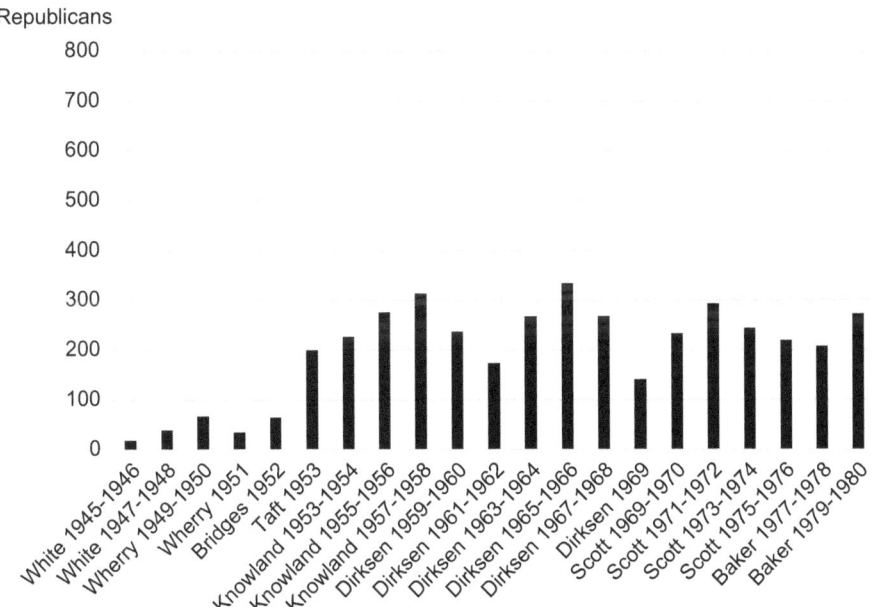

FIGURE 8.5 Frequency of *Washington Post* stories mentioning Senate leaders, 1945–80
Source: ProQuest Historical Newspapers.

media relations, leaders since the early 1950s exhibited remarkable continuity in the aggregate coverage they received. Even the self-effacing Mansfield was second in the ranking of senators covered in Associated Press stories in 1973–74 (Hess 1986, 134).

In Figure 8.5 we show that, with the exception of Lucas, the *Washington Post* in the 1940s and early 1950s did not regularly mention floor leaders in its coverage of the Senate. Only with Taft and Knowland, in 1953–54, and Johnson, in 1955–56, did this change decisively. For the majority leaders in the 1955–80 period, all Democrats, the average number of *Post* stories for the two-year period of a Congress, excluding 1959–60 when much of the coverage of Johnson was devoted to his presidential candidacy, was 284. The average number of days in session per Congress was 322 for the same period. In that period, minority leaders, all Republicans, averaged 267 stories, only slightly less than majority leaders.[57]

In the 1960s and 1970s, however, news coverage of Congress shrank as the news media, particularly television, gave more attention to the White House and less to Capitol Hill (Robinson and Appel 1979; Hess 1981, 1994; Ornstein 1989). Dirksen could not do much about this. On the Democratic side, Mansfield was considerably and deliberately less visible than Johnson had been in the 1950s (Oberdorfer 2003, 405). Mansfield's low-key, laconic style created opportunities for other senators to attract media attention, usually through television coverage of committee hearings, but it was a shrinking news hole that during this period did not include cable news—CNN began in 1980—or television coverage of the Senate floor. (The Senate did not allow television coverage of the floor until 1986.) By the late 1970s, the declining coverage of Congress and the stable number of mentions of Senate floor leaders meant that the media presence of leaders was growing increasingly important.

CONCLUDING OBSERVATIONS

Party competition drove organizational innovation in the 1940s and early 1950s. The reinvention of the Republican party organization by Taft and the addition of critical staff operations by the Democrats' Johnson were explicitly justified by the parties' needs to improve legislative and electoral effectiveness. To be sure, even though by the measures of Senate party budgets and number of staff, party infrastructure was small in comparison to subsequent decades, leaders' efforts to address the coordination and collective action challenges with staffing innovations were nevertheless viewed as important by contemporary observers and proved lasting. It is noteworthy that the Mansfield era,

---

[57] *Washington Post* stories are counted from a search of ProQuest, Jan. 1–Dec. 31, for each Congress or period of service within a Congress as floor leader, using these search terms: "lastname near/2 firstname" AND "Senate." In the case of death, counts were stopped two days before death. The number of Senate session days is available at www.brookings.edu/multi-chapter-report/vital-statistics-on-congress/.

1961–77, was a period of dominance by the Democratic party. With no serious threat of losing their Senate majority, the Democrats could afford a leader who was not assertive in setting a direction for the party and instead focused on maintaining peace among party factions. Mansfield played a leading role in opposition to President Nixon's Vietnam policies, but, as a general rule, he did not have to mobilize his party and fashion public relations strategies to retain majority party status in the Senate.

Notably, the development of a party-based infrastructure was symmetric—but only over the long run. Republicans, usually in the minority, more fully exploited appropriations for party staff. It is easy to point to the motivation of gaining majority status as the primary reason, but the full story appears to be more complicated. Minority committee leaders had less to lose from policy interventions by party leaders and their staff, loosening the constraints on building a party staff, and minority party senators had less reliable access to committee staff, making the accessible party staff more important to them than to majority party senators.

The organizational development of Senate parties has strong cumulative tendencies. As a rule, Senate parties retain their organization—including leadership posts and staff arrangements—from Congress to Congress. New leaders or new circumstances, such as a change in party control or the party of the president, are usually required for the parties to accept significant change. Once organizational arrangements are adjusted, staff are added, and daily patterns of behavior are established, expectations of continuity quickly form. New resources are seldom voluntarily forfeited.

Intraparty factionalism always played a role in intraparty development. For the Republicans, the election of floor leaders, conference chairs, and even policy committee chairs often involved factional contests, usually won by the more conservative elements of the party after McNary's death. Conflict over the direction of the party, in addition to competition for party control of the Senate and a new media and campaign environment, shaped the development of the party's organizational and staff infrastructure. For Senate Democrats, deep splits within the party delayed the development of a party apparatus that some conference members, usually southern conservatives, believed would be used to advance liberal legislation. Johnson and Mansfield, very different leaders but both sensitive to the divisions within their party, hired staff to meet their needs as managers of floor activity and routine party affairs, but neither leader built a staff capable of writing legislation on a regular basis. Only when Byrd took over did Democrats begin to build a larger party-based staff, responding to the example set by Republicans and the growing demands of liberals within the party.

The record of factionalism and party development has implications for the "conditional party government" (CPG) thesis (Aldrich, Berger, and Rhode 2002). CPG contends that a factionalized, heterogeneous majority party produces a policymaking process that relies little on central party leaders and instead turns to standing committees to take the initiative. By most measures, factionalism ran deep and partisan polarization was low from the late 1930s until the 1980s (Sinclair 2012). Indeed, during most of this era, the organizational capacity of the top leaders to devise policy was limited and reliance on standing committees to write legislation was nearly universal, as the CPG thesis posits. For the majority party, exceptions to the rule, such as the way in which civil rights bills and Vietnam War measures were written under the guidance of party leaders and their staff, were rare. Until the end of the period, the policy committee and conference staffs were process-oriented, with a focus on serving the leader in his performance of floor management duties.

The minority party was a different matter and is largely ignored in CPG accounts. Under Taft's leadership, the Republicans proved to be remarkably centralized in responding to a Democratic president and Senate majority. Yet the Republican conference was factionalized. Taft led a majority of Republicans who were conservative on domestic issues against an eastern, more moderate group that supported Dewey and Eisenhower. Taft, initially labeled an isolationist, also opposed the internationalism of Dewey and Eisenhower. Not all Republicans supported Taft's policy pronouncements, but the press assumed that Taft spoke for most Republicans, and on many issues he rallied his colleagues to make life difficult for the majority Democrats.

Finally, ambitious senators, seeking leadership posts or even the presidency, advocated new approaches to achieving party electoral and policy goals and expressed a willingness to assume the burden to plan and implement party strategy. Senate parties are small enough to enable a single senator to have a substantial impact on a party's performance. Senators recognize this and reward colleagues who perform these duties reasonably well with reelection or election to Senate party offices.

Minority Whip John Cornyn (R, Tex.), Minority Leader Mitch McConnell (R, Ky.), and Majority Leader Harry Reid (D, Nev.) head to the front of the chamber together before President Barack Obama delivers his State of the Union speech in 2014.

9

Polarization, Competition, and Centralization, 1981–2024

About an hour after receiving the news of the unexpected death of Supreme Court Justice Antonin Scalia in February 2016, Republican majority leader Mitch McConnell (R, Ky.) announced that the Senate would not act on any nomination by Democratic president Barack Obama until after the November elections. McConnell, out of town on a vacation, did not have time to consult with party colleagues; he assumed that he could speak for most of them and that his decision would stand. McConnell was right. Few Senate Republicans questioned him when he asserted that "the vacancy should not be filled until we have a new president."[1] Republicans' refusal to act, even to hold hearings, on the president's nomination was momentous. And it was the direct consequence of McConnell's quick decision. Not for another few days, until he returned to Washington, did McConnell find precedents to justify his announcement. "We discovered some useful facts. It had been 80 years since a vacancy on the Supreme Court occurring in a presidential year, an election year, had been filled," McConnell recounted learning. "You'd have to go back to 1888— Grover Cleveland in the White House—to find the last time a vacancy on the Supreme Court occurring in an election year was confirmed by the Senate of a different party of the president."[2] But these references to precedent were ad hoc, the historical facts meticulously chosen and phrased. Ten times since the Civil War a seat on the Supreme Court had stood vacant in a presidential election year, and every time that seat had been filled before the election.[3]

---

[1] Burgess Everett and Glenn Thrush, "McConnell Throws Down the Gauntlet: No Scalia Replacement under Obama," *Politico*, Feb. 13, 2016.

[2] Authors' interview with Senator Mitch McConnell, Jan. 9, 2018.

[3] Russell Wheeler, "McConnell's Fabricated History to Justify a 2020 Supreme Court Vote," Brookings, Sept. 24, 2020. Wheeler identifies nine cases. The tenth is Frank Murphy, who was confirmed by voice vote in January 1940.

As recently as 1988—a presidential election year—a Democratic Senate had unanimously confirmed Anthony Kennedy (whose nomination by Republican president Ronald Reagan had come late in 1987) to the Supreme Court. In fact, not since the presidency of Andrew Johnson, in 1866, and for reasons that had nothing to do with elections, had the Senate refused to act on a nomination to the Supreme Court.[4]

Four years later, when Justice Ruth Bader Ginsburg died six weeks before the 2020 elections, on September 18, McConnell again moved swiftly to stake out the position of the Republican Senate majority. In the terse press release, issued by his office on the day of Ginsburg's death, McConnell simultaneously noted that "the Senate and the nation mourn" Ginsburg and vowed that "President Trump's nominee will receive a vote on the floor of the United States Senate," presumably before the election.[5] The Republican majority moved immediately to hold hearings and confirm Amy Coney Barrett to the Supreme Court. McConnell argued that there was one set of precedents when Senate majorities aligned with the president, as in 2020, and another set of precedents for times of divided government, as in 2016. "No Senate has failed to confirm a nominee in the circumstances that face us now," McConnell explained, in justifying his decision.[6]

The notion of competing precedents was an invention of the moment. For 150 years, from 1866 until 2016, in election years and non-election years alike, the Senate had never before failed to act on a president's Supreme Court nomination, except when the nomination had been withdrawn. So the case for proceeding with the nomination was clear: apart from the Senate's decision not to take up the nomination of Merrick Garland in 2016, there was no instance in the modern era of the Senate rejecting a nominee without a hearing. But the case against was also strong. First, there was the matter of timing. The confirmation vote in 2020 took place on October 26, just eight days before Election Day. While 10 other Supreme Court Justices had been seated during presidential election years since the Civil War, none had been confirmed by the Senate later in the year than July.[7] Second, there was the speed of the process: 27 days, the fastest-moving confirmation process since the mid-1970s.[8] And,

[4] "Supreme Court Nominations (1789–Present)," United States Senate, www.senate.gov/legislative/nominations/SupremeCourtNominations1789present.htm (accessed Mar. 2025).

[5] Office of the Senate Majority Leader, "McConnell Statement on the Passing of Justice Ruth Bader Ginsburg," press release, Sept. 18, 2020.

[6] Marianne LeVine, "McConnell Fends Off Accusations of Hypocrisy over Holding Supreme Court Vote," *Politico*, Sept. 21, 2020. See also Jane Chong, "Senate Republicans Are Playing a Dangerous Game with the Court's Legitimacy," *The Atlantic*, Oct. 11, 2020.

[7] Russell Wheeler, "McConnell's Fabricated History to Justify a 2020 Supreme Court Vote," Brookings, Sept. 24, 2020. William Brennan was not confirmed by the Senate until 1957, but he was named to the Court as a recess appointment by President Dwight Eisenhower in October 1956.

[8] "Supreme Court Nominations (1789–Present)," United States Senate, www.senate.gov/legislative/nominations/SupremeCourtNominations1789present.htm (accessed Mar. 2025).

third, there was McConnell's own principle, articulated in 2016, that voters should have the opportunity to weigh in on election-year vacancies. But McConnell knew his caucus: all but two Senate Republicans sided with him in the decision to confirm Barrett before the election.[9] With all Democrats in opposition, it was the first entirely partisan confirmation vote approving a Supreme Court Justice since 1869.[10]

Senators of the mid-twentieth century would be disoriented in McConnell's Senate. Between 1981 and 2020, the Senate had moved from a highly individualistic institution with fluid coalitions to an institution dominated by partisan teams with strong leaders and sizable staffs. This transformation was accompanied by great changes in the expectations of senators about the role of parties, in the nature of party organization, and in the everyday activity of floor leaders. Over the four decades, senators shifted much of their attention away from committee rooms to party venues. In this same period, they doubled the number of staff in party offices. Perhaps most dramatically, floor leaders assumed unprecedented responsibility for setting party strategy on a wide range of legislation and procedural decisions.

The Senate of the late 1970s and 1980s had been difficult for contemporary observers of Congress to characterize. What appeared to be runaway individualism, a surge in obstructive uses of Senate rules, and often hyperactive subcommittees led some observers to fear that Congress could not act coherently and expeditiously on a range of policy challenges (Deering and Smith 1985). Some legislators—primarily strong liberals among Democrats and strong conservatives among Republicans—were demanding more team play by their party colleagues, calling for procedural reform and more effective leadership to make it happen. Outside observers were not optimistic that party leaders were up to it. "Senate leadership in the 1980s remains an unformed commodity. Despite certain imperatives, the post still depends largely on the personality and priorities of the individual occupant," Roger Davidson (1985, 249) wrote. "Leadership positions have shifted in accord with personal skills, preferences, and styles; they are not yet institutionalized, in the sense that incumbents have to conform to rigorous models or sets of expectations."

The 1980s proved to be transitional years. Partisan conflict intensified during the decade, and senators demanded more effective party organizations and leadership. Robert Byrd (D, W.Va.) was challenged for Democratic floor leader in 1986, and two years later gave up his post because he was not meeting his colleagues' expectations as a team leader and party spokesman. By the mid-1990s, not only did party leaders serve as their parties' chief strategists on floor procedure, but they also increasingly guided the tandem tasks of writing important legislation and fashioning media strategies. Procedural maneuvering intensified on the Senate floor, which placed floor leaders in the middle of every legislative battle. In the 2010s and early 2020s, intense partisan conflict produced a policymaking "process" that was remarkably centralized in the floor leaders—with "process" in quotation marks because it was, in fact, an ad hoc legislative process that varied from bill to bill. The two floor leaders not only acted to address obstacles that committee leaders could not manage, as they had for decades previously, they also took charge of the legislative process and guided action from beginning to end on the most important legislation. The Senate reached 2024 with more elaborate organizations than ever before, its most assertive leaders since Lyndon Johnson in the 1950s, and, in McConnell and Charles Schumer (D, N.Y.) the most powerful, centralized leaders in its history.

Developments in this period lead us to qualify otherwise persuasive accounts of congressional parties offered by other scholars. Partisan polarization and electoral competition motivate leaders and innovations in party organization, but there also is a cumulative character to the roles and resources of party leaders. Leaders rarely give up resources that they have inherited. More commonly, they use what they are given and make incremental improvements, and then, occasionally, exhibit a willingness to remodel party organization and resources when their colleagues allow or even demand it. The centralized leadership structures of 2024 represent, then, not only the intense polarization of the early decades of the twenty-first century but also the steady accumulation of powers extending back to the first stirrings of elected leadership in the 1890s.

PARTY BATTLES: INDIVIDUALISM, ENTREPRENEURS, AND FACTIONS

Partisanship deepened and broadened in the more than four decades between 1981 and 2024. After a 26-year period when the Democrats enjoyed uninterrupted control of the Senate, with low levels of partisan polarization and deep factionalism in both parties, the 1980 elections inaugurated a period, now 44 years long, of intense partisan conflict over issues and constant competition for majority control of Congress. Aggressive individuals and, particularly among Republicans, organized factions pushed for full exploitation of parliamentary procedures to block the other party's initiatives and enact their own, often by forcing a stalemate to gain leverage over the other side. Partisan polarization, procedural tactics on the floor, and the never-ending battle for majority control pushed more decisions into party meetings and onto the shoulders of Senate leaders.

Ferocious competition for control of the Senate, House, and White House shaped the political context (Lee 2016; Gamm and Smith 2002a). After half a

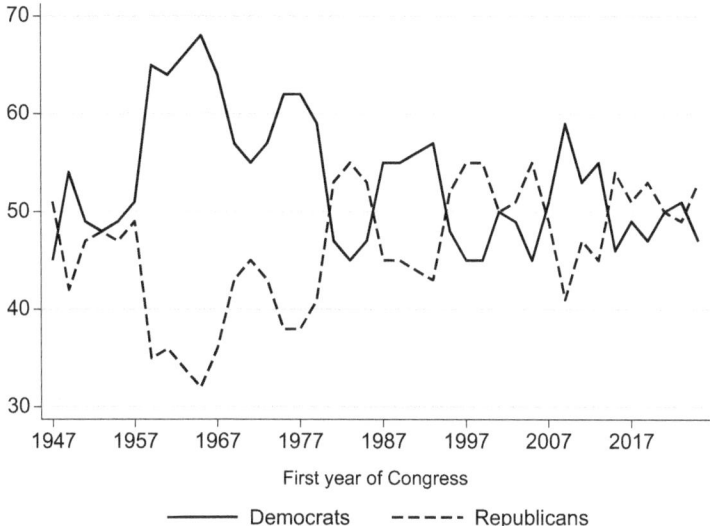

FIGURE 9.1 Size of parties, 1947–2025

century of Democratic dominance, senators experienced frequent changes of party control in the long era that started with the 1980 elections (Figure 9.1)—three shifts between 1981 and 2001, four between 2001 and 2003, and four between 2003 and 2025. Only for one six-month period (in the second half of 2009) did either party have as many as 60 seats, the cloture threshold, and the Democrats passed Obamacare during that period. Including that Congress, the 12 Democratic majorities averaged 53.6 seats and the 14 Republican majorities averaged 52.9 seats. Neither party controlled the Senate for more than four consecutive Congresses in this era. The mean number of Congresses in which a party held a majority was less than three—shorter than a senator's term. Uncertainty about majority control became senators' normal condition for an exceptionally long period of time. With few exceptions, senators serving in this period experienced minority party status and the lack of control over floor and committee agendas that came with it. Legislative strategies have been geared toward maintaining or gaining a Senate majority, and more party resources were devoted to public relations and fundraising.

Associated with the competition for control of the national policymaking institutions were major changes in the campaign finance and media environments (Sinclair 2006) that encouraged partisanship and electoral competitiveness. The cost of campaigns and the flow of money through outside organizations made incumbent senators more vulnerable to effective challengers and increased the incentives for the Senate parties to bolster their campaign committee efforts. At the same time, the rise of more partisan outlets on radio, television, and online, coupled with the demise of newspapers and network news, altered how voters received their news and how party elites communicated with them. Perhaps in response to all of these developments, the number of genuine independent voters fell as the proportion of Americans identifying with one of the two parties increased. The political environment became sharply partisan, and the resources engaged in influencing election outcomes climbed exponentially.

Partisan Polarization

While continuing to struggle with individualism, Senate leaders in the 1980s and 1990s appealed to their party colleagues to harmonize differences. Those appeals became more successful as each party became less heterogeneous in policy preferences, as partisan battles erupted over fiscal policy and social issues, as Republicans and Democrats routinely and fiercely fought for control of the Senate, and as senators became convinced that party discipline on the floor was critical to winning elections. The range of issues consumed by partisan conflict widened. The size of government and taxation were longtime partisan issues and remained so in these years. The new feature of the party agenda was the rise of social issues. Nearly absent, at least as partisan issues, until the late 1970s, social issues—abortion, school prayer, guns, LGBTQ rights, family structure, religious freedom, immigration—came to define both parties in subsequent decades (Claasen 1973; Smith 1981; Hare and Poole 2014). The conflict extended to judicial nominations in the 1990s and the early twenty-first century.

The parties grew sharply polarized in this period. In the 1970s and 1980s, Republicans picked up southern seats, lost their moderate and liberal members in the Northeast and Midwest, and nominated more conservative candidates elsewhere. In 1981, eight Republican senators, all conservative, represented states of the old Confederacy, up from none in 1961 and four in 1971. The number of southern Republicans then doubled again over the next 40 years. In 2021, southern senators were overwhelmingly Republican, most of them located on the conservative side of the party. As the Republican party grew increasingly conservative, the number of moderate and conservative voices in the Democratic conference went into a steady decline. Ideologically, the parties lurched apart.

A common way to demonstrate the polarization of the Senate parties is to consider the aggregate pattern of senators' roll-call voting decisions. Figure 9.2 illustrates the overall pattern. The solid line represents the difference between the two parties in mean liberal-conservative scores. The full scale runs from −1.0 to 1.0, so the difference of over 0.9 near the end of the period represents almost half of the scale. The upward trend is plain to see, but the sharp increase in the 2010s is worth special notice. The voting patterns reflect what comes to the floor for a vote, which is a product of several factors, including the agenda-setting tactics of the majority party, the proposals offered by leaders and rank-and-file senators, and obstructionist tactics and responses to them. In 2021–22, due to minority obstruction, a majority of votes were cast on nominations and

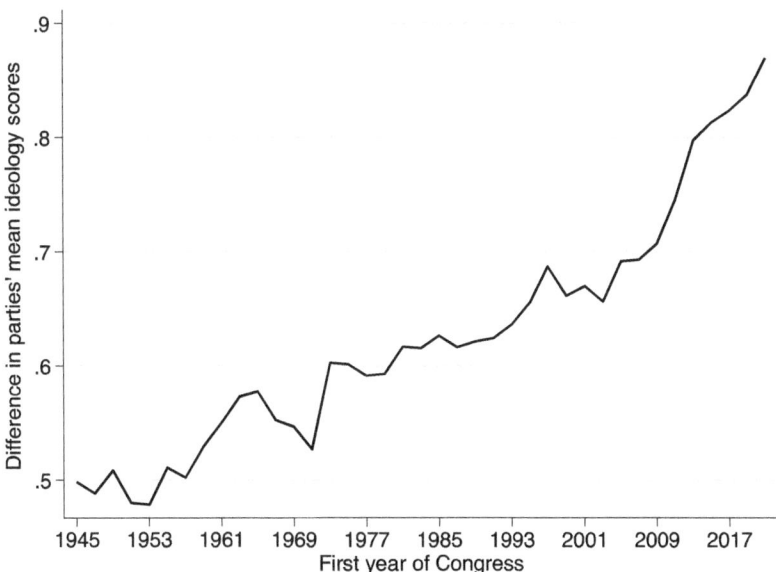

FIGURE 9.2 Party polarization in the Senate, 1945–2019
Source: https://voteview.com/articles/party_polarization. Difference in the mean DW-NOMINATE score for the two parties.

cloture motions related to nominations. Taken together, policy preferences and legislative strategies have yielded a strong pattern of deepening partisan polarization.

The aggregate patterns in the figure mask the fact that average Republican scores shifted farther right than Democratic scores shifted to the left. In fact, Republican leaders Howard Baker (R, Tenn.) and Robert Dole (R, Kans.) found their party moving to the right of them. By the 1990s, Dole and his whip, Alan Simpson (R, Wyo.), were held in suspicion by more conservative colleagues. Many of these insurgent Republicans had recently arrived in the Senate from service in the House, where they supported the uncompromising, partisan strategies of Newt Gingrich (Daschle 2007, 12; Theriault and Rohde 2011; Theriault 2013). Trent Lott (R, Miss.), Jim DeMint (R, S.C.), and Rick Santorum (R, Pa.) were central to the group of former House members who viewed themselves as revolutionaries and intended to sharpen the partisan edge to their party's legislative and political strategies. About the same time, a number of Republicans with a record of working with Democrats—William Cohen (R, Maine), Nancy Kassebaum (R, Kans.), Robert Packwood (R, Ore.) —retired from the Senate (Loomis 2019, 122). Lott's election as floor leader in 1996 represented a victory of aggressive ideologues over the pragmatists who had led the party since the 1950s (Lott 2005, 117–18; Daschle 2007, 12; Simpson 2007, 8, 34; Loomis 2019, 116). Lott had been House Republican whip for eight years before his election to the Senate in 1988, during which time he became closely associated with Gingrich and his "Conservative Opportunity Society." In the Senate, the strategies of Lott's faction took root among Republicans and were pursued even more rigorously by Lott's successors, Bill Frist (R, Tenn.) and Mitch McConnell.

Factionalism is represented in the uptick in both parties' standard deviations in the 2010s (data not shown). This is a product of the opposition of the most conservative Republicans and most liberal Democrats to the few legislative measures that represented a compromise between the two highly polarized parties.[11] That is, while the distance between the party means was increasing, there were occasions on which the more extreme senators refused to go along with the rest of their parties. These sometimes-defiant senators contributed to the widening distance between the parties' mean scores. At times, the renegades represented a serious problem for floor leaders trying to find majorities and control their parties' messages.

Factions, Ambition, and Electing Leaders

A strong floor leader in this era possessed energy, intelligence, interpersonal skills, public relations skills, good judgment, and creative ideas about how to pursue the policy and electoral goals of the party (Campbell 2019; Smith 2019). High expectations helped to make a record of service to the party—as whip or as chair of a major committee, the campaign committee, or the policy committee—a necessary condition for election as party leader. But the ability to pursue a multifaceted party strategy has been central to leadership contests. In 1988, public relations was the primary issue in Byrd stepping down as Democratic leader and the election of George Mitchell (D, Maine).[12] Mitchell's retirement in 1994 led to a contest between Tom Daschle (D, S.Dak.) and Christopher Dodd (D, Conn.) that focused on whether Daschle would be sufficiently aggressive as a strategist for the minority party.[13] Similar concerns on the other side of the aisle were central to Lott beating Simpson (R, Wyo.) to become Republican whip in 1995 (Simpson 2007, 34), followed

---

[11] In the Congresses of the 2010s, conservative senators Tom Coburn (R, Okla.), Ted Cruz (R, Tex.), Mike Lee (R, Utah), Rand Paul (R, Ky.), James Risch (R, Idaho), and Pat Toomey (R, Pa.) frequently voted against the rest of their party. During the same period, liberal senators Tammy Baldwin (D, Wisc.), Cory Booker (D, N.J.), Kamala Harris (D, Calif.), Mazie Hirono (D, Hawaii), Ed Markey (D, Mass.), Bernie Sanders (D, Vt.), and Elizabeth Warren (D, Mass.) broke from their party more often than other Democrats.

[12] While Byrd stepped down voluntarily in late 1988, he had wanted to remain leader. Mitchell reports that Byrd asked him to drop out of the race, believing that Mitchell could not win and that Byrd would be reelected once Mitchell's supporters swung to him. The conversation, Mitchell notes, "was one of the most intense and difficult of my Senate career" (Mitchell 2015, 160–61).

[13] Carroll J. Doherty, "Daschle, Dodd Fight to Stand Out in Senate Democrats' Race," *CQ Magazine*, Nov. 26, 1994, 3393; "Daschle Faces Tough Challenge in Sculpting Stronger Party," *CQ Magazine*, Dec. 3, 1994, 3436.

the next year by Lott's succession to floor leader.[14] And Schumer's promotion to leader over Dick Durbin (D, Ill.) in 2016 resulted from Schumer's success in leading the campaign committee and public relations "war room" in previous Congresses.

In most, but not all, leadership contests, factional conflict over party strategy was involved. The individualism of the 1970s continued into the 1980s and 1990s, taking on strongly ideological and partisan coloration.[15] If the parties were not yet fully effective teams, individuals and small groups of senators could exploit Senate rules and practices (Ehrenhalt 1982; Sinclair 1989; Smith 1989; Oleszek and Oleszek 2019). A succession of senators—perhaps most famously, Jesse Helms (R, N.C.), Jim McClure (R, Idaho), Howard Metzenbaum (D, Ohio), and Jim DeMint (R, S.C.)—seemed to revel in their ability to obstruct floor action and force leaders to anticipate their moves (Simpson 2007, 8). The "Steering Committee," which formed in the mid-1970s and was led primarily by McClure into the 1980s and later by Jeff Sessions (R, Ala.) and DeMint, was comprised of more than a dozen conservative Republicans who pooled resources to hire staff to facilitate their work. Motivated by the strategies of counterparts in the House, particularly Representatives Bob Walker (R, Pa.) and Newt Gingrich (R, Ga.), the group pressed for action on conservative legislation and often pursued floor strategies without the cooperation of Republican floor leaders (Bailey 1988, 75–76; Mitchell 2007, 22). Steering committee members' assertive partisanship generated filibusters, threatened filibusters, and produced holds, often in ways that reflected poorly on the influence of their own party's floor leader. Republican floor leaders of the 1980s and 1990s struggled mightily to manage the affairs of their caucus under these conditions, with leaders often pursuing strongly partisan tactics to avoid appearing to be timid and out of touch with their colleagues.

A major triumph of this conservative faction was Lott's ascendancy in party ranks—his election as conference secretary in 1993, as whip in 1995, and as leader in 1996.[16] As Lott explained, he was backed by the most conservative Republicans, including several Gingrich allies who had moved from the House to the Senate: "I could rely on a tight, conservative clique of relatively young senators and former representatives—some who preceded me to the upper

---

[14] Jackie Koszcuk, "Lott Trying to Elbow Simpson Out of Majority Whip Post," *CQ Magazine,* Nov. 26, 1994, 3396; Jackie Kosczuk and Alissa J. Rubin, "With Lott Victory, Senate GOP Chooses a Bolder Approach," *CQ Magazine,* Dec. 3, 1994, 3437.

[15] Individualism and decentralization are the dominant themes of a collection of scholarly essays on congressional leadership published in 1981 (Mackaman 1981) and again in 1992 (Hertzke and Peters 1992). Daschle (2003, 77) notes the metaphors used by leaders of the 1980s and 1990s to describe the individualism of the Senate: George Mitchell referred to the Senate as "a collection of 'independent contractors,'" Byron Dorgan referred to his colleagues as "one hundred bad habits," and Daschle said that his job "is like loading frogs into a wheelbarrow." Lott used the most common phrase, "herding cats," in the title of his own autobiographical account of his leadership years.

[16] Richard Cohen, "Seismic Power Shift in the Senate," *National Journal,* May 17, 1996.

chamber, some who arrived with me, some who soon followed," Lott (2005, 117–18) recalled. "We were conservative, we were hungry, and we intended to make a difference and to eventually capture the leadership." Lott's conservative faction persuaded the Republican conference to adopt a six-year term limit for elected party leaders, except the floor leader and president pro tempore, and for committee chairs. While the idea was borrowed from House conservatives, their immediate concerns were to remove moderate Mark Hatfield (R, Ore.) as Appropriations chair and to free up more leadership posts for conservative senators. Once in place, the term-limit rule was maintained in subsequent Congresses. The result has been regular turnover in, and more frequent contests for, lesser leadership posts—assistant floor leader (whip), conference chair and vice chair, and chairs of the policy and campaign committees.

In the late twentieth and early twenty-first centuries, Senate Democrats did not experience factionalism as deep as the Republicans did (Mitchell 2007, 22). White southern conservatives—who had been the foundation of the Democratic caucus since the party's organization in the 1820s and 1830s and who remained a formidable bloc into the 1970s—had largely disappeared from party ranks by the 1980s, some seats taken by moderate Democrats but the largest share taken by conservative Republicans. Moderate Democrats formed the Senate New Democratic Coalition (SNDC) in 2000, after a similar group formed in the House in 1997, and initially challenged liberals on a few issues. Just after the 2000 elections, an aide to Daschle described the major groups within the party as the New Democrats, progressives, women, and committee leaders (Hanson 2019, 165), none of which were as potent a force as Lott's backers in the Republican conference. Within a few years, the New Democrats faded as a recognized faction.

While the Democrats did not adopt term limits for party leaders or committee chairs, they dramatically increased the number of leadership positions. For a full century, dating back to the time of Arthur Pue Gorman, the Democrats had distilled leadership into a single position: their floor leader served simultaneously as chair of the caucus, chair of the steering committee, and chair of the policy committee. This changed with Mitchell's election as floor leader in late 1988, when he named Daschle co-chair of the policy committee and Daniel Inouye (D, Hawaii) chair of the steering committee, the body responsible for committee assignments (Daschle 2009, 2; Pope, Paone, and Saffold 2009, 19–20). When Daschle became leader in 1995, he established separate communications and outreach chairmanships as well as the position of assistant floor leader. Harry Reid (D, Nev.) created a new elective post, vice chair of the conference, in late 2006 to reward Schumer for his service as campaign chair.[17] Then, in 2017, Schumer created the position of "assistant leader," separate from the whip position, to retain Patty Murray (D, Wash.), conference secretary for the

[17] Carl Hulse, "G.O.P. in House Gears Up for New Leadership Fight," *New York Times*, Nov. 15, 2006, A24.

last decade, in a leadership position. By 2023, a total of 12 Democrats held elective or appointive positions in party leadership, up from three in 1988—when there had been just the leader, the whip, and the caucus secretary.

Party Developments

The increasingly intense partisan polarization and unrelenting competition for majority control had a palpable effect on legislators. As Daschle, the Democratic floor leader, wrote in 2003, just after the Congress in which the two Senate parties started at a 50–50 tie, "We have arrived at a time in our culture where the alignment of politics, of power, of ideologies, and of beliefs is arrayed so incredibly evenly that, while the visions and views of one group or another may be a universe apart, only the narrowest of margins separates them" (Daschle 2003, 2–3). The resulting conflict and incivility even infected leaders who had long taken pride in maintaining a level of legislative professionalism and preserving Senate traditions (Packwood 2007, 50). Lott wrote his party leaders about the need to go to "war" in 2002 to win back a Senate majority; in 2005, Reid named his public relations push a "war room" (Annis 2019, 222).[18]

As time passed, strategies to fully exploit parliamentary rules in the interest of the party were more likely to win the support of nearly all members of a party conference. Policy stalemate, created by frequent divided party control of the House, Senate, and presidency and the Senate's own rules, sharply reduced the incentives for legislators to dedicate their time to legislating. Campaigning, fundraising, and public relations became higher priorities and were more fully coordinated by top leaders. Floor leaders assumed responsibility for guiding party strategies, working for good election outcomes for their parties' candidates, and managing a burgeoning support staff. Within each party, the desire to enhance the party's effectiveness in the legislative and electoral arenas encouraged innovation. One party's innovations motivated responses by the other party, which, over time, generated party organizations of size and complexity without any precedent in Senate history.

MANAGING THE PARTY

By the time Baker became majority leader in 1981, leaders recognized that individualism and the demise of deference to senior committee leaders during the 1960s and 1970s required that they involve more senators in meaningful discussions of party strategy, which encompassed policy priorities, public relations, and floor tactics. Their colleagues demanded it. Abby Saffold, who served

---

[18] Richard L. Berke, "Lott Takes Parting Shot on Eve of Senate Power Shift," *New York Times*, June 3, 2001, A22; Philip Shenon, "Lott Steps Aside, Making a Pledge of Cooperation," *New York Times*, June 8, 2001, A23.

as the Democrats' secretary for the majority under Byrd and Mitchell, described Mitchell's experience: "If he consulted them seven times the previous week but didn't consult them this week on something they cared about, then he wasn't being consultative" (Pope, Paone, and Saffold 2009, 19). At the same time, leaders needed to coordinate committee activity and resources to realize the goals of their caucus. The challenge was to give everyone a voice in party deliberations, keep committee leaders working cooperatively with the leadership, and avoid individual initiatives that undermined party objectives. A "more of everything" approach—more meetings for the floor leader with committee leaders, task forces, and conferences, as well as stronger connections between committee staff and the leader's staff—was the result. These developments required careful scheduling of the leader's time and an expansion of the leader's staff.

Venues and Leaders

Party venues multiplied in this era and did so largely at the direction of the floor leaders. The initiative was usually taken by minority leaders, who created retreats, conference meetings, and task forces in an effort to lift spirits and unify the party, respond to demands for change in party strategy, address public image challenges, and create more opportunities for rank-and-file senators and some factions to have a voice in developing conference priorities. The Republicans of the mid-twentieth century took the lead and then the Democrats followed after losing a Senate majority in the 1980 elections. The effect of these innovations was to shift more responsibility for deciding legislative strategy from committees to party leadership.

Republicans took the lead in holding *party retreats*, which started in 1978 when the party was in the minority and without the presidency. These retreats, especially in early years, included some governors and House members. The first Democratic retreat was held in 1981. Minority Leader Byrd responded to the frustrations of his fellow Democrats that year after they suffered legislative defeats at the hands of President Ronald Reagan and the new Republican Senate majority.[19] Retreats were held over weekends at resorts or large hotels at which senators and their families could socialize in off-hours. Republicans held their early retreats in sessions open to the media, but Democrats started and continued with closed sessions. Retreat sessions often included outside policy experts and political consultants and, among Democrats, were so well-received that Mitchell and Daschle held them twice a year (Daschle 2009, 4).

---

[19] David S. Broder, "Senate Democrats Invited to Parley on Party Politics," *Washington Post*, July 24, 1981, A10; Martin Tolchin, "Democrats Assail Military Program: On Weekend Retreat, Senators Criticize Reagan's Missile Proposals as 'Political,'" *New York Times*, Oct. 4, 1981, 40.

Majority Leader Robert Dole (R, Kans.) and Minority Leader Robert Byrd (D, W.Va.), conferring with President Ronald Reagan in the Cabinet Room of the White House in 1985. Bill Fitz-Patrick—White House via Consolidated News Photos/Newscom

As Republicans assumed majority status in 1981, they continued their *weekly luncheons* for all members of the party conference, held under the auspices of their policy committee, a practice dating back to the 1950s. Byrd and the Democrats began holding their own luncheons, also under the auspices of their policy committee, only after becoming the minority party in the aftermath of the 1980 elections (Davidson, Oleszek, and Davis 1982, 24; Bailey 1988, 103; Scott and Wyatt 2019, 92). Daschle's appointment as co-chair of the policy committee in 1989 led him to start weekly sessions that began as roundtable seminars on major issues, often with outside experts, and all Democrats were usually welcome to attend (Pope, Paone, and Saffold 2009, 20). For both parties, these weekly meetings were, and continue to be, the primary place that floor leaders vet strategies and mobilize support for issues before the Senate. Along with senators, only a handful of leadership staff attend the luncheons. The parties frequently have a guest or two, often an administration official for the party holding the presidency.[20]

---

[20] Byrd also began to use the Democratic policy committee in 1981, but eventually discontinued regular meetings. Policy committee meetings restarted in 1989 after George Mitchell replaced Byrd as leader and Tom Daschle was appointed co-chairman.

Once in the majority in 1981, Baker met with a *"chairmen's committee"* regularly, usually after his weekly meeting with the president at the White House, to report on the meeting, learn of developments in committees, and set priorities in moving legislation to the floor.[21] Baker had started this practice with ranking minority members a few years earlier. He added a freshman and a sophomore senator to every meeting to give junior senators an introduction to the strategic challenges he faced.[22] Baker and his successors held these sessions just before the party lunches or later in the week (Miller 1986, 80; Bailey 1988, 97–98; Baker 2007, 8; McCluney 2008, 4; McConnell and Brownell 2019, 105–7). Democratic leaders, dating back to McFarland in 1951, had been holding regular meetings with committee chairmen or ranking members, and Byrd and his successors continued the practice, either before the Tuesday luncheons or on another day (Daschle 2009, 3, 6; Pope, Paone, and Saffold 2009, 19; Hanson 2019, 158).

Upon becoming Republican minority leader in 1977, Baker appointed several *task forces*—groups of a half dozen or more party colleagues—as a means of crafting policy proposals and rallying party support for them. Dole and Lott rarely appointed task forces. Frist appointed task forces in areas in which he and other Republicans wanted to pull together multi-committee proposals and advertise the party's activity, but McConnell, who placed strategy in his own hands, appointed only a few. In 1981, after the Democrats became a Senate minority, Byrd created task forces on several issues (Davidson, Oleszek, and Davis 1982, 24; Davidson 1985, 237; Bailey 1988, 103). At first, the recommendations of task forces were reviewed by Byrd's policy committee.[23] Subsequent leaders used task forces from time to time, but with less fanfare, as leaders' central role in setting legislative strategy was taken for granted. Reid ended the long run of task forces for the Democrats in favor of giving committee chairs a more central role (Reid 2008, 138). Thus, for both parties, the task force era phased out in the 2010s.

For a floor leader who sees nearly all of their colleagues on the floor every day there are floor votes, the need for more formal meetings is not obvious. For the Democrats, a regular *leadership meeting* did not happen until after the 1994 elections, when the party lost its majority status and Daschle was elected floor leader to replace the retiring Mitchell. Through the late 1980s, under Byrd and his predecessors, the leader had chaired the conference, policy committee, and steering committee, so the leader and the whip were the only top leaders and they could meet informally at will. Mitchell, who created committee co-chairs, did not organize regular meetings of these party leaders. But Daschle scheduled weekly leadership meetings of his larger set of leaders (Daschle 2003, 82),

[21] Irwin B. Arieff, "Under Baker's Leadership Senate Republicans Maintain Unprecedented Voting Unity," *CQ Weekly Report*, Sept. 12, 1981, 1747.

[22] Martin Tolchin, "Howard Baker: Trying to Tame an Unruly Senate," *New York Times Magazine*, Mar. 28, 1982, 74. Surely unknown to Baker, McFarland also included one or two junior senators in his meetings with committee chairs in 1951 and 1952.

[23] Phil Gailey, "From Majority Leader to Minority Leader," *New York Times*, Mar. 9, 1982, A20.

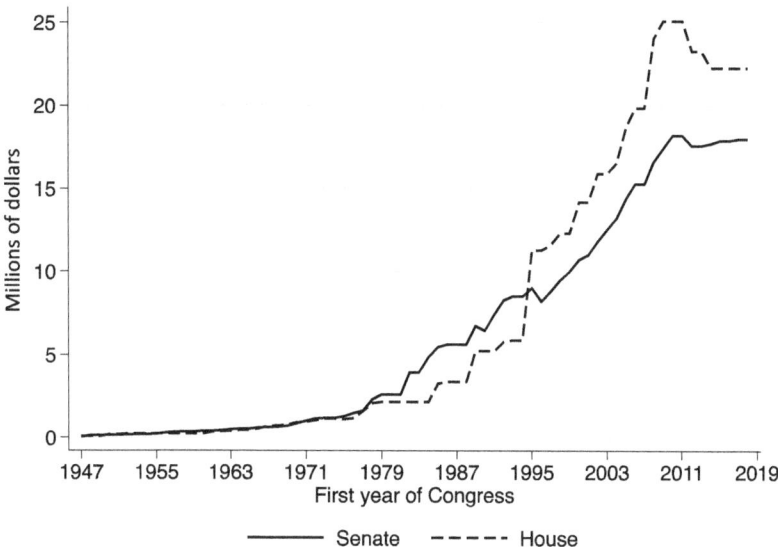

FIGURE 9.3 Appropriations for party offices, in millions of dollars, House and Senate, 1947–2018

a practice his successors have continued. Republicans took a different path. Baker and Dole met frequently but irregularly with other leaders. Lott chose to meet almost daily with a handpicked "Council of Trent" comprised of his strongest allies who backed him in leadership contests and some of whom held leadership posts themselves (Lott 2005, 125). Frist had weekly meetings with other elected and appointed leaders, as did McConnell, who often also named another senator as "counsel" to the leadership who would attend his leadership meetings (McConnell and Brownell 2019, 55). These sessions typically focused on the legislative plans for the week and often involved gaining a consensus among leaders before the Tuesday luncheons, giving McConnell a stronger hand in guiding discussions of strategy at the luncheons.

Party Staff

While leaders' attentiveness to staffing matters varied, a common thread in personal accounts of floor leaders' operations is the importance of talented staff and, usually implicitly, of the growth of the staff of both the floor leaders and the party committees.[24] Scheduling in this era grew increasingly difficult, as leaders grappled with the demands of senators, rising obstructionism, and a large

---

[24] Dole, for example, paid less attention to staffing matters than most other recent leaders: see interview with Al Lehn, Office of the Minority Leader, Dec. 5, 1990, with the authors.

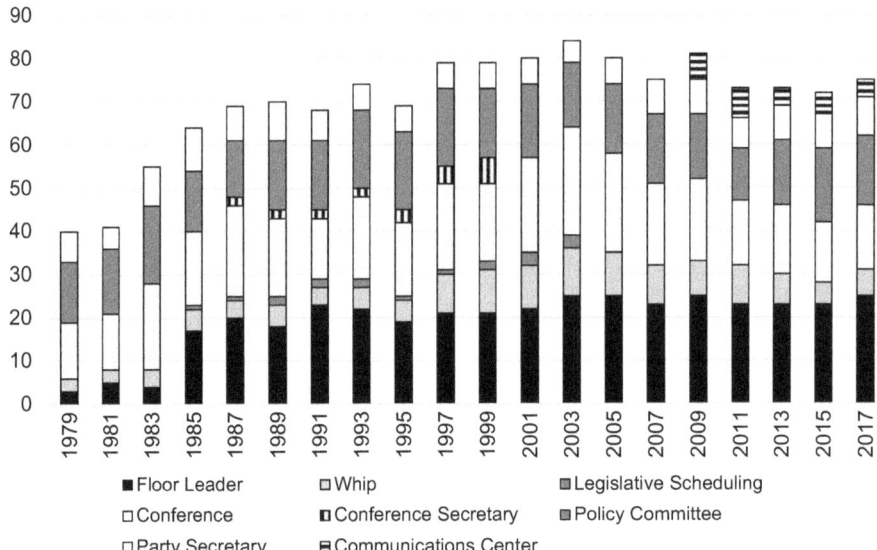

FIGURE 9.4 Number of Republican staff members by party office, 1979–2017
Source: Congressional Directories.

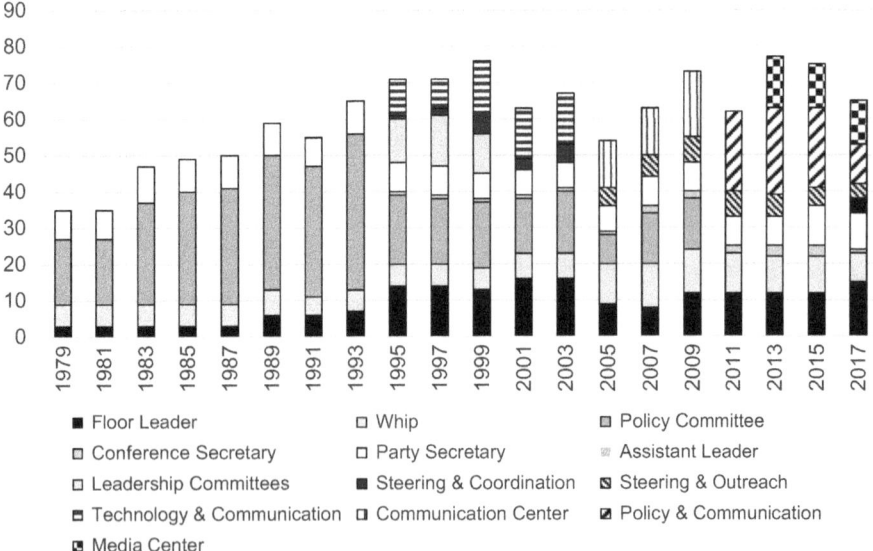

FIGURE 9.5 Number of Democratic staff members by party office, 1979–2017
Source: Congressional Directories.

legislative agenda. Consequently, responding to scheduling requests from committee chairs and the administration, managing holds, and implementing strategies that served the party's interests required a degree of intelligence gathering and coordination that no leader could manage effectively by himself. In addition to addressing scheduling needs, staff were also expanded to improve the parties' ability to formulate policy proposals and pursue public relations strategies.

Funding for party staff in legislative appropriations bills went equally to the two parties and began an upward trajectory in the 1970s.[25] In Figure 9.3, we show total spending for party staff in both houses of Congress. In the four decades after 1977, when Byrd and Baker became floor leaders, spending on party staff climbed at a rapid pace under both Democratic and Republican majorities. In fact, there was a near-linear increase in party funding that represented a rate of increase 10 times the rate of the previous three decades (not adjusted for inflation). Since 2010, conflicts over spending and multi-year budget deals flattened spending on most line items in the legislative appropriations bills.

The trend in the number of party staff differs from the trend in spending. The number of staff for the two parties grew in the 1980s but leveled off in the 1990s, as we show in Figures 9.4 and 9.5.[26] In the 1980s, Dole quadrupled the number of staff in the Republican leader's office over his predecessor, and Byrd increased the size of the policy committee staff by about 50 percent. Spending on non-salary expenses, including technology and office operations, and increases in average salaries, both of which reflect the expanding duties of party staff, account for the rise in spending after the number of staff leveled off.

Republicans expanded party staff within the previously established structure of a policy committee staff, conference staff, leader staff, and party secretary staff. Under Baker in the late 1970s and early 1980s, the policy and conference staffs grew, which was followed by an expansion of the floor leader's staff under Dole in the mid-1980s (Dove 2008, 21; McCluney 2008, 23). McConnell elaborated on the structure by creating the Republican communications center staff in 2007, to bring the number of staff under the leader's direct supervision to about 30 and total party staff to about 70, up from four and 36, respectively, in 1981.

Democrats, under Byrd's leadership in the 1980s, continued their established pattern of centralized control of party staff by placing most party staff in the policy committee he chaired; there was no separate conference staff. The election of Mitchell as Byrd's successor began a period of two decades of elaboration and experimentation with the Democratic party committees (Kelly 1995; Crespin, Madonna, Sievert, and Ament-Stone 2015). By the early 2010s, the Democratic staff was housed in several locations: the leader's office, a media center, and party secretary operations, all supervised by the floor leader; a whip's staff of 10 or 12 people; a policy and communications center

---

[25] In the House, the two parties receive equal funds with the important exception of the speaker's office, which is the primary reason House spending on party offices is shown to be larger than Senate spending.
[26] Excluded from these counts are the campaign staffs of the two parties.

staff that was run by a senator appointed by the leader; and a small steering and outreach committee staff under the supervision of a chair appointed by the leader. There have been few changes in the years since.

Campaign Committees

This is an era in which the floor leaders assumed personal responsibility for strategies to gain or maintain majority party status. The competitiveness of the parties became clear when the Republicans took majority control of the Senate after the 1980 elections, an event that appeared to clarify the importance of party strategy for winning elections. Senator Richard Lugar (R, Ind.) noted in 1987 that Byrd, Baker, and Dole, leaders of both parties in the 1980s, "have taken on an additional role of fundraising, of party management, of sort of the grand strategy of how you get 51 votes."[27] This included more travel to attend campaign and fundraising events, the creation of political action committees ("leadership PACs"), and more involvement in the activities of the party campaign committees.

The parties' campaign operations—the Democratic senatorial campaign committee (DSCC) and the national Republican senatorial committee (NRSC) —were transformed in this period in response to major changes in the electoral landscape. In the years since 1980, the committees' efforts became more fully focused on winning and maintaining a Senate majority. While they continued to transfer funds to state parties and directed private campaign contributions to candidates, they engaged in more fundraising of their own in order to assist incumbents in close contests, defeat opposition party incumbents, and win open seats. The campaign chairs and their staffs sought to maximize their direct contributions to candidates' campaigns and engage in even more independent spending (Kolodny 1998, 146–95). The committees increased the money raised from tens of millions of dollars in the 1980s and 1990s to nearly $180 million for the Democrats in the 2018 election cycle.[28]

Campaign committee staffs, which are funded with private money raised by the committees, grew in size to enable the committees to expand training and technical services provided to candidates. By 2000, the Republicans' staff had grown to 75 and the Democrats' to over 50, up from a dozen staff members in the early 1980s (Baumer and Gold 2010, 14–15), exceeding the number of all other party staff combined. With the NRCC leading the way in the 1990s, the committees hired consulting firms, often run by former campaign committee staffers, to provide services to their candidates.

Experience as campaign committee chairs gained new importance in both parties. As the post became a steppingstone to other leadership positions, the

[27] Brookings Institution interviews with senators, June 2, 1987, 16 (transcript in possession of the authors).

[28] www.opensecrets.org.

Democratic leader was often heavily lobbied about the appointment of the campaign committee chair, and factional fights for the chairmanship were common among Republicans, whose chair was elected by the caucus (Kolodny 1998, 166–67). Before becoming floor leaders, Republicans McConnell and Frist and Democrats Mitchell and Schumer served as campaign committee chairs, as did Bob Packwood (R, Ore.), Donald Nickles (R, Okla.), John Cornyn (R, Tex.), Wendell Ford (D, Ky.), and Patty Murray (D, Wash.), all of whom were later elected to other party leadership posts.[29]

Beyond playing a role in selecting campaign committee chairs, floor leaders have always had a significant place in their parties' campaign efforts. They planned the legislative schedule and floor tactics to the advantage of colleagues running for reelection, made themselves available for fundraising and other events in Washington and across the country, made some efforts to recruit good candidates, and frequently directed donors to support candidates in need. Beginning in the 1980s, leaders had political action committees through which they directed contributions to the campaigns of their parties' Senate candidates. While these "leadership PAC" contributions represented a small part of most Senate campaigns, they could be important at early stages of a campaign. Over the 1990s and into the new century, leaders' campaign activities intensified, and the fundraising and spending of their PACs expanded (Hernnson 2009).

A noteworthy event in 2004 reflected the deepening involvement of leaders in candidate recruitment and the creation of obligations to the party that superseded a recognized bipartisan norm. A longstanding norm guiding floor leaders' campaign activities was that the two leaders did not campaign against each other. After all, it was observed, they needed to work together daily on the floor, which required a degree of deference and civility. That year, however, Republican majority leader Frist flew to South Dakota to appear at events with John Thune, who was running for the Senate seat held by Democratic leader Tom Daschle. Notifying Daschle in advance, Frist explained that he felt obligated to Thune because he had recruited Thune to run for the Senate two years earlier, and Frist promised that he would be campaigning for Thune rather than against Daschle. Frist also directed substantial campaign donations from his PAC and other contributors to Thune. Most observers, and Daschle, viewed Frist's South Dakota visit and funding efforts as a clear violation of the norm and a sign of intensifying partisanship in the Senate.[30]

[29] Mitchell stands out for acquiring the admiration of his colleagues for his success as campaign chair in the 1980s and then serving as a model for other senators: see David S. Cloud, "Turned Tables on Defeats: Resiliency, Persistence Helped New Leader Rise," *CQ Weekly Report*, Dec. 3, 1988, 3434–36.
[30] Sheryl Gay Stoberg, "The 2004 Campaign: The Senate; Daschle Has Race on His Hands and Interloper on His Turf," *New York Times*, May 23, 2004, 20; Paul Kane, "Daschle Is Frist's Top Priority," *Roll Call*, Apr. 19, 2004. For Frist's perspective, see Annis 2019, 221.

The Supreme Court's 2010 *Citizens United* decision and subsequent Federal Election Commission rulings stimulated major changes in the financing of congressional campaigns and spurred floor leaders to expand their role in the campaign finance game. These rulings enabled unlimited fundraising and spending by organizations independent of campaigns, leading to the creation of super PACs that outspent all party and regulated political organizations combined by 2016. Leaders of both parties endorsed super PACs that supported Senate candidates they favored with independent spending that could match the spending of the Senate campaign committees. Over the decade following *Citizens United*, the Senate parties' super PACs spent hundreds of millions of dollars. In the 2018 election cycle alone, the Senate Democrats' main super PAC spent about $160 million and the Republicans' super PAC spent about $130 million.[31] Overall, super PAC spending advantaged Republicans.[32] The result is that nearly all senators elected in the late 2010s received funding from super PACs under the direction of the floor leaders.

Committee Assignments

The influence of floor leaders over committee assignments increased in this period. On the Democratic side, seniority had not been a firm rule in making committee assignments for many years, and floor leaders continued to be proactive in seeking to influence committee assignments in a way that rewarded allies and party service.[33] In 1989 Mitchell expanded the jurisdiction of the steering committee beyond committee assignments to include developing better relations with outside groups important to the party and appointed Inouye its chair. With Mitchell's move, another Democrat gained status as a party leader, and the committee gained a year-round responsibility to mobilize interest group support.

The most important developments occurred in the Republican conference, which at the turn of the twenty-first century still adhered to seniority in allocating assignments, with automatic decision rules in cases of ties, severely limiting the influence of party leaders.[34] The Republican committee on committees, which once made all assignments to the standing committees, had long ago become a shadow of its former self. In late 2004, however, power shifted decisively to the leader. Just after the Republican majority won four more Senate seats and George W. Bush was reelected president, Frist was eager to

---

[31] www.opensecrets.org.

[32] www.opensecrets.org/news/reports/a-decade-under-citizens-united#super-pacs; see also Baker 2019, 263, on Reid's creation of Senate Majority PAC in response to the rise of conservative super PACs.

[33] David M. Herszenhorn and Carl Hulse, "Among Democrats' Leadership Questions: What to Do with Lieberman?" *New York Times*, Nov. 7, 2008, A26.

[34] Phil Weaver, "Briefing," *New York Times*, Jan. 10, 1983, A16.

advance a large legislative agenda. Thus he proposed and the conference adopted a rule that "the leader shall have the authority to appoint half of all vacancies of each 'A' committee, and where there are an odd number of vacancies the leader appoints half plus one of all vacancies" (Republican Conference Rule V).[35] The "A" committees are the 13 most important committees—and the leader appoints all Republicans for the important Committee on the Budget.[36] Frist intended the rule to increase his ability to shape the composition of committees, particularly when the party was in the majority, and guide the construction of legislation to meet the party's needs.[37]

McConnell inherited Frist's committee assignment authority and exercised it aggressively. Still, he chafed at the limits on his office. "I'm told the Democratic leader has more power. I don't have much. I can put people on committees but I can't take them off," McConnell observed. "They're elected chairmen by the members of the committee which are ratified by the conference. A strong tradition of seniority. I can't think of a single time we haven't just given the chairmanship to the most senior person. So my job, except for scheduling, is basically all carrot and no stick."[38] Yet, in the vantage of any of his Republican predecessors, McConnell's powers were now vast.

MANAGING THE FLOOR

Party-driven agendas and strategies—as opposed to agendas and strategies designed by committees, chairs, and bill managers—came to dominate Senate floor action during this period. Moves and countermoves by the parties propelled floor leaders to a more central role. Floor leaders continued to maintain firm control over floor proceedings for their parties, assisted by their whips and bill managers, but they became more deeply involved in the substance of policymaking and designing party strategies for both individual legislative measures and whole Congresses. By the 1990s, floor leaders' offices, just a few yards from the Senate floor, became command centers.

Between 1981 and 2001, the individualism and factionalism that was associated with more holds and obstructionism in the 1970s became more deeply partisan. Although at first the minority leader tended to be a bystander to the obstructive moves of his party colleagues, obstruction from someone in the minority party became the norm for significant legislation. Over time, though, the obstruction was more frequently orchestrated by the minority leader.

---

[35] Carl Hulse, "Larger Majorities and the Itch to Stretch G.O.P. Muscles," *New York Times*, Nov. 19, 2004, A18; "Editor's Notebook: Power Trap," *CQ Magazine*, Nov. 20, 2004, 2716.

[36] Judy Schneider, "Committee Assignment Process in the U.S. Senate: Democratic and Republican Party Procedures," Congressional Research Service, Nov. 3, 2006, RL30743, 5.

[37] Allison Stevens, "More Power to the Senate's Majority Leader," *CQ Magazine*, Nov. 6, 2004, 2605–6; David M. Herszenhorn and Carl Hulse, "Among Democrats' Leadership Questions: What to Do with Lieberman?" *New York Times*, Nov. 7, 2008, A26.

[38] Authors' interview with Senator Mitch McConnell, Jan. 9, 2018.

Denying the majority party legislative successes became a routine minority strategy. As McConnell observed, the "60-vote Senate" had arrived by the 2010s: action on nearly any bill of significance would require a three-fifths majority to gain cloture and pass (Smith 2014, 224).

Floor Strategy and the Senate Syndrome

As the Republicans took majority control in 1981, obstructionism—in the form of filibusters, threatened filibusters, and holds—already was considered a serious problem. A series of actions had been taken in the 1970s in response (Sinclair 1989; Smith 1989). The 1974 Budget Act enabled simple majorities to avoid filibusters on budget resolutions and reconciliation measures. The 1975 change in Rule XXII, reducing the threshold for cloture from two-thirds of senators voting to three-fifths of all senators, was negotiated by Mansfield—although liberals, but not Mansfield, had been demanding a lower cloture threshold. Moves to prevent post-cloture filibusters in 1977 and 1979 were spearheaded by Byrd (Smith 2014, 129–37). When the issue of televising Senate floor sessions came to a head in 1986, Dole and Byrd proposed rules that would have limited debate on motions to proceed, allowed a germaneness requirement for amendments to be imposed by a three-fifths majority, and reduced post-cloture debate to 30 hours. Only the 30-hour limit on post-cloture debate was adopted (Smith 2014, 146).

Obstructionism began to change character when party control of the Senate flipped after the 1986 elections, giving Democrats control of both houses in Reagan's last two years as president. Byrd, the Democratic majority leader, attempted to expedite action on the Democrats' agenda by tightening up floor proceedings. He instituted early morning votes to get senators to the Capitol, limited roll-call votes to the 15 minutes provided in the rules, and lengthened daily sessions. Appearing to be influenced by the rise of organized conservatives in the House, Republicans began to block action on the Democrats' major legislative initiatives. Byrd responded by trying and failing to overcome Republican obstruction by using Morning Hour to avoid filibusters on motions to proceed and, when that did not work, by forcing Republicans to conduct an old-fashioned filibuster. The result was an uptick in the number of filibusters and cloture motions, with Dole, the minority leader, voting against cloture 29 times on 37 motions (Smith 2014, 153–70). Holds continued to plague majority leaders seeking to clear legislation with their colleagues and the minority leader. Senators' ability to threaten to object to unanimous consent requests to bring up legislation, particularly legislation of only modest importance, had to be taken seriously. Dozens of holds could be placed on measures at any one time and hundreds over the course of a Congress, consuming the attention of at least two staff members working under the party secretary and making planning for everyday floor activity a constant struggle (Greene 2007, 20–21; Mitchell 2008, 19; Mitchell 2010, 11–12; Howard and Roberts 2015).

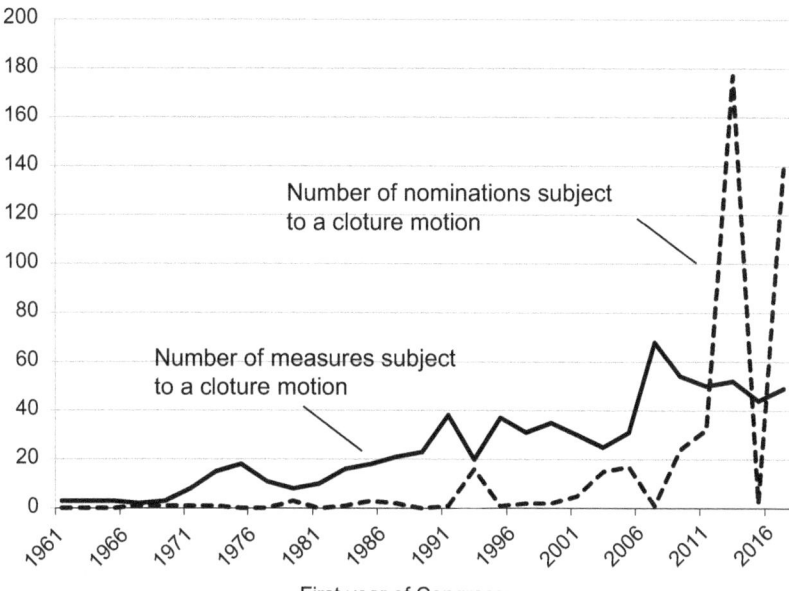

FIGURE 9.6 Number of measures and nominations subject to cloture motions, 1961–2020

Source: https://www.senate.gov/legislative/cloture/clotureCounts.htm.

Although obstructionism was already becoming partisan by the late 1980s, these tactics became qualitatively different in the early 1990s. For Dole, the minority leader, filibustering initially had been a matter of bill-by-bill tactics and seldom defined a medium- or long-term strategy (Packwood 2007, 39). That changed at the end of the George H. W. Bush administration and the beginning of the Clinton administration. As Figure 9.6 shows, the Republican minority filibustered a record 38 measures in 1991–92, threatened filibusters on others, and began filibustering the motion to proceed much more frequently. In 1993 and 1994, Republicans blocked action on a record number of presidential nominations and worked to prevent the Democrats from establishing a good legislative record (Mitchell 2008, 16). Denying the majority party legislative successes and even the opportunity to bring a bill to the floor became a routine minority strategy, often implemented by Dole, which Byrd considered a "basic change" in minority behavior.[39]

[39] Janet Hook, "Extensive Reform Proposals Cook on the Front Burner," *CQ Weekly Online*, June 6, 1992, 1579.

Majority Leader Trent Lott (R, Miss.), Former Majority Leader Howard Baker (R, Tenn.), and Minority Leader Tom Daschle (D, S.Dak.) in 1998.
Photo by Heather Moore, U.S. Senate Historical Office

The Republican obstructionism in the early 1990s established a new plateau in obstructionism, as Figure 9.6 suggests. After the 1994 elections, when Republicans gained a new majority, they faced a comparable level of obstruction from Democrats, which generated talk among Republicans about forcing a change in the threshold for cloture from 60 to a simple majority. Republican leader Lott complained about the minority Democrats engaging in a "rolling filibuster on every issue" and "planned gridlock"; Daschle complained that the Republicans refused to negotiate and had a quick trigger with cloture (Smith 2014, 178–80). Taking a lesson from the Republicans of the early 1990s, Daschle, who became Democratic leader in 1995, forced Republicans to vote repeatedly on amendments providing for a minimum wage hike, a strategy that drew public attention to a popular cause and persuaded his party colleagues that he could play hardball. Of course, nongermane amendments had been used as a tactic by minority senators for many decades. What distinguished Daschle's effort was his persistence in orchestrating this process as floor leader. The response of majority leaders Dole and Lott, from the mid-1990s through the early 2000s, was to invoke cloture earlier in the process in order to impose a germaneness requirement and, at times, to fill the amendment tree and negotiate over what amendments would be allowed (Hanson 2019, 160–62).

By 2007, when McConnell became the new leader of a Republican caucus now back in the minority, he made obstruction to acquire concessions for the minority the standard operating procedure. In his first month in the post,

McConnell asked for and received the trust of his party colleagues to pursue this strategy and proved its utility, setting a pattern of regular obstruction that would last until the Republicans gained a majority in the 2014 elections.[40] This was not McConnell acting in isolation. He was building on years of precedents and he was responding to his conference. In part, McConnell was trying to stay ahead of the parade—other Republicans showed an eagerness to filibuster when he didn't take the lead. His effort was redoubled when Democrat Barack Obama became president in 2009. McConnell recognized that allowing bipartisan support for major legislation would benefit the majority Democrats and the president; legislative failure would be blamed on them (Dyche 2009, 206–8; MacGillis 2014, 85–109).

During the 1990s, then increasingly in the twenty-first century, majority leaders adopted innovations in floor tactics to overcome the obstruction that challenged them so frequently (Smith 2014). They employed an array of tactics—filing cloture motions even before a filibuster had materialized or before seeking unanimous consent to proceed to consideration of a bill; filling the amendment tree, which precluded amendments by the minority; finding ways to combine bills in order to circumvent filibusters and to reserve time for other measures; negotiating "side-by-side" amendments, allowing votes on opposing amendments in order to gain unanimous consent to proceed; transforming tax bills into reconciliation measures, which could not be filibustered and were protected from nongermane amendments; agreeing to 60-vote requirements for amendments or bills in unanimous consent agreements; and forging agreements directly with House leadership rather than sending bills to conference, which avoided obstruction on conference committee reports. This obstruct-and-restrict pattern—the "Senate syndrome"—became the norm after McConnell became minority leader in 2007, pursued by him and by Democratic leaders Reid and Schumer, with each side playing its respective roles in the majority and minority (Smith 2014). As Figure 9.7 indicates, this "Senate syndrome" is associated with historically high levels of minority obstruction, placing ever more responsibility for party strategy in the hands of the floor leaders.

Minority obstruction and the majority response have altered the character of floor decision-making in a fundamental way. This is illustrated by the radical decline in the number of amendments receiving a roll-call vote of some kind—to adopt, to table, and so on—on the floor, a place where a senator could count on having an opportunity to make a mark on the substance of legislation. As shown in Figure 9.7, the number of amendments dropped to a couple of dozens in some years of the 2010s and beyond.

Floor leaders are central to this process. On regular legislation, minority leaders refuse unanimous consent to act on bills and force cloture votes that

---

[40] "McConnell Takes the Inside Track," *Roll Call*, Jan. 30, 2007; Emily Pierce, "McConnell Tactic Roils 9/11 Debate," *Roll Call*, Mar. 7, 2007.

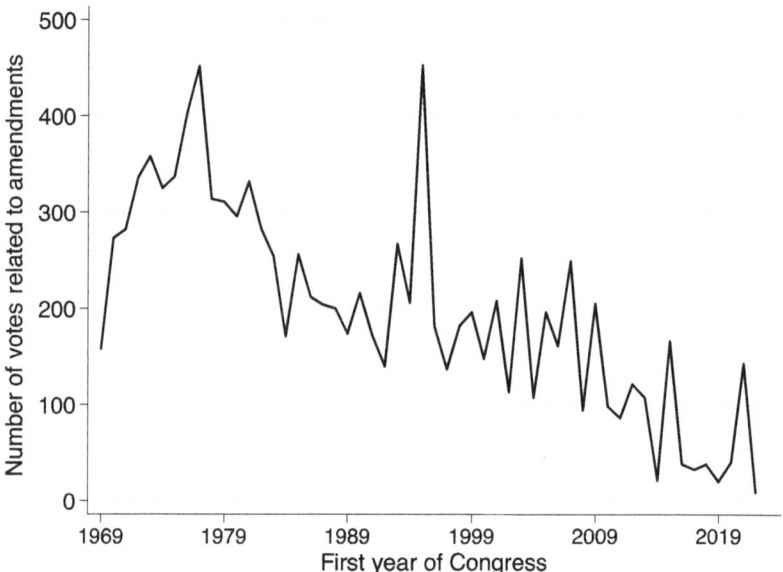

FIGURE 9.7 Number of floor votes related to amendments, by year, 1969–2022

Source: Jason Roberts, David Rohde, and Michael H. Crespin. Political Institutions and Public Choice Senate Roll-Call Database. Retrieved from https://ou.edu/carlalbertcenter/research/pipc-votes/.

often are unsuccessful. Majority leaders block minority amendments by filling the amendment tree or negotiating unanimous consent agreements that limit amendments to a handful that are sure to lose. More outcomes are the product of off-the-floor negotiations, often spearheaded by floor leaders, who then protect the outcome of those negotiations with agreements that limit further amendments in open floor consideration of the measure.

Leaders and the Nuclear Option

Until the twenty-first century, floor leaders were cautious about reform of the Senate's cloture rule. Democrats Johnson and Byrd blocked significant changes to a rule that was ardently defended by the southern wing of the party. Mansfield relented to reducing the threshold for cloture to a three-fifths majority of all senators, but held off more radical change and retained the two-thirds threshold for changes in the standing rules. Most Democratic leaders also were pessimistic about the prospects of meaningful reform and concerned that the time devoted to the issue would divert attention away from policy issues that were more important to their party. Republican leaders, serving in the minority or representing the conservative view that blocking new government initiatives is a high priority for conservatives, also opposed most filibuster reform.

The issue of filibuster reform had long created special problems for Democratic leaders. Dating back at least to the 1930s, liberal Democrats had sought to reduce the cloture threshold—most insisted on simple-majority cloture—to overcome filibusters led by southern Democrats or Republicans that prevented Senate passage of civil rights and other legislation. Because Rule XXII, the cloture rule, provided that a two-thirds majority is required to invoke cloture on a measure changing the rules, the minority party could easily block a change in the rule. Reformers argued that this self-reinforcing feature of the rule violated the Constitution's provision (Art. I, Sec. 5) empowering the Senate to make its own rules. They argued that, because the Senate decided other matters by a simple majority (like passing a bill), a simple majority must be allowed to consider rules changes and a supermajority obstacle cannot be placed in the way. They urged leaders to support a point of order to settle the matter. Democratic leaders steadily resisted through the 1980s.

But Mitchell, who lamented that obstruction had become a matter of Republican party strategy in the 1990s, proposed other reforms. He advocated a rule that limited debate on motions to proceed to two hours and other changes to reduce delay in floor proceedings, but was unsuccessful in effecting these changes. In 2002 Lott, the Republican leader—urged to use a point of order to impose simple-majority cloture to facilitate passage of Republican measures—predicted that the minority Democrats would "go nuclear" in response, meaning that they would bring the Senate to a crawl by objecting to every unanimous consent request. The term "nuclear option" was born, although it quickly came to be used to describe the parliamentary move of the majority (Smith 2014, 200–201).

Presidential nominations for lifetime appointments to the federal courts proved to be the issue that brought a dramatic rupture to Senate practice. The obstruction of action on nominations came to a near-breaking point in 2005 when minority Democrats under Harry Reid blocked votes on a set of judicial nominations made by Republican president George W. Bush. The majority leader, Bill Frist, threatened the nuclear option but found his effort blocked by the "Gang of 14," a group of seven Democrats and seven Republicans who refused to support simple-majority cloture for judicial nominations and agreed to move forward on some of the nominees.

In 2013, with the minority Republicans obstructing action on a set of Obama's judicial nominees, Reid used a point of order, backed by his party's Senate majority, to impose simple-majority cloture on all nominations except Supreme Court nominations. No "gang" of senators seeking to avoid such a radical step emerged to block the move. McConnell, who as majority leader subsequently blocked action on Obama's Supreme Court nomination in 2016, "went nuclear" in 2017 to impose simple-majority cloture for Supreme Court nominations and gain confirmation for President Donald Trump's first Supreme Court nominee. McConnell used the same tool again in 2019 to reduce the post-cloture debate time from 30 hours to two hours on most executive branch and all district court nominations, which further limited the ability of a minority to slow Senate proceedings. Notably, neither Reid nor McConnell used the constitutional argument to gain a vote on a change in Rule XXII. Instead, they imposed a new cloture threshold through a point of order, overturning a ruling of the chair by a simple majority, without argument. The point of order was contrary to the plain meaning of the rule, which was left untouched. Reid justified his move by observing the importance of acting on nominations and the harm that party-orchestrated obstruction was doing to the process. McConnell merely observed that the Democrats had done it first.

DETERIORATING PERSONAL RELATIONS

It is hardly surprising that, as longstanding norms of restraint and civility were crushed under the weight of partisan conflict, personal relations between the floor leaders suffered serious strains. Respect for the institution and for each other were the essential features of relations between majority and minority leaders until the time of Frist, McConnell, and Reid (Daschle 2003; Mitchell 2015, 164). The mutual understanding between the leaders of the two parties included, most prominently and explicitly, a promise not to surprise each other in their parliamentary moves on the floor and to maintain a courteous and respectful timbre to their rhetoric about each other (Baker 2007, 10; Daschle 2007, 13; Dole 2009, 4; Pope, Paone, and Saffold 2009, 16–18; Mitchell 2010, 12–13). Good relations between the two leaders facilitated communication with each other about floor scheduling and allowed both floor leaders to keep lines of communication open to all senators, whose forbearance was required to acquire unanimous consent for most floor activity. Through the 1990s, with few exceptions, leaders observed this practice and took pride in doing so. Even in the case of Daschle and Lott, with the latter considering himself a revolutionary when he became leader in 1996, a "hotline" between their offices allowed them to consult frequently without the participation of others or the knowledge of staff (Lott 2005, 178; Rae 2019, 200). This relationship survived intensifying partisanship in the 1980s, 1990s, and early 2000s—even when the Senate was divided 50–50 in 2001, when Lott and Daschle negotiated a power-sharing arrangement (Daschle 2003, 33–35; Hanson 2019; Rae 2019).

Nevertheless, partisan sensitivities to developments on the floor were already growing as Republicans assumed majority control of the Senate in 1981. Byrd, as Democratic majority leader in 1977–80, had used points of order to crack down on post-cloture filibusters and to limit the places at which filibusters could develop. These moves involved parliamentary rulings by the presiding officer, who followed the advice of the parliamentarian. When Republicans assumed the majority in 1981, Baker, the Republican leader, replaced the parliamentarian, Murray Zweben, with Robert Dove, Zweben's assistant. It was the first time the parliamentarian was fired and replaced for any reason; it was partisan and done by the majority leader. Dove's promotion did not end the matter. In 1987, when Byrd was again majority leader, he replaced Dove with Alan Frumin, Dove's assistant, and Dove moved to Minority Leader Dole's leadership office. Dove moved back to the parliamentarian's post after the Republicans regained majority status in 1995. Remarkably, Dove was removed from office by Trent Lott in 2001 because of his recommended rulings on sensitive budget measures (Ritchie 2000; Dove 2008, 9–11; Smith 2014, 156–58). But Dove's departure in 2001 led to a truce between the party leaders, at least on that issue. Dove was replaced by Frumin, who then served under leaders of both parties—Lott, Daschle, Frist, Reid, and McConnell—as party control of the Senate swung back and forth. After Frumin retired in 2012, he was succeeded by Elizabeth MacDonough, who continued to serve under majority leaders of both parties.

Relations between the two floor leaders deteriorated in late 2001 after the 9/11 crisis and was reflected in public and personal criticism of each other (Sinclair 2006). The Daschle-Lott relationship became testy after the Senate passed a wave of bipartisan measures in response to the 9/11 attacks and the Republicans, then in the minority and eager to undermine the Democratic majority's reputation for effectiveness, chose to block action on an economic stimulus bill (Daschle 2003, 140). The relationship between Frist, who had campaigned for Daschle's opponent in 2004, and Reid was strained from the start (Reid 2008, 195–217). McConnell, replacing Frist, began on much better terms with Reid but chose not to continue weekly meetings with his counterpart. Their relationship became distinctly cold in the 2010s, in part because McConnell blocked action on a flood insurance measure important to Reid and then Reid's super PAC ran ads against McConnell (MacGillis 2014, 123; Baker 2019, 262–63).[41] Partisan interests came to overwhelm a commitment to maintaining an effective, businesslike relationship.

The McConnell-Schumer relationship appears to have been more civil and constructive, but was sometimes strained and even acrimonious.[42] Negotiations between the two leaders occasionally occurred alongside threats and counterthreats. The confirmation vote for Justice Amy Coney Barrett in 2020 was unusually contentious, since it took place eight days before a presidential election and four years after the Republican majority, led by McConnell, had refused to consider the nomination of Merrick Garland, nominated by President Obama to the Supreme Court. Days before the vote, in October

---

[41] Julie Hirschfeld Davis and Laura Litvan, "Reid Friendship with McConnell Helps Bridge Gap Between Parties," *Bloomberg Business*, Jan. 18, 2011; Steven T. Dennis, "Reid: Gentleman's Agreement Is Broken," *Roll Call*, Oct. 18, 2011; Martin Kady II, "The War Against Mitch McConnell," *Politico*, Apr. 20, 2010.

[42] Alexander Bolton, "McConnell and Schumer's Relationship Shredded After Court Brawl," *The Hill*, Oct. 28, 2020; Alexander Bolton, "Schumer Discussed Tense Relationship with McConnell," *The Hill*, May 1, 2020; John Bresnahan, Burgess Everett, and Marianne LeVine, "Schumer-McConnell Clash Defines the Impeachment Trial," *Politico*, Feb. 5, 2019.

2020, Schumer attempted, with little success, to slow down the Senate's proceedings, arguing that Republicans were doing great damage to Senate norms. But McConnell had no patience for Democratic efforts to derail the nomination. "Every new escalation, every new step, every new shattered precedent, every one of them was initiated over there," McConnell argued, referring to the Democratic side of the aisle. "I hope our colleague from New York is happy with what he's built. I hope he's happy with where his ingenuity has gotten the Senate." Schumer, of course, rejected McConnell's apportioning of blame. "We have just heard a tit-for-tat convoluted version of history that the majority leader uses to justify steering the Senate toward one of the lowest moments in its history," Schumer retorted. "The Republicans, as we all know, as the nation knows, are running the most partisan, most hypocritical, least legitimate process in the history of Supreme Court nominations ... Might does not make right."[43]

BUILDING COALITIONS

Since 1980, floor leaders' roles as coalition leaders within their parties have been transformed. With small majority parties in most Congresses in the 1981–2024 era, party discipline became more important in both parties. Successful minority obstruction to gain leverage with the majority party or to simply prevent the majority party from winning legislative battles required that few or no minority party senators support cloture. To avoid an embarrassing loss on salient amendments or procedural motions and to avoid the blame for legislative stalemate, the majority party had to keep its members united. Floor leaders who for decades often left legislative priorities, the details of legislation, and efforts to build floor majorities to committee leaders—assisting them when requested and taking a more central role only occasionally—became the architects of legislative agendas, the overseers of legislative drafting, and chief coalition builders for their parties on most major legislation. Even in foreign policy, floor leaders were taking a significant role in establishing party positions and negotiating the most important congressional action (Smith 1994). For major issues, the model of committee-oriented policymaking was replaced by party-oriented policymaking in the late twentieth century.

This transformation occurred incrementally and without significant changes in the formal powers of floor leaders, either in party or chamber rules. For the most part, it occurred as leaders devised strategies to meet changing circumstances, meeting their party colleagues' expectations in doing so and thrusting them into a more central role in the legislative affairs of the Senate. Leaders often explicitly wed their centrality to legislating to their responsibility to gain

---

[43] Nicholas Fandos, "Democrats Try to Shut Down Senate, Seeking to Stain Barrett Confirmation," *New York Times*, Oct. 23, 2020.

or maintain majority party status for their party.[44] Their activities were facilitated by the addition of staff and the addition of venues through which party strategy could be formulated, aired, and adjusted, but it was primarily a matter of floor leaders adapting to intensifying partisan competition and floor maneuvers that committee leaders were unable to manage.

The centrality of the leaders to coalition building was quite apparent with Daschle and Lott in the late 1990s.[45] Daschle and Lott began to adopt agendas that emphasized issues that united their parties and divided the opposition (Hanson 2019, 151, 168). This was not a new tactic, but it became a standard strategy. The approach reduced opportunities for bipartisan legislative work and increased the share of floor action that was characterized by partisan rhetoric. When both parties pursued this strategy, the leaders were bound to clash over legislative priorities, partisan rhetoric was sharpened, the minority was likely to be obstructionist, and opportunities for bipartisan work were limited. Even policy proposals with broad support in both parties were blocked by the minority at times to avoid handing the majority party a legislative victory.

The Whips and Whip Organizations

The role of the whips in managing the floor has always depended on the interest of the whip in serving as a stand-in for the floor leader and the leader's need to have someone take floor duties. Many, but not all, whips have taken the title of "assistant leader" to reflect their role.[46] The uncertainty of floor activity, particularly the possibility that rogue senators would make unexpected motions, start a filibuster, or otherwise disrupt the plans of the majority leader, increased the importance of carefully monitoring the floor. The party secretaries and other staff have nearly always been present. Since the 1960s, whips also acquired a role in marshaling and counting votes—a task previously assigned to bill managers, often assisted by the floor leader and party floor staff (Evans 2018).

On the Republican side, Baker gave his whip, Ted Stevens (R, Alaska), a regular turn at floor duties, which Stevens hoped would serve as a springboard to his own election as leader. Dole and Lott, in contrast, were not strong teammates—Lott defeated incumbent whip Alan Simpson (R, Wyo.), a close friend of Dole—so Lott spent more time on other whip activities than he did on the floor. As leaders, Lott and McConnell preferred to be present on the floor

---

[44] The priority given to party electoral interests in the legislative arena was particularly transparent in 1985 and 1986, just before Republicans lost their majority in the 1986 elections: see Andy Plattner, "Dole on the Job: Keeping the Senate Running," *CQ Weekly Report*, June 29, 1985, 1269, and Jacqueline Calmes, "Majority Leader Dole: Determined to Do It All," *CQ Weekly Report*, Sept. 6, 1986, 2075–79.

[45] Carroll J. Doherty, "A Study in Clashes and Contrasts," *CQ Weekly Report*, July 27, 1996, 2092.

[46] For a brief history of the use of the titles of whip and assistant leader, see McConnell and Brownell 2019, 187–89.

rather than turn over floor activity to their whips. Similarly, Democratic leaders Byrd and Mitchell covered the floor personally, with only modest dependence on their whips to handle routine activities on the floor. Whips Harry Reid (D, Nev.) and Dick Durbin (D, Ill.), on the other hand, dedicated themselves to floor activities and leaders Daschle, Reid, and Schumer were quite dependent on them to manage routine business for many hours (Reid 2008, 63; Baker 2019, 244; McConnell and Brownell 2019, 185–92).

For the Democrats, Alan Cranston (D, Calif.), who served as whip from 1977 until 1990, set a standard for intelligence gathering and head counts, conducting about two dozen whip counts a year. While his successor, Wendell Ford (D, Ky.), was less active, Reid and Durbin conducted whip counts frequently. Reid also expanded the whip office staff, who served primarily as liaisons to senators and their committee and personal staff and gathered information about sentiment within the party about floor agendas and strategies (Reid 2008, 63). When Durbin became whip in 2005, he found his role limited by the rising importance of public relations in shaping legislative tactics. Durbin remained a head counter, floor manager, and important liaison to the leadership for his party colleagues, but Schumer assumed responsibility for party messaging efforts.

On the Republican side, Dole did not rely on the whip for counting votes until 1995, when Lott became whip. For Lott, counting heads became a personal responsibility. He assumed this role as whip, shifting responsibility for head counts from the party secretary, and he kept this a personal responsibility once he was elected leader in 1996 (Lott 2005, 120–21; Lott 2007, 9–10). As whip under Frist, McConnell rejuvenated head-counting duties, a function that his whips—Jon Kyl (R, Ariz.), Cornyn, and John Thune (R, S.Dak.)—continued to perform (McConnell and Brownell 2019, 190).[47]

Tempered Centralization

The centralization of coalition-building activity in floor leaders was well underway by 2009, but the Obama health care legislation illustrates how far the process had moved away from committee-centered policymaking in both parties by then. Democratic leader Reid, consistent with his practice since becoming majority leader in 2007, had initially deferred to the two Senate committees with jurisdiction over health-care programs: the Committee on Health, Education, Labor, and Pensions (HELP) and the Committee on Finance. The HELP Committee bill was constructed and approved with little participation by minority Republicans, but Max Baucus (D, Mont.), chair of Finance, hoped to fashion a proposal with enough Republican support to

[47] Helen Dewar, "Wielding Power Behind the Scenes," *Washington Post*, July 9, 2001, A15; Niels Lesniewski, "John Thune's New Whip Office Staff Learning the Ropes and Getting to Work," *Roll Call*, Jan. 15, 2019.

overcome a Republican filibuster when the issue was on the floor. After long discussions between Baucus and committee Republicans, the Republicans abruptly ended negotiations, under pressure from the new Tea Party and guidance from Republican leader McConnell. Reid then took over and brought the two committee chairs, a few other Democrats, and administration representatives into his conference room to construct a bill that was brought to the floor (Baker 2019, 252–53). Responding to a pattern of Republican obstructionism, Reid took charge of the agenda and legislative strategy until 2015, when Democrats lost their majority. "Reid is still not willing to take any blame for the Senate's deterioration, something that veteran senators in both parties are willing to discuss," Paul Kane, the experienced Senate reporter for the *Washington Post*, later observed. "His last couple years as majority leader saw almost no major work done by Senate committees, with his leadership team in charge of every decision."[48]

Centralized construction of major policy proposals remained the norm under McConnell. In 2017, after Donald Trump was first elected president, a Republican majority with only 51 Senate seats sought to enact a major tax cut bill. McConnell took charge from the start. During committee deliberations, McConnell and four handpicked Finance Committee Republicans met in his conference room to discuss and guide committee developments. They regularly invited a few other Republicans into the discussions to inform them of developments, adjust the bill to address their concerns, and keep the party united. Last-minute changes to acquire the necessary votes were made at McConnell's direction. After the tax bill passed—as a reconciliation bill that could not be filibustered—McConnell, not the committee chair, gathered the Republicans he intended to name to the conference committee and gained their commitment to support the conference report before they were appointed by the Senate. "I pick the conferees. That's another thing that's really important: the leader gets to pick the conferees," McConnell recalled. "I had my conferees in here, and sat around the table, and I said to them, 'I want to ask each of you a question. I want you to answer it separately. Will you sign the conference report no matter what?' 'Yes.' 'Yes.' 'Yes.' 'Yes.' ... On a really important bill like that, you don't want to take chances." He directed the negotiations with the House, which were completed quickly, and the bill was enacted.[49] Nearly every Republican senator understood that McConnell was responsible for fashioning most major bills.[50] While the details varied from bill to bill, the central role of

---

[48] Paul Kane, "Harry Reid in Retirement: Railing Against Trump, Bemoaning a Broken Senate and Making Peace with Romney," *Washington Post*, Feb. 22, 2020.
[49] Account from authors' interview with Senator Mitch McConnell, Jan. 9, 2018.
[50] Benjamin Wallace-Wells, "The Republican Tax Bill and Mitch McConnell's Wonderful, Terrible Year," *The New Yorker*, Dec. 20, 2017; Seung Min Kim, "How McConnell Got a Win on Taxes," *Politico*, Dec. 2, 2017.

the leader's office in constructing omnibus spending bills and responses to the Covid-19 pandemic in 2019 and 2020 remained the same.

PUBLIC RELATIONS AND OUTREACH

Managing public relations was probably the last of their major functions that leaders fully recognized as their responsibility and tried to master. Beginning in the 1980s, the media and campaign landscape changed radically. The domination of the newspapers and three major television networks gave way to talk radio, cable television, and eventually the internet and social media. The result by the 2010s was a 24/7 news cycle and hyperpartisan networks and shows. Advertising by independent groups and super PACS, only loosely connected to candidates and the two major parties, added to the explosive growth of media efforts. This fractured media environment made it more difficult for congressional parties to get their messages heard through traditional press conferences, media appearances, and floor statements. For years, leaders like Mansfield, Scott, and Byrd expressed the view that committee leaders and other senators could take turns speaking for the party in the mass media. But competition for control of the Senate and their colleagues' demands for more effective messaging efforts motivated leaders to place greater emphasis on public relations.

Republican leaders Baker and Dole were not shy about making television appearances or interacting with reporters, but they were not aggressive. Rather, they responded to circumstances tactically, selectively making appearances on news programs and using their daily contact with Capitol Hill reporters to try to get their message out. The most regular exchange between floor leaders and reporters occurred in "dugout chatter" sessions, a continuation of a practice dating back to at least the 1940s, in which reporters met with Democratic and Republican leaders on the floor before daily sessions began.[51] Lott was considerably more skilled in media engagements and made more regular appearances on television programs (Rae 2019). Lott also worked harder to coordinate the legislative agenda and floor tactics of his party with the media message effort of party leaders (Evans and Oleszek 2001).

Byrd, who gave up regular press conferences when the Democrats fell into the minority in 1981, saw public relations duties as a chore, took the view that "the less I said within what was required of me, the better," and ended the dugout sessions (Scott and Wyatt 2019, 86, also 87–92).[52] Under pressure from colleagues, he started Saturday press conferences in 1982 and hired a former aide to President Carter to be director of communications for the policy

[51] Warren Weaver, Jr., "Dugout Chatter, a Senate Tradition," *New York Times*, Jan. 27, 1982, A20.

[52] Janet Hook, "The Byrd Years: Surviving in a Media Age Through Details and Diligence," *CQ Weekly Report*, Apr. 16, 1988, 976–78.

Minority Leader Tom Daschle (D, S.Dak.) speaks at a press conference in 1998. To the left of Daschle is newly elected Minority Whip Harry Reid (D, Nev.). To the right of Daschle is Barbara Mikulski (D, Md.), Democratic conference secretary. Other Democratic senators with party posts attended.

Ron Sachs—Consolidated News Photos/Newscom

committee.[53] Nevertheless, Byrd gained little attention on the television networks (Foote and Davis 1987). Following Byrd's decision to step down as leader in 1988, Democrats elected Mitchell and Daschle in succession with their media skills in mind. They returned to occasional dugout sessions and strengthened the communications staff and technology of the party. Daschle established the Democratic technology and communications committee, appointed Jay Rockefeller (D, W.Va.) as chair, allocated funding for television and satellite technology, and formed a "message team" to orchestrate the party's themes on the floor and in the media. He also held frequent "Daschle dugouts," press briefings around a table in a room off the Senate floor.[54] In the 2000s, leaders of both parties phased out dugout chatter and held more "stakeout" sessions, usually after Tuesday lunches. Stakeouts are brief press conferences held in the Ohio Clock corridor just off the Senate floor, a location where television cameras and electronic recording are allowed.[55]

---

[53] Phil Gailey, "From Majority Leader to Minority Leader," *New York Times,* Mar. 9, 1982, A20; Nadine Cohodas and Dale Tate, "Senate Democrats Re-Elect Byrd as Leader," *CQ Weekly Report,* Dec. 15, 1984, 3087–89.
[54] Daniel J. Parks, "An Unassuming Authority," *CQ Weekly Report,* May 26, 2001, 1213.
[55] Martin Paone, long-term Democratic floor aide and secretary of the Senate, and James Manley, communications director for Senator Harry Reid, personal communications, Mar. 2021. For

Just after taking over from Daschle in 2005, Reid went a step further in staffing a "war room" to provide quick responses to the Republicans, who controlled the White House and both houses of Congress. The war room was to coordinate the party's legislative and messaging strategies with the specific purpose of offering proposals on the floor that made the Republicans look inattentive to the needs of Americans while the Democrats were offering attractive alternatives (Reid 2008, 150; Annis 2019, 222). Reid, who spoke softly but had a sharp tongue, avoided media appearances himself and used the war room to encourage senators like Schumer to speak for the party (Baker 2019, 246).[56] Moreover, Reid encouraged the policy committee, headed by Byron Dorgan (D, N.Dak.) in 2007, to hold hearings and other public events to attract media attention to Democrats' critique of developments in the Republican administration.[57] In 2010, Reid gave Schumer control of communications and messaging operations in Schumer's capacity as chair of the new policy and communications committee.[58] After replacing Reid as leader following the 2016 elections, Schumer hired additional communications staff, including people experienced in presidential campaigns.[59] Schumer planned media campaigns for his party and made almost daily appearances with reporters.

Reid's war room motivated McConnell to greatly expand the Republican communications staff in 2007, just after replacing Frist as Republican leader. The new "communications center" was placed directly under the control of McConnell and his top staff and substantially increased the ability of the floor leader to personally coordinate legislative and public relations efforts for the party.[60] It contributed to the most centralized leadership operation for Senate Republicans since the time of Robert Taft in the first half of 1953—even more tightly managed than the traditionally centralized Democratic operation in the Senate.

The coordinated legislative-messaging efforts of the two parties contributed to intensified partisan conflict in the 2010s and 2020s. Public relations opportunities were given far more emphasis in leaders' calculations, so that claiming credit and attributing blame were planned before serious legislative efforts were given a chance to succeed. The sizable staffs poised to flood social media and the airwaves were activated before senators had time to resolve differences. Neither party in 2024 dared delay going public for fear of losing an edge in the public relations battle.

---

more background on communications efforts in the 1990s and early years of the new century, see Sinclair 2006, 265–83.

[56] Emily Pierce, "Reid Turns Messaging Over to Schumer, Stabenow," *Roll Call*, Nov. 15, 2010.

[57] Byron Dorgan, "Senate DPC's Role Expands as It Begins New Decade," *Roll Call*, Jan. 29, 2007.

[58] Carl Hulse, "In Wake of Losses, New Powers for a Political Master," *New York Times*, Nov. 21, 2010, 25; Jackie Kucinich, "Senate Democrats Unveil New Message Operation," *Roll Call*, Jan. 5, 2011; Emily Pierce, "For Durbin, Small Majority Means Whip Smart," *Roll Call*, Dec. 1, 2010.

[59] Niels Lesniewski, "Schumer Builds Press Team for Leader's Office," *Roll Call*, Jan. 4, 2017.

[60] Authors' interview with Senator Mitch McConnell, Jan. 9, 2018.

INTERMEDIARY WITH THE PRESIDENT

Presidents, from Reagan through Trump, were the dominant political forces in this era, continuing a long period of a strong presidency that commanded policymaking and public attention. Most of the time, presidents' policy agendas shaped the congressional agenda, and their media presence overshadowed media efforts on Capitol Hill. Leaders of the president's party continued to champion the president's program and consulted with the president weekly while Congress was in session (Smith 1994, 144–52).

Two factors shaped the relationship between Senate party leaders and the president: first, the frequency of divided party control of the White House and Senate, and, second, the deepening partisanship of the Senate. Every president in the 1981–2024 period except Donald Trump and Joe Biden experienced a Senate majority of the other party for at least one Congress. Since the late 1990s, the ideological gulf between the parties combined with public relations gamesmanship to make divided party control quite debilitating to legislative action. Even when the president's party controlled the Senate, minority obstruction proved a major challenge to action on controversial measures.

Perhaps the last concerted effort between a president and an opposition Senate leader to pass more than an isolated measure in this period occurred after Lott replaced Dole as majority leader in 1996, at a time that President Clinton was running for reelection. Lott wanted a solid legislative record for his Senate party colleagues who were also on the ballot. A Clinton aide approached Lott about the possibility of swift legislative action on a set of bills of modest policy significance. Agreement was reached—Lott called it a "backstairs arrangement"—and a wave of measures made it through Congress and to the president, to the chagrin of Dole, Clinton's opponent in the presidential contest (Lott 2005, 129–33; Rae 2019, 196–97). The relationship continued to be important when a large budget compromise was reached the next year (Lott 2005, 142–44).

In the 2000s, though, cooperation like this became a distant memory. Senate Democrats regularly obstructed Republican initiatives and appointments during the George W. Bush presidency. However, it was the Republicans, during the Obama presidency, who went further to obstruct a president and his Senate party than any previous minority in modern times. "The single most important thing we want to achieve is for President Obama to be a one-term president," McConnell, the Senate Republican minority leader, stated in 2010, just before the first midterm election. "Our single biggest political goal is to give our nominee for president the maximum opportunity to be successful … We need to work smarter than we did [in the mid-1990s], and not become the foil off which [President Obama] pivots."[61] In practice, this meant preventing significant legislative victories for the president's party, forcing the majority Democrats to rely on party-line votes to pass critical bills, and making the

---

[61] Andy Barr, "The GOP's No-Compromise Pledge," *Politico*, Oct. 28, 2010; Emily Pierce, "GOP Complains Reid Filing Cloture Too Often," *Roll Call*, Apr. 17, 2007; Glenn Kessler, "When Did McConnell Say He Wanted to Make Obama a 'One-Term President'?" *Washington Post*, Sept. 25, 2012; "After the Wave," *National Journal*, Oct. 25, 2010.

president's party appear either inept at governing or highly partisan. Although McConnell's statement lacked nuance, this same strategy was pursued by the minority Democrats under President Trump.

The united front that an opposition party maintained since the 1990s proved a source of frustration for presidents. It meant that presidents could not circumvent the opposition leader in the Senate to build bridges with factions whose support they often needed to overcome obstruction on their legislation. It also gave floor leaders some bargaining leverage with the president that they would not have had otherwise, forcing presidents to shrink their legislative agendas. Not surprisingly, personal relations between presidents and leaders of the opposite party grew more strained. Partisan rhetoric sharpened and intensified in the twenty-first century. Democratic leaders' relationships with Republican presidents Bush and Trump were "cool," "stormy," and even "acidic," and McConnell's relationship with Obama was at various times "frosty" or "frigid" (McConnell 2016; Baker 2019; Olezsek and Olezsek 2019).[62] Nevertheless, through the end of the Obama administration in 2017, presidents maintained civil relations with opposition Senate leaders. That changed with the Trump presidency, as Schumer's relationship with Trump bristled with hostility on both sides. Meetings between Trump and Democratic congressional leaders were few, and direct communication rarely constructive.

While the president's party leaders in the Senate usually worked to support presidential initiatives, the preeminent role of McConnell as his party's chief strategist put him in a position to fill voids that were created by President Trump's lack of attention to legislative matters. Not only did McConnell take the lead in designing the 2017 tax bill, but he successfully insisted that Trump nominate Judge Amy Coney Barrett to the Supreme Court in late 2020 following the death of Justice Ruth Bader Ginsburg. Barrett was McConnell's choice on the basis of her policy views, the desire to firm up the conservative majority on the Court, and his interest in generating enthusiasm for the party in its electoral base just before the election. "If Trump even thought of picking someone else," according to *Politico* reporters Burgess Everett and Marianne LeVine, "he needed to call McConnell and give him a chance to change the president's mind." Trump met with no other candidates and he announced Barrett's nomination eight days after the vacancy occurred.[63]

---

[62] Christi Parsons and Michael A. Memoli, "Obama, Mitch McConnell Start Anew to Warm Up Their Relationship," *Los Angeles Times*, Dec. 3, 2014; James R. Carroll, "The Obama–McConnell Cold War," *U.S. News*, June 22, 2016; Carl Hulse, "McConnell, With Majority at Risk, Turns to an Old Target: Obama," *New York Times*, May 12, 2020.

[63] Burgess Everett and Marianne LeVine, "How the Senate GOP's Right Turn Paved the Way for Barrett," *Politico*, Oct. 26, 2020; Paul Kane, "McConnell Says Barrett Nomination Helped Some Vulnerable GOP Incumbents, Gives Even Odds on Holding the Senate," *Washington Post*, Oct. 27, 2020; Carl Hulse, "How Mitch McConnell Delivered Justice Amy Coney Barrett's Rapid Confirmation," *New York Times*, Oct. 27, 2020.

CONCLUSION

The developments described in this chapter—escalating competition for partisan control of the Senate, more polarized parties, the rise of systematic party-motivated obstructionism—placed the two floor leaders squarely in the middle of action on all major legislation in the late twentieth and early twenty-first centuries. Factionalism and personal ambition continued to play a role in organizational innovations within the parties, but the overwhelming influence was party competition in the legislative and electoral arenas. Party competition drove the proliferation of party venues and committees, the expansion of party staffs, and the centralization of legislative and electoral strategies in the hands of floor leaders. Partisan competition drove a surprising degree of centralization in Senate policymaking.

Weakening factional divisions also played an important role in these years. The loss of liberal Republicans and the loss of an even larger number of conservative Democrats over the 1980s and 1990s facilitated unified party action. These developments motivated and enabled innovation in party organization. Improving the ability of the party to generate fresh policy proposals and to sell the party message to the public served both a party's interest in winning legislative battles and its interest in winning elections. As they were intended to do, these developments contributed to more disciplined and polarized parties.

The leader-led partisanship of the 2010s drew considerable commentary (Baker 2019; Shapiro 2018). Much of the commentary expressed frustration that supermajority rule in the Senate was more frequently generating gridlock than forcing compromise. As a conservative trying to lead colleagues who were willing to exploit Senate rules on their own, Republican leader Mitch McConnell took much of the blame. But both McConnell and Harry Reid expanded party staffs and enhanced the ability of the leadership offices to wage legislative and public relations war against each other in the 2010s (Smith 2017). In the 2020s, this chapter of Senate party development is not over.

These developments are consistent with political science arguments that partisan polarization and electoral competition motivate innovations in party organization and place top leaders in a more central place in the legislative and electoral efforts of their parties. Both factors—the degree of partisan polarization and the intensity of party competition for control of the Senate—shape the incentives for improving the capacity of parties to compete. What matters, too, we argue, is the cumulative character of the roles and resources of party leaders. Leaders and parties rarely give up resources that improve their ability to compete. The centralized leadership structures of 2025 reflect not only the intense partisan competition in the legislative and electoral arenas of the early decades of the twenty-first century but also the steady accumulation of leadership roles, committees, and staff since the late nineteenth century.

Former senator Barbara Mikulski (D, Md.) is seen with Amy Klobuchar (D, Minn.), Majority Leader Charles Schumer (D, N.Y.), and Minority Leader Mitch McConnell (R, Ky.), during a ceremony to name rooms on the Senate side of the U.S. Capitol after Mikulski and former senator Margaret Chase Smith (R, Maine), in June 2022.

IO

Conclusion

Looking over the broad sweep of Senate history, we have found that senators elaborated party organization and leadership in response to party competition in the legislative and electoral arenas. They adopted innovations as they were looking for an advantage, in organization and resources, that would allow them to win legislative battles and elections. Factional and entrepreneurial motivations often sparked proposals for change and gave direction to the kind of organizational arrangements adopted, but party competition propelled the most dramatic moments of institutional innovation in the Senate. It is *the other party*, we have witnessed, that is the primary obstacle to the achievement of the collective goals of a legislative party—and it is in competition with the other party that Senate caucuses first arose, then began, through the years, to articulate the institutions that came to define and organize the entire chamber.

SENATE PARTY DEVELOPMENT

Organizational innovation in Senate parties is not continuous. When it occurs, much of it is visible only to the closest observers of Senate politics. Innovation is time-consuming and causes rifts among senators and so has been most likely to occur when the short-term payoff, in terms of the goals of majority party control and winning legislative battles, is substantial. The payoff is likely to be greatest when party strength is close to parity: when party control may switch because the parties are of nearly equal strength, a party is most likely to look to its own organization, rules, or leadership to improve its competitiveness. A majority party's weakness in size or cohesiveness can stimulate innovation, as can fear of losing a Senate majority. For a minority party, the drive to overcome its limitations with more effective legislative and electoral strategies encourages innovations.

Our central theme has been that modern party leaders advance their parties' legislative and electoral goals by managing their party organization, coordinating party activities on the floor, serving as intermediaries with the president, building coalitions, and serving as party spokespersons. In Table 10.1, we indicate when party caucuses and steering committees emerged in the Senate, then, beginning with Arthur Pue Gorman, when Democratic floor leaders assumed responsibility to perform key functions for the party. We focus in this table on Democratic leaders, since Republicans lagged Democrats in creating the position of elected floor leader and in assigning significant powers to the position.

Our historical account has demonstrated the winding path taken by Senate parties to create formal organizations, acquire resources, and assign a variety of important tasks to elected or appointed leaders. Managing a few basic party activities—presiding over caucus meetings and naming members to caucus committees—was the responsibility of caucus chairs beginning in the mid-nineteenth century. With the creation of the Republican steering committee in the 1880s and 1890s, Republicans created a powerful model of collective leadership, which assumed responsibility for managing the party and assembling policy coalitions. For the Democrats, Gorman invented the position of floor leader in 1890, then subsequently took charge of floor battles on important occasions. After he was elected chair in 1913, John Kern instantly became an even more regular coalition leader, a task still shared with bill managers, and was the primary, but not sole, intermediary with the president. Joe Robinson performed all of these functions but was more proactive than his predecessors in articulating his party's position. With Robinson, a fully modern floor leader emerged. Republicans exhibited a similar pattern of development, beginning with Jacob Gallinger in 1913, at first appearing to mimic the Democrats. In 1924, Charles Curtis became the first Republican conference chair chosen for reasons other than seniority.

We have emphasized throughout this book that legislative and electoral goals are usually pursued in tandem. Leaders are expected to devise strategies when tradeoffs between these goals are required. In the early twenty-first century, with the expansion of party organizations and staff, floor leaders have more direct control over the resources to implement those strategies than ever before. Placing supervisory responsibility for these functions in the hands of floor leaders allows Senate caucuses to more efficiently initiate and coordinate party activities.

Through our account of major developments in Senate parties, we have identified several institutional innovations that have been either ignored or given insufficient attention in past accounts. These include:

- the prominent role of presiding officers during the first decades of the nineteenth century;
- the rise of party caucuses in the 1840s, spurred by Henry Clay and the Whigs, as a regular institution to manage legislative business;

TABLE 10.1 *Functions of Senate leaders*

Democratic Caucus	Party Management	Coalition Leader	Floor Management	Party Spokesperson	Intermediary with President
Caucuses form, select chairs (1841–79)	✓				
Steering committees (1870s–1913)	✓				
Gorman to Martin (1890–1913)	✓	✓			
Kern (1913–17)	✓	✓	✓	✓	
Martin (1917–19)	✓	✓	✓	✓	✓
Underwood (1920–23)	✓	✓	✓	✓	✓
Robinson (1923–37)	✓	✓	✓	✓	✓

✓ Assumed primary responsibility

- the maturation of party caucuses between the 1850s and the 1870s;
- the creation of the first campaign committees and ad hoc committees on the order of business;
- the origins of the Republican steering committee in 1882–83 and the strengthening of its role 10 years later;
- the invention of elected floor leadership in 1890, with the central role played by Arthur Pue Gorman and the battle to stop passage of the Federal Elections Bill;
- the interpretation of unanimous consent agreements in the nineteenth century and the foundations of Rule 12(4);
- the story behind the "right of first recognition" in 1937;
- the importance of Lyndon B. Johnson and Robert Taft in developing the foundations for party staff in the middle of the twentieth century;
- the rapid expansion of party leadership posts and staff since 1990; and
- the centralization of communications operations under central leaders in the first decade of the twenty-first century.

That list illustrates an important theme: the cumulative character of party building. With the important exception of the Republican steering committee at the turn of the last century, Senate parties seldom reversed developments that added to the capability of party leaders or the collective capacity of the party organizations. The *use* of that capacity waxes and wanes in response to political circumstances and personalities, but a party rarely unilaterally reduces its ability to compete with the other party. The process of organizational invention is sporadic. But it is also one of nearly monotonic increases in the organizational capability of the two parties since the creation of party caucuses in 1841.

A NEW PERSPECTIVE ON THEORIES OF CONGRESSIONAL
PARTIES

In our attention to the cumulative nature of Senate party organization and leadership posts, we emphasize a feature of Senate party history that is largely ignored in theories of legislative parties. The importance of party competition in driving this process is a feature of Senate politics we observed in our earliest papers on this project. This fundamental process—the elaboration of Senate parties in response to their competition over legislation and elections—seems obvious but had not been a central focus of previous studies. Still, this process is closely related to those that are featured in previous theories of legislative parties.

The House and the "Standard" Account

Existing studies of congressional parties are, quite disproportionately, focused on the House of Representatives. It is in the House that variation in the role of parties in the policymaking process has been so conspicuous. The key elements of House history were the emergence of a strong speaker and the creation of the modern Rules Committee in the 1880s, culminating in the adoption of the Reed rules in 1890; the revolt against Speaker Joseph Cannon in 1909–10; the establishment of strong committee chairs in the mid-twentieth century; the reforms of the early 1970s that revitalized the Democratic caucus, enhanced the powers of the speaker, and weakened committee chairs; and the sharp centralization of power following the arrival of Speaker Newt Gingrich and his Republican majority after the 1994 elections. Most political science characterizations of House policymaking have emphasized the degree to which the legislative process of the House was centralized in majority party leadership or decentralized in the standing committees.

Since the 1980s, political scientists have offered persuasive accounts of the forces that drive variation in the policymaking process of the House. Several key arguments are now part of a standard account. First, legislators exhibit a meaningful level of partisan loyalty at most times as a function of their common party label and interest in being in the majority party (Cox and McCubbins 1993; Lee 2009). Second, the majority party maintains at least some control over outcomes, acting like a cartel to prevent proposals not favored by most party members and to limit the number of floor votes on which the majority party loses (Cox and McCubbins 1993, 2005; Pearson and Schickler 2009; Schickler and Pearson 2011). Third, it took decades for a true cartel to develop. It was only in the middle of the nineteenth century that majority party legislators in the House began to recognize their common interests and organize themselves to gain control of basic organizational activities of the House (Jenkins and Stewart 2013). Fourth, party leaders are licensed to be assertive when the parties are polarized on major issues; they recede to a role supportive of committees when the parties are not polarized and internally divided (Aldrich and Rohde 2000). And fifth and finally, by electing its leader to the speakership, the House majority party enhances its control over the legislative process by allowing its leader to exercise power through both party and chamber rules and practices. This general account emphasizes that members of a congressional party exhibit at least some minimal level of support for the party—quite high on procedural matters. Above that minimal level, parties vary over time in their cohesiveness and willingness to empower their leaders. They are imperfect cartels.

A variety of studies have applied these themes to the Senate (Lee 2009; Den Hartog and Monroe 2011; Smith, Ostrander, and Pope 2013). For recent decades, Sinclair (2006) emphasized how the mutually reinforcing influences of polarized parties and keen party competition for control of Congress have generated a more thoroughly partisan policymaking process in Congress (see also Lee 2016). In many ways, this view of legislative parties as teams fits the Senate as well as the House. The Senate majority party in the twenty-first century enjoys several advantages over the minority party, such as the right of first recognition for its floor leader and the ability to offer motions to table unfriendly amendments, and the Senate majority can exploit other tactics, such as filling the amendment tree, that are central to its efforts to set the agenda and block minority initiatives.

But, overall, the standard account fits Senate parties much less well than House parties. This is due, in part, to the size of Senate parties—generally 40–60 members—in comparison to the 180–240 common in the House. It is simply easier for members of Senate parties to be consulted and to coordinate activity in response to changing circumstances. But there are many other ways in which the chambers differ. The Senate minority's ability to filibuster and offer amendments, even if a majority might be able to overcome filibusters at times and can prevent action on unfriendly proposals, affords the minority bargaining leverage with the majority that far exceeds what the House minority enjoys. A majority party that wants to enhance its ability to move legislation by giving its own leader stronger procedural prerogatives usually finds the minority party obstructing its effort to do so. Moreover, while the right of first recognition is vital to the ability of the Senate majority leader to attempt to set the agenda, it is limited in impact by the ability of a large minority to block action, which makes the ability of the Senate majority party leader to structure floor activity substantially weaker than that of the House speaker. In this respect, the fact that the majority leader does not preside over the Senate, as does the House speaker, limits the powers enjoyed by the party leader. In both houses, of course, a small majority party may have difficulty creating majority coalitions for controversial legislation on the floor, but the supermajority cloture rule frequently limits floor wins for the Senate's majority party even when it acts as a cartel and is unified in its goals.

The Minority Party

These observations about the distinctiveness of the Senate force more attention to the minority party than is given in studies of the House. As we have noted, many innovations in party organization were initiated when a party was in the minority but carried over into Congresses in which it held a Senate majority. The important but narrow fixation on parliamentary rules and the centralization of power in majority party leadership leads to the standard account's emphasis on cycles of party influence above some floor of party loyalty. Also, studies of the House appropriately focus attention on the chamber itself, where rules are made and the speaker is chosen by the majority. As we discovered in our own work, however, the secret maneuverings of both party caucuses, which in the Senate have been the wellsprings of institutional change, are much harder to discern and uncover than public floor proceedings. Our focus on party organization and leadership structures leads us to see party capacity as cumulative, in majority *and* minority parties, even if a party's capacity of collective action is not fully exploited by a party and its leaders as political circumstances evolve. And we have needed to develop tools, much less necessary in studies of the House, to understand the institutions that have come to govern the Senate, most of which have grown up out of public view and in two discrete, secretive party arenas.

Attention to the minority party also brings more attention to party size. Party size plays a secondary role in the standard account of the House, but it is central to a more complete understanding of the incentives for the elaboration of Senate party organizations and leadership. A Senate minority party's size, along with the majority party's cohesiveness, determines the chances of legislative success and the value of investing in collective party efforts.

In the Senate, of course, minority party strategies are quite variable. Not until the late twentieth and early twenty-first centuries did the minority party object to motions to proceed and votes on measures so routinely that the cloture threshold became the de facto standard for passing legislation and confirming nominations of any significance. Minority obstructionism generated majority party responses that are described in the previous chapter and have been called a "Senate syndrome" (Smith 2014). These developments, we have observed, are associated with polarizing parties, intense partisan competition in legislative and electoral arenas, the elaboration of party organizations and staffs, multiplication of leadership posts, and more assertive leaders. The interplay of the parties generated this process—as much a minority party process as a majority party one.

The standard account represents several separate and distinct efforts to provide a theoretical foundation for understanding the role of parties in Congress. In the interest of developing parsimonious theory with some deductive power, most theorists have opted to assert that legislators focus on either their own reelection or the adoption of their policy preferences. This is an approach with which we have great sympathy. Legislators' reelection interests motivate concern about their parties' reputations, which may be best cultivated through the collective action facilitated by leadership and organization and, for the majority party, by controlling the floor agenda. Legislators' policy interests may at times be served by strong party leaders and at other times by weak party leaders, making "party government" conditional on the way legislators' policy preferences are distributed within and between the parties. These are insightful arguments about fundamental political processes that find ample confirmation in everyday legislative activity.

By focusing on either policy goals or reelection efforts, these accounts intentionally simplify legislators' personal goals and therefore their purposes for organizing legislative parties. This makes it easier to generate predictions about the kind of parties that legislators organize. While none of these accounts ignores policy or reelection goals, they tend to treat one type of goal as derivative of the other. Winning elections may demand addressing policy; winning legislative battles over policy may require the election of fellow partisans. Nevertheless, it is generally assumed that the actions of party leaders reflect the primary goal, policy or election, of party members, which yields credible and readily confirmed expectations about party behavior.

However useful the simplification is for building a theory, it has costs. In practice, we argue throughout this book, parties, as well as individual senators, have both electoral and policy interests. Parties have electoral and policy goals that need to be prioritized, balanced, and even compromised. Doing so is not easy and often subject to conflict within a party. There is nothing automatic about agreeing to strategies among legislators of the same party. Successfully managing these conflicts over a party's policy and electoral interests *is itself* a public or collective good for members of the party, and the choice of strategies and their implementation can be a critical coordination problem. Addressing collective action and coordination challenges may involve such strategies as the delegation of tasks, new methods of communication, and expanded staff resources, which may not be feasible in the short run. Addressing these challenges is most important when party competition is intense. Once adopted, organizational innovations are apt to be retained. Parties tend to keep their internal leadership posts, committees, and staffs from one Congress to the next, and reversion or retraction is met by resistance from legislators who benefit from them. This cumulative pattern—which, in our view, probably characterizes both houses of Congress and is not readily explained by the standard account—is essential to understanding the parties' behavior and influence at any moment.

Incorporating into our account two non-identical goals that may dictate different strategies has the consequence of making predictions about party development less precise. Theories are tools for improving our understanding of how people govern themselves. We gain by both drawing out the implications of a simple assumption of legislative motivation and appreciating the reinforcing and conflicting effects of two or more motivations. We have found that managing efforts in pursuit of both goals so frequently challenges senators in parties and yields organizational innovation that we cannot confidently assume that any one goal dominates.

Historical Patterns

The two houses of Congress exhibit different patterns of centralization and decentralization. For the House, Jenkins and Stewart (2013) describe how House majority parties came to control the election of chamber officers in the nineteenth century. There is some question about the strength of that cartel during the middle decades of the twentieth century because of factionalism among House Democrats (Oppenheimer 1977; Aldrich and Rohde 2000; Pearson and Schickler 2009), but there is little doubt that the speaker's assertion of control over the agenda in the late nineteenth century created at least the potential for majority party control of the agenda through the twentieth and into the twenty-first centuries. The move to majority party procedural control of the House in 1890 represented a lasting regime change; it allowed cohesive majority parties to run the House as they wanted.

Nothing quite like the regime change of the late-nineteenth-century House occurred in the Senate. Perhaps the closest parallels are the adoption of a rule providing for a motion to table, the invention of the modern rule governing unanimous consent agreements in 1914, the adoption of supermajority cloture in 1917, the use of the nuclear option in 2013 and 2017 to reduce the threshold for cloture on nominations, and the use of reconciliation procedures on tax measures to avoid filibusters and nongermane amendments. As important as these developments were to Senate majorities, they were all narrow in scope compared with the assertion of the House speaker's powers under the Reed rules and transformation of the use of special rules to control floor proceedings.

Even within the "majority party regime" in the House since the late nineteenth century, there has been considerable variation in the speaker's control over the policymaking process. This variation is properly associated with the majority party's evolving internal factionalism. There is a significant minimum level of party activity and allegiance that appears to generate some majority party influence over outcomes and, for long stretches associated with either polarized parties or closely balanced parties in the House, there is more concerted majority control over procedure and policy outcomes.

The Senate, again, is different. Senators may share with their House colleagues an incentive to see that their party is successful in defining and pursuing party goals and, for the majority party senators, they may share with their House counterparts a desire to have their leaders control the agenda and pass their legislative program. However, the House majority party can change chamber or party rules to enhance or reduce the speaker's powers, while the Senate majority party is historically much more constrained in its ability to change chamber rules and usually finds that a change in party rules will not deal with the most important problem—an obstructionist minority. As a result, the amplitude of the pattern of decentralization and centralization of the policymaking process—the responsiveness to polarization and party competition—can be much greater in the House than in the Senate.

Nevertheless, Senate legislating became more party-oriented and centralized in the 2010s than most long-time observers of Congress would have expected. Leaders in the twenty-first century have taken the initiative to set legislative strategy more independently and more frequently than at any time in the past, even at the heyday of Taft and Johnson. In support of their activities, the top leaders have direct control over more staff than ever before. Polarized parties, promoted by organized interests, monied outsiders, partisan media, and all-out efforts to win majority control have changed expectations about the role of leaders. Nevertheless, even in 2024 the Senate's majority party leadership cannot gain Senate approval for its favored legislation nearly as readily as the House majority party leadership does.

We have emphasized in this book and elsewhere that far more than incremental change has occurred in legislative parties over the last half-century (Gamm and Smith 2000, 2002a, 2002b; Smith and Gamm 2001, 2020).

These developments were built upon organizational foundations that were established over centuries—and, once created, never contracted in any significant way. The result is a set of imperfect generalizations about the development of Senate parties. First, the common partisan interests that serve as the basis for congressional parties took time to crystallize and produce concerted action by party caucuses. Second, once a stable, two-party system emerged in the 1860s, the longevity of the parties and continuity in membership allowed organizational changes to accumulate more specialized party organs and staff. Third, periods of cohesive majority parties often resulted in more aggressive majority party leadership. Fourth, intraparty factions have always looked for ways to strengthen their influence over party strategies by promoting organizational changes, parliamentary rules, and leaders that advantaged them. And finally, organizational innovations tended to be produced in periods of sharp party competition in the legislative and electoral arenas and have usually been cumulative.

For the Senate, both party polarization *and* keen party competition can vary and often creates incentives for organizational innovation. This does not produce a tidy pattern: neither a cycle nor a smooth cumulative pattern of organizational change characterizes legislative party committees and leadership. Organizational capacity, however, has tended to be one-directional, even if sporadic and in response to evolving political circumstances.

THE REMARKABLE 2010S AND 2020S

The extraordinary party competition of the twenty-first century and the obvious assertiveness of the Senate floor leaders deserve special notice. Partisanship began intensifying in the Senate in the 1980s, but it appeared to sharpen greatly just after the turn of the new century, as Trent Lott and Tom Daschle prepared to leave the Senate and were replaced by Bill Frist and Harry Reid. A partisan "syndrome" came to engulf the Senate (Smith 2014). Each party began to more fully exploit its parliamentary prerogatives. The minority blocked action by refusing unanimous consent to take up legislation and opposing cloture motions, and the majority responded by attempting to limit the minority's opportunities to obstruct or amend legislation. The Senate frequently reached points of legislative gridlock, which were circumvented at times only by invoking cloture, setting aside legislation, or accepting lowest-common-denominator legislation, often in the form of short-term authorizations and appropriations that left most senators unhappy with the outcome. In the 1993–98 period about half of all major legislation was subject to filibusters or threatened filibusters, many times the rate that was typical of previous decades. The pace accelerated into the new century, when the vast majority of major bills were affected by a filibuster or cloture. In the 107th Congress (2001–2), 61 cloture votes were taken; in the 111th (2009–10), 91 cloture votes were taken.

As we emphasized in Chapter 9, majority party leadership in the first two decades of the new century has been forced to adjust its strategy to respond to and anticipate minority moves. On both sides of the aisle, party leaders in the twenty-first century are taking more initiative in setting party strategy. The two parties have elaborated and expanded their party organizations and staff. The political and media environment reward quick responses to the legislative and public relations moves of the other party and the president, which only leaders and staff under their direction could provide. The process may have intensified partisanship as party members supported their leaders' responses to the tactics of the other side, often derided as unfair. Unfortunately for the majority party, if the minority is reasonably cohesive, as it is in a highly polarized Senate, the majority cannot readily translate its own cohesiveness into significant policy accomplishments. Often, the majority can only hope that its dedicated floor leader can improve efficiency and persuade the public of the value of its program.

In the eyes of many senators, these developments have altered the nature of their institution. Calls for a return to "regular order"—meaning more reliance on standing committees, more amending activity on the floor, fewer filibusters, and more inter-party negotiation—have been common in recent years, but the return to the standard operating procedures of the mid-twentieth century has not materialized. While neither party's leaders can dictate party strategy entirely on their own, they now routinely take the initiative that once was in the hands of committee leaders. Rather than being the legislative chamber that operated informally and readily accommodated individual legislators' desire to debate and offer amendments, as senators calling for regular order seem to be yearning for, the Senate is now bogged down by full exploitation of formal rules and precedents, as the two parties seek every legislative and public relations advantage over the other.

Scholars—surely including the two of us when we began this project many years ago—were wrong in thinking that the Senate parties in the late 1990s, under leaders Lott and Daschle, was as centralized as they could ever be. Considering only the legislative process, we would have considered it pointless in the 1990s for the majority party to enhance the power of its leader over party affairs when the other party could so easily block its proposals on the floor. Over the preceding decades, the lesson of Senate history had seemed to impose strict limits on how centralized policymaking in the majority leadership could become in the Senate, making modern Senate parties chronically less centralized than House parties. However, in the twenty-first century, as messaging and winning elections has become more important in a chamber that struggles to legislate, the value of more assertive party leaders who can act with greater speed and agility in public relations has justified the creation of new venues for coordinating public relations strategies and expanding staff. These developments have sharply reduced reliance on committee leaders to set legislative priorities, choose and implement political tactics, and represent the party to the media and public.

A time may yet come when the pendulum swings back, when Senate party leaders are again less central to policymaking. But it will not happen soon. As the historical account laid out in this book suggests, Senate parties will not easily dismantle the organizational apparatuses that they have built over two centuries' time. Organizational elaboration has always been sporadic. While some party units have fallen into disuse for a period of years, Senate parties have rarely unilaterally discarded innovations that have enhanced their capacity to compete in the legislative or electoral arenas. Even when factionalism has reduced the ability of a party to act cohesively and undermined deference to a floor leader, the party organization has seldom withered away. When a party did radically cut back on formal party organization—as the Democrats did in the 1860s (during the Civil War and the first years of Reconstruction) and the Republicans did in the 1930s (at the height of the New Deal)—it was due entirely to the party's depleted ranks, not to any internal factionalism, and, in the years following, the party reconstituted its institutions and leadership positions as soon as it began recovering substantial numbers of Senate seats.

Understanding the development of Senate party organization and leadership adds a new layer to long-held ways of viewing congressional institutions. One important pattern, we have noted, is a steady level of party loyalty that comes with party caucus membership. Another is the rise and fall of party-oriented policymaking, associated with the strength of factionalism within the majority party. The layer that we have discovered is the organizational sediment within Senate parties. Going back to the Whig caucuses of 1841, extending to the proliferation of caucus committees through the rest of the nineteenth century, embracing the rise of floor leadership in 1890, and including a multitude of new party institutions in the twentieth and twenty-first centuries, Senate parties have grown, almost inexorably, in their capacity. Over nearly two centuries, since senators first turned from the presiding officer to their own caucuses for direction, Senate parties have, steadily if intermittently, expanded the capacity of caucus organizations and leadership. They have done this, at times of party competition, to meet legislative and electoral challenges and they then retained their organizational innovations. The Senate parties of 2025, the conferences led by Chuck Schumer and John Thune, contain within them ancient seeds, many of them dating back to the first generations of Senate history and still stubbornly sprouting new shoots in our own time.

Appendix

TABLE A.1 *Senate Republican leadership*

Chairs of the Senate Republican caucus

John P. Hale (N.H.), *Dec. 1857*–Dec. 1862
Henry B. Anthony (R.I.), Dec. 1862–Sept. 2, 1884
John Sherman (Ohio), Dec. 1, 1884–Dec. 10, 1885
George Edmunds (Vt.), Dec. 11, 1885–Nov. 1, 1891
John Sherman (Ohio), Dec. 7, 1891–Mar. 4, 1897
William Boyd Allison (Iowa), Mar. 6, 1897–Aug. 4, 1908
Eugene Hale (Maine), Dec. 9, 1908–Mar. 3, 1911
Shelby Cullom (Ill.), Apr. 4, 1911–Mar. 3, 1913
Jacob Gallinger (N.H.), Mar. 5, 1913–Aug. 17, 1918
Henry Cabot Lodge (Mass.), Aug. 24, 1918–Nov. 9, 1924
Charles Curtis (Kans.), Nov. 28, 1924–Mar. 3, 1929
James Watson (Ind.), Mar. 5, 1929–Mar. 3, 1933
Charles McNary (Ore.), Mar. 7, 1933–Feb. 25, 1944
Arthur H. Vandenberg (Mich.), Feb. 25, 1944–Dec. 29, 1946
Eugene D. Millikin (Colo.), Dec. 30, 1946–Jan. 2, 1957
Leverett Saltonstall (Mass.), Jan. 3, 1957–Jan. 2, 1967
Margaret Chase Smith (Maine), Jan. 10, 1967–Jan. 2, 1973
Norris Cotton (N.H.), Jan. 3, 1973–Dec. 31, 1974
Carl T. Curtis (Nebr.), Jan. 14, 1975–Jan. 2, 1979
Robert Packwood (Ore.), Jan. 15, 1979–Jan. 4, 1981
James A. McClure (Idaho), Jan. 5, 1981–Jan. 2, 1985
John Chafee (R.I.), Jan. 3, 1985–Jan. 2, 1991
Thad Cochran (Miss.), Jan. 3, 1991–Jan. 6, 1997
Connie Mack (Fla.), Jan. 7, 1997–Jan. 2, 2001
Richard J. Santorum (Pa.), Jan. 3, 2001–Jan. 2, 2007
Jon Kyl (Ariz.), Jan. 4–Dec. 17, 2007
Lamar Alexander (Tenn.), Dec. 18, 2007–Jan. 22, 2012
John Thune (S.Dak.), Jan. 23, 2012–Jan. 2, 2019
John Barrasso (Wyo.), Jan. 3, 2019–Jan. 2, 2025
Tom Cotton (Ark.), Jan. 3, 2025–

(continued)

TABLE A.1 (*continued*)

Senate Republican floor leaders

Jacob Gallinger (N.H.), Mar. 5, 1913–Aug. 17, 1918
Henry Cabot Lodge (Mass.), Aug. 24, 1918–Nov. 9, 1924
Charles Curtis (Kans.), Nov. 28, 1924–Mar. 3, 1929
James Watson (Ind.), Mar. 5, 1929–Mar. 3, 1933
Charles McNary (Ore.), Mar. 7, 1933–Feb. 25, 1944
Wallace White (Maine), Feb. 25, 1944–Jan. 2, 1949
Kenneth Wherry (Nebr.), Jan. 3, 1949–Nov. 29, 1951
Styles Bridges (N.H.), Jan. 8, 1952–Jan. 2, 1953
Robert Taft (Ohio), Jan. 3–July 31, 1953
William Knowland (Calif.), Aug. 4, 1953–Jan. 2, 1959
Everett Dirksen (Ill.), Jan. 7, 1959–Sept. 7, 1969
Hugh Scott (Pa.), Sept. 24, 1969–Jan. 2, 1977
Howard Baker (Tenn.), Jan. 4, 1977–Jan. 2, 1985
Robert Dole (Kans.), Jan. 3, 1985–June 11, 1996
Trent Lott (Miss.), June 12, 1996–Dec. 20, 2002
William H. Frist (Tenn.), Dec. 23, 2002–Jan. 2, 2007
Mitch McConnell (Ky.), Jan. 4, 2007–Jan. 2, 2025
John Thune (S.Dak.), Jan. 3, 2025–

TABLE A.2 *Senate Democratic leadership*

Chairs of the Senate Democratic caucus (since 1873) and Senate Democratic floor leaders (since 1890)

John W. Stevenson (Ky.), Dec. 1873–Mar. 3, 1877
William A. Wallace (Pa.), Mar. 5, 1877–Mar. 3, 1881
George Pendleton (Ohio), Mar. 5, 1881–Mar. 3, 1885
James Beck (Ky.), Mar. 5, 1885–May 3, 1890
Arthur Pue Gorman (Md.), May 12, 1890–Apr. 28, 1898
David Turpie (Ind.), Apr. 29, 1898–Mar. 3, 1899
James K. Jones (Ark.), Dec. 5, 1899–Mar. 3, 1903
Arthur Pue Gorman (Md.), Mar. 6, 1903–June 4, 1906
Joseph Blackburn (Ky.), June 9, 1906–Mar. 3, 1907
Charles Culberson (Tex.), Dec. 3, 1907–Dec. 8, 1909
Hernando Money (Miss.), Dec. 9, 1909–Mar. 3, 1911
Thomas S. Martin (Va.), Apr. 7, 1911–Mar. 3, 1913
John Kern (Ind.), Mar. 4, 1913–Mar. 3, 1917
Thomas S. Martin (Va.), Mar. 6, 1917–Nov. 12, 1919
Oscar Underwood (Ala.), Apr. 27, 1920–Dec. 2, 1923
Joseph Robinson (Ark.), Dec. 3, 1923–July 14, 1937
Alben Barkley (Ky.), July 22, 1937–Jan. 19, 1949
Scott Lucas (Ill.), Jan. 20, 1949–Jan. 2, 1951
Ernest McFarland (Ariz.), Jan. 3, 1951–Jan. 2, 1953
Lyndon B. Johnson (Tex.), Jan. 3, 1953–Jan. 2, 1961

Mike Mansfield (Mont.), Jan. 3, 1961–Jan. 2, 1977
Robert Byrd (W.Va.), Jan. 4, 1977–Jan. 2, 1989
George Mitchell (Maine), Jan. 3, 1989–Jan. 2, 1995
Thomas Daschle (S.Dak.), Jan. 4, 1995–Jan. 2, 2005
Harry Reid (Nev.), Jan. 4, 2005–Jan. 2, 2017
Charles E. Schumer (N.Y.), Jan. 3, 2017–

Notes and sources for Tables A.1 and A.2

The listings in this table of nineteenth and early twentieth-century caucus chairs and floor leaders are thoroughly original to this project. Before we began this research, no accurate lists of early caucus leaders had existed. We are happy to report that, as we go to press in 2025, both the *Biographical Directory of the United States Congress* and various websites maintained by the Senate have been updated to incorporate the research reflected in this table: see, for example, U.S. Senate Historical Office (2024a, 2024b). As we document in Chapters 5 and 6, Democrats have regarded their caucus chair as their elected floor leader since 1890 and Republicans have done so since 1913. This table includes precise dates of service for every caucus chair and leader, including twentieth-century leaders whose dates of service have been reported erroneously in other sources.

Caucus chairs and floor leaders are not routinely identified in the *Senate Journal*, in the *Congressional Record*, or in older accounts of congressional debates and proceedings. Formerly, the most reliable sources of information on congressional leadership—records of the Senate, the Senate Historical Office, and the Congressional Research Service; *History, Rules, and Precedents of the Senate Republican Conference, 105th Congress* (1997) and *117th Congress* (2022); previous websites of the Senate Majority Leader; the *Biographical Directory of the United States Congress, 1774–1989* (1989); Riddick's 1971 study; Munk's 1974 study; Byrd's 1993 volume of historical statistics and tables—relied on incomplete and inaccurate lists of caucus leaders. Riddick (1971, 6–8), drawing on the then-unpublished caucus minutes, reported two lists of Senate Democratic and Republican leaders for the period since 1893. His first list, which includes pre-1903 Democrats and pre-1911 Republicans, is fragmentary and based on unidentified, "unofficial," sources, while his second list was "determined from the caucus minutes of the two major parties." Munk (1974, 25), who compiled a somewhat different list than Riddick, noted, like Riddick, that the "identities, titles, and terms of service" of leaders in the 1890s and 1900s were "difficult to define with certainty." Of his two lists, only Riddick's second list—the list of Democrats since 1903 and of Republicans since 1911—is accurate. Though Riddick placed greater confidence in this second list, various students of the chamber subsequently republished the two Riddick lists as a single, authoritative list of Senate leaders. The *Biographical Directory of the United States Congress, 1774–1989* (1989) changed its biographies to reflect the data in Riddick's two lists, while tables in Byrd (1993) and Vincent et al. (1996) directly reproduce Riddick's listings.

To create this table, we searched for contemporary accounts of caucus meetings for each Congress since the 1820s. Entries are based on accounts of Democratic and Republican caucus meetings published in various newspapers. We also rely on *Minutes of the Senate Democratic Conference, 1903–1964* (Ritchie 1998a) and *Minutes of the Senate Republican Conference, 1911–1964* (Wolff and Ritchie 1999). Caucus minutes do not survive from the nineteenth century and are not available for the period after 1964. Since newspaper accounts of caucus meetings accurately report caucus business for the period for which we have access to conference minutes, we regard newspaper accounts as accurate for the other periods as well. We have located accounts of the election (and, in most cases, biennial reelection) of each leader in this table as well as accompanying references to the death or retirement of the preceding leader. We have italicized the initial entries in the table—the beginning of John P. Hale's term as Republican caucus chair and of John W. Stevenson's term as Democratic caucus chair—because we are not certain when their terms began. In these two cases, we have listed the date of the earliest references that we have found to their roles as chairs.

We do not include acting caucus chairs and acting leaders on this list, since their dates of service were usually brief and uncertain. (The one exception we make is for Arthur H. Vandenberg and

(*continued*)

TABLE A.2 (*continued*)

Wallace White, who were elected to leadership positions in the Republican conference in February 1944, immediately before the death of Charles McNary. Unlike others who served as acting leaders, these two men were formally elected to their positions as acting chair and acting leader, and both were reelected to their positions with permanent titles at the start of the next Congress.) Thus we do not include Aaron Cragin (N.H.), who was acting chair of the Republican caucus when Henry B. Anthony (R.I.) fell briefly ill in January 1877, or John Sherman (Ohio), who served as acting chair during Anthony's terminal illness, in 1883–84. Neither Isham Harris (Tenn.) nor Arthur Pue Gorman (Md.), who served as acting Democratic caucus chairs during the final two years of James Beck's (Ky.) term, is listed in this table until May 1890, when Beck died and Gorman assumed the chairmanship in his own right. Similarly, Gilbert Hitchcock (Nebr.), who, as caucus vice chair, served as acting Democratic caucus chair in 1919–20, is not on this list. (We note that various published lists include Hitchcock as a leader, but nothing distinguished his case from those of others who served in a temporary way before him.) And Warren Austin (Vt.), who served as acting Republican leader at various times in the early 1940s, is not included here. Since the establishment of caucus chairmanships in the middle of the nineteenth century, it appears that no other senators served as acting caucus chairs or acting leaders for any significant length of time.

TABLE A.3 *Presidents pro tempore of the Senate*

Cong.	President pro tempore	Party and state	Rank	First day	Last day
1st	John Langdon	Pro-Admin, N.H.	n/a	Ballot	Apr. 6, 1789	Apr. 21, 1789
	John Langdon			Ballot	Aug. 7, 1789	Aug. 9, 1789
2nd	Richard Henry Lee	Anti-Admin, Va.	n/a	Ballot	Apr. 18, 1792	Oct. 8, 1792
	John Langdon	Pro-Admin, N.H.	n/a	Ballot	Nov. 5, 1792	Dec. 4, 1792
	John Langdon			Ballot	Mar. 1, 1793	Mar. 3, 1793
3rd	John Langdon	Anti-Admin, N.H.	n/a	Resumed	Mar. 4, 1793	Dec. 2, 1793
	Ralph Izard	Pro-Admin, S.C.	n/a	Ballot	May 31, 1794	Nov. 9, 1794
	Henry Tazewell	Anti-Admin, Va.	n/a	Ballot	Feb. 20, 1795	June 7, 1795
4th	Henry Tazewell	R, Va.	8	Ballot	Dec. 7, 1795	Dec. 8, 1795
	Samuel Livermore	F, N.H.	10	Ballot	May 6, 1796	Dec. 4, 1796
	William Bingham	F, Pa.	16	Ballot	Feb. 16, 1797	Mar. 3, 1797
5th	William Bradford	F, R.I.	5	Ballot	July 6, 1797	Oct. 1797
	Jacob Read	F, S.C.	9	Ballot	Nov. 22, 1797	Dec. 12, 1797
	Theodore Sedgwick	F, Mass.	16	Ballot	June 27, 1798	Dec. 5, 1798
	John Laurance	F, N.Y.	20	Ballot	Dec. 6, 1798	Dec. 27, 1798
	James Ross	F, Pa.	7	Ballot	Mar. 1, 1799	Dec. 1, 1799
6th	Samuel Livermore	F, N.H.	3	Ballot	Dec. 2, 1799	Dec. 29, 1799
	Uriah Tracy	F, Conn.	13	Ballot	May 14, 1800	Nov. 16, 1800
	John E. Howard	F, Md.	14	Ballot	Nov. 21, 1800	Nov. 27, 1800
	James Hillhouse	F, Conn.	10	Ballot	Feb. 28, 1801	Mar. 3, 1801

(continued)

TABLE A.3 (continued)

Cong.	President pro tempore	Party and state	Rank		First day	Last day
7th	Abraham Baldwin	R, Ga.	9	Ballot	Dec. 7, 1801	Jan. 14, 1802
	Abraham Baldwin			Ballot	Apr. 17, 1802	Dec. 13, 1802
	Stephen R. Bradley	R, Vt.	5	Ballot	Dec. 14, 1802	Jan. 18, 1803
	Stephen R. Bradley			Ballot	Feb. 25, 1803	Feb. 25, 1803
	Stephen R. Bradley			Ballot	Mar. 2, 1803	Oct. 16, 1803
8th	John Brown	R, Ky.	1	Ballot	Oct. 17, 1803	Dec. 6, 1803
	John Brown			Ballot	Jan. 23, 1804	Feb. 26, 1804
	Jesse Franklin	R, N.C.	7	Ballot	Mar. 10, 1804	Nov. 4, 1804
	Joseph Anderson	R, Tenn.	4	Ballot	Jan. 15, 1805	Feb. 3, 1805
	Joseph Anderson			Ballot	Feb. 28, 1805	Mar. 2, 1805
	Joseph Anderson			Ballot	Mar. 2, 1805	Dec. 1, 1805
9th	Samuel Smith	R, Md.	10	Ballot	Dec. 2, 1805	Dec. 15, 1805
	Samuel Smith			Ballot	Mar. 18, 1806	Nov. 30, 1806
	Samuel Smith			Ballot	Mar. 2, 1807	Oct. 25, 1807
10th	Samuel Smith	R, Md.	6	Ballot	Apr. 16, 1808	Nov. 6, 1808
	Stephen R. Bradley	R, Vt.	2	Ballot	Dec. 28, 1808	Jan. 8, 1809
	John Milledge	R, Ga.	21	Ballot	Jan. 30, 1809	Mar. 3, 1809
11th	John Milledge	R, Ga.	16	Resumed	Mar. 4, 1809	May 21, 1809
	Andrew Gregg	R, Pa.	17	Ballot	June 26, 1809	Dec. 18, 1809
	John Gaillard	R, S.C.	10	Ballot	Feb. 28, 1810	Mar. 2, 1810
	John Gaillard			Ballot	Apr. 17, 1810	Dec. 11, 1810
	John Pope	R, Ky.	17	Ballot	Feb. 23, 1811	Nov. 3, 1811

Congress	President pro tempore	Party, State	No.	Type	Elected	Term end
12th	William H. Crawford	R, Ga.	16	Ballot	Mar. 24, 1812	Mar. 23, 1813
13th	Joseph B. Varnum	R, Mass.	21	Ballot	Dec. 6, 1813	Feb. 3, 1814
	John Gaillard	R, S.C.	5	Ballot	Apr. 18, 1814	Nov. 25, 1814
	John Gaillard			Ballot	Nov. 25, 1814	Dec. 3, 1815
14th	John Gaillard	R, S.C.	2	Resumed	Dec. 4, 1815	Mar. 3, 1817
15th	John Gaillard	R, S.C.	1	Resumed	Mar. 4, 1817	Mar. 4, 1817
	John Gaillard			Ballot	Mar. 6, 1817	Feb. 18, 1818
	John Gaillard			Ballot	Mar. 31, 1818	Jan. 5, 1819
	James Barbour	R, Va.	8	Ballot	Feb. 15, 1819	Dec. 5, 1819
16th	James Barbour	R, Va.	3	Resumed	Dec. 6, 1819	Dec. 26, 1819
	John Gaillard	R, S.C.	1	Ballot	Jan. 25, 1820	Dec. 2, 1821
17th	John Gaillard	R, S.C.	1	Resumed	Dec. 3, 1821	Dec. 27, 1821
	John Gaillard			Ballot	Feb. 1, 1822	Dec. 2, 1822
	John Gaillard			Ballot	Feb. 19, 1823	Nov. 30, 1823
18th	John Gaillard	CrR, S.C.	1	Resumed	Dec. 1, 1823	Jan. 20, 1824
	John Gaillard			Ballot	May 21, 1824	Mar. 3, 1825
19th	John Gaillard	J, S.C.	1	Ballot	Mar. 9, 1825	Dec. 4, 1825
	Nathaniel Macon	J, N.C.	2	Ballot	May 20, 1826	Dec. 3, 1826
	Nathaniel Macon			Ballot	Jan. 2, 1827	Feb. 13, 1827
	Nathaniel Macon			Ballot	Mar. 2, 1827	Dec. 2, 1827

(continued)

TABLE A.3 (continued)

Cong.	President pro tempore	Party and state	Rank		First day	Last day
20th	Samuel Smith	J, Md.	1	Ballot	May 15, 1828	Dec. 18, 1828
21st	Samuel Smith	J, Md.	1	Ballot	Mar. 13, 1829	Dec. 10, 1829
	Samuel Smith			Ballot	May 29, 1830	Dec. 31, 1830
	Samuel Smith			Ballot	Mar. 1, 1831	Dec. 4, 1831
22nd	Samuel Smith	J, Md.	1	Resumed	Dec. 5, 1831	Dec. 11, 1831
	Littleton Tazewell	J, Va.	5	Ballot	July 9, 1832	July 16, 1832
	Hugh L. White	J, Tenn.	7	Ballot	Dec. 3, 1832	Dec. 1, 1833
23rd	Hugh L. White	J, Tenn.	4	Resumed	Dec. 2, 1833	Dec. 15, 1833
	George Poindexter	AJ, Miss.	15	Ballot	June 28, 1834	Nov. 30, 1834
	John Tyler	AJ, Va.	7	Ballot	Mar. 3, 1835	Dec. 6, 1835
24th	William R. King	J, Ala.	1	Ballot	July 1, 1836	Dec. 4, 1836
	William R. King			Ballot	Jan. 28, 1837	Mar. 3, 1837
25th	William R. King	D, Ala.	1	Ballot	Mar. 7, 1837	Sept. 3, 1837
	William R. King			Ballot	Oct. 13, 1837	Dec. 3, 1837
	William R. King			Ballot	July 2, 1838	Dec. 18, 1838
	William R. King			Ballot	Feb. 25, 1839	Dec. 1, 1839
26th	William R. King	D, Ala.	1	Resumed	Dec. 2, 1839	Dec. 26, 1839
	William R. King			Ballot	July 3, 1840	Dec. 15, 1840
	William R. King			Ballot	Mar. 3, 1841	Mar. 3, 1841

Congress	President pro tempore	Party, State	Ballots	Method	Date	Date
27th	William R. King	D, Ala.	1	Resolution	Mar. 4, 1841	Mar. 4, 1841
	Samuel Southard	W, N.J.	2	Ballot	Mar. 11, 1841	May 31, 1842
	Willie P. Mangum	W, N.C.	1	Ballot	May 31, 1842	Dec. 3, 1843
28th	Willie P. Mangum	W, N.C.	1	Resumed	Dec. 4, 1843	Mar. 3, 1845
29th	Willie P. Mangum	W, N.C.	1	Resumed	Mar. 4, 1845	Mar. 4, 1845
	David R. Atchison	D, Mo.	21	Ballot	Aug. 8, 1846	Dec. 6, 1846
	David R. Atchison			Ballot	Jan. 11, 1847	Jan. 13, 1847
	David R. Atchison			Resolution	Mar. 3, 1847	Dec. 5, 1847
30th	David R. Atchison	D, Mo.	16	Resolution	Feb. 2, 1848	Feb. 8, 1848
	David R. Atchison			Resolution	June 1, 1848	June 14, 1848
	David R. Atchison			Resolution	June 26, 1848	June 29, 1848
	David R. Atchison			Resolution	July 29, 1848	Dec. 4, 1848
	David R. Atchison			Resolution	Dec. 26, 1848	Jan. 1, 1849
	David R. Atchison			Resolution	Mar. 2, 1849	Mar. 4, 1849
31st	David R. Atchison	D, Mo.	6	Resolution	Mar. 5, 1849	Mar. 5, 1849
	David R. Atchison			Resolution	Mar. 16, 1849	Dec. 2, 1849
	William R. King	D, Ala.	2	Resolution	May 6, 1850	May 19, 1850
	William R. King			Resolution	July 11, 1850	Mar. 3, 1851
32nd	William R. King	D, Ala.	1	Resumed	Mar. 4, 1851	Dec. 20, 1852
	David R. Atchison	D, Mo.	1	Resolution	Dec. 20, 1852	Mar. 3, 1853
33rd	David R. Atchison	D, Mo.	2	Resolution	Mar. 4, 1853	Dec. 4, 1854
	Lewis Cass	D, Mich.	4	Resolution	Dec. 4, 1854	Dec. 4, 1854
	Jesse D. Bright	D, Ind.	3	Ballot	Dec. 5, 1854	Dec. 2, 1855

(continued)

Cong.	President pro tempore	Party and state	Rank		First day	Last day
34th	Jesse D. Bright	D, Ind.	1	Resumed	Dec. 3, 1855	June 9, 1856
	Charles E. Stuart	D, Mich.	24	Ballot	June 9, 1856	June 10, 1856
	Jesse D. Bright	D, Ind.	1	Resolution	June 11, 1856	Jan. 6, 1857
	James M. Mason	D, Va.	5	Ballot	Jan. 6, 1857	Mar. 3, 1857
35th	James M. Mason	D, Va.	5	Resolution	Mar. 4, 1857	Mar. 4, 1857
	Thomas J. Rusk	D, Tex.	3	Ballot	Mar. 14, 1857	July 29, 1857
	Benjamin Fitzpatrick	D, Ala.	9	Ballot	Dec. 7, 1857	Dec. 20, 1857
	Benjamin Fitzpatrick			Ballot	Mar. 29, 1858	May 2, 1858
	Benjamin Fitzpatrick			Ballot	June 14, 1858	Dec. 5, 1858
	Benjamin Fitzpatrick			Resolution	Jan. 19, 1859	Jan. 19, 1859
	Benjamin Fitzpatrick			Resolution	Jan. 25, 1859	Feb. 9, 1859
36th	Benjamin Fitzpatrick	D, Ala.	9	Resolution	Mar. 9, 1859	Dec. 4, 1859
	Benjamin Fitzpatrick			Ballot	Dec. 19, 1859	Jan. 15, 1860
	Benjamin Fitzpatrick			Resolution	Feb. 20, 1860	Feb. 26, 1860
	Jesse D. Bright	D, Ind.	2	Resolution	June 12, 1860	June 13, 1860
	Benjamin Fitzpatrick	D, Ala.	9	Resolution	June 26, 1860	Dec. 2, 1860
	Solomon Foot	R, Vt.	1	Resolution	Feb. 16, 1861	Feb. 17, 1861
37th	Solomon Foot	R, Vt.	2	Resolution	Mar. 23, 1861	July 3, 1861
	Solomon Foot			Resolution	July 18, 1861	Dec. 1, 1861
	Solomon Foot			Resolution	Jan. 15, 1862	Jan. 15, 1862
	Solomon Foot			Resolution	Mar. 31, 1862	May 21, 1862
	Solomon Foot			Resolution	June 19, 1862	Dec. 12, 1862
	Solomon Foot			Resolution	Feb. 18, 1863	Mar. 3, 1863

Congress	Name		Number		Date	Date
38th	Solomon Foot	R, Vt.	1	Resolution	Mar. 4, 1863	Dec. 6, 1863
	Solomon Foot			Resolution	Dec. 18, 1863	Dec. 20, 1863
	Solomon Foot			Resolution	Feb. 23, 1864	Feb. 23, 1864
	Solomon Foot			Resolution	Mar. 11, 1864	Mar. 13, 1864
	Solomon Foot			Resolution	Apr. 11, 1864	Apr. 13, 1864
	Daniel Clark	R, N.H.	9	Resolution	Apr. 26, 1864	Jan. 4, 1865
	Daniel Clark			Resolution	Feb. 9, 1865	Feb. 19, 1865
39th	Lafayette S. Foster	R, Conn.	5	Resolution	Mar. 7, 1865	Mar. 2, 1867
	Benjamin F. Wade	R, Ohio	1	Resolution	Mar. 2, 1867	Mar. 3, 1867
40th	Benjamin F. Wade	R, Ohio	1	Resumed	Mar. 4, 1867	Mar. 3, 1869
41st	Henry B. Anthony	R, R.I.	7	Resolution	Mar. 23, 1869	Mar. 28, 1869
	Henry B. Anthony			Resolution	Apr. 9, 1869	Dec. 5, 1869
	Henry B. Anthony			Resolution	May 28, 1870	June 2, 1870
	Henry B. Anthony			Resolution	July 1, 1870	July 5, 1870
	Henry B. Anthony			Resolution	July 14, 1870	Dec. 4, 1870
42nd	Henry B. Anthony	R, R.I.	6	Resolution	Mar. 10, 1871	Mar. 12, 1871
	Henry B. Anthony			Resolution	Apr. 17, 1871	May 9, 1871
	Henry B. Anthony			Resolution	May 23, 1871	Dec. 3, 1871
	Henry B. Anthony			Resolution	Dec. 21, 1871	Jan. 7, 1872
	Henry B. Anthony			Resolution	Feb. 23, 1872	Feb. 25, 1872
	Henry B. Anthony			Resolution	June 8, 1872	Dec. 1, 1872
	Henry B. Anthony			Resolution	Dec. 4, 1872	Dec. 8, 1872
	Henry B. Anthony			Resolution	Dec. 13, 1872	Dec. 15, 1872
	Henry B. Anthony			Resolution	Dec. 20, 1872	Jan. 5, 1873
	Henry B. Anthony			Resolution	Jan. 24, 1873	Jan. 24, 1873

(continued)

TABLE A.3 (continued)

Cong.	President pro tempore	Party and state	Rank		First day	Last day
43rd	Matthew H. Carpenter	R, Wisc.	20	Resolution	Mar. 12, 1873	Mar. 13, 1873
	Matthew H. Carpenter			Resolution	Mar. 26, 1873	Nov. 30, 1873
	Matthew H. Carpenter			Ballot	Dec. 11, 1873	Dec. 6, 1874
	Matthew H. Carpenter			Ballot	Dec. 23, 1874	Jan. 4, 1875
	Henry B. Anthony	R, R.I.	3	Resolution	Jan. 25, 1875	Jan. 31, 1875
	Henry B. Anthony			Resolution	Feb. 15, 1875	Feb. 17, 1875
44th	Thomas W. Ferry	R, Mich.	18	Ballot	Mar. 9, 1875	Mar. 10, 1875
	Thomas W. Ferry			Resolution	Mar. 19, 1875	Dec. 20, 1875
	Thomas W. Ferry			Resolution	Dec. 20, 1875	Mar. 4, 1877
45th	Thomas W. Ferry	R, Mich.	12	Resolution	Mar. 5, 1877	Mar. 5, 1877
	Thomas W. Ferry			Resolution	Feb. 26, 1878	Mar. 3, 1878
	Thomas W. Ferry			Resolution	Apr. 17, 1878	Dec. 1, 1878
	Thomas W. Ferry			Resolution	Mar. 3, 1879	Mar. 17, 1879
46th	Allen G. Thurman	D, Ohio	2	Resolution	Apr. 15, 1879	Nov. 30, 1879
	Allen G. Thurman			Resolution	Apr. 7, 1880	Apr. 14, 1880
	Allen G. Thurman			Resolution	May 6, 1880	Dec. 5, 1880
47th	Thomas F. Bayard	D, Del.	1	Resolution	Oct. 10, 1881	Oct. 13, 1881
	David Davis	I, Ill.	n/a	Resolution	Oct. 13, 1881	Mar. 3, 1883
	George F. Edmunds	R, Vt.	2	Resolution	Mar. 3, 1883	Dec. 2, 1883
48th	George F. Edmunds	R, Vt.	2	Resumed	Dec. 3, 1883	Jan. 14, 1884
	George F. Edmunds			Resolution	Jan. 14, 1884	Mar. 3, 1885

49th	John Sherman	R, Ohio	Resolution	1	Dec. 7, 1885	Feb. 26, 1887
	John J. Ingalls	R, Kans.	Resolution	4	Feb. 26, 1887	Dec. 4, 1887
50th	John J. Ingalls	R, Kans.	Resumed	4	Dec. 5, 1887	Mar. 3, 1889
51st	John J. Ingalls	R, Kans.	Resolution	4	Mar. 7, 1889	Mar. 17, 1889
	John J. Ingalls		Resolution		Apr. 2, 1889	Dec. 1, 1889
	John J. Ingalls		Resolution		Dec. 5, 1889	Dec. 10, 1889
	John J. Ingalls		Resolution		Feb. 28, 1890	Mar. 18, 1890
	John J. Ingalls		Resolution		Apr. 3, 1890	Mar. 2, 1891
	Charles F. Manderson		Resolution	22	Mar. 2, 1891	Dec. 6, 1891
52nd	Charles F. Manderson	R, Nebr.	Resumed	20	Dec. 7, 1891	Mar. 3, 1893
53rd	Charles F. Manderson	R, Nebr.	Resumed	14	Mar. 4, 1893	Mar. 22, 1893
	Isham G. Harris	D, Tenn.	Resolution	3	Mar. 22, 1893	Jan. 7, 1895
	Matt W. Ransom	D, N.C.	Resolution	1	Jan. 7, 1895	Jan. 10, 1895
	Isham G. Harris	D, Tenn.	Resolution	3	Jan. 10, 1895	Mar. 3, 1895
54th	William P. Frye	R, Maine	Resolution	9	Feb. 7, 1896	Mar. 3, 1897
55th	William P. Frye	R, Maine	Resumed	7	Mar. 4, 1897	Dec. 3, 1899
56th	William P. Frye	R, Maine	Resumed	5	Dec. 4, 1899	Mar. 3, 1901
57th	William P. Frye	R, Maine	Resolution	5	Mar. 7, 1901	Mar. 4, 1903
58th	William P. Frye	R, Maine	Resumed	5	Mar. 5, 1903	Mar. 3, 1905

(*continued*)

TABLE A.3 (*continued*)

Cong.	President pro tempore	Party and state	Rank	Resolution	First day	Last day
59th	William P. Frye	R, Maine	3	Resumed	Mar. 4, 1905	Mar. 3, 1907
60th	William P. Frye	R, Maine	2	Resolution	Dec. 5, 1907	Mar. 3, 1909
61st	William P. Frye	R, Maine	1	Resumed	Mar. 4, 1909	Apr. 3, 1911
62nd	William P. Frye	R, Maine	1	Resumed	Apr. 4, 1911	Apr. 27, 1911
	Augustus O. Bacon	D, Ga.	1	Resolution	Aug. 14, 1911	Aug. 14, 1911
	Charles Curtis	R, Kans.	23	Resolution	Dec. 4, 1911	Dec. 12, 1911
	Augustus O. Bacon	D, Ga.	1	Resolution	Jan. 15, 1912	Jan. 17, 1912
	Jacob H. Gallinger	R, N.H.	2	Resolution	Feb. 12, 1912	Feb. 14, 1912
	Augustus O. Bacon	D, Ga.	1	Resolution	Mar. 11, 1912	Mar. 12, 1912
	Frank B. Brandegee	R, Conn.	21	Resolution	Mar. 25, 1912	Mar. 26, 1912
	Augustus O. Bacon	D, Ga.	1	Resolution	Apr. 8, 1912	Apr. 8, 1912
	Jacob H. Gallinger	R, N.H.	2	Resolution	Apr. 26, 1912	Apr. 27, 1912
	Jacob H. Gallinger			Resolution	May 7, 1912	May 7, 1912
	Augustus O. Bacon	D, Ga.	1	Resolution	May 10, 1912	May 10, 1912
	Henry Cabot Lodge	R, Mass.	4	Resolution	May 25, 1912	May 25, 1912
	Augustus O. Bacon	D, Ga.	1	Resolution	May 30, 1912	June 3, 1912
	Augustus O. Bacon			Resolution	June 13, 1912	July 5, 1912
	Jacob H. Gallinger	R, N.H.	2	Resolution	July 6, 1912	July 31, 1912
	Augustus O. Bacon	D, Ga.	1	Resolution	Aug. 1, 1912	Aug. 10, 1912
	Jacob H. Gallinger	R, N.H.	2	Resolution	Aug. 12, 1912	Aug. 26, 1912
	Augustus O. Bacon	D, Ga.	1	Resolution	Aug. 27, 1912	Dec. 15, 1912
	Jacob H. Gallinger	R, N.H.	2	Resolution	Dec. 16, 1912	Jan. 4, 1913
	Augustus O. Bacon	D, Ga.	1	Resolution	Jan. 5, 1913	Jan. 18, 1913
	Jacob H. Gallinger	R, N.H.	2	Resolution	Jan. 19, 1913	Feb. 1, 1913
	Augustus O. Bacon	D, Ga.	1	Resolution	Feb. 2, 1913	Feb. 15, 1913
	Jacob H. Gallinger	R, N.H.	2	Resolution	Feb. 16, 1913	Mar. 3, 1913

63rd	James P. Clarke	D, Ark.	6	Resolution	Mar. 13, 1913	Mar. 3, 1915
64th	James P. Clarke	D, Ark.	5	Resolution	Dec. 6, 1915	Oct. 1, 1916
	Willard Saulsbury	D, Del.	35	Ballot	Dec. 14, 1916	Mar. 4, 1917
65th	Willard Saulsbury	D, Del.	27	Resumed	Mar. 5, 1917	Mar. 3, 1919
66th	Albert B. Cummins	R, Iowa	12	Resolution	May 19, 1919	Mar. 3, 1921
67th	Albert B. Cummins	R, Iowa	12	Resolution	Mar. 7, 1921	Dec. 2, 1923
68th	Albert B. Cummins	R, Iowa	9	Resumed	Dec. 3, 1923	Mar. 3, 1925
69th	Albert B. Cummins	R, Iowa	5	Resumed	Mar. 4, 1925	Mar. 6, 1925
	George H. Moses	R, N.H.	16	Resolution	Mar. 6, 1925	Mar. 4, 1927
70th	George H. Moses	R, N.H.	12	Resolution	Dec. 15, 1927	Mar. 3, 1929
71st	George H. Moses	R, N.H.	10	Resumed	Mar. 4, 1929	Dec. 6, 1931
72nd	George H. Moses	R, N.H.	9	Resumed	Dec. 7, 1931	Mar. 3, 1933
73rd	Key Pittman	D, Nev.	5	Resolution	Mar. 9, 1933	Jan. 2, 1935
74th	Key Pittman	D, Nev.	5	Resolution	Jan. 7, 1935	Jan. 4, 1937
75th	Key Pittman	D, Nev.	4	Resumed	Jan. 5, 1937	Jan. 2, 1939

(continued)

TABLE A.3 (continued)

Cong.	President pro tempore	Party and state	Rank		First day	Last day
76th	Key Pittman	D, Nev.	4	Resumed	Jan. 3, 1939	Nov. 10, 1940
	William H. King	D, Utah	4	Resolution	Nov. 19, 1940	Jan. 3, 1941
77th	Pat Harrison	D, Miss.	4	Resolution	Jan. 6, 1941	June 22, 1941
	Carter Glass	D, Va.	3	Resolution	July 10, 1941	Jan. 5, 1943
78th	Carter Glass	D, Va.	3	Resolution	Jan. 14, 1943	Jan. 2, 1945
79th	Kenneth McKellar	D, Tenn.	1	Resolution	Jan. 6, 1945	Jan. 2, 1947
80th	Arthur H. Vandenberg	R, Mich.	2	Resolution	Jan. 4, 1947	Jan. 2, 1949
81st	Kenneth McKellar	D, Tenn.	1	Resolution	Jan. 3, 1949	Jan. 2, 1951
82nd	Kenneth McKellar	D, Tenn.	1	Resumed	Jan. 3, 1951	Jan. 2, 1953
83rd	Styles Bridges	R, N.H.	1	Resolution	Jan. 3, 1953	Jan. 4, 1955
84th	Walter F. George	D, Ga.	1	Resolution	Jan. 5, 1955	Jan. 2, 1957
85th	Carl Hayden	D, Ariz.	1	Resolution	Jan. 3, 1957	Jan. 6, 1959
86th	Carl Hayden	D, Ariz.	1	Resumed	Jan. 7, 1959	Jan. 2, 1961
87th	Carl Hayden	D, Ariz.	1	Resumed	Jan. 3, 1961	Jan. 8, 1963
88th	Carl Hayden	D, Ariz.	1	Resolution	Jan. 9, 1963	Jan. 3, 1965
89th	Carl Hayden	D, Ariz.	1	Resumed	Jan. 4, 1965	Jan. 9, 1967

91st	Richard B. Russell	D, Ga.	1	Resolution	Jan. 3, 1969	Jan. 20, 1971
92nd	Richard B. Russell	D, Ga.	1	Resumed	Jan. 21, 1971	Jan. 21, 1971
	Allen J. Ellender	D, La.	1	Resolution	Jan. 22, 1971	July 27, 1972
	James O. Eastland	D, Miss.	1	Resolution	July 28, 1972	Jan. 2, 1973
93rd	James O. Eastland	D, Miss.	1	Resolution	Jan. 3, 1973	Jan. 13, 1975
94th	James O. Eastland	D, Miss.	1	Resumed	Jan. 14, 1975	Jan. 3, 1977
95th	James O. Eastland	D, Miss.	1	Resumed	Jan. 4, 1977	Dec. 27, 1978
96th	Warren G. Magnuson	D, Wash.	1	Resolution	Jan. 15, 1979	Dec. 4, 1980
	Milton R. Young	R, N.Dak.	1	Resolution	Dec. 5, 1980	Dec. 5, 1980
	Warren G. Magnuson	D, Wash.	1	Resumed	Dec. 6, 1980	Jan. 4, 1981
97th	Strom Thurmond	R, S.C.	1	Resolution	Jan. 5, 1981	Jan. 2, 1983
98th	Strom Thurmond	R, S.C.	1	Resumed	Jan. 3, 1983	Jan. 2, 1985
99th	Strom Thurmond	R, S.C.	1	Resolution	Jan. 3, 1985	Jan. 5, 1987
100th	John C. Stennis	D, Miss.	1	Resolution	Jan. 6, 1987	Jan. 2, 1989
101st	Robert C. Byrd	D, W.Va.	1	Resolution	Jan. 3, 1989	Jan. 2, 1991
102nd	Robert C. Byrd	D, W.Va.	1	Resumed	Jan. 3, 1991	Jan. 4, 1993
103rd	Robert C. Byrd	D, W.Va.	1	Resumed	Jan. 5, 1993	Jan. 3, 1995

(continued)

TABLE A.3 (continued)

Cong.	President pro tempore	Party and state	Rank		First day	Last day
104th	Strom Thurmond	R, S.C.	1	Resolution	Jan. 4, 1995	Jan. 6, 1997
105th	Strom Thurmond	R, S.C.	1	Resumed	Jan. 7, 1997	Jan. 5, 1999
106th	Strom Thurmond	R, S.C.	1	Resumed	Jan. 6, 1999	Jan. 2, 2001
107th	Robert C. Byrd	D, W.Va.	1	Resolution	Jan. 3, 2001	Jan. 20, 2001
	Strom Thurmond	R, S.C.	1	Resolution	Jan. 20, 2001	June 6, 2001
	Robert C. Byrd	D, W.Va.	1	Resolution	June 6, 2001	Jan. 6, 2003
108th	Ted Stevens	R, Alaska	1	Resolution	Jan. 7, 2003	Jan. 3, 2005
109th	Ted Stevens	R, Alaska	1	Resumed	Jan. 4, 2005	Jan. 3, 2007
110th	Robert C. Byrd	D, W.Va.	1	Resolution	Jan. 4, 2007	Jan. 5, 2009
111th	Robert C. Byrd	D, W.Va.	1	Resumed	Jan. 6, 2009	June 28, 2010
	Daniel K. Inouye	D, Hawaii	1	Resolution	June 28, 2010	Jan. 4, 2011
112th	Daniel K. Inouye	D, Hawaii	1	Resumed	Jan. 5, 2011	Dec. 17, 2012
	Patrick J. Leahy	D, Vt.	1	Resolution	Dec. 17, 2012	Jan. 2, 2013
113th	Patrick J. Leahy	D, Vt.	1	Resumed	Jan. 3, 2013	Jan. 5, 2015
114th	Orrin Hatch	R, Utah	1	Resolution	Jan. 6, 2015	Jan. 2, 2017
115th	Orrin Hatch	R, Utah	1	Resumed	Jan. 3, 2017	Jan. 2, 2019
116th	Chuck Grassley	R, Iowa	1	Resolution	Jan. 3, 2019	Jan. 2, 2021

117th	Chuck Grassley	R, Iowa	1	Resumed Resolution	Jan. 3, 2021	Jan. 19, 2021
	Patrick J. Leahy	D, Vt.	1		Jan. 20, 2021	Jan. 2, 2023
118th	Patty Murray	D, Wash.	1	Resolution	Jan. 3, 2023	Jan. 2, 2025
119th	Chuck Grassley	R, Iowa	1	Resolution	Jan. 3, 2025	

Notes and sources for Table A.3.

No list previously existed of presidents pro tempore with their dates of service. Several lists of presidents pro tempore, without dates of service, did exist. Although we found inaccuracies in these other lists, they were helpful in laying a groundwork for this table. The best of these compilations are Gilfry (1911) and the *Senate Manual.* These two sources, which rely on the *Senate Journal* and the various records of congressional debates, contain relatively comprehensive lists of presidents pro tempore, including dates of election. Both sources, though, contain several omissions and one erroneous inclusion (Ambrose Sevier, in the 29th Congress, who, like many other senators, presided over the Senate for a day but was never elected president pro tempore). More important, the two sources are inconsistent in their treatment of presidents pro tempore who resume the chair without a new election, and neither source lists the dates that terms end. (Other lists of presidents pro tempore are based entirely on one or the other of these two sources, including Byrd 1993, iv: 647–53; Sachs 1995; Vincent et al. 1996; and the *Congressional Directory.* Thus they duplicate the flaws of the originals, while introducing new inaccuracies.) An entirely different source for a list of presidents pro tempore—drawing data not from the *Senate Journal* but from the signatures attached to enrolled bills—is contained in the volumes of *U.S. Statutes at Large.* Because weeks often elapsed in the nineteenth century without enrolled bills, these data are less reliable than the day-to-day proceedings recorded in the *Journal.*

To compile this table, we turned directly to the original sources—the *Senate Journal,* the records of debates (the *Annals,* the *Register of Debates,* the *Congressional Globe,* and the *Congressional Record*), and, in cases where neither the *Journal* nor the debates indicated the last day of a president pro tempore's term, the signatures on original copies of enrolled bills. Scott Amrozowicz and Jeff Jackson did most of the work for this massive research project, patiently compiling independent versions of this table, then reconciling their two lists. Drawing on an unpublished draft of the table we present here, the Senate Historical Office updated its own records and website (though retaining the erroneous inclusion of Sevier in the 29th Congress). The table now appears online at www.senate.gov/artandhistory/history/common/briefing/President_Pro_Tempore.htm#5.

Until Mar. 12, 1890, the term of the president pro tempore ended whenever the vice president appeared in the Senate. Since Mar. 12, 1890, the president pro tempore has held his office at the pleasure of the Senate; he keeps his office whether or not the vice president is in attendance, though he exercises the duties of the office only in the absence of the vice president. In determining terms of service, we include recesses when a president pro tempore sat in the chair at the adjournment of a session. Also, we consulted Byrd (1993, iv: 75–188) to identify accurate end dates for presidents pro tempore who died, left office, or were ending a six-year Senate term. For the first 76 Congresses, "rank" is determined according to cumulative years of Senate service, as reported in the ICPSR biographical data file. Beginning with the 77th Congress, we define "rank" by years of consecutive service in the Senate. Dates written in *italics* are not precise.

TABLE A.4 *Senate Republican committee on the order of business (through 1913)*

Date	Committee
Feb. 10–Mar. 3, 1863	Fessenden, Trumbull, Wilson, Collamer, Grimes
Mar. 8–10, 1869	Trumbull, Sherman, Edmunds, Pool, Stewart
Apr. 24–29, 1872	Scott (chair), Hamlin, Morrill of Vt., Morton, Sawyer, Logan, Sherman
Feb. 10–14, 1873	*Three-person committee, membership unknown*
May 11–18, 1874	Edmunds (chair) *and four others*
Dec. 8–9, 1874	*Membership unknown*
Apr.–May 3, 1878	Edmunds (chair), Blaine, Hoar, Oglesby, Cameron of Wisc., Sargent
Dec. 3–11, 1878	Blaine, Edmunds, Dawes, Howe, Christiancy ("an advisory committee … in all political matter")
Feb. 5–13, 1879	*Membership unknown*
Apr. 27–May 3, 1881	Dawes (chair), Rollins, Ingalls, Jones of Nev., Cameron of Wisc., Miller of Calif., Sewell
Oct. 8, 1881	Edmunds (chair), Sherman, Allison, McMillan, Logan ("to confer … upon the organization of the Senate")
Dec. 4, 1882–Mar. 3, 1883	Allison, Edmunds, Sherman, Morrill, Hawley, Hill, Miller of Calif., Harrison, Aldrich, Logan, Ingalls
Mar. 31–July 7, 1884	*Nine-person committee, membership unknown*
Dec. 2, 1884–Mar. 3, 1885	*Same committee, continued in new session*
Apr.–Aug. 5, 1886	**Edmunds**, Allison, Conger
Dec. 1886	*Membership unknown*
Feb. 5–Mar. 3, 1887	Sherman, Allison, *and others*
Mar. 31–Oct. 20, 1888	Sherman (chair), Allison, Teller, Hiscock, Stewart, Chandler, Morrill, Plumb, Aldrich, Jones of Nev., Hoar
Mar. 19–May 1890	**Edmunds** (chair), Sherman, Allison, Platt, Teller, Cullom, Dolph
July 10–Aug. 1890	Hoar, Spooner, Frye, Moody, Platt, Aldrich, Sherman, Ingalls, **Edmunds** (on cloture and the order of business)
Aug. 21–Oct. 1, 1890	Hoar (chair), Allison, Evarts, Plumb, Spooner, Hale, Allen
Dec. 1, 1890–Mar. 3, 1891	*Same committee, continued in new session*
June–Aug. 5, 1892	*Membership unknown*
Dec. 15, 1892–Jan. 5, 1893	Hoar (chair), McMillan, Chandler, Teller, Mitchell (special "steering committee" on state elections) "To take into consideration the wisdom and propriety of Senatorial interference in the [electoral] contests." "To advise on any measures necessary to be taken to defend Republican interests." "To determine what action … [to] take in regard to the election of Senators in the doubtful States." "To watch every move made by the Democrats with a view to securing Democratic Senators."
Jan. 1893	Teller (chair), Hoar, Mitchell, Chandler, Higgins (same committee reconstituted, all on Privileges and Elections) "To take special charge of the subject of organization" and promote Republican interests in doubtful states. "[To] see that nothing is done to 'jeopardize the chances of the Republicans.'" "[To watch] the Senatorial elections in the West and … meet any contests arising out of the disputes."

Jan. 5–Mar. 3, 1893	**Sherman** (chair), Frye, Dolph, Cullom, Platt, Washburn, Quay
Dec. 5, 1893–Aug. 28, 1894	Allison (chair), Aldrich, Hale, Cullom, Dolph, Manderson, Quay, Washburn, Dubois
Dec. 3, 1894–Mar. 3, 1895	*Same committee, continued in new session*
Mar. 4–Dec. 1, 1895	*Same committee, continued through the recess*
Apr. 23–June 11, 1896	Allison (chair), Hale, Aldrich, Davis, Quay, McMillan, Dubois, Perkins, Pritchard
June 12–Dec. 7, 1896	*Same committee, continued through the recess*
Dec. 8, 1896–Mar. 3, 1897	Allison (chair), Aldrich, Hale, McMillan, Cullom, Perkins, Quay, Davis, Hansbrough, Shoup
Mar. 9–July 24, 1897	**Allison** (chair), Hale, Aldrich, Cullom, Davis, Sewell, Carter
Mar.–Apr. 1898	Allison (chair), Aldrich, Spooner, Hawley, Burrows, Hanna, Wolcott
Dec. 1898–Mar. 3, 1899	Allison (chair), Cullom, *and others*
Mar. 4–Dec. 3, 1899	*Same committee, continued through the recess*
Feb. 24–June 7, 1900	Allison (chair), Hale, Aldrich, Cullom, Wolcott, Sewell, Spooner, McBride, Hanna
June 8–Dec. 2, 1900	*Same committee, continued through the recess, with Elkins replacing Cullom*
Dec. 3, 1900–Mar. 3, 1901	*Same committee, continued in new session*
Mar. 4–9, 1901	*Same committee, continued in new Congress*
Feb. 7–July 1, 1902	Allison (chair), Aldrich, Hale, Cullom, Lodge, Perkins, Clark of Wyo., Elkins, Spooner, Hanna, Beveridge
July 2–Nov. 30, 1902	*Same committee, continued through the recess*
Dec. 1, 1902–Mar. 3, 1903	*Same committee, continued in new session*
Mar. 5–19, 1903	*Same committee, continued in new Congress*
Mar. 20–Nov. 8, 1903	*Same committee, continued through the recess*
Jan. 6–Feb. 15, 1904	Allison (chair), Hale, Aldrich, Cullom, Lodge, Perkins, Clark of Wyo., Elkins, Spooner, Hanna, Beveridge
Feb. 16–Apr. 28, 1904	*Same committee, with Kean replacing Hanna*
Apr. 29–Dec. 4, 1904	*Same committee, continued through the recess*
Dec. 5, 1904–Mar. 3, 1905	*Same committee, continued in new session*
Mar. 4–18, 1905	*Same committee, continued in new Congress*
Mar. 19–Dec. 4, 1905	*Same committee, continued through the recess*
Jan.–June 30, 1906	**Allison** (chair), Hale, Aldrich, Cullom, Lodge, Perkins, Clark of Wyo., Elkins, Spooner, Kean, Beveridge
Dec. 3, 1906–Mar. 3, 1907	*Same committee, continued in new session*
Jan.–May 30, 1908	Allison (chair), Hale, Aldrich, Cullom, Lodge, Perkins, Clark of Wyo., Elkins, Nelson, Kean, Beveridge
Dec. 9, 1908–Mar. 3, 1909	*Same committee, continued in new session, with* **Hale** *succeeding* **Allison** *as chair*
Mar. 22–Aug. 5, 1909	**Hale** (chair), Aldrich, Cullom, Lodge, Perkins, Clark of Wyo., Elkins, Nelson, Kean, Beveridge, Nixon
Dec. 6, 1909–June 25, 1910	*Same committee, continued in new session*
Dec. 5, 1910–Mar. 3, 1911	*Same committee, continued in new session*

(continued)

425

TABLE A.4 (continued)

Apr. 5–Aug. 22, 1911	**Cullom** (chair), Gallinger, Clark of Wyo., Nelson, Gamble, Brandegee, Smith, Borah, Brown, Briggs, Jones
May–Aug. 26, 1912	Crane (chair), Gallinger, Smoot, Heyburn, Warren, *and others*
Feb. 7–Mar. 3, 1913	Oliver (chair), Smoot, La Follette, Cummins, Root

Notes and sources for Table A.4

Caucus chair appears in **bold**. Where a specific date is uncertain, it appears in *italics*. In these cases, we lack any evidence to suggest the committee existed before this month (for starting dates) or beyond this month (for ending dates).

Sources: Except for some scattered information, the emergence and development of the Republican steering committee has been entirely unknown to congressional scholars. This table contains all references we have located to Senate Republican caucus committees on the order of business until 1913 (apart from references to committees named on Jan. 11, 1879 and Jan. 17, 1881, which, upon closer scrutiny, appeared, despite the terminology in some newspapers, to be caucus committees unrelated to the order of business). Most of these committees were termed "committees on the order of business" or, in later years, "steering committees"; where the language differs from this, we indicate the committee's responsibility. In assembling the list, we consulted various sources to determine whether the Senate Republican caucus named any sort of committee on the order of business and, where we find such a committee, to identify the committee's membership. We began this work by searching the *New York Times*, *Washington Post*, *Wall Street Journal*, and *Christian Science Monitor*, then expanded the search to include the *Congressional Record* and the digital archives of the following newspapers: *Arizona Republican*, *Atlanta Constitution*, *Austin American Statesman*, *Baltimore Sun*, *Boston Globe*, *Boston Herald**, *Chicago Tribune*, *Cincinnati Enquirer*, *Detroit Free Press*, *Los Angeles Times*, *Louisville Courier Journal*, *Minneapolis Star Tribune*, *Nashville Tennessean*, *New York Tribune*, *Philadelphia Inquirer**, *San Francisco Chronicle*, *St. Louis Post Dispatch*, *St. Petersburg Times*, and *Washington Evening Star**. All but three of these newspapers are available through ProQuest Historical Newspapers; the others, identified with asterisks, are in America's Historical Newspapers, the U.S. Northeast Collection in ProQuest Historical Newspapers, and Chronicling America: Historic American Newspapers. Redd Brown, Hugh Curran, and Zach Lawlor did outstanding work searching these databases. What follows are our sources for each of the Republican committees: "Republican Caucus," *New York Tribune*, Feb. 11, 1863, 4; "From Washington," *Chicago Tribune*, Feb. 11, 1863, 1; "Secretary Seward's Private Confidential Dispatches," *New York Tribune*, Mar. 2, 1863, 1; "Appearances indicate …," *Cincinnati Commercial Tribune*, Mar. 9, 1869, 4; "Republican Senatorial Caucus," *New York Herald*, Mar. 9, 1869, 3; "Business of Congress," *Cincinnati Daily Gazette*, Mar. 10, 1869, 3; "Personal and Political," *Burlington Daily Free Press and Times*, Mar. 11, 1869, 2; "Republican Caucus," *Cincinnati Daily Gazette*, Mar. 11, 1869, 3; "Republican Caucus," *New York Times*, Mar. 11, 1869, 1; "Senate Republican Caucus," *Chicago Tribune*, Mar. 11, 1869, 1; "Current Topics at the Capital," *New York Tribune*, Apr. 25, 1872, 1; "A Senate Republican Caucus," *Chicago Tribune*, Apr. 25, 1872, 2; "Work for the Senate Caucus," *New York Times*, Apr. 29, 1872, 1; "Order of Business in the Senate," *Louisville Courier Journal*, Apr. 30, 1872, 1; "Business in the Senate," *National Republican*

(Washington, D.C.), Feb. 11, 1873, 1; "Caucus of Republican Senators," *New York Times*, Feb. 11, 1873, 1; "Senatorial Republican Caucus," *Commercial Advertiser (New York, N.Y.)*, Feb. 14, 1873, 4; "Republican Senatorial Caucus," *Cincinnati Daily Gazette*, Feb. 15, 1873, 1; "Washington: Radical Senators in Labor," *Cincinnati Enquirer*, May 12, 1874, 1; "Later as to the Civil-Rights Bill," *Richmond Daily Dispatch*, May 13, 1874, 2; "The Adjournment of Congress," *Burlington Daily Free Press and Times*, May 19, 1874, 3; "The Caucus of the Republican Senators," *New York Times*, Dec. 9, 1874, 5; "Senatorial Conference," *Chicago Tribune*, Dec. 9, 1874, 1; "The Caucus of Republican Senators," *Boston Evening Traveller*, Dec. 9, 1874, 4; "The Republican Senatorial Caucus," *Boston Journal*, May 4, 1878, 4; "The Coming Campaign: What the Republicans Are Doing," *Inter Ocean (Chicago, Ill.)*, May 4, 1878, 2; "The Proposed Outrage Inquiry," *New York Times*, Dec. 4, 1878, 1; "Two Senate Caucuses," *National Republican*, Dec. 4, 1878, 1; "Righteous Retaliation," *National Republican*, Dec. 7, 1878, 1; "Washington," *Nashville Tennessean*, Jan. 12, 1879, 1; "The Caucus of Senators," *New York Tribune*, Jan. 13, 1879, 1; "A Caucus of Republican Senators," *Washington Evening Star*, Feb. 5, 1879, 1; "Order of Business in the Senate," *Washington Evening Star*, Feb. 13, 1879, 1; "Washington," *St. Louis Post Dispatch*, Feb. 13, 1879, 4; "Republican Senatorial Caucus," *New York Times*, Feb. 14, 1879, 1; "The Kellogg Case: Programme of the Republican Senators," *Minneapolis Tribune*, Jan. 18, 1881, 1; "The Kellogg Case," *New Haven Evening Register*, Jan. 18, 1881, 1; "Republican Senators Consulting," *New York Tribune*, Jan. 18, 1881, 1; "The Kellogg Plot Fails," *New York Times*, Jan. 18, 1881, 1; "Caucus of Republican Senators," *Baltimore Sun*, Jan. 18, 1881, 1; "The Republican Caucus," *New York Times*, Apr. 28, 1881, 1; "The Senatorial Caucus," *Washington Post*, Apr. 28, 1881, 1; "Notes from Washington," *New York Times*, Apr. 29, 1881, 1; "Troubles of the Senate," *New York Times*, May 3, 1881, 1; "The Dead-Lock Broken," *Washington Post*, May 4, 1881, 1; "Garfield at the Front," *Washington Post*, May 7, 1881, 1; "The New York Patronage," *New York Times*, May 9, 1881, 5; "The New Administration," *New York Times*, Oct. 9, 1881, 1; "The Situation: It Is Bad," *Chicago Tribune*, Oct. 9, 1881, 9; "Agree to Disagree," *Louisville Courier Journal*, Oct. 9, 1881, 2; "Organization of the Senate," *New York Tribune*, Oct. 9, 1881, 1; "Senate Republicans," *Boston Herald*, Dec. 15, 1882, 4; "Christmas Holidays," *Boston Herald*, Dec. 20, 1882, 2; "Prospects of Mr. Pendleton's Bill," *Public Ledger (Memphis, Tenn.)*, Dec. 26, 1882, 2; "Caucus of Republican Senators," *New York Tribune*, Feb. 7, 1883, 1; "Notes from Washington," *New York Times*, Feb. 11, 1883, 8; "Business before the Senate," *New York Times*, Feb. 23, 1883, 1; "Two Republican Caucuses," *Washington Post*, Feb. 23, 1883, 1; "Washington: News Gathered about the Capital City," *Austin American Statesman*, Feb. 23, 1883, 1; "News from Washington: The Senate Organization," *Baltimore Sun*, Feb. 28, 1883, 1; "Order of Business," *Boston Herald*, Apr. 1, 1884, 1; "Republican Senators in Caucus," *New York Times*, Apr. 1, 1884, 5; "Congressional Notes," *Washington Post*, Dec. 3, 1884, 1; "Washington Notes," *New York Tribune*, Dec. 3, 1884, 1; "Republican Senatorial Caucus," *Baltimore Sun*, Dec. 3, 1884,1; "Postal Telegraphy: Some Queer Work in the Senate," *Chicago Tribune*, Dec. 10, 1884, 6; "Order of Business in the Senate," *Washington Evening Star*, Feb. 6, 1885, 1; "Republican and Democratic Conference," *St. Louis Post Dispatch*, Apr. 19, 1886, 2; "Business in the Senate," *Washington Post*, Apr. 20, 1886, 1; "In Congress Yesterday," *Washington Post*, May 28, 1886, 2; "Notes from Washington," *New York Times*, June 10, 1886, 3; "Logan Shakes His Mane," *Boston Herald*, July 22, 1886, 8; "Caucus of Republican Senators," *Baltimore Sun*, Dec. 18, 1886, 1; "Republican Senatorial Caucus," *St. Louis Post Dispatch*, Feb. 5, 1887, 3; "A Fruitless Caucus," *New York Times*, Feb. 6, 1887, 6; "Washington: Steering Committee Appointed by Republican Senators," *Nashville Tennessean*,

Feb. 6, 1887, 1; "Pension Agents at Work," *New York Times*, Feb. 17, 1887, 5; "What the Week May Bring Forth," *New York Herald*, Feb. 21, 1887, 2; "Work for Congress to Do," *New York Times*, Feb. 21, 1887, 2; *but see also* "A Senate Steering Committee," *New York Herald*, Feb. 16, 1887, 3; which names a three-person committee that includes neither Allison nor Sherman; *and, from the next day in the same newspaper,* "Washington Notes," *New York Herald*, Feb. 17, 1887, 3; which identifies Sherman as the committee chair; "Senators in Caucus: Solving a Republican Dilemma," *New York Tribune*, Mar. 30, 1888, 2; "The republican senators held a caucus this morning …," *Burlington Free Press*, Mar. 31, 1888, 3; "The Senate Order of Business," *St. Louis Post Dispatch*, Mar. 31, 1888, 2; "General Washington News," *Louisville Courier Journal*, Apr. 1, 1888, 12; "Badly Mixed," *Minneapolis Tribune*, Apr. 2, 1888, 1; "The Bond Bill in the Senate," *Washington Post*, Apr. 3, 1888, 2; "Republican Senators," *Louisville Courier Journal*, Apr. 14, 1888, 2; "Republican Caucus," *Washington Evening Star*, May 18, 1888, 3; "Democratic Senators in Caucus," *Washington Critic*, June 28, 1888, 1; "Order of Business,'" *Washington Critic*, Aug. 9, 1888, 1; "Clearing the Senate Calendar," *Washington Post*, Aug. 16, 1888, 2; "Fighting for Life," *Nashville Tennessean*, Aug. 16, 1888, 1; "Republican Senators in Caucus," *New York Tribune*, Aug. 16, 1888, 1; "Republican Senators Caucus," *Pittsburg Dispatch*, Mar. 19, 1890, 1; "The Leaders Alarmed," *Pittsburg Dispatch*, Mar. 21, 1890, 1; "Mr. Chipman Protests," *New York Times*, Mar. 24, 1890, 5; "The Week in Congress: The Montana Senatorial Question to Be Considered," *Atlanta Constitution*, Mar. 31, 1890, 1; "The Committee on the Order of Business …," *New York Times*, Mar. 31, 1890, 4; "Is Ready for Use," *Minneapolis Tribune*, May 1, 1890, 1; "Silver Legislation," *Wall Street Journal*, May 2, 1890, 1; "The Radicals' Programme," *Louisville Courier Journal*, July 11, 1890, 1; "Plan for a Closure of Debate," *Rochester Democrat and Chronicle*, July 12, 1890, 1; "From Washington," *Baltimore Sun*, July 12, 1890, 1; "The Senate Conference," *New York Tribune*, July 12, 1890, 2; "Business in the Senate," *Boston Herald*, July 20, 1890, 6; "National Capital Gossip," *Detroit Free Press*, July 20, 1890, 1; "The Force Bill Goes Over," *New York Times*, Aug. 23, 1890, 1; "Republican Plans," *Louisville Courier Journal*, Aug. 23, 1890, 1; "The Force Bill To Be Rushed," *Atlanta Constitution*, Dec. 2, 1890, 1; "Getting Down to Work," *Atlanta Constitution*, Jan. 28, 1891, 1; "Radicals Accept Defeat," *New York Times*, Jan. 28, 1891, 5; "New Mexico's Needs," *Washington Post*, Feb. 24, 1891, 4; "Morgan Stands All Alone," *New York Times*, June 30, 1892, 4; "Senators Talking Business," *Pittsburg Dispatch*, June 30, 1892, 1; "Republican Senatorial Caucus," *Washington Evening Star*, Dec. 15, 1892, 1; "Doubtful Senate Seats," *New York Times*, Dec. 16, 1892, 5; "All Sections Now in Line," *Washington Post*, Dec. 16, 1892, 1; "Conferring on the Western Senatorships," *New York Tribune*, Dec. 16, 1892, 2; "Republican Senatorial Caucus," *Washington Evening Star*, Dec. 21, 1892, 1; "Republican Steering Committee," *Baltimore Sun*, Dec. 21, 1892, 2; "'Tis Greek Meet Greek," *Washington Post*, Dec. 21, 1892, 1; "Watching the Doubtful States," *Chicago Tribune*, Dec. 22, 1892, 9; "The Republican Senate Steering Committee," *Washington Evening Star*, Dec. 29, 1892, 6; "No New 'Steering' Committee," *New York Tribune*, Dec. 30, 1892, 2; "A Republican Caucus," *Washington Evening Star*, Jan. 5, 1893, 6; "The Republican Senatorial Caucus," *Washington Post*, Jan. 6, 1893, 1; "No Surrender Intended," *New York Times*, Jan. 6, 1893, 3; "Will Fight for Control," *Atlanta Constitution*, Jan. 6, 1893, 1; "To Fix a Programme for the Senate," *New York Tribune*, Jan. 6, 1893, 5; "May Vote on Anti-Option," *Chicago Tribune*, Jan. 11, 1893, 10; "A Programme Arranged," *New York Tribune*, Jan. 25, 1893, 5; "Senate Republicans," *Boston Herald*, Dec. 5, 1893, 2; "Will Fight Cleveland," *Washington Post*, Dec. 6, 1893, 7; "Mr. Harris's Motion Prevails," *New York Times*, Aug. 17, 1894, 2; "Derelict in Its Duty," *Baltimore Sun*, Dec. 6, 1894, 1;

"Republicans Say No to Tariff," *Wall Street Journal*, Jan. 7, 1895, 1; "To Agree Upon a Policy," *New York Times*, Jan. 7, 1895, 1; "More Bolts on the Door," *Washington Post*, Jan. 8, 1895, 1; "Tariff and Finance," *Washington Evening Star*, Jan. 9, 1895, 3; "Committees Will Hold Over," *New York Times*, Mar. 3, 1895, 3; "Republican Senate Caucus," *New York Times*, Nov. 29, 1895, 7; "Senate Reorganization," *New York Tribune*, Dec. 6, 1895, 1; "Washington News," *Wall Street Journal*, Mar. 18, 1896, 1; "A Republican Caucus," *Washington Evening Star*, Apr. 23, 1896, 2; "Preparing To Adjourn," *New York Times*, Apr. 24, 1896, 2; "For an Order of Business," *Washington Post*, May 27, 1896, 4; "To-Day's Caucus," *Wall Street Journal*, Dec. 8, 1896, 1; "The Dingley Bill," *Washington Evening Star*, Dec. 8, 1896, 1; "Ready for Its Quietus," *Washington Post*, Dec. 9, 1896, 2; "Republican Senate Caucus," *New York Times*, Dec. 9, 1896, 1; "Dingley Bill Doomed," *Philadelphia Inquirer*, Dec. 9, 1896, 1; "Silver Rules the Senate," *New York Tribune*, Dec. 9, 1896, 1; "Allen Sprung a Mine," *Baltimore Sun*, Dec. 10, 1896, 1; "Steering Committee Meeting," *Washington Post*, Jan. 7, 1897, 4; "No Bargain, Says Mr. Kyle," *New York Times*, Feb. 20, 1897, 2; "Democratic Senators Will Go Slow," *New York Tribune*, Mar. 10, 1897, 2; "Dubois as Secretary," *Washington Post*, Mar. 10, 1897, 4; "Steering Committee," *Austin American Statesman*, Mar. 10, 1897, 2; "Had Hot Words," *New York Times*, Boston Herald, May 27, 1897, 2; *Cong. Rec.*, July 7, 1897, 2428; *Cong. Rec.*, July 22, 1897, 2817; "Foreign Relations Committee," *New York Times*, Mar. 31, 1898, 3; "Must Know by Monday," *Boston Globe*, Mar. 31, 1898, 1; "Cannot Avert War," *Washington Post*, Apr. 9, 1898, 1; "Still Undecided," *Washington Evening Star*, Apr. 11, 1898, 1; "Beer Tax Will Remain," *Bay City (Mich.) Times*, Dec. 11, 1898, 1; "Spanish Theft Aids Carlists: Cullom's Senatorial Duties," *Chicago Tribune*, Jan. 9, 1899, 7; "To Force Extra Session," *Chicago Tribune*, Feb. 23, 1899, 7; "To Reorganize Senate," *Boston Herald*, Mar. 24, 1899, 2; "Without Precedent," *Biloxi (Miss.) Herald*, Dec. 31, 1899, 6; "Caucus of Senators," *Washington Evening Star*, Feb. 14, 1900, 1; "Quay Case Is Buried," *Boston Herald*, Feb. 17, 1900, 2; "Order of Business in the Senate," *New York Tribune*, Feb. 25, 1900, 4; "Senate Steering Committee," *New York Tribune*, Feb. 25, 1900, 5; "Senator Allison's Views," *New York Tribune*, June 8, 1900, 1; "Fifty-sixth Congress Bare of Great Results," *New York Times*, June 10, 1900, 28; "Will Provoke a Fight," *Washington Post*, Nov. 24, 1900, 1; "Anxious for Subsidy," *Washington Post*, Dec. 1, 1900, 3; "Aldrich on Shipping Bill," *Washington Post*, Jan. 2, 1901, 6; "Says It Cannot Pass," *Washington Post*, Feb. 16, 1901, 4; "Big Money Measures," *Boston Herald*, Feb. 16, 1901, 12; "The Army Bill's Chances," *New York Times*, Mar. 1, 1901, 5; "Democrats Object," *Washington Evening Star*, Mar. 6, 1901, 1; "Business of Senate," *Washington Post*, Feb. 8, 1902, 2; Jos. Ohl, "Steering Committee Led by Allison," *Los Angeles Times*, Sept. 21, 1902, 1; "Mr. Quay's Fight for the Statehood Bill," *New York Times*, June 25, 1902, 8; "Clears Fog Away," *Los Angeles Atlanta Constitution*, Feb. 13, 1902, 6; "Caucus about Statehood," *Washington Post*, Jan. 13, 1903, 4; "Compromise on Statehood Bill," *Boston Globe*, Feb. 23, 1903, 14; "Panama and Cuban Treaties," *Wall Street Journal*, Mar. 7, 1903, 2; "Cuban Treaty," *Wall Street Journal*, Mar. 14, 1903, 2; "Congress Will Not Be Called in Early Fall," *Philadelphia Inquirer*, Mar. 14, 1903, 1; "To Save Cuban Treaty," *New York Tribune*, Nov. 7, 1903, 1; "Allison Announces Steering Committee," *Washington Post*, Jan. 7, 1904, 3; "Hanna as a Senator," *Washington Post*, Feb. 16, 1904, 4; "Steering Committee Meets," *Washington Post*, Apr. 28, 1904, 4; "W. D. Crum Reappointed," *Baltimore Sun*, Apr. 29, 1904, 1; Henry Loomis Nelson, "President Does Not Make Laws," *Boston Herald*, Nov. 21, 1904, 6; "Plan for Two States," *Washington Post*, Dec. 8, 1904, 1; "Subsidy a 'Stop-Gap,'" *New York Tribune*, Dec. 2, 1905, 9; "Caucus of Senators," *Washington Post*, Dec. 5, 1905, 1; "Senate Chairmanships," *New York Tribune*, Dec. 5, 1905, 2; "Congress Has Begun Making of History," *Washington Post*, Dec. 5, 1905, 5; "Senate's Programme," *New York Tribune*, Dec. 6, 1905, 2; "Rate Control Put at Calendar's End," *Tucson Citizen*, Feb. 2, 1906, 1; "House Has Hustled," *Washington Post*, Feb. 12, 1906, 4; "Plan Rate Compromise with Senate

(continued)

TABLE A.4 (continued)

Democrats," *New York Times*, Feb. 26, 1906, 1; "May Adjourn June 28," *Washington Post*, June 14, 1906, 1; "Case of Negro Troops up in Congress," *Boston Herald*, Dec. 4, 1906, 1; "Senate's Programme," *New York Tribune*, Dec. 6, 1906, 1; "Smile, and Talk Subsidy to Death," *New York Times*, Mar. 4, 1907, 4; "Spooner Will Retire," *Washington Evening Star*, Mar. 4, 1907, 14; "Coming of Message Tricked Wise Ones," *Boston Herald*, Feb. 2, 1908, 6; "Legislative Briefs," *Washington Post*, Apr. 21, 1908, 5; Smith D. Frye, "'The Lucky Thirteen,'" *Los Angeles Times*, July 12, 1908, II:11; "Hale Now Senate Leader," *New York Times*, Dec. 10, 1908, 5; "Senate Places Filled," *Washington Post*, Mar. 24, 1909, 3; "Holds Senate to Tariff," *Washington Post*, Mar. 27, 1909, 4; "Coffee Futures Are Still Quiet," *Boston Herald*, May 10, 1909, 13; "Lawmaking Sags," *Washington Evening Star*, Jan. 21, 1910, 2; "Senate Steering Board in Action," *Boston Herald*, Mar. 9, 1910, 3; "Senate Changes Vital to the West," *Chicago Tribune*, Apr. 20, 1910, 2; "Insurgents Get Places," *Washington Post*, Apr. 6, 1911, 4; *Cong. Rec.*, July 12, 1911, 2856; "Congress Talks of Adjournment," *Atlanta Constitution*, May 20, 1912, 5; "Senator Crane To Quit," *Baltimore Sun*, May 22, 1912, 1; "Utah to the Front," *Boston Globe*, Aug. 22, 1912, 10; "Republican Plan to Revive Party," *Chicago Tribune*, Feb. 8, 1913, 4; "Oliver Heads Steering Committee," *Philadelphia Inquirer*, Feb. 8, 1913, 4; "The Day in Washington," *New York Tribune*, Feb. 16, 1913, 6.

Date	Committee
July 7–Aug. 18, 1856	Weller, Stuart, Douglas, Mallory, Hunter, Toombs
Mar.–Apr. 1878	Wallace (chair), Ransom, McDonald, Eaton, Cockrell ("the Executive Committee of the Senate Caucus")
Mar. 17–July 1, 1879	Thurman (chair), Saulsbury, Whyte, Kernan, Jones of Fla., Bailey, Lamar, Voorhees, Vance
Dec. 1879	*Same committee, continued in new session*
Oct. 8, 1881	Pendleton (chair), Garland, Voorhees, Pugh, Davis of W.Va. ("to confer … upon the organization of the Senate")
Apr. 1886	*Membership unknown*
June 1886	Beck, Harris, Cockrell
Feb. 15–Mar. 3, 1887	Harris (chair), Cockrell, Kenna
Apr. 2–Oct. 20, 1888	Harris (chair), Cockrell, Voorhees, Coke, Beck, Jones of Ark., McPherson, Morgan, Butler, Gorman, Walthall
Jan. 1891	Gorman *and others*
June 29–Aug. 5, 1892	Gorman (chair), Harris, Cockrell, Voorhees, Hill
Dec. 7, 1892–Jan. 1893	*Same committee, continued in new session*
Dec. 7, 1892–Jan. 1893	Gorman (chair), Brice, Carlisle ("special caucus committee" on state elections, the "Senatorial steering committee")
	"[To] act as a law-advisory body to Democratic members of Western and Northwestern legislatures."
	"[To work with] Democrats of the western states … to secure the fruits of victory in the shape of senators."
	"To look after contested election cases and close Legislatures in North-western States."
	"To do all that could be done to aid in bringing about the choice of democratic Senators [from those states]."
	"[To plan] for circumventing the attempts of the Republicans to steal the doubtful Legislatures in the West."
Mar. 4–7, 1893	Gorman, Cockrell, Harris, Brice, Ransom
Mar. 7–Apr. 15, 1893	Gorman (chair), Cockrell, Harris, Brice, Ransom, Blackburn, White of La. (on reorganization of the Senate)
Aug. 10–Nov. 3, 1893	Gorman (chair), Cockrell, Blackburn, Walthall, Ransom, Vilas, Gray, White of La.
Feb.–Aug. 28, 1894	Gorman (chair), Cockrell, Harris, Blackburn, Jones of Ark., Brice, Ransom, Gray, Faulkner
Aug. 29–Dec. 2, 1894	*Same committee, continued through the recess*
Dec. 3, 1894–Mar. 3, 1895	*Same committee, continued in new session*
Mar. 4–Dec. 1, 1895	*Same committee, continued through the recess*
Dec. 10, 1895–June 11, 1896	Gorman (chair), Cockrell, Harris, Blackburn, Jones of Ark., Brice, Walthall, Murphy, White
Dec. 7, 1896–Mar. 3, 1897	Gorman (chair), Cockrell, Blackburn, Walthall, Murphy, White, Faulkner, Smith
Mar. 9–10, 1897	*Same committee, continued in new session*
Mar. 15–July 8, 1897	*Same committee, continued in new session*
July 9–July 24, 1897	Gorman (chair), Cockrell, Harris, Jones of Ark., Walthall, Murphy, White, Faulkner, Smith
Dec. 6, 1897–May 1898	*Same committee, continued in new session*
	Same committee, continued in new session, with seat of Harris vacant
	Same committee, continued in new session

(*continued*)

TABLE A.5 (continued)

Date	Committee
Dec. 7, 1899–June 7, 1900	**Jones of Ark.** (chair), Cockrell, Martin, Bacon, Rawlins, Turley, Money
Dec. 3, 1900–Mar. 3, 1901	Same committee, continued in new session
Mar. 4–9, 1901	Same committee, continued in new Congress, with seat of Turley vacant
Mar. 10–Dec. 1, 1901	Same committee, continued through the recess
Dec. 11, 1901–July 1, 1902	**Jones of Ark.** (chair), Cockrell, Martin, Bacon, Rawlins, Money, Dubois
Dec. 1, 1902–Mar. 3, 1903	Same committee, continued in new session
Mar. 6–19, 1903	**Gorman** (chair), Cockrell, Martin, Bacon, Money, Dubois, Bailey, Blackburn, Tillman
Nov. 9–Dec. 7, 1903	Same committee, continued in new session
Dec. 7, 1903–Apr. 28, 1904	Same committee, continued in new session
Dec. 5, 1904–Mar. 3, 1905	Same committee, continued in new session
Dec. 8, 1905–June 4, 1906	**Gorman** (chair), Martin, Bacon, Money, Dubois, Bailey, Blackburn, Tillman, Teller
June 9–30, 1906	**Blackburn** (chair), Martin, Bacon, Money, Dubois, Bailey, Tillman, Teller, Overman
Dec. 3, 1906–Mar. 3, 1907	Same committee, continued in new session
Dec. 8, 1907–May 30, 1908	**Culberson** (chair), Martin, Bacon, Money, Tillman, Stone, Simmons, Newlands, Clarke
Dec. 7, 1908–Mar. 3, 1909	Same committee, continued in new session
Mar. 5–6, 1909	**Culberson** (chair), Martin, Bacon, Money, Tillman, Stone, Simmons, Newlands, Clarke
Mar. 15–Aug. 5, 1909	Same committee, continued in new session
Dec. 9, 1909–June 25, 1910	Same committee, continued in new session, with **Money** succeeding **Culberson** as chair
Dec. 5, 1910–Mar. 3, 1911	Same committee, continued in new session
Apr. 11–Aug. 22, 1911	**Martin of Va.** (chair), Culberson, Simmons, Clarke, Bankhead, Fletcher, Williams, Kern, Hitchcock
Dec. 4, 1911–Aug. 26, 1912	Same committee, continued in new session
Dec. 2, 1912–Mar. 3, 1913	Same committee, continued in new session

Notes and sources for Table A.5

Caucus chair appears in **bold**. Where a specific date is uncertain, it appears in *italics*. In these cases, we lack any evidence to suggest the committee existed before this month (for starting dates) or beyond this month (for ending dates).

Sources: Except for some scattered information, the emergence and development of the Democratic steering committee has been entirely unknown to congressional scholars. This table contains all references we have located to Senate Democratic caucus committees on the order of business through 1892 and steering committees from 1893 to 1913; it was in 1893 that the Democratic steering committee assumed responsibility for committee assignments and a separate committee on committees ceased to exist. Most of these committees were termed "committees on the order of business" or, in later years, "steering committees"; where the language differs from this, we indicate the committee's responsibility. In assembling the list, we consulted various sources to determine whether the Senate Democratic caucus named any sort of committee on the order of business or steering committee and, where we find such a committee, to identify the committee's membership. (We do not include any committee for December 1882: although newspapers reported that the caucus authorized the appointment of a five-person committee, we find no evidence that the committee was named or that it ever met. We also do not include the "steering committee" named on Jan. 17, 1899, which appears to have been an ad hoc committee organized around a treaty ratification vote.) We began this work by searching the *New York Times*, *Washington Post*, *Wall Street Journal*, and *Christian Science Monitor*, then expanded the search to include the *Congressional Record* and the digital archives of the following newspapers: *Arizona Republican*, *Atlanta Constitution*, *Austin American Statesman*, *Baltimore Sun*, *Boston Globe*, *Boston Herald**, *Chicago Tribune*, *Cincinnati Enquirer*, *Detroit Free Press*, *Los Angeles Times*, *Louisville Courier Journal*, *Minneapolis Star Tribune*, *Nashville Tennessean*, *New York Tribune*, *Philadelphia Inquirer**, *San Francisco Chronicle*, *St. Louis Post Dispatch*, *St. Petersburg Times*, and *Washington Evening Star**. All but three of these newspapers are available through ProQuest Historical Newspapers; the others, identified with asterisks, are in America's Historical Newspapers, the U.S. Northeast Collection in ProQuest Historical Newspapers, and Chronicling America: Historic American Newspapers. Redd Brown, Hugh Curran, and Zach Lawlor did outstanding work searching these databases. What follows are our sources for each of the Democratic committees: *Cong. Globe*, July 23, 1856, 1719–23; "The Three Million Armament Bill in the Senate," *New York Times*, July 23, 1856, 1; "Caucus of Democratic Senators," *New York Times*, Apr. 14, 1878, 1; "A meeting of Democratic Senators . . ," *Washington Post*, Apr. 15, 1878, 2; "Washington," *Louisville Courier Journal*, Apr. 15, 1878, 3; "Caucuses of Democratic Senators," *Washington Evening Star*, Mar. 17, 1879, 1; "The Senatorial Caucus," *Minneapolis Tribune*, Mar. 17, 1879, 1; "Details of the Democratic Caucus: Election of Senate Officers," *Baltimore Sun*, Mar. 21, 1879, 1; "Washington: Lengthy Session of the Democratic Conference Committees," *Detroit Free Press*, Mar. 23, 1879, 2; "Democratic Caucus," *Nashville Tennessean*, May 26, 1879, 1; "A Caucus in Deep Secrecy," *New York Times*, May 1, 1879, 1; "A Conference To-Day," *Minneapolis Tribune*, May 27, 1879, 1; "Caucus Action on the Veto Message," *New York Times*, June 3, 1879, 1; "Democratic Council," *Chicago Tribune*, June 17, 1879, 1; "The Senate Patronage," *Washington Evening Star*, Dec. 4, 1879, 1; "Returning Reason," *Chicago Tribune*, Dec. 11, 1879, 2; "The New Administration," *New York Times*, Oct. 9, 1881, 1; "The Situation: It Is Bad," *Chicago Tribune*, Oct. 9, 1881, 9; "Agree to Disagree," *Louisville Courier Journal*, Oct. 9, 1881, 2; "Organization of the Senate," *New York Tribune*, Oct. 9, 1881, 1; "Notes from Washington," *New York Times*, Dec. 15, 1882, 1; "Steering Committee," *Chicago Tribune*, Dec. 15, 1882, 1; "Senator Pendleton," *Chicago Tribune*, Dec. 17, 1882, 17; "Republican and Democratic Conference," *St. Louis Post Dispatch*, Apr. 19, 1886, 2; "Business in the Senate," *Washington Post*, Apr. 20, 1886, 1; "Notes from Washington," *New York Times*, June 10, 1886, 3; "Order of Business in the Senate," *New York Tribune*, June 10, 1886, 2; "A Senate Steering Committee," *New York Herald*, Feb. 16, 1887, 3; "Pension Agents at Work," *New York Times*, Feb. 17, 1887, 5; "Work for Congress to Do," *New York Times*, Feb. 21, 1887, 2; "The Bond Bill in the Senate," *Washington Post*, Apr. 3, 1888, 2; "Caucus Committee on Business," *Louisville Courier Journal*, Apr. 3, 1888, 3; "The Senatorial Tangle," *New York Times*, Apr. 3, 1888, 1; "The Delayed Appropriations Bills," *Washington Evening Star*, June 28, 1888, 1; "Democratic Senators in Caucus," *Washington Critic*, June 28, 1888, 1; "The Democratic Senators Had a Caucus," *Washington Evening Star*, Aug. 15, 1888, 1; "No Intention to Filibuster," *Baltimore Sun*, Aug. 16, 1888, 1; "Democrats Not to Filibuster," *New York Tribune*, Aug. 16, 1888, 3; "Democratic Senators Caucus," *Nashville Daily American*, Aug. 16, 1888, 1; "Republican Senatorial Programme," *Plainfield (N.J.) Evening News*, Aug. 17, 1888, 2; "Republicans Sit It Out," *Chicago Tribune*, Jan. 17, 1891, 1; "All After the Gavel," *Washington Evening Star*, Nov. 28, 1891, 13; "Morgan Stands All Alone," *New York Times*, June 30, 1892, 4; "Senators Talking Business," *Pittsburg Dispatch*, June 30, 1892, 1; "After the Senate," *Washington Evening Star*, Dec. 8, 1892, 3; "Democratic Conference," *Boston Herald*, Dec. 8, 1892, 2; "The News from Washington: Democratic Senators Caucus," *Springfield (Mass.) Republican*, Dec. 8, 1892,

(continued)

433

4; "To Watch Republicans," *Washington Post*, Dec. 8, 1892, 7; "Looking After the Next Senate," *New York Times*, Dec. 8, 1892, 5; "Want To Talk with Cleveland," *Boston Herald*, Dec. 9, 1892, 5; "A Bad Steering Committee," *Philadelphia Inquirer*, Dec. 9, 1892, 6; "Senators Off to New York," *Washington Post*, Dec. 9, 1892, 1; "Gorman's Bugaboo," *Los Angeles Times*, Dec. 9, 1892, 6; "Czarism," *Cincinnati Enquirer*, Dec. 9, 1892, 2; "The Democratic Advisory Committee," *Washington Post*, Dec. 10, 1892, 1; "Hatching the Conspiracy," *New York Tribune*, Dec. 10, 1892, 1; "Hill Will Be Absent," *San Francisco Chronicle*, Dec. 10, 1892, 2; "Growing Nervous about the Senate," *New York Tribune*, Jan. 7, 1893, 5; "May Vote on Anti-Option," *Chicago Tribune*, Jan. 11, 1893, 10; "Republicans in Caucus," *New York Times*, Jan. 17, 1893, 2; "The latest advices from Wyoming . . . ," *Washington Post*, Jan. 18, 1893, 4; "Democrats Alarmed over Montana," *Chicago Tribune*, Jan. 24, 1893, 2; "The Democrats in Caucus," *Washington Post*, Mar. 8, 1893, 5; "Democrats in Caucus," *New York Times*, Mar. 8, 1893, 2; "The Democratic Senators," *Baltimore Sun*, Mar. 8, 1893, 2; "The Majorities," *Los Angeles Times*, Mar. 14, 1893, 5; "The Senate Chairmanships," *New York Tribune*, Mar. 14, 1893, 3; "The Democratic Caucus," *Washington Evening Star*, Mar. 21, 1893, 6; "The Senate's Employes," *New York Times*, Mar. 22, 1893, 2; "Democrats Offer Compromise," *New York Times*, Mar. 23, 1893, 5; "Failed To Agree," *Baltimore Sun*, Aug. 10, 1893, 2; "Repeal Is Far Off," *Chicago Tribune*, Aug. 10, 1893, 1; "Senator Gorman," *Baltimore Sun*, Aug. 11, 1893, 1; "The Silver Fight," *Washington Evening Star*, Aug. 11, 1893, 1; "Repeal Men Give up the Long Fight," *Philadelphia Inquirer*, Oct. 13, 1893, 1; "Working on the Compromise," *Chicago Tribune*, Oct. 13, 1893, 1; "Majority Rule Rejected," *New York Tribune*, Oct. 19, 1893, 1; "Repeal in Danger," *Boston Herald*, Oct. 20, 1893, 1; "Unconditional Repeal," *Boston Herald*, Oct. 24, 1893, 1; "The Time for Delay Gone," *New York Times*, Oct. 27, 1893, 3; "The New Senator," *Washington Evening Star*, Feb. 16, 1894, 1; "Will Be Missed from the Senate," *Maysville (Ky.) Evening Bulletin*, Feb. 21, 1894, 1; "They Rise to Explain," *Washington Post*, Mar. 7, 1894, 1; "Mr. Mills's Speech," *Baltimore Sun*, Apr. 25, 1894, 1; "Getting Down to Work," *Washington Post*, May 18, 1894, 1; "Democratic Plans," *Los Angeles Times*, Apr. 30, 1894, 2; "Mr. Harris Backed Down," *New York Tribune*, May 18, 1894, 1; "That Coal Syndicate," *Philadelphia Inquirer*, July 24, 1894, 1; "Democratic Leaders Confer," *Baltimore Sun*, July 24, 1894, 1; "Fate of the Tariff Bill," *Boston Herald*, Aug. 12, 1894, 6; "No Choice Left," *Boston Globe*, Aug. 12, 1894, 1; A. Maurice Low, "Law against Law," *Boston Globe*, Aug. 20, 1894, 1; "Our Washington dispatches have directed attention . . . ," *New York Times*, Aug. 27, 1894, 4; "Democratic Leaders in a Muddle," *Chicago Tribune*, Nov. 19, 1894, 2; "Democrats Caucus," *Nashville American*, Dec. 5, 1894, 1; "A Do Nothing Programme," *New York Times*, Dec. 7, 1894, 1; "Situation in Congress," *Baltimore Sun*, Dec. 8, 1894, 2; "Export Trade Suffering," *New York Times*, Dec. 21, 1894, 13; "Republicans Plan to Prevent Action," *Chicago Tribune*, Feb. 1, 1895, 3; *Cong. Rec.*, Feb. 23, 1895, 2625; "Railroads and Pooling," *New York Times*, Feb. 24, 1895, 3; "Committees Will Hold Over," *New York Times*, Mar. 3, 1895, 3; "Alabama," *New York Times*, Mar. 4, 1895, 1; "Bitter Fight On," *Boston Herald*, May 4, 1895, 2; "Senator Vest Talks," *Washington Evening Star*, Nov. 18, 1895, 1; "The Senate Organization," *Washington Post*, Nov. 23, 1895, 3; "Wanted: A Policy," *Philadelphia Inquirer*, Nov. 23, 1895, 1; "Democratic Caucus," *Washington Evening Star*, Dec. 5, 1895, 2; "Situation in the Senate," *New York Times*, Dec. 6, 1895, 2; "Democratic Steering Committee," *Washington Evening Star*, Dec. 10, 1895, 2; "Democratic Steering Committee," *Philadelphia Inquirer*, Dec. 11, 1895, 7; "Quay the Politicians' Idol," *Boston Herald*, Dec. 22, 1895, 26; "The Senatorial Caucus," *Washington Post*, Feb. 13, 1896, 3; "To Divide the Offices," *New York Times*, Apr. 2, 1896, 4; "Good Times," *Boston Globe*, May 10, 1896, 16; "The Charities Commission," *Washington Evening Star*, June 11, 1896, 1; "The Senate Programme," *New York Times*, Jan. 8, 1897, 4; "The Pacific Railroad Bill," *Washington Post*, Jan. 8, 1897, 1; *Cong. Rec.*, Jan. 28, 1897, 1249;

"This Week in Congress," *New York Times*, Feb. 8, 1897, 5; *Cong. Rec.*, Feb. 24, 1897, 2201; "Dubois as Secretary," *Washington Post*, Mar. 10, 1897, 4; "Democratic Caucus," *Philadelphia Inquirer*, Mar. 10, 1897, 2; "Tariff Question First, Then the Currency," *Philadelphia Inquirer*, Mar. 31, 1897, 2; "Senate Committee Places," *Boston Herald*, Apr. 30, 1897, 3; "Two Hours' Debate," *Washington Evening Star*, Dec. 13, 1897, 2; "Democrats Disagree," *Washington Evening Star*, Jan. 14, 1898, 2; "Foreign Relations Committee," *New York Times*, Mar. 31, 1898, 3; "Cannot Avert War," *Washington Post*, Apr. 9, 1898, 1; "In Congress," *Philadelphia Inquirer*, May 3, 1898, 6; Henry MacFarland, "Pledges on Treaty," *Boston Herald*, Jan. 18, 1899, 3; "Democratic Caucus Committee," *Washington Post*, Dec. 8, 1899, 4; Jos. Ohl, "Cost of the War in the Philippines," *Atlanta Constitution*, Dec. 13, 1899, 1; "Minority Committee Places," *Chicago Tribune*, Dec. 16, 1899, 9; "Clay's Good Assignments," *Savannah Morning News*, Dec. 16, 1899, 5; "Pressed for Time," *Dallas Morning News*, Feb. 8, 1901, 1; "Democrats Object," *Washington Evening Star*, Mar. 6, 1901, 1; "Jones To Be Retained," *Baltimore Sun*, Mar. 9, 1901, 2; "Democratic Leadership," *Boston Herald*, Mar. 9, 1901, 14; "M'Laurin Has Read Himself Out of Party," *Atlanta Constitution*, Mar. 11, 1901, 1; "No Longer Democrat," *Boston Herald*, Mar. 11, 1901, 3; "Idaho Senators at the White House," *New York Tribune*, Nov. 17, 1901, 11; "What Bacon Saw in Philippine Islands," *Atlanta Constitution*, Nov. 25, 1901, 1; "M'Laurin Put on Black List," *Atlanta Constitution*, Dec. 6, 1901, 7; "Tillman Jabs Pitchfork into Writhing M'Laurin," *Atlanta Constitution*, Dec. 10, 1901, 1; "Democratic Rumpus: Jones Bumps against Teller," *Los Angeles Times*, Dec. 11, 1901, 2; "A Hard Craft To Steer," *New York Tribune*, Dec. 11, 1901, 4; "Democratic Senate Caucus," *New York Tribune*, Dec. 12, 1901, 3; "Posts for Minority," *Baltimore Sun*, Dec. 15, 1901, 9; "Capitol Chat," *Washington Post*, Feb. 19, 1902, 6; "Democrats Put Gorman at Helm," *Atlanta Constitution*, Mar. 7, 1903, 1; "Gorman Chosen Leader," *New York Times*, Mar. 7, 1903, 9; "Gorman To Lead Party in Nation," *Chicago Tribune*, Mar. 7, 1903, 1; "Harmony Fest for Democrats," *Atlanta Constitution*, Mar. 20, 1903, 5; "In the Senate," *New York Tribune*, Nov. 10, 1903, 2; "Think Charges True," *Washington Post*, Nov. 10, 1903, 4; "Senator Hanna Chosen," *New York Tribune*, Nov. 11, 1903, 2; "Committee Work of Bacon," *Washington Post*, Atlanta Constitution, Nov. 18, 1903, 1; "Democracy's New Leader," *New York Times*, Nov. 30, 1903, 7; "To Offer No Amendments," *Washington Post*, Dec. 13, 1903, 3; "Where Gorman Stands," *New York Tribune*, May 27, 1904, 2; "Combine against Parker," *Kansas City Star*, June 5, 1904, 13; "Gorman Again Chosen as the Minority Leader," *Washington Post*, Dec. 9, 1905, 4; "It Was a Swell Dinner," *Daily Silver State (Winnemucca, Nev.)*, Feb. 10, 1906, 1; Ritchie 1998a, 9–10; "Role of Filibuster Assumed by Bacon on Immigration Bill," *Atlanta Constitution*, Feb. 15, 1907, 1; Ritchie 1998a, 11–12; "Meet To Fill Vacancies," *Washington Post*, Dec. 10, 1907, 4; "Cannon Names a Committee," *Chicago Tribune*, Dec. 17, 1907, 6; "Inattentive Senators," *Washington Evening Star*, Mar. 14, 1908, 1; "Prod Democratic Senators," *New York Times*, Mar. 15, 1908, 8; "Seek President's Idea," *Washington Post*, Apr. 14, 1908, 3; Ritchie 1998a, 21–22; "Senate Committees," *New York Tribune*, Mar. 18, 1909, 5; Ritchie 1998a, 30–32; "Nepotism Run to Seed," *Goldsboro (N.C.) Semi-Weekly Argus*, Dec. 22, 1909, 3; "Mobile Men Are Heard," *Montgomery (Ala.) Advertiser*, Jan. 6, 1910, 2; "Taft Too Busy To Give Plums," *Montgomery (Ala.) Advertiser*, Jan. 10, 1910, 1; "Terrell Given His Committees," *Atlanta Constitution*, Dec. 8, 1910, 3; "Senate Democrats Appear Divided," *Dallas Morning News*, Apr. 6, 1911, 6; Ritchie 1998a, 39–40; "Favors Low Tariff Senators," *New York Times*, Apr. 12, 1911, 2; "Will Steer Minority," *Washington Post*, Apr. 12, 1911, 2; "Honor for Williams," *Gulfport (Miss.) Daily Herald*, Apr. 12, 1911, 5; "Democratic Steering Committee Named," *Philadelphia Inquirer*, Apr. 12, 1911, 16; "Regulars Reject Insurgent Demands," *New York Tribune*, Apr. 27, 1911, 4; "New Inquiry Made Sure in Lorimer Case," *Chicago Tribune*, May 20, 1911, 1; "For Martin Resolution," *Boston Globe*, May 26, 1911, 3; *Cong. Rec.*, June 1, 1911, 1680; "Senators Change Places," *Washington Evening Star*, Jan. 23, 1912, 5; "Senate Amendments Rejected by House," *Dallas Morning News*, July 31, 1912, 3; "Simmons' Party Rank," *Charlotte Daily Observer*, Aug. 2, 1912, 4; "Garber's Nomination Confirmed by Senate," *Montgomery (Ala.) Advertiser*, Aug. 18, 1912, 9; Ben F. Allen, "Wilson to Shape Senate's Course," *Cleveland Plain Dealer*, Dec. 25, 1912, 1; "Defend Seniority Rule," *Washington Post*, Dec. 31, 1912, 4; "O'Gorman Succeeds Rayner," *Washington Evening Star*, Jan. 3, 1913, 2.

References

Abbott, Richard H. 1986. *The Republican Party and the South, 1855–1877.* Chapel Hill: University of North Carolina Press.

Acheson, Sam Hanna. 1932. *Joe Bailey: The Last Democrat.* New York: Macmillan.

Aldrich, John H. 1993. "Rational Choice Theory and the Study of American Politics." In *The Dynamics of American Politics,* eds. Lawrence C. Dodd and Calvin Jillson. Boulder, Colo.: Westview Press.

——— 1995. *Why Parties? The Origin and Transformation of Political Parties in America.* Chicago, Ill.: University of Chicago Press.

Aldrich, John H., Mark M. Berger, and David W. Rohde. 2002. "The Historical Variability in Conditional Party Government, 1877–1994." In *Parties, Procedure and Policy: Essays on the History of Congress,* eds. David W. Brady and Mathew D. McCubbins. Stanford, Calif: Stanford University Press, 17–35.

Aldrich, John H., and David W. Rohde. 1997. "Balance of Power: Republican Party Leadership and the Committee System in the 104th House." Paper presented at the Annual Meeting of the American Political Science Association, Chicago, Ill.

——— 1998. "Measuring Conditional Party Government." Paper presented at the Annual Meeting of the Midwest Political Science Association, Chicago, Ill.

——— 2000. "The Consequences of Party Organization in the House: The Role of the Majority and Minority Parties in Conditional Party Government." In *Polarized Politics: Congress and the President in a Partisan Era,* eds. Jon R. Bond and Richard Fleisher. Washington, D.C.: CQ Press, 31–72.

Alexander, DeAlva Stanwood. 1916. *History and Procedure of the House of Representatives.* Boston, Mass.: Houghton Mifflin.

Altman, O. R. 1937. "First Session of the Seventy-fifth Congress, January 5, 1937, to August 21, 1937." *American Political Science Review* 31 (6): 1071–93.

Annis, J. Lee. 1995. *Howard Baker: Conciliator in an Age of Crisis.* Lanham, Md.: Madison Books.

——— 2019. "William H. 'Bill' Frist, MD: 'The Doctor as Leader.'" In *Leadership in the U.S. Senate: Herding Cats in the Modern Era,* ed. Colton C. Campbell. New York: Taylor & Francis, 209–40.

Arrow, Kenneth Joseph. 1951. *Social Choice and Individual Values*. New York: Wiley.

Bach, Stanley. 1991. "The Senate's Compliance with Its Legislative Rules: The Appeal of Order." *Congress & the Presidency* 18 (1): 77–92.

1997. "Rules, Rulings, and the Rule of Law in Congress." Paper presented at the Annual Meeting of the Midwest Political Science Association, Chicago, Ill.

Bach, Stanley, and Steven S. Smith. 1988. *Managing Uncertainty in the House of Representatives: Adaptation and Innovation in Special Rules*. Washington, D.C.: Brookings Institution Press.

Bacon, Donald C. 1991. "Joseph Taylor Robinson: The Good Soldier." In *First Among Equals: Outstanding Senate Leaders of the Twentieth Century*, eds. Richard A. Baker and Roger H. Davidson. Washington, D.C.: Congressional Quarterly, 63–97.

Bailey, Christopher J. 1988. *The Republican Party in the U.S. Senate: 1974–1984, Party Change and Institutional Development*. Manchester: Manchester University Press.

Bair, Sheila. 2007. Interview, December 17, 2007. Robert J. Dole Oral History Project, Robert J. Dole Institute for Politics, Lawrence, Kans.

Baker, Bobby. 2013. "Oral History Interview with Bobby Baker." *Politico Magazine*, November 19, 2013.

Baker, Howard. 2007. Interview with Senator Howard Baker, Jr., March 1, 2007, April 13, 2007, May 7, 2007. Robert J. Dole Oral History Project, Robert J. Dole Institute for Politics, Lawrence, Kans.

Baker, Richard A. 1988. *The Senate of the United States: A Bicentennial History*. Malabar, Fla.: Robert E. Krieger.

Baker, Richard A., and Roger H. Davidson. 1991. "Introduction." In *First Among Equals: Outstanding Senate Leaders of the Twentieth Century*, eds. Richard A. Baker and Roger H. Davidson. Washington, D.C.: Congressional Quarterly, 1–6.

Baker, Robert Gene. 1978. *Wheeling and Dealing: Confessions of a Capitol Hill Operator*. New York: W. W. Norton.

2009. Oral history interviews with Robert G. Baker. Senate Historical Office, Washington, D.C.

Baker, Ross. 1991. "Mike Mansfield and the Birth of the Modern Senate." In *First Among Equals: Outstanding Senate Leaders of the Twentieth Century*, eds. Richard A. Baker and Roger H. Davidson. Washington, D.C.: Congressional Quarterly, 264–96.

2018. *Is Bipartisanship Dead? A Report from the Senate*. New York: Routledge.

2019. "Leave It to Harry: Harry Reid as Democratic Leader." In *Leadership in the U.S. Senate: Herding Cats in the Modern Era*, ed. Colton C. Campbell. New York: Taylor & Francis, 240–71.

Barfield, Claude E. 1965. "The Democratic Party in Congress, 1909–1913." Ph.D. diss., Department of History, Northwestern University.

1970. "'Our Share of the Booty': The Democratic Party, Cannonism, and the Payne-Aldrich Tariff." *Journal of American History* 57 (2): 308–23.

Barkley, Alben W. 1954. *That Reminds Me*. New York: Doubleday & Company.

Bateman, David A., Ira Katznelson, and John S. Lapinski. 2018. *Southern Nation: Congress and White Supremacy after Reconstruction*. New York and Princeton, N.J.: Russell Sage Foundation and Princeton University Press.

Baumer, Donald C. 1992. "Senate Democratic Leadership in the 101st Congress." In *The Atomistic Congress*, eds. Allen D. Hertzke and Ronald M. Peters. Armonk, N.Y.: M.E. Sharpe.

Baumer, Donald C., and Howard J. Gold. 2010. *Parties, Polarization and Democracy.* New York: Routledge.

Baumol, William. 1952. *Welfare Economics and the Theory of the State.* Cambridge, Mass.: Harvard University Press.

Bawn, Kathleen. 1998. "Congressional Party Leadership: Utilitarian versus Majoritarian Incentives." *Legislative Studies Quarterly* 23 (2): 219–43.

Beard, Charles A. 1910. *American Government and Politics.* New York: Macmillan.

Beeman, Richard R. 1968. "Unlimited Debate in the Senate: The First Phase." *Political Science Quarterly* 83 (3): 419–34.

Benedict, Michael Les. 1974. *A Compromise of Principle: Congressional Republicans and Reconstruction, 1863–1869.* New York: Norton.

Bensel, Richard R. 1984. *Sectionalism and American Political Development, 1880–1980.* Madison: University of Wisconsin Press.

Benton, Thomas Hart. 1856. *Thirty Years' View; or, a History of the Working of the American Government for Thirty Years, from 1820 to 1850.* Vol. 2. New York: D. Appleton and Company.

Berdahl, Clarence A. 1949. "Some Notes on Party Membership in Congress, I." *American Political Science Review* 43 (2): 309–21.

Berg, A. Scott. 2013. *Wilson.* New York: G.P. Putnam's Sons.

Binder, Sarah. 1996. "The Partisan Basis of Procedural Choice: Allocating Parliamentary Rights in the House, 1789–1990." *American Political Science Review* 90 (1): 8–20.

1997. *Minority Rights, Majority Rule: Partisanship and the Development of Congress.* Cambridge: Cambridge University Press.

2020. "How We (Should?) Study Congress and History." *Public Choice* 185: 415–27.

Binder, Sarah, Anthony J. Madonna, and Steven S. Smith. 2007. "Going Nuclear, Senate Style." *Perspectives on Politics* 5 (4): 729–40.

Binder, Sarah, and Steven S. Smith. 1997. *Politics or Principle? Filibustering in the United States Senate.* Washington, D.C.: Brookings.

Biographical Directory of the United States Congress, 1774–1989. 1989. Washington, D.C.: Government Printing Office.

Biographical Directory of the United States Congress, 1774–Present. 2021. https://bioguideretro.congress.gov

Black, Duncan. 1958. *The Theory of Committees and Elections.* Cambridge: Cambridge University Press.

Bogue, Allan G. 1981. *The Earnest Men: Republicans of the Civil War Senate.* Ithaca, N.Y.: Cornell University Press.

1989. *The Congressman's Civil War.* Cambridge: Cambridge University Press.

Bogue, Allan G., and Mark Paul Marlaire. 1975. "Of Mess and Men: The Boardinghouse and Congressional Voting, 1821–1842." *American Journal of Political Science* 19 (2): 207–30.

Bond, Jon R., and Richard Fleisher. 1990. *The President in the Legislative Arena.* Chicago, Ill.: University of Chicago Press.

Bone, Hugh A. 1956a. "An Introduction to the Senate Policy Committees." *American Political Science Review* 50 (2): 339–59.

1956b. "Some Notes on the Congressional Campaign Committees." *Western Political Quarterly* 9 (1): 116–37.

1968. *Party Committees and National Politics*. Seattle: University of Washington Press.

Bowers, Claude G. 1918. *The Life of John Worth Kern*. Indianapolis, Ind.: Hollenbeck Press.

1932. *Beveridge and the Progressive Era*. Boston, Mass.: Houghton Mifflin.

Bradley, Phillips. 1925. "The Farm Bloc." *Journal of Social Forces* 3 (4): 714–18.

Brady, David W. 1973. *Congressional Voting in a Partisan Era: A Comparison of the McKinley House to the Modern House*. Lawrence: University Press of Kansas.

1988. *Critical Elections and Congressional Policy Making*. Stanford, Calif.: Stanford University Press.

Brady, David, Richard Brody, and David Epstein. 1989. "Heterogeneous Parties and Political Organization: The U.S. Senate, 1880–1920." *Legislative Studies Quarterly* 14 (2): 205–23.

Brady, David, and David Epstein. 1997. "Intraparty Preferences, Heterogeneity, and the Origins of the Modern Congress: Progressive Reformers in the House and Senate, 1890–1920." *Journal of Law, Economics, and Organization* 13 (1): 26–49.

Brands, H. W. 2018. *Heirs of the Founders: The Epic Rivalry of Henry Clay, John Calhoun and Daniel Webster, the Second Generation of American Giants*. New York: Doubleday.

Brant, Irving. 1953. *James Madison: Secretary of State, 1800–1809*. Indianapolis, Ind.: Bobbs-Merrill.

Brown, Everett Somerville, ed. 1923. *William Plumer's Memorandum of Proceedings in the United States Senate, 1803–1807*. New York: Macmillan.

Brown, George Rothwell. 1922. *The Leadership of Congress*. Indianapolis, Ind.: Bobbs-Merrill.

Browne, William P. 1988. *Private Interests, Public Policy, and American Agriculture*. Lawrence: University of Kansas Press.

Bryce, James. 1891. *The American Commonwealth*. 2nd ed., rev. New York: Macmillan.

Bullock, Charles S., III. 1976. "Motivations for U.S. Congressional Committee Preferences: Freshmen of the 92nd Congress." *Legislative Studies Quarterly* 1 (2): 201–12.

Burdette, Franklin L. 1940. *Filibustering in the Senate*. Princeton, N.J.: Princeton University Press.

Burke, Sheila. 2016. "Sheila Burke Oral History: Chief of Staff to Robert Dole, Senate Finance Committee Aide." Edward M. Kennedy Institute.

Burnham, James. 1959. *Congress and the American Tradition*. Chicago, Ill.: Henry Regnery Company.

Byrd, Robert C. 1988. *The Senate, 1789–1989*. Vol. 1. *Addresses on the History of the United States Senate*. 100th Cong., 1st Sess. S. Doc. 100-20. Washington, D.C.: Government Printing Office.

1991. *The Senate, 1789–1989*. Vol. 2. *Addresses on the History of the United States Senate*. 100th Cong., 1st. Sess. S. Doc. 100-20. Washington, D.C.: Government Printing Office.

1993. *The Senate, 1789–1989*. Vol. 4. *Historical Statistics, 1789–1992*. 100th Cong., 1st Sess. S. Doc. 100-20. Washington, D.C.: Government Printing Office.

Calhoun, Charles W. 2005. *Benjamin Harrison.* New York: Times Books.

Calvert, Randall L. 1987. "Coordination and Power: The Foundation of Leadership Among Rational Legislators." Paper presented at the Annual Meeting of the American Political Science Association, Chicago, Ill.

Campbell, Colton C. 2019. *Leadership in the U.S. Senate.* New York: Taylor & Francis.

Cannon, Clarence. 1944. *Democratic Manual of the Democratic National Convention,* 5th ed. Washington, D.C.: Democratic National Committee.

Canon, David T., and Charles Stewart III. 2002. "Parties and Hierarchies in Senate Committees, 1789–1946." In *U.S. Senate Exceptionalism,* ed. Bruce I. Oppenheimer. Columbus: Ohio State University Press, 157–81.

Caro, Robert A. 2002. *The Years of Lyndon Johnson: Master of the Senate.* New York: Alfred A. Knopf.

Carroll, E. Malcolm. 1925. *Origins of the Whig Party.* Durham, N.C.: Duke University Press.

Carter, Jimmy. 1982. *Keeping Faith: Memoirs of a President.* New York: Bantam Books.

Carter, Richard B. 2001. *Clearing New Ground: The Life of John G. Townsend, Jr.* Dover: Delaware Heritage Press.

Chambers, William Nisbet. 1963. *Political Parties in a New Nation: The American Experience, 1776–1809.* New York: Oxford University Press.

Chilton, Horace. 1908. "Portraits of U.S. Senators." Papers, unpublished. Dolph Briscoe Center for American History, University of Texas at Austin.

Claasen, Aage. 1973. *How Congressmen Decide: A Policy Focus.* New York: St. Martin's Press.

Coase, Ronald H. 1960. "The Problem of Social Cost." *Journal of Law and Economics* 3 (1): 1–44.

Coleman, Charles H. [1933] 1971. *The Election of 1868: The Democratic Effort to Regain Control.* New York: Octagon Books.

Collier, Ken. 1994. "Eisenhower and Congress: The Autopilot Presidency." *Presidential Studies Quarterly* 24 (2): 309–25.

Committee on Rules, U.S. House of Representatives. 1983. *A History of the Committee on Rules.* 97th Cong., 2nd Sess. Washington, D.C.: Government Printing Office.

Congressional Quarterly. 1976. *Origins and Development of Congress.* Washington, D.C.: Congressional Quarterly.

Connelly, William P., Jr. 1991. "Party Policy Committees in Congress." Paper presented at the Annual Meeting of the Western Political Science Association, Seattle, Wash.

Coolidge, L. A. 1901. "Senator Aldrich: The Most Influential Man in Congress." *Ainslee's Magazine* 8 (5): 405–13.

Cooper, Joseph. 1970. *The Origins of the Standing Committees and the Development of the Modern House.* Typescript: Rice University.

Cooper, Joseph, and David W. Brady. 1981. "Institutional Context and Leadership Style: The House from Cannon to Rayburn." *American Political Science Review* 75 (2): 411–25.

Corbin, David A. 2012. *The Last Great Senator: Robert C. Byrd's Encounters with Eleven U.S. Presidents.* Washington, D.C.: Potomac Books.

Cox, Gary W., and Mathew D. McCubbins. 1993. *Legislative Leviathan: Party Government in the House.* Berkeley and Los Angeles: University of California Press.

2005. *Setting the Agenda: Responsible Party Government in the U.S. House of Representatives*. Cambridge: Cambridge University Press.

Crespin, Michael H., Anthony Madonna, Joel Sievert, and Nathaniel Ament-Stone. 2015. "The Establishment of the Party Policy Committees in the U.S. Senate: Coordination, Not Coercion." *Social Science Quarterly* 96 (1): 34–48.

Cullom, Shelby M. 1911. *Fifty Years of Public Service*. Chicago, Ill.: A. C. McClurg & Co.

Cunningham, Noble E., Jr. 1957. *The Jeffersonian Republicans: The Formation of Party Organization, 1789–1801*. Chapel Hill: University of North Carolina Press.

1963. *The Jeffersonian Republicans in Power: Party Operations, 1801–1809*. Chapel Hill: University of North Carolina Press.

ed. 1965. *The Making of the American Party System, 1789 to 1809*. Englewood Cliffs, N.J.: Prentice-Hall.

Dailey, Jane. 2004. "White Supremacy." In *The American Congress: The Building of Democracy*, ed. Julian E. Zelizer. Boston, Mass.: Houghton Mifflin, 250–67.

Darilek, Richard E. 1976. *A Loyal Opposition in Time of War*. Westport, Conn.: Greenwood Press.

Daschle, Tom. 2003. *Like No Other Time: Two Years that Changed America*. New York: Three Rivers Press.

2007. Interview with Sen. Tom Daschle, May 25, 2007. Robert J. Dole Oral History Project, Robert J. Dole Institute for Politics, Lawrence, Kans.

2009. Interview, by Brien Williams, April 20, 2009. George J. Mitchell Oral History Project, 70, Bowdoin College.

Davidson, Roger H. 1985. "Senate Leaders: Janitors for an Untidy Chamber?" In *Congress Reconsidered*, 3rd ed., eds. Lawrence C. Dodd and Bruce I. Oppenheimer. Washington, D.C.: Congressional Quarterly, 225–52.

Davidson, Roger H., and Walter J. Oleszek. 1977. *Congress Against Itself*. Bloomington: Indiana University Press.

Davidson, Roger H., Walter J. Oleszek, and Edward M. Davis III. 1982. "Changing the Guard in the United States Senate, 1981." Paper presented at the Annual Meeting of the American Political Science Association, Denver, Colo.

Davis, Christopher M. 2015. *The President Pro Tempore of the Senate: History and Authority of the Office*. CRS Report RL30960. Washington, D.C.: Congressional Research Service.

Davis, Lula J. 2009. Interview, by Brien Williams, August 17, 2009. George J. Mitchell Oral History Project, 70, Bowdoin College.

Davis, Polly Ann. 1979. *Alben W. Barkley: Senate Majority Leader and Vice President*. New York: Garland Publishing.

DeArment, Roderick A. 2007. Interview, March 1, 2007, April 13, 2007, August 17, 2007. Robert J. Dole Oral History Project, Robert J. Dole Institute for Politics, Lawrence, Kans.

Deason, Brian. 2019. *Proud Democrat: Scott Lucas of Illinois, Senate Majority Leader*. Published by CreateSpace Independent Publishing Platform (Kindle Direct Publishing).

Deering, Christopher J., and Steven S. Smith. 1985. "Subcommittees in Congress." In *Congress Reconsidered*, 3rd ed., eds. Lawrence C. Dodd and Bruce I. Oppenheimer. Washington, D.C.: Congressional Quarterly, 189–210.

Democratic National Committee. 1876. *The Campaign Textbook*. New York: Democratic National Committee.

——— 1952. *Democratic Manual*. Prepared by Clarence Cannon. Washington, D.C.: Democratic National Committee.

Democratic Policy Committee, U.S. Senate. 2007. *A History of the Democratic Policy Committee: 1947–2007*. Democratic Policy Committee. www.dpc.senate.gov/pdf/dpchistory.pdf

Den Hartog, Chris, and Nathan W. Monroe. 2011. *Agenda Setting in the U.S. Senate*. Cambridge: Cambridge University Press.

Dion, Douglas. 1997. *Turning the Legislative Thumbscrew: Minority Rights and Procedural Change in Legislative Politics*. Ann Arbor: University of Michigan Press.

DiSalvo, Daniel. 2009. "Party Factions in Congress." *Congress & the Presidency* 36 (1): 27–57.

Doherty, Brendan J. 2007. "Meeting the Challenges of Senate Leadership." *PS: Political Science and Politics* 40 (2): 422–24.

Dole, Bob. 1989. *Historical Almanac of the United States Senate*. 100th Cong., 2nd Sess. S. Doc. 100-35.

Dole, Robert J. 2007. Interview, December 14, 2007. Robert J. Dole Oral History Project, Robert J. Dole Institute for Politics, Lawrence, Kans.

——— 2009. Interview, by Brien Williams, September 22, 2009. George J. Mitchell Oral History Project, 70, Bowdoin College.

Donnelly, Thomas Claude. 1930. "Party Leadership in the United States Senate." Ph.D. diss., New York University.

Dove, Bob. 2008. Interview, March 27, 2008. Robert J. Dole Oral History Project, Robert J. Dole Institute for Politics, Lawrence, Kans.

Drury, Allen. 1963. *A Senate Journal*. New York: McGraw-Hill.

Dyche, John David. 2009. *Republican Leader: A Political Biography of Senator Mitch McConnell*. Wilmington, Del.: ISI Books.

Ehrenhalt, Alan. 1982. "In the Senate of the 1980s, Team Spirit Has Given Way to the Rule of Individuals." *Congressional Quarterly Weekly Report* (September 4): 2175–79.

Evans, C. Lawrence. 2018. *The Whips: Building Coalitions in Congress*. Ann Arbor: University of Michigan Press.

Evans, C. Lawrence, and Daniel Lipinski. 2005. "Holds, Legislation, and the Senate Parties." Paper presented at the Conference on Senate Parties, Oxford University.

Evans, C. Lawrence, and Walter Olezsek. 1997. *Congress under Fire: Reform Politics and the Republican Majority*. Boston, Mass.: Houghton Mifflin.

——— 2001. "Message Politics and Senate Procedure." In *The Contentious Senate: Partisanship, Ideology, and the Myth of Cool Judgment*, eds. Colton C. Campbell and Nicol C. Rae. Lanham, Md.: Rowman and Littlefield, 107–27.

Evans, Roland, and Robert D. Novak. 1966. *Lyndon B. Johnson: The Exercise of Power, A Political Biography*. New York: New American Library.

Farley, James A. 1948. *The Jim Farley Story: The Roosevelt Years*. New York: McGraw-Hill.

Farrand, Max, ed. 1966. *The Records of the Federal Convention of 1787*. 4 vols. New Haven, Conn.: Yale University Press.

Fenno, Richard F., Jr. 1973. *Congressmen in Committees.* Boston: Little Brown.
———. 1989. "The Senate through the Looking Glass: The Debate over Television." *Legislative Studies Quarterly* 14 (3): 313–48.
———. 1997. *Learning to Govern: An Institutional View of the 104th Congress.* Washington, D.C.: Brookings.
Ferris, Charles D. 2004. Oral history interviews with Charles D. Ferris, Staff Director, Senate Democratic Policy Committee (1963–77), April 5, 2004–September 23, 2009. Senate Historical Office, Washington, D.C.
Fess, Simeon. 1910. *History of Political Theory and Party Organization in the United States.* Boston, Mass.: Ginn & Co.
Fiorina, Morris P., and Kenneth Shepsle. 1989. "Formal Theories of Leadership: Agents, Agenda-Setters, and Entrepreneurs." In *Leadership and Politics: New Perspectives in Political Science,* ed. Bryan D. Jones. Lawrence: University of Kansas Press, 17–40.
Foer, Franklin. 2004. "Center Forward? The Fate of the New Democrats." In *Varieties of Progressivism in America,* ed. Peter Berkowitz. Stanford, Calif: Hoover Institution Press, 87–104.
Foley, Michael. 1980. *The New Senate: Liberal Influence on a Conservative Institution, 1959–1972.* New Haven, Conn.: Yale University Press.
Foote, Joe S., and David J. Weber. 1984. "Network Evening News Visibility of Congressmen and Senators." Paper presented at the Annual Meeting of the Association for Education in Journalism and Mass Communication, Gainesville, Fla.
Foote, Joe S., and Dennis K. Davis. 1987. "Network Visibility of Congressional Leaders, 1969–1985." Paper presented at the Annual Meeting of the International Communication Association, Montreal, Canada, May 22–25.
Fowler, Dorothy Ganfield. 1961. *John Coit Spooner: Defender of Presidents.* New York: University Publishers.
Franken, Al. 2019. "A Conversation with Former Senate Majority Leader Harry Reid." The Al Franken Podcast, October 6, 2019.
Freeman, Joanne B. 2018. *The Field of Blood: Violence in Congress and the Road to Civil War.* New York: Farrar, Straus and Giroux.
Frist, William H. 1999. *Tennessee Senators, 1911–2001: Portraits of Leadership in a Century of Change.* Lanham, Md.: Madison Books.
Frohlich, Norman, Joe Oppenheimer, and Oran Young. 1971. *Political Leadership and Collective Goods.* Princeton, N.J.: Princeton University Press.
Fry, William Henry. 1860. *Republican "Campaign" Text-Book, for the Year 1860.* New York: A. B. Burdick.
Furber, George P. 1893. *Precedents Relating to the Privileges of the Senate of the United States.* 52nd Cong., 2nd Sess. S. Misc. Doc. 68.
Galloway, George. 1953. *The Legislative Process in Congress.* New York: Thomas Y. Crowell Company.
Galston, William. 2004. "Incomplete Victory." In *Varieties of Progressivism in America,* ed. Peter Berkowitz. Stanford, Calif.: Hoover Institution Press, 59–85.
Gamm, Gerald, and Kenneth Shepsle. 1989. "Emergence of Legislative Institutions: Standing Committees in the House and Senate, 1810–1825." *Legislative Studies Quarterly* 14 (1): 39–66.
Gamm, Gerald, and Steven S. Smith. 2000. "Last Among Equals: The Senate's Presiding Officer." In *Esteemed Colleagues: Civility and Deliberation in the U.S. Senate,* ed. Burdett A. Loomis. Washington, D.C.: Brookings, 105–37.

2002a. "Emergence of Senate Party Leadership." In *U.S. Senate Exceptionalism*, ed. Bruce I. Oppenheimer. Columbus: Ohio State University Press, 212–38.

2002b. "Policy Leadership and the Development of the Modern Senate." In *Party, Process, and Political Change in Congress: New Perspectives on the History of Congress*, eds. David W. Brady and Mathew D. McCubbins. Stanford, Calif: Stanford University Press, 287–311.

Garraty, John A. 1953. *Henry Cabot Lodge: A Biography*. New York: Knopf.

Gilfry, Henry H. 1911. *President of the Senate Pro Tempore*. 62nd Cong., 1st. Sess. S. Doc. 104.

Goldstein, Warren. 1989. *Playing for Keeps: A History of Early Baseball*. Ithaca, N.Y.: Cornell University Press.

Gonzalez, Darryl J. 2010. *The Children Who Ran for Congress: A History of Congressional Pages*. Santa Barbara, Calif.: Praeger.

Goodwin, Doris Kearns. 1976. *Lyndon Johnson and the American Dream*. New York: Harper and Row.

2005. *Team of Rivals: The Political Genius of Abraham Lincoln*. New York: Simon & Schuster.

Gould, Lewis L. 2005. *The Most Exclusive Club: A History of the Modern United States Senate*. New York: Basic Books.

Granat, Diane. 1983. "Ruling Rambunctious Senate Proves to Be Thorny Problem for Republican Leader Baker." *Congressional Quarterly Weekly Report* (July 16): 1427–32.

Granthan, Dewey W. 1958. *Hoke Smith and the Politics of the New South*. Baton Rouge: Louisiana State University Press.

Greene, Howard O. 2007. Interview, July 11, 2007. Robert J. Dole Oral History Project, Robert J. Dole Institute for Politics, Lawrence, Kans.

Greenstein, Fred. 1982. *The Hidden-Hand Presidency: Eisenhower as Leader*. New York: Basic Books.

Griffin, Patrick. 2009. Interview, by Brien Williams. George J. Mitchell Oral History Project, Bowdoin College.

Gross, Donald A. 1984. "Changing Patterns of Voting Agreement Among Senatorial Leadership, 1947–1976." *Western Political Quarterly* 37 (1): 120–42.

Groves, Charles S. 2012. *Henry Cabot Lodge: The Statesman*. Boston, Mass.: Small, Maynard & Company.

Gugin, Linda C., and James E. St. Clair. 1997. *Sherman Minton: New Deal Senator, Cold War Justice*. Indianapolis: Indiana Historical Society.

Hale, Jon F. 1995. "The Making of the New Democrats." *Political Science Quarterly* 110 (2): 207–32.

Hansen, John Mark. 1991. *Gaining Access: Congress and the Farm Lobby, 1919–1981*. Chicago, Ill.: University of Chicago Press.

Hanson, Peter. 2019. "Senate Democratic Leader Tom Daschle." In *Leadership in the U.S. Senate: Herding Cats in the Modern Era*, ed. Colton C. Campbell. New York: Taylor & Francis, 150–87.

Hare, Christopher, and Keith T. Poole. 2014. "The Polarization of Contemporary American Politics." *Polity* 46 (3): 411–29.

Harlow, Ralph V. 1917. *The History of Legislative Methods in the Period before 1825*. New Haven, Conn.: Yale University Press.

Hatch, Louis C. 1934. *A History of the Vice-Presidency of the United States*. New York: American Historical Society.

Hatcher, Andrea C. 2010. *Majority Leadership in the U.S. Senate*. Amherst, N.Y.: Cambria Press.

Hatfield, Mark O. 1997. *Vice Presidents of the United States, 1789–1993*. 104th Cong., 2nd Sess. S. Doc. 104-126. Washington, D.C.: Government Printing Office.

Hathorn, Guy B. 1956. "Congressional and Senatorial Campaign Committees in the Midterm Election Year 1954." *Southwestern Social Science Quarterly* 37 (3): 207–21.

Haughton, Virginia F. 1973. "John Worth Kern and Wilson's New Freedom: A Study of a Senate Majority Leader." Ph.D. diss., University of Kentucky.

Haynes, George H. 1906. *The Election of Senators*. New York: Henry Holt and Company.

1938. *The Senate of the United States: Its History and Practice*. 2 vols. Boston, Mass.: Houghton Mifflin.

Hechler, Kenneth W. 1940. *Insurgency: Personalities and Politics of the Taft Era*. New York: Columbia University Press.

Herring, E. Pendleton. 1932. "American Government and Politics: First Session of the Seventy-second Congress, December 7, 1931, to July 16, 1932." *American Political Science Review* 26 (5): 846–74.

1933. "American Government and Politics: Second Session of the Seventy-second Congress, December 5, 1932, to March 4, 1933." *American Political Science Review* 27 (3): 404–22.

1934. "American Government and Politics: First Session of the Seventy-third Congress, March 9, 1933, to June 16, 1933." *American Political Science Review* 28 (1): 65–83.

Herrnson, Paul S. 2009. "The Roles of Party Organizations, Party-Connected Committees, and Party Allies in Elections." *Journal of Politics* 71 (4): 1207–24.

Hertzke, Allen D., and Ronald Peters. 1992. *The Atomistic Congress*. Armonk, N.Y.: M.E. Sharpe.

Hess, Stephen. 1981. *The Washington Reporters*. Washington, D.C.: Brookings Institution.

1986. *The Ultimate Insiders: U.S. Senators in the National Media*. Washington, D.C.: Brookings.

1991. *Live from Capitol Hill: Studies of Congress and the Media*. Washington, D.C.: Brookings.

1994. "The Decline and Fall of Congressional News." In *Congress, the Press, and the Public*, eds. Thomas Mann and Norman J. Ornstein. Washington, D.C.: Brookings and American Enterprise Institute, 151–56.

Hildenbrand, William F. 1985. Oral history interviews, March 20, 1985–May 6, 1985. Senate Historical Office, Washington, D.C.

History, Rules, and Precedents of the Senate Republican Conference, 105th Congress. 1997.

History, Rules, and Precedents of the Senate Republican Conference, 117th Congress. 2022.

Hoar, George F. 1903. *Autobiography of Seventy Years*. 2 vols. New York: Charles Scribner's Sons.

Hollingsworth, J. Rogers. 1963. *The Whirligig of Politics: The Democracy of Cleveland and Bryan*. Chicago, Ill.: University of Chicago Press.

Holt, James. 1967. *Congressional Insurgents and the Party System, 1909–1916.* Cambridge, Mass.: Harvard University Press.

Holt, Michael F. 1999. *The Rise and Fall of the American Whig Party: Jacksonian Politics and the Onset of the Civil War.* New York: Oxford University Press.

Holt, W. Stull. 1933. *Treaties Defeated by the Senate.* Baltimore, Md.: Johns Hopkins University Press.

Holt, Wythe W., Jr. 1975. "The Senator from Virginia and the Democratic Floor Leadership." *Virginia Magazine of History and Biography* 83 (1): 3–21.

Howard, Nicholas O., and Jason M. Roberts. 2015. "The Politics of Obstruction: Republican Holds in the U.S. Senate." *Legislative Studies Quarterly* 40 (2): 273–94.

Howe, Daniel Walker. 2007. *What Hath God Wrought: The Transformation of America, 1815–1848.* New York: Oxford University Press.

Huitt, Ralph K. 1961. "Democratic Party Leadership in the Senate." *American Political Science Review* 55 (2): 333–44.

Hulsey, Byron C. 2000. *Everett Dirksen and His Presidents.* Lawrence: University Press of Kansas.

Humbert, W. H. 1932. "The Democratic Joint Policy Committee." *American Political Science Review* 26 (3): 552–54.

Inaugural Addresses of the Presidents of the United States: From George Washington, 1789, to Lyndon Baines Johnson, 1965. 1965. 89th Cong., 1st Sess. H. Doc. 51. Washington, D.C.: Government Printing Office.

Jenkins, Jeffery A., Nolan McCarty, and Charles Stewart III. 2020. "Learning from Each Other: Causal Inference and American Political Development." *Public Choice* 185: 245–51.

Jenkins, Jeffery A., and Justin Peck. 2013. "Building Toward Major Policy Change: Congressional Action on Civil Rights, 1941–1950." *Law and History Review* 31 (1): 139–98.

———. 2021. *Congress and the First Civil Rights Era, 1861–1918.* Chicago, Ill.: University of Chicago Press.

Jenkins, Jeffery A., and Charles Stewart III. 2013. *Fighting for the Speakership: The House and the Rise of Party Government.* Princeton, N.J.: Princeton University Press.

Jentleson, Adam. 2021. *Kill Switch: The Rise of the Modern Senate and the Crippling of American Democracy.* New York: Liveright.

Jewell, Malcolm E. 1962. *Senatorial Politics and Foreign Policy.* Lexington: University of Kentucky Press.

Johnson, Evans C. 1980. *Oscar W. Underwood: A Political Biography.* Baton Rouge: Louisiana State University Press.

Johnson, Roger T. 1964. *Robert M. La Follette, Jr., and the Decline of the Progressive Party in Wisconsin.* Madison: State Historical Society of Wisconsin, for the Department of History, University of Wisconsin.

Johnstone, Robert M., Jr. 1978. *Jefferson and the Presidency: Leadership in the Young Republic.* Ithaca, N.Y.: Cornell University Press.

Jones, Charles O. 1970. *The Minority Party in Congress.* Boston, Mass.: Little, Brown.

———. 1976. "Senate Party Leadership in Public Policy." In *Policymaking Role of Leadership in the Senate.* Compilation of papers prepared for the Commission on the Operation of the Senate, 94th Cong., 2nd Sess. Washington, D.C.: Government Printing Office, 18–33.

Josephy, Alvin M., Jr. 1979. *On the Hill: A History of the American Congress.* New York: Simon and Schuster.

Katznelson, Ira. 2005. *When Affirmative Action Was White: An Untold History of Racial Inequality in Twentieth-Century America.* New York: W.W. Norton.

———. 2011. "Historical Approaches to the Study of Congress: Toward a Congressional Vantage on American Political Development." In *The Oxford Handbook of the American Congress,* eds. Eric Schickler and Frances E. Lee. New York: Oxford University Press, 115–38.

———. 2013. *Fear Itself: The New Deal and the Origins of Our Time.* New York: Liveright.

Katznelson, Ira, and John S. Lapinski. 2006. "At the Crossroads: Congress and American Political Development." *Perspectives on Politics* 4 (2): 243–60.

Keith, Robert. 1977. "The Use of Unanimous Consent in the Senate." In U.S. Senate, *Committees and Senate Procedures.* 94th Cong., 2nd Sess.

Keller, Morton. 1977. *Affairs of State: Public Life in Late Nineteenth Century America.* Cambridge, Mass.: Harvard University Press.

Kelly, Howard A., and Walter L. Burrage. 1920. *American Medical Biographies.* Baltimore, Md.: Norman, Remington Co.

Kelly, Sean Q. 1995a. "Democratic Leadership in the Modern Senate: The Emerging Roles of the Democratic Policy Committee." *Congress & the Presidency* 22 (2): 113–39.

———. 1995b. "Passing the Torch: Generational Change and the Selection of the Senate Democratic Leader in the 104th Congress." Paper presented at the Annual Meeting of the Midwest Political Science Association, Chicago, Ill.

Kerr, Clara Hannah. 1895. *The Origin and Development of the United States Senate.* Ithaca, N.Y.: Andrus & Church.

Kiepper, James J. 2001. *Styles Bridges: Yankee Senator.* Sugar Hill, N.H.: Phoenix Publishing.

Kiewiet, D. Roderick, and Mathew D. McCubbins. 1991. *The Logic of Delegation: Congressional Parties and the Appropriations Process.* Chicago, Ill.: University of Chicago Press.

Kimmitt, J. Stanley. 2001. Oral history interviews with J. Stanley Kimmitt, Secretary for the Majority (1965–76) and Secretary of the Senate (1977–81), February 15, 2001– October 9, 2002. Senate Historical Office, Washington, D.C.

Kinney, Charles L. 2009. Interview, by Diane Dewhirst, July 27, 2009. George J. Mitchell Oral History Project, 70, Bowdoin College.

Kirsch, George B. 1989. *The Creation of American Team Sports: Baseball and Cricket, 1838–72.* Urbana: University of Illinois Press.

Klinkner, Philip. 1999. "Democratic Party Ideology in the 1990s: New Democrats or Modern Republicans?" In *The Politics of Ideas: Intellectual Challenges Facing the American Political Parties,* eds. John K. White and John C. Green. Albany: State University of New York Press, 113–31.

Klotz, Robert. 2022. *Thomas Brackett Reed: The Gilded Age Speaker Who Made the Rules for American Politics.* Lawrence: University Press of Kansas.

Koger, Gregory. 2010. *Filibustering: A Political History of Obstruction in the House and Senate.* Chicago, Ill.: University of Chicago Press.

Koger, Gregory, and Matthew J. Lebo. 2017. *Strategic Party Government: Why Winning Trumps Ideology.* Chicago, Ill.: University of Chicago Press.

Kolodny, Robin. 1998. *Pursuing Majorities: Congressional Campaign Committees in American Politics*. Norman: University of Oklahoma Press.

Kravitz, Walter. Circa 1971. "The United States Senate: An Interpretive History." Unpublished manuscript, Senate Historical Office.

Krout, John A., ed. 1928. "Henry J. Raymond on the Republican Caucuses of July, 1866." *American Historical Review* 33 (4): 835–42.

Lambert, John R., Jr. 1953. *Arthur Pue Gorman*. Baton Rouge: Louisiana State University Press.

    ed. 1963. "The Autobiographical Writings of Senator Arthur Pue Gorman." *Maryland Historical Magazine* 58 (2, 3): 93–122, 233–46.

Latner, Richard B. 1978. "The Kitchen Cabinet and Andrew Jackson's Advisory System." *Journal of American History* 65 (2): 367–88.

Lee, Frances. 2009. *Beyond Ideology: Politics, Principles, and Partisanship in the U.S. Senate*. Chicago, Ill.: University of Chicago Press.

    2016. *Insecure Majorities: Congress and the Perpetual Campaign*. Chicago, Ill.: University of Chicago Press.

Letchworth, Elizabeth. 2010. Oral history interviews with Elizabeth Letchworth, Page Floor Assistant, Republican Party Secretary, 1975–2001, October 5, 2010–March 21, 2012. Senate Historical Office, Washington, D.C.

Lewis, Jeffrey B., Keith Poole, Howard Rosenthal, Adam Boche, Aaron Rudkin, and Luke Sonnet. 2020. *Voteview: Congressional Roll Call Votes Database*. https://voteview.com/

Lewis-Beck, Michael S., and Tom W. Rice. 1992. *Forecasting Elections*. Washington, D.C.: Congressional Quarterly.

Libbey, James K. 2016. *Alben Barkley: A Life in Politics*. Lexington: University Press of Kentucky.

Lodge, Henry Cabot. 1893. "The Struggle in the Senate: Obstruction in the Senate." *North American Review* 157 (444): 523–29.

Loomis, Burdett. 1991. "Everett M. Dirksen: The Consummate Minority Leader." In *First Among Equals: Outstanding Senate Leaders of the Twentieth Century*, eds. Richard A. Baker and Roger H. Davidson. Washington, D.C.: Congressional Quarterly, 236–63.

    2019. "Bob Dole's Leadership: The Partisan Dealmaker." In *Leadership in the U.S. Senate: Herding Cats in the Modern Era*, ed. Colton C. Campbell. New York: Taylor & Francis, 103–26.

Lott, Trent. 2005. *Herding Cats: A Life in Politics*. New York: William Morrow.

    2007. Interview, June 20, 2007. Robert J. Dole Oral History Project, Robert J. Dole Institute for Politics, Lawrence, Kans.

Luce, Robert. 1922. *Legislative Procedure: Parliamentary Practices and the Course of Business in the Framing of Statutes*. Boston, Mass.: Houghton Mifflin.

Lynch, Michael, Anthony Madonna, Mark Owens, and Ryan D. Williamson. 2018. "The Vice President in the U.S. Senate: Examining the Consequences of Institutional Design." *Congress & the Presidency* 45 (2): 145–65.

MacGillis, Alec. 2014. *The Cynic: The Political Education of Mitch McConnell*. New York: Simon & Schuster.

Mackaman, Frank H. 1981. *Understanding Congressional Leadership*. Washington, D.C.: Congressional Quarterly Press.

Maclay, Edgar S., ed. 1890. *Journal of William Maclay: United States Senator from Pennsylvania, 1789–1791*. New York: D. Appleton and Company.

Macmahon, Arthur W. 1930. "First Session of the Seventy-first Congress." *American Political Science Review* 24 (1): 38–59.

MacNeil, Neil. 1970. *Dirksen: Portrait of a Public Man*. New York: World Publishing.

MacNeil, Neil, and Richard A. Baker. 2013. *The American Senate: An Insider's History*. New York: Oxford University Press.

Macy, Jesse. 1918. *Party Organization and Machinery*. New York: The Century Co.

Madden, James William. 1929. *Charles Allen Culberson: His Life, Character and Public Service*. Austin, Tex.: Gammel's Book Store.

Madonna, Anthony J. 2012. "Senate Rules and Procedure: Revisiting the Bank Bill of 1841 and the Development of Senate Obstruction." In *New Directions in Congressional Politics*, ed. Jamie L. Carson. New York: Routledge, 126–42.

Magleby, David B. 2011. "How the 2008 Elections Were Financed." In *The Change Election*, ed. David B. Magleby. Philadelphia, Pa.: Temple University Press, 27–51.

Malbin, Michael. 1980. *Unelected Representatives*. New York: Basic Books.

Malsberger, John W. 1987. "The Transformation of Republican Conservatism: The U.S. Senate, 1938–1952." *Congress & the Presidency* 14 (1): 17–31.

Martin, Janet M. 2019. "George J. Mitchell: Majority Leader." In *Leadership in the U.S. Senate: Herding Cats in the Modern Era*, ed. Colton C. Campbell. New York: Taylor & Francis, 127–49.

Matthews, Donald. 1960. *U.S. Senators & Their World*. New York: Vintage Books.

Mayhew, David R. 1974. *Congress: The Electoral Connection*. New Haven, Conn.: Yale University Press.

McCluney, Joyce. 2008. Interview, January 23, 2008. Robert J. Dole Oral History Project, Robert J. Dole Institute for Politics, Lawrence, Kans.

McConachie, Lauros G. 1898. *Congressional Committees: A Study of the Origins and Development of Our National and Local Legislative Methods*. New York: Thomas Y. Crowell.

McConnell, Mitch. 2016. *The Long Game: A Memoir*. New York: Sentinel.

McConnell, Mitch, and Roy E. Brownell II. 2019. *The U.S. Senate and the Commonwealth: Kentucky Lawmakers and the Evolution of Legislative Leadership*. Lexington: University Press of Kentucky.

McCormick, Richard P. 1982. *The Presidential Game: The Origins of American Presidential Politics*. New York: Oxford University Press.

McFarland, Ernest W. 1979. *Mac: The Autobiography of Ernest W. McFarland*. S.l.: McFarland.

McKenna, Brian. n.d. "Arthur Gorman." SABR Baseball Biography Project, Society for American Baseball Research.

McMillan, James Elton. 2004. *Ernest W. McFarland: Majority Leader of the Senate, Governor and Chief Justice of Arizona*. Prescott, Ariz.: Sharlot Hall Museum Press.

McPherson, James M. 1988. *Battle Cry of Freedom: The Civil War Era*. New York: Oxford University Press.

Menefee-Libey, David J. 1989. "The Politics of National Party Organization: The Democrats from 1968 to 1986." Ph.D. diss., University of Chicago.

Merk, Frederick. 1967. *The Oregon Question: Essays in Anglo-American Diplomacy and Politics*. Cambridge, Mass.: Harvard University Press.

Merriam, Charles Edward, and Harold Foote Gosnell. 1929. *The American Party System: An Introduction to the Study of Political Parties in the United States.* New York: Macmillan.

Merrill, Horace Samuel, and Marion Galbraith Merrill. 1971. *The Republican Command: 1897–1913.* Lexington: University Press of Kentucky.

Merry, Robert W. 1991. "Robert A. Taft: A Study in the Accumulation of Legislative Power." In *First Among Equals: Outstanding Senate Leaders of the Twentieth Century,* eds. Richard A. Baker and Roger H. Davidson. Washington, D.C.: Congressional Quarterly, 163–98.

Miller, James A. 1986. *Running in Place: Inside the Senate.* New York: Simon & Schuster.

Mitchell, George J. 2007. Interview, April 7, 2007. Robert J. Dole Oral History Project, Robert J. Dole Institute for Politics, Lawrence, Kans.

———. 2008. Interview (2), by Andrea L'Hommedieu and Mike Hastings, September 11, 2008. George J. Mitchell Oral History Project, 70, Bowdoin College.

———. 2010. Interview (3), by Andrea L'Hommedieu, December 20, 2010. George J. Mitchell Oral History Project, 70, Bowdoin College.

———. 2015. *The Negotiator.* New York: Simon & Schuster.

Mitnick, Barry M. 1975. "The Theory of Agency: The Policing 'Paradox' and Regulatory Behavior." *Public Choice* 24: 27–42.

Montgomery, Gayle B., and James W. Johnson. 1998. *One Step from the White House: The Rise and Fall of William F. Knowland.* Berkeley: University of California Press.

Mooney, Booth. 1956. *The Lyndon Johnson Story.* New York: Farrar, Straus and Cudahy.

Moore, Betty J. 1986. "The Majority Leader of the United States Senate: The Leader's Effectiveness as a Major Determinant in the Leadership Model." Ph.D. diss., University of Maryland.

Morgan, H. Wayne. 1963. *William McKinley and His America.* Syracuse, N.Y.: Syracuse University Press.

Morgan, William G. 1969. "The Origin and Development of the Congressional Nominating Caucus." *Proceedings of the American Philosophical Society* 113 (2): 184–96.

Morris, Dick. 2001. "Bush Must Deal To Win Tax Cut." *The Hill.* March 14.

Muller, Ernest Paul. 1957. "Preston King: A Political Biography." Ph.D. diss., Columbia University.

Munk, Margaret. 1970. "Origin and Development of the Party Floor Leadership in the United States Senate." Ph.D. diss., Department of Government, Harvard University.

———. 1974. "Origin and Development of the Party Floor Leadership in the United States Senate." *Capitol Studies* 2 (2): 23–41.

Murphy, Thomas P. 1974. *The New Politics Congress.* Lexington, Mass.: Lexington Books.

Murray, Robert K. 1976. *The 103rd Ballot: Democrats and the Disaster in Madison Square Garden.* New York: Harper & Row.

National Republican Congressional Committee. 1966. *One Hundred Years: A History of the National Republican Congressional Committee.* Washington, D.C.: Judd and Detweiler.

Neal, Steve. 1985. *McNary of Oregon: A Political Biography.* Portland, Ore.: Oregon Historical Society.

1991. "Charles L. McNary: The Quiet Man." In *First Among Equals: Outstanding Senate Leaders of the Twentieth Century*, eds. Richard A. Baker and Roger H. Davidson. Washington, D.C.: Congressional Quarterly, 98–126.

Nelson, Garrison. 1980. "Senate Leadership Changes: A Theory of Institutional Interaction." Paper presented at the Conference on Understanding Congressional Leadership: The State of the Art, sponsored jointly by the Everett McKinley Dirksen Congressional Leadership Research Center and the Sam Rayburn Library, Georgetown University Law Center, Washington, D.C.

Neustadt, Richard E. 1955. "Presidency and Legislation: Planning the President's Program." *American Political Science Review* 49 (4): 980–1021.

Nevins, Allan. 1932. *Grover Cleveland: A Study in Courage*. New York: Dodd, Mead.

Newberry, Farrar. 1913. *James K. Jones, The Plumed Knight of Arkansas*. Arkadelphia, Ark.: Siftings-Herald.

Nickles, Donald. 2007. Interview with Sen. Don Nickles, March 27, 2007. Robert J. Dole Oral History Project, Robert J. Dole Institute for Politics, Lawrence, Kans.

Niven, John. 1983. *Martin Van Buren: The Romantic Age of American Politics*. Newtown, Conn.: American Political Biography Press.

North, Douglass C. 1990. *Institutions, Institutional Change, and Economic Performance*. Cambridge: Cambridge University Press.

Oberdorfer, Don. 2003. *Senator Mansfield: The Extraordinary Life of a Great American Statesman and Diplomat*. Washington, D.C.: Smithsonian Books.

Oleszek, Mark J. 2017. *"Holds" in the Senate*. CRS Report R43563. Congressional Research Service, January 24, 2017.

Oleszek, Mark J., and Walter J. Oleszek. 2019. "Legislating in the Senate: From the 1950s into the 2000s." In *Leadership in the U.S. Senate: Herding Cats in the Modern Era*, ed. Colton C. Campbell. New York: Taylor & Francis, 1–40.

Oleszek, Walter J. 1971. "Party Whips in the United States Senate." *Journal of Politics* 33 (4): 955–79.

1985. *Majority and Minority Whips of the Senate*. S. Doc. 98-45. 98th Cong., 2nd Sess. Washington, D.C.: Government Printing Office.

1991. "John Worth Kern: Portrait of a Floor Leader." In *First Among Equals: Outstanding Senate Leaders of the Twentieth Century*, eds. Richard A. Baker and Roger H. Davidson. Washington, D.C.: Congressional Quarterly, 7–37.

Olson, Mancur. 1965. *The Logic of Collective Action*. Cambridge, Mass.: Harvard University Press.

Oppenheimer, Bruce I. 1977. "The Rules Committee: New Arm of Leadership in a Decentralized House." In *Congress Reconsidered*, eds. Lawrence C. Dodd and Bruce I. Oppenheimer. New York: Praeger, 96–116.

1985. "Changing Time Constraints on Congress: Historical Perspectives on the Use of Cloture." In *Congress Reconsidered*, 3rd ed., eds. Lawrence C. Dodd and Bruce I. Oppenheimer. Washington, D.C.: CQ Press, 393–413.

Ornstein, Norman J. 1989. "What TV News Doesn't Report about Congress—and Should." *TV Guide* (October 21): 11.

Ornstein, Norman J., Robert L. Peabody, and David W. Rohde. 1977. "The Changing Senate: From the 1950s to the 1970s." In *Congress Reconsidered*, eds. Lawrence C. Dodd and Bruce I. Oppenheimer. New York: Praeger, 3–20.

Ostrogorski, M[oisey]. 1899. "The Rise and Fall of the Nominating Caucus, Legislative and Congressional." *American Historical Review* 5 (2): 253–83.

1902. *Democracy and the Organization of Political Parties.* 2 vols. New York: Macmillan.

Packwood, Bob. 2007. Interview with Sen. Bob Packwood, July 20, 2007. Robert J. Dole Oral History Project, Robert J. Dole Institute for Politics, Lawrence, Kans.

Page, William Tyler. 1922. "Political Organization of Congress Explained." *Congressional Digest* 1 (11): 23.

Paone, Martin P. n.d. Oral history interviews with Martin P. Paone, Senate Democratic Cloakroom Staff to Majority Secretary, 1979–2008. Senate Historical Office, Washington, D.C.

Park, Hong Min, Ryan J. Vander Wielen, and Steven S. Smith. 2017. *Politics Over Process: Partisan Conflict and Post-Passage Processes in the U.S. Congress.* Ann Arbor: University of Michigan Press.

Patterson, James T. 1967. *Congressional Conservatism and the New Deal: The Growth of the Conservative Coalition in Congress, 1933–1939.* Lexington: University of Kentucky Press.

1972. *Mr. Republican: A Biography of Robert A. Taft.* Boston, Mass.: Houghton Mifflin.

Patterson, Samuel C. 1989. "Party Leadership in the U.S. Senate." *Legislative Studies Quarterly* 14 (3): 393–413.

Patterson, Samuel C., and Thomas H. Little. 1992. "The Organizational Life of the Congressional Parties." Paper presented at the Annual Meeting of the Midwest Political Science Association, Chicago, Ill.

Peabody, Robert L. 1966. *The Ford-Hallack Leadership Contest, 1965.* Eagleton Institute Cases in Practical Politics. New York: McGraw-Hill.

1976. *Leadership in Congress: Stability, Succession, and Change.* Boston, Mass.: Little, Brown.

1981. "Senate Leadership: From the 1950s to the 1980s." In *Understanding Congressional Leadership*, ed. Frank H. Mackaman. Washington, D.C.: CQ Press, 261–92.

Pearson, Kathryn, and Eric Schickler. 2009. "Discharge Petitions, Agenda Control, and the Congressional Committee System, 1929–76." *Journal of Politics* 71 (4): 1238–56.

Petersen, R. Eric. 2007. *Senate Policy Committees.* CRS Report RL32015. Congressional Research Service, April 25, 2007.

Peterson, Merrill D. 1987. *The Great Triumvirate: Webster, Clay, and Calhoun.* New York: Oxford University Press.

Pinchot, Amos. 1958. *History of the Progressive Party, 1912–1916.* New York: New York University Press.

Polsby, Nelson W. 1989. "Tracking Changes in the U.S. Senate." *PS: Political Science and Politics* 22 (4): 789–93.

Poole, Keith T., and Howard Rosenthal. 1997. *Congress: A Political-Economic History of Roll Call Voting.* New York: Oxford University Press.

Poore, Benjamin Perley. 1886. *Perley's Reminiscences of Sixty Years in the National Metropolis.* 2 vols. Philadelphia, Pa.: Hubbard Brothers and J. W. Keeler & Co.

Pope, Martha, Martin P. Paone, and C. Abbott Saffold. 2009. Interview, by Diane Dewhirst, May 26, 2009. George J. Mitchell Oral History Project, 70, Bowdoin College.

Price, H. Douglas. 1975. "Congress and the Evolution of Legislative Professionalism." In *Congress in Change: Evolution and Reform*, ed. Norman J. Ornstein. New York: Praeger, 316–36.

Rae, Nicol C. 2019. "Ambition and Achievement: The Senate Republican Leadership of Trent Lott." In *Leadership in the U.S. Senate: Herding Cats in the Modern Era*, ed. Colton C. Campbell. New York: Taylor & Francis, 188–208.

Reedy, George E. 1986. *The U.S. Senate: Paralysis or a Search for Consensus?* New York: Crown Publishers.

Reeves, Paschal. 1960. "Thomas S. Martin: Committee Statesman." *Virginia Magazine of History* 68 (3): 344–64.

Reid, Harry. 2008. *The Good Fight: Hard Lessons from Searchlight to Washington.* New York: Berkley Books.

Remini, Robert V. 1991. *Henry Clay: Statesman for the Union.* New York: W.W. Norton.

1997. *Daniel Webster: The Man and His Time.* New York: W.W. Norton.

2001. *The Life of Andrew Jackson.* New York: Harper Perennial Modern Classics.

Republican Executive Congressional Committee. 1860. *The Poor Whites of the South: The Injury Done Them by Slavery.* Washington, D.C.: Republican Congressional Committee.

Riddick, Floyd M. 1941. "American Government and Politics: Third Session of the Seventy-sixth Congress, January 3, 1940, to January 3, 1941." *American Political Science Review* 35 (2): 284–303.

1949. *The United States Congress: Organization and Procedure.* Manassas, Va.: National Capitol Publishers.

1971. "Majority and Minority Leaders of the Senate: History and Development of the Offices of the Floor Leaders." 92nd Cong., 1st Sess. S. Doc. 92-42. Washington, D.C.: Government Printing Office.

1977. "Majority and Minority Leaders of the Senate." 95th Cong., 1st Sess. S. Doc. 95-24. Washington, D.C.: Government Printing Office.

1992. *Riddick Senate Procedure.* www.riddick.gpo.gov. Accessed March 2025.

Riedel, Richard Langham. 1969. *Halls of the Mighty: My 47 Years at the Senate.* Washington, D.C.: Robert B. Luce.

Rienow, Robert, and Leona Train Rienow. 1965. *Of Snuff, Sin and the Senate.* Chicago, Ill.: Follett.

Riker, William H. 1955. "The Senate and American Federalism." *American Political Science Review* 49 (2): 452–69.

Ripley, Randall B. 1969a. *Majority Party Leadership in Congress.* Boston, Mass.: Little, Brown.

1969b. *Power in the Senate.* New York: St. Martin's Press.

1976. "Party Leaders, Policy Committees, and Policy Analysis in the United States Senate." In Commission on the Operation of the Senate, *Policymaking Role of Leadership in the Senate*, 94th Cong., 2nd Sess. Washington, D.C.: Government Printing Office, 5–11.

Ritchie, Donald A. 1991a. "Alben W. Barkley: The President's Man." In *First Among Equals: Outstanding Senate Leaders of the Twentieth Century*, eds. Richard A.

Baker and Roger H. Davidson. Washington, D.C.: Congressional Quarterly, 127–62.

1991b. *Press Gallery: Congress and the Washington Correspondents.* Cambridge, Mass.: Harvard University Press.

1997. *A History of the United States Senate Republican Policy Committee, 1947–1997.* S. Doc. 105-5. Washington, D.C.: Government Printing Office.

ed. 1998a. *Minutes of the Senate Democratic Conference: Fifty-eighth Congress through Eighty-eighth Congress, 1903–1964.* 105th Cong. S. Doc. 105-20. Washington, D.C.: Government Printing Office.

1998b. "The Senate of Mike Mansfield." *Montana: The Magazine of Western History* 48 (4): 50–62.

2000. "Charles Lee Watkins." In *Arkansas Biography*, ed. Nancy A. Williams. Fayetteville: University of Arkansas Press.

2009. "Oral History Interview with Bobby Baker." *Politico Magazine*, November 19, 2013.

Roberts, Jason M. 2010. "The Development of Special Orders and Special Rules in the U.S. House, 1881–1937." *Legislative Studies Quarterly* 35 (3): 307–36.

Roberts, Jason M., and Steven S. Smith. 2007. "The Evolution of Agenda-Setting Institutions in Congress: Path Dependency in House and Senate Institutional Development." In *Process, Party and Policy Making: Further New Perspectives on the History of Congress*, eds. David Brady and Mathew McCubbins. Stanford, Calif.: Stanford University Press, 182–204.

Robertson, David. 1994. *Slay and Able: A Political Biography of James F. Byrnes.* New York: W.W. Norton.

Robinson, Donald A. 1976. "If Senate Democrats Want Leadership: An Analysis of the History and Prospects of the Majority Party Policy Committee." In *Policymaking Role of the Leadership in the Senate*, papers compiled for the Commission on the Operation of the Senate, 94th Cong., 2nd Sess. Washington, D.C.: Government Printing Office, 40–57.

Robinson, George Lee. 1954. "The Development of the Senate Committee System." Ph.D. diss., Department of Government, New York University.

Robinson, James A. 1963. *The House Rules Committee.* Indianapolis, Ind.: Bobbs-Merrill.

Robinson, Michael J., and Kevin R. Appel. 1979. "Network News Coverage of Congress." *Political Science Quarterly* 94 (3): 407–18.

Rogers, Lindsay. 1920. "American Government and Politics." *American Political Science Review* 14 (1): 74–92.

1922. "American Government and Politics: The First (Special) Session of the Sixty-seventh Congress, April 11, 1921–November 23, 1921." *American Political Science Review* 16 (1): 41–52.

1925. "First and Second Sessions of the Sixty-eighth Congress." *American Political Science Review* 19 (4): 761–72.

Rohde, David W. 1991. *Parties and Leaders in the Postreform House.* Chicago, Ill.: University of Chicago Press.

Rohde, David W., Norman J. Ornstein, and Robert L. Peabody. 1985. "Political Change and Legislative Norms in the U.S. Senate, 1957–1974." In *Studies of Congress*, ed. Glenn R. Parker. Washington, D.C.: CQ Press, 147–88.

Rohde, David W., and Kenneth A. Shepsle. 1987. "Leaders and Followers in the House of Representatives: Reflections on Woodrow Wilson's *Congressional Government*." *Congress & the Presidency* 14 (2): 111–33.

Roper, Burns W. 1983. *Trends in Attitudes Toward Television and Other Media*. New York: Roper Organization.

Ross, Stephen A. 1973. "The Economic Theory of Agency: The Principal's Problem." *American Economic Review* 62 (2): 134–39.

Rothman, David J. 1966. *Politics and Power: The United States Senate, 1869–1901*. Cambridge, Mass.: Harvard University Press.

Rovere, Richard H. 1956. *Affairs of State: The Eisenhower Years*. New York: Farrar, Straus, and Cudahy.

Russo, David J. 1972. "The Major Political Issues of the Jacksonian Period and the Development of Party Loyalty in Congress, 1830–1840." *Transactions of the American Philosophical Society* 62(5): 3–51.

Sabato, Larry J. 1985. *PAC Power: Inside the World of Political Action Committees*. New York: W.W. Norton.

Sachs, Richard C. 1995. "The President Pro Tempore of the Senate: History and Authority of the Office." CRS Report for Congress. Washington, D.C.: Congressional Research Service.

Sarasohn, David. 1989. *The Party of Reform: Democrats in the Progressive Era*. Jackson: University Press of Mississippi.

Sasser, James. 2010. Interview with Jim Sasser, by Diane Dewhirst, April 27, 2010. George J. Mitchell Oral History Project, 70, Bowdoin College.

Schapsmeier, Edward L., and Frederick H. Schapsmeier. 1977. "Scott W. Lucas of Havana: His Rise and Fall as Majority Leader in the United States Senate." *Journal of the Illinois State Historical Society* 70 (4): 302–20.

1985. *Dirksen of Illinois: Senatorial Statesman*. Urbana: University of Illinois Press.

Schickler, Eric. 2001. *Disjointed Pluralism: Institutional Innovation and the Development of the U.S. Congress*. Princeton, N.J.: Princeton University Press.

Schickler, Eric, and Kathryn Pearson. 2011. "Agenda Control, Majority Party Power, and the House Rules Committee." *Legislative Studies Quarterly* 34 (4): 455–91.

Schiller, Wendy J., and Charles Stewart. 2014. *Electing the Senate: Indirect Democracy before the Seventeenth Amendment*. Princeton, N.J.: Princeton University Press.

Schiller, Wendy, and Cory Manento. 2019. "Howard Baker and the Conditional Use of Parliamentary Procedure in the U.S. Senate." In *Leadership in the U.S. Senate: Herding Cats in the Modern Era*, ed. Colton C. Campbell. New York: Taylor & Francis, 41–67.

Schriftgiesser, Karl. 1944. *The Gentleman from Massachusetts: Henry Cabot Lodge*. Boston, Mass.: Little, Brown.

Scott, Katherine, and James Wyatt. 2019. "Robert C. Byrd: Tactician and Technician." In *Leadership in the U.S. Senate: Herding Cats in the Modern Era*, ed. Colton C. Campbell. New York: Taylor & Francis, 68–102.

Shaffer, Samuel. 1980. *On and Off the Floor: Thirty Years as a Correspondent on Capitol Hill*. New York: Newsweek Books.

Shanley, Robert A. 1988. "Franklin D. Roosevelt and Water Pollution Control Policy." *Presidential Studies Quarterly* 18 (2): 319–30.

Shapiro, Ira. 2018. *Broken: Can the Senate Save Itself and the Country?* Lanham, Md.: Rowman and Littlefield.

Shepsle, Kenneth A. 1989. "The Changing Textbook Congress." In *Can the Government Govern?*, eds. John E. Chubb and Paul E. Peterson. Washington, D.C.: Brookings Institution, 238–66.

Shuman, Howard E. 1991. "Lyndon B. Johnson: The Senate's Powerful Persuader." In *First Among Equals: Outstanding Senate Leaders of the Twentieth Century*, eds. Richard A. Baker and Roger H. Davidson. Washington, D.C.: Congressional Quarterly, 199–235.

Silbey, Joel H. 1967. *The Shrine of Party: Congressional Voting Behavior, 1841–1852.* Pittsburgh, Pa.: University of Pittsburgh Press.

1991. *The American Political Nation, 1838–1893.* Stanford, Calif.: Stanford University Press.

2002. *Martin Van Buren and the Emergence of American Popular Politics.* Lanham, Md.: Rowman & Littlefield Publishers.

Simpson, Alan K. 2007. Interview with Sen. Alan Simpson, October 9, 2007. Robert J. Dole Oral History Project, Robert J. Dole Institute for Politics, Lawrence, Kans.

Sinclair, Barbara. 1983. *Majority Leadership in the House.* Baltimore, Md.: Johns Hopkins University Press.

1989. *The Transformation of the U.S. Senate.* Baltimore, Md.: Johns Hopkins University Press.

1990. "Congressional Leadership: A Review Essay and a Research Agenda." In *Leading Congress: New Styles, New Strategies*, ed. John J. Kornacki. Washington, D.C.: CQ Press, 97–162.

1995. *Legislators, Leaders, and Lawmaking: The U.S. House of Representatives in the Postreform Era.* Baltimore, Md.: Johns Hopkins University Press.

2002. "The '60-Vote Senate': Strategies, Process and Outcomes." In *U.S. Senate Exceptionalism*, ed. Bruce I. Oppenheimer. Columbus: Ohio State University Press, 241–61.

2006. *Party Wars: Polarization and the Politics of National Policy Making.* Norman: University of Oklahoma Press.

2012. "Senate Parties and Party Leadership, 1960–2010." In *The U.S. Senate: From Deliberation to Dysfunction*, ed. Burdette A. Loomis. Washington, D.C.: CQ Press, 85–109.

Smith, Elbert. 1958. *Magnificent Missourian: The Life of Thomas Hart Benton.* Philadelphia, Pa.: Lippincott.

Smith, Oliver Hampton. 1858. *Early Indiana Trials and Sketches: Reminiscences by Hon. O. H. Smith.* Cincinnati, Ohio: Moore, Wilstach, Keys & Co.

Smith, Steven S. 1981. "The Consistency and Ideological Structure of U.S. Senate Voting Alignments, 1957–1976." *American Journal of Political Science* 25 (4): 780–795.

1989. *Call to Order: Floor Politics in the House and Senate.* Washington, D.C.: Brookings Institution.

1993. "Forces of Change in Senate Party Leadership and Organization." In *Congress Reconsidered*, 5th ed., eds. Lawrence C. Dodd and Bruce I. Oppenheimer. Washington, D.C.: Congressional Quarterly, 259–90.

1994. "Congressional Party Leaders." In *The President, the Congress, and the Making of Foreign Policy*, ed. Paul E. Peterson. Norman: University of Oklahoma Press, 129–57.

2007. *Party Influence in Congress*. Cambridge: Cambridge University Press.
2014. *The Senate Syndrome: The Evolution of Procedural Warfare in the Modern U.S. Senate*. Norman: University of Oklahoma Press.
2017. "Leadership and Partisanship in the Modern Senate." In *Leadership in American Politics*, eds. Jeffery A. Jenkins and Craig Volden. Lawrence: University of Kansas Press, 41–64.
2019. "Recent Senate Party Leaders in Historical Perspective." In *Leadership in the U.S. Senate: Herding Cats in the Modern Era*, ed. Colton C. Campbell. New York: Taylor & Francis, 272–92.
Smith, Steven S., and Christopher J. Deering. 1990. *Committees in Congress*, 2nd ed. Washington, D.C.: Congressional Quarterly.
Smith, Steven S., and Marcus Flathman. 1989. "Managing the Senate Floor: Complex Unanimous Consent Agreements since the 1950s." *Legislative Studies Quarterly* 14 (3): 349–74.
Smith, Steven S., and Gerald Gamm. 2001. "The Dynamics of Party Government in Congress." In *Congress Reconsidered*, 7th ed., eds. Lawrence C. Dodd and Bruce I. Oppenheimer. Washington, D.C.: CQ Press, 245–68.
2020. "The Dynamics of Party Government in Congress." In *Congress Reconsidered*, 12th ed., eds. Lawrence C. Dodd and Bruce I. Oppenheimer. Washington, D.C.: CQ Press, 197–224.
Smith, Steven S., Ian Ostrander, and Christopher M. Pope. 2013. "Majority Party Power and Procedural Motions in the U.S. Senate." *Legislative Studies Quarterly* 38 (2): 205–36.
Socolofsky, Homer E., and Allan B. Spetter. 1987. *The Presidency of Benjamin Harrison*. Lawrence: University Press of Kansas.
Sorensen, Theodore C. 1965. *Kennedy*. New York: Harper and Row.
Stephenson, Nathaniel Wright. 1930. *Nelson W. Aldrich: A Leader in American Politics*. New York: Charles Scribner's Sons.
Stewart, Charles, III. 1992. "Responsiveness in the Upper Chamber: The Constitution and the Institutional Development of the Senate." In *The Constitution and American Political Development: An Institutional Perspective*, ed. Peter F. Nardulli. Urbana: University of Illinois Press, 63–96.
Stewart, Charles, III, and Barry R. Weingast. 1992. "Stacking the Senate, Changing the Nation: Republican Rotten Boroughs, Statehood Politics, and American Political Development." *Studies in American Political Development* 6 (2): 223–71.
Stewart, John G. 1971. "Two Strategies of Leadership: Johnson and Mansfield." In *Congressional Behavior*, ed. Nelson W. Polsby. New York: Random House, 61–92.
1975. "Central Party Organs in Congress." *Proceedings of the Academy of Political Science* 32 (1): 20–33.
Stromer, Marvin E. 1969. *Making of a Political Leader: Kenneth S. Wherry and the United States Senate*. Lincoln: University of Nebraska Press.
Strother, Ernest S., Jr. 1966. "Thomas Staples Martin: His Senatorial Career." M.A. thesis, Department of History and Political Science, University of Richmond.
Sundquist, James L. 1981. *The Decline and Resurgence of Congress*. Washington, D.C.: Brookings.
Swanstrom, Roy. 1988. *The United States Senate, 1787–1801: A Dissertation on the First Fourteen Years of the Upper Legislative Body*. 100th Cong., 1st Sess. S. Doc. 100–31. Washington, D.C.: Government Printing Office.

Swift, Elaine K. 1989. "Reconstitutive Change in the U. S. Congress: The Early Senate, 1789–1841." *Legislative Studies Quarterly* 14 (2): 175–203.

1996. *The Making of an American Senate: Reconstitutive Change in Congress, 1787–1841*. Ann Arbor: University of Michigan Press.

Thelen, David P. 1976. *Robert M. La Follette and the Insurgent Spirit*. Boston, Mass.: Little, Brown.

Theriault, Sean M. 2013. *The Gingrich Senators: The Roots of Partisan Warfare in Congress*. New York: Oxford University Press.

Theriault, Sean M., and David W. Rohde. 2011. "The Gingrich Senators and Party Polarization in the U.S. Senate." *Journal of Politics* 73 (4): 1011–24.

Thompson, Charles Willis. 1906. *Party Leaders of the Time*. New York: G. W. Dillingham.

Thorn, John. 2011. *Baseball in the Garden of Eden: The Secret History of the Early Game*. New York: Simon and Schuster.

Truman, David B. 1959. *The Congressional Party: A Case Study*. New York: John Wiley & Sons.

Upchurch, Thomas Adams. 2004. *Legislating Racism: The Billion Dollar Congress and the Birth of Jim Crow*. Lexington: University Press of Kentucky.

U.S. Senate Historical Office. 2024a. "About Parties and Leadership: Conference Chairs." www.senate.gov/about/parties-leadership/conference-chairs.htm

2024b. "About Parties and Leadership: Majority and Minority Leaders." www.senate .gov/about/parties-leadership/majority-minority-leaders.htm

Valelly, Richard M. 2004. *The Two Reconstructions: The Struggle for Black Enfranchisement*. Chicago, Ill.: University of Chicago Press.

2007. "Partisan Entrepreneurship and Policy Windows: George Frisbie Hoar and the 1890 Federal Elections Bill." In *Formative Acts: American Politics in the Making*, eds. Stephen Skowronek and Matthew Glassman. Philadelphia: University of Pennsylvania Press, 126–52.

2009. "The Reed Rules and Republican Party Building: A New Look." *Studies in American Political Development* 23 (2): 115–42.

Valeo, Francis R. 1985. Oral history interviews with Francis R. Valeo, Secretary of the Senate, 1966–1977. Senate Historical Office, Washington, D.C.

1999. *Mike Mansfield, Majority Leader: A Different Kind of Senate, 1961–1976*. Armonk, N.Y.: M.E. Sharpe.

Van Deusen, Glyndon G. 1967. *William Henry Seward*. New York: Oxford University Press.

Vincent, Carol Hardy, Paul S. Rundquist, Richard C. Sachs, and Faye M. Bullock. 1996. "Party Leaders in Congress, 1789–1996: Vital Statistics." CRS Report for Congress. Washington, D.C.: Congressional Research Service.

Wallach, Philip A. 2023. *Why Congress*. New York: Oxford University Press.

Waller, Douglas. 2002. "Capitol Grudge Match." *Time*. June 10: 29–30.

Walton, Brian G. 1973. "Ambrose Hundley Sevier in the United States Senate, 1836–1848." *Arkansas Historical Quarterly* 32 (1): 25–60.

Watkins, Charles L., and Floyd M. Riddick. 1964. *Senate Procedure: Precedents and Practices*. 88th Cong. S. Doc. 88-44. Washington, D.C.: Government Printing Office.

Watson, James E. 1936. *As I Knew Them: Memoirs of James E. Watson*. Indianapolis, Ind.: Bobbs-Merrill.

Wawro, Gregory J., and Eric Schickler. 2006. *Filibuster: Obstruction and Lawmaking in the U.S. Senate*. Princeton, N.J.: Princeton University Press.

Weaver, David H., and G. Cleveland Wilhoit. 1974. "News Magazine Visibility of Senators." *Journalism Quarterly* 51 (1): 67–72.

———. 1980. "News Media Coverage of U.S. Senators in Four Congresses, 1953–1974." *Journalism Monographs* 67 (April): 1–34.

Weisberger, Bernard A. 1994. *The La Follettes of Wisconsin: Love and Politics in Progressive America*. Madison: University of Wisconsin Press.

Welch, Richard E., Jr. 1965. "The Federal Elections Bill of 1890: Postscripts and Prelude." *Journal of American History* 52 (3): 511–26.

———. 1971. *George Frisbie Hoar and the Half-Breed Republicans*. Cambridge, Mass.: Harvard University Press.

———. 1988. *The Presidencies of Grover Cleveland*. Lawrence: University Press of Kansas.

Weller, Cecil Edward. 1998. *Joe T. Robinson: Always a Loyal Democrat*. Fayetteville: University of Arkansas Press.

White, William S. 1954. *The Taft Story*. New York: Harper & Brothers.

———. 1957. *Citadel: The Story of the U.S. Senate*. New York: Harper & Row.

Widenor, William C. 1980. *Henry Cabot Lodge and the Search for an American Foreign Policy*. Berkeley: University of California Press.

———. 1991. "Henry Cabot Lodge: The Astute Parliamentarian." In *First Among Equals: Outstanding Senate Leaders of the Twentieth Century*, eds. Richard A. Baker and Roger H. Davidson. Washington, D.C.: Congressional Quarterly, 38–62.

Wilentz, Sean. 2005. *The Rise of American Democracy: Jefferson to Lincoln*. New York: W. W. Norton.

Wilhoit, G. Cleveland, and Kenneth S. Sherrill. 1968. "Wire Service Visibility of U.S. Senators." *Journalism Quarterly* 45 (1): 42–48.

Williams, Brien. 2009. Interview with Patrick J. Griffin, George J. Mitchell Oral History Project, Bowdoin College.

Williams, Christine. 2008. Interview, by Brien Williams, November 21, 2008. George J. Mitchell Oral History Project, 70, Bowdoin College.

Wilson, Woodrow. 1885. *Congressional Government: A Study in American Politics*. Boston, Mass.: Houghton Mifflin.

———. 1908. *Constitutional Government in the United States*. New York: Columbia University Press.

Wolff, Wendy, and Donald A. Ritchie, eds. 1999. *Minutes of the Senate Republican Conference: Sixty-second Congress through Eighty-eighth Congress, 1911–1964*. 105th Cong. S. Doc. 105–19. Washington, D.C.: Government Printing Office.

Woodburn, James Albert. 1903. *Party Politics in Indiana during the Civil War*. Washington, D.C.: Government Printing Office.

Young, James Sterling. 1966. *The Washington Community: 1800–1828*. New York: Columbia University Press.

Zelizer, Julian E. 2004. *On Capitol Hill: The Struggle to Reform Congress and Its Consequences, 1948–2000*. Cambridge: Cambridge University Press.

Index

For EU product safety concerns, contact us at Calle de José Abascal, 56–1°,
28003 Madrid, Spain or eugpsr@cambridge.org.

www.ingramcontent.com/pod-product-compliance
Ingram Content Group UK Ltd.
Pitfield, Milton Keynes, MK11 3LW, UK
UKHW011003090725
460592UK00004B/7